Theory of Knowledge for the IB Diploma

SECOND EDITION

Richard van de Lagemaat

Cambridge University Press's mission is to advance learning, knowledge and research worldwide.

Our IB Diploma resources aim to:

- encourage learners to explore concepts, ideas and topics that have local and global significance
- help students develop a positive attitude to learning in preparation for higher education
- assist students in approaching complex questions, applying critical-thinking skills and forming reasoned answers.

CAMBRIDGE
UNIVERSITY PRESS

University Printing House, Cambridge CB2 8BS, United Kingdom

Cambridge University Press is part of the University of Cambridge.

It furthers the University's mission by disseminating knowledge in the pursuit of education, learning and research at the highest international levels of excellence.

education.cambridge.org

First published 2005
Full-colour edition 2011
Second edition 2015

Printed in the United Kingdom by Latimer Trend

A catalogue record for this publication is available from the British Library

ISBN 978-1-107-61211-2 Paperback

According to the philosopher Martin Heidegger, 'in all teaching, the teacher learns the most'. This book is dedicated to the countless students and teachers I have met whose ideas have informed, inspired and delighted me.

Contents

Introduction

This textbook is designed to be used with the theory of knowledge course in the International Baccalaureate Diploma Programme, but it may also be useful for students following other critical thinking courses.

The main question in theory of knowledge (TOK) is 'How do you know?' The course encourages you to think critically about the subjects you are studying rather than passively accepting what you are taught. Critical thinking involves such things as asking good questions, using language with care and precision, supporting your ideas with evidence, arguing coherently and making sound judgements. You are, of course, encouraged to think critically in every subject that you study. TOK is designed to help you to reflect on and further develop the thinking skills you have acquired in your other subjects.

Knowledge claims and knowledge questions

The TOK course is built around analysing knowledge claims by formulating and exploring knowledge questions.

A *knowledge claim* is an assertion that something is the case. Any statement that can be true or false makes a knowledge claim. For example: 'Santiago is the capital of Chile'; 'I'm in love'; 'It's raining'; 'The universe is expanding'; 'Hitler was a monster'; '2 + 2 = 4'; 'Cats grow on trees'. Our everyday conversation is riddled with knowledge claims and we are bombarded by such claims at school, in the media and on the internet.

A *knowledge question* is, as the name suggests, a question about knowledge. Such questions have three key features:

1. *They are second-order questions.* A first-order question is a question about the world; a second-order question is a question about knowledge. In relation to academic subjects, first-order questions arise *within* a subject whereas second-order questions are *about* a subject. For example, 'Is the universe expanding?' is a first-order question which is dealt with by physics, whereas 'How certain is scientific knowledge?' is a second-order question and is part of TOK.
2. *They are contested questions.* Knowledge questions do not have straightforward answers and they are open to discussion and debate. Since they are contested, such questions require personal thought and judgement. The fact that there are rarely definitive answers in TOK is sometimes a source of frustration, but it can also be intellectually exhilarating.
3. *They are general questions.* Knowledge questions are concerned not so much with specific examples, such as the ethics of the Milgram experiment on human obedience (see page 387), as with underlying principles and criteria. A good knowledge question here might be: 'How can we know what ethical constraints to put on experiments in the human sciences?'

An additional feature of knowledge questions is that they are often *comparative*. We might, for example, compare the reliability of different sources of knowledge, such as reason and intuition, or different areas of knowledge such as mathematics and ethics.

As you work through the TOK course, you might find it useful to keep in mind the following 'high altitude' knowledge questions:

1. *Meaning:* what does it mean?
2. *Evidence:* what counts as evidence?
3. *Certainty:* how certain is it?
4. *Perspective:* how else can we look at it?
5. *Limitations:* what are the limitations?
6. *Value:* why does it matter?
7. *Connections:* how similar/different is it to/from…?

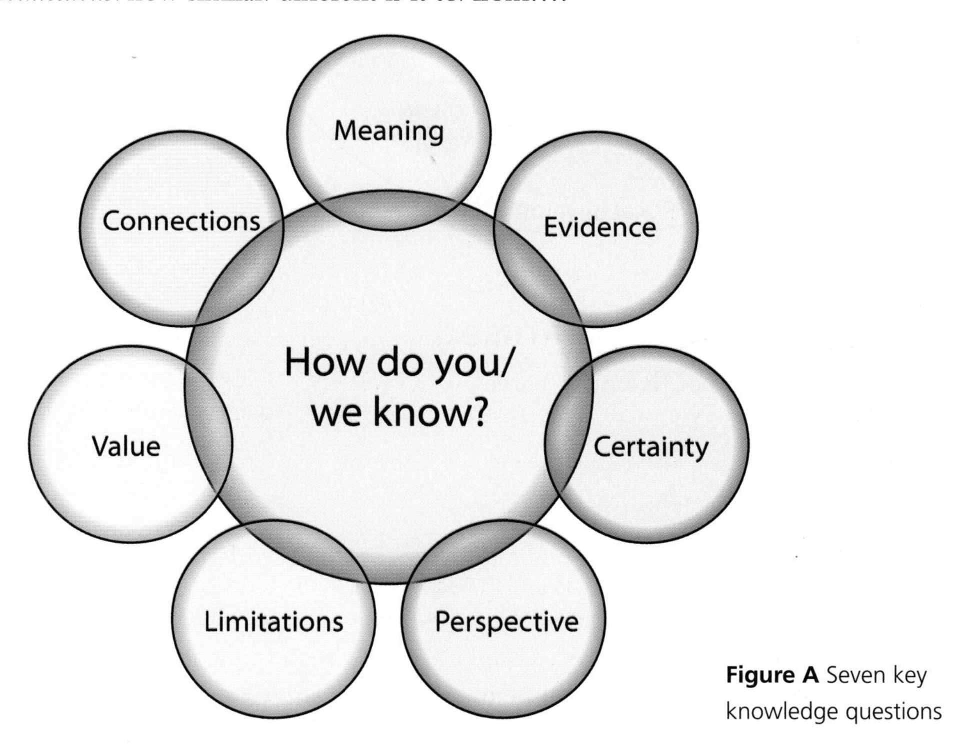

Figure A Seven key knowledge questions

A TOK diagram

There is no 'official' TOK diagram, but as will be discussed in Chapter 1, diagrams and maps are useful ways of making sense of the corresponding territory – as long as we do not take them too literally. Teachers using this textbook should keep in mind that the IB *TOK subject guide* explicitly states that it 'offers a framework rather than prescribed content' and that teachers should 'construct their own unique TOK course around key TOK concepts'. With that in mind, Figure B presents one way of making sense of the course and integrating its key elements in a single diagram. (These elements are explained after the diagram.)

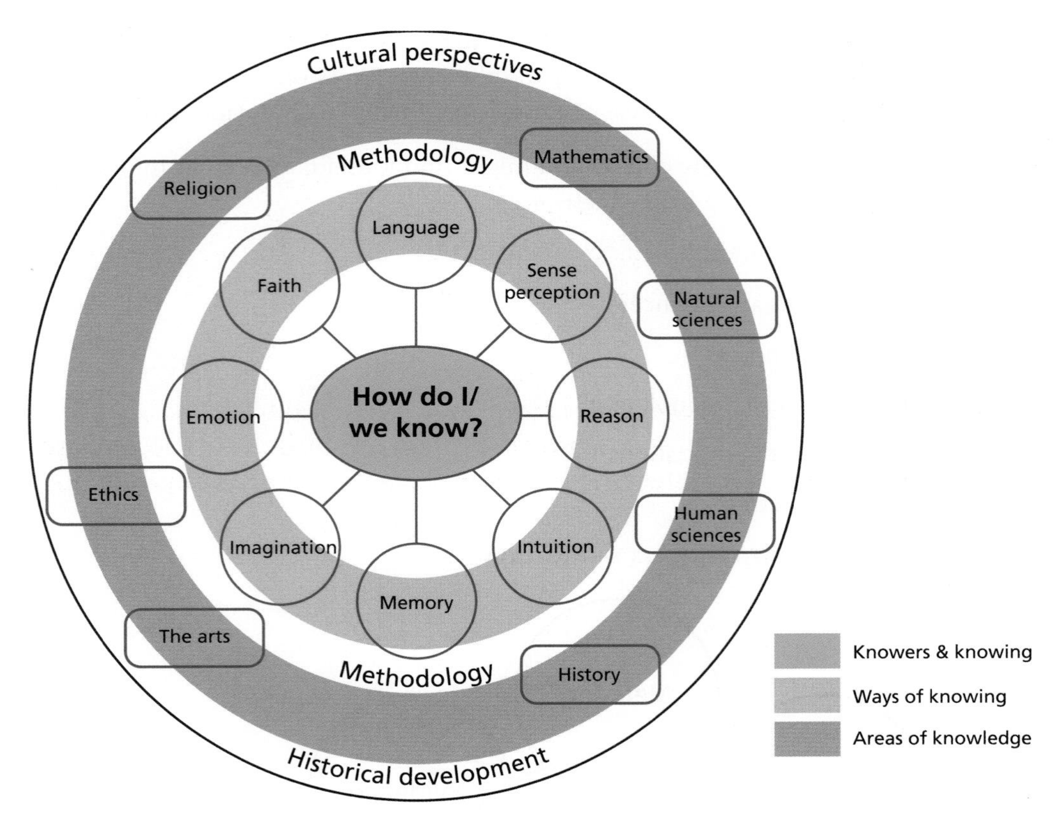

Figure B A TOK diagram

How this book is organised

This textbook consists of five main parts:

1. Knowers and knowing
2. Ways of knowing
3. Areas of knowledge
4. The big picture
5. Assessment

The first three parts reflect the three main elements as shown in Figure B.

1. *Knowers and knowing.* Since TOK is concerned with the question 'How do you know?', we need to say something about the nature of knowledge. Among the questions we shall be asking are:

    What is knowledge?
    How does knowledge differ from belief?
    What is the difference between knowledge and information?
    Is knowledge primarily a personal or a shared phenomenon?
    How does practical knowledge differ from theoretical knowledge?
    How reliable are second-hand sources of knowledge such as school, the internet and the news media?

2. *Ways of knowing (WOKs).* The TOK course suggests that there are eight main ways of acquiring knowledge about the world: language, perception, reason, emotion, intuition, imagination, memory, and faith. Take anything that you claim to know and ask yourself how you know it and you can probably trace it back to one of these eight sources. Despite their value, none of these ways of knowing is infallible. In fact, they are all *double-edged* in the sense that they can be both a source of knowledge and an obstacle to it. For example, your senses may generally be reliable, but your eyes can sometimes deceive you. So we will need to evaluate the strengths and weaknesses of each of these ways of knowing.

3. *Areas of knowledge (AOKs).* We then consider the various areas of knowledge – mathematics, the natural sciences, the human sciences, history, the arts, ethics and religion. These areas are ultimately based on the ways of knowing, but each one has its own distinctive scope, method and history. In addition to analysing the different AOKs, we also touch on some of the 'big questions' that lie at the frontiers of knowledge. For example:

   Why is mathematics so useful?

   Does science prove things?

   What makes human beings different?

   Can the past be known?

   Do we have free will?

   Are there any universal values?

   Is everyone selfish?

   What is the purpose of art?

   Does life have a meaning?

   We will also consider the similarities and differences between the above areas of knowledge and raise various comparative questions that will help you to think about how different subjects are related to one another and to develop a more coherent and inclusive picture of the world.

4. *The big picture.* Finally, we try to pull together the various strands in our exploration of knowledge. We look at cultural perspectives on knowledge and ask how, for example, 'western', 'eastern' and 'indigenous' cultures contribute to our understanding of the world. We then raise more abstract questions about the nature of truth, such as:

   To what extent are we able to know the truth?

   Should we seek the truth at any price?

   This leads on to a discussion about the difference between knowledge and wisdom. Perhaps the most important element of wisdom is a sense of humility and an understanding that there may be limits to knowledge.

5. *Assessment.* Following the main text, there are two chapters which give detailed support and guidance on all aspects of the TOK essay and TOK presentation.

   Although the chapters in this book are arranged to be consistent with the diagram shown in Figure B, they do not have to be read in the order in which they appear in the book; there may be other equally valid paths through the material.

Chapter features

In addition to the main body of the text, each chapter contains the following features:

- *Quotations* appear at the beginning of each chapter and may provoke your own thoughts about the topic.
- *Activity questions* appear regularly throughout the text and encourage you to engage with the issues under discussion and reflect on them.
- *Key terms* are helpfully defined in the margins and listed at the end of each chapter. They are indicated by the initials 'KT' and are coloured green.
- *Linking questions* encourage you to make connections with other ways of knowing and other areas of knowledge. They are indicated by the initials 'LQ' and are coloured purple.
- *Real-life situations* appear at regular intervals and help you to relate theory to practice. Most consist of brief headlines which you can research online to get the full story. Some may give you ideas for a TOK presentation. They are indicated by the initials 'RLS' and are coloured blue.
- *Knowledge framework focus*, which appears at the end of each chapter in Part 3, highlights some of the main characteristics of each area of knowledge.
- *Key points* are summarised at the end of each chapter and are useful for quick reference.
- *Further reading* includes books for in-depth exploration and stimulating articles which can be found online.
- *IB prescribed essay titles* are provided at the end of each chapter in Parts 1–4 so that you can relate the material covered to possible essay questions.

Personal thought

The vast majority of the questions raised in this book do not have definite answers, but this does not make them any less important. My aim in writing this book is not to save you the effort of thinking about these issues, but to provoke you to think about them for yourself. My hope is that you will be able to relate what I have written to your own experience and that this book will help you to find your way to your own conclusions.

Part 1

KNOWERS AND KNOWING

The problem of knowledge

1

The greatest obstacle to progress is not the absence of knowledge but the illusion of knowledge.

Daniel Boorstin, 1914–2004

The familiar is not understood simply because it is familiar.

Georg Wilhelm Friedrich Hegel, 1770–1831

By doubting we are led to enquire, and by enquiry we perceive the truth.

Peter Abélard, 1079–1142

All men have opinions, but few think.

George Berkeley, 1685–1753

Properly speaking, there is no certainty; there are only people who are certain.

Charles Renouvier, 1815–1903

A very popular error – having the courage of one's convictions; rather it is a matter of having the courage for an attack upon one's convictions.

Friedrich Nietzsche, 1844–1900

Common sense consists of those layers of prejudice laid down before the age of 18.

Albert Einstein, 1879–1955

It is the customary fate of new truths to begin as heresies and to end as superstitions.

T. H. Huxley, 1825–95

There are two ways to slide easily through life: to believe everything, or to doubt everything; both ways save us from thinking.

Alfred Korzybski, 1879–1950

We know too much to be sceptics and too little to be dogmatists.

Blaise Pascal, 1623–62

Introduction

We live in a strange and perplexing world. Despite the explosive growth of knowledge in recent decades, we are confronted by a bewildering array of contradictory beliefs. We are told that astronomers have made great progress in understanding the universe in which we live, yet many people still believe in astrology. Scientists claim that the dinosaurs died out 65 million years ago, yet some insist that dinosaurs and human beings lived simultaneously. Apollo 11 landed on the moon in 1969, but it is rumoured in some quarters that the landings were faked by NASA. A work of art is hailed as a masterpiece by some critics and dismissed as junk by others. Some people support capital punishment, while others dismiss it as a vestige of barbarism. Millions of people believe in God, yet atheists insist that 'God is dead'. Faced with such a confusion of different opinions, how are we to make sense of things and develop a coherent picture of reality?

Given your school education, you might think of knowledge as a relatively unproblematic commodity consisting of various facts found in textbooks that have been proved to be true. But things are not as simple as that. After all, if you had attended school one hundred or five hundred years ago, you would have learned a different set of 'truths'. This suggests that knowledge is not static, but has a history and changes over time. Yesterday's revolution in thought becomes today's **common sense**, and today's common sense may go on to become tomorrow's superstition. So what guarantee is there that our current understanding of things is correct? Despite the intellectual progress of the last five hundred years, future generations may look back on our much-vaunted achievements and dismiss our science as crude, our arts as naive, and our ethics as barbaric.

KT – common sense: cultural beliefs and practices generally considered to be true without need for any further justification

When we consider ourselves from the perspective of the vast reaches of time and space, further doubts arise. According to cosmologists, the universe has been in existence for about 13.7 billion (13,700,000,000) years. If we imagine that huge amount of time compressed into one year running from January to December, then the earliest human beings do not appear on the scene until around 10.30 p.m. on 31 December, fire was only domesticated at 11.46 p.m., and the whole recorded history occupies only the last ten seconds of the cosmic year. Since we have been trying to make sense of the world in a systematic way for only a minute fraction of time, there is no guarantee that we have got it right. Furthermore, it turns out that in cosmic terms we are also fairly small. According to astronomers, there are ten times more stars in the night sky than grains of sand in *all* the world's deserts and beaches. Yet we flatter ourselves that we have discovered the laws that apply to *all* times and *all* places. Since we are familiar with only a minute fraction of the universe, this seems like a huge leap of faith. Perhaps it will turn out that some of the deeper truths about life, the universe and everything are simply beyond human comprehension.

Common sense

Most people do not think that there is a problem of knowledge and they see knowledge as nothing more than organised common sense. While there may be something to be said for this view, the trouble is that much of what passes for common sense consists of little more than vague and untested beliefs that are based on such things as prejudice, hearsay and blind appeals to authority. Moreover, many things that at first seem obvious to common sense become less and less obvious the closer you look at them.

Yet we need some kind of picture of what the world is like if we are to cope with it effectively, and common sense at least provides us with a starting point. We all have what might be called a **mental map** of reality, which includes our ideas of what is true and what is false, what is reasonable and what is unreasonable, what is right and what is wrong, etc. Although only a fool would tell you to rip up your mental map and abandon your everyday understanding of things, you should – at least occasionally – be willing to subject it to critical scrutiny.

KT – mental map: a personal mental picture of what is true and false, reasonable and unreasonable, right and wrong, beautiful and ugly

To illustrate the limitations of our common-sense understanding of things, let us make an analogy between our mental maps and real geographical maps. Consider the map of the world shown below, which is based on what is known as the Mercator Projection. If you were familiar with this map as you grew up, you may unthinkingly accept it as true and be unaware of its limitations.

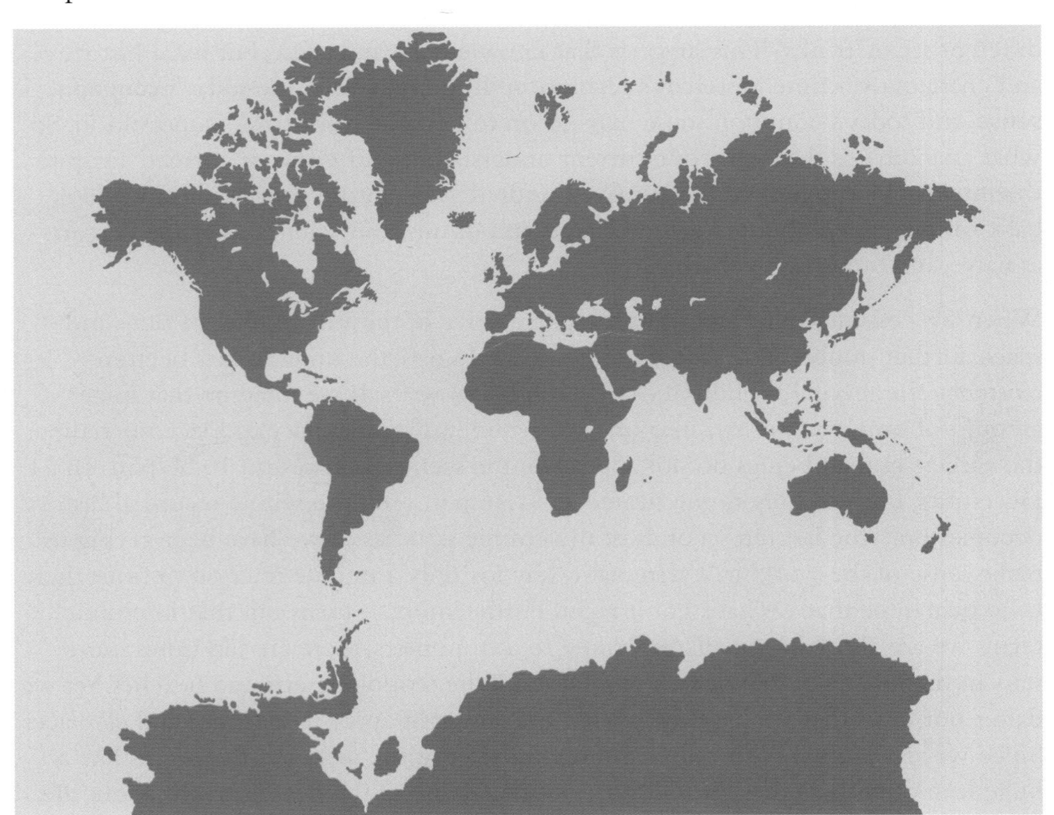

Figure 1.1 The Mercator Projection

ACTIVITY 1.1

1. Think of as many different ways as you can in which the world map shown in Figure 1.1 is:
   a. inaccurate
   b. based on arbitrary conventions
   c. culturally biased.
2. Do you think it would be possible to make a perfect map of a city? What would such a map have to look like? How useful would it be?

Among the weaknesses of the map in Figure 1.1 are the following:

1. It distorts the relative size of the land masses, so that areas further from the equator seem larger than they are in reality. The distortion is most apparent when we compare Greenland to Africa. According to the map they are about the same size, but in reality Africa is fourteen times bigger than Greenland.
2. It is based on the convention that the northern hemisphere is at the top of the map and the southern hemisphere at the bottom. Although we are used to this way of representing things, the reality is, of course, that the world does not come with a label saying 'This way up'!
3. The map is Eurocentric in that it not only exaggerates the relative size of Europe, but also puts it in the middle of the map.

Now compare the Mercator Projection with another map of the world, known as the Hobo-Dyer Equal Area Projection (Figure 1.2).

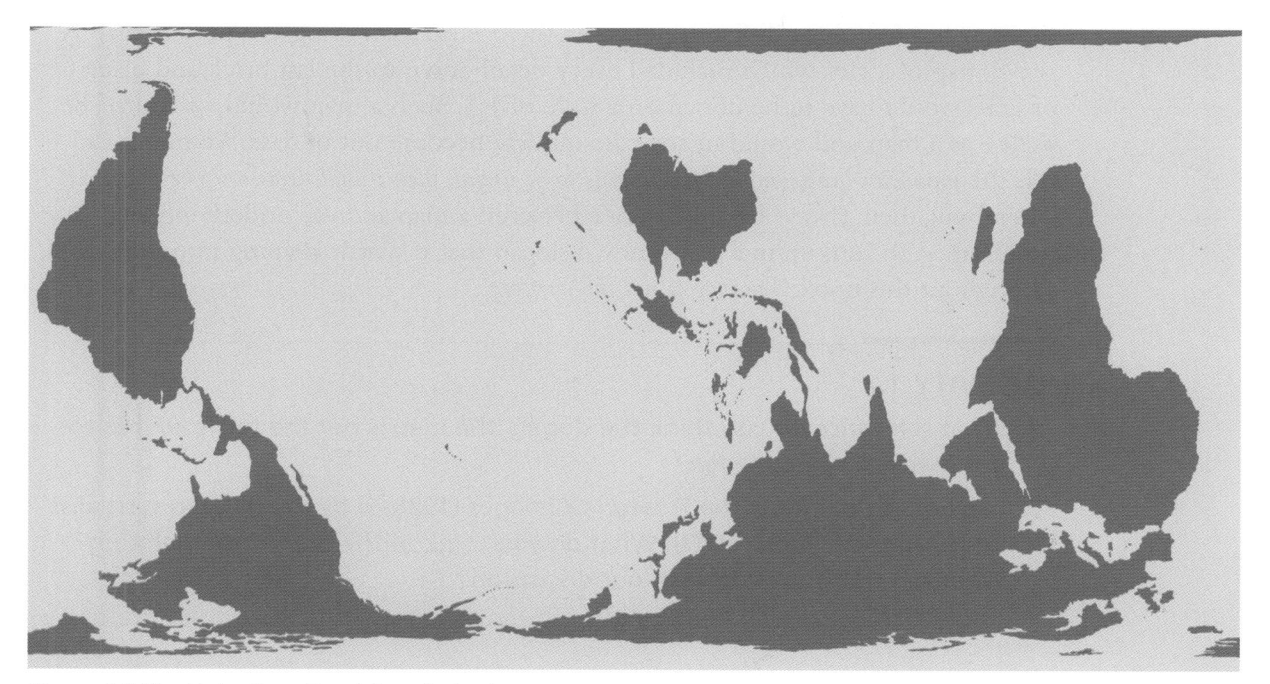

Figure 1.2 The Hobo-Dyer Equal Area Projection

Figure 1.3 *The Treason of Images*

This projection accurately reflects the relative sizes of the land masses (although it distorts their shape); it has the southern hemisphere at the top and the northern hemisphere at the bottom; and it is centred on the Pacific rather than Europe. The fact that most people find this map disorienting illustrates the grip that habitual ways of thinking have on our minds and how difficult it is to break out of them.

The point of this excursion into maps is to suggest that, like the Mercator Projection, our common-sense mental maps may give us a distorted picture of reality. Our ideas and beliefs come from a variety of sources, such as our own experience, parents, friends, teachers, books, the news media – and, of course, the internet. Since we don't have time to check up on everything to make sure that it is true, there are likely to be all kinds of inaccuracies, half-truths and falsehoods woven into our mental maps. Furthermore, it can be difficult for us to think outside the customs and conventions with which we are familiar and see that there may be other ways of looking at things. Finally, there may be all kinds of cultural biases built into our picture of the world. If you ask an English person to name the greatest writer and greatest scientist of all time, they will probably say Shakespeare and Newton. If you ask the same question to an Italian, they are more likely to say Dante and Galileo. Meanwhile in China they will boast about their four great inventions – the compass, gunpowder, paper-making and printing – and urge you to read *The Dream of the Red Chamber* by Cao Xueqin (1715–1763).

One final point to draw out of this discussion is that, while different maps may be more or less useful for different purposes, there is no such thing as a perfect map. A *perfect* map of a city which included every detail down to the last brick and blade of grass would have to be drawn on a scale of 1:1. Such a map would, of course, be useless as a map, and would in any case quickly become out of date. We might call this the *paradox of cartography*: *if a map is to be useful, then it will necessarily be imperfect.* There will, then, always be a difference between a map and the underlying territory it describes. To sum up in a well-known slogan that is worth keeping in mind throughout this book: '*the map is not the territory*'.

ACTIVITY 1.2

1. What relevance do you think the slogan 'the map is not the territory' has to our search for knowledge?
2. Look at the painting *The Treason of Images* (1928–9) by the Belgian surrealist René Magritte (1898–1967). What do you think of the title of the painting? What has this got to do with our discussion?

Certainty

If there are problems with our common-sense picture of the world, perhaps we should abandon our everyday understanding of things and limit ourselves to what is certain. For it has often been thought that certainty is what distinguishes knowledge from mere belief. The idea here is that when you know something you are certain it is true and have no doubts about it; but when you merely believe it, you may think it is true, but you are not certain. At first sight, this seems reasonable enough; but when you start to look critically at the things we normally claim to know, you may begin to wonder if any of them are completely certain!

ACTIVITY 1.3

List in order the five things in life that you are most certain of. Compare your list with someone else's. Can you come to any agreement?

RLS – Headline: 'Mysterious UFO over Denver Puzzles Aviation Experts'. Is it reasonable to believe in UFOs?

Consider, for example, the following four statements:

1. I know that Neil Armstrong landed on the moon in 1969.
2. I know that strawberries are red.
3. I know that if *a* is bigger than *b* and *b* is bigger than *c*, then *a* is bigger than *c*.
4. I know that murder is wrong.

KT – ways of knowing: the eight possible ways of acquiring knowledge outlined by the Theory of Knowledge – language, reason, perception, intuition, emotion, memory, imagination, faith

I imagine you would say that all of the above statements are true. But how do you know? You might say that you know that Neil Armstrong landed on the moon in 1969 because you read about it in an encyclopaedia or online; you know that strawberries are red because you can see that they are red; you know that if *a* is bigger than *b* and *b* is bigger than *c*, then *a* is bigger than *c* because you can reason it out; and you know that murder is wrong because it is intuitively obvious. However, if you ask yourself whether you are 100 per cent certain that these statements are true, doubts may begin to creep in. A quick look at four key **ways of knowing** – language, sense perception, reason and intuition – suggests that they cannot simply be taken at face value.

Figure 1.4 How sure are you that the Americans landed on the moon?

1 Language

Language enables us to acquire knowledge from other people, and we claim to know a great many things because we have been told them or we have read them somewhere. However, the authority of other people is not always a reliable source of knowledge, and even the so-called experts sometimes 'get it wrong'. If you are into conspiracy theories, you might ask how we can be sure that the alleged American moon landings were not an elaborate CIA-inspired hoax.

2 Sense perception

Much of our knowledge is based on personal experience, but our senses sometimes deceive us. For example, if you are colour blind, you might not see strawberries as red. We shall have more to say about this in Chapter 5. For the time being, you might like to consider Figure 1.5.

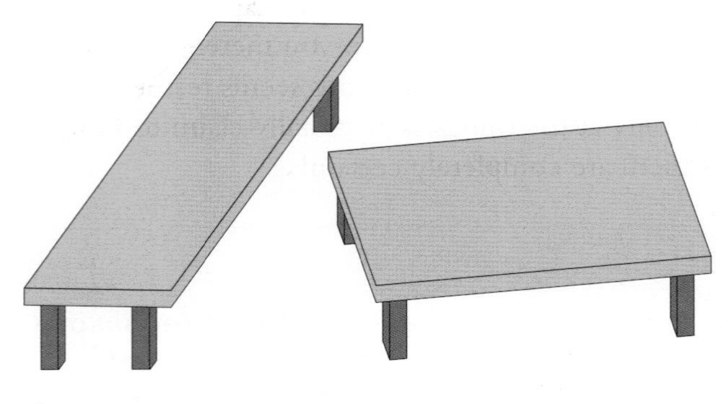

Figure 1.5

Believe it or not, the two table tops are exactly the same shape and size. This suggests that we should not blindly trust our perception and assume that it gives us certainty.

3 Reason

Statement 3 above might seem less open to doubt than the others, and some philosophers have claimed that reason gives us greater certainty than perception. In practice, however, people do not seem to be very good at abstract reasoning and they are liable to make all kinds of errors. To illustrate, assuming that some dentists are drunkards and no cyclists are drunkards, does it follow that some cyclists are dentists? The answer is that it does not – but we may well struggle to see that this is true.

4 Intuition

Some of the things that we claim to know strike us as intuitively obvious. The trouble is that what is intuitively obvious to me may not be intuitively obvious to you. You only have to consider debates about such things as abortion or capital punishment to see the extent to which people may have conflicting intuitions on important issues. And it would surely be arrogant simply to assume that my intuitions are right and yours are wrong.

We can mention four other possible ways of knowing which, like those listed above, are important sources of knowledge, but may not be entirely reliable.

5 Memory

Our knowledge about the past is based on memory. Indeed, there is a sense in which *all* of our knowledge – intellectual as well as autobiographical – is based on memory. If we literally forgot everything, we would know nothing. Despite their importance, our memories are notoriously unreliable and we often complain about them. We quickly forget the details of many of our experiences and sometimes even 'remember' things that never happened.

6 Emotion

Emotions play a crucial role in our lives and they shape and colour our perceptions and values. A person without emotions who was, say, unable to see a terrorist attack as frightening would surely be deficient in knowledge. At the same time, emotions can easily distort our perception of reality and act as an obstacle to, rather than a source of, knowledge. When angry people argue with one another, they produce a great deal of heat but very little light.

7 Imagination

Imagination is relevant to knowledge in that it is the source of creative ideas. A great deal of intellectual progress is the result not of discovering new things but of new ways of looking at existing things. Consider, for example, the famous insight by Copernicus (1473–1543) that the earth revolves around the sun rather than vice versa. However, when imagination is not tested against reality, there is a danger that we end up replacing public facts with private fantasies. The claim that the singer Michael Jackson faked his own death and is in fact still alive would seem to fit into this category.

8 Faith

For many people, faith is the basis for at least some of their knowledge claims about reality. Indeed, it could be argued that our most fundamental beliefs are ultimately matters of faith. Nevertheless, such knowledge claims contradict one another and what one person calls faith, another person might call superstition. In general, we may worry that, unless they are informed by reason, appeals to faith can be used to justify any belief.

RLS – Headline: 'Superstitions and Beliefs of Indian Space Scientists'. Are superstitions irrational?

Radical doubt

So far, we have raised some preliminary doubts about knowledge based on the eight ways of knowing mentioned above. But, following the French philosopher René Descartes (1596–1650), there is perhaps one statement that you think is absolutely certain – namely that 'I exist'. Surely that is something that cannot sensibly be doubted?

It could be argued that we cannot even be sure about that! In the 1998 movie *The Truman Show* a character called Truman Burbank lives on an island called Seahaven and leads an apparently ordinary life. As the movie progresses, we learn that Truman's entire life is being filmed 24 hours a day and broadcast live on TV, and that his wife, family, friends and acquaintances are all paid actors. Truman himself is unaware of this and he mistakes his illusory world for reality. So how can you be certain that you are not living a Truman-Show-type life and that the people around you are not simply actors? Some philosophers have even speculated that the whole of life might be a dream. Perhaps you will awake in a few minutes and realise that you have been having the strangest dream in which you were a creature called a human being, living on a planet called Earth. Although such a radical supposition does not prove that you do not exist, it *does* suggest that your life might be completely different from what you thought.

ACTIVITY 1.4

1. Do you think it is seriously possible that you could be dreaming right now?
2. Do you think that some areas of knowledge are more certain than others?

Relativism

KT – relativism: the theory that people's ideas of what is true or valuable are not absolute but depend on their culture

Sometimes people react to this lack of certainty by swinging to the opposite extreme and embracing a position known as **relativism**. According to relativism, there is no such thing as absolute truth that exists in an objective way independent of what anyone happens to believe is true. Instead, truth is relative and may be different for different individuals or for different cultures. So rather than say that something is true or false in an unqualified way, the most we can do is say that it is 'true for me' or 'false for you'. Since there are no grounds for saying that one opinion is better than another, we must therefore conclude that all points of view are of equal value.

Since there are disputed questions in all areas of knowledge, relativism might at first seem an attractive position. Rather than insist that I am right and you are wrong, it is surely more attractive to say that one and the same knowledge claim can be true for me and false for you?

Despite its attractions, relativism leads to as many difficulties as equating knowledge with certainty. Consider the question of whether or not the earth is round. According to a relativist we would have to say it is true for me and false for a

Figure 1.6 Is everything relative?

member of the Flat Earth Society. But surely there is an objective fact of the matter independent of what I or anyone else may happen to think? After all, the earth cannot be both round and flat. In view of this, what people may really mean when they say that something is 'true for them' is that they believe it is true. You are, of course, entitled to believe what you like, but the mere fact that you believe that something is true doesn't mean that it actually is true. A young child might believe that Santa Claus exists, but it only confuses the issue to say that it is 'true for the child'. For, no matter what the child believes, Santa Claus does not in fact exist.

The fact that we take seriously the idea that someone might be wrong in their beliefs suggests that relativism is false. Indeed, it could be argued that the statement 'All truth is relative' is self-contradictory. For if we ask ourselves about the status of the statement itself, we seem to run into difficulties – as can be seen from the dialogue in Figure 1.8. On the one hand, if it is absolutely true that all truth is relative, then there is at least one absolute truth – namely the truth that all truth is relative. On the other hand, if it is only relatively true that all truth is relative, then if a consistent relativist meets someone who says 'It is *not* true for me that all truth is relative', they are hardly in a position to argue with them!

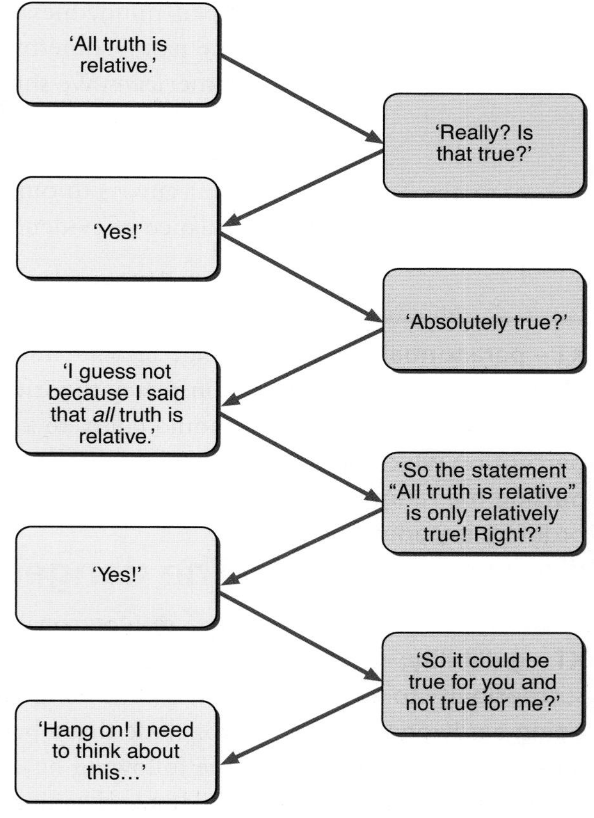

Figure 1.7 The dialogue of relativism

ACTIVITY 1.5

Read the dialogue taken from the novel *White Noise* by Don DeLillo (see page 20). What doubts does Heinrich cast on his father's claim that it is raining? Which, if any, of these doubts do you think are reasonable?

What should we believe?

We have seen that neither common sense, nor certainty, nor relativism can give us a quick solution to the problem of knowledge. So what should we believe? There is no simple answer to this question, and TOK is, in any case, more concerned with *how* you believe something than with *what* you believe. Whatever you believe, you should, for example, try to support your beliefs with evidence and be able to consider and respond to criticisms of your views.

The role of judgement

Since we live in a world in which there are few absolute certainties, you will probably have to rely more on judgement than proof in deciding what to believe. One important aspect of good judgement is the ability to balance **scepticism** with

KT – scepticism: a philosophical position which doubts or denies that knowledge is possible open-mindedness. Take the claim that aliens have visited the earth at some time in the past – something which opinion polls suggest is believed by around one-third of Americans. We should be sceptical enough to question some of the flimsy evidence that has been put forward to support this claim, but open-minded enough to allow that it is possible that a technologically advanced civilisation may have evolved and sent envoys to our planet. We must then engage in the difficult task of assessing the balance of evidence and coming to a provisional conclusion.

The great marketplace of beliefs in the so-called information age is, of course, the internet. Surfing around, you can quickly find websites devoted not only to a whole range of academic subjects, but also to a dizzying array of **paranormal phenomena**, conspiracy theories and urban legends. Since we are naturally credulous, we should cultivate a healthy scepticism as an antidote to intellectual – and financial – **gullibility**. (If you are too gullible, you will find plenty of charlatans and hucksters out there who will be only too willing to relieve you of your money!)

KT – paranormal phenomena: phenomena such as extra-sensory perception which lie outside the range of ordinary experience and defy current scientific explanation

KT – gullibility: susceptibility to being easily deceived; inclination to believe things on insufficient evidence

The danger of gullibility

You may personally believe in some paranormal phenomenon or conspiracy theory, and at some point it may even be shown to be true. However, no one is willing to believe *everything* they read on the internet, and we all have limits beyond which we conclude that a belief is absurd. It is doubtful that you would take seriously any of the following headlines from the *Weekly World News*, which styles itself as 'America's wildest and zaniest supermarket tabloid':

'Faith Healer Cures Sick Pets with the Power of Prayer' (August 1999)

'Washington Think Tanks are Riddled with Space Aliens' (October 1999)

'First Marriage Between Human and Space Alien Still Going Strong' (October 1999)

'Dog Reincarnation: Five Ways to Tell if Your Dog was a Human in a Past Life' (November 1999)

'Your Dead Pet's Ghost May be Peeing on Your Carpet' (May 2000)

'Researchers Discover Language That Only Women Understand!' (March 2001)

'Teen's Hair Changes Color . . . With her mood!' (November 2001)

'Ventriloquist is in Coma – But His Dummy's Still Talking!' (January 2002)

'Man Eats Books – And Remembers Every Word!' (May 2002)

'Zebra Born With Horizontal Stripes' (February 2006)

'Woman Delivers Own Baby While Skydiving!' (November 2006)

'Flying Witches Arrested in Kansas' (May 2013)

The danger of scepticism

Despite the above comments, there is also a danger in being *too* sceptical; for you may then close your mind to new ideas that challenge the conventional wisdom. There are many examples of ideas that were ridiculed when they first appeared but were later shown to be true. For example, until the early nineteenth century, scientists dismissed as superstition the idea that stones could fall from the sky; but we now take the existence of meteorites for granted. Similarly, when Alfred Wegener (1880–1930) suggested the theory of continental drift in 1912, it was rejected by his contemporaries, but it was resurrected in the 1960s as part of the theory of plate tectonics. The moral of the tale is that just because an idea does not fit our currently accepted theories does not necessarily mean that it is wrong. It is always possible that it is our theories that need to be changed. Thus if we are too sceptical there is a danger that intellectual progress will grind to a halt and knowledge stagnate.

So we need to find a balance between being open to new ideas that challenge our current way of thinking, and keeping in mind that human beings are credulous animals who are sometimes willing to believe strange things on the basis of slender evidence.

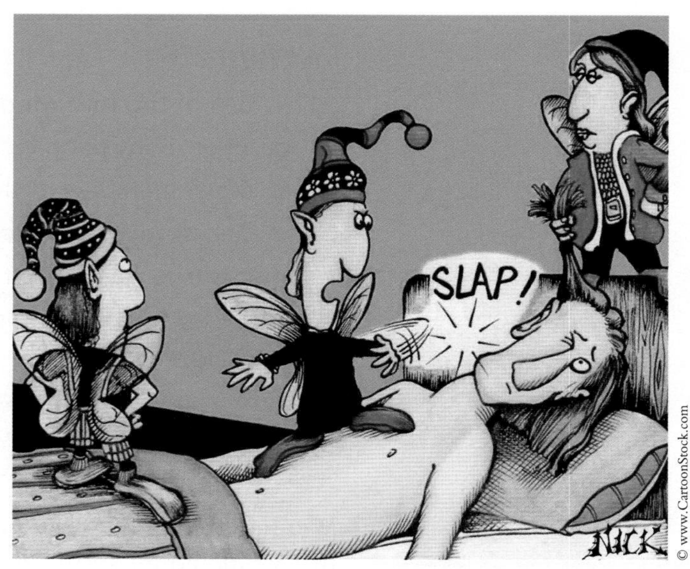

"For goodness sake, man, SNAP OUT OF IT..!!! We're NOT Aliens from outer space!! We're PIXIES! Pixies from your GARDEN! IS THAT SO DIFFICULT TO UNDERSTAND..?!?"

Figure 1.8

ACTIVITY 1.6

Comment on the following quotation, and explain why you either agree or disagree with it:

'My view is that there is such a thing as being too open-minded. I am *not* open-minded about the earth being flat, about whether Hitler is alive today, about claims by people to have squared the circle, or to have proven special relativity wrong. I am also not open-minded with respect to the paranormal. And I think it is wrong to be open-minded with respect to these things, just as I think it is wrong to be open-minded about whether or not the Nazis killed six million Jews in World War II.' [Douglas Hofstadter]

RLS – Headline: 'Silenced: the Writer who Dared to Say Chiropractice is Bogus'. Do we have a right to criticise beliefs we consider to be absurd?

Reasonable knowledge

In trying to determine whether or not a knowledge claim is reasonable, two preliminary criteria may serve as useful guides: (1) evidence and (2) coherence.

1 Evidence

For a belief to be reasonable there should be some positive evidence in support of it. Imagine someone claiming that there are little green men living on Mars. When you challenge them to support their belief, they say 'Well, you can't prove that there aren't.' This is a bad argument because the person has given no positive evidence to support their belief; and although it is difficult to prove that there are definitely not little green men on Mars, this simply reflects the fact that it is always difficult to prove a negative. The fact that you can't prove that something *isn't* true does nothing to show that it *is* true. The fallacy of thinking that it does is called ***argument ad ignorantiam***.

KT – argument *ad ignorantiam*: the fallacy of assuming that a proposition is true simply because it has not been proved false, or false because it has not been proved true

ACTIVITY 1.7

1. Which of the following is an example of argument *ad ignorantiam*?
   a. Since many people claim to have seen ghosts, it is likely that they exist.
   b. Many members of the Society for the Paranormal believe in ghosts.
   c. Ghosts must exist because no one has proved that they do not.
   d. It is true for me that ghosts exist.
2. Make up three examples of your own to illustrate the fallacy of argument *ad ignorantiam*.
3. How would you go about trying to prove that a species has become extinct? What has this got to do with our discussion?

KT – confirmation bias: the tendency to notice evidence which supports your position and ignore evidence which contradicts it

We should look not only for evidence in favour of our beliefs, but also for evidence that would count against them. For, according to psychologists, we have a disturbing tendency, known as **confirmation bias**, to notice only evidence that supports our beliefs. For example, if you believe in astrology, you will tend to notice the times your horoscope is right and overlook the times it is wrong. To counter this tendency, you should keep a record not only of how often the horoscope is right but also of how often it is wrong.

2 Coherence

A second criterion for deciding whether or not a belief is reasonable is whether it coheres, or fits in, with our current understanding of things. Despite appearances, I don't think that this criterion contradicts what we said earlier about the need to question common sense. When it comes to examining our beliefs, our position is like that of a sailor who has to rebuild his ship while still at sea. If he dismantles the ship completely and tries to rebuild it from scratch, he will drown. His only option is to rebuild it piece by piece. Similarly, we cannot cast doubt on all of our beliefs at the same time. The best we can do is examine them one at a time against the background of our other beliefs. If we don't want to drown, there is simply no other way to proceed.

What this criterion implies is that, although we should be open to new ideas, the more unlikely something is relative to the current state of knowledge, the stronger the evidence in its favour should be before we take it seriously. Consider, for example, the claims of people such as Uri Geller – 'the world's most famous paranormalist' – to be able to bend spoons using only mental energy. Given our current knowledge of the way the world works, it seems unlikely that a spoon can be bent through non-physical means simply by focusing one's mind on it. So before accepting such a belief we should demand good evidence in support of it. As far as I know, no such evidence currently appears to exist.

ACTIVITY 1.8

1. According to the astronomer Carl Sagan (1934–96), 'extraordinary claims require extraordinary evidence'. Explain what he meant by this. Do you agree?
2. Explain, with reasons, which of the following statements you think is less likely to be true.
   a. The Loch Ness monster exists.
   b. Some mystics are able to levitate.
3. In a book entitled *The Appalling Fraud* (*L'effroyable imposture*), the French author Thierry Meyssan makes the extraordinary claim that a passenger jet did not hit the Pentagon on 11 September 2001, and that the explosion was instead caused by a truckload of explosives. Using the criterion mentioned above, how much evidence would you need in order to be convinced of the truth of Meyssan's claim?

Who cares?

At this point, you might ask whether it really matters what we believe. We may laugh at some of the crazy ideas people hold, but what harm do they do? Don't people have the right to believe what they like? I am as in favour of freedom of belief as the next person, but I think it matters what you believe; and although it may sound undemocratic I think some beliefs are more worthy of respect than others.

One reason why your beliefs and opinions matter is that they are an important – perhaps defining – part of who you are as a person. So if you want to be something more than a 'second-hand self' who mindlessly repeats the opinions of other people, you need to make your beliefs and opinions genuinely your own by subjecting them to critical scrutiny. Socrates (470–399 BCE) once famously said that 'The unexamined life is not worth living.' Although it would make little sense to be constantly examining your beliefs, if you never examine them you may end up leading a life that is not genuinely your own.

A second reason why beliefs matter is that people's beliefs affect their actions; and, in some cases at least, beliefs can literally be a matter of life and death. For example, between the fifteenth and seventeenth centuries in Europe, an estimated half a million people were burnt to death because they were believed to be guilty of the 'crime' of witchcraft. Fortunately, we no longer burn people to death for witchcraft; but there is no shortage of dangerous and misguided beliefs in circulation. Here are two examples:

1. A former chief executive of an international tobacco company once claimed that cigarettes are no more addictive than gummy bears candy. But the statistical evidence suggests that every cigarette you smoke shortens your life by about the amount of time it takes to smoke it.

Figure 1.9 Marshall Applewhite

2. In 1997, Marshall Applewhite, the leader of an American religious cult called 'Heaven's Gate', persuaded his followers that if they 'shed their bodies' they would be beamed on board a spaceship behind the Hale–Bopp comet and taken to a new world. Thirty-nine people committed suicide as a result.

ACTIVITY 1.9

1. Do you think we should respect the beliefs of a racist or sexist person? Give reasons.
2. Find some examples of beliefs that you think are both misguided and dangerous.

The French philosopher Voltaire (1694–1778) once said that 'People who believe absurdities will commit atrocities'. Although most people who hold eccentric beliefs show no interest in massacring their neighbours, you may think there may be an element of truth in Voltaire's comment. A society in which 'anything goes' is a fertile breeding ground for fanatics and extremists of all kinds. Some historians have observed that the rise of Hitler in Germany was accompanied by a growing interest in various kinds of pseudo-science. The psychologist Viktor Frankl (1905–1997), who was a survivor of a Nazi concentration camp, sees a direct link between the two: 'I am absolutely convinced that the gas chambers of Auschwitz, Treblinka, and Maidanek were ultimately prepared not in some ministry or other in Berlin, but rather at the desks and in the lecture halls of nihilistic scientists and philosophers'. If there is any truth in this claim, then each of us has the responsibility, at least occasionally, to take a critical look at our own beliefs and prejudices.

Conclusion

"Or, failing that, the virtual truth as you imagine it to be."

Figure 1.10

At the beginning of this chapter, we saw that it is difficult to form a coherent picture of reality in the modern world. The way we see the world is shaped by our history, and by culture and psychology; and since in cosmic terms humans have not been around very long, we may wonder if we have any privileged access to the truth. We then looked at three possible solutions to the problem of knowledge – common sense, certainty and relativism – and we saw that none of them is entirely adequate. Since the problem of knowledge has no easy solution we must use our judgement in trying to decide what to believe.

I hope that after working through this chapter you will agree that there is a problem of knowledge and that it is worth spending some time thinking about it. The next stage is to look in more detail at what we mean by the word 'knowledge'. This will be explored in Chapter 2.

Key points

- The world is a confusing place in which we find a bewildering variety of different opinions.
- Our common-sense picture of reality probably contains inaccuracies and biases that we are not aware of.
- We acquire knowledge about the world through various ways of knowing, such as language, perception, reason and intuition, but none of these ways of knowing can give us certainty.
- According to relativism, truth is relative to the individual; but the fact that we take seriously the idea that someone may be wrong in their beliefs suggests that relativism is false.
- Since there are few absolute certainties in the world, we have to rely more on our own judgement.
- An important aspect of good judgement is finding the right balance between scepticism and open-mindedness.
- Two preliminary criteria for deciding whether a knowledge claim is plausible are evidence and coherence.
- Since we are what we believe and our beliefs affect our actions, if we want to be authentic and responsible we should occasionally subject our beliefs to critical scrutiny.

Key terms

argument *ad ignorantiam*

common sense

confirmation bias

gullibility

mental map

paranormal phenomena

relativism

scepticism

ways of knowing

IB prescribed essay titles

1. 'Doubt is the key to knowledge.' (Persian proverb) To what extent is this true in two areas of knowledge? (November 2010 / May 2011)
2. To what extent do we need evidence to support our beliefs in different areas of knowledge? (November 2010 / May 2011)

Further reading

Books

André Comte-Sponville, *The Little Book of Philosophy* (Heinemann, 2004), Chapter 5, 'Knowledge'. A beautifully written chapter on knowledge, scepticism and certainty. Since it is written by a philosopher, it is quite challenging, but it is worth reading, thinking about, and then reading again!

Carl Sagan, *The Demon Haunted World* (Ballantine, 1997). This classic text written from a scientific and sceptical point of view contains many thought-provoking chapters. Try Chapter 12, 'The Fine Art of Baloney Detection', Chapter 17, 'The Marriage of Skepticism and Wonder' and Chapter 19, 'No Such Thing as a Dumb Question'.

Online articles

- Isaac Asimov, 'The Relativity of Wrong', *The Skeptical Inquirer*, Fall 1989.
- Edward Harrison, 'The Uncertainty of Knowledge', *New Scientist*, 24 September 1987, page 78.

Some problems of knowledge

LANGUAGE

Does some knowledge lie beyond language?

PERCEPTION

How trustworthy are our senses?

REASON

How can we justify logic?

INTUITION

When intuitions conflict, which ones should we trust?

EMOTION

How reliable are our feelings and emotions?

MEMORY

How can we distinguish accurate from false memories?

IMAGINATION

How does imagination contribute to knowledge?

FAITH

Should we trust knowledge claims based on faith?

MATHEMATICS

How does mathematics relate to the world?

NATURAL SCIENCES

How certain is scientific knowledge?

HUMAN SCIENCES

Can human behaviour be predicted?

HISTORY

Can history be unbiased?

THE ARTS

Do the arts give us knowledge?

ETHICS

Are values objective or subjective?

RELIGION

Can we know what the meaning of life is?

CULTURAL PERSPECTIVES

How are our beliefs shaped by our culture?

Reading resources

Dialogue: SCIENCE'S FINEST HOUR

The following dialogue is taken from a novel called *White Noise* by Don DeLillo. A father is driving his 14-year-old son, Heinrich, to school. Heinrich begins the conversation.

'It's going to rain tonight.'

'It's raining now', I said.

'The radio said tonight.' . . .

'Look at the windshield', I said. 'Is that rain or isn't it?'

'I'm only telling you what they said.'

'Just because it's on the radio doesn't mean we have to suspend belief in the evidence of our senses.'

'Our senses? Our senses are wrong a lot more often than they're right. This has been proved in the laboratory. Don't you know about all those theorems that say nothing is what it seems? There's no past, present or future outside our own mind. The so-called laws of motion are a big hoax. Even sound can trick the mind. Just because you don't hear a sound doesn't mean it's not out there. Dogs can hear it. Other animals. And I'm sure there are sounds even dogs can't hear. But they exist in the air, in waves. Maybe they never stop. High, high, high-pitched. Coming from somewhere.'

'Is it raining', I said, 'or isn't it?'

'I wouldn't want to have to say.'

'What if someone held a gun to your head?'

'Who, you?'

'Someone. A man in a trenchcoat and smoky glasses. He holds a gun to your head and he says, "Is it raining or isn't it? All you have to do is tell the truth and I'll put away my gun and take the next flight out of here."'

'What truth does he want? Does he want the truth of someone traveling at almost the speed of light in another galaxy? Does he want the truth of someone in orbit around a neutron star? Maybe if these people could see us through a telescope we might look like we were two feet two inches tall and it might be raining yesterday instead of today.'

'He's holding the gun to your head. He wants your truth.'

'What good is my truth? My truth means nothing. What if this guy with a gun comes from a planet in a whole different solar system? What we call rain he calls soap. What we call apples he calls rain. So what am I supposed to tell him?'

'His name is Frank J. Smalley and he comes from St Louis.'

'He wants to know if it's raining now, at this very minute?'

'Here and now. That's right.'

'Is there such a thing as now? "Now" comes and goes as soon as you say it. How can I say it's raining now if your so-called "now" becomes "then" as soon as I say it?'

'You said there was no past, present, or future.'

'Only in our verbs. That's the only place we find it.'

'Rain is a noun. Is there rain here, in this precise locality, at whatever time within the next two minutes, that you choose to respond to the question?'

'If you want to talk about this precise locality while you're in a vehicle that's obviously moving, then I think that's the trouble with this discussion.'

'Just give me an answer, okay, Heinrich?'

'The best I could do is make a guess.'

'Either it's raining or it isn't', I said.

'Exactly. That's my whole point. You'd be guessing. Six of one, half dozen of the other.'

'But you see it's raining.'

'You see the sun moving across the sky. But is the sun moving across the sky or is the earth turning?'

'I don't accept the analogy.'

'You're so sure that's rain. How do you know it's not sulfuric acid from factories across the river? How do you know it's not fallout from a war in China? You want an answer here and now. Can you prove, here and now, that this stuff is rain? How do I know that what you call rain is really rain? What is rain anyway?'

'It's the stuff that falls from the sky and gets you what is called wet.'

'I'm not wet. Are you wet?'

'All right', I said. 'Very good.'

'No, seriously, are you wet?'

'First-rate', I told him. 'A victory for uncertainty, randomness and chaos. Science's finest hour.'

'Be sarcastic.'

'The sophists and the hairsplitters enjoy their finest hour.'

'Go ahead, be sarcastic, I don't care.'

The nature of knowledge

2

A man with only one theory is a lost man.

Bertolt Brecht, 1898–1956

The will to a system is a lack of integrity.

Friedrich Nietzsche, 1844–1900

Knowledge is the small part of ignorance that we arrange and classify.

Ambrose Bierce, 1842–1914

Man is a credulous animal, and must believe something; in the absence of good grounds for belief, he will be satisfied with bad ones.

Bertrand Russell, 1872–1970

Information is acquired by being told, whereas knowledge can be acquired by thinking.

Fritz Machlup, 1902–83

It is the mark of an educated man to look for precision in each class of things just so far as the nature of the subject admits; it is evidently foolish to accept probable reasoning from a mathematician and to demand from a rhetorician scientific proofs.

Aristotle, 384–322 BCE

The more connections and interconnections we ascertain, the more we know the object in question.

John Dewey, 1859–1952

The world can only be grasped by action, not by contemplation . . . The hand is the cutting edge of the mind.

Jacob Bronowski, 1908–74

The learned man who is helpless in practical affairs is analogous to the miser, in that he has become absorbed in a means.

Bertrand Russell, 1872–1970

Introduction

Having looked at the problem of knowledge, we now need to say something about the nature of knowledge. The word 'knowledge' is what might be described as a **thick concept** in that it is not exhausted by a short definition and can only be understood through experience and reflection. Indeed, the whole of this book is, in a sense, a reflection on the meaning of the word 'knowledge'. Having said that, a definition can still give us a useful preliminary hook for thinking about the meaning of a word. We shall begin this chapter by exploring a definition of knowledge as **justified true belief**. It is, however, important to note that this is a starting point for reflection. With that in mind, we will then consider the idea that there are different levels of knowledge depending on one's depth of understanding. Finally, we will distinguish between three main types of knowledge: (1) knowledge by acquaintance, (2) practical knowledge (or 'know-how'), and (3) knowledge by description. In this chapter, we focus on (1) and (2), which together make up experiential knowledge.

KT – thick concept: a concept that can only be understood through experience and reflection

KT – justified true belief: the standard definition of knowledge dating back to the time of Plato (428–348 BCE) – to know that something is true we not only have to believe it but also need to have justification for our belief

Knowledge as justified true belief

Taking our preliminary definition of knowledge as *justified true belief*, let us consider the three elements that make it up.

Truth

The most obvious thing that distinguishes knowledge from belief is truth. If you know something, then what you claim to know *must* be true, but if you merely believe it, then it may be true or it may be false. This is why you cannot *know* that Rome is the capital of France, or that pigs have wings, or that the earth is flat.

Truth is another thick concept, which we shall have a lot to say about in Chapter 20. For the time being we can say that, as traditionally understood, truth is independent of what anyone happens to believe is true, and that simply believing that something is true does not make it true. Indeed, even if *everyone* believes that something is true, it may turn out to be false. For example, during the Middle Ages, everyone thought they knew that there were seven 'planets' orbiting the earth (Sun, Moon, Mercury, Venus, Mars, Saturn and Jupiter). They were wrong: we now know that there are nine planets orbiting the sun. Or do we? Some astronomers argue that Pluto should not count as a planet at all.

This raises the question of how can we ever be sure that what we think we know really is true. Perhaps in the future they will discover a tenth planet, and what we

Figure 2.1 How many planets are there in our solar system?

thought we knew will turn out to be false. Since we are fallible beings, this is indeed possible. But, as we saw in Chapter 1, this simply shows that knowledge requires something less than certainty. In practice, when we say that something is true, we usually mean that it is 'beyond reasonable doubt'. Since we are willing to imprison – and in some cases execute – people on the basis of evidence that is beyond reasonable doubt, this is surely an acceptable criterion for saying that we know something.

Belief

RLS – Headline: 'IBM's Watson Supercomputer Crowned Jeopardy King'. In what sense, if any, can a computer be said to know and understand things?

If you know something, then what you claim to know must not only be true, but you must also *believe* it to be true. We might say that, while truth is an objective requirement for knowledge, belief is a subjective requirement for it. If you have no conscious awareness of something, then it makes little sense to say that you know it. That is why encyclopaedias do not *know* that Paris is the capital of France, and pocket calculators do not *know* that 2 + 2 = 4.

ACTIVITY 2.1

1. Can you think of any cases in which someone might be said to know something without knowing that they know it?
2. As technology develops, do you think it will ever make sense to say that a computer knows things?

Since the time of Plato (428–348 BCE), some philosophers have argued that when you know something you are in a completely different mental state to when you merely believe it. For when you know something you are certain of it, and when you merely believe it you are not. However, we shall adopt a less demanding standard of knowledge. Rather than think of knowledge as being completely different from belief, it may make more sense to think in terms of a belief – knowledge continuum,

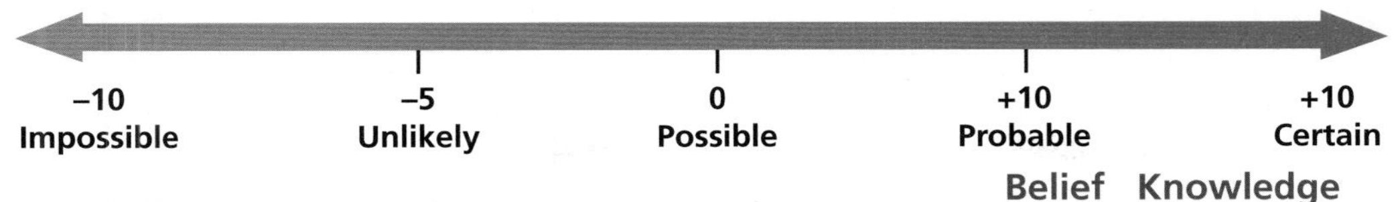

Figure 2.2 The belief–knowledge continuum

with unjustified beliefs at one end of the continuum, beliefs for which there is some evidence in the middle, and beliefs which are 'beyond reasonable doubt' at the other end.

RLS – Headline: 'Donald Trump Says Obama Birth Certificate Fake'. How strong must evidence be for us to be able to say that we know?

Here are three examples of various kinds of belief:

- *A vague belief.* I may vaguely believe that eating tomatoes helps to reduce the risk of heart disease, but have no idea where I came across this idea and readily abandon it in the light of counter-evidence.
- *A well-supported belief.* I may believe that Smith killed Jones, and be able to give evidence for my belief, but still be unwilling to say that I know that this is the case.
- *A belief that is beyond reasonable doubt.* I may find the evidence which supports the claim that the Americans landed on the moon in 1969 so convincing and the counter-evidence of conspiracy theorists so flimsy that I am willing to say that I know the Americans landed on the moon.

Given this way of looking at things, the question of exactly where we should draw the line between belief and knowledge does not appear to be a very interesting one. It is like asking where, in a spectrum of shades running from black to white, black ends and white begins. The important thing, surely, is to try to develop as reasonable and well-supported a set of beliefs as possible.

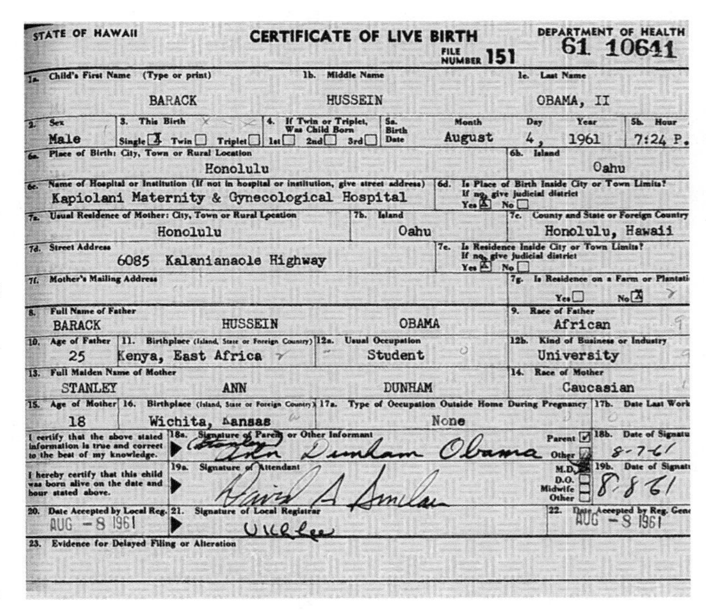
STATE OF HAWAII CERTIFICATE OF LIVE BIRTH DEPARTMENT OF HEALTH
FILE NUMBER 151 61 10641

1a. Child's First Name (Type or print): BARACK
1b. Middle Name: HUSSEIN
1c. Last Name: OBAMA, II
2. Sex: Male
3. This Birth: Single ☒ Twin ☐ Triplet ☐
4. If Twin or Triplet, Was Child Born 1st ☐ 2nd ☐ 3rd ☐
5a. Birth Date: Month August Day 4, Year 1961
5b. Hour: 7:24 P.
6a. Place of Birth: City, Town or Rural Location: Honolulu
6b. Island: Oahu
6c. Name of Hospital or Institution (If not in hospital or institution, give street address): Kapiolani Maternity & Gynecological Hospital
6d. Is Place of Birth Inside City or Town Limits? If no, give judicial district. Yes ☒ No ☐
7a. Usual Residence of Mother: City, Town or Rural Location: Honolulu
7b. Island: Oahu
7c. County and State or Foreign Country: Honolulu, Hawaii
7d. Street Address: 6085 Kalanianaole Highway
7e. Is Residence Inside City or Town Limits? If no, give judicial district. Yes ☒ No ☐
7f. Mother's Mailing Address:
7g. Is Residence on a Farm or Plantati[on] Yes ☐ No ☒
8. Full Name of Father: BARACK HUSSEIN OBAMA
9. Race of Father: African
10. Age of Father: 25
11. Birthplace (Island, State or Foreign Country): Kenya, East Africa
12a. Usual Occupation: Student
12b. Kind of Business or Industry: University
13. Full Maiden Name of Mother: STANLEY ANN DUNHAM
14. Race of Mother: Caucasian
15. Age of Mother: 18
16. Birthplace (Island, State or Foreign Country): Wichita, Kansas
17a. Type of Occupation Outside Home During Pregnancy: None
17b. Date Last Work
I certify that the above stated information is true and correct to the best of my knowledge.
18a. Signature of Parent or Other Informant: Ann Dunham Obama
Parent ☑ Other ☐
18b. Date of Signatu[re]: 8-7-61
I hereby certify that this child was born alive on the date and hour stated above.
19a. Signature of Attendant: David A Sinclair
M.D. ☒ D.O. ☐ Midwife ☐ Other ☐
19b. Date of Signat[ure]: 8-8-61
20. Date Accepted by Local Reg.: AUG − 8 1961
21. Signature of Local Registrar
22. Date Accepted by Reg. Gen[eral]: AUG − 8 1961
23. Evidence for Delayed Filing or Alteration

Figure 2.3 Barack Obama's birth certificate

ACTIVITY 2.2

Where on the belief–knowledge continuum, running from −10 to +10, would you put the following propositions?

a. Christopher Columbus 'discovered' America in 1492.

b. If A is bigger than B and B is bigger than C, then A is bigger than C.

c. Human beings are descended from apes.

d. Murder is wrong.

e. Aliens have visited the earth at some time during its history.

f. All metals expand when heated.

g. Human beings have an immortal soul.

h. It is possible to construct a square with the same area as a given circle.

Justification

You might think that true belief is a sufficient condition for knowledge, and that if you believe something and your belief is true, then you can be said to know it. However, something more is in fact required – your belief must also be justified in the right kind of way. Imagine that someone claims to know that there are nine planets in the solar system. When you ask how they know, they reply that there is an analogy between the 'microcosmos' of the human body and the 'macrocosmos' of the solar system, and that, just as there are nine 'windows' in the temple of the body – two nostrils, two ears, two eyes, a mouth, and two windows in the lower portion of the body – so there must also be nine planets in the solar system. This person believes that there are nine planets in the solar system, and his belief is true, but we would not want to say that he *knows* this because his belief has not been justified in the right kind of way. To us it makes no sense to talk of an analogy between the 'windows' in the human body and the planets in the solar system.

The point, in short, is that in order to be able to say that you know something you must be able to justify your belief, and your justification must be of the right kind. We usually justify our knowledge claims by appealing to one of the ways of knowing that are distinguished in TOK. If someone asks you how you know, you might reply:

'Someone told me' (language)

'I saw it' (perception)

'I worked it out' (reason)

'It's obvious' (intuition)

'It feels right' (emotion)

'I remember it' (memory)

'Empathy' (imagination)

'I have faith' (faith)

With respect to our planetary example, you might be said to *know* that there are nine planets in the solar system if you are part of a team of astronomers that have made the relevant observations, or if you came across this fact in a reputable encyclopaedia or science magazine.

You might ask why some kinds of justification, such as perception, are usually considered acceptable, while others, such as telepathy, are not. Imagine that a psychic asks you to think of an animal, and then correctly says that you are thinking of a zebra. When you ask her how she knew, she replies that she read your mind. Most people would not find this an acceptable justification, and would say that the psychic did not really know that you were thinking of a zebra, but simply made a lucky guess.

The key thing that distinguishes acceptable from unacceptable justifications seems to be *reliability*. Although it is not infallible, perception is a generally reliable source of knowledge. Telepathy, by contrast, is unreliable, and the scientific evidence to date suggests that psychics do no better than chance when it comes to trying to read

Figure 2.4

other people's minds. The sceptic and magician James Randi has offered a prize of $1 million to anyone who can demonstrate psychic powers. At the time of writing, the prize remains unclaimed. This does not prove that telepathy is false, but it does suggest that it cannot be appealed to as a reliable justification for our knowledge claims.

Whether or not you are justified in saying that you *know* something also depends on context. For example, you might claim to know that Mr Thompson is in his office because you just saw him go in, and you can hear his voice through the wall. But if, for some extraordinary reason, the future of the planet depended on whether or not Mr Thompson really is in his office, you might begin to feel less sure. Perhaps what you saw was only an actor who looked like Mr Thompson, and perhaps what you can hear is only a recording of his voice. This is the stuff of Hollywood dramas, and you are never likely to find yourself in such a situation. Since life is too short to raise sceptical doubts about everything you see, you have to make a judgement about when doubt is appropriate and when it is inappropriate. While *indiscriminate* scepticism has little to commend it, you would probably be more cautious about saying 'I know' in a court of law than you would in everyday life.

When you say you *know* something you are, in a sense, taking *responsibility* for its being true. If, for example, you say that you *know* the bridge across the chasm will support my weight, there is a sense in which you are responsible for what happens to me if I cross it. And if you say you *know* that Apollo 11 landed on the moon, you are implying that if other people look at the evidence with an open mind they *ought* to come to the same conclusion. Although we tend to think of facts as being completely different from values, this suggests that there is an ethical element built into the pursuit of knowledge.

Levels of knowledge

There is a lot more we can say about knowledge than simply that it is justified true belief. For a start, there are also different levels of knowledge. You may, for example, have a superficial grasp, a good understanding, or complete mastery of a subject. When five-year-old Jimmy says 'My mum's a doctor' his understanding of what this means is clearly not the same as his mother's. Much of what we claim to 'know' is in fact second-hand knowledge that we have acquired from other people and do not understand in any great detail. You might, for example, struggle to explain to another

Figure 2.5

person what gravity is, or why the sky is blue, or how a mobile phone works. Young children who are continually asking 'Why?' are sometimes irritating precisely because they bring to light the superficial nature of our understanding.

If you study a subject in depth, your understanding of it is likely to grow and develop over time. For example, if you study the *theory of relativity* in your physics class, revisit it as a university student, specialise in it when studying for a doctorate, and finally teach courses on it as a university professor, your knowledge of the theory as a university professor will be deeper and more sophisticated than it was as a first-year physics student. You may already have had the experience of revisiting a topic several years after you first studied it and realising how superficial your previous understanding of it was!

Knowledge and information

KT – information: disconnected facts which have not been organised into systematic knowledge

At this point, we should make a distinction between *knowledge* and **information**. Imagine sitting a child down one afternoon and teaching them some disconnected facts: 'nine times seven is sixty-three'; 'the chemical formula for water is H_2O'; 'aardvarks live in Africa'; 'the heroine in *Pride and Prejudice* is called Elizabeth Bennett', and so on. By the end of the afternoon, the child may be said to have acquired some knowledge in the limited sense of information. After all, each of these statements is true, the child (we assume) believes they are true, and she is justified in taking them as true because you are a reliable authority. However, if the child does not know how to multiply, knows nothing about atoms and molecules, does not know where Africa is, and has never read *Pride and Prejudice*, there is clearly something missing from her knowledge. Drilling random facts into someone's mind may be good for quiz shows, but it does not lead to genuine understanding.

A person with genuine knowledge of a subject does not merely have information about it, but understands how the various parts are related to one another to form a meaningful whole. To clarify with an analogy, we might say that information is to knowledge as bricks are to a building. While you cannot have a building without bricks, a building is more than just a heap of bricks. Similarly, while you cannot have knowledge without information, an area of knowledge is more than just a heap of information. The point is that when you study a subject you are not simply taught endless lists of facts, but you also learn various background assumptions, theories and informing ideas that help you to make sense of the facts.

So, if you wish to understand something, it is not enough to merely acquire information about it – you also need to think about the information and see how it hangs together. In a well-known Sherlock Holmes story, the famous detective and his trusty assistant, Dr Watson, are at the scene of a murder surveying the evidence. Holmes turns to Watson and says 'I see it all now, I know who did it.' Watson says with astonishment 'My dear Holmes, I've examined this same room with you and I see nothing at all!' To which Holmes replies 'No Watson, you "see" everything, but you "observe" nothing.' While Watson has at his disposal exactly the same information as Holmes, he cannot see the pattern which has allowed Holmes to solve the crime. What this story shows is that you can sometimes acquire knowledge simply by reflecting on the information you already have at your disposal rather than by looking for more information. This is a point worth keeping in mind in the internet age when many people have access to vast amounts of information.

ACTIVITY 2.3

1. Have you ever passed an exam by 'cramming' the week before, but felt that you did not really understand the subject? What does this suggest to you about the difference between knowledge and information?
2. What is the difference between knowing, in the sense of understanding, and knowing in the sense of being able to recite the relevant facts and theories without understanding them?

Types of knowledge

Thinkers and philosophers commonly distinguish three main types of knowledge, which are distinct but connected:

1. **Knowledge by acquaintance.** First-hand knowledge based on perceptual experience, which can be thought of as *knowledge of*. For example, you may have direct knowledge of Buenos Aires because you live there.
2. **Practical knowledge.** Skills-based knowledge which can be thought of as *knowledge how*. For example, you may know how to dance the tango because you took lessons.
3. **Knowledge by description.** Second-hand knowledge which comes in the form of language and which can be thought of as *knowledge that*. For example, you may know that Buenos Aires is the capital of Argentina because you read it in an encyclopaedia.

Most academic knowledge that you find in textbooks consists of 'knowledge by description' and we will explore that idea further in the course of this book. In this chapter, we focus on the first two kinds of knowledge, which together constitute **experiential knowledge**. As we shall see in Chapter 3, experiential knowledge is, in turn, an important part of *personal knowledge*.

KT – experiential knowledge: knowledge gained through experience, either by acquaintance or as practical knowledge

Figure 2.6 How do these people know?

Knowledge by acquaintance

Acquaintance with things is one of the basic ingredients out of which knowledge is constructed. We are most obviously acquainted with such things as colours, sounds, smells, people and places. Some languages mark the distinction between knowledge by acquaintance and knowledge by description by using a different verb for each of them. For example, French uses *connaître* for the former and *savoir* for the latter; German has the verbs *kennen* and *wissen*; and a native American language called Wintu has different verb forms for knowledge based on direct observation and knowledge based on hearsay.

ACTIVITY 2.4

1. Do any other languages with which you are familiar use different words for different kinds of knowing?
2. Could someone who has never visited New York know more about it than someone who lives there?
3. Could a male doctor know more about childbirth than a woman who has had children?
4. What problems arise when female novelists try to represent male characters, or vice versa?
5. If you have never gone without food, how might that affect your attitude towards the estimated 925 million hungry people in the world?
6. Since you have no direct experience of it, can you really know what it is like to be elderly? How might doing social service in a retirement home help?
7. How might your knowledge of, say, land use or soil erosion change as the result of going on a geography field trip?

To see the difference between acquaintance and description, consider the contrast between someone who has visited the Amazon rain forest and someone who has simply read about it in a book. Most people would say that this difference is not simply one of *degree*, but one of *kind*. If you visit the rain forest, you don't simply know more facts about it than someone who has not; you also know it in a different way which you may find difficult to communicate to them. When you try to explain such an experience, you might end up saying 'You had to be there!' Of course, acquaintance itself may also be experienced by degrees. There is a difference between someone who goes to the Amazon on a two-week jungle adventure, an anthropologist who lives and works with a tribal community for a year, and an indigenous person who was born and raised in the Amazon. According to a well-known saying, 'Travel broadens the mind', but the extent to which this is true will depend on how much people engage with the places they visit. We may all be familiar with tourists who seem to have been everywhere but seen nothing!

The difference between acquaintance and description is especially clear in the case of our knowledge of people. When you meet someone you have previously only heard about, you might find yourself saying, 'You are not at all as I imagined you to be.' Once again, there are degrees of acquaintance. You may, for example, be acquainted with someone, but not well-acquainted with them, and form a superficial – and perhaps misleading – impression of them after meeting them briefly. This is very different from the way good friends know each other.

The relation between acquaintance and description

Knowledge by acquaintance and knowledge by description are related to each other in various ways:

1. *Description depends on acquaintance.* According to a widely held view, known as **empiricism**, knowledge by description must ultimately be based on knowledge by acquaintance. The common-sense idea is that if a description of, say, the Amazon is to count as knowledge, you must be able to trace it back to someone who has first-hand experience of it.

KT – empiricism: the belief that all knowledge is ultimately based on sense experience

2. *Acquaintance spills beyond description.* We can never fully capture our first-hand experiences in language. It is, for example, hard to describe the taste of coffee or chocolate to someone who has never had them. Similarly, we often struggle to pin our emotions down in words. Sometimes a work of art can express a feeling such as love more accurately than a factual description; but no matter how moving a poem or a piece of music is, it can still never perfectly describe what you are feeling.

3. *Description colours acquaintance.* You are likely to see things differently if they have been described to you in advance. Such **verbal overshadowing** can easily distort perception. To prevent this happening, you might refuse to describe someone to a friend who has not met them because you don't want to prejudice their opinion: 'I'll let you meet them and then you can make up your own mind.'

KT – verbal overshadowing: the tendency of a verbal description to influence and distort perception

4. *Acquaintance fades with time.* We are more likely to remember things if we can capture them in words; but the uniqueness of our first-hand experiences fades with time and they can easily be replaced by general descriptions which simplify and distort them.

ACTIVITY 2.5

1. Try describing the following experiences to someone who has never had them:
   a. The taste of an onion
   b. Toothache
   c. The smell of freshly cut grass
   d. Hunger
2. Can a work of art capture the uniqueness of an experience better than words? Explore this question with reference to a specific example.
3. Animals and pre-linguistic infants are acquainted with many things; but in what sense, if any, can they be said to *know* anything?

"I keep thinking it's Tuesday"

Figure 2.7

Knowledge by acquaintance is connected not only with sense perception, but also with emotion and intuition. Some people claim that, just as we have external senses which acquaint us with the world outside, we also have an internal sense which acquaints us with our own thoughts, feelings and moods, and an intellectual sense which acquaints us with abstract things such as numbers and values. What is allegedly common to each of these 'senses' is that they enable us to *see* directly that something is the case without our needing to give any further justification. We will look in detail at sense perception, emotion and intuition in Part 2 of this book.

Practical knowledge

When we discuss knowledge, we often focus on theoretical 'knowledge of the head' and overlook practical 'knowledge of the hand'. Indeed, there seems to be something of a prejudice against the latter. For example, the abstract knowledge of the scientist is generally held in higher esteem than the practical knowledge of the car mechanic or the craftsman. This prejudice may derive from the widespread assumption that our capacity for reason is what distinguishes us from the rest of the animal kingdom. However, it could be argued that our ability to manipulate things is just as unique, and that the hand with its opposable thumb is as good a symbol of human intelligence as the head with its bulging cranium. Indeed, there is a sense in which know-how is prior to, and more fundamental than, know-that. After all, we need basic skills, such as the ability to speak and the ability to manipulate objects, before we can acquire any kind of knowledge.

Know-how across the curriculum

Although we naturally associate know-how with physical skills and manual dexterity, it covers a wide spectrum of activities ranging from the more physical to the more cerebral. You may, for example, know how to swim, know how to play the trumpet, know how to play chess, know how to speak Swahili, know how to solve a quadratic equation – and know how to write a TOK essay! Indeed, it could be argued that the real test of knowledge is the ability to put what you have learned into practice by applying it to the real world. That is why enlightened school systems stress the value of acquiring skills rather than memorising facts.

To see the importance of know-how, consider the role it plays in the following four areas of knowledge.

- *The Arts.* We naturally associate the arts with practical knowledge and speak of knowing *how* to draw, or weave, or play a musical instrument.
- *Language.* In studying a second language, you must learn how to put your theoretical knowledge of grammar and vocabulary together so that you can communicate with people.
- *The Sciences.* Although we tend to think of the sciences as theoretical, they are based on *experimentation* – which is a form of know-how.
- *Ethics.* A person's ethical knowledge could be said to show itself less in what they say than in the way they live their life.

Figure 2.8

ACTIVITY 2.6

1. Which of the following would you say are genuine examples of know-how and which are not? Give reasons.
   - a. I know how to digest food.
   - b. I know how to play the guitar.
   - c. Birds know how to fly.
   - d. Leo Messi knows how to play soccer.
   - e. Joe Average knows how to play soccer.
   - f. I know how to speak English.
   - g. Calculators know how to multiply.
   - h. I know how to write a TOK essay.
2. What role does practical know-how play in the IB subjects you study? Consider, in particular, languages, sciences and the arts.
3. Do you think that education puts too much emphasis on theoretical knowledge and not enough on practical knowledge?

Doing and explaining

Practical know-how is often difficult to put into words. You would probably find it very hard to write simple instructions on how to tie your shoelaces, or how to ride a bicycle, or how to swim. Following someone else's instructions can be equally difficult. If you ask a stranger for directions in an unfamiliar town, they may know where you should go and yet be unable to explain it to you. Similarly, if you buy an electronic device or some flat-pack furniture you may find the allegedly 'easy to follow' instruction manual incomprehensible; and it's a strange fact that no matter how carefully you follow grandma's recipe for a cake, it never tastes quite the same as it does when she makes it! When it comes to sport, the writer David Foster Wallace once complained that the autobiographies of great athletes are often boring because the athletes themselves are 'stunningly inarticulate' about precisely those skills 'that constitute their fascination'.

We should not, however, exaggerate the difficulty of communicating know-how. You only have to think of the number of self-help and how-to-do-it books on the market to see that, in some cases, at least, we can benefit from verbal guidance. Moreover, there are plenty of websites, such as wikiHow, which give helpful advice on how to do just about anything (there is even an entry for 'How to wiggle your ears'!). While there is doubtless a discrepancy between words and the reality that they seek to convey, the internet has made it increasingly easy to supplement explanations with pictures and videos.

ACTIVITY 2.7

1. Many people can speak their own language fluently, but cannot explain its underlying grammar. What does this suggest about the relation between know-how and know-that?
2. Write a paragraph explaining as clearly as you can how to do one of the following. How useful do you think your instructions would be to a novice?
   a. How to turn left on a bicycle
   b. How to use chopsticks
   c. How to roll your Rs
   d. How to catch a ball
   e. How to tie a necktie
   f. How to whistle
3. Take a skill you possess – such as speaking a language, playing the guitar, or skiing – and explain what role theoretical knowledge played in your acquisition of it.

RLS – Headline: 'Omani Football Cameraman Performs Spectacular Back Flick'. How can we assess know-how and distinguish skill from luck?

Theory and practice

You cannot acquire know-how without practice. To achieve mastery of a skill, you need to engage in what is known as *deliberative practice*. This requires that you break it into manageable chunks, focus on your weaknesses, get feedback on how you are doing, and gradually increase the level of challenge. Failure to engage in deliberative practice may explain why some people who practise a skill regularly never improve beyond a certain level.

While there is no substitute for practice, it is clear that skill can benefit from theory. To see this, consider a classic experiment in which children practised throwing darts at targets submerged under water. Half the children were taught the theory of refraction, which explains why a submerged target is not where it seems to be; the other half were not. In subsequent trials the first group did much better than the second at hitting targets at a variety of different depths. This is because their behaviour was guided by theory rather than being based on trial and error. So if you understand why you are doing what you are doing, it is generally easier to adjust your behaviour to different contexts.

When you first learn a skill, you need the guidance of rules in the same way that a child learning to ride a bicycle needs the guidance of training wheels. A beginner skiing down a slope may say to themselves 'Lean forward!', 'Bend your knees!', 'Keep it smooth!' As they progress, they will gradually acquire 'muscle memory', and eventually, if all goes well, their body will simply 'know' what to do without their consciously having to think about it. At the highest level, a skilled performer makes what they do appear effortless. The state of grace in which one is completely absorbed in and at one with what one is doing is known as **flow**.

KT – flow: a mental state in which one is completely absorbed in an activity

Analysis paralysis

Sometimes, when you think too much about what you are doing, theory disrupts practice. For example, if you are speaking a foreign language and you focus too much on the rules of grammar, your conversation loses its fluency and spontaneity; and if you think about what your fingers are doing when you type or play the piano you make more mistakes. In sport, **analysis paralysis** is known as *choking* and is usually attributed to over-thinking. As the American baseball legend Yogi Berra once asked: 'How can you think and hit at the same time?' We can also choke in everyday life when we think too much about an important decision and are unable to make up our minds. If we were to give the title of 'patron saint of chokers' to anyone, it would have to be Shakespeare's Hamlet.

KT – analysis paralysis: over-analysis of a problem which results in the inability to take action

ACTIVITY 2.8

1. Assuming that you know how to type and are familiar with a standard keyboard, take a piece of paper and reproduce the layout of the alphabet from memory. What does this task suggest to you about the relation between know-how and 'knowledge that'?
2. How would you try to avoid analysis paralysis in deciding which university to attend? Is there an optimal amount of information?

Assessing know-how

When someone says they know how to do something, we cannot simply take *their* word for it and their knowledge claim needs to be justified. While some people are unduly modest about what they can do, others are overconfident and have an exaggerated sense of their talents and abilities.

At the beginning of this chapter, we gave a preliminary definition of knowledge as justified true belief. When it comes to practical skills, we might say that genuine know-how requires a *successful performance* (similar to justification) judged against a *standard of excellence* (similar to truth) with some kind of *conscious awareness* (similar to belief).

1. *Successful performance.* You must be able to justify your claim to practical knowledge by giving a successful performance. Furthermore, if you claim to be, say, a good batter in baseball, you must show that you can *reliably* hit the ball well. Anyone can get lucky and hit a home run once, but it requires a great deal of skill to achieve a consistently high standard.

Figure 2.9 Hamlet: Is thought the enemy of action?

2. *Standard of excellence.* We have a standard of excellence for any skill against which we judge a person's performance. Sometimes people have an inflated view of their abilities because they are not aware how good it is possible to be. If you are a keen swimmer you may think your freestyle is pretty fast, but once you've seen Michael Phelps perform you will probably revise your opinion. You may be a good swimmer, but you are not that good!

3. *Conscious awareness.* Know-how also requires some kind of conscious awareness. We saw above that thinking can sometimes interfere with expert performance. Nevertheless, the ability to step back and reflect on what one is doing is what distinguishes the intelligent activity of a human being from the blind activity of a machine. In 1997 an IBM chess-playing computer called Deep Blue beat the then world champion Gary Kasparov in a six-match series. Despite its success, you would probably not want to say that Deep Blue *knew* how to play chess. This is because, unlike Kasparov, it was simply following a program and had no idea what it was doing.

Conclusion

We began this chapter by defining knowledge as justified true belief, and then suggested that the difference between knowledge and belief is one of degree rather than kind. We then saw that knowledge consists of more than a jumble of isolated facts, and that its various parts are related to one another in a systematic way. You only have to think of the way in which a textbook is organised to see that this is the case. This suggests that, in order to gain a deeper understanding of an area of knowledge, you need a mixture of *detail* and *context*. (If the mind is like a camera, we could say that you need both a zoom and a wide-angle function.)

We then distinguished between knowledge by acquaintance, practical knowledge, and knowledge by description, and we focused on the first two, which together make up experiential knowledge. Such knowledge is hugely important, but it can be difficult to express in words and communicate to other people. This may explain why it is sometimes overlooked. In Chapter 3 we will look at a related distinction that also plays a key role in Theory of Knowledge – namely that between *personal knowledge* and *shared knowledge*.

Key points

- A good preliminary definition of knowledge is to say that it is justified true belief.
- According to the traditional view, truth is independent, and simply believing that something is true does not make it true.
- Rather than say that belief and knowledge are two completely different things, it may make more sense to think of there being a belief–knowledge continuum.
- Knowledge is more than true belief, for your belief must be justified in the right kind of way.
- The main thing that seems to distinguish an acceptable from an unacceptable justification is reliability.
- Whether or not you are justified in saying you know something depends on context.
- When you say you know something you are in a sense taking responsibility for its truth.
- There are different levels of knowledge ranging from a superficial grasp of a subject to complete mastery of it.
- The difference between knowledge and information is that knowledge is information organised into a meaningful whole.
- Three different types of knowledge can be distinguished: (1) *knowledge by acquaintance*, (2) *practical knowledge*, (3) *knowledge by description*. (The first two make up *experiential knowledge*.)
- Knowledge by acquaintance – that is, direct knowledge based on personal experience – is held by empiricists to be the basis of all knowledge.
- Although it is often overlooked, one might argue that practical 'know-how' is prior to, and more fundamental than, knowledge-that.

Key terms

analysis paralysis
empiricism
experiential knowledge
flow
information
justified true belief
knowledge by acquaintance
knowledge by description
practical knowledge
thick concept
verbal overshadowing

IB prescribed essay titles

1. 'Knowledge is nothing more than the systematic organisation of facts.' Discuss this statement with reference to two areas of knowledge. (May 2014)
2. 'The knowledge that we value the most is the knowledge for which we can provide the strongest justifications.' To what extent would you agree with this claim? (November 2008 / May 2009)

Further reading

Books

Stephen Law, *The Philosophy Gym* (Hodder, 2003), Chapter 19: 'What is Knowledge?' Law helps you to exercise your intellect by considering some problems with the definition of knowledge as justified true belief and considering an alternative which also runs into problems. Such is TOK!

Charles van Doren, *A History of Knowledge* (Ballantine, 1992). A fascinating book to dip into; van Doren weaves a coherent narrative of the people and events that advanced knowledge from ancient times up to the present.

Online articles

A. C. Grayling, 'The Importance of Knowing How', *New Scientist*, 6 August 2008.

Jason Stanley, 'The Practical and the Theoretical', *New York Times*, Opinionator blog, 6 May 2012.

The nature of knowledge: some questions

TRUTH
Can we ever be certain of the truth?

BELIEF
Where does belief end and knowledge begin?

AUTHORITY
To what extent should we accept knowledge by authority?

JUSTIFICATION
What distinguishes a good justification from a bad one?

PARADIGMS
What role do paradigms play in knowledge?

INFORMATION
What is the difference between knowledge and information?

CONTEXT
Does knowledge depend on context?

WISDOM
What is the difference between knowledge and wisdom?

ACQUAINTANCE
How does acquaintance differ from second-hand knowledge?

KNOW-HOW
What is the relation between theory and practice?

Personal and shared knowledge

3

Knowledge is of two kinds. We know a subject ourselves, or we know where we can find information upon it.

Samuel Johnson, 1709–84

A society which wants to preserve a fund of personal knowledge must submit to tradition.

Michael Polanyi, 1891–1976

We can never be sure of anything that only we ourselves know and no one else.

Hannah Arendt, 1906–75

Everyone is entitled to his own opinions, but not to his own facts.

Daniel Patrick Moynihan, 1927–2003

Culture isn't knowing when Napoleon died. Culture means knowing how I can find out in two minutes.

Umberto Eco, 1932–

When information is cheap, attention becomes expensive.

James Gleick, 1954–

Science is the belief in the ignorance of experts.

Richard Feynman, 1918–88

If 50 million people say a foolish thing, it is still a foolish thing.

Anatole France, 1844–1924

Education: That which discloses to the wise and disguises from the foolish their lack of understanding.

Ambrose Bierce, 1842–1914

If you believe everything you read, better not read.

Japanese proverb

When all think alike, then no one is thinking.

Walter Lippmann, 1889–1974

Propaganda is to democracy what violence is to dictatorship.

Noam Chomsky, 1929–

Introduction

Imagine that a strange new virus suddenly appeared which destroyed our ability to communicate with one another. Speech lapsed into meaningless noise, sign language into incomprehensible gestures, and writing into a nonsense of inky blobs and squiggles. The consequences of the virus would be devastating. Within a few decades vast areas of knowledge would evaporate since we would no longer be able to pass on our accumulated wisdom to the next generation. If you grew up in such a world, your knowledge would be limited to the tiny circle of your own experience.

As the above thought experiment suggests, the pursuit of knowledge is an essentially collective enterprise. If we were solitary creatures, subjects such as physics, economics and history – as well as language itself – would be impossible. Given this, we should be wary of what might be called *the myth of the lonely thinker* – the idea that knowledge is the heroic achievement of brilliant thinkers working in isolation. For even the greatest minds have huge – and sometimes unacknowledged – intellectual debts to their predecessors and the culture from which they spring. At the same time, individuals play a key role in sustaining, refining and developing culture. In the modern era, such contributions are often made by groups of thinkers, and the internet – which makes it easy to connect and share information – has undoubtedly accelerated this development.

This chapter is concerned with personal and shared knowledge and the relation between them. We begin by clarifying what they are and then consider their respective strengths and weaknesses. As we shall see, the interaction between them can help to ensure that knowledge does not degenerate into private fantasy on the one hand or mindless conformity on the other. We then look at five key sources of shared knowledge which come to us 'second-hand' from other people and assess their reliability.

Figure 3.1 Rodin's *The Thinker*

Clarifying the distinction

Somewhat confusingly, the distinction that the Theory of Knowledge makes between personal and shared knowledge cuts across the threefold division of knowledge we made in Chapter 2. We shall see how these two sets of distinctions are related in what follows. To start with, we might take Auguste Rodin's famous sculpture *The Thinker* as a symbol of personal knowledge and a digital library as a symbol of shared knowledge. We can also mark the distinction by contrasting the verb 'to know' with the noun 'knowledge', the point being that what any one individual knows is only a tiny subset of the total amount of knowledge that exists in the world.

ACTIVITY 3.1

1. What does Rodin's famous sculpture *The Thinker* suggest to you about the nature of knowledge? How would you critique it?
2. Who do you think was the last person to know pretty much everything there was to know at the time they lived?
3. If you were to write a 'personal encyclopaedia' summarising everything you know, how extensive do you think it would be? And how accurate?

What is personal knowledge?

KT – personal knowledge: experiential knowledge (personal acquaintance and practical know-how) plus those parts of academic and informal knowledge which you have made your own

As the name suggests, **personal knowledge** is the knowledge that a particular individual has of the world. This consists of two main overlapping components:

1. *Experiential knowledge.* Knowledge based on personal acquaintance or practical know-how – both of which were explored in detail in Chapter 2.
2. *Second-hand knowledge.* Knowledge acquired 'second-hand' from sources such as your culture, school, the internet, and the news media. This has two main components:
   a. *Academic knowledge.* Your understanding of academic subjects – such as physics, economics and history – which you have acquired from school and personal research.
   b. ***Informal knowledge***. Your (second-hand) stock of cultural and local knowledge, random facts and trivia.

KT – informal knowledge: any knowledge which is not organised into an academic discipline, such as cultural and local knowledge, random facts and trivia

As mentioned, experiential knowledge and second-hand knowledge overlap with one another. Much of what you learn at school is conveyed second-hand through words, but it is also supplemented by first-hand experience. Consider, for example, doing a science experiment or playing in the school orchestra.

LQ – Arts: To what extent can the arts help us to share emotional experiences that cannot be expressed in factual language?

Much of your personal knowledge consists of 'common knowledge' about prevailing facts, theories and values; but some may be 'common' only in your culture or community, or particular circle of friends. At the limit, you also have 'secret knowledge' that is known only to you. Some of your experiences you *choose* not to share with other people because they are too trivial or embarrassing. Others – such as intense emotional experiences – you may feel you are *unable* to share because they are incommunicable. Whether or not the latter can be thought of as knowledge is a matter of debate. Some people believe that the highest truths are private and lie beyond language; others insist that knowledge must be justified in a way that is publicly verifiable.

ACTIVITY 3.2

1. Do you think there can be personal knowledge in the strong sense – i.e. knowledge that cannot in principle be communicated to other people?
2. When you look at social networking sites such as Facebook and Twitter, are you struck more by the uniqueness of each individual's worldview or by the similarities between them?

What is shared knowledge?

Shared knowledge is the sum total of knowledge which we can communicate to one another. This includes academic knowledge, informal knowledge, and that part of practical know-how that we can communicate verbally or non-verbally. (A wordless exchange between a master and an apprentice with the former demonstrating and the latter imitating is an example of non-verbal communication.) Some shared knowledge derives from individuals working alone and some from groups of people working together.

KT – shared knowledge: the stock of academic knowledge, informal knowledge and practical know-how which can be communicated verbally or non-verbally to other people

A key component of shared knowledge is academic knowledge, and the whole of Part 3 of this book will be devoted to looking at the various areas of knowledge – such as mathematics, the natural sciences and history. An important feature of these subjects is that they have a generally accepted *method* (or methods), and there are agreed standards and procedures for assessing knowledge claims and determining what counts as knowledge. As this suggests, *there is more to knowledge than what an uninformed individual happens to think.* This does not mean that we should blindly accept what we are taught, but we cannot simply dismiss it either. Rather we need to engage with the various areas of knowledge and have some understanding of them before we can make any meaningful contributions to and/or informed criticisms of them.

Most of the things that surround us in daily life are also the products of shared knowledge. To illustrate, economist Tim Harford (1973–) considers a humble cappuccino. No one person, he says, has the knowledge to grow and process the coffee beans, extract the milk from the cow, make the espresso machine, fashion the coffee cup, and so on. What seems like a simple drink turns out to be the product of the collective know-how of hundreds – perhaps thousands – of people. And what is true of cappuccinos is even truer of computers and the other technological gadgets we take for granted.

LQ – Ethics: How are our beliefs about right and wrong influenced by the beliefs of those around us?

Communities of knowledge

While shared knowledge can in theory be shared by everyone, in practice it is often shared only by groups, for example:

- *Friends.* Friends are typically bound together by shared experiences and knowledge known only to them. This is why 'in' jokes are so difficult to explain to outsiders.

- *Subject specialists.* Subject specialists, such as philosophers, physicists or photographers, might be thought of as *tribes*, each with their own set of assumptions, specialist language and distinctive way of looking at the world.
- *Cultures.* Every culture has its own hidden assumptions and unwritten rules which may be difficult to explain to outsiders. Some people claim that you have to be born into a culture to fully understand it.

ACTIVITY 3.3

1. What, if anything, do you think everyone *does* know? What, if anything, do you think everyone *should* know?
2. What kind of groups and cliques exist in your school? What kind of knowledge do they have which binds them together and excludes others?
3. To what extent do you think it is possible to know another culture if you were not raised in it?

Summary

We can summarise the relation between personal and shared knowledge in the following diagram. We might begin by thinking of shared knowledge as the sum total of everyone's personal knowledge. (So there should be more than eight billion dots in the shared knowledge circle.) However, some 'knowledge' is never thought, used or accessed by anyone, and it only exists in libraries or on computer servers. This is the pink segment on the left. Some people argue that this is not really knowledge and that just as a word must be used to be part of a language, so knowledge needs a knower to be properly alive. Others disagree. Either way, as information piles up,

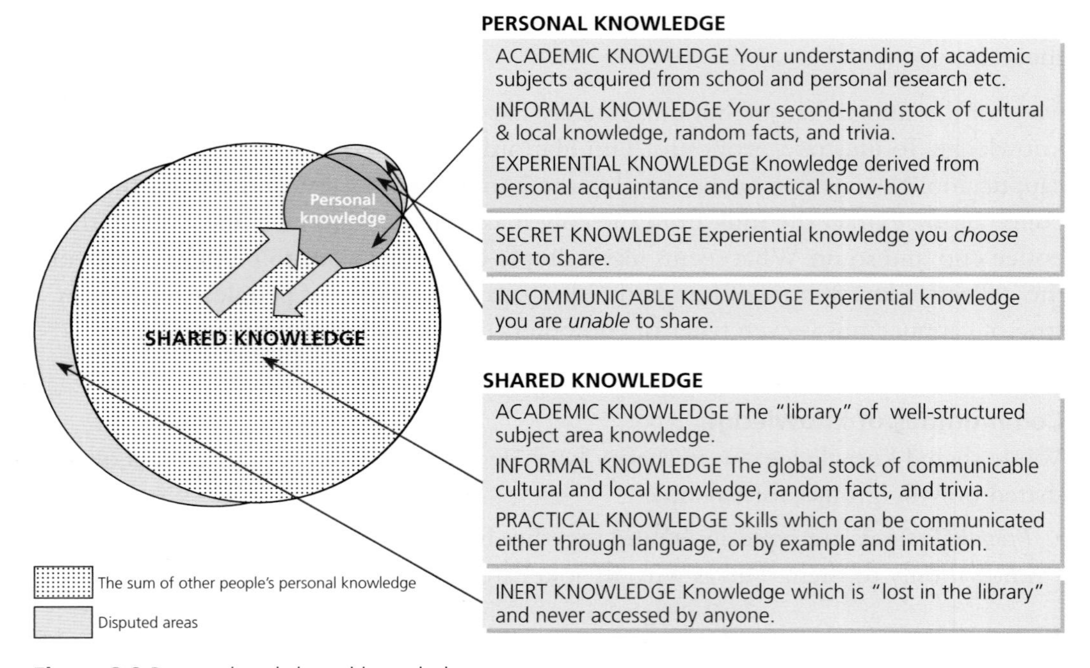

Figure 3.2 Personal and shared knowledge

the amount of 'inert knowledge' is likely to increase rapidly in the future. Most of the personal knowledge circle intersects the shared knowledge circle. This is because most of it either comes from or is shared with the community. (We get far more knowledge from the community than we give to it.) How much personal knowledge people keep secret is by its nature hard to know, but our obsession with texting, tweeting and blogging (as well as talking) suggests that we like to 'share' even the most trivial details of our lives. Since people disagree about whether there can be personal knowledge we are *unable* to communicate, this is again shown in pink.

ACTIVITY 3.4

1. What would your estimate be of the relative sizes of the five different parts of Figure 3.2?
2. To what extent does a photo-sharing and networking service such as Instagram enable us to bypass language and share our experiences directly with other people?
3. If someone told you they had discovered the meaning of life but it lies beyond language, what, if anything, would convince you that they *really knew* the meaning of life?
4. If a deadly virus wiped out the human race, but left all of the libraries – both physical and digital – intact, in what sense, if any, would knowledge still exist?

Personal knowledge

We looked at two important components of personal knowledge in Chapter 2 – knowledge by acquaintance and practical knowledge. The majority of personal knowledge is, however, derived second-hand from other sources. While the value of such knowledge might seem obvious, some people argue that in the internet age we no longer need to pack our minds with trivial facts and figures. All that matters is knowing where to find information when we need it. Such *know-where* is clearly useful, and it makes sense to outsource trivial information to our gadgets and free up mental space for more important tasks. Nevertheless, this does not mean that we no longer need our own store of mental knowledge. On the contrary, background knowledge plays a key role in critical thinking. If, for example, you know nothing about Nazi Germany and you stumble on a *holocaust denial* site, you may end up being taken in by it. To the ignorant mind, nothing is surprising and all knowledge claims – no matter how outlandish or bizarre – will seem equally plausible.

"That's the guy I hired to read Proust for me."

Figure 3.3

ACTIVITY 3.5

1. Do you agree or disagree with the claim that in the internet age what matters is not so much knowing the answers as knowing where to find the answers?
2. Which of the following do you think an educated person should know without having to use the internet?
   a. The periodic table
   b. Key dates in history
   c. Mental arithmetic
   d. Correct spelling
   e. Capital cities
   f. Common fallacies
   g. Newtonian physics
   h. Great literature
3. Despite the growth of knowledge, what evidence, if any, is there that the average person is less gullible and superstitious than their ancestors were five hundred years ago?
4. 'Even if we could be learned with other men's learning, at least wise we cannot be except by our own wisdom' (Montaigne, 1533–92). What do you think Montaigne meant by this? Do you agree?

KT – illusion of explanatory depth: the illusion that you understand something in detail when in fact you do not

Some obstacles to personal knowledge

If we want to be effective critical thinkers, it is important that we are well informed. However, we can all too easily confuse our own opinions and beliefs with genuine knowledge, and a mixture of ignorance, apathy, fantasy, bias and peer pressure can distort our picture of reality.

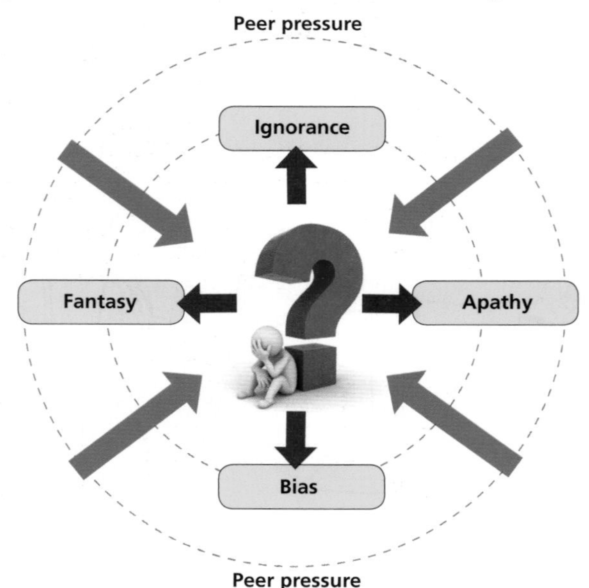

Figure 3.4 Peer pressure

Ignorance

Given the vast amount of knowledge in the world, we are inevitably ignorant of many things. The real danger, however, is not so much our ignorance as *our ignorance of our ignorance*. This can lead to overconfidence and the belief that we know more than we do. Such overconfidence is widespread. When people are asked trivia questions such as 'Is Rome north or south of New York' they are often certain that they know the correct answer when in fact they do not. (Rome is *north* of New York.) Similarly, you may think you know how a zipper or a bicycle works, or what causes rainbows or earthquakes; but when someone asks you to explain, you discover that your knowledge is quite superficial. You may have experienced the **illusion of explanatory depth** in the middle of an exam when you belatedly realised that you did not understand something as well as you thought!

Apathy

We may be naturally curious animals, but once we have formed an opinion about something we are reluctant to change our minds. We are attached to our beliefs partly because they are familiar, partly because they reflect our identity, and partly because we dislike the uncertainty that comes from questioning them. ('I know what I think, so please don't confuse me with the facts.') We also tend to prefer 'common-sense' falsehoods to complex, difficult-to-understand truths. While such intellectual laziness may be understandable, it means that when we are confronted with evidence that threatens our opinions we sometimes find it easier to reject – and then forget – the evidence than revise our opinions. As you may have noticed, when people lose an argument, they rarely change their minds.

Figure 3.5 How dangerous is overconfidence?

Fantasy

Our personal beliefs can also be clouded by fantasy, and it is easy for us to slip from *wanting* something to be true to *believing* it is true. Such **wishful thinking** may explain why so many people rate themselves as significantly above average when it comes to desirable traits such as rationality, open-mindedness, sociability, generosity and sense of humour. (How many people do you know that admit to being irrational, closed-minded, anti-social, mean and humourless?) It may also account for the popularity of pseudo-science and conspiracy theories which people want to believe even though there is little evidence for them.

KT – wishful thinking: convincing yourself that something is true simply because you want it to be true

ACTIVITY 3.6

1. Look at the four drawings in Figure 3.6. Which would you say is the most accurate portrayal of a real bicycle?

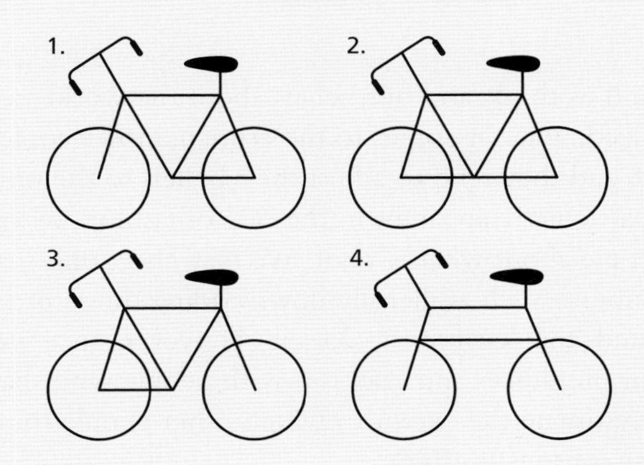

Figure 3.6

2. Do you know how the flushing mechanism on a toilet works? If so, write a short paragraph of explanation.

Figure 3.7

ACTIVITY 3.7

Which of the following beliefs would you like to be true, and which do you think are in fact true?

a. 'I am special.'
b. 'You can achieve anything with the right attitude.'
c. 'We are governed by reason rather than emotion.'
d. 'The scientific world-view can explain everything.'
e. 'My culture has made a unique contribution to world civilisation.'
f. 'History shows that progress is inevitable.'
g. 'People get what they deserve.'
h. 'There is life after death.'
i. 'Everyone's opinion is of equal value.'
j. 'Human beings are naturally good.'

Figure 3.8 Three kinds of people

Bias

Since our beliefs are influenced by such things as our character, cultural background and experience, bias is inescapable and it is impossible to achieve a 'God's eye' view of reality. Nevertheless, it is difficult to resist the feeling that our own way of looking at the world is uniquely perceptive and insightful. When we exhort other people to 'Be reasonable!' often what we really mean is 'Think like me!' (The writer Gore Vidal once impishly observed: 'There is not one human problem that could not be solved if people would simply do as I advise.') While we are quick to spot the errors and biases in other people's opinions, we tend to be blind to our own intellectual shortcomings. We will have more to say about the nature and extent of cognitive biases in Chapter 8 (page 214).

Peer pressure

We all care what those around us think, and our beliefs about the world are strongly influenced by our peers. Indeed, when it comes to the crunch, most people would rather be liked than be right, and they tend to adjust their beliefs to the norms of those around them. This is particularly apparent in the case of fashion, where we take our cues from other people about what is 'cool'. We may also think that various forms of questionable behaviour – such as illegally downloading music or tax evasion – are acceptable on the grounds that 'everybody does it'. However, since we tend to read things that reflect our prejudices and associate with people who share our attitudes, we sometimes overestimate the extent to which other people think as we do. This is known as the **false consensus effect.**

KT – false consensus effect: the tendency to overestimate the extent to which other people agree with your point of view

Towards objectivity

If we seek a more objective picture of reality, one of the best antidotes to the obstacles outlined above is to subject our opinions to the critical scrutiny of other people. Without such an external check, personal knowledge can easily degenerate

Figure 3.9 To what extent are our beliefs influenced by peer pressure?

into private fantasy. More often than not, those who work in complete isolation from their peers end up not with the dazzling insights of the genius but with the crazy convictions of the crank. As has often been observed, even smart people can end up believing dumb things. This is because, like skilful lawyers, they are good at defending bad cases and are able to convince themselves that what they want to believe is true. Somewhat ironically, Sir Arthur Conan Doyle, creator of the highly uber-rational detective Sherlock Holmes, was himself taken in by a hoax which convinced him of the existence of fairies.

ACTIVITY 3.8

1. The motto of the Royal Society is 'On the word of no one'. How good is this advice? What problems are there with it?
2. 'Art is I; Science is We' (Claude Bernard, 1813–78). Does personal knowledge play a greater role in some areas of knowledge than in others?
3. Does personal knowledge and understanding develop with age and experience, or can it equally well degenerate?
4. How do attitudes to the elderly in modern societies differ from attitudes to the elderly in indigenous groups?

Shared knowledge

The vast majority of our knowledge is shared knowledge. Such knowledge is closely connected with language, which makes possible a *division of intellectual labour.* If Smith goes north and Jones goes south, and Bloggs goes east and Brown goes west, and they then share what they have learnt, they will do much better than if they each try to discover everything for themselves. Language also enables us to pass on beliefs and practices from one generation to the next in the form of **culture**. So rather than constantly reinventing the wheel, we can make progress by building

KT – culture: a 'map' of beliefs and practices through which a group of people try to make sense of reality on the accumulated achievements of past generations. The scientist Isaac Newton (1642–1727) once remarked: 'If I have seen further it is by standing on the shoulders of giants.' His point was that he was able to make his discoveries only because he was building on the contributions of other brilliant minds.

Since Newton's time, knowledge has grown at an extraordinary rate; but whether or not this will continue remains an open question. Some people worry that all of the 'easy discoveries' have already been made and that in the future it will be increasingly difficult to push back the frontiers of knowledge. Others think that the sheer number of people engaged in research, together with rapid advances in computer technology, will lead to a cognitive golden age.

A great deal of academic research is now conducted by teams rather than by individuals working alone. When people work together, they can discuss, check, and critique one another's ideas, and creative new approaches and solutions may arise as a result of such cross-fertilisation. There is, of course, a danger that the ideas of a particularly creative individual will be snuffed out by an unimaginative group, but in general it seems that the pros outweigh the cons. The benefits of teamwork are particularly apparent in the sciences. If we judge the importance of a scientific paper by the number of times it is cited by other scientists, it turns out that papers which are cited at least a hundred times are six times more likely to be written by teams than by individual scientists.

ACTIVITY 3.9

1. 'Conversation doesn't shuffle the cards – it creates new cards' (Theodore Zeldin, 1933–). To what extent do you find that discussing your ideas with friends helps you to come up with new ideas?
2. According to a well-known saying, 'The many are smarter than the few.' Are there any circumstances in which they are dumber than the few?

Since it comes to us 'second-hand' from other people, most knowledge must be taken on trust – for we have neither the time nor the ability to check up on other people's research. So the question 'What should I believe?' often comes down to the question, 'Who should I trust?' Trust operates as a default setting in the sense that we tend to trust people unless we have reason to believe they are wrong. If you stop a stranger and ask for directions you usually assume that they are not *trying* to deceive you. You can, of course, be *too* trusting, and put your faith in someone who is misinformed or malicious. But you would not get very far if you were universally suspicious and refused to trust anyone.

Some dangers with shared knowledge

Although it is immensely important, shared knowledge cannot always be taken on trust and it is as liable to distortion as personal knowledge. We will consider four related dangers below.

Authority worship

Despite the obvious advantages of trusting other people and accepting knowledge 'second-hand' from them, we must be careful not to fall into **authority worship** and blindly accept what we are told without thinking about it. For hundreds of years people believed that the earth was the centre of the universe, that everything was made up of four elements – fire, water, earth and air, that maggots spontaneously generated out of rotting meat, that women were inferior to men, and that some people were natural slaves. But they were wrong. While it would be nice to think that we are moving closer to the truth, perhaps every generation has its own 'conventional wisdom' of unquestioned assumptions and false beliefs. Given this, it could be argued that we have an intellectual duty not only to respect what we are taught but also to question it. After all, the mere longevity of a belief is no guarantee of its truth; and if we are unwilling to question what we inherit from the past, we will be unable to augment what we bequeath to the future.

KT – authority worship: uncritically accepting something as true simply because an authority says it is true

The key thing to keep in mind here is that, since authority is not an original source of knowledge, nothing should be accepted as true just because someone says so. In the end, claims based on authority must be validated in terms of something more fundamental, such as evidence and argument. For example, you may claim to know that Napoleon was defeated at the battle of Waterloo on 18 June 1815 because you read it in a textbook; and the writer of the textbook may claim to know it because he read it in some other book; but sooner or later this chain of authority-based claims must terminate in the account of one or more eye-witnesses who were actually at Waterloo on that fateful day. Moreover, the evidence for the claim must be verifiable – at least by the relevant experts. For example, mathematicians must be able to check proofs, scientists must be able to repeat experiments, and historians must be able to authenticate primary sources. In practice we still have to take a great deal on trust; but in theory at least we could verify things for ourselves if we made the time or acquired the relevant expertise.

ACTIVITY 3.10

1. When, if ever, would you be willing to trust the authority of other people rather than the evidence of your own senses?
2. Have you ever done a science experiment and got a result that differed from the textbook? If so, which did you trust – your own result, or the textbook? Why?
3. What 'sacred cows' – i.e. beliefs you are not supposed to question – exist in your society? Should we be willing to question everything, or are some things 'beyond question'?

LQ – Faith: Are we obliged to take the opinions of experts on faith?

Groupthink

Groupthink is a form of peer pressure which leads everyone in a group to think in the same way. It is widespread in politics and business where leaders are inclined to surround themselves with 'yes-people' who follow the 'party line', but it can also be found in science and other areas of academic life. When you look at the history of

Figure 3.10

ideas, you can find many examples of scientific breakthroughs which were initially ridiculed by the scientific community because they rejected the prevailing consensus. Recent examples include the Israeli chemist Dan Shechtman (1941–) who discovered 'quasi-crystals', and the Australian physician Barry Marshall (1951–) who showed that stomach ulcers are caused by bacteria rather than by stress or diet. Both men initially encountered strong resistance to their ideas. Shechtman's work was dismissed by the eminent US chemist Linus Pauling (1901–94) with the words 'There is no such thing as quasi-crystals, only quasi-scientists.' Meanwhile, Marshall resorted to deliberately infecting himself by drinking a petri dish of pathogens in order to prove his point! Both Shechtman and Marshall went on to be awarded the Nobel Prize in their respective fields.

KT – vested interest: an ulterior motive, acknowledged or unacknowledged, for claiming that something is true or false

Power distortions

Governments and corporations sometimes have a **vested interest** in influencing our beliefs and values. A government may 'massage' data about the state of the economy, or a pharmaceutical company may exaggerate the health benefits of a particular drug. Since knowledge can easily be distorted by power, this is another reason for questioning authority. Power can not only distort the content of knowledge but also influence the direction of academic research and the kind of information people are exposed to. For example, a great deal of scientific research is connected with military interests; and governments around the world often decide what students are taught in history. At the limit, repressive regimes may resort to tight censorship and systematic indoctrination to ensure that people know only what they want them to know.

Figure 3.11 Julian Assange

RLS – Headline: 'Julian Assange Defends Leaking Government Secrets'. How can knowledge be abused by those in power?

ACTIVITY 3.11

1. How might powerful interest groups try to influence and distort people's beliefs about the following:
   a. The threat of terrorism
   b. Gender roles
   c. Income distribution
   d. The theory of evolution
   e. Global warming
2. Do you think that modern technology is making it easier or more difficult for the rich and powerful to influence ordinary people's beliefs?

Fragmentation

While intellectual specialisation has doubtless helped to promote the growth of knowledge, it has also led to fragmentation. Today, even the most conscientious of professional mathematicians, scientists or historians struggles to keep up with the deluge of new articles and developments in their own narrow field of expertise. The result is that depth is increasingly bought at the expense of breadth. Already in the nineteenth century, the Russian novelist Fyodor Dostoevsky was complaining about the scholars 'who have only analysed the parts and overlooked the whole'. We may worry about a situation in which each individual holds one tiny piece of the jigsaw, but no one is able to see the whole picture. Given this, one might argue that a genuinely educated person should have not only a depth of specialist knowledge but also a breadth of general understanding. Ideally, we should have a sense of what it means to think like a statistician, and a scientist, and a historian, and a literary critic and moral philosopher. Such an ideal may be unattainable, but we can perhaps move closer to it.

Summary

We have seen that there are pros and cons with shared knowledge as there are with personal knowledge. We might think of the relation between the two in terms of a *dialogue*. As individuals, our job is not only to acquire the shared knowledge of the community, but also to question and critique it. For it is only by daring to question things that we can push back the frontiers of knowledge. At the same time, our personal claims to knowledge cannot be accepted at face value and must be open to the critical scrutiny of the community.

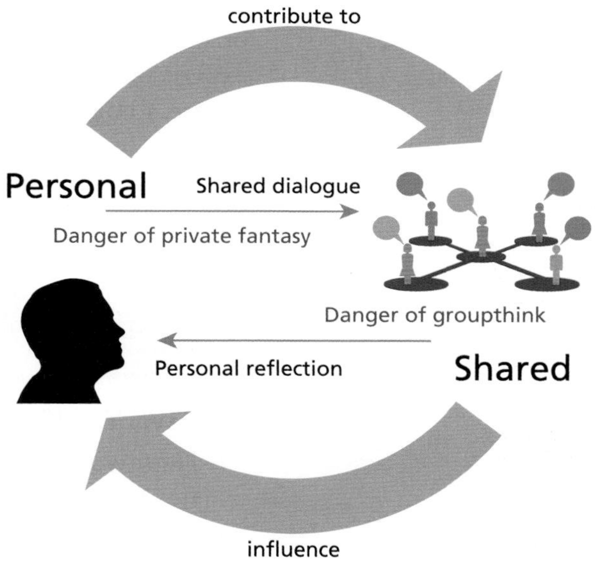

Figure 3.12 Dialogue and reflection

In the rest of this chapter, we focus on five key sources of shared knowledge:

- the internet
- cultural tradition
- school
- expert opinion
- the news media.

While each of these can be a valuable source of knowledge, they are not infallible, and we need to be aware of their limitations.

The internet

Within the space of twenty years, the internet has become by far the most important channel for the delivery of shared knowledge. Among its key advantages, compared with books, are its size, speed and accessibility. As mobile devices become more widely used, we are moving towards a world in which we will be able to access anything, anywhere, any time. Moreover, it has never been easier for individuals to share ideas by setting up websites and blogs, posting academic papers, and contributing to online discussion forums. Far from being a neutral means of delivery, some people claim that the internet is changing our conception of knowledge from a changeless, disconnected, conformist one to a more fluid, hyperlinked, pluralistic one. Knowledge, we might say, is not so much an *individual product* as an *interactive process*. We might even compare the internet to a global brain in which each individual represents a single neuron. If the aliens ever make contact perhaps they will see us as a single organism rather than a world of eight billion individuals!

Some possible drawbacks

Despite the many advantages of the internet, we should also be aware of its alleged drawbacks, which are said to include lack of quality control, superficiality and filter bubbles.

Lack of quality control

The upside of the internet is that it is democratic – anyone can say what they like – but the downside is that there is no quality control. Far from being an electronic oracle infallibly dispensing wisdom, it contains the views not only of credentialed experts but also of uninformed idiots – and everything in between. There is, of course, a huge amount of useful, accurate and trustworthy information online, but it is not always easy to find. Search engines like Google may help, but it is important to keep in mind that page rankings are determined by popularity rather than truth. Since conspiracy theories surrounding events such as 9/11 are popular, they are likely to appear high on such rankings, but this does not mean they are true. So if we are to avoid being misled, we need not only the ability to locate information, but also the critical thinking skills to evaluate it.

ACTIVITY 3.12

1. Find two articles from the internet: one that you believe and one that you do not believe. Give your reasons.
2. What criteria would you use for distinguishing generally trustworthy websites from generally untrustworthy ones?
3. Do some research to determine which of the following commonly held beliefs is true:
   a. The dinosaurs became extinct because they were slow-moving and stupid.
   b. The Inuit have hundreds of different words for snow.
   c. American astronauts conducted sex experiments while orbiting the earth in the space shuttle in 1996.
   d. Waterproof sun-screen can cause blindness in children.
   e. Human beings are the only animals that kill their own kind.
   f. Christopher Columbus' contemporaries believed that the earth was flat.
4. What evidence, if any, is there that the average person in your country is generally better informed than they were fifty years ago?

Superficiality

Some people worry that the internet is 'making us dumb' and promoting a superficial approach to learning and understanding. The claim is that in a world of online distractions – which are available at the click of a mouse or the swipe of a screen – we find it increasingly difficult to concentrate on one particular thing for any length of time. Instead we resort to **multi-tasking**, or flit restlessly from one thing to the next. Since we are always in a rush, we demand knowledge in simple, easy-to-digest chunks. The problem is that you cannot reduce a complex argument to a series of tweets, or capture the nuances of a real-life situation in a soundbite. Scanning chunks of information online is no substitute for the immersive reading and deep processing that is required for genuine understanding; and cutting and pasting chunks of text is no substitute for expressing things in your own words – which is a good way of finding out if you really understand something.

KT – multi-tasking: trying to perform more than one task at the same time

While there may be an element of truth in the above concerns, it is worth noting that we do not need electronic devices in order to to be distracted, or a cut-and-paste function to copy information. In the days before the internet, students could easily daydream their way through several pages of a textbook without taking in a word and then mindlessly copy chunks of it in their notes! Perhaps all that is required to improve concentration is a little self-discipline? One obvious way to avoid electronic distractions is occasionally to work offline. However, given the addictive nature of the internet, this might be easier said than done.

ACTIVITY 3.13

1. On average, how long do you spend on a particular task without any kind of interruption?
2. What evidence, if any, is there that multi-tasking works – in the sense of being more efficient than doing one thing at a time?
3. Working with a partner, time each other on the following three exercises. (The aim is to complete each task as quickly as possible.)
   a. Recite the alphabet from A to J.
   b. Recite the numbers from 1 to 10.
   c. Recite letters followed by numbers from A, 1 to J, 10.

   How long did each task take? What light does this throw on question 2 above?
4. According to the American internet analyst Clay Shirky, there is no such thing as *information overload* – only *filter failure*. What do you think he meant by this? Do you agree?
5. 'If you want to think seriously about something, you need to disconnect from the internet.' Do you agree or disagree with this claim?

LQ – Cultural perspectives: Is the internet reducing cultural diversity?

"One question: If this is the Information Age, how come nobody knows anything?"

Figure 3.13

Filter bubbles

Despite the huge variety of opinions that can be found online, some critics worry that the internet is not broadening our horizons but making us more narrow-minded. Since we like to have our opinions confirmed, the fear is that, once we are in the grip of a particular way of thinking, we will only visit websites and blogs that reflect rather than question our prejudices. We then end up in a 'filter bubble' of auto-propaganda and illusory consensus. If, for example, you believe that adopting the 'paleo diet' of our hunter-gatherer ancestors is the road to health and happiness you can spend your time with the online paleo crowd. If you believe that Barack Obama was born in Kenya rather than Hawaii you can avoid inconvenient facts by only reading the blogs of true-believing 'birthers'. Most ominously of all, if you advocate political violence of any description, you can hook up with like-minded extremists and find a ready-made support structure for your views.

KT – filter bubble: a situation in which we surround ourselves with information that confirms our pre-existing prejudices

While the above dangers cannot be ignored, it is worth keeping in mind that, for most of human history, people were trapped in the *de facto* **filter bubble** of their own culture and were exposed to an incredibly narrow range of ideas and opinions. Now, they have unprecedented access to the views of people from different cultures, social classes and political groups. While some people find this disorienting and retreat into filter bubbles, others find it liberating and welcome the opportunity to be challenged by new ways of thinking.

ACTIVITY 3.14

1. Do you think the 'free market in ideas' found on the internet will take us closer to the truth or further away from it?
2. Since it is such an important source of information, should internet access be classified as a basic human right?
3. Under what circumstances, if any, are governments justified in censoring websites?

Cultural tradition

A culture can be thought of as a map through which a group of human beings try to make sense of the world, and it consists of the beliefs and practices that are passed on from one generation to another. The culture you grow up in has a strong influence on the way you see the world. You may be familiar with the saying 'Familiarity breeds contempt', but research suggests that the opposite is true: *familiarity breeds fondness*. We have a natural attachment to our own beliefs and practices and they help to determine what we consider to be 'normal' or 'reasonable'. To see the power of traditional ways of thinking, you only have to look at the clock face in Figure 3.14. While it might seem more rational to divide a day into ten equal hours, most people would not want to decimalise time – simply because they are used to dividing a day into two 12-hour periods, and it therefore feels right.

Figure 3.14 Ten-hour clock

Since a culture embodies 'the inherited wisdom of the community', we should approach different traditions with respect, and be open to the fact that we may have something to learn from them. Cultural diversity reminds us that there are many ways of being human and many different perspectives on reality. Some people fear that the internet is eroding this diversity and leading to a more homogenised 'world culture' in which we will all end up watching the same movies, listening to the same music and reading the same books. This fear may be exaggerated, but it is understandable. We should, however, distinguish between diversity *across* cultures and diversity *within* cultures. For it could be argued that, while cultures are becoming more alike, we now have greater choice within cultures and it is easier to escape the 'tyranny of place' and the straitjacket of a single way of looking at things.

We should also keep in mind that *living* traditions change and develop over time and that we do not have to be imprisoned by our cultural inheritance. Cultures are not museum pieces, and, as we discussed earlier, the longevity of a belief is no guarantee of its truth. A person living in Britain in the nineteenth century might have argued that it was a long British tradition, sanctified by time, to exclude women from political power. Fortunately, some people were willing to question this inherited belief. If we are to make progress in any area of knowledge, we need to find the right balance between respecting traditional ways of thinking and being willing to question them. We will explore the concept of culture further when we look at cultural perspectives on knowledge in Chapter 19.

ACTIVITY 3.15

1. 'Cultures are not distinct but overlapping, and it is impossible to say where one culture ends and another culture begins.' Discuss.
2. How would you characterise your own cultural identity? Can you belong to more than one culture?

3. Which of the following is natural and which is simply a matter of tradition or convention?
   a. A seven-day week
   b. A 365-day year
   c. A base 10 number system
   d. The value of pi
   e. Reading from left to right
   f. Wearing clothes
4. Which of the following statements do you think are true only in certain cultures, and which do you think are or should be true in all cultures?
   a. When you are introduced to someone you should kiss them on both cheeks.
   b. When your boss is talking to you, you should look him or her straight in the eye.
   c. It is rude to ask an adult you hardly know how old they are.
   d. It is acceptable for women to sunbathe topless at holiday resorts.
   e. It is fine to arrive at an appointment ten or fifteen minutes late.
   f. If you belch after a good meal, it is a sign of appreciation.
   g. You should be allowed to carry a concealed weapon, such as a gun, for protection.
   h. When a woman gets married she should adopt her husband's surname.
   i. There is nothing wrong with parents smacking their children when they behave badly.
   j. It is OK to live with someone before marrying them.
5. On balance, do you think that the internet is making cultures more similar to each other or more diverse?

LQ – Reason: To what extent are our ideas about what is 'reasonable' shaped by our education?

KT – literary canon: a list of literary works considered by experts to have the greatest literary and cultural value

School

Since the introduction of universal education, schools have played a key role in the transmission of knowledge from one generation to the next. The roughly 14,000 hours you spend at school are supposed not only to give you mastery of various subjects, but also to prepare you for life. Since it is impossible to teach literally *everything*, any school curriculum will inevitably be selective and cover only a limited number of topics. This raises questions not only about how we should decide what to include in the curriculum, but also about the difference between education and indoctrination. In many countries governments determine what is taught and they are sometimes more influenced by political considerations than academic ones.

The danger of bias is most apparent in the humanities where arguments rage about nationalist distortions of history, which authors to include in the **literary canon**, and

Figure 3.15 What is the difference between education and indoctrination?

the place of religion – if any – in the curriculum. But there are equally fierce debates about how science should be taught. Allegedly contentious issues include:

- whether or not the 'theory of **intelligent design**' should be taught alongside the theory of evolution
- whether or not environmental science students are being brainwashed with a hidden 'green agenda'
- and whether or not science in general is indoctrinating students with a materialist world-view.

KT – intelligent design: a view held by some people which rejects the theory of evolution and claims that each species was uniquely created by God

KT – spurious balance: giving equal weight to both sides of an alleged controversy when the evidence strongly suggests that one side is wrong

The difference between education and indoctrination may concern not so much *what* is taught as the *way* it is taught. According to this view, schools should not shy away from controversial issues, but teach them in a balanced way which shows both sides and allows students to make up their own minds. This sounds reasonable, but it can sometimes result in **spurious balance**. Some people still believe the earth is flat, but no one would argue that to ensure 'balance' you should look at the 'flat earth theory' alongside the standard 'round earth' view. Similarly, if you are studying the Holocaust in history class, you would not expect equal time to be given to the Holocaust denial position which – against all the evidence – denies that it ever happened. As these examples show, the fact that some people disagree with a mainstream view does not make a controversy a genuine one. How, then, can we distinguish real controversies, which are worth studying, from spurious ones which are not? In the end, we can only look at the consensus among experts and go with their judgement.

"If nothing else, school has prepared me for a lifetime of backpacking."

Figure 3.16

ACTIVITY 3.16

1. 'In most countries certain ideas are recognised as correct and others as dangerous. Teachers whose opinions are not correct are expected to keep silent about them' (Bertrand Russell, 1872–1970). What opinions, if any, are teachers in your country expected to keep silent about?
2. What qualities would you look for if you were appointing a new teacher to your school? How much would these qualities vary according to the subject to be taught?
3. If you were asked to design a curriculum for students aged 14 to 18 living in a colony on the moon, what would you include in the curriculum and why?
4. How would you rate the IB Diploma as an educational programme? In particular, to what extent do you think:
   a. it strikes the right balance between acquiring specialist knowledge and retaining academic breadth?
   b. its curriculum and teaching methods are genuinely international rather than culturally biased?
5. Some people predict that the internet will eventually make school as an institution obsolete. Do you agree or disagree? Would it matter?

RLS – Headline: 'Couple Cleared of Killing Son after Doctors Failed to Diagnose Rickets'. To what extent should we trust experts?

Expert opinion

We live in an increasingly specialised world and have to rely on expert opinion to justify many of our knowledge claims. For example, we may be willing to say that we know that the sun is 93 million miles (150 million kilometres) from the earth even though we have no idea how to prove this ourselves. But we could, if necessary, refer you to an astronomer who could support this knowledge claim with a wealth of evidence. On a practical level, we show our confidence in other people's expertise every time we get on a plane, visit a doctor or call a plumber.

Figure 3.17

The fallibility of experts

Despite the obvious value of relying on experts, we should keep in mind that they are fallible and sometimes get it wrong. For example, from 1923 until 1955 it was widely agreed by experts that human beings had twenty-four pairs of chromosomes. This was known to be 'true' because a Texan biologist called Theophilus Painter (1889–1969) had counted them under a microscope. Unfortunately, Painter miscounted and no one got round to checking his data for more than thirty years! (We in fact have twenty-three pairs of chromosomes.) To take another example, when the skulls of 'Piltdown Man' were discovered in Sussex, England, in 1912, anthropologists thought they were the 'missing link' between human beings and apes, but in 1953 chemical tests proved that the fossils were frauds.

Predicting the future

Experts are particularly unreliable when it comes to predicting the future; and there may be some truth in the wry observation that 'An expert is someone who will tell you tomorrow why what happened today is what you should have expected yesterday'! Consider the following examples:

- In 1894, the eminent American physicist Albert Michelson (1852–1931) said 'It seems probable that most of the grand underlying principles [of physical science] have been firmly established.' Eleven years later, Albert Einstein (1879–1955) burst onto the scene and changed the nature of physics forever.
- In 1933 another famous physicist, Ernest Rutherford (1871–1937), said 'Anyone who expects a source of power from the transformation of [. . .] atoms is talking moonshine.' Twelve years later atomic bombs were dropped on Hiroshima and Nagasaki.
- On the eve of the Wall Street Crash of 1929, the economist Irving Fisher (1867–1947) famously predicted that stock prices would continue to rise.
- In 1973, the population biologist Paul Ehrlich (1932–) predicted that by 1990 more than 65 million Americans would be suffering from starvation – which, ironically, turned out to be roughly the number of Americans who were obese in 1990.

Given these examples, we would be well advised to look carefully at the track records of experts and only trust those with a history of making accurate predictions.

Range of competence

We should also keep in mind that experts have a limited range of competence and there is no evidence to suggest that they have any great wisdom about things outside their own specialised area. The physicist Richard Feynman (1918–88) once said: 'I believe that a scientist looking at non-scientific problems is just as dumb as the next guy.' That is, while you might take Einstein as an authority on physics, he is not necessarily a competent guide in areas such as politics, ethics and religion. In modern celebrity-driven culture, people sometimes defer to the rich and famous and treat them as experts on all kinds of issues. However, there is no particular reason to think that rock singers or movie stars have any privileged insight into, say, how to save the planet.

ACTIVITY 3.17

1. Which of the following would you consider to be a reasonable appeal, and which an unreasonable appeal, to expert opinion? Give reasons.
   a. My maths teacher said Fermat's Last Theorem has recently been proved by someone called Andrew Wiles.
   b. *Gosh*, a popular men's magazine, quotes the pop star Jacob Johnson as saying that for good dental hygiene you should floss your teeth three times a day.
   c. The Oxford historian Trevor Pickard says that the newly discovered Hitler Diaries are genuine: but this is disputed by fellow historian Camille Tchoungui of the Sorbonne.
   d. There is broad agreement among art critics that Pablo Picasso was one of the greatest painters of the twentieth century.
   e. According to Dr Keiji Kaku, head of scientific research at Cigarettes R Us, the health hazards associated with tobacco have been greatly exaggerated.
   f. Mona Jakes, a well-known astrologer, says that Vivek and Chloe will be happy together because they have compatible star signs.
2. Advertisers sometimes appeal to the authority of science in order to sell their products. Find and analyse two such examples.
3. Name three experts – one from each of the higher-level subjects that you study – whose opinion you trust. Explain why.
4. Can we speak of expert opinion in all areas of knowledge, or only in some of them? Give reasons.

When should we trust experts?

We have seen that we are reliant on experts but we cannot simply *assume* that they are right. So we need some criteria for deciding when to trust them. Among the factors that might strengthen an expert's credibility are:

- *Credentials*: they have the relevant expertise.
- *Evidence*: they support their position with evidence and argument (some of which may be accessible to non-experts).
- *Corroboration*: their views are supported by other experts in the field.
- *Track record*: they have a good record of honesty and reliability.
- *Neutrality*: they do not have biases that might colour their opinion – such as strong political or religious beliefs, or connections with big business.

The above criteria can be helpful, but they are not foolproof. An expert's good track record is no guarantee that they will be right next time; the fact that experts agree could simply mean that they are all wrong; and neutrality may be an impossible ideal. Moreover, experts may disagree with each other on controversial issues such as climate change, how to run the economy, or whether intelligence can be inherited. Perhaps the best strategy here is to 'go with the numbers' and adopt the opinion held by the *majority* of experts. But we should keep in mind that dissenting experts who reject the consensus view sometimes turn out to be right!

ACTIVITY 3.18

The New Age thinker Deepak Chopra (1947–) claims to be an expert in 'quantum mysticism'. Given the five criteria mentioned above, to what extent would you trust his pronouncements?

Experts, amateurs and algorithms

Some people think that the 'democratisation of knowledge' made possible by the internet means that we no longer need to rely on experts and can appeal directly to the collective intelligence of amateurs. As evidence for this, they point to the online encyclopaedia Wikipedia – which is written largely by amateurs. Its science articles, in particular, are said to be remarkably accurate. However, it is important to note that Wikipedia is not in the business of content creation, but of summarising content that has been created elsewhere – usually by experts. Moreover, the much-vaunted accuracy of its articles can itself only be judged by experts (who else could we ask?). This is not to criticise Wikipedia, but to point out that there is no escape from appealing to experts. The broad spectrum of topics covered by Wikipedia is in many ways to be welcomed, and it is sometimes a good place to begin your research. It is, however, a bad place to end it.

RLS – Headline: 'Quant Trading: How Mathematicians Rule the Markets'. Are computer algorithms more reliable than human judgement?

Another threat to expert judgement arising out of the computer revolution comes from what is known as 'big data'. In many areas ranging from online shopping to medicine, to crime, to sport, it is now common for organisations to mine huge amounts of data and look for patterns from which rules can be extracted in order to make predictions. Such rules are known as **algorithms**. To give a simple example, if many online customers who bought A, B and C also bought D and you have bought A, B and C, they will probably recommend D to you. More sophisticated algorithms may help a doctor to diagnose an illness, or a parole board to predict which criminals are likely to reoffend, or the manager of a sports team to decide on the best player to buy. In many cases, such algorithms make better predictions than the experts. However, this does not mean that we can simply replace experts by computer programs. While the latter may help improve decision making, we still need experts to provide context and interpretation. Indeed, it could be argued that if we are to make any sense of big data then we also need *big judgement*.

KT – algorithm: a set of step-by-step rules found in computer programs (and elsewhere) which is designed to achieve a specific task

ACTIVITY 3.19

1. Some schools ban the use of Wikipedia as a reference source in written assignments. What are the pros and cons of this policy?
2. Choose a Wikipedia entry on a topic you consider to be controversial. How would you go about trying to assess its accuracy and objectivity?
3. What role, if any, do you think there is for literary critics in an age of automatically generated book recommendations?
4. Would you be willing to trust an algorithm over the judgement of a parole officer about whether or not a criminal is likely to reoffend? What ethical issues does this example raise?

LQ – History: 'News is the first draft of history.' What does this mean and what are the implications?

The news media

The news media play a key role in shaping our picture of the world. However, many people now regard daily print newspapers and television news bulletins at set times as a thing of the past; they consume the news online at their own convenience. Technology is also revolutionising not only the consumption but also the production of news. While professional journalists still gather a great deal of news, their work is often supplemented by user-generated content. With the rise of mobile devices, it is now possible for individuals who are present at news hot-spots to share video clips, photos, and tweets as a story unfolds. Such **citizen journalists** are said to have played a particularly important role in the 'Arab Spring' uprisings in Tunisia and Egypt in 2011.

KT – citizen journalists: ordinary people who actively gather, report and spread news via social networking websites

Despite these developments, the mainstream news media continue to be central to the production of news. Indeed, it could be argued that only organisations such as the

Figure 3.18 To what extent are the news media biased?

BBC, Al Jazeera and CNN have the resources to investigate and authenticate breaking stories, provide the relevant context and deliver the news to a mass audience. In some countries, however, news outlets are closely controlled by governments, and in others 'media moguls' – who are in the business of making money – have a disproportionate influence on public opinion. Given this, it is hardly surprising that many people treat the news with suspicion and question its objectivity. Sometimes, journalists and politicians cooperate with each other and the latter may be willing to trade access – such as interviews and inside information – for sympathetic coverage. Any journalists who refuse to 'play the game' are likely to find themselves cut out of the information loop. Meanwhile, private-sector media giants often have a vested interest in reflecting business priorities. This might explain why the price of cotton is more likely to receive media coverage than the plight of cotton workers.

ACTIVITY 3.20

1. Why might trained journalists be more accurate sources of news than citizen journalists? Why might they be less accurate?
2. Compare and contrast the way three different newspapers cover a major news story. How easy is it to distinguish between fact and opinion in order to establish the truth?

Two main types of media bias are commonly distinguished: **agenda setting**, which is concerned with the *selection* of stories; and framing, which is concerned with their *treatment*.

KT – agenda setting: the tendency of the news media to influence which stories the public consider important

Setting the agenda

When a news presenter opens a bulletin with the words 'Here is the news', the little word 'the' does a great deal of work. This is because it creates a misleading sense of objectivity. The truth, of course, is that there is no one objective view on events: the news consists of a *selection* of stories from around the world. In practice, there seem to be three common criteria for deciding what to put into a news bulletin: sensational news, bad news and national news. Each of these can be thought of as a kind of bias.

1. Sensationalism bias

KT – sensationalism bias: the news media's tendency to focus on sensational news stories to the detriment of less dramatic but equally important ones

The media have an incentive to focus on sensational stories to attract our attention. There is some truth in the adage that if a dog bites a man it isn't news, but if a man bites a dog – that's news. Focusing on the extraordinary can result in the exception being seen as the rule. For example, obsessive media coverage of terrorism can lead people to vastly exaggerate its threat. The media also focus on dramatic human-interest stories at the expense of other arguably more important news. For example, a story about attempts to rescue a child trapped down a well may be given huge coverage while the fact that an estimated 1.2 million people die of malaria every year is hardly reported. The media also crave pictures and, other things being equal, a story accompanied by dramatic video footage is more likely to attract coverage than one without images.

ACTIVITY 3.21

1. How do the news media influence people's assessment of the risk of being the victim of violent crime?
2. What are the pros and cons of the media's desire to 'put a face on a problem' when it comes to the reporting of humanitarian disasters?
3. Using specific examples, explain how media sensationalism distorts the reporting of (a) science, (b) the arts. How might such reporting be improved?

2. Bad news bias

A TV news bulletin typically contains far more bad news than good news and it usually consists of a catalogue of crimes, wars and natural disasters. This may give people an unduly pessimistic view of the state of the planet and help to create and sustain a climate of fear. In a world of eight billion people, there will always be a plentiful supply of bad news even if things are generally going well. **Bad news bias** may reflect our in-built tendency to focus on the negative rather than the positive. We remember the humiliation of failure better than the triumph of success and feel the sting of criticism more strongly than the balm of praise. There could be good evolutionary reasons for this asymmetry. If we ignore good news, we will live to fight another day; but if we ignore bad news we could be dead.

KT – bad news bias: the tendency of the news media to focus on bad news rather than good news

3. National bias

If you glance at the front pages of newspapers from around the world, you will be struck by the extent of national bias in the media. Every country views global events through the lens of its own interests. So if a plane crashes in dense fog in a distant country killing everyone on board, the coverage it gets will probably depend on how

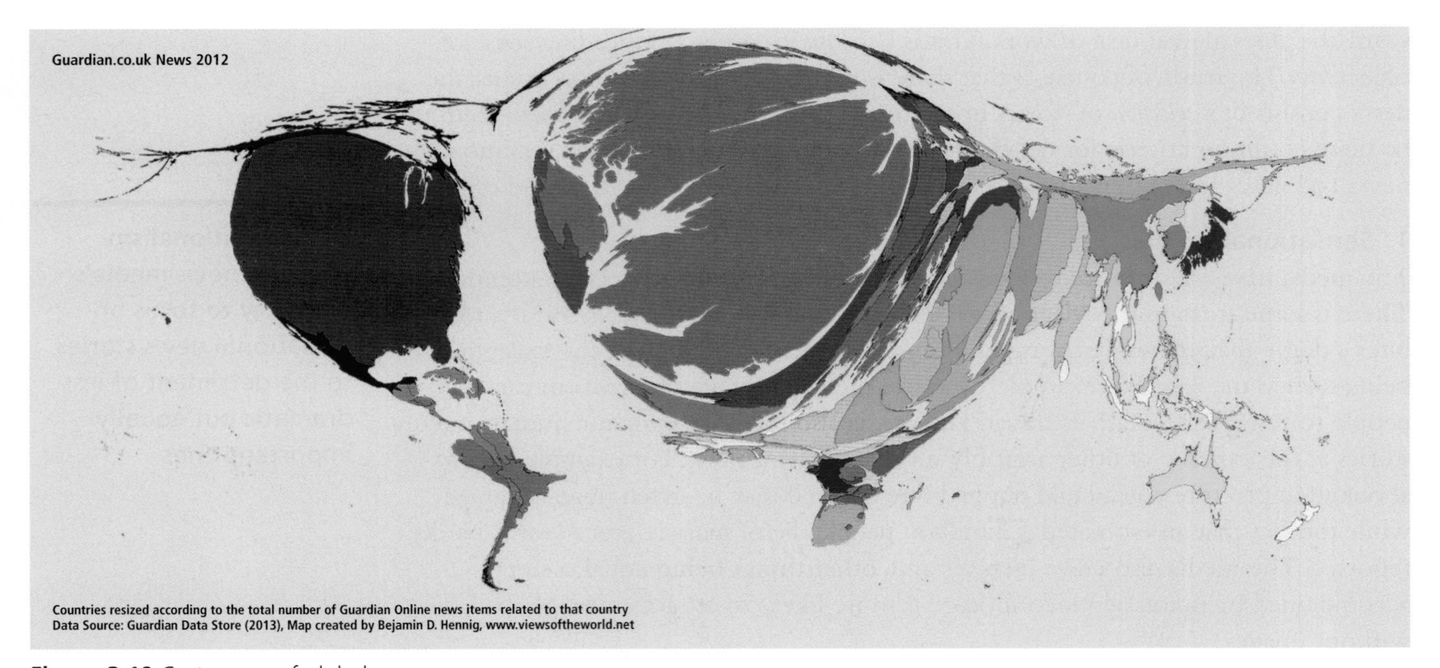

Figure 3.19 Cartogram of global news coverage

many national citizens are on the flight. The cartogram below illustrates the extent of national bias in the UK. It shows the countries of the world resized according to the coverage they were given on the website of the *Guardian* newspaper in 2012. Given such biased coverage, it is hardly surprising that many people in the world are unaware that, for example, an estimated 5.4 million people died in a civil war in the Democratic Republic of the Congo (formerly called Zaire) in the period 1998–2008.

LQ – Natural and human sciences: To what extent do the news media oversimplify and sensationalise scientific findings?

ACTIVITY 3.22

1. 'Since we are naturally most interested in our own sphere of action, it is reasonable for national news media to focus more on domestic than on foreign news.' Discuss.
2. Some foreign journalists working in the Middle East are unable to speak Arabic. How do you think this is likely to affect their reporting?
3. To what extent do you think that world news is distorted by the alleged dominance of the English-language media?

Some people argue that the rise of social media has reduced the ability of traditional news organisations to set the agenda. Readers can increasingly decide which stories matter to them, and news often spreads via Facebook, trends on Twitter and goes viral on YouTube. On some social media aggregation sites, such as Reddit, the prominence given to a particular story is determined by users, who can vote it up or down. However, the fact that the death of singer Michael Jackson in 2009 received more coverage on media websites than the 2011 Japanese tsunami – which killed an estimated 15,000 people – suggests that the popularity of a story may not be an accurate reflection of its importance.

ACTIVITY 3.23

1. Is it obvious that the Japanese tsunami was a more important story than the death of Michael Jackson? Give your reasons.
2. What criteria, if any, can be used to determine the objective importance of a news story?

Framing

While agenda-setting is concerned with the *choice* of story, **framing** is concerned with its *presentation*. As the name suggests, it consists in putting a story into some kind of framework or loose theory which makes sense to readers and influences the way they see it. For example, during a military conflict, a story might be framed in terms of patriotism – 'Support our troops!' – or peace – 'No more war!' The media are particularly interested in determining responsibility for events and may use a number of different 'blame frames'. Thus a story about prisoner abuse might be framed in terms of 'a few bad apples' among the prison guards, or in terms of systematic institutional failures. Who gets blamed will also be influenced by national bias.

KT – framing: the news media's use of pictures and language to shape the way a story is presented

Figure 3.20 Is media coverage biased?

The media critic Robert Entman once compared US media coverage of two apparently similar events: the 1983 shooting down of a Korean civilian plane by the Soviet Union, and the 1988 shooting down of an Iranian civilian plane by the USA. The former was framed as an act of aggression, the latter as a tragic accident.

As the above examples show, framing is largely a matter of how language is used to shape perceptions this will be explored further in Chapter 4 (see page104). Even small words can make a difference. While the US broadcaster CNN spoke of the 2003 conflict in the Middle East as the 'war *in* Iraq', the pan-Arab newspaper *Al Hayat* described it as the 'war *on* Iraq'. Pictures, too, play a role. A flattering or unflattering photo of someone in the media spotlight may influence the amount of sympathy we have for them. At the limit, the media sometimes cross an ethically important line and manipulate images with the intention of misleading readers.

ACTIVITY 3.24

With reference to two specific examples, show how photos can be used to support the way in which a news story is framed.

Who should you trust?

Some years ago a radio station had as its slogan, 'Don't trust anyone – not even us!' This was doubtless designed to encourage listeners to think critically about the news. While it would be naive to believe everything you hear in the media, it would be equally foolish to reject everything. If we are going to find out what is going on in the world then we have to trust someone, and this requires that we engage in the difficult task of trying to establish criteria for distinguishing between more and less reliable sources of news.

Conclusion

In this chapter you have explored the ways in which personal knowledge and shared knowledge are two important perspectives on knowledge which mutually inform one another. The vast majority of our knowledge in fact comes to us second-hand via sources such as the internet, culture, school, experts and the news media. This raises the question of whom we should trust. The following diagram, based on the well-known CARS checklist for evaluating sources, may be helpful in this context. But there is no foolproof way of determining credibility and we need to find the right balance between taking knowledge on authority and relying on our own resources. Hopefully, the dialogue between personal and shared knowledge can help us to steer a middle course between private fantasy on the one hand and mindless conformity on the other.

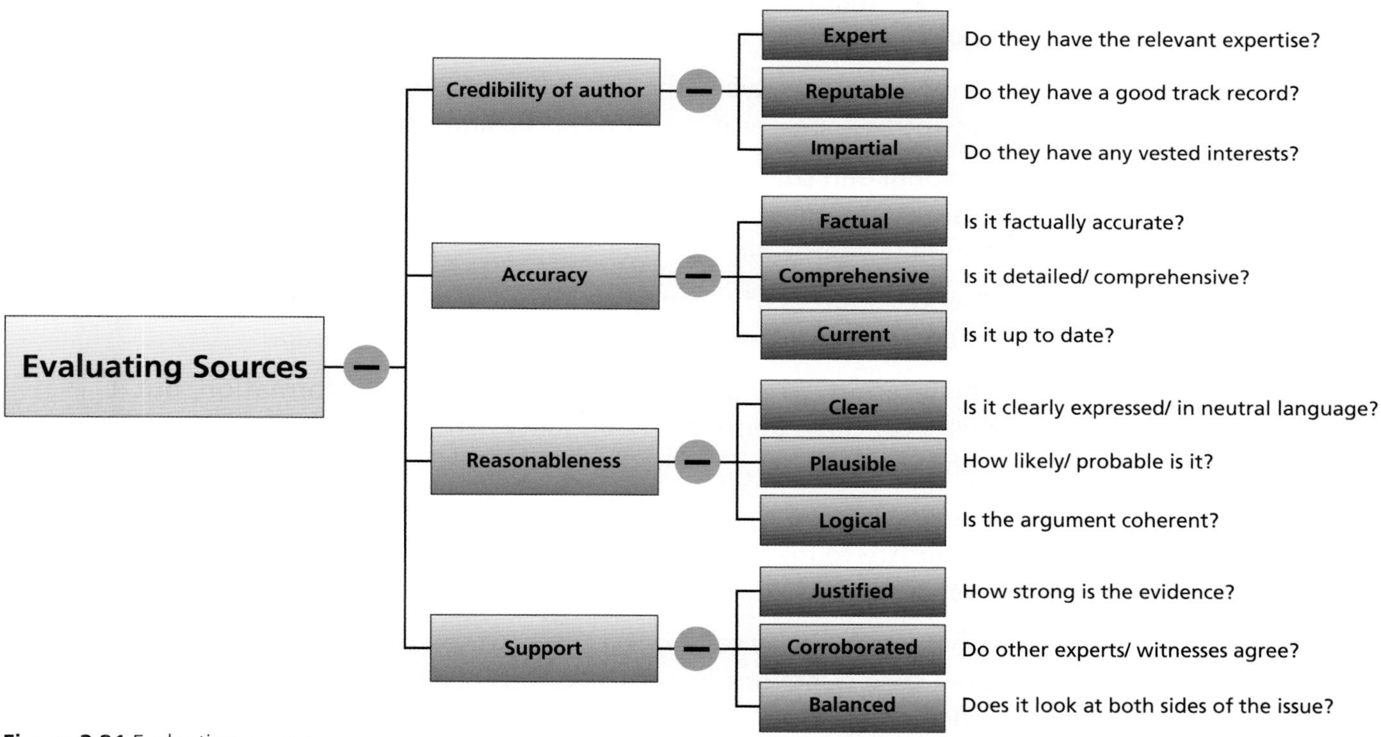

Figure 3.21 Evaluating sources

Key points

- The pursuit of knowledge is a collective enterprise, but individuals and groups help to refine, critique and develop the culture they inherit.
- Personal knowledge is acquired through personal experience (direct acquaintance and practical know-how), formal education and other second-hand sources such as the internet.
- An individual's knowledge claims can be distorted by ignorance, apathy, fantasy, bias and peer pressure.
- Shared knowledge consists of the (justified) beliefs and practices which can be communicated verbally or non-verbally to other people.
- The fact that we can share our knowledge means that we can all know vastly more than if we relied purely on our own resources.
- Among the dangers with shared knowledge are authority worship, groupthink, power distortions and fragmentation.
- Personal and shared knowledge can discipline each other and help to ensure that knowledge does not degenerate into private fantasy or mindless conformity.
- Five key sources of second-hand knowledge are the internet, cultural tradition, school, expert opinion and the news media.
- The internet gives us unprecedented access to information, but it raises concerns about lack of quality control, superficiality and filter bubbles.
- Cultures can be thought of as maps through which groups of human beings try to make sense of the world, but they change and develop over time.
- Schools play a key role in the transmission of knowledge, but they raise questions about the difference between education and indoctrination.
- In the modern age, we are increasingly reliant on expert opinion, but experts are fallible – particularly when it comes to predicting the future.
- The news media help to shape our picture of the world, but bias arises in both the *selection* and *treatment* of stories.

Key terms

agenda setting

algorithm

authority worship

bad news bias

citizen journalists

culture

false consensus effect

filter bubble

framing

illusion of explanatory depth

informal knowledge

intelligent design

literary canon

multi-tasking

personal knowledge

sensationalism bias

shared knowledge

spurious balance

vested interest

wishful thinking

IB prescribed essay titles

1. How important are the opinions of experts in the search for knowledge? (November 2010 / May 2011)
2. What sources of knowledge – books, websites, the media, personal experience, authorities or some other – do you consider most trustworthy, and why? (November 2002 / May 2003)

Further reading

Books

Michael Polanyi, *Personal Knowledge* (Routledge, 1958). A challenging and highly influential book in which the author argues that personal participation and individual judgement play a crucial role in the construction of knowledge.

David Weinberger, *Too Big to Know* (Basic Books, 2012). In this timely book Weinberger explores how the internet is changing our conception of knowledge. 'There's always been too much to know, but now we know there's too much to know, and that has consequences.'

Online articles

Cordelia Fine, 'The Vain Brain', *The Guardian*, 26 January 2006.

John Naughton, 'The Internet: Is It Changing the Way We Think?', *The Observer*, 15 August 2010.

Part 2

WAYS OF KNOWING

Introduction

The Theory of Knowledge course lists eight ways of knowing (WOKs). They are:

- language
- perception
- reason
- emotion
- memory
- intuition
- imagination
- faith.

These can be thought of as *possible sources of knowledge*. You will find a chapter in this book devoted to each WOK. This introduction makes some preliminary comments about WOKs in general.

Blurred borders

The borders between WOKs are somewhat blurred. This is partly because we cannot divide mental activity into distinct, watertight compartments; and it is partly because *all* borders – including those between *areas of knowledge* (AOKs) – are blurred. Making distinctions is extremely useful as it enables us to focus on one thing at a time, but you should keep in mind that WOKs overlap and interact with one another. Here are some examples:

a. After something has happened, *perception* blurs into *memory*, so they are both relevant to assessing, say, the reliability of eye-witness testimony.

b. *Language* infiltrates *perception*, and the way in which something is described can affect the way we see it.

c. *Emotions* can sharpen (or distort) *perception*. For example, when you are frightened you tend to notice real (or imaginary) threats.

d. We naturally think of *reason* and *emotions* as opposed to one another, but our emotions can themselves be more or less rational.

e. Your ability to tell at a glance what a friend is feeling is part of *emotional intelligence*, but it could be classified as an *intuition*.

f. We typically think of empathy as a feeling or *emotion*, but it also requires *imagination* to project yourself into someone else's situation.

g. Our most fundamental 'core *intuitions*' – for example, your intuition that you are not dreaming right now – can be thought of as matters of *faith*.

As regards Part 2 of this book, one implication of the blurred borders between WOKs is that it is sometimes arbitrary whether a particular topic is dealt with in one chapter rather than another. We do not need to get involved in sterile debates about whether, say, empathy should properly be classified under imagination or emotion – for it clearly involves elements of both.

Shared knowledge

We might naturally think of WOKs as forms of personal knowledge, but they also have a crucial shared dimension. Language, for example, only makes sense as a shared phenomenon and it enables us to acquire knowledge from other people. Reason, too, is something we share in the sense that if something is a reason it must be a reason for everyone. In the case of perception and memory, we may all have our own perspective on things but these perspectives presuppose a shared world and a shared history. Emotion, intuition, imagination and faith might seem the most personal WOKs and we sometimes find it difficult to express our deepest or most creative thoughts and feelings in words. But here, too, we should be cautious about saying we know something on their basis unless we have further, shareable evidence for our claim.

Double-edged tools

We should not take the name 'ways of knowing' too literally. In particular, it should not be taken to imply that each of the WOKs gives us unproblematic access to knowledge. In fact, any alleged *way of knowing* can just as easily be a *way of distorting things*. One of the aims of TOK is precisely to assess the pros and cons of WOKs as reliable sources of knowledge. On the one hand, communication, sensory evidence, logic, intuitive insight, access to the past, creativity, gut feelings and trust can all contribute positively to the search for truth; on the other hand, deception, illusions, fallacies, prejudice, false memories, fantasy, emotional distortion and dogmatism can all be barriers to it. Given this, you may find it helpful to think of WOKs as double-edged knowledge tools. Although they play a key role in justifying knowledge claims, their fallibility means that we will often need to test them against each other and see if they are confirmed by other people.

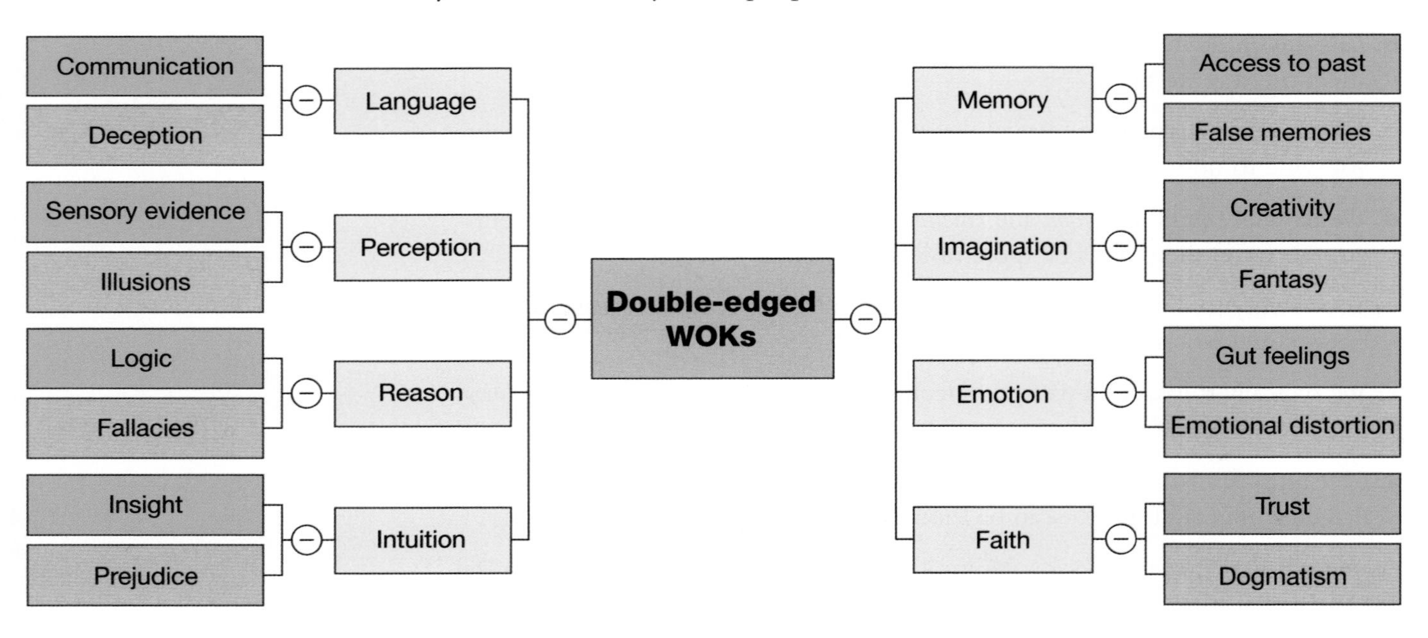

Ranking WOKs

Although there are eight ways of knowing, they are not necessarily equally important. Many people think that the two key WOKs are reason and sense perception, but opinions differ about the relative merits of all eight. For example, while some people believe that faith is a key source of knowledge, others think that it does not give us knowledge at all. The IB suggests that you study four of the eight WOKs in depth, but it also encourages you to take seriously the idea that every WOK has something to contribute to knowledge.

Schools of thought

Historically, there have been different schools of thought associated with different WOKs. You can get a sense of four key movements from the following one-sentence descriptions and quotations.

a. *Empiricism.* Empiricism claims that all knowledge is ultimately based on perceptual experience. 'No man's knowledge can go beyond his experience' (John Locke, 1632–1704).

b. *Rationalism.* Rationalism holds that reason rather than experience is the most important source of knowledge. 'Reason is an universal instrument that is... available on every occasion' (René Descartes, 1596–1650).

c. *Romanticism.* Romanticism emphasises the importance of intuitions, emotions and imagination for making sense of the world. 'Axioms in philosophy are not axioms until they are proved upon our pulses' (John Keats, 1795–1821).

d. *Fideism.* Fideism holds that knowledge is ultimately based on faith. 'It is an act of faith to assert that our thoughts have any relation to reality at all' (G. K. Chesterton, 1874–1936).

You might be interested to research the above views further online to see if you find any of them plausible.

WOKs and AOKs

Since the eight WOKs seemingly cover all sources of knowledge, it follows that the various areas of knowledge are ultimately based on them. However, it would be a mistake to think that each AOK is simply an amalgam of different WOKs; for this overlooks the fact that each one has a distinctive scope, method and history. (We will say more about this when we discuss the Knowledge Framework at the beginning of Part 3.) Nevertheless, you might still think that some WOKs are more closely connected with some AOKs than with others – for example, sense perception with science, reason with mathematics, imagination with the arts, and faith with religion. There may be an element of truth in this, but we should avoid simplistic caricatures. We should, for example, ask ourselves what role imagination and faith might have in the sciences. By thinking in this way we can gain a more sophisticated understanding of the various AOKs.

WOKs in the world

Beyond school, reflection on the nature, strengths and weaknesses of the various WOKs can help you think more critically in everyday life. Consider the following examples:

- You are trying to decide which university to attend and wonder whether you should trust your intuitions.
- A friend is describing a shared experience and you find yourself saying 'That's not how I remember it.'
- You listen to a politician making a speech and suspect that her argument is flawed.
- You misinterpret something a friend says and start thinking about the ambiguity of language.
- You are frightened of flying and you wonder whether your fear is rational or irrational.
- An eye-witness claims to have seen a UFO, but you think their senses must have deceived them.
- You attribute a fellow student's indifference to other people's feelings to their lack of imagination.
- A close friend is accused of shoplifting, but you have faith that they did not do it.

Given the points made above, it makes sense to devote a separate chapter to each WOK, but you should not think of them in isolation. Instead, you should constantly be asking yourself how the various WOKs are related to each other, to AOKs, and to everyday life.

Language

4

Speech is but a broken light upon the depth / Of the unspoken.

George Eliot, 1819–80

Man is an animal suspended in webs of significance he himself has spun.

Clifford Geertz, 1923–2006

The word is half his that speaks, and half his that hears it.

Michel de Montaigne, 1533–92

Language was given to man to disguise his thoughts.

Talleyrand, 1754–1838

Almost all education is language education.

Neil Postman, 1931–2003

Who does not know another language does not know his own.

Goethe, 1749–1832

Words are like sheepdogs herding ideas.

Daniel Dennett, 1942–

When you're learning a new language, you're not simply learning a new way of talking, you are also inadvertently learning a new way of thinking.

Lera Boroditsky, 1976–

Language is not merely a reproducing instrument for voicing ideas but rather is the shaper of ideas [. . .] We dissect nature along lines laid down by our native languages.

Benjamin Whorf, 1897–1941

Language was the real innovation in our biological evolution; everything since has just made our words travel faster or last longer.

Steven Pinker, 1954–

Philosophy is a battle against the bewitchment of our intelligence by means of language.

Ludwig Wittgenstein, 1889–1951

Introduction

Like the air we breathe, language is something that so completely surrounds us that we rarely think about it or are consciously aware of it. Yet it has a central function in human life. We use language for a variety of purposes, such as describing things, expressing our feelings, persuading people, telling jokes, writing literature and speculating about the meaning of life.

As explored in Chapter 3, language plays a key role in Theory of Knowledge because it is one of the main ways in which we acquire knowledge about the world. By communicating with one another, we are able to break out of the small circle of our own experience and tap into the collective experience of the community. The division of intellectual labour that this makes possible has been a key factor in our success as a species.

ACTIVITY 4.1

How much could you know about the world if you had no language or means of communicating with other people?

KT – communication: exchanging information by speaking, writing, or by some other (perhaps non-verbal) means

Despite its importance, language is not a perfect medium of **communication**, and it has drawbacks as well as benefits. One problem is that what one person means when they say something may not be what another person understands when they hear it. (How often have you found yourself saying to someone 'No, that's not what I meant at all'?) Furthermore, language is sometimes used to deliberately deceive and manipulate people – as, for example, in propaganda. So we cannot simply take language for granted, but must look in more detail at what it is and how it affects our knowledge of the world.

Figure 4.1 Why can't we remember anything before we learn to speak?

What is language?

Since language is a complex phenomenon, we should begin by saying more about its nature. In this section, we shall consider three key features which might be said to distinguish it from non-language.

1. Language is rule-governed.
2. Language is intended.
3. Language is creative and open-ended.

Figure 4.2 What is language?

Language is rule-governed

When you learn another language, one of the main things you have to learn is **grammar**. Grammar gives the rules for how to combine words in the correct order, and it helps to determine the meaning of a sentence. For example, if someone asks who did what to whom in the sentence 'Jill hit Jack', we can say that Jill is the active 'hitter', and Jack the passive 'hittee'. How do we know this? Well, in English there is a rule which says that the noun before the verb is the subject, and the noun after the verb is the object. There is no deep reason why the rule is the way it is, and English might easily have evolved so that the noun before the verb is the object and the noun after the verb the subject. All that really matters is that everyone agrees on the rules.

KT – grammar: the rules for constructing meaningful phrases and sentences out of words

The other main element in language – vocabulary – is also governed by arbitrary rules. For a native English speaker, it feels as if there is a natural – almost magical – connection between the word 'dog' and the animal it stands for. But there is of course no deep reason why this noise should be associated with *that* animal. It could just as well be *quan* (Chinese), *koira* (Finnish), *chien* (French), *Hund* (German), *kutta* (Hindi), *inu* (Japanese), *gae* (Korean), *sobaka* (Russian), *perro* (Spanish), or *köpek* (Turkish). For communication to work, it does not matter what noises or squiggles we correlate with objects, so long as there is general agreement within the linguistic community.

ACTIVITY 4.2

Take any familiar word of your choice, such as 'table' or 'chair', and repeat it twenty times. What happens? What does this suggest to you about the relation between words and things?

Language is intended

Although language is a form of communication, not all communication is language. To see the difference between the two, consider the following two situations.

- You are bored in class and, while the teacher is looking at their computer, you catch someone's eye across the room and make a yawning gesture by putting your hand to your mouth.
- You are trying to look interested in what someone says and to your horror find yourself starting to yawn.

KT – body language: conscious or unconscious body movements and positions that communicate our attitudes and feelings

While both of these yawns communicate information – and might loosely be called **body language** – only the first can really be described as language. This is because the first is intended and the second is not. This suggests that a key thing that distinguishes the subset of communication that is language from other forms of communication is that the former is intended while the latter are not.

ACTIVITY 4.3

1. How would you interpret the body language in the two pictures in Figure 4.3? What do you think is being communicated?
2. How easy is it to misunderstand the body language of someone from a different culture?

There are many situations in which information is communicated, but no one would describe it as language. For example, if you put a coin in a vending machine and press the button which says 'coffee white with sugar', you get coffee white with sugar. Although information has clearly been communicated, you would not say the vending machine *understood* that you wanted a cup of coffee. Vending machines – and other mechanical devices – are simply not in the business of understanding things.

Figure 4.3 Body language

Language is creative and open-ended

A final distinguishing feature of language is that the rules of grammar and vocabulary allow us to make an almost infinite number of grammatically correct sentences. We are able to create and understand sentences that have never been written or said before. For example, you have probably never seen the following sentence before, 'The wise cow seeks shelter when it snows at dusk', but you have no problem understanding what it means and conjuring up a mental picture corresponding to it. The creative resources of language are, in fact, staggering. The psychologist Steven Pinker (1954–) has calculated that there are at least 10^{20} grammatically correct English sentences up to twenty words long. (This is a huge number: if you said one sentence every five seconds, it would take you one hundred trillion, 10^{14}, years to utter them all – that's 10,000 times longer than the universe has been in existence!)

LQ – Human sciences: Is language unique to human beings?

Moreover, languages are not static entities, but change and develop over time. William Shakespeare (1564–1616) introduced many new words into the English language, such as 'dwindle', 'frugal' and 'obscene'. As well as inventing new words, languages also borrow words from one another. English is full of such borrowed words: 'algebra' is Arabic, 'Kindergarten' is German and 'chutzpah' Yiddish. Many new words continue to appear with the arrival of new technology.

ACTIVITY 4.4

1. Make up a meaningful – though not necessarily true – English sentence which to the best of your knowledge has never in the history of the universe been written before.
2. Give some examples of words that have entered the English language as a result of the technological revolution.
3. Do you think animals have language? Read the 'Dialogue on Animal Language' at the end of this chapter. Who do you think gets the better of the argument – Dolly or Guy?

One thing that comes out of our discussion is that, although we usually associate language with meaningful sounds or squiggles, it could in principle express itself in any medium. The sign language used by deaf people is a language in the full sense of the word because it has rules (grammar and vocabulary), is intended and is creative and open-ended. Indeed, if we could emit distinct sequences of smells by controlling our sweat glands, then we could develop a scent language!

Figure 4.4

The problem of meaning

Since much of our knowledge comes to us in the form of language, we need to be clear about the meanings of words if we are to understand the information that is being communicated to us.

LQ – Reason: How many arguments turn out to be about the meaning of words?

ACTIVITY 4.5

Read the following passage, attributed to Judy Lanier, which is called 'The Montillation of Traxoline', and answer the questions below.

'It is very important that you learn about traxoline. Traxoline is a new form of zionter. It is montilled in Ceristanna. The Ceristannians gristeriate large amounts of fevon and then bracter it into quasel traxoline. Traxoline may well be one of our most lukized snezlaus in the future because of our zionter lescelidge.'

1. What is traxoline?
2. Where is traxoline montilled?
3. How is traxoline quaselled?
4. Why is it important to know about traxoline?

You probably had no difficulty in answering the above questions – traxoline is a new form of zionter, it is montilled in Ceristanna, and so on. However, you have not really learned anything from this passage because you have no idea what words such as 'montillation' and 'traxoline' mean. (In fact, they don't mean anything!)

The above example shows that if you do not know what the key words in a passage mean you will not understand it. This raises the question of what it is to know the meaning of a word. Meaning is important in our search for knowledge because *you must know what a sentence means before you can decide whether it is true or false.* You can repeat parrot-fashion that traxoline is montilled in Ceristanna, but if you do not know what 'traxoline' and 'Ceristanna' refer to, you will have no idea whether the statement is true or false.

RLS – Headline: 'Last speaker of ancient language of Bo dies in India'. What knowledge, if any, is lost when a language becomes extinct?

We tend to assume that pinning down meaning is a relatively straightforward business, and that every word has a fixed meaning that is understood and accepted by everyone. While life might be easier if this were true, we could argue that there is a *problem of meaning* and that words are often ambiguous and open to a variety of interpretations.

Theories of meaning

We will briefly look at three theories of what distinguishes meaningful words from meaningless ones. The first theory says that meanings are to be found in dictionaries, the second that they are found in the world, and the third that they are found in the mind.

1 Definition theory

The most obvious way of trying to resolve confusions about what a word means is to consult a dictionary. However, coming up with a good definition of a word can be more difficult than it seems.

ACTIVITY 4.6

1. Define as precisely as you can the following three words:
   a. triangle, **b.** table, **c.** love.
2. How would you try to explain to a blind person what the word 'red' means? What does this suggest to you about the limitation of definitions?

If you tried the above exercise, you probably had no difficulty in defining a triangle. 'Three straight lines that define an area' might do it. When it comes to the word 'table', things are more difficult. Perhaps you came up with something similar to the following dictionary definition: 'a piece of furniture with a flat top and one or more legs, providing a level surface for eating, writing, working at, playing games etc.'. That seems fairly good, but it is not difficult to think of borderline cases and counter-examples. What about a flat surface that is built into an alcove and doesn't have any legs, or a flat surface that is suspended by chains from the ceiling? Where exactly does a table end and a desk begin? What if you regularly use an old tea chest as a table – does that make it a table? A good response to these questions might be: who cares? Life is too short to worry about exactly where tables end and non-tables begin!

Love is probably the most difficult of the three words in the above exercise to define. My dictionary says it is 'an intense feeling of deep affection or fondness for a person or thing' (although it also offers 'zero score in games such as tennis'). The trouble with a word such as 'love' is that it seems to have depths that cannot be neatly captured in a few well-chosen words. If Angie turns to Jake and says 'I don't think you really know the meaning of the word "love"', you are not going to solve Jake's problem by handing him a dictionary!

RLS – Headline: 'Psychiatric Group Push to Redefine Mental Illness Sparks Revolt'. Why are some things difficult to define and why does it matter?

What comes out of this discussion is that the only words that we can define in a clear and unambiguous way are mathematical ones, such as 'triangle', 'circle', 'straight line', etc. When it comes to other words, they have a fuzziness at their borders that is hard – if not impossible – to eliminate.

Criticisms

The main problem with the idea that the meaning of a word is its dictionary definition is not simply that most definitions are vague and imprecise, but, more fundamentally, that they only explain the meanings of words by using other words. If we are to avoid being trapped in an endless circle of words, language must surely connect with the world.

2 Denotation theory

According to the **denotation** theory what distinguishes a meaningful word from a meaningless one is that the former stands for something while the latter does not.

KT – denotation: the literal meaning of a word

Thus 'France' means something because it stands for the country in Europe that is north of the Pyrenees and west of the Rhine, while 'mibulous' is meaningless because there is nothing in the world that corresponds to it. Since the following lines from the opening of Lewis Carroll's (1832–98) poem 'Jabberwocky' do not refer to anything, they are considered nonsense poetry:

Twas brillig, and the slithy toves
Did gyre and gimble in the wabe:
All mimsy were the borogoves,
And the mome raths outgrabe.

Criticisms

While the denotation theory might work in the case of names such as 'France' or 'Socrates', it seems to fall down in the case of abstract words – such as 'multiplication', 'freedom' and 'wisdom' – which do not seem to stand for any *thing*. Admittedly, you may be able to point to examples of wisdom, but you cannot point to wisdom itself.

On reflection, problems arise even in the case of proper names. The meaning of a name such as 'Socrates' cannot literally be Socrates – for otherwise the word would have become meaningless when Socrates died. If we took the denotation theory literally, then people would be unable to talk about you after you were dead.

RLS – Headline: 'Child Named Hitler is Refused Cake Request'. What's in a name? Should parents have complete freedom to choose their children's names?

3 Image theory

According to the image theory, the meaning of a word is the mental image it stands for, and you know the meaning of a word when you have the appropriate concept in your mind. For example, you know what the word 'freedom' means when you associate it with the concept of freedom – being able to do what you like, not being imprisoned and so on. This view also has something to be said for it. For the difference between my speaking English and a parrot 'speaking English' is surely that, while my speech is accompanied by the appropriate mental activity, the parrot quite literally does not know what it is talking about. Rather than *speaking* English, the parrot is merely making noises that *sound* like the noises made by an English speaker.

Criticisms

The problem with the image theory is that if meanings are in the mind then we can never be sure that someone else understands the meaning of a word in the same way that we do – or, indeed, that they understand it at all. For you can never get into another person's mind and find out what is going on in it.

ACTIVITY 4.7

1. To what extent is your use of language accompanied by images? Does every word conjure up an image or only some of them?
2. How do you know that what we both call 'red' I don't experience as what you would call 'green' if you were looking out of my eyes, and what we both call 'green' I don't experience as what you would call 'red' if you were looking out of my eyes?
3. What difference, if any, would it make in real life if the above were the case?

Figure 4.5 We sometimes fail to understand what someone else is saying to us

Meaning as know-how

Rather than think of meanings as something that can be found in dictionaries, or in the world, or in the mind, perhaps it would be better to say that meaning is a matter of *know-how*, and that you know the meaning of a word when you know how to use it correctly. For example, if you can use the word 'red' appropriately when discussing such things as traffic lights, red peppers and Rudolph the red-nosed reindeer, you surely know what it means. At the same time, it is hard to resist the idea that there must be something appropriate going on in our heads when we mean and understand things.

ACTIVITY 4.8

If a robot could use and respond appropriately to language would it make sense to conclude that it could think? Give reasons.

Problematic meaning

When we consider how language is used in practice, things start to get complicated. We often use language in all kinds of non-literal ways. As the poet Robert Frost (1874–1963) observed, we rarely say exactly what we mean, for 'we like to talk in parables and in hints and in indirections – whether from diffidence or some other instinct'. In what follows, we will consider five kinds of problematic meaning that can be found in everyday language: vagueness, ambiguity, secondary meanings, metaphor and irony.

1 Vagueness

Many words, such as 'fast' and 'slow', are intrinsically vague, and their meaning depends on context. For example, 'fast' means something different to a long-distance runner than to a Formula 1 driver. And, even in a specific context, people may have quite different ideas of what a vague word implies.

ACTIVITY 4.9

1. Without thinking too much about it, write a figure down for each of the following:
   a. John lives close to his school. How near does he live?
   b. Janet is a heavy smoker. How many cigarettes does she smoke a day?
   c. Mr Smith is middle-aged. How old is he?
   d. Nafisha's mother earns a lot of money. What is her annual income?
2. Do you think that communication would be improved if we got rid of vague words, or do you think they sometimes serve a useful purpose?
3. 'It is easy to be certain – one only has to be sufficiently vague' (Charles Sanders Peirce, 1839–1914). What do you think Peirce meant by this? Give examples.

Despite their disadvantages, vague words are in fact very useful; for, although they may fail to pin things down, they can at least point us in the right direction. It is, in any case, impossible to make words completely precise. Ask yourself, for example, how little hair a man must have before you can describe him as bald? Does the loss of one particular hair change him from being non-bald to bald? The answer is, of course, that the concept is inherently vague. Some men are balder than others, but it is impossible to say exactly where non-baldness ends and baldness begins. Many other concepts are similarly vague – even ones that might appear quite precise. For example, if you say that an object is exactly 4 centimetres long, the vagueness comes in when we ask to how many decimal places you made the measurement.

2 Ambiguity

Many words and phrases are ambiguous. For example, 'The duchess cannot bear children' can mean either that the duchess is unable to have children, or that she does not like them. 'The author lives with his wife, an architect and amateur musician in Hampshire' would usually be taken to mean that the author lives with his wife *who* is an architect and amateur musician; but it could also mean that the author lives with his wife *and* an architect *and* an amateur musician.

Ford: You should prepare yourself for the jump into hyperspace; it's unpleasantly like being drunk.

Arthur: What's so unpleasant about being drunk?

Ford: Just ask a glass of water.

[From Douglas Adams, *The Hitchhiker's Guide to the Galaxy*]

While ambiguity is sometimes amusing, it can also be used to mislead people. A politician might deliberately exploit an ambiguous sentence so that it is understood in different ways by different listeners. For example, 'I am opposed to taxes which damage incentives' could be taken to mean 'I am opposed to all taxes because they damage incentives' or 'I am opposed only to those taxes which damage incentives'.

ACTIVITY 4.10

1. Each of the following sentences is ambiguous. Give two different meanings for each of them:
   a. Flying planes can be dangerous.
   b. They saw Mrs Jones and the dog sitting under the table.
   c. Bob tickled the man with a feather duster.
   d. Refuse to be put in the basket.
   e. Mia wanted to hear the pop star sing very badly.
   f. Visiting relatives can be boring.
   g. Many poor students are on scholarships.
   h. Johnny ate the bacon on the sofa.
   i. I didn't sleep with my spouse before we were married. Did you?
   j. As Imran came in to bowl I saw her duck.
2. To what extent can punctuation help to reduce the ambiguity of a sentence? Give some examples.
3. Many jokes are based on ambiguity (see the dialogue on the previous page). Give some examples and analyse them.

Context can again help us to determine the meaning of an ambiguous sentence. In (b) above the most reasonable interpretation of the sentence is 'They saw Mrs Jones and *the-dog-sitting-under-the-table*' rather than 'They saw *Mrs-Jones-and-the-dog* sitting under the table'. This is because people do not usually sit under tables with dogs.

3 Secondary meaning

Words have not only a primary meaning or denotation, but also a secondary meaning or **connotation**. The denotation of a word is what it refers to, the connotation is the web of associations that surrounds it. While the denotation of a word is public, its connotations vary from person to person. Words such as 'love', 'death', 'school' and 'priest' may have different connotations for different people. Sometimes we use **euphemisms** for harsh words because they have more acceptable connotations. For example, 'passed away' is a euphemism for 'died'. Both expressions have the same denotation, but 'passed away' brings with it associations of peace and serenity that 'died' lacks.

KT – connotation: the ideas and associations a word evokes in addition to its literal meaning

KT – euphemism: a softer-sounding word or phrase used to disguise something unpleasant

ACTIVITY 4.11

1. When Bill Clinton entered the White House in 1993, his wife Hillary Rodham Clinton wanted to be known not as the 'First Lady' but as the 'Presidential Partner'. What is the difference in connotation between 'First Lady' and 'Presidential Partner'?
2. If a married woman becomes president of the USA, what do you think would be an appropriate title for her husband?

3. Explain the different connotations of each of the following sets of words:
   a. slender, skinny, thin
   b. stubborn, steadfast, firm
   c. praise, flatter, commend
   d. energetic, spirited, frenzied
   e. stench, smell, fragrance
4. Think of as many different words or expressions for each of the following. What is the difference in their connotations?
   a. Vomit
   b. Drunk
   c. Stupid

KT – metaphor: a figure of speech which makes an implicit comparison between two things

4 Metaphor

We use language not only literally, but also metaphorically. You might say that 'Miranda has got her *head in the clouds*', or 'Marvin is a *pillar* of the community', or 'Agnes has *put her roots down* in Canada'. Despite being literally false, each of these sentences might still be metaphorically true. Miranda does not have an unusually long neck, but she may walk around in a dreamlike state; Marvin is not made of stone, but he may be an important figure in his community; Agnes has not grown roots, but she may have settled permanently in Canada.

When trying to decide whether a sentence is meant literally or metaphorically, we might get a hint from the context. Compare, for example, the following two sentences:

(1) 'My brother is a butcher.'

(2) 'My dentist is a butcher.'

Most people would interpret (1) literally and (2) metaphorically. For while your brother may well make his living as a butcher, there is probably no one who divides their professional life between dentistry and butchery.

In practice it can be difficult to determine where literal meaning ends and metaphorical meaning begins. For ordinary language is riddled with *dead metaphors*. Consider, for example, the following expressions: 'night*fall*'; '*sharp* tongue', '*brilliant* mind', 'chair *leg*', '*in* love'. All of these phrases are, strictly speaking, metaphorical, but they are so familiar that we have forgotten their metaphorical origin.

ACTIVITY 4.12

1. Explain the difference between the following two sentences. Is either of them true? If so, in what sense?
   a. 'No man is an island' (John Donne, 1572–1631)
   b. 'No man is a banana' (Richard van de Lagemaat, 1958–)
2. Take a paragraph from a newspaper or magazine, and identify as many metaphors in it as you can. Try to rewrite the piece without using any metaphors.
3. Birds fly and planes fly. Since fish swim, why don't we say that submarines also swim? What do submarines do?

5 Irony

Irony – the saying of one thing in order to mean the opposite – shows just how problematic language in action can be. Despite the oddity of using a sentence which literally means *X* in order to suggest not-*X*, irony is something that is found in all cultures. If the weather forecast predicted sunshine and it is pouring with rain outside, you might look out of the window and say 'Nice weather, heh?' Or if your friend makes a dumb suggestion, you might say 'Any more bright ideas, Einstein?' Irony means that we cannot necessarily take a statement at face value, and it adds another layer of ambiguity to language.

KT – irony: a figure of speech in which words are used to say one thing and mean the opposite

Meaning and interpretation

We could perhaps summarise our discussion of problematic meaning in three words: *language is ambiguous*. For vagueness, secondary meaning, metaphor and irony can all be seen as different kinds of ambiguity. The implication is that there is an element of *interpretation* built in to all communication. Although language is governed by rules, and you cannot make words mean anything you like, many of the rules are quite loose and there is often more than one way of interpreting a sentence. As we have seen, *context* may help you to decide what someone 'really means'. If a friend says 'It was so funny that I nearly died laughing', you do not ask if they were rushed to intensive care or chalk it up as another near-death experience. But you cannot always rely on context. If someone says 'I am so angry I could kill him', you would probably not alert the police; but perhaps this time they really mean it!

Rather than think of meaning as an all-or-nothing concept – either you understand it or you don't – it might make better sense to think in terms of levels of meaning. As we discussed in Chapter 2, a physics professor is likely to have a much clearer idea of what 'the theory of relativity' means than a non-physicist. And a forty-year-old adult is likely to have a more sophisticated understanding of what 'love' means than a six-year-old child.

ACTIVITY 4.13

What problems are there in trying to interpret the following sentences?

a. 'If John works hard, he should do himself justice in the final exam.'

b. 'It is as difficult for a rich man to enter the kingdom of heaven as it is for a camel to pass through the eye of a needle.'

c. 'After he had said this, he left her as on the previous evening.'

d. 'What's up?'

e. '$E = mc^2$'

Why should we care about the meanings of words?

We have spent some time exploring the problem of meaning, but you may wonder why we should care about it. Does it really matter if we cannot pin down the meaning of a word? In some cases, it does. For an accused person, the difference between 'murder' and 'manslaughter' may be literally a matter of life and death; and if we want a war on terrorism, we need to be clear about what we mean by 'terrorist'.

It probably comes as no surprise to you that politicians sometimes manipulate the meanings of words in order to deceive the public. If the government wants to reduce poverty in a country the most painless way of doing it is to redefine what is meant by the word 'poverty'. Unemployment too high? Simple! Just change what the word means. Want to raise taxes without anyone noticing? Try calling it 'revenue enhancement'! If we want our politicians to be genuinely accountable, it pays to keep an eye on the way they use language.

"Congratulations, Dave! I don't think I've read a more beautifully evasive and subtly misleading public statement in all my years in government."

Figure 4.6

Another group of people who exploit vague language are tricksters who claim to have psychic powers or to be able to predict the future. In the 1940s, the eminent psychologist B. R. Forer gave each of his students the following 'individualised' horoscope, and asked them to rate how well it described their character:

> *You have a strong need for other people to like you and for them to admire you. At times you are extroverted, affable, and sociable, while at other times you are introverted, wary, and reserved. You have a great deal of unused energy which you have not turned to your advantage. While you have some personality weaknesses, you are generally able to compensate for them. You prefer a certain amount of change and variety and become dissatisfied when hemmed in by restrictions and limitations. You pride yourself on being an independent thinker and do not accept other opinions without satisfactory proof. You have a tendency to be critical of yourself. Some of your aspirations tend to be pretty unrealistic.*

Almost all of Forer's students rated the description as 'good' or 'excellent'. Forer concluded that 'people tend to accept vague and general personality descriptions as uniquely applicable to themselves without realising that the same description could be applied to just about anyone'. If we are not to be taken in by tricksters and charlatans, it is worth keeping this example in mind.

Language and translation

Up until now we have been speaking about 'language' as if there were only one such thing, but there are, of course, many different languages in the world. (The most commonly quoted figure is 3,000, but they are disappearing fast.)

Each of us has a privileged relation to our own native language, and we tend unthinkingly to assume that it fits reality like a glove. According to one apocryphal story, the US senate was once debating whether the constitution should be amended to state that English is the official language of the United States. A senator who supported the amendment allegedly finished his speech with the rousing words, 'And if English was good enough for Jesus, then it's good enough for me!' Whether or not the story is true, it illustrates the dangers of unthinking linguistic chauvinism. As well as enabling you to communicate with other people, one of the benefits of learning a second language is that it gives you a perspective on your own.

ACTIVITY 4.14

1. What would be the advantages and disadvantages if everyone in the world spoke a single common language? What would be gained by this, and what would be lost?
2. 'Who does not know another language does not know his own' (Goethe, 1749–1832). What can you learn about your own language by studying a second language?
3. In what other ways does learning a second language contribute to, and expand, your knowledge of the world?

4

Language

When you learn a second language, one of the things you discover is that different languages divide the world up in different ways. If words were simply labels we stuck on objects and the only difference between languages was that they used different words to refer to these objects, then translation would be a relatively straightforward matter. But it does not work like that. If you make a word-for-word translation from one language to another, you will not get a workable translation but nonsense. That is why translation is more of an art than a science.

Problems of translation

There are three problems that arise in translating something from one language to another that are particularly worth mentioning: context, untranslatable words and **idioms**.

KT – idiom: a colloquial expression whose figurative meaning cannot be deciphered from its literal meaning

Context

The meaning of a word in a language is partly determined by its relation to other words. For example, to understand what the word 'chat' means in English, you also need to be aware of related words such as 'talk', 'gossip' and 'discuss', each of which has a different shade of meaning. When we move from one language to another, such subtle differences can easily get lost in translation.

Untranslatable words

Every language contains words that have no equivalent in other languages, and can only be translated by a lengthy and inelegant paraphrase. For example, the English word 'quaint' has no very precise equivalent in other languages. Here are some examples from other languages:

- *Schlimmbesserung* (German), 'an "improvement" that actually makes things worse'
- *Aware* (Japanese), 'the feeling engendered by ephemeral beauty'
- *Rojong* (Indonesian), 'the relationship among a group of people committed to accomplishing a task of mutual benefit'
- *Jayus* (Indonesian), a joke so unfunny that it becomes funny
- *Puijilittatuq* (Inuktitut, Canadian Arctic), 'he does not know which way to turn because of the many seals he has seen come to the ice surface'
- *Mamihlapinatapai* (Terra del Fuegan), 'to look at each other, each hoping the other will offer to do something which both parties much desire done but which neither is willing to do' (According to *The Guinness Book of Records*, this is the most succinct word in the world.)

Translation problems can even arise at a relatively simple level. For example, German and French – together with many other languages – have two forms of 'you' – *du* and *Sie*, and *tu* and *vous*. When both are translated into English as 'you', something is clearly lost.

Idioms

An idiom is a colloquial expression whose meaning cannot be worked out from the meanings of the words it contains: for example, 'I was over the moon'; 'Don't beat about the bush'; 'He was born with a silver spoon in his mouth'. Such idiomatic expressions are common – there are said to be more than 25,000 in English – and they are particularly difficult to translate from one language to another. According to one story, when the sentence 'Out of sight is out of mind' was translated into Russian, and then re-translated into English, it came back as 'invisible idiot'. And 'The spirit is willing, but the flesh is weak' came back as 'The vodka is agreeable, but the meat is inferior'.

ACTIVITY 4.15

1. Give some examples of words in your own language, or your second language, which have no precise English equivalent.
2. How would you go about trying to translate the following idioms into another language?
   a. 'David is barking up the wrong tree.'
   b. 'Tina threw a spanner in the works.'
   c. 'Samuel was only pulling your leg.'
   d. 'Daniela is resting on her laurels.'
3. Give some examples of idiomatic expressions in other languages that are difficult to translate into English.
4. What kinds of text do you think are easiest to translate from one language to another and what kinds of text do you think are most difficult to translate?

There are many amusing anecdotes about mistranslations. When Pepsi-Cola ran an advertising campaign in Taiwan, they translated the slogan 'Come Alive with Pepsi' into Chinese. The campaign was a flop. When the slogan was translated back into English, it read 'Pepsi brings your ancestors back from the dead!': understandably a failure. And the Swedish company Electrolux were no more successful when they tried to advertise their vacuum cleaners in the United States with the slogan 'Nothing sucks like an Electrolux'. Here are some other entertaining examples of mistranslations:

'The manager has personally passed all the water served here.' (Mexican hotel)

'The lift is being fixed for the next day. During that time we regret that you will be unbearable.' (Romanian hotel)

'Ladies may have a fit upstairs.' (Hong-Kong tailor shop)

'You are invited to take advantage of the chambermaid.' (Japanese hotel)

'Ladies, leave your clothes here and spend the afternoon having a good time.' (Italian laundry)

'Visitors are expected to complain at the office between the hours of 9:00 a.m. and 11:00 a.m. daily.' (Athens hotel)

'Take one of our horse-driven city tours – we guarantee no miscarriages.' (Czech tourist agency)

'We take your bags and send them in all directions.' (Danish airline ticket office)

'Ladies are requested not to have children in the bar.' (Norwegian cocktail lounge)

Lost in translation

Perhaps not surprisingly, most linguists would say that there is no such thing as a perfect translation and that something is always lost when we move from one language to another. As an Italian saying has it, *Traduttore traditore* – 'the translator is a traitor'. (Something is lost even in this translation!) So what makes one translation better than another? There are three commonly agreed criteria:

- *Faithfulness* – the translation should be faithful to the original text.
- *Comprehensibility* – the translation should be comprehensible.
- ***Back translation*** – when we retranslate a translation back into its original language, it should approximate to the original.

KT – back translation: translating something which has been translated into a target language back into the original language

To take some simple examples, consider how one might translate the following sentences:

(a) '*Guten Tag.*' (German → English)

(b) '*S'il vous plaît.*' (French → English)

(c) 'How do you do?' (English → any language)

The literal translation of '*Guten Tag*' is 'Good day', but people in Britain do not usually say 'Good day' (although it is more common in Australia). So a better translation might be 'Good morning', 'Good afternoon', or 'Hello'. Similarly, we do not translate '*S'il vous plaît*' as 'If it pleases you', but as 'Please'. Finally, 'How do you do?' would sound absurd in German and French if translated literally – how do you do what? Perhaps it is best translated as '*sehr erfreut*' and '*enchanté*'.

These examples show in microcosm the tension between going with the letter and going with the spirit of a text when you are making a translation. The more faithful you are to the letter – or literal meaning – of the text, the stranger the translation is likely to sound in the target language. The more natural the translation sounds in the target language, the more likely you are to have strayed from the literal meaning of the original text.

Poetry raises particular problems for the translator. When some of his poems were translated from Spanish into French, the Chilean poet Pablo Neruda (1904–73) commented: 'If I had been a French poet, I would not have said what I did in that poem, because the value of the words is so different. I would have written something else.' Given that Spanish and French are closely related languages, imagine how difficult it would be to translate one of Neruda's poems into Chinese!

ACTIVITY 4.16

Find a copy of Lewis Carroll's poem 'Jabberwocky' and translate it into another language. What difficulties are involved in doing this? How would you decide that one translation was better than another?

Although we should not overstate the problem of translation, it could in fact be said that there is an element of translation involved in all communication. For even when native speakers are talking together, they understand one another's words in slightly different ways. Indeed, getting to know another person could be said to be partly a matter of getting to know how they use language.

Labels and stereotypes

Our discussions about language, meaning and translation in the previous three sections have focused on the problematic nature of human communication and shown that we cannot simply take the meanings of words for granted. We will now explore the way in which language affects the way we see and think about the world. In this section, we will focus on labels and stereotypes; and we will then go on to consider how language affects the way we think and the kinds of value-judgements that we make about things.

Language consists of two main kinds of words: proper names and general words. We give proper names to such things as people, places and pets. But the vast majority of words in a language – such as 'reticent', 'rhinoceros', 'riddle', 'river' and 'run' – do not describe one unique thing, characteristic or action, but are general in nature. For this reason, we can think of language as being essentially a labelling system.

Labels

Putting labels on things has advantages and disadvantages. On the plus side, using labels is efficient and economical. If, for example, there was no general word for 'sand' and we were standing on a beach and had to give each individual grain a proper name, communication would quickly become impossible. A good label enables you to predict how the object in question will behave. For example, if you take an object from a box labelled apples, you can be confident that it will look, smell and taste like an apple, and that it will nourish rather than poison you.

ACTIVITY 4.17

What predictions can you make from the following labels?

a. Dog **b.** Tiger **c.** Teacher **d.** Bread **e.** Mushroom

On the negative side, labelling creates the danger that you mislabel things. If you treat similar things as if they were different, or different things as if they were similar, you are likely to run into trouble. Imagine, for example, that there are three glasses, A, B and C; filled with liquid; A and C are colourless, and B is red (Figure 4.7); and you are asked which liquid is the odd one out.

You might naturally say that liquid B is the odd one out. But not if you are thirsty, and liquid A is water, liquid B is water coloured with a harmless red vegetable dye, and liquid C is hydrochloric acid! This shows that if you classify things on the basis

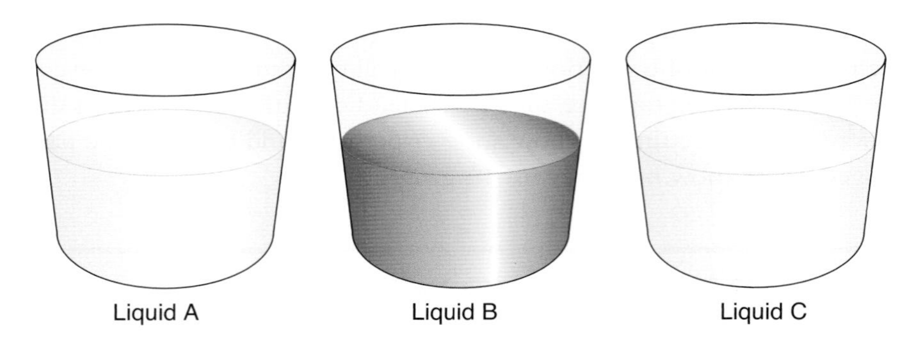

Figure 4.7

of superficial resemblance, you may overlook important underlying differences between them.

Since it is always possible to find similarities or differences between things, there are in fact many different ways of labelling or classifying a group of objects. Consider, for example, luggage at an airport: you can classify it according to shape, size, weight, colour, material, make, owner, country of origin, destination, etc. The most useful way of classifying luggage is likely to vary with context. A designer is likely to classify it in one way, a baggage handler in another way, and a traveller in a third way.

ACTIVITY 4.18

Using any system of classification that you like, divide the following eight objects into two groups, each numbering four items. How many different ways of doing this can you think of?

a. Typewriter **b.** Cake **c.** Car **d.** Hen

e. Horse **f.** Pencil **g.** Snake **h.** Paint

Since there are many different ways of classifying things, you might ask why we classify things the way we do. According to one view the labels we use reflect natural classes of things that exist 'out there'. According to another, labels are essentially social constructions that we impose on the world. While the first view says that labels are *natural* and there are objective similarities between things, the second says that labels are *cultural* and that similarity is in the eye of the beholder. Since we classify things using words, what is at issue here is the role played by language in the way we see the world. To what extent do our labels passively describe reality, and to what extent do they actively structure it?

The idea that our labels reflect the natural order of things is supported by the fact that there really do seem to be elements – such as gold and silver – and species – such as dogs and cats – out there corresponding to our categories. However, other labels – especially those used to classify human beings – might seem to be more cultural than natural.

ACTIVITY 4.19

1. What are the main advantages and disadvantages of classifying people according to their nationality?
2. What are the main advantages and disadvantages of classifying people according to their star sign?
3. What other ways of classifying people are there? Are some more natural than others? Are some better than others?

Stereotypes

One danger with putting labels on people is that our labels can easily harden into **stereotypes**. A stereotype arises when we make assumptions about a group of people purely on the basis of their membership of that group. The use of stereotypes is particularly apparent in the case of nationality. Since Giovanni is Italian, he must love wine, pasta and ice cream, throw his hands around when he talks, and enjoy opera. And since Fritz is German, he must love beer, sausages and sauerkraut, work hard, and be very serious.

KT – stereotype: a fixed, oversimplified and usually negative picture of an individual or group based on their membership of that group

Despite the dangers of stereotyping people, some generalisations contain an element of truth in them. If you visit a restaurant in Rome and one in Berlin, you will notice a difference in atmosphere and the way people typically behave. According to one witty observation, students go to international schools with prejudices about other cultures and leave realising they are all true!

What, then, distinguishes damaging stereotypes from harmless generalisations? Typically, a stereotype is a caricature which exaggerates the negative features of a group and assumes they are possessed by *all* members of the group. Furthermore, it is usually based on prejudice rather than fact and is difficult to change in the light of contrary evidence. For example, if a racist who believes that all immigrants are lazy is shown an example of a hard-working immigrant, he will probably insist that the example is not typical, and quickly forget it.

LQ – Ethics: Should offensive language be censored?

ACTIVITY 4.20

1. What stereotypes, if any, do you think exist in your culture concerning the following groups?
   a. Americans
   b. Islamic fundamentalists
   c. Feminists
   d. Environmental activists
   e. Lawyers
   f. Buddhists
   g. Scientists
   h. Computer hackers
2. What other common stereotypes exist in your culture? To what extent do you think they affect the way people see things?

3. Which of the following pairs of sentences sounds normal, and which sounds a bit strange? What does this have to do with stereotypes?
   - **a1** 'She's a mother, but she isn't a housewife.'
   - **a2** 'She's a mother, but she is a housewife.'
   - **b1** 'He's a father, but he doesn't work.'
   - **b2** 'He's a father, but he does work.'
4. In your culture, which of the following adjectives are associated more with men and which are associated more with women? How much truth do you think there is in these stereotypes?
   - **a.** Emotional
   - **b.** Reckless
   - **c.** Active
   - **d.** Aggressive
   - **e.** Sensitive
   - **f.** Tough
   - **g.** Affectionate
   - **h.** Cautious
5. Some believers in astrology say that Leos and Cancers are incompatible – that is, if you are a Leo, there is no point in dating a Cancer, and vice versa. To what extent could this be seen as the astrological equivalent of racism?

What comes out of our discussion of labels and stereotypes is that we need to be aware of the disadvantages as well as the advantages of using general words to label things. Despite their obvious value, labels can trap us into one particular way of looking at things. Moreover, as we discussed in Chapter 3, it is difficult – if not impossible – to capture the uniqueness and individuality of things in words. If you try to describe one of your friends to someone who does not know them, you will see how hard it is to paint a verbal portrait of them. It is equally difficult to capture the taste of a strawberry, or the colour of the sea, or falling in love in the butterfly net of language. Reality, it seems, always spills beyond any description that we are able to give of it.

Language and thought

In this section we will consider the extent to which language affects the way we think about the world.

The Sapir–Whorf hypothesis

KT – Sapir–Whorf hypothesis: the claim that the language you speak influences or determines the way you see the world

According to the **Sapir–Whorf hypothesis**, language determines our experience of reality, and we can see and think only what our language allows us to see and think. To give a well-known example, the Inuit are said to have many different words for snow, and their sophisticated snow vocabulary helps them to make finely grained snow discriminations. As a result, they see and experience snow-covered landscapes quite differently from the rest of us. According to Edward Sapir (1884–1939), one of the proponents of the hypothesis:

Figure 4.8 Do Inuit languages show that the Sapir–Whorf hypothesis is true?

> *The 'real world' is to a large extent unconsciously built upon the language habits of the group. No two languages are ever sufficiently similar to be considered as representing the same social reality. The worlds in which different societies live are distinct worlds, not merely the same world with different labels attached... We see and hear and otherwise experience very largely as we do because the language habits of our community predispose certain choices of interpretation.*

Benjamin Whorf (1879–1941), the other proponent of the hypothesis, studied the difference between the language of the Hopi Indians of North America and European languages, and came to the surprising conclusion that the Hopi language contains 'no words, grammatical forms, constructions or expressions that refer directly to what we call "time", or to past, present, or future, or to enduring or lasting'. Since the Hopi have no words for it, Whorf came to the conclusion that they have no concept of abstract time. In his fascinating book *The Language Instinct*, Steven Pinker gives several examples of Whorf's translations of Hopi language:

> 'He invites people to a feast' → 'He, or somebody, goes for eaters of cooked food.'
>
> 'The boat is grounded on the beach.' → 'It is on the beach, pointwise as an event of canoe motion.'

ACTIVITY 4.21

1. Could the above examples simply be bad translations? To test this idea, translate something word-for-word from a foreign language into English. Does the result sound equally bizarre?
2. If you are fluent in more than one language, to what extent do you think differently when you switch between languages?

Language

KT – linguistic determinism: the idea that our language and its structures limit and determine what and how we think

Since the Sapir–Whorf hypothesis claims that language determines the way we think, it can be described as a form of **linguistic determinism**. A well-known fictional example of this can be found in George Orwell's dystopian novel, *1984*. Orwell imagines a totalitarian government called *Ingsoc* which seeks to control not only how people behave but also what they think, by inventing a new language called Newspeak:

> *The purpose of Newspeak was not only to provide a medium of expression for the world-view and mental habits proper to devotees of Ingsoc, but to make all other modes of thought impossible. It was intended that when Newspeak had been adopted once and for all and Oldspeak forgotten, a heretical thought – that is, a thought diverging from the principles of Ingsoc – should be literally unthinkable, at least so far as thought is dependent on words. Its vocabulary was so constructed as to give exact and often very subtle expression to every meaning that a Party member could properly wish to express, while excluding all other meanings and also the possibility of arriving at them by indirect methods. This was done partly by the invention of new words but chiefly by eliminating undesirable words and by stripping such words as remained of unorthodox meanings, and so far as possible of all secondary meanings whatever. To give a single example. The word 'free' still existed in Newspeak, but it could only be used in such statements as 'This dog is free from lice' or 'This field is free from weeds'. It could not be used in its old sense of 'politically free' or 'intellectually free', since political and intellectual freedom no longer existed even as concepts, and were therefore of necessity nameless. Quite apart from the suppression of definitely heretical words, reduction of vocabulary was regarded as an end in itself, and no word that could be dispensed with was allowed to survive. Newspeak was designed not to extend but to diminish the range of thought, and this purpose was indirectly assisted by cutting the choice of words down to a minimum.*

Testing the hypothesis

Several attempts have been made to test the Sapir–Whorf hypothesis. In his book *Word Play: What Happens When People Talk* the anthropologist Peter Farb discussed an experiment which used as test subjects bilingual Japanese women who had married American servicemen and were living in the USA.

> *The women spoke English to their husbands, children, and neighbours, and in most everyday speech situations; they spoke Japanese whenever they came together to gossip, reminisce, and discuss the news from home. Each Japanese woman thus inhabited two language worlds – and according to the predictions of the hypothesis, the women should think differently in each of these worlds. The experiment consisted of two visits to each woman by a bilingual Japanese interviewer. During the first interview he chatted with them only in Japanese; during the second he carried on the same discussion and asked the same questions in English. The results were quite remarkable; they showed that the attitudes of each woman differed markedly, depending upon whether she spoke Japanese or English. Here, for example, is the way the same woman completed the same sentences at the two interviews:*
>
> *When my wishes conflict with my family's …*
>
> *… it is a time of great unhappiness. (Japanese)*
>
> *… I do what I want. (English)*

Real friends should ...

... help each other. (Japanese)

... be very frank. (English)

Clearly, major variables in the experiment had been eliminated – since the women were interviewed twice by the same person in the same location of their homes, and they discussed the same topics – with but one exception. And that sole exception was language. The drastic differences in attitudes of the women could be accounted for only by the language world each inhabited when she spoke.

Despite the above evidence, some people are not convinced by the Sapir–Whorf hypothesis. According to critics, the fact that the Inuit have many different words for snow does not show that language determines reality, but instead suggests that reality determines language. For the Inuit presumably developed their snow vocabulary in response to their environment. The reason there are not many words for 'snow' in English is that it doesn't snow very often in England. But when people such as skiers require a more discriminating snow vocabulary, they don't have much difficulty in inventing words, or borrowing them from other languages. To say that the Inuit have a different experience of reality because they have lots of different words for snow is surely no more plausible than saying that printers have a different experience of reality because they have lots of different words for print fonts.

Furthermore, although the Sapir–Whorf hypothesis says that language determines thought, there is in fact evidence to suggest that thought is possible without language:

1. Psychologists have discovered that babies and animals are able to think without the benefit of language. Some clever experiments have shown that babies as young as five months can do a simple form of mental arithmetic. And pigeons have been trained to recognise general classes such as trees, human beings, bodies of water, dogs and fish.

2. Some creative people claim that language plays only a secondary role in their thinking and that their ideas first come to them in images. Albert Einstein once observed:

   The words of a language as they are written and spoken do not seem to play any role in the mechanisms of my thought. The physical entities which seem to serve as elements in thought are certain signs and more or less clear images which can be voluntarily reproduced and combined. The above mentioned elements are, in my case, of visual, and some of muscular type. Conventional words or other signs have to be sought for laboriously only in a secondary stage.

3. We sometimes struggle to find the right words to express thoughts that feel as if they are already there. You have probably had the experience of saying something, and then adding in frustration 'No, that's not quite what I want to say', and then trying to express yourself with greater clarity. This suggests that our thoughts are there prior to language and that we are simply trying to find the right words with which to express them.

4. If language determines thought, it is unclear how new words ever enter a language, or, indeed, how language could have arisen in the first place. The most obvious explanation is that some kind of pre-linguistic thought is possible for which we later find words.

While the above points count against a strong version of the Sapir–Whorf hypothesis, there is a weaker version of the hypothesis, which says that language *influences* rather than *determines* thought. For complex thinking does seem to be closely connected to language. A baby may have a basic concept of number before it can talk, but it is hard to see how someone could do multiplication if they did not have the appropriate mathematical vocabulary. The American cultural critic Neil Postman (1931–2003) gave a good example to illustrate the point:

> *The process by which words and other symbols give shape and substance to our thoughts can be suggested by your trying to multiply 495 by 384. Except in this instance you must use only Roman numerals. I think you will find the operation quite impossible to do. Without access to the symbol 0 and a system of positional notation, the answer is literally inconceivable, i.e., you cannot think it.*

More generally, it might be hard to have various abstract ideas if you did not have the appropriate vocabulary. Admittedly, we sometimes think in images and then struggle to find the appropriate words, but we usually know what we think only after we have put it into language. While language may not determine thought, it might be said to predispose it, in the sense that we tend to think along the lines of our linguistic categories. This is not to say that we are trapped in our own language. For, as we saw earlier, it is always possible to borrow words from another language. Nevertheless, to come up with a new way of thinking usually requires the development of a new vocabulary – and this is one of the hallmarks of genius.

> *. . . As imagination bodies forth*
> *The forms of things unknown, the poet's pen*
> *Turns them to shapes, and gives to airy nothing*
> *A local habitation and a name.*

William Shakespeare, A Midsummer Night's Dream, *V, i*

Figure 4.9 Is gossip universal?

Language and values

We use language not only to describe the world, but also to persuade and influence one another. When we gossip, for example, we don't just tell stories about people, but negotiate with one another about how to describe them. Would you say that John is a good storyteller or a liar? Is Maurice a fluent conversationalist or a wind bag? Do you see Melissa as self-confident or arrogant? Is Paul's refusal to show emotion a sign of inner strength or of insensitivity? Which of these competing descriptions you settle on is likely to affect the way you think about the person in question.

ACTIVITY 4.22

The philosopher Bertrand Russell pointed out that we tend to interpret our own behaviour in the best possible light, and are less charitable when it comes to other people. To illustrate the point, he 'conjugated' the following 'irregular verbs':

'I am firm; you are obstinate; he is a pig-headed fool.'

'I am righteously indignant; you are annoyed; he is making a fuss about nothing.'

'I have reconsidered it; you have changed your mind; he has gone back on his word.'

Working in pairs, suggest how some of the following verbs might be 'conjugated' in a similar way:

1. 'I speak my mind . . .'
2. 'I am unlucky . . .'
3. 'I compromise . . .'
4. 'I take calculated risks . . .'
5. 'I am eloquent . . .'
6. 'I am idealistic . . .'
7. 'I am spontaneous . . .'
8. 'I am tolerant . . .'

Advertisers have long been aware of the power of language to influence and persuade. Here are two examples:

- It was a stroke of marketing genius on someone's part to brand water with bubbles in it as '*sparkling* water'. If it had been marketed as 'gassy water', it would probably never have become so popular.
- Since airlines have something called 'first class', it would be natural to think that the next two classes should be called 'second class' and 'third class'. Wrong! It's 'business class' and 'economy class'. Now even 'economy class' is becoming unfashionable. If you travel economy, British Airways now describes you as a 'world traveller'. This may sound impressive, but it makes no difference to the quality of the food or the leg room!

Figure 4.10 Why are advertisers so fond of the word 'natural'?

ACTIVITY 4.23

1. Take two advertising slogans of your choice – such as the classic 'A diamond is forever' (DeBeers) or 'Just do it' (Nike) – and explain why you think they are effective.
2. Why do you think so many advertisers describe their products as 'natural'? Are natural things always good? Can you give any examples of things which are natural and bad?

Using language to influence and persuade

We have already come across the power of language when we discussed the way the media 'frame' stories in Chapter 3 (see page 67). To explore the connection between language and values further, consider four ways in which language can be used to influence and persuade.

KT – emotive meaning: the aura of favourable or unfavourable feeling that hovers about a word

1 Emotionally laden language

Some words have not only a descriptive meaning, but also an **emotive meaning**. Emotive meaning can be defined as 'the aura of favourable or unfavourable feeling that hovers about a word'. While some words such as 'hero', 'peace' and 'democracy' have positive connotations, others such as 'thief', 'liar' or 'pervert' have negative ones. That is why everyone claims to be in favour of peace, and no one likes to be labelled a liar.

ACTIVITY 4.24

1. Analyse the way language is being used in each of the following pairs of expressions:
   a. Terrorist / freedom fighter.
   b. Pro life / pro choice.
   c. Genetically modified food / Frankenstein food.
   d. Free speech / hate speech
   e. 'Blocking your child's access to objectionable material on the internet is not called CENSORSHIP, it is called PARENTING' (Al Gore).
2. In 1947 the United States Department of War was renamed the Department of Defense. What difference, if any, do you think this makes? What is the corresponding department of state called in your country?

Euphemisms, which substitute mild or neutral-sounding words for a negative-sounding one, are a widely used form of emotive language. We sometimes resort to euphemisms in order to avoid taboo subjects, or to protect people's feelings. Thus, we may speak of the 'rest room' rather than the toilet. In addition to such benign uses, people sometimes use euphemisms to deliberately mislead people. For example, the timber industry no longer speaks of 'clear cutting' – an ugly-sounding expression – when it cuts down old-growth forest, but of 'landscape management'. This may serve to hide the reality of what is happening and make an unacceptable practice sound acceptable.

Although the influence of emotionally laden language is a matter of continuing debate, there is evidence to suggest that how people respond to survey questions depends on how they are phrased. In one US survey, when people were asked if more money should be spent on 'assistance to the poor', 68 per cent replied 'yes'; but when they were asked if more money should be spent on 'welfare', the number dropped to 24 per cent. In another survey, people were far more willing to spend money on 'national defence' than on the 'military'.

2 Weasel words

Weasel words are words such as 'many', 'should' and 'probably' which people slip into sentences to give themselves an escape route. For example, a manufacturer might say, 'Our product will work for you if you simply follow the instructions carefully.' You buy the product; it doesn't work; and when you phone up to complain, you are told that you clearly didn't follow the instructions *carefully enough*.

KT – weasel words: words that qualify a seemingly clear and precise statement and make it vague or ambiguous

ACTIVITY 4.25

Explain how weasel words are used in each of the following cases:

1. 'Our product can restore up to 25% of lost hair.'
2. 'Probably the best lager in the world.'
3. 'Dentifresh toothpaste helps fight tooth decay.'
4. 'If Timothy works hard, he should do himself justice in the final exam.'

3 Grammar

Grammar can also affect the way people see things. For example, the passive voice may be used to cover up someone's responsibility for something. Compare the following two sentences:

(a) 'Many villages were bombed.'

(b) 'We bombed many villages.'

While the first sentence makes the bombing sound like a natural disaster, the second puts the spotlight on the perpetrators.

4 Revealing and concealing

Language can be used not only to *reveal* certain aspects of reality, but also to conceal other aspects by diverting attention away from them. Consider, for example, the following four descriptions:

(a) 'I have invited an attractive blonde to the party.'

(b) 'I have invited a cellist to the party.'

(c) 'I have invited a marathon runner to the party.'

(d) 'I have invited a feminist to the party.'

Each description carries with it a different set of connotations, but it is possible that they all refer to the same person. Which description we use is likely to affect the way other people see the person in question.

Figure 4.11

ACTIVITY 4.26

1. According to a well-known children's rhyme, 'Sticks and stones may break my bones, but names will never hurt me.' Do you agree or disagree with this? Give your reasons.
2. Find out something about the political correctness (PC) movement, which seeks to use language to change attitudes to the oppressed or disadvantaged. What arguments are there in favour of political correctness and what arguments are there against it?

Language at war

The fact that language is not innocent and can be used to manipulate the way we see things is particularly apparent in times of war. Military training camps have long been aware that to get 'our boys' to kill their troops, *they* need to be dehumanised. During the Vietnam war, enemy soldiers were known as 'Gooks' by US servicemen. And in the first Gulf War (1991), an American pilot described firing on Iraqi soldiers as a 'turkey shoot'. Whatever your views about the rights and wrongs of these military campaigns, you would probably agree that it is psychologically easier to kill 'gooks' and 'turkeys' than human beings. Here are some more examples of 'warspeak', which is often used to cover up the reality on the ground.

Warspeak	Real meaning
security assistance	arms sales
neutralise	kill
no longer a factor	dead
take out	destroy
inoperative combat personnel	dead soldiers
pacification	bombing
service a target	dropping bombs on a target
collateral damage	bombed cities
friendly fire	accidentally firing on your own troops
strategic redeployment	retreat
liberate	invade
reporting guidelines	censorship
pre-emptive	unprovoked
ethnic cleansing	genocide

Language is power

While opinions differ about the relation between language and values, the fact that political parties and businesses invest so heavily in media consultants and spin doctors suggests that they, at least, think that it plays an important role in shaping our attitudes. At the limit, the seductive eloquence of demagogues such as Adolf Hitler reminds us that language can be used not only to educate and enlighten, but also to fuel the flames of hatred. So we would be well-advised to take seriously the slogan that 'language is power'.

LQ – Religion: Does religious experience lie beyond language?

Conclusion

Since much of our knowledge comes to us in words, our discussion of language in this chapter is clearly relevant to our quest for knowledge. Perhaps the key thing you will have discovered is that language is not as simple or straightforward as you first thought. We need to know what a statement means before we can decide whether it is true or false, but in practice it is difficult to fix the meanings of words with complete precision.

As a final point, brief mention should be made of two different views about the relationship between language and knowledge. On one side, some people claim that in order to know something you must be able to put it into words, and that 'if you can't say it then you don't know it' (Hans Reichenbach, 1891–1953). Such a robust view suggests that the only way to demonstrate your understanding of something is to put it into words and share it with other people. Against this, other people insist that some of our knowledge is personal and lies beyond words; and that, as the Hungarian thinker Michael Polanyi (1891–1976) claimed, we know more than we can say. Advocates of this view argue that our practical knowledge and knowledge of things we are acquainted with goes beyond our ability to describe them. This takes us back to the slogan mentioned in Chapter 1: 'the map is not the territory'.

Interestingly, mystics in all the great world religions have held that the deepest truths cannot be expressed in language. The Taoist sage Lao Tzu (*c.* 600 BCE) observes that 'Those who speak do not know; those who know do not speak'; the Buddhist *Lankaatara Sutra* tells us that 'Truth is beyond letters and words and books'; and in Judaism the Talmud says that 'If silence be good for the wise, how much the better for fools.'

One thing, however, is certain: if the deepest truths about life, the universe and everything do lie beyond words, then there is nothing we can say about them! With that in mind, I leave the last word to the philosopher Ludwig Wittgenstein (1889–1951) who at the end of his great book *Tractatus Logico-Philosophicus* wrote: 'What we cannot speak about we must pass over in silence.'

Key points

- A great deal of our knowledge comes through language and this makes possible an intellectual division of labour.
- Language is a subset of communication and is rule-governed, intended and creative.
- We need to understand what a sentence means before we can decide whether it is true or false.
- Since the definition, denotation and image theories of meaning all have shortcomings, perhaps we should say that meaning is a matter of know-how.
- A great deal of language is ambiguous and there is an element of interpretation built into all communication.
- Since different languages divide the world up in different ways, translation is more of an art than a science.
- We use language to label and classify, and this brings with it the danger that we misclassify or stereotype things.
- Although language may not *determine* our experience of reality, as claimed by the Sapir–Whorf hypothesis, it seems likely that it *influences* it.
- We use language not only to describe, but also to influence, persuade and sometimes *manipulate* the way people see things.
- Whether or not there are some truths that lie beyond language is a matter of continuing debate.

Key terms

ambiguity
back translation
body language
communication
connotation
denotation
emotive meaning
euphemism
grammar
idiom
irony
linguistic determinism
metaphor
Sapir–Whorf hypothesis
stereotype
weasel words

IB prescribed essay titles

1. Does language play roles of equal importance in different areas of knowledge? (November 2007 / May 2008)
2. Are truths obscured by the languages in which we express them? (November 2000 / May 2001)

Further reading

Books

Donna Jo Napoli and Vera Lee-Schoenfeld, *Language Matters* (Oxford University Press, 2010). Written by two professors of linguistics, this short, accessible and entertaining book has chapters on such things as how we acquire language, whether animals have language, translation, and the relation between language and thought.

George Lakoff and Mark Johnson, *Metaphors We Live By* (University of Chicago Press, 1980). According to the authors, metaphors pervade our language and often shape our thinking without our being aware of it. If you only dip into Chapters 1 and 2 you will already get a sense of the power of such metaphors as 'argument is war' and 'time is money'.

Online articles

Guy Deutscher, 'Does Your Language Shape How You Think?', *New York Times*, 26 August 2010.

Ryan Bloom, 'Lost in Translation: What the First Line of "The Stranger" Should Be', *The New Yorker*, 15 May 2012.

Dialogue: On animal language

The following dialogue by Richard van de Lagemaat explores the question of whether or not any animals can be said to possess language.

Dolly: I have just been to the zoo, and I was wondering: do you think that animals have language?

Guy: Animals? Hmm ... Well, as it stands that is a badly formulated question.

Dolly: What do you mean?

Guy: The word 'animal' covers a spectrum of living beings, ranging from amoebae and worms at one end to apes and human beings at the other. When you ask, 'Do animals have language?', I could answer that since we are animals, and since what we do is *by definition* language, then it is trivially true that animals have language. Nevertheless, I doubt that amoebae have a lot to say for themselves.

Dolly: Well, apart from human beings, you would surely agree that most animals communicate with each other in one way or another – either through noises, or scents, or bodily movements. To take a well-known example, bees perform a 'dance' to convey information about the distance and direction of nectar sources to their fellow workers. And that surely is a rudimentary form of language.

Guy: I think we need to make a distinction here between language and communication. I would say that while bees certainly communicate with one another, they do not have language.

Dolly: What is the difference?

Guy: Well, language is a *subset* of communication, and while all language is a form of communication, it is not the case that all forms of communication are language.

Dolly: I would have said that the words 'language' and 'communication' are pretty much synonymous.

Guy: No! There are many forms of communication that no one would call language. For example, when you turn your car key in the ignition, the car starts, but no one would say the car *understands* that you want it to start. While information is certainly communicated, the communication in question is purely mechanical and has nothing to do with language.

Dolly: As sometimes happens, our disagreement here seems to be about the meanings of words. My understanding of the word 'communication' is derived from the *Encyclopaedia Britannica* which defines it as 'the exchange of meanings between individuals through a common system of symbols'. You seem to be using it in a much broader sense to include purely mechanical communication.

Guy: Well, let's not get bogged down in semantics. My point is that bees respond to one another in an essentially mechanical way. In any case, since all they can 'talk' about is nectar, it would, to say the least, be misleading to describe their dance as a form of language.

Dolly: But how do you know that nectar is all they can talk about?

Guy: Well, given that bees have only primitive brains, I think it's a safe bet that they don't spend much time discussing the meaning of life.

Dolly: OK. To move the discussion forward, why don't we focus on higher animals, such as monkeys? Do you think that monkeys have language?

Guy: No! I believe that language is unique to human beings.

Dolly: But given that we evolved from chimpanzees and share 99% of our genes with them, we should surely take seriously the idea that they might have abilities similar to our own?

Guy: The fact that we share 99% of our genes with chimpanzees doesn't tell us anything – the remaining 1% could make all the difference. Moreover, our brains account for a much bigger proportion of our body weight than do chimp brains, and a bigger relative brain size is a good indication of greater intelligence.

Dolly: Well, let's take a look at some of the scientific evidence. Take the case of vervet monkeys. Scientists have discovered that their alarm calls vary according to the predator that threatens them. The leopard alarm call, eagle alarm call, and snake alarm call are all different from each other, and elicit different responses from members of the group. When the monkeys hear the leopard alarm call they climb into the trees, when they hear the eagle alarm call they hide in the undergrowth, and when they hear the snake alarm call they look around in the grass. This surely proves that they have *words* for 'leopard', 'eagle', and 'snake', and that they understand what these words mean.

Guy: It proves no such thing! What your example shows is that vervet monkeys can communicate with one another about matters that are important for their survival. Rather than attribute understanding to them, I think their behaviour is best explained in terms of stimulus and response. Just as Pavlov's dogs were conditioned to salivate whenever they heard a bell ring, so the monkeys are reacting automatically to various alarm calls. Understanding does not come into it – it is simply a matter of a particular call triggering a particular response.

Dolly: OK, so what about the various experiments in which chimpanzees have been taught American sign language? One of the first stars of such experiments was a chimp called Washoe who successfully learnt more than a hundred words of sign language.

Guy: Well, from what I've read about this experiment, Washoe's main concern was with getting food and being tickled. Drilling a chimpanzee in a few bits of sign language doesn't seem so very different from training a hungry rat to press a lever that releases food.

Dolly: You are not doing justice to the remarkable linguistic abilities shown by these chimps. For example, their ability to talk about absent objects shows that they are not simply reacting automaton-like to things in their immediate environment. Similarly, the fact that they sometimes tell lies in order to mislead their trainers suggests that rather than responding instinctively to various cues, they are using signs intentionally. Perhaps most impressive of all, they demonstrate genuine creativity by inventing new combinations of signs. To give a few examples, Washoe came up with the constructions 'open food eat' for a refrigerator, 'hot metal blow' for a cigarette lighter, and 'listen drink' for Alka-Seltzer. Such creativity proves that far from responding mechanically, Washoe had a genuine understanding of the meanings of these signs.

Guy: I think you will find that more recent research has cast doubt on the validity of these experiments. According to some observers, Washoe's trainers became so emotionally involved with their subject that they lost the ability to be objective and were often simply *projecting* sign language onto Washoe's random hand movements. In the view of Steven Pinker of MIT, Washoe may actually have known as few as 20 signs. Compare that with human beings whose vocabularies consist of literally thousands of words.

Dolly: Your talk about lack of objectivity shows that you don't really understand how social science works. You simply cannot study apes with the same dispassionate objectivity with which you can study rocks – at least, not if you want to teach them language. If you were trying to teach your child language, how far do you think you would get if you tried to do it objectively and without emotional involvement? Not very far, I'll bet! It's the same with apes. You can only teach them language if you have some kind of emotional rapport with them.

Guy: Perhaps you are right about that; but my point is that once you have made an emotional connection with an ape, you may be too keen to attribute skills to it that it does not really possess. Just as I think parents are not the best judges of their children's intelligence, so I doubt that someone who has spent years working with an ape can look at what is happening dispassionately.

Dolly: You know, I'm beginning to think that you do not really have an open mind on this topic, that you have already decided that chimps do not have language, and that you are not willing to accept any evidence that goes against your belief.

Guy: Not at all! I am sceptical about the claims concerning primate language because I know that people have a tendency to project human qualities on to animals and that they find it difficult to be objective about them.

Dolly: Well, let's take the more recent experiments conducted by Sue Savage-Rumbaugh on bonobo chimps. Rather than sign language, she taught her chimps to communicate using a keyboard with more than 200 symbols on it, each representing a particular word; and she has achieved results with her star pupil, Kanzi, at least as impressive as those of Washoe. Since replacing signs with a keyboard gets rid of any ambiguity about how we interpret what is going on, I don't think you can dismiss this evidence so easily.

Guy: But what exactly does it prove?

Dolly: It proves that Kanzi has a grasp of semantics and understands the meanings of words. When his trainers say to him things like, 'Please go to the office and bring back the red ball', he does just that. What's that if it is not understanding?

Guy: Once again, I would say that it is the ability to respond to signals as the result of training.

Dolly: Listen, they set up an experiment in which Kanzi was given 600 sentences *he had never heard before*, and he was able to respond correctly to them in over 75% of cases. That is as good as what is achieved by a two-and-a-half-year-old child. You can't explain that away in terms of mere training.

Guy: Even so, there is still a huge gulf between what a two-year-old child can do, and what a mature user of the language can do.

Dolly: Well, at least you seem to be admitting that these chimps have a rudimentary form of language similar to that possessed by children.

Guy: I am admitting no such thing! Look, I don't think you have grasped my main point. Sure, these chimps are clever, and their trainers are dedicated; but basically they've just been taught a bunch of party tricks that don't have a whole lot to do with language. All they are doing is responding to cues from their trainers in order to get rewards. Language proper has something called syntax – rules for joining words together to form complex sentences – words like 'but', 'and', 'or', 'not' and 'because' which enable us to articulate complex thoughts. Animals don't have language because they don't have syntax. When we use language, we don't just talk about our immediate desires or objects in our environment. We can formulate abstract thoughts, talk about the distant past and future, and meditate on the meaning of life. Even the people who work with chimps and gorillas readily admit that their subjects can do none of these things.

Dolly: You know, you keep raising the bar. You said vervet monkeys were just reacting to signs, so I gave the example of Washoe and his creative use of language. You questioned the validity of that evidence, so I then gave you the example of Kanzi where the evidence is beyond question. Now you suddenly redefine what you mean by language. I am not claiming that what the chimps can do is the same as what you and I can do: I am claiming that it is *sufficiently similar* to deserve the name of language.

Guy: Sufficiently similar? I don't think so! To describe what these chimpanzees do as a form of language is like describing what champion long jumpers do as a form of flight. The best athletes may be able to jump more than 8 metres, but no matter how hard they train – or how many illegal drugs they take – they will never be able to fly like an eagle flies. And just as human beings are not built for flight, so chimpanzees are not built for language.

Dolly: I think your analogy is misleading and simply confuses the issue. As I said earlier, my impression is that you have decided in advance of the evidence that animals do not have language, and this makes me wonder about your motives. Perhaps you will feel more comfortable about exploiting animals if you can convince yourself that there is an unbridgeable gulf between human beings and the rest of the animal kingdom.

Guy: Listen, I, too, am opposed to the exploitation of animals and I believe in animal rights. However, the reason that animals have rights derives from the fact that they are able to feel pain, and it has nothing to do with whether or not they have language. So instead of trying to project human qualities onto animals, why don't you just accept that they are different from us?

Dolly: Well, perhaps you should remember what you said at the beginning of the discussion – namely, that we, too, are animals. In any case, this particular animal is getting tired. Perhaps it is time to stop.

Sense perception

5

It's not what you look at that matters, it's what you see.

Henry David Thoreau, 1817–62

Two-thirds of what we see is behind our eyes.

Chinese proverb

A fool sees not the same tree that the wise man sees.

William Blake, 1757–1827

The greatest calamity that can befall people is not that they should be born blind, but rather that they should have eyes and yet fail to see.

Helen Keller, 1880–1968

Whilst part of what we perceive comes through our senses from the object before us, another part (and it may be the larger part) always comes out of our own mind.

William James, 1842–1910

Things do not seem the same to those who love and those who hate, nor to those who are angry and those who are calm.

Aristotle, 384–322 BCE

The greatest thing a human soul ever does is to see something, and to tell what it saw in a plain way . . . To see clearly is poetry, prophecy and religion – all in one.

John Ruskin, 1819–1900

It is only with the heart that one can see rightly; what is essential is invisible to the eye.

Antoine de Saint–Exupéry, 1900–44

Every man takes the limits of his own field of vision for the limits of the world.

Arthur Schopenhauer, 1788–1860

If the doors of perception were cleansed, everything would appear to man as it is – infinite.

William Blake, 1757–1827

Introduction

Our senses play a fundamental role in giving us knowledge of the world. They are 'the gates and windows' of the mind – channels of communication between ourselves and the outside world, which effortlessly present us with the rich, and often pleasurable, variety of the world: the beautiful colours of a New England autumn, the sound of waves breaking on a shore, the tickle of a feather, the taste of hot soup on a cold day, the smell of freshly cut grass.

KT – empiricism: a school of thought which claims that all knowledge must ultimately be based on sense perception

Almost everyone would agree that our senses are important sources of knowledge. Indeed, according to one major school of philosophy, known as **empiricism**, *all* knowledge is ultimately based on perceptual experience. This may be too extreme, but sense perception clearly plays a key role in almost all subject areas, ranging from the sciences through history to the arts. Think, for example, of the role played by observation in biology, or eye-witness accounts in history, or the ability to see things with new eyes in the visual arts.

ACTIVITY 5.1

1. Leonardo da Vinci (1452–1519) once reflected that the average human being 'looks without seeing, listens without hearing, touches without feeling, eats without tasting, moves without physical awareness, inhales without awareness of odour or fragrance, and talks without thinking'. Do you agree with his assessment?
2. Is perception a more important source of knowledge in some subjects than others? Are there any areas of knowledge in which perception plays no role?

KT – common-sense realism: the belief that the world is more or less as we perceive it to be

Our default understanding of perception is a position known as **common-sense realism**. According to this view, perception is a passive and relatively straightforward process which gives us an accurate picture of reality. Colours and sounds and smells exist 'out there', and the act of observation does not affect what is observed. This view of the relation between perception and the world is probably adequate for the practical demands of everyday life; if our senses were not generally reliable, we would probably not have survived as a species.

LQ – Human sciences: When studying human beings, how does the act of observation influence what is observed?

Nevertheless, we will suggest in this chapter that there is more to perception than meets the eye, and that it is a more active process than common-sense realism allows. Rather than our senses passively reflecting an independent reality, our experience of the world is affected not only by what is 'out there', but also by the structure of our sense organs and our minds. As we shall see, this has implications for the reliability of sense perception as a source of knowledge. While it generally makes sense to trust our senses, we should keep in mind that they cannot always be trusted and may sometimes deceive us.

The senses

We are usually taught that we have five senses: sight, sound, touch, taste and smell. This may strike you as common sense, but, depending on the criteria used, the number can vary. Some people claim that we have as few as three types of senses: mechanical (touch and hearing), chemical (tastes and smells) and light (vision). Others say that we have more than five senses and they include such things as the following:

Proprioception: awareness of the position of your limbs in space

Equilibroception: sense of balance

Interoception: awareness of stimuli originating inside the body

Thermoception: awareness of temperature

ACTIVITY 5.2

1. Imagine that you are on a roller coaster at an amusement park. Describe in detail everything you are experiencing. To what extent can these experiences be slotted into the traditional five senses model of perception?
2. If for some reason you had to sacrifice one of your senses, which would you be most willing to lose and which would you be least willing to lose? Give reasons.
3. What do the following imply about the relative importance of our different senses?
   a. When people go on holiday they usually take photos of what they see rather than make recordings of what they hear.
   b. We commonly speak of 'eye-witnesses' rather than 'ear-witnesses' or 'nose-witnesses'.
   c. We have art forms associated with vision and hearing, but none associated with smell.
4. Give some examples of figures of speech in English, or any other language, that connect knowledge and the senses. For example: 'Seeing is believing'.

Hierarchy of senses

The traditional five human senses are not necessarily of equal value; some are believed to be more important than others. Most people would agree that vision is our most dominant sense and a large part of the human brain is devoted to visual processing. Indeed, we naturally tend to connect vision with knowledge. For example, we say that seeing is believing rather than smelling is believing; when we understand someone we say 'I see what you mean', not 'I smell what you mean'; and we speak of someone having in*sight* not in*smell*. However, there are also some metaphors for knowledge deriving from other senses. For example, you might say that someone has lost *touch* with reality, or that an argument *smells* fishy; and there is a well-known Sufi saying, 'He who *tastes*, knows.'

Figure 5.1 How different would our experience of the world be if smell were our dominant sense?

The sense most people say they would sacrifice if they had to lose one of them is smell. As this suggests, smell is usually seen as the poor relation of the senses, and it is sometimes called the mute sense. While we have many different words for colours, our smell vocabulary does not extend much beyond 'smells good', 'smells bad' and 'smells like'. Despite its lowly status, we are in fact able to distinguish more than ten thousand different odours. And our sense of smell has a more direct route to our brains than any of our other senses. This may explain why evocative smells can sometimes trigger powerful emotional memories, and why the perfume industry is worth millions of dollars a year.

Our senses are, in theory at least, remarkably acute. For example, on a clear, dark night you can see a candle flame from several miles away; when it is quiet you can hear the wind rustling in distant trees; and you can apparently detect a teaspoon of sugar dissolved in eight litres of water. Furthermore, if you lose one of your senses, evidence suggests that your other senses compensate and that the part of your brain originally devoted to the lost sense gets rewired so that it can process information from the others. This might appear to justify the claim that, for example, deafness should be seen not as 'hearing impairment' but as 'vision enhancement'.

Despite their acuity, our senses have a limited range of sensitivity, and they capture only certain kinds of data. For example, our eyes are sensitive only to light of a certain wavelength, and we are unable to see such things as ultraviolet and infrared which lie beyond the visible spectrum. Similarly, our ears can detect only certain kinds of sound and our noses only certain kinds of smell. Given this, we should not assume that the map of human sense perception is identical with the underlying territory of reality.

ACTIVITY 5.3

1. Compare human sense perception with the sense perception of one of the following:
   a. an octopus; **b.** a bat; **c.** a hawk; **d.** a dog.
2. To what extent do you think our senses give us an accurate picture of reality? Give reasons.
3. How can technology help us to overcome the limits of our senses and extend the frontiers of knowledge?

Integrated senses: synaesthesia

Synaesthesia is an unusual condition in which two or more of the senses we normally experience separately are experienced together. For example, a synaesthete might see sounds, or smell sights. The most common form of synaesthesia is perceiving letters and numbers as inherently coloured. This condition is thought to be the result of cross-wiring of the brain and it is often associated with 'creative types', such as artists, novelists, poets and composers. Well-known artistic synaesthetes include the painter Vassily Kandinsky (1866–1944), the novelist Vladimir Nabokov (1899–1977) and the jazz musician Miles Davis (1926–91).

Figure 5.2 Bouba-kiki

Some people claim that we are all partially synaesthetes. For example, we naturally associate phenomena from one sense with those from another, as can be seen in common cross-sensory metaphors such as 'smooth voice', 'loud shirt', 'cold light', 'sharp taste', 'bitter wind', 'light music', 'heavy silence'. As further support for this claim, consider the bouba-kiki test. Imagine that the two shapes above are letters from the Martian alphabet, one is called bouba and the other is called kiki. Your task is to guess which is which.

Interestingly, almost everyone guesses that the figure on the right is kiki and the one on the left bouba – irrespective of their native language. The psychologist V. S. Ramachandran suggests that this is because the sharpness of the sound 'kiki' reflects the jaggedness of the shape on the right; while the roundness of the word 'bouba' – our lips adopt a rounded shape in enunciating it – mimics the figure on the left.

Alternative senses: animals

Some animals have senses which extend beyond the limits of our own. Dogs, for example, can smell and hear things of which we are completely unaware.

Other animals have completely different senses:

- *Echolocation.* Bats famously navigate using a system of echolocation which gives them a form of 'acoustic vision'. They emit high-frequency sounds and are able to judge the shape, size and distance of objects in their environment by the echo that is reflected back to their ears. (Dolphins, too, have a *biological sonar* for navigating through turbid waters.)
- *Magnetic sense.* Birds are able to travel thousands of miles with complete accuracy without the aid of satellite navigation. This is probably because they are sensitive to the earth's magnetic field.
- *Heat detection.* Some snakes have temperature-sensitive organs which allow them to locate their prey in the dark and strike with complete accuracy.

Figure 5.3 Can we ever really know how a bat experiences the world?

Figure 5.4 *"And only you can hear this whistle?"*

Interestingly, some people have developed their senses beyond the normal range. Two extraordinary individuals, one deaf and one blind, are worth mentioning:

> *Evelyn Glennie* is a world-famous percussionist who has been profoundly deaf since childhood. Glennie performs without shoes and picks up on subtle changes in the vibrations of her instruments to which her body is extremely sensitive.
>
> *Daniel Kish* was born blind, but as a child taught himself echolocation. By clicking his tongue and listening for echoes, he can identify objects and obstacles and successfully navigate his way around in the world. Indeed, so effective is his 'onboard sonar' that he can confidently hike and mountain bike in the wilderness.

Figure 5.5 Evelyn Glennie: Can we develop senses beyond the normal range?

Extending our senses: technology

We are not completely restricted by the senses given to us by nature. As well as being able to train our senses, we can also extend their range with the help of technology. The most obvious examples are microscopes and telescopes which enable us to study subatomic particles on the one hand and distant galaxies on the other. More dramatically, some commentators predict that we are currently on the verge of a new era in which machines will significantly enhance our senses. Already, scientists have given rats brain-implants and taught them to see infrared; and human vision could, in theory, be similarly extended. Some people speculate that superhuman hearing is on the horizon and that one day we will be able to hear sounds that are currently inaudible. Meanwhile, 'wearable electronic fingertips' have been developed which enhance the sense of touch and which could benefit surgeons conducting operations. These developments may sound like science fiction, but some of them could easily become scientific fact.

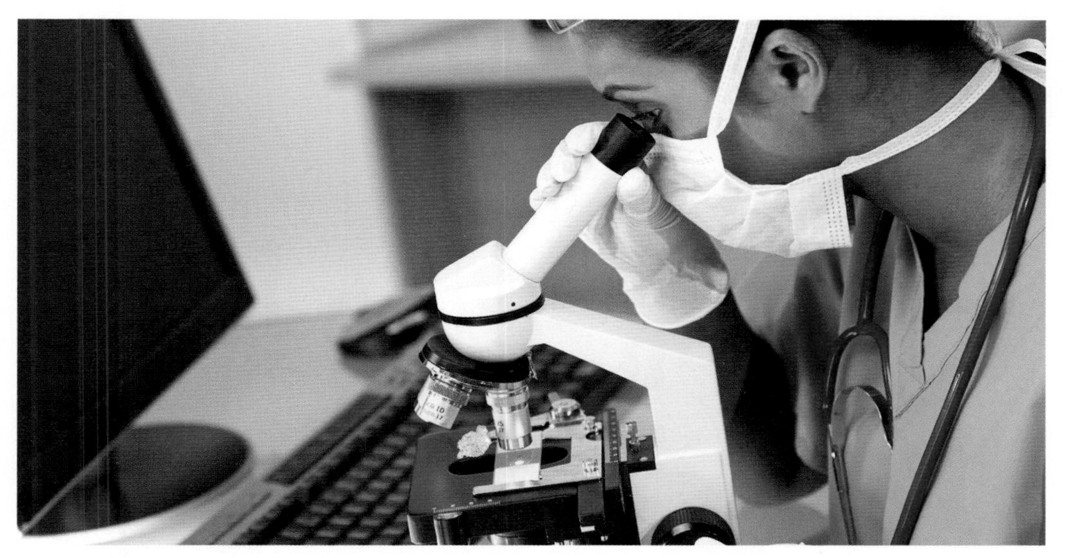

Figure 5.6 How can technology extend our senses?

Perceptual illusions

Despite the ease with which we perceive the world, perception is a complex process in which many things are going on below the level of conscious awareness. In simple terms, it can be thought of as consisting of two distinct elements:

- ***sensation***, which is provided by the world
- *interpretation*, which is provided by our minds.

KT – sensation: raw uninterpreted perceptual information which floods into our senses from the world around us

In everyday life, we are not usually aware of our minds interpreting the sensations that flood into our senses, and we simply experience the familiar world of tables and chairs and cats and dogs and family and friends. A good way of becoming more aware of such interpretations is to look at visual illusions. In what follows we will look at four kinds of visual illusion, all of which arise not from sensations as such, but from the interpretation we put on them.

Context

The way we see something depends partly on the context in which we see it. Look at the three men in Figure 5.7. While the figure on the right looks a lot bigger than the figure on the left, the reality is that they are both the same size. How can we explain this illusion? The answer has something to do with perspective. Relative to the background, the man on the left is small and the man on the right is big.

In everyday life, we are constantly making such contextual judgements without being consciously aware of it. If you look at Figure 5.8 and focus on the figure on the left and the figure in the middle, they appear to be two normal-sized people, one some distance away and the other in the foreground. However, the two-dimensional 'reality' is that the figure originally on the left is much smaller than the one in the middle – as can be clearly seen when it is moved to the right of the picture.

What both of the above illusions illustrate is that we usually judge the size of an object by looking at the overall context.

Figure 5.7

Figure 5.8

Figure and ground

When we look at something, we tend to highlight certain aspects of what we see ('figure'), and treat other parts of it as background ('ground'). For example, when you look at a page of writing, the black parts stand out and you pay no attention to the white background. Sometimes we can make different aspects of what we see stand out as the figure. This is best illustrated by the well-known Rubin face/vase illusion. Figure 5.9 can be interpreted either as a symmetrical vase, or as two identical silhouettes looking at one another.

KT – figure and ground: our natural tendency to focus on certain aspects of what we perceive and treat the rest as background

There are many examples of ambiguous figures which rely on the **figure and ground** phenomenon. If you try slightly blurring your vision, you should be able to find two different interpretations of each of the pictures in Figures 5.10 and 5.11.

Figure 5.9

Figure 5.10 Young man–old man

Figure 5.11 Young woman–old woman

Visual grouping

KT – visual grouping: the tendency to group sensory data together and see them as shapes and patterns

We have a natural tendency to look for meaning in what we see and to group our perceptual experiences together into shapes and patterns. If you look at Figure 5.12, you have no difficulty in seeing a dog. What is striking is how little information is actually given to us – just a few patches of black. But our minds – specifically our imaginations – have no difficulty in filling in the missing parts to create a meaningful picture. We will explore further the role imagination plays in sense perception in Chapter 9 (see page 232).

In some cases, however, it can be more difficult to find any meaning in what we see. The first time people see Figure 5.13 they are usually unable to make any sense of it. (If you want to know what this is, look at page 137.)

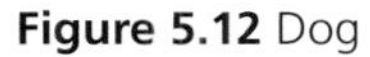

Figure 5.12 Dog

Figure 5.13 Hidden face

Expectations

LQ – Natural sciences: To what extent do expectations influence observations in the natural sciences?

Our expectations can also influence how we see things. For example, in a well-known experiment, people were asked to identify playing cards that were briefly flashed before them. However, irregular cards, such as a red six of Spades or a black nine of Diamonds were included in the pack. When people saw an irregular card, most of them misperceived it in accordance with their expectations. For example, the red six of Spades was seen as either a regular red six of Diamonds or a regular black six of Spades.

You might think *you* would not make such a mistake, but look at Figure 5.14 and read the message contained in it. If you have not seen this before, you probably read 'Paris in the spring', but it actually says 'Paris in the *the* spring'. When you look again you may think to yourself 'How could I have missed that second "the"?' The reason, of course, is that, since you did not expect to see two 'the's in a row, your mind simply blanked out one of them. If you think how difficult it is to spot your own spelling errors, then you can understand that this kind of perceptual error is far from uncommon.

Figure 5.14

While we can experience many other kinds of illusion, the examples of the role played by context, figure–ground, visual grouping and expectations should be enough to convince you that there is an important element of interpretation built into our perception of the world.

Illusions with other senses

We suffer not only from visual illusions, but also from illusions with other senses. The mobile phone era has brought with it two related illusions: the phantom ringing illusion and the phantom vibration illusion – mistakenly believing that your phone is ringing or vibrating when it isn't. You may have experienced both of these illusions yourself! Here are some other examples:

Figure 5.15 Why do so many people suffer from phantom vibration syndrome?

1. *Hearing: the McGurk effect.* The sounds 'bah' and 'dah' are usually easy to distinguish. But if you watch a video clip of someone seeming to mouth the syllable 'bah' while the soundtrack plays 'dah', you will hear the 'dah' as a 'bah'. The effect is very powerful, as you will discover if you look at an online video clip of it.
2. *Touch: the size–weight illusion.* If you lift two objects of equal weight but different size, you will find that the larger one feels much lighter than the smaller one – even though they weigh the same. The explanation for this illusion is that there is interference between your senses of vision and touch which affects your *expectations*. Your brain naturally expects the larger object to weigh more than the smaller one. Relative to this (disappointed) expectation, the larger object then feels light.
3. *Taste: the soundbite effect.* Our perception of taste can easily be influenced by our other senses. In one intriguing experiment, subjects ate crisps while the sound was picked up by a microphone and simultaneously played back to them through headphones. However, what was played back was modified to sound more or less crispy. The crispier the sound, the tastier the subjects reported the crisps to be – even though they were identical. This again shows the influence of expectations on perception: if crisps *sound* fresher, you expect them to taste better – so they *do* taste better!

LQ – Language: How does the way we describe something affect the way we see it?

RLS – Headline: 'Joshua Bell: No Ordinary Busker'. How is our interpretation of what we are hearing influenced by context?

ACTIVITY 5.4

1. How can the taste of food be influenced by:
   a. what you have eaten immediately beforehand
   b. its smell
   c. its appearance
   d. the way it is described?
2. Do we suffer more from illusions with some senses than with others, or are they equally unreliable?

As the above illusions suggest, our senses are interconnected, and the information we receive from one sense can affect our interpretation of the information we receive from another. Our brains, it seems, are less concerned with discrete colours, sounds, tastes, smells and feels than with building up one integrated picture of the world.

The role of the unconscious

According to psychologists, many of the interpretations we routinely make about the world happen at an unconscious level. When you look at something, what actually appears on your retina are two small inverted two-dimensional images. Yet, without any conscious effort on your part, you see one life-size right-way-up three-dimensional world.

In an interesting psychology experiment, which illustrates the power of unconscious interpretation, subjects were asked to put on spectacles which inverted their image of the world. For the first few days they were completely disoriented and saw everything as being upside down. But, interestingly, their brains soon flipped the images round so that they saw the world the right way up again. When the spectacles were removed at the end of the experiment they again experienced everything as upside down for a while until their vision returned to normal.

In fact, we are constantly making all kinds of unconscious inferences about what we experience. For example, your image in the bathroom mirror is actually about half the size of your head; but when you stumble out of bed in the morning and look at yourself in the mirror, you never have the impression that your head has shrunk in the night. It always *looks* the right size. Similarly, if someone walks towards you from the other end of a corridor, the image on your retina steadily expands, but you do not see them as slowly inflating like a balloon. As far as you are concerned, they remain the same size.

More generally, although vision is simply a matter of light of various wavelengths falling on your retina, you do not experience the world as so many blobs of colour. You never, for example, have to think to yourself 'Ah, those patches of colour over there must be a desk, and these patches must be someone's face.' You just see the world of familiar everyday objects.

KT – visual agnosia: a visual impairment in which a sufferer is able to see things but is unable to recognise or interpret them

Sadly, some people who have suffered brain damage experience a condition known as **visual agnosia** in which they lose the ability to interpret what they see. There is nothing wrong with their vision or sense of language as such, but they have no sense of how things hang together. For example, they may see a smooth metal rod with three elongated prongs at the end of it, but be unable to recognise it as a fork. As this suggests, they have the same sensations as people with regular vision but they are unable to give them any coherent interpretation. We can get a sense of what this might be like by looking again at Figure 5.12. Although you have no problem seeing the various patches of black, if this is the first time you have seen this image, you may not be able to make any sense of it. To suffer from visual agnosia is to be permanently trapped in such a world.

Selectivity of perception

Apart from visual illusions, another reason for being cautious about what our senses tell us is that perception is *selective*. A vast amount of data is constantly flooding in to our senses, and our minds would overload if we were consciously aware of everything. So we only notice some things in our perceptual field and overlook others. The selectivity of perception can be seen as a generalisation of the figure–ground phenomenon mentioned above. Certain aspects of a situation engage our attention and 'stand out', and the rest fade away into a more or less indeterminate background. For example, if we are having a conversation at school, I may notice your facial expression, yet have no conscious awareness of the picture on the wall behind you; or I may hear what you are saying, yet be oblivious to the quiet hum of the computer. While the light reflected from the picture affects my eyes, and the air vibrations caused by the computer hit my ears, my conscious mind treats these things as the background against which what I am interested in stands out.

If we consider what kind of stimuli we usually notice, intensity and contrast are two important factors. The ticking clock may sometimes go unheard, but you would hear if a bomb exploded in the building next door. Drop a small object on a patterned carpet and it can sometimes be hard to find again; but a tiny drop of blood on a white carpet will be immediately apparent. For good evolutionary reasons, we are also sensitive to moving objects. If you work at a desk by a window, your attention may suddenly be caught by something which makes you look up without quite knowing why – only to realise a second later that there is a distant bird passing over the trees. Since it may be moving towards you, such an object represents a potential threat and you therefore notice it.

What you tend to notice in a particular environment is partly a matter of biological nature, but it is also influenced by your interests, emotions and culture.

Interests

The particular interests that you have can be thought of as filters that determine what shows up as you scan the world around you. If three friends go for a walk in the countryside, one may focus mainly on nature and the variety of the wildlife; a second may attend to what his friends are wearing and talking about; and a third may notice very little because her mind is on something completely different. The following question, which I owe to an anonymous colleague, shows how our perspective on something affects the way we see it.

ACTIVITY 5.5

Take one of the following phenomena and describe how it might be seen through the eyes of the following people:

a. A child dying in poverty as seen by a doctor, an economist, a social worker, the child's father.

b. A sunset as seen by a religious figure, a physicist, a painter, a farmer.

c. A tree as seen by a biologist, a logger, an environmentalist, a native American.

As the pattern of our interests changes, so does what we tend to notice. It is striking that if your family buys a new car you will begin to see cars of the same model and colour everywhere. Similarly, if a woman becomes pregnant, she begins noticing pregnant women wherever she goes.

Emotions

Our feelings and emotions also shape and colour our perceptions. When you are in a good mood you see the world in quite a different way to when you are in a bad mood. While an optimist sees a glass as half-full, a pessimist sees the same glass as half-empty. An emotion such as love can have a particularly strong effect on our perception. When you fall in love with someone you may unconsciously project your dreams and fantasies onto them so that they seem to possess every imaginable perfection. If you later fall out of love, you may look at your 'ex' and wonder what you ever saw in

LQ – Emotion: How does your mood affect your perception of things?

them. Perhaps not surprisingly, it has been said that at the beginning of a relationship you tend to notice the things you have in common with someone, and at the end of a relationship you tend to notice the things that make you different. Our perception can also be distorted by fear. If you are alone on a dark and stormy night you may be frightened by sounds that you wouldn't normally notice. As a Persian proverb has it, 'He who has been bitten by a snake fears a piece of string.'

Culture

The culture we grow up in also shapes our perceptions. There is, for example, evidence to suggest that Asians tend to perceive things more holistically (that is, as a whole) while Westerners tend to focus more on individual objects. There are other interesting differences in sense perception across cultures. Here are two:

1. *Vision*. Whatever their own race, human beings seem to find it difficult to distinguish between individuals of other races. They may have the feeling that 'they all look the same'. This is not necessarily due to racism; nor is it because some races are objectively more homogeneous than others (they are not). Rather it seems to be due to the fact that we tend to focus on the facial differences of people in our own culture and become blind to other differences. This effect is known as the **other-race effect**.

KT – other-race effect: the tendency to recognise individuals of one's own race more easily than those of other races

2. *Sound*. Culture can also affect the way we distinguish certain sounds and overlook others. For example, Japanese people struggle to distinguish the letters 'l' and 'r' in English. Meanwhile, the English are deaf to subtle tonal differences which play a key role in the Chinese language. We are born with the ability to distinguish sounds in *any* language, but this ability quickly disappears as we tune in to our own.

LQ – Cultural perspectives: How does the culture in which you grow up influence your perception?

ACTIVITY 5.6

1. Take one of the following and explain how education and training can affect what we perceive:
   a. A biologist looking down a microscope
   b. A dentist looking at an X-ray
   c. A professional wine taster
   d. A lifeguard
   e. An artist
   f. An indigenous person in a rainforest
2. In what emotional state do you think we see the world with the greatest clarity and objectivity?

Change blindness

KT – change blindness: the tendency not to notice what, retrospectively, seem to be obvious changes in our environment

The selectivity of perception may explain why we are remarkably poor at noticing what retrospectively seem to be obvious changes in our environment. The following two well-known experiments – videos of which can be found online – illustrate the extent of such **change blindness**:

1. If a subject is talking to a stranger and their vision is obstructed for a moment – say, by two people passing between them carrying a wooden door – in about 50 per cent of cases the subject fails to notice when the original stranger is replaced by another different-looking stranger.
2. When an audience watch a video of a group of people throwing a basketball around and are asked to count the number of passes, the vast majority fail to notice a man in a gorilla suit walk straight across their field of vision.

RLS – Headline: 'Driver Didn't See Schoolboy Cyclist Until It Was "Too Late", Inquest Hears'. What does change blindness suggest about the reliability of perception?

Our inattention in the above cases is to some extent understandable, as we do not *expect* the changes in question. However, at an everyday level, change blindness may help to explain traffic accidents in which drivers fail to notice, say, pedestrians or cyclists who are directly in their path. It should also make us cautious about uncritically accepting eye-witness testimony, as discussed in the next section.

Seeing and believing

At the start of this chapter, we considered the idea that 'seeing is believing' but, since our beliefs and expectations can affect the way we see things, sometimes it might be more accurate to say that 'believing is seeing'. Here are three examples from different subject areas of the way in which our beliefs can affect our perception.

- *Science.* In the nineteenth century some scientists speculated that an undiscovered planet – which they named Vulcan – existed between Mercury and the sun. With this belief in mind, some astronomers claimed to have seen Vulcan through their telescopes. But it turned out that no such planet exists.
- *History.* 'Bloody Sunday' is an infamous day in the history of Northern Ireland. On 30 January 1972 there was a violent confrontation between British troops and Catholic demonstrators which left thirteen Catholics dead. According to the British soldiers, they came under attack from terrorist elements and returned fire. But Catholic witnesses said the army opened fire on a peaceful demonstration without provocation. Perhaps one of the two sides was deliberately lying; but it is equally possible that, as a result of the 'fog of battle', each side genuinely believed its own version of events.
- *Art.* In the visual arts, people have a tendency to draw and paint, not what they see, but what they think is there. For example, in antiquity some artists portrayed horses with eyelashes on the upper and lower lids of their eyes even though horses in fact have eyelashes only on their upper lids.

LQ – Arts: To what extent do the arts help us to see the world with new eyes?

ACTIVITY 5.7

We are all very good at seeing only what we want to see. Can you give some examples of the way in which our beliefs affect the way we see things?

Eye-witness testimony

LQ – History: How reliable is eye-witness testimony as a primary source in history?

As implied above, the fallibility of sense perception is not only of theoretical interest but also has important implications in the real world. In criminal trials, juries tend to put a great deal of faith in eye-witness testimony, and such evidence can determine whether or not a person is found guilty. However, according to psychologists, the uncorroborated evidence of a single witness should be treated with great caution. In recent years, a number of cases have come to light of people convicted of crimes on the basis of eye-witness accounts that subsequent DNA testing showed they could not have committed. What emerges from recent research is that the eye is not a camera and visual memories are not photographs that can be universally relied on to give an accurate record of what we have seen. The reliability of eye-witness testimony will be explored further when we discuss memory in Chapter 10 (see page 261).

ACTIVITY 5.8

Imagine you witness a violent crime and get a brief but clear glimpse of the assailant. How confident would you be that you could correctly identify one of the following three men?

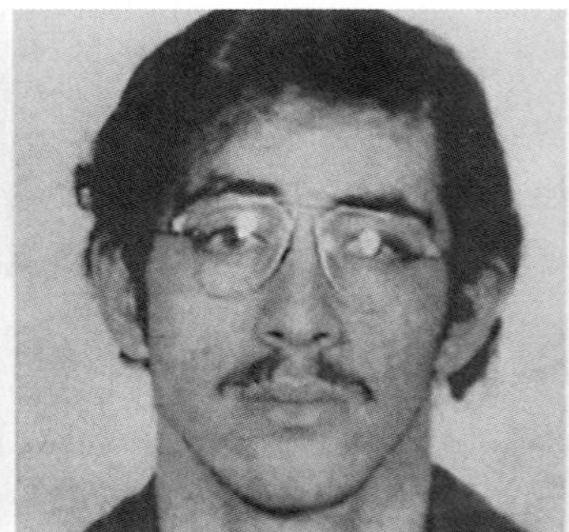

Figure 5.16 Suspects

Distinguishing appearance from reality

RLS – Headline: '"Did You See That?": Heathrow Jet Pilot Saw High-Speed "UFO" That "Passed Within Feet of his Plane"'. Are people who claim to have witnessed UFOs simply misinterpreting what they saw?

Although perception is an important source of knowledge, our discussion has shown that there are at least three reasons for treating it with caution:

1. we may misinterpret what we see

2. we may fail to notice something

3. we may misremember what we have seen.

However, we should not conclude from this that we can *never* trust our senses. After all, we take some things to be illusions only relative to other things that we assume to be true. For example, I can say that the three men in Figure 5.7 (see page 122) are *really* the same height only because I trust my senses when I measure them. If I were uniformly suspicious, I could not even trust the evidence which tells me that some of my perceptions are illusions!

How, then, do we distinguish between appearance and reality in everyday life?

Confirmation by another sense

One way to distinguish appearance from reality is to use a second sense to confirm the evidence of a first. If something looks like an apple and tastes like an apple, then it seems reasonable to conclude that it really *is* an apple. If, on the other hand, there is a conflict between two of our senses, then we may suspect that we are experiencing an illusion. For example, if a pencil is half-immersed in a beaker of water it appears bent to the eye, but if you run your hand along it you can feel that it is straight. So you are likely to conclude that the pencil is not *really* bent but merely *looks* bent.

If you want to be awkward, you might ask why in this example we have given our sense of touch priority over that of sight. Why not say instead that when I half-immerse a pencil in water, it bends, but I suffer a peculiar tactile illusion that makes me think it is still straight? The answer is that, as a matter of brute fact, touch takes priority in determining the reality of something. If you are unsure whether the wall in front of you is real or an illusion, try banging your head against it. If you think that you may be hallucinating the fire in the hearth, try putting your hand in it. For common sense at least, pain is proof enough of the reality of an object. In short, if it hurts then it is real!

Coherence

A second way of distinguishing appearance from reality is in terms of coherence. If you see something that does not 'fit' with your overall experience of the world, then the chances are that you are mistaken. If a man sees a pig flying over the rooftops one evening, he is unlikely to believe what he saw. Since pigs lack the aerodynamic wherewithal to fly, it makes more sense to dismiss a flying pig as an hallucination.

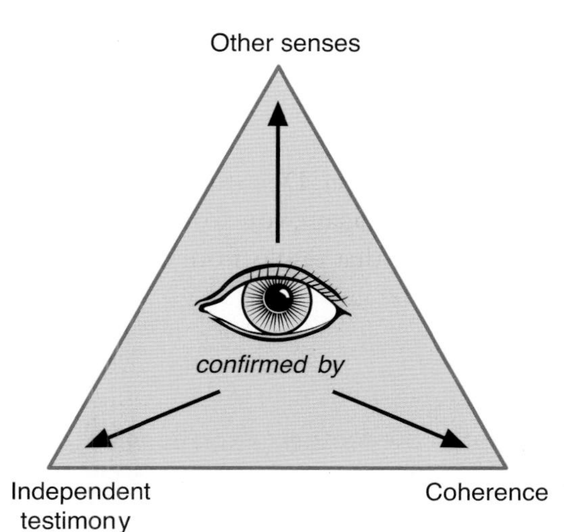

Coherence also explains why in the pencil example (above) it makes more sense to say that we suffer a visual rather than a tactile illusion. The point is that, while the hypothesis that objects bend every time you half-immerse them in water contradicts the known laws of physics, we can explain why they appear to bend in terms of physical theories about the refraction of light.

Figure 5.17 Checking evidence

Independent testimony

A final criterion for distinguishing appearance from reality is the testimony of other people. As discussed on page 130, the evidence of a single eye-witness cannot always be taken at face value; but the credibility of such evidence is greatly increased if it is confirmed by other people. If dozens of independent witnesses claim to have seen a plane crash into a building, then, unless you are in the grip of a conspiracy theory, there is a high – 'beyond reasonable doubt' – probability that such testimony is true.

To summarise, we can say that, while our senses are liable to error, we are in many cases able to correct our mistakes by appealing to such things as a second sense, coherence and the testimony of other people. Of course, we can never be certain that we are right but, as discussed in Chapter 2, knowledge requires something less than certainty. Perception may be fallible, but in many cases it is a reliable enough foundation on which to base our knowledge claims.

Ultimate reality

The final topic in this chapter is a philosophical one concerning the extent to which perception gives us knowledge of ultimate reality. As discussed earlier, we are only able to capture some information in the butterfly-net of our senses. Imagine if we had evolved so that our eyes were sensitive to light in a different range of wavelengths, or that we used echolocation rather than vision. Our experience of the world would presumably be very different from what it is now. This may lead us to wonder what reality is actually like once we strip away the interpretation that our sense-organs impose on it.

What is really out there?

To explore the question of what is really 'out there', consider the following three examples.

1 Pain, taste and colour

If by accident you burn your hand in a fire, you think of the resulting pain as being in your hand rather than in the fire. You do not think that the pain is somehow in the fire, independent of your experience of it. The pain that you feel is surely nothing more than the subjective experience that results from the interaction between your hand and the fire.

Take another example: if you drink a can of cola it tastes sweet. Does the sweetness exist in the cola, or does it exist only in your mouth? Well, again, you would probably agree that the sweetness is simply a subjective experience that results from the interaction between your taste buds and the cola.

ACTIVITY 5.9

Galileo (1564–1642) once said 'The tickle is not in the feather.' Explain what you think he meant by this. What relevance does it have to our discussion?

While you may accept the idea that pain and taste are merely subjective experiences, you probably feel less sure about this way of thinking when it comes to such things as colours. Surely the sky is blue and snow is white and grass is green? Well, for *us* all of these things are of course true. But if we apply the same reasoning that we used in the cola example, we seem forced to admit that the green is no more in the grass than the sweetness is in the cola or the pain is in the fire. The green that you see when you look at the grass is, once again, simply the result of the interaction between your eyes and the underlying structure of the grass. And if our eyes had evolved differently and were sensitive to light of a different wavelength we would not see grass as green at all. We seem to be pushed towards the unsettling conclusion that the world in itself has no colour at all – reality is colourless.

2 The tree in the forest

Consider the well-known question 'If a tree falls in a forest and there is no one there to hear it, does it make a sound?' The common-sense answer is to say that of course it makes a sound. Falling trees are noisy things. You may conjure up in your mind a picture of a huge tree falling and the tremendous crash it makes as it falls to the ground. But if you think that sound is nothing more than the effect of air vibrations on our ears, then it would seem to follow that if there are no ears in the neighbourhood, then the tree does not make a sound.

One way of trying to resolve the above puzzle is to make a distinction between two senses of the word 'sound'. Sound_1, we might say, is *physical* sound – that is, the vibrations in the air that are caused by things like falling trees. Sound_2, by contrast, is *experienced* sound – the actual crash, bang, wallop that we hear when trees hit the ground. We can now say that if a tree falls in a forest and there is no one there to hear it, there is sound_1 but no sound_2.

This solves the problem, but it may leave you with a somewhat eerie feeling. For it means that, if the phone rings after everyone has left my apartment in the morning, there may be vibrations in the air, but there is no distinctive 'ring-ring' sound. The most we can say is that if I were in my apartment then I would hear the phone ring. More dramatically, this way of thinking means that, millions of years ago before the emergence of life on Earth, our planet was a silent place. Breaking waves and storms and volcanoes set up vibrations in the air, but there were no crashes or bangs or wallops. And if right now we were to surgically remove the ears from all sentient beings, the world would again revert to silence.

Now consider another question: if a rose flowers and dies in an uninhabited garden and there is no one there to see it, does it have a colour? We might again distinguish between physical and experienced colour, and say that in the former sense it has a colour, and in the latter sense it does not. This seems to lead us to the conclusion that, before there were any eyes in the world, the sky was not blue, and the roses were not red, and the grass was not green – at least not in the experiential sense of these words.

The examples we have considered above suggest that we cannot say that colours, sounds and tastes exist out there independent of our experience of them. So we may begin to wonder whether *anything* can be said to exist independent of our experience of it.

3 The tables in the classroom

As a final example, consider the tables in your classroom at school. After you leave the room at the end of the day, how do you know the tables are still there? If you had nothing better to do, you could sneak back to school in the evening and take a look. I am confident that you would find the tables quietly sitting there just as you left them. But how do you know the tables are still there when no one is looking at them? (This is similar to the child's question: 'How do you know the light goes out when you close the fridge door?')

This may sound like a stupid question, and common sense will of course say that unobserved tables look much the same as observed tables. But how do you *know*? Perhaps tables only behave like decent, law-abiding tables when we are there to keep an eye on them; and perhaps when no one is around they dance around the room and turn somersaults.

You might think that there is a conclusive way to put an end to such surreal speculations. All you have to do is set up a video camera in the classroom, switch it on before you go home for the evening, and leave it running overnight. You will produce the most boring movie ever made: *Tables! The Motion Picture* – a movie in which absolutely nothing happens. This surely proves that unobserved tables behave in the same way as tables that are observed. But in fact your use of the video has not solved the problem, but merely relocated it. For the question now arises: 'How do you know that the images stay on the film when you are not watching it?'

This discussion may confirm your suspicion that philosophers spend their time asking useless questions that have no practical value. Surely life is too short to worry about what tables do when there is no one around to see them? Who really cares? Although we may be unable to *prove* that tables behave in standard table-like ways when we are not around, perhaps all that really matters is that they behave like tables when we are around. Perhaps we should conclude that what tables do in their spare time is no concern of ours!

Theories of reality

There are three different theories about the relationship between perception and reality:

1. common-sense realism

2. scientific realism

3. phenomenalism.

1 Common-sense realism

This is the common-sense idea, mentioned at the beginning of this chapter, that the way we perceive the world mirrors the way the world actually is. However, since what we perceive is determined in part by the nature of our sense-organs, we have seen that there are good reasons for rejecting common-sense realism.

ACTIVITY 5.10

In your own words, outline the main arguments against common-sense realism.

2 Scientific realism

According to **scientific realism**, the world exists as an independent reality, but it is very different from the way we perceive it. The physicist Sir Arthur Eddington (1882–1944) once compared the common-sense description of a table with the scientific description of it. According to common sense, a table has extension and colour, and is comparatively permanent and substantial. But the scientific table is quite different:

KT – scientific realism: the view that the real world is not the world as it appears to our senses, but as it is described by science

> *It does not belong to the world previously mentioned – that world which spontaneously appears around me when I open my eyes ... My scientific table is mostly emptiness. Sparsely scattered in that emptiness are numerous electric charges rushing about with great speed; but their combined bulk amounts to less than a billionth of the bulk of the table itself. Notwithstanding its strange construction it turns out to be an entirely efficient table. It supports my writing paper as satisfactorily as [an ordinary table] for when I lay the paper on it the little electric particles with their headlong speed keep on hitting the underside, so that the paper is maintained in shuttlecock fashion at a nearly steady level. If I lean upon this table I shall not go through; or, to be strictly accurate, the chance of my scientific elbow going through my scientific table is so excessively small that it can be neglected in practical life.*
>
> *Arthur Eddington,* The Nature of the Physical World, *London: Dent, 1935*

This brief description draws attention to the strangeness of the scientific picture of reality. The familiar, comfortable, sensuous world of our everyday experience vanishes and is replaced by a colourless, soundless, odourless realm of atoms whizzing around in empty space.

3 Phenomenalism

At the beginning of this chapter, we discussed a philosophical position known as empiricism, according to which all knowledge must ultimately be based on experience. If we take this idea seriously, then we seem to arrive at a more radical position known as **phenomenalism**. According to this view, matter is simply *the permanent possibility of sensation*, and it makes no sense to say that the world exists independent of our experience of it. A phenomenalist would take the statement 'There are tables in the classroom at school' to mean not that the tables are in some deep sense there but simply that if you go to the classroom you will have various table-experiences. The Irish philosopher George Berkeley (1685–1753) summed up the phenomenalist position with the famous slogan 'To be is to be perceived'.

KT – phenomenalism: an extreme form of empiricism which claims that physical objects are 'bundles of sense-data' that cannot be said to exist in themselves independently of our experience

Despite its counter-intuitive nature, phenomenalism seems to follow logically from the idea that all knowledge must ultimately be based on experience. For, if this is true, then we obviously cannot know what the world is like independent of our experience of it. This does not mean that the world does *not* exist independent of our experience of it – for that, too, is to make a claim that goes beyond the limits of experience. The point is rather that, beyond our experience of reality, there is simply nothing to be said. Understood in this way, phenomenalism could be seen as a call to humility; for it insists that we can only know the world from our distinctively human perspective and have no right to pontificate about the nature of ultimate reality.

ACTIVITY 5.11

1. If you believed in phenomenalism, what difference, if any, would it make to practical life?
2. Does it bother you to think that we cannot know anything about what the universe is like independent of our experience of it?

What should we believe?

The three theories of reality we have discussed can be summarised in the following three slogans.

Common-sense realism: 'What you see is what is there'

Scientific realism: 'Atoms in the void'

Phenomenalism: 'To be is to be perceived'

One interesting thing that comes out of this rather surreal discussion about the nature of ultimate reality is that if we push empiricism to its limits we end up with counter-intuitive conclusions. At this point we have a choice. We can either stick with empiricism and insist that we can know nothing about ultimate reality, or reject strict empiricism and insist that there is a world out there independent of our experience of it.

Deep down, most people are probably realists about the existence of the world. Despite the doubts we have raised about realism, there are perhaps two ways of trying to rescue it:

1. Although we cannot prove the existence of an independent reality, we might argue that it is the most reasonable hypothesis to account for the regularity of our experience. If, for example, you light a fire and return some hours later to find only a pile of ashes, the simplest way to explain what happened is to say that the fire was burning continuously in your absence.
2. The vast majority of people have a strong intuition that the world exists independent of our perception of it. As our discussion of scientific realism has shown, it may be very different from our everyday picture of it, but most scientists are intuitive realists and believe that they are making discoveries about an independently existing reality.

Conclusion

We began this chapter by stressing that perception is an important way of knowing which plays a key role in most areas of knowledge. However, as our discussion has progressed we have seen that there is more to perception than meets the eye, and that we cannot simply take the evidence of our senses for granted. For not only do they sometimes deceive us, but they are also selective and can be distorted by our beliefs and prejudices. In everyday life, there are ways of distinguishing between appearance and reality, and moving towards a more accurate picture of the world. We can, for example, use a second sense to check up on a first, or appeal to the testimony of other people.

"Don't you understand? This is life, this is what is happening. We can't switch to another channel."

Figure 5.18

On a practical level, you would be mad to simply ignore the evidence of your senses. If you want to survive when you cross the road, it pays to go with the hypothesis that if something looks and sounds like a 20-tonne truck speeding towards you then it really is a 20-tonne truck. As a general rule of thumb, it probably makes sense to doubt our senses only if there are good reasons for doing so. Admittedly, perception cannot give us certainty but, as we saw in Chapter 2, knowledge requires something less than certainty. If the perceptual evidence is consistent with other ways of knowing, such as reason and intuition, then it is probably a good enough foundation for reliable knowledge.

Key to Figure 5.13

Figure 5.19 Face: the image of Figure 5.13, clarified

Key points

- Our five senses are an important source of knowledge about the world, but rather than passively reflecting reality, they actively structure it.
- Perception consists of two elements, sensation and interpretation, but we are often not consciously aware of the latter element.
- Looking at visual illusions can help make us aware of the role that interpretation plays in perception.
- Perception is selective and what we notice in a given environment is influenced by factors such as intensity, contrast, interest, mood and expectations.
- The fallibility of perception is relevant to issues in the real world such as eye-witness testimony in criminal trials.
- We usually distinguish between appearance and reality by using a second sense to confirm the evidence of the first, or by appealing to coherence or the testimony of other people.
- The way we experience the world is partly determined by the structure of our sense-organs.
- If we accept that pain and taste are subjective, we might conclude that colour and sound are also subjective.
- There are three main theories about the relationship between perception and reality: common-sense realism, scientific realism and phenomenalism.
- Despite our sceptical doubts, the existence of the external world is the most reasonable hypothesis to account for the regularity of our experience.
- Although perception cannot give us certainty, if the evidence of our senses is consistent with what reason and intuition tell us, it can still provide a good foundation for reliable knowledge.

Key terms

change blindness
common-sense realism
empiricism
figure and ground
other-race effect
phenomenalism
scientific realism
sensation
visual agnosia
visual grouping

IB prescribed essay titles

1. When should we trust our senses to give us truth? (November 2008 / May 2009)
2. To what extent may the subjective nature of perception be regarded as an advantage for artists but an obstacle to be overcome for scientists? (November 2004 / May 2005)

Further reading

Books

Diane Ackerman, *A Natural History of the Senses* (Vintage, 1995). In this book, the author takes us on a rich journey through each of the five senses. She skilfully weaves insights from the sciences, arts and personal experience into a fascinating synthesis.

V. S. Ramachandran, *Phantoms in the Brain* (Quill, 1999), Chapter 4: 'The Zombie in the Brain'. V. S. Ramachandran is a neuroscientist who has studied brain-damaged patients. In this chapter he focuses on a strange condition known as 'blindsight' to analyse and speculate about the nature of perception.

Online articles

Beau Lotto, 'Optical Illusions Show How We See', *Huffington Post*, 6 November 2012.

6 Reason

You are not thinking. You are merely being logical.

Niels Bohr, 1885–1962, to Albert Einstein

Logic is the beginning of wisdom, Valeris, not the end.

Spock, *Star Trek*

The head is always fooled by the heart.

La Rochefoucauld, 1613–80

Two extravagances: to exclude reason, to admit only reason.

Blaise Pascal, 1623–62

We are never more true to ourselves than when we are inconsistent.

Oscar Wilde, 1854–1900

All generalizations are false – including this one.

Henry David Thoreau, 1817–62

Critical reason is the only alternative to violence so far discovered.

Karl Popper, 1902–94

You do not reason a man out of something he was not reasoned into.

Jonathan Swift, 1667–1745

It is better to debate a question without settling it than to settle a question without debating it.

Joseph Joubert, 1754–1824

Man has such a predilection for systems and abstract deductions that he is ready to distort the truth intentionally, he is ready to deny the evidence of his senses only to justify his logic.

Fyodor Dostoevsky, 1821–81

He that will not reason is a bigot; he that cannot reason is a fool; and he that dares not reason is a slave.

William Drummond, 1585–1649

Introduction

According to Sherlock Holmes, that most English of fictional detectives, 'crime is common, logic is rare'. Holmes prided himself on having made the 'faculties of deduction and logical synthesis' his 'special province'. In one mystery concerning the theft of an expensive race horse, a police officer asks Holmes if any aspect of the crime strikes him as significant. 'Yes', he says, 'the curious incident of the dog in the night time'. 'The dog did nothing in the night time', says the hapless police officer. 'That was the curious incident', replies Holmes. The solution to the crime hinges on the fact that the watchdog guarding the horse did not bark in the night, and from this Holmes deduces that the thief must have been known to the dog. Formally, we can lay out Holmes' reasoning process as follows:

Figure 6.1 Sherlock Holmes

> Watchdogs bark at strangers.
>
> The watchdog did not bark at the thief.
>
> Therefore the thief was not a stranger.

This is a good example of the way in which we can acquire new knowledge about the world by using reason. Although we may not have Sherlock Holmes' power of **deduction**, we are constantly using reason to go beyond the immediate evidence of our senses. You notice that the pavement is wet when you go out in the morning and conclude that it has been raining during the night. You know that you left your mobile phone either in your coat pocket or on your desk; it is not in your coat pocket, therefore it must be on your desk. You know that Lake Geneva is a fresh-water lake, and you know that sharks don't like fresh water; therefore there cannot be any sharks in Lake Geneva.

KT – deduction: reasoning from the general to the particular

The benefits of this kind of reasoning are obvious. Take the last example: assuming that your initial assumptions are correct, you don't need to waste your time checking every freshwater lake you come across to see if it has any sharks in it. Reason tells you that you can safely swim in any freshwater lake happy in the knowledge that you will not be attacked by a shark. Similarly, Holmes did not need to base his knowledge that the dog knew the thief directly on sense experience, but was able to infer it from what he already knew.

One of the great attractions of reason as a source of knowledge is that it seems to give us certainty. To take a well-known example, given that all human beings are mortal, and given that Socrates is a human being, it *necessarily* follows that Socrates is mortal. There are no 'if's or 'but's about it, and it is not a matter of personal opinion or the culture in which you were brought up. Given the assumptions – which in logic are called **premises** – the conclusion *has* to follow. There is no way you can wriggle out of it. After discussing the fallibility of sense perception in the last chapter, this kind of certainty might seem refreshing, and it is perhaps not surprising that there is a school of philosophy, called **rationalism**, according to which reason is the most important source of knowledge.

KT – premises: assumptions on which an argument is based or from which a conclusion is drawn

KT – rationalism: a school of thought which says that reason is the most important source of knowledge

The central tenet of rationalism is that we can discover important truths about reality through the use of reason alone. Rationalists are particularly impressed with areas of knowledge such as logic and mathematics, which seem to be both certain and useful; and, unlike their empiricist rivals, they are suspicious of knowledge based on sense perception on the grounds that our senses can all too easily mislead us. One of the most famous rationalists in history was René Descartes (1596–1650) who tried to build a system of philosophy on his famous, and allegedly self-evident, starting point, '*Cogito ergo sum*' ('I think therefore I am'). Curiously enough, in one of his books Descartes tells us that the idea of building a rational system of philosophy first came to him in a dream!

LQ – Cultural perspectives: Are there universal standards of reasoning, or does the way people reason vary from culture to culture?

Whether it is actually possible to build a system of philosophy based purely on reason may be doubted, but reason is clearly an important way of knowing. In this chapter, we will look at three kinds of reasoning:

- deductive reasoning
- inductive reasoning
- informal reasoning.

In our discussion, we shall encounter a variety of well-known and commonly committed **fallacies** (i.e. invalid patterns of reasoning) that it is important to guard against. We will then try to come to a balanced assessment of the value and limitations of logic.

KT – fallacy: an invalid pattern of argument

ACTIVITY 6.1

1. Which of our faculties do you think is more reliable – reason or sense perception? Give reasons.
2. The following text is taken from a *Calvin & Hobbes* cartoon and is an amusing exchange between Calvin and his father. Analyse what Dad says and determine whether or not it is internally consistent.

   CALVIN: Dad, how come old photographs are always black and white? Didn't they have color film back then?

   DAD: Sure they did. In fact, those old photographs are in color. It's just the world was black and white then.

   CALVIN: Really?

   DAD: Yep. The world didn't turn color until some time in the 1930s, and it was pretty grainy color for a while, too.

   CALVIN: That's really weird.

   DAD: Well, truth is stranger than fiction.

LQ – Sense perception: Compare and contrast the reliability of reason and perception as possible sources of knowledge. If they conflict, which would you trust?

CALVIN: But then why are old paintings in color? If the world was black and white, wouldn't artists have painted it that way?

DAD: Not necessarily. A lot of great artists were insane.

CALVIN: But – but how could they have painted in color anyway? Wouldn't **their paints** have been shades of grey back then?

DAD: Of course, but they turned color like everything else did in the '30s.

CALVIN: So why didn't old black and white photos turn color too?

DAD: Because they were color pictures of black and white, remember?

Figure 6.2 In general, do people reason more like Mr Spock or Homer Simpson?

Deductive reasoning

Deductive reasoning is any form of reasoning that moves from the general to the particular. For example:

All dogs are mammals.

Fido is a dog.

Therefore Fido is a mammal.

As you can see, the argument moves from a general claim about *all* dogs to a particular conclusion about Fido.

Syllogisms

The above kind of deductive argument is known as a **syllogism**. A syllogism consists of the following items:

1. two premises and a conclusion
2. three terms, each of which occurs twice ('dogs', 'mammals' and 'Fido')
3. **quantifiers**, such as 'all', or 'some' or 'no', which tell us the quantity that is being referred to.

KT – syllogism: a deductive argument with two premises and a conclusion

KT – quantifier: a word used with a noun to tell us the quantity of the thing being referred to

Truth and validity

KT – validity: the property of an argument in which the conclusion follows logically from the premises

Before looking at some more examples of syllogisms, we need to make a distinction between truth and **validity.** These two words are sometimes used interchangeably, but they do not mean the same thing. Truth is concerned with what is the case, validity with whether conclusions follow from premises; truth is a property of statements, validity of arguments. To avoid confusion, you should not say that an argument is true or false, but rather that it is valid or invalid.

More formally, we can say that an argument is valid if the conclusion follows logically – that is, necessarily – from the premises; and it is invalid if the conclusion does *not* follow logically from the premises. The main point to grasp is that *the validity of an argument is independent of the truth or falsity of the premises it contains.* Consider, for example, the following syllogism:

> All panthers are pink.
>
> Che Guevara is a panther.
>
> Therefore Che Guevara is pink.

Both the premises and the conclusion of this argument are false, but *the argument itself is valid.* To see this, *imagine* a world – call it planet Zog – where all panthers are pink, and Che Guevara is a panther. You can immediately conclude that on planet Zog Che Guevara must be pink!

So, if you want to determine the validity of an argument, imagine that the first premise is true on planet Zog, and imagine that the second premise is true on planet Zog – it doesn't matter whether or not the premises are true on Earth – and then ask yourself whether, on planet Zog, the conclusion must necessarily be the case. If the answer is 'yes', then the argument is valid; if it is 'no', then the argument is invalid. What logic enables you to do is draw conclusions about planet Zog that may not have been obvious from the information you were initially given (the premises).

Figure 6.3

It is worth noting that an argument can be valid, not only when its premises and conclusion are false – as in the above example – but also when premises are false and the conclusion is true. For example:

All ostriches are teachers.

Richard is an ostrich.

Therefore Richard is a teacher.

In fact, we can construct valid arguments for almost any combinations of true and false premises and conclusions. *The only situation that is impossible is a valid argument with true premises and a false conclusion.*

ACTIVITY 6.2

Make up your own valid syllogisms to illustrate each of the following.

1. Two true premises and a true conclusion
2. One true premise, one false premise and a true conclusion
3. One true premise, one false premise, and a false conclusion
4. Two false premises and a true conclusion
5. Two false premises and a false conclusion

The structure of arguments

As our discussion has suggested, pure logic is concerned only with the *structure* of arguments. It doesn't matter if the premises are false, or even meaningless. All that matters is that the conclusion logically follows from the premises. Consider, for example, the following syllogism:

All blims are blams.

Some blims are bloms.

Therefore some blams are bloms.

Although 'blim', 'blam' and 'blom' are meaningless words, we can still say with total confidence that if all blims are blams and some blims are bloms, then some blams are bloms. What this means is that, once you have determined that the structure of an argument is valid (or invalid), you can say that any other argument with the same structure will also be valid (or invalid). The argument structure for the above syllogism is:

All *A*s are *B*s.

Some *A*s are *C*s.

Therefore some *B*s are *C*s.

We can substitute anything we like for *A*, *B* and *C* and the argument will always be valid.

KT – belief bias: the tendency to think an argument is valid simply because you agree with the conclusion

Abstracting from the content of an argument and focusing on its structure can help to avoid the danger of **belief bias**. This refers to the tendency we have to believe that an argument is valid simply because we agree with the conclusion. Consider the following argument: 'Democrats are in favour of free speech, and since dictators are not democrats, they are obviously opposed to free speech.' Since you probably agree with the conclusion, you might be tempted to say that the argument is valid. But it is not. The point to remember from this example is *just because you agree with a conclusion does not mean that the argument for it is a sound one.*

Using Venn diagrams

KT – Venn diagram: a diagram which shows the logical relations between sets of things

Trying to decide whether or not a syllogism is valid is no easy matter. A useful way to picture what is going on is to draw a **Venn diagram**. The example above can be represented in terms of three overlapping circles. To represent 'All *A*s are *B*s', put the circle of *A*s inside the circle of *B*s; and to represent 'Some *A*s are *C*s', have the circle of *C*s intersect the circle of *A*s. You can now see that to the extent that circles *A* and *C* intersect, circles *B* and *C* must also intersect. It therefore follows that 'Some *B*s are *C*s'. The argument is valid.

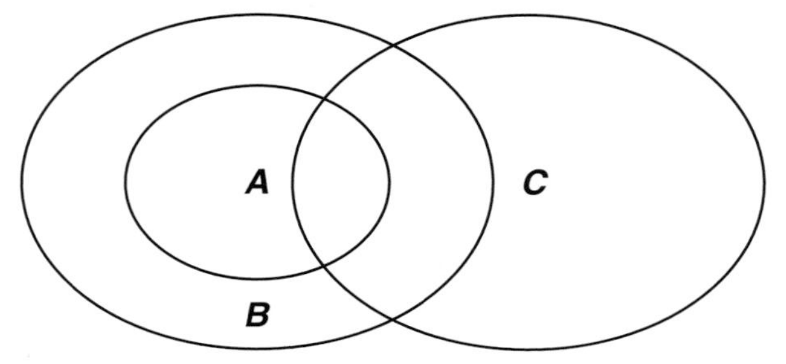

Figure 6.4

You can also use Venn diagrams to show invalid argument structures. For example, the following argument structure is invalid.

All *As* are *Bs*.
All *Bs* are *Cs*.
Therefore all *Cs* are *As*.

This can be pictured as in Figure 6.5.

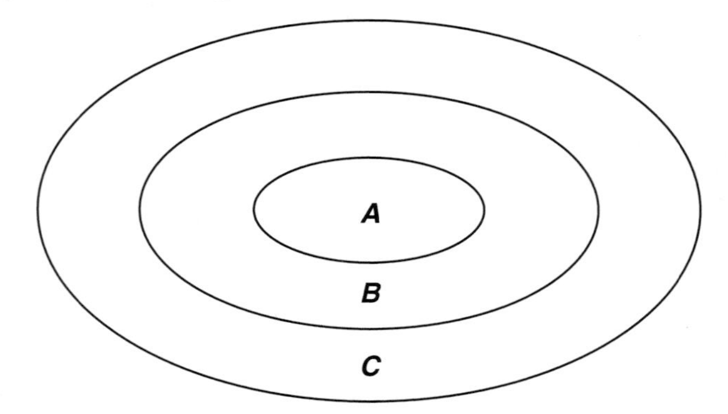

Figure 6.5

You can now see that just because the circle of *A*s falls inside the circle of *B*s, and the circle of *B*s falls inside the circle of *C*s, it does not follow that 'All *C*s are *A*s'. The argument is invalid.

ACTIVITY 6.3

How would you have to change the conclusion in the above example to make the argument structure valid?

When using Venn diagrams to judge the validity of arguments, you need to be careful about the way you interpret them. Despite appearances, you cannot conclude from Figure 6.4 that 'Some *C*s are not *A*s'. Nor can you conclude from Figure 6.5 that 'Some *C*s are not *A*s'. (Can you see why in each case?) Using Venn diagrams, then, is no substitute for careful thinking; but it can still be a help in solving these kinds of problem.

ACTIVITY 6.4

Using Venn diagrams, state whether each of the following arguments is valid or invalid:

1. All Italians eat spaghetti.
   Giovanni Rossi eats spaghetti.
   Therefore Giovanni Rossi is an Italian.
2. No Martians have red noses.
   Rudolph has a red nose.
   Therefore Rudolph is not a Martian.
3. All bull-fighters are brave people.
   Some brave people are compassionate.
   Therefore some bull-fighters are compassionate.
4. Some monks are Tibetans.
   All Tibetans meditate.
   Therefore some monks meditate.
5. Some astrologers are frauds.
   Some frauds are poor.
   Therefore some astrologers are poor.
6. All bobos have dogs.
   No doctors have dogs.
   Therefore no bobos are doctors.
7. All rookies are red-heads.
   All red-heads are runners.
   Therefore all rookies are runners.
8. No alphas are betas.
   No gammas are betas.
   Therefore no gammas are alphas.

Deductive reasoning preserves truth

We have seen that the validity of an argument has nothing to do with the truth or falsity of its premises. So *just because an argument is valid, it does not follow that the conclusion is true*. To be sure that the conclusion of an argument is true, you must be able to answer 'yes' to both of the following questions:

1. Are the premises true?

2. Is the argument valid?

Figure 6.6

In practice, logic is most useful when we begin with true premises; for if we then reason validly we can be sure that the conclusion is true. Logical reasoning can therefore be seen as a technique for *preserving truth* in the sense that if you begin with truth you will end up with truth. (If, on the other hand, you begin with falsehood, you can end up with anything.)

When people argue in everyday life, they rarely set their arguments out in a formal way, and if a premise strikes them as obvious, they may simply assume it and not bother explicitly stating it. Such an incomplete argument is known as an **enthymeme**.

KT – enthymeme: an incomplete argument in which one of the premises is assumed but not stated

ACTIVITY 6.5

Supply the missing premise for each of the following enthymemes:

1. Jenny goes to Oxford University, so she must be very intelligent.
2. Drugs should be legalised because they only harm the addict.
3. Graham is a politician so he is probably lying.
4. Cheerleading should be an Olympic event because cheerleaders compete, train and have a high level of physical fitness.
5. Since it is natural to eat meat, there is nothing morally wrong with it.

We have seen that deductive reasoning is an instrument for the *preservation* of truth but this does not mean that it is a *source* of truth. If you go back to the syllogism about Socrates, the conclusion that 'Socrates is mortal' is true only if the premises are true. But how do you know that the premises are true? How, for example, can you be sure that 'All human beings are mortal'? Your knowledge that all human beings are mortal cannot be conjured out of logic, but is based on *experience*. This brings us to the topic of inductive reasoning.

ACTIVITY 6.6

How sure are you that some day you will die? What evidence do you have for your belief?

Inductive reasoning

While deductive reasoning goes from the general to the particular, another kind of reasoning, known as **induction**, goes in the opposite direction – from the particular to the general. With reference to the above example, my belief that all human beings are mortal is a generalisation from a vast number of particular instances. In history, every human being I know of eventually died, and I have never heard of a historical human being who *didn't* die. Therefore, I can say with confidence that 'All *observed* human beings throughout history have died.' But when we reason inductively we typically go further than this and generalise – or make an *inductive inference* – from the observed to the unobserved. Thus, in this example, we move from 'All *observed* human beings are mortal' to 'All human beings are mortal.'

KT – induction: reasoning from the particular to the general

Since inductive reasoning typically moves from the observed to the unobserved, it enables us to make generalisations about the world, and we are constantly using such reasoning in everyday life. Since apples have nourished me in the past, I assume that they will nourish me in the future. Since my neighbour's dog has been friendly to me in the past, I am confident that he will not bite me today. And since my chair has supported my weight in the past, I expect it to continue to do so in the future. In each of these cases past experience shapes our expectations about the (unobserved) future. If you think about it, you will see that you make literally thousands of such inferences every day, and that life would be impossible if you did not assume that most of the regularities that have held in the past will continue to hold in the future.

Indeed, there is a sense in which the whole of language is based on inductive generalisations. For, as we saw in Chapter 4, when we put labels, such as 'teacher', 'dog' or 'table', on things we are implicitly organising them into general classes so that we can make predictions about them. If you call something a 'table' you have different expectations about its behaviour than if you call it a 'dog'. For example, tables aren't interested in being stroked, and dogs don't like having objects put on them. Thus language might be thought of as the inherited wisdom of the community about how the world is organised; and our tendency to look for regularities in our environment and put labels on them has obvious survival value.

LQ – Language: How can vague language lead to bad reasoning?

ACTIVITY 6.7

1. If someone says 'You should never generalise', there is a sense in which they are contradicting themselves. Why is this, and what conclusion do you draw from it?
2. My dog, Fido, gets excited when I get his leash out, and seems to know that he is about to go for a walk. Do you think he is using inductive reasoning to predict what is going to happen in the future? Does this mean that he is able to reason?

Science also uses inductive reasoning and typically formulates general laws on the basis of a limited number of observations. For example, if metal *A* and metal *B* and metal *C* expand when heated, at some point a scientist is likely to conclude that *all* metals expand when heated.

ACTIVITY 6.8

What percentage of the metal existing on our planet would you guess scientists have tested to see if it expands when heated? What does this suggest to you about the certainty or otherwise of scientific laws?

Deduction and induction compared

When we compare induction with deduction we can say that the former gives us more information in that it enables us to make generalisations about the world, but the latter is more certain. The difference between the two kinds of reasoning can be summarised in the table below.

DEDUCTION	INDUCTION
Definition	
Reasoning from general to particular	Reasoning from particular to general
Example	
All metals expand when heated. A is a metal. Therefore A expands when heated.	Metal A expands when heated; metal B expands when heated; metal C expands when heated. Therefore all metals expand when heated.
Value	
More certain, but less informative than induction	More informative, but less certain than deduction

In practice, however, deduction turns out to be no more certain than induction. This is because the premises on which deductive reasoning about the world is based must be derived from induction. To see this, go back to the example at the beginning of this chapter. The validity of Sherlock Holmes' conclusion that the thief was known to the dog depends on the truth of the premise that all watchdogs bark at strangers. And we can know that only by induction! Watchdogs *A, B, C, D, E, …* bark at strangers. Therefore all watchdogs bark at strangers. So Holmes' conclusion is only as certain as the inductive premises on which it is based.

How reliable is inductive reasoning?

Since induction goes beyond the immediate evidence of our senses, we cannot always rely on it. This is because we tend to make *hasty generalisations* and jump to conclusions on the basis of insufficient evidence. For example, if a tourist is served by a rude French waiter, he may conclude that all French people are rude; and if a female fighter pilot crashes a jet her male colleague may conclude that women are unfit to fly. Neither of these conclusions is justified by the evidence, and this kind of faulty reasoning can easily lead to racist or sexist attitudes. The trouble, as the psychologist Gordon Allport (1897–1967) observed, is that, 'Given a thimbleful of facts, we rush to make generalizations as large as a tub.'

RLS – Headline: 'White House Says No Evidence of Aliens'. When is absence of evidence, evidence of absence?

Sometimes even well-established generalisations can let us down. With reference to the examples mentioned above, it is always possible that tomorrow apples make me sick, my neighbour's dog savages me, and my chair collapses. Europeans used to believe that all swans are white until they went to Australia and discovered that some swans are black. You might even question a well-established regularity, such as 'Water boils at 100 degrees centigrade.' After all, it is not true if you are at the top of a mountain!

Figure 6.7 When can we trust inductive reasoning?

The tendency to make hasty generalisations is made worse by a phenomenon known as *confirmation bias*. As we saw in Chapter 1, this suggests that people tend to remember only evidence that supports their beliefs and to forget evidence that goes against them. Thus once you have decided that the French are arrogant or that the English are cold, you may notice only examples that confirm your prejudice and overlook those that go against it. This may explain why it is so difficult to change the mind of someone who is in the grip of a prejudice.

ACTIVITY 6.9

1. Give three examples of your own of some hasty generalisations.
2. Why do you think that people are so quick to jump to conclusions?
3. What is the difference between a prejudice, a generalisation, and a scientific law?

To illustrate the extent to which we jump to conclusions on the basis of insufficient evidence, consider the following story, which was devised by the psychologist William V. Haney to illustrate precisely this point:

> *A businessman had just turned off the lights in the store when a man appeared and demanded money. The owner opened a cash register. The contents of the cash register were scooped up, and the man sped away. A member of the police force was notified promptly.*

ACTIVITY 6.10

Given the information in the story, respond to each of the statements below by making a note of your response to each one: 'T' if the statement is definitely true, 'F' if the statement is definitely false, and 'U' if the statement is unknown.

1. A man appeared after the owner had turned off his store lights.
2. The robber was a man.
3. The man did not demand money.
4. The man who opened the cash register was the owner.
5. The store owner scooped up the contents of the cash register and ran away.
6. Someone opened a cash register.
7. After the man who demanded the money scooped up the contents of the cash register, he ran away.
8. While the cash register contained money, the story does not state how much.
9. The robber demanded money of the owner.
10. The story concerns a series of events in which only three persons are referred to: the owner of the store, a man who demanded money, and a member of the police force.
11. The following events in the story are true: someone demanded money, a cash register was opened, its contents were scooped up, and a man dashed out of the store.

If you check your responses with the answers given at the end of this chapter, you may be surprised by the extent to which you jumped to various false conclusions on the basis of the information that was given to you.

What distinguishes good generalisations?

Since generalisations sometimes lead us into trouble, we need to think about how to distinguish good ones from bad ones. Here are some relevant general criteria:

- *Number.* You should look at a reasonable number of instances. If you see one example of a dog swimming, this is clearly not enough to conclude that 'all dogs can swim', and you should look at a lot more cases.
- *Variety.* You should look at a variety of circumstances. In the above example, you might look at different breeds of dogs, young dogs, old dogs, etc.

- *Exceptions.* You should actively look for counter-examples. You might, for example, ask if anyone has a dog that cannot swim. This will help to guard against confirmation bias.
- *Coherence.* You should demand more evidence to support surprising claims than unsurprising ones. It would take more to convince me that all dogs can walk on their hind legs than that all dogs can swim.
- *Subject area.* You should be aware of the subject area you are dealing with, and keep in mind that generalisations tend to be more reliable in the natural sciences than in the human sciences. For example, if you heat copper sulphate crystals they always turn from blue to white; but when you do experiments with dogs, the results are much less predictable. Indeed, according to the so-called Harvard law of animal behaviour, 'Under carefully controlled experimental circumstances an animal will behave as it damned well pleases.' And the behaviour of human beings – the most complex and contrary of animals – is, of course, the most difficult to predict of all. That is why there are a greater number of reliable generalisations in chemistry than in economics.

LQ – Human sciences: What role does the assumption that human beings are 'rational animals' play in economics? How justified is this assumption?

Although the above criteria can help us to distinguish between more and less reasonable generalisations, they are not precise rules. How many times should a team of scientists repeat an experiment before concluding that they have discovered a new law of nature? We can give some general advice, such as 'Many times if the experiments deal with complex phenomena or give unexpected results'. But there is not a number we can stipulate such as seven or twenty-three. All we can say is that the greater the number of confirming instances the more confident we can be about the generalisation.

Informal reasoning

In the previous section we considered examples of fallacies associated with deduction and induction, such as invalid syllogisms and hasty generalisations. We will now consider some other fallacies that crop up frequently in arguments and discussions.

Post hoc ergo propter hoc

The fallacy of *post hoc ergo propter hoc* (literally, 'after this, therefore on account of this') consists of assuming that because one thing, *B*, follows another thing, *A*, then *A* must be the cause of *B*. For example, just because the murder rate in a country goes up after the abolition of capital punishment, it does not necessarily follow that capital punishment is an effective deterrent. The increase in the murder rate could be explained by other factors – such as a rise in poverty or the greater availability of guns. Notice that we said 'it does not *necessarily* follow that capital punishment is an effective deterrent'. The point is that while it *could be* the case, we cannot jump to this conclusion simply from the fact that the murder rate has gone up. We need more evidence.

Even when one event, A, is *regularly* followed by another event, B, it still does not necessarily mean that A is the cause of B. For example night is *regularly* followed by day, but night is not the *cause* of day. The evening weather forecast is *regularly* followed by the next day's weather, but the forecast does not *cause* the weather. The purchase of wedding rings is regularly followed by weddings, but the rings do not cause people to marry. In each of the above cases, the event in question is caused by some other factor – the rotation of the earth on its axis, pre-existing weather conditions, the decision to marry.

ACTIVITY 6.11

1. 'Crime Down Since New Police Commissioner Took Over.' What does this headline *imply* about the cause of the drop in crime? How reasonable is it to draw this implication?
2. How would you explain the well-known observation – supported by statistical evidence – that as the number of churches in American cities increases, so does the number of prostitutes?

RLS – Headline: 'Drink More Milk – You Could Win a Nobel Prize! Nations That Consume More of the White Stuff Have More Laureates'. What distinguishes a causal connection from a coincidental correlation?

We need to be careful not to claim that this fallacy is being committed when in fact it is not. For example, for many years the American tobacco industry admitted that there was a statistical correlation between smoking and cancer, but denied that there was a causal connection. They implied that people who said 'Smoking causes cancer' were committing the *post hoc ergo propter hoc* fallacy. A clever ploy, but the fact is that, in addition to this statistical correlation, there is a large amount of other evidence that smoking causes cancer.

In general, we can say that a correlation between two things may be a *preliminary* indication that there is a causal connection between them. If, for example, I notice that the incidence of heart disease is lower in people who eat fruit every day than in the general population, it may be worth investigating this further. A fallacy is only being committed if we immediately jump to the conclusion that fruit prevents heart disease.

Figure 6.8

Ad hominem fallacy

The *ad hominem* fallacy (literally, 'against the man') consists in attacking or supporting the person rather than the argument. If, for example, you make an argument for world government, and are told that you are too young and idealistic to know what you are talking about, that is *ad hominem*. Rather than critiquing your argument, your opponent is simply attacking *you*. Similarly, if I make a case for higher salaries for teachers, and you reject what I say on the grounds that as a teacher I *would* say that, then that, too, is *ad hominem*. The fact that as a teacher I might have a *vested interest* in teachers getting higher salaries may, of course, make you *suspicious* of my argument, but it is not in itself a reason for rejecting it. You need to think about what I actually say.

Although the *ad hominem* fallacy is usually committed by *criticising* someone, it can also be committed by *supporting* them. For example, if you say 'Einstein was in favour of world government, so it must be a good thing', you are again focusing on the speaker rather than the argument. The same mistake arises when we appeal to what 'most people' or the 'vast majority' believe in order to justify something. As we saw in our discussion of *authority worship* in Chapter 3 (see page 51), just because the vast majority of people believe something doesn't make it true. After all, there was a time when most people believed that it was acceptable to keep slaves and that women shouldn't be allowed to vote.

The above discussion raises the question of whether we are *ever* justified in taking an argument on trust from someone else. The ideal would be to always work everything out for ourselves; but in practice we lack the time and expertise to do this. Given this, it seems more reasonable to take an argument on trust from someone if they are an *authority* in the relevant area than if they are not. So if you say, 'It must be true because Einstein said so', this carries more weight if we are discussing relativity theory than if we are discussing politics or religion – areas in which Einstein has no particular authority. In this context, it is worth bearing in mind Hans Eysenck's comment:

> *Scientists, especially when they leave the particular field in which they have specialised, are just as ordinary, pig-headed and unreasonable as anybody else, and their unusually high intelligence only makes their prejudices all the more dangerous.*

We might now ask whether we are ever justified in *rejecting* what someone says solely on the basis of who they are. If, for example, you were a juror in a criminal trial and discovered that one of the eye-witnesses had a history of telling lies, would you be committing the *ad hominem* fallacy if you rejected his evidence out of hand? Well, if someone has a history of lying, you should clearly not take what he says at face value. But since it is at least possible that *this time* he is telling the truth, you should at least listen to his testimony and see how consistent it is with the rest of the evidence.

Circular reasoning

Circular reasoning (also known as 'vicious circle' and 'begging the question') consists in assuming the truth of something that you are supposed to be proving. When someone commits this fallacy, what at first sight looks like an argument, turns out to be nothing more than a reassertion of their position. Imagine that someone says, 'I know that

Jesus was the Son of God because he said he was, and the Son of God would not lie.' They are begging the question because they are *assuming* the very thing that they are supposed to be *proving* – namely that Jesus was the Son of God. The philosopher Anthony Flew gives another nice example of circular reasoning:

> *Three thieves are arguing about how to divide up the seven pearls they have stolen. One of them picks up the pearls and gives two to each of the other two, keeping the remaining three for himself. One of the other men says 'How come you have kept three?' 'Because I am the leader.' 'Oh. But how come you are the leader?' 'Because I have more pearls.'*

Special pleading

The fallacy of 'special pleading' involves the use of double standards – making an exception in your own case that you would not find acceptable if it came from someone else. For example, if your neighbour says 'I know there is a drought and we need to save water, but I am putting my prize flowers in a competition next week and I need to give them plenty of water', this is an example of special pleading. He is giving a justification for his behaviour that he would not accept if it were given by somebody else.

ACTIVITY 6.12

Imagine in the example given here that you accuse your neighbour of special pleading, and he says 'No I'm not. Despite the drought, I think that everyone with prize flowers should be allowed to water them.' Is he still engaging in special pleading?

Human beings tend to be rather good at special pleading – perhaps because there are many situations in which it would be convenient if everyone followed the rules *except me*. We will look in more detail at our tendency to make exceptions in our own case when we consider ethics in Chapter 17.

Equivocation

Equivocation is a fallacy that occurs when a word is used in two different senses in an argument. Consider the following syllogism:

A hamburger is better than nothing.
Nothing is better than good health.
Therefore a hamburger is better than good health.

Although this argument is formally valid in the sense that the conclusion follows from the premises, there is clearly something wrong with it. The problem lies with the word 'nothing' because it has a different meaning in each of the premises. In the first premise, it means 'not having anything'; in the second, it means 'there is not anything'. The second premise is clearly not intended to mean that 'not having anything' is better than having good health. In practice, it is not always easy to tell if someone is using a word consistently or not. This may be why so many arguments end up being about the meanings of words.

Argument *ad ignorantiam*

You commit the fallacy of argument *ad ignorantiam* if you claim that something is true on the grounds that there is no evidence to disprove it. We discussed this fallacy in Chapter 1, but here is an example to refresh your memory. During the 'witch hunt' against communists in the USA in the early 1950s, Senator Joe McCarthy's case against one alleged communist was that 'there is nothing in the files to disprove his communist connections'. The point is, of course, that to show that someone is a communist – which is, in any case, no crime – we need *positive* evidence of their political affiliation.

ACTIVITY 6.13

In most legal systems, someone who is accused of a crime is considered to be innocent until proved guilty. Is this an example of argument *ad ignorantiam*? If so, does this mean that we should abandon the assumption that someone is innocent until proved guilty?

RLS – Headline: 'Umberto Eco Compares Berlusconi with Hitler'. How can we decide whether an analogy is appropriate or misleading?

Figure 6.9 Argument *ad ignorantiam*

The particular relevance of this fallacy to TOK is nicely expressed by the biologist Richard Dawkins (1941–): 'There is an infinity of possible things that one might believe – unicorns, fairies, millions of things – and just because you can't disprove them it doesn't mean there is anything plausible about them.'

False analogy

In trying to persuade people of something, you might use various analogies to support your argument, and this can be an effective rhetorical device. A false analogy arises when you assume that because two things are similar in some respects they must also be similar in some further respect. Consider the following syrupy example: 'Just as in time the gentle rain can wear down the tallest mountains, so, in human life, all problems can be solved by patience and quiet persistence.' Well, maybe and maybe not. The point is that there is not much of a similarity between the action of rain

Figure 6.10 'To me, boxing is like a ballet, except there's no music, no choreography and the dancers hit each other.' [Jack Handey, 1949–]

on mountains and that of patience on problems. For one thing, it takes millions of years for mountains to be worn down by the action of rain, and when it comes to solving problems we don't have that kind of time.

False dilemma

This is the fallacy of assuming that only two alternatives exist when there is in fact a wider range of options. If, for example, someone says 'Do those who advocate an increase in military expenditure really want to see our schools and hospitals close?' they are implying that we have only two choices: *either* we increase military expenditure *or* we keep our schools and hospitals open. Since you are probably in favour of keeping schools and hospitals open, you seem forced to conclude that we should not support an increase in military expenditure. But there may in fact be more than two choices. For example, if we raise taxes we might be able to increase military expenditure *and* keep our schools and hospitals open. (Of course, if there really are only two choices, then this kind of reasoning is perfectly valid. If John Smith is either alive or dead, and he is not dead, then it follows that he must be alive.)

One reason that false dilemma is a common fallacy is that we tend to see the world in black and white terms. (Someone once said that, 'The world is divided into those who divide things into two types and those who don't.') Such *binary thinking* may have served our ancestors well; for their survival must often have depended on making quick friend-or-foe, fight-or-flight types of decision. However, it may not be as useful in the modern world where many issues are not black and white, but various shades of grey.

Loaded questions

A loaded question is one that contains a built-in assumption that has not been justified and may be false. For example, if someone says 'Do you always cheat in exams?', then if you answer 'yes', you are admitting that you always cheat, and if you answer 'no' you are implying that you *sometimes* cheat. What you have to do is challenge the assumption built into the question and say 'I *never* cheat in exams.'

When governments hold referenda, or social scientists or polling organisations seek to gather data of various kinds, they should try to avoid loaded questions. But in practice it may be difficult to decide whether a question is biased or not; for, as we saw in Chapter 4, it is difficult to express anything in a completely neutral way. We shall explore the problem of loaded questions when we discuss the human sciences in Chapter 14.

Statements may also contain built-in assumptions. A sentence such as 'The headteacher was not drunk today' may in a narrow sense be true. But it carries with it the implication that this is unusual and that he or she is often drunk – and, in most schools at least, this is likely to be false!

ACTIVITY 6.14

Imagine that the Norwegian government has decided to hold a referendum about whether or not Norway should join the European Union. Your job is to phrase the referendum question in as neutral and unbiased a way as possible. What is your question? And why did you choose to phrase it the way you did?

Fallacies: a summary

We have now considered nine informal fallacies. If we add to these the fallacy of hasty generalisation from the previous section, we can speak of the 'ten deadly fallacies' of informal reasoning, which are summarised in the table below.

THE TEN DEADLY FALLACIES	
Ad ignorantiam	Claiming something is true because it cannot be proved to be false
Hasty generalisation	Generalising from insufficient evidence
Post hoc ergo propter hoc	Confusing a correlation with a causal connection
Ad hominem	Attacking/supporting the person rather than the argument
Circular reasoning	Assuming the truth of what you are supposed to be proving
Special pleading	Using double standards to excuse an individual or group
Equivocation	Using language ambiguously
False analogy	Assuming that because two things are alike in some respects they are alike in other respects
False dilemma	Assuming that only two black and white alternatives exist
Loaded question	A question that is biased because it contains a built-in assumption

As we have seen, it requires an element of judgement to determine whether or not one of the above fallacies has been committed; and it is worth noting that one of the most common fallacies is to falsely claim that someone has committed a fallacy!

ACTIVITY 6.15

In each of the twenty cases described below, state which of the following best applies to the argument:

A Valid
B Invalid syllogism
C Hasty generalisation
D *Post hoc ergo propter hoc*
E Circular reasoning
F *Ad hominem* fallacy
G Special pleading
H Argument *ad ignorantiam*
I False dilemma
J False analogy
K Equivocation
L Loaded question

1. Since strict gun control laws were introduced in Dodge City, the crime rate has risen. This shows that gun control does nothing to reduce crime.
2. Arisa said she trusted me, and she must be telling the truth because she wouldn't lie to someone that she trusted.
3. The ends justify the means. After all, if you want to make omelettes, you have to break eggs.
4. Since the English always talk about the weather, if you meet someone who talks about the weather you can be sure they are from England.
5. That can't be right. None of my friends would believe it.
6. Since many great scientists have believed in God, there must be some truth in religion.
7. We got on very well on both of our dates together. We are clearly well suited. Let's get married!
8. Do you want to be part of the solution or part of the problem?
9. I agree that everyone should pay their taxes. But since I'm short of money this year and want to take my family on a much-needed holiday, it's OK if I don't declare my full income.
10. The average UK family has 2.5 children. The Smiths are very average people. Therefore they must have 2.5 children.
11. Since no one has been able to prove that we are alone in the universe, we must conclude that alien life-forms exist.
12. Are all your family stupid, or is it just you?
13. Many great artists were not recognised in their own lifetimes. Since my work has not been recognised, I must be a great artist.

14. Since there are two candidates for student president – Boris and Bertha – and I know he did not vote for Boris, he must have voted for Bertha.
15. As no one succeeds without hard work, the fact that you failed your exams shows how idle you have been.
16. No breath of scandal has ever touched the senator. So he must be an honest man.
17. Just as you are more likely to take care of a car that you own than one that you rent, so a slave owner is more likely to take care of his slave than an employer is of his worker.
18. To ignore the possibility that America was discovered by Africans simply because these explorers are unknown is irresponsible and arrogant. If we are unaware of an event, it does not mean it never happened.
19. In the fight against terrorism, you are either with us or against us.
20. The English can't cook. If he really is English, then obviously he won't be able to cook.

Causes of bad reasoning

If we ask ourselves why we sometimes reason poorly, and commit, or fail to recognise, the above kinds of fallacy, I think there are four main reasons: *ignorance, laziness, pride* and *prejudice*. In some cases, we do not realise that a particular form of reasoning is fallacious, and are taken in by it. In other cases, we have developed fixed habits of thinking and are too lazy to check the argument or see if it has supporting evidence. Perhaps it is psychologically easier to hold simple beliefs with confidence than get bogged-down with confusing details. Pride also plays a role in bad reasoning; for although we all like to think we are open-minded, once we get involved in an argument we can become more interested in winning than in establishing the truth. Unfortunately logic, the art of reasoning, can all too easily give way to **rhetoric**, the art of persuasion. And we may then be tempted to resort to any argument – valid or invalid – to defend our position. Indeed, on some occasions, we may simply begin with our prejudices, and then manufacture bad reasons in order to justify them. This is known as **rationalisation**, and we shall explore this further when we discuss the emotions in Chapter 7.

LQ – History: What kinds of bad reasoning can typically be found in history?

KT – rhetoric: the art of persuasive speaking or writing

KT – rationalisation: the manufacturing of reasons to justify your pre-existing belief

ACTIVITY 6.16

Take any editorial or opinion article from a newspaper and see how many of the above fallacies you can find in it.

Reason and certainty

We have considered three different kinds of reasoning – deductive reasoning, inductive reasoning and informal reasoning. The fact that fallacies can arise with each of these suggests that we cannot always rely on reason to give us knowledge. Furthermore, we have seen that, when it comes to reasoning about the world, the conclusions of deductive arguments are no more certain than the premises they are based on. In practice, then, it would seem that, at best, reason is a means of preserving truth in the sense that if you begin with truth and reason validly then you will end with truth.

KT – laws of thought: the fundamental assumptions on which logic is based

We might, however, say that, *as a way of thinking*, logical reasoning cannot really be doubted. Such reasoning is based on the following three **laws of thought**.

1. *The law of identity*. If *A*, then *A*. For example, 'If something is a banana, then it is a banana.'
2. *The law of non-contradiction*. Nothing can be both *A* and not-*A*. For example, 'Nothing can be both a banana and not-a-banana.'
3. *The law of the excluded middle*. Everything is either *A* or not *A*. For example, 'Everything is either a banana or not a banana.'

These three laws probably strike you as self-evident. If something is a banana, then it must be a banana. And given that it's a banana then it cannot *not* be a banana. Finally, if you put all the bananas in the universe on your left, and all the non-bananas on your right, there is nothing left in the middle hovering uncertainly between being and not being a banana. (A banana with an identity crisis, perhaps? A banana that has gone bananas?)

What, then, should we say to someone who asks 'Why should I be logical?' At one level, the question is self-defeating because in asking for reasons you are implicitly presupposing the value of logic. A statement such as 'Logic isn't useful' is equally self-defeating; for, in making it, you presumably wish to exclude the contrary idea that logic *is* useful, and you are therefore presupposing the usefulness of the principle of non-contradiction. The fact is that logic is presupposed in all meaningful communication, and any assertion *p* that you care to make must – if it is to say anything – exclude the contrary assertion *non-p*.

'But can't two people have a love–hate relationship?' you might ask. 'And, if so, doesn't that mean that you can both love and not-love someone?' Well, this is true in a sense, but not in a way that undermines logic. For you cannot love and not love the same person in the same way at the same time. What you really mean when you say you have a love–hate relationship with someone is that you love them in certain ways or at certain times, but not in other ways or at other times. And this, of course, does nothing to invalidate logic. (A man once explained his love–hate relationship with his wife as follows. 'It's quite simple', he said. 'I love her and she hates me!')

'You still haven't proved that the laws of logic are true', you might persist – 'you have just assumed that they are true'. This is admittedly true; but this follows from the fact that *all proof must end somewhere*. And since we cannot prove everything, where better to start than with principles that seem self-evident and are the basis for meaningful communication? In the end if someone ignores logic and keeps contradicting themselves, we are likely to get frustrated and will probably stop talking to them.

ACTIVITY 6.17

1. Find out what is meant by the phrase 'infinite regress' and explain why all proof must end somewhere.
2. What is the difference between being irrational and being insane? How irrational must someone be before you classify them as insane?

Can deductive reasoning be doubted?

Despite what has been said in the previous paragraphs, some philosophers have in fact been willing to question the truth of the basic principles of logic. Here are three possible reasons for doubt:

1. We cannot be sure that the laws of logic do not simply describe the way we *think* rather than the way the universe *is*. G. K. Chesterton (1874–1936) claimed that 'It is an act of faith to assert that our thoughts have any relation to reality at all' and he concluded from this that 'Reason is itself a matter of faith.'

LQ – Faith: Is faith rational or irrational?

2. Logic depends on language in that it presupposes that we can organise the world into precise, clear-cut categories. But in reality this is never possible. For example, who can say where 'day' begins and 'night' ends? Even the concept of a banana is fuzzy round the edges; for if we genetically modified a banana one cell at a time, we can imagine a borderline case where it would be impossible to say whether it was still a banana. This point was well summarised by the philosopher Bertrand Russell (1872–1970):

   The law of excluded middle is true when precise symbols are employed, but it is not true when symbols are vague, as, in fact, all symbols are.

3. If we take seriously the idea that everything is constantly changing, then nothing stays the same long enough to be identical with itself, and there is nothing for logic to be true of. This is probably what the Greek philosopher Heraclitus (c. 540–470 BCE) was drawing attention to when he famously observed that 'You can never step in the same river twice.' The emphasis on change is also characteristic of Eastern ways of thinking such as the Chinese nature religion Taoism. While Western logic is typically black and white either – or thinking as represented by circle (a) on the right, we can get a sense of Taoist thinking about logic in the famous taijitu symbol – circle (b). As you can see, this symbol suggests that opposites flow into each other and that there is some white inside the black and some black inside the white.

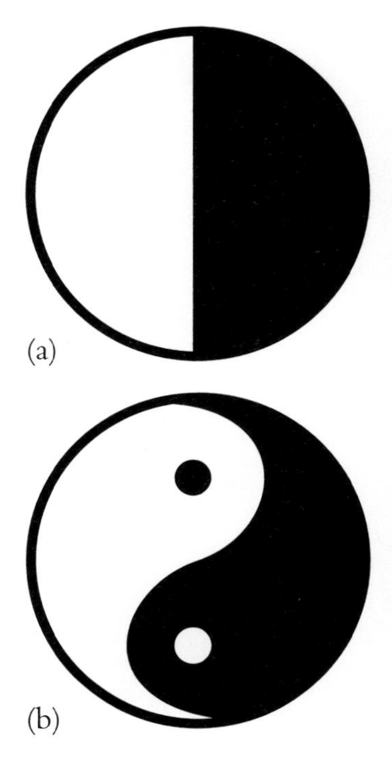

Figure 6.11 Western and Eastern logic

The above doubts are quite abstract in nature, but they show that it is possible to doubt even the basic laws of logic. In practice, however, it is difficult to imagine abandoning logic without bringing down the entire structure of knowledge.

Can inductive reasoning be doubted?

In this section we will consider how far inductive reasoning can be doubted. We saw earlier that induction cannot give us certainty because it involves a jump from 'All observed *X*' to 'All *X*'. To illustrate the extent to which well-confirmed generalisations can sometimes let us down, consider the following story about some 'inductive turkeys' that arrive on a farm one January. They are well looked after, and every morning after breakfast the farmer comes and feeds them. After a few weeks, some of the more philosophical turkeys begin to notice that *whenever* the farmer appears they get fed. As good inductive turkeys they continue to observe patiently, and as January turns to February they become increasingly confident of the truth of the generalisation that 'Whenever the farmer comes, we get fed.' The months pass, and as spring turns to summer, and summer turns to autumn, this generalisation acquires the status of a law of nature. The connection between the farmer's appearance and the arrival of food is, the turkeys decide, a brute fact about reality, and to question it would be a clear sign of insanity. Things continue in much the same way until one cold December morning – 24 December to be precise – the farmer breaks the neck of the first turkey that comes up to him to be fed. (British people traditionally eat turkey for lunch on Christmas day.)

ACTIVITY 6.18

1. To what extent do human beings sometimes act like the turkeys in this story?
2. The turkeys turned out to be wrong, but do you think that their belief was reasonable? What does this suggest to you about the relationship between reason and truth?

The story about the inductive turkeys may be a fairy tale, but it alerts us to the fact that even well-confirmed generalisations can fail us. For example, Newton's laws of motion were confirmed by observational evidence on countless occasions and were believed to be true for more than 200 years. Nevertheless, they eventually turned out to be false (or, at best, approximations to a deeper truth).

Despite the obvious survival value of inductive reasoning, we might ask how we can know that the future will be similar to the past *in any respect*. How can you be sure that the laws of physics, together with the countless everyday regularities that you take for granted, won't suddenly break down tomorrow? Imagine, for example, that you wake up tomorrow morning and discover that you have been transformed into an insect, like the character in Franz Kafka's novel *Metamorphosis*. This is the stuff of nightmares, and you might reasonably insist that you *know* that this will not happen. After all, the world exhibits demonstrable regularities that prohibit you from turning into an insect. This has certainly been true up until now; but how can you be sure that the laws of nature won't suddenly break down tomorrow?

Most people do not lie awake at night worrying about whether or not the laws of physics will continue to hold in the future; but the question is whether we can *justify* our confidence in the comforting regularities of nature. You might argue that we know the future will be similar to the past on the basis of experience. For example, last Tuesday I predicted that on Wednesday – which was then in the future – the laws of physics would continue to hold true – and they did. And on Wednesday I predicted that they would continue to hold true on Thursday. And you know what? They did again! So it would seem that there is in fact a huge amount of evidence that the future will be like the past. The problem, however, is that, although the laws of nature held true in *past* futures, this does not prove that they will continue to hold true in *future* futures. From a logical point of view, it is possible that tomorrow, for the first time, they will break down.

Since inductive reasoning moves from the observed to the unobserved, there is in fact no way we can justify our belief in it on the basis of experience. And since it lacks the certainty of deduction, we cannot give a logical justification of it either. Therefore, it would seem that we cannot justify induction at all. So perhaps we should conclude that it is simply an *instinct* that we share with animals.

However, we might look at the situation in another way, and argue that *using inductive reasoning is simply part of what it means to be rational.* For, although we sometimes question the validity of a particular generalisation, it makes no real sense to question the general idea of using the past as a guide to the future. To see this, just imagine someone sticking their hand in a fire every day on the grounds that, although it has always hurt in the past, they have no reason to think that it will hurt them this time. You would surely say they are foolish – and rightly so! For as the Scottish philosopher David Hume (1711–76) observed: 'None but a fool or madman will ever pretend to dispute the authority of experience.'

Lateral thinking

In the previous section, we saw that, although philosophical doubts can be raised about both deductive and inductive reasoning, it would be difficult if not impossible to survive without making use of them. Having said that, it is worth pointing out that we can sometimes become trapped in what has been called 'the prison of consistency'. The point is that once you have taken a position on something, you may find it difficult to change your mind without losing face. As the Russian novelist Leo Tolstoy once observed:

> *I know that most men, including those at ease with problems of the greatest complexity, can seldom accept even the simplest and most obvious truth if it is such as would oblige them to admit the falsity of conclusions which they have delighted in explaining to colleagues, which they have proudly taught to others, and which they have woven, thread by thread, into the fabric of their lives.*

So perhaps it would be better if we all had a little more intellectual flexibility, and followed the example of the economist John Maynard Keynes (1883–1946). When a critic complained that he had changed his opinion about something, Keynes retorted 'When I discover I am wrong, I change my mind. What do you do?'

LQ – Ethics: How important is consistency in moral reasoning?

ACTIVITY 6.19

1. Which do you think is easier: having the courage of your convictions, or having the courage to question your convictions?
2. 'The madman is not the man who has lost his reason. The madman is the man who has lost everything but his reason' (G. K. Chesterton, 1874–1936). Should you always try to be as rational as possible, or are there dangers in being too rational?

KT – lateral thinking: thinking 'outside the box' and coming up with creative solutions to problems

According to Edward de Bono (1933–) if we are to escape from the 'prison of consistency', then we must learn to 'think outside the box' and come up with more creative ways of looking at problems. To help us to do this, he has developed a way of reasoning called **lateral thinking** which complements traditional, 'vertical' logic. De Bono describes the difference between the two ways of thinking as follows:

Vertical thinking [i.e. traditional logic] is digging the same hole deeper; lateral thinking is trying elsewhere.

His point is that, since we cannot rely on traditional logic to give us new ideas, we need to adopt a more creative way of thinking that encourages us to search actively for better solutions to problems.

"Never, ever, think outside the box."

Figure 6.12

ACTIVITY 6.20

1. Give a rational explanation for each of the following situations. In each case you will need to question your assumptions and try to 'think outside the box'.
   a. A man walks into a bar and asks the barman for a glass of water. The barman pulls out a gun and points it at the man. The man says 'Thank you' and walks out.
   b. A man is lying dead in a field. Next to him there is an unopened package. There is no other creature in the field. How did he die?
   c. Anthony and Cleopatra are lying dead on the floor of a villa in Egypt. Nearby is a broken bowl. There is no mark on either of their bodies and they were not poisoned. How did they die?
   d. A man rode into town on Friday. He stayed three nights and then left on Friday. How come?

2. Two boxers are in a boxing match (regular boxing, not kick boxing). The fight is scheduled for 12 rounds but ends after 6 rounds, after one boxer knocks out the other boxer. Yet no man throws a punch. How is this possible?
3. In your cellar there are three light switches in the OFF position. Each switch controls one of three light bulbs on the floor above. You may move any of the switches but you may only go upstairs to inspect the bulbs one time. How can you determine the switch for each bulb with one inspection?
4. A landscape gardener is given instructions to plant four special trees so that each one is exactly the same distance from each of the others. How would you arrange the trees?
5. Connect the nine crosses below using only four straight lines and without taking your pen off the paper.

Figure 6.13

Conclusion

At the beginning of this chapter, we saw that rationalist philosophers such as René Descartes believed that reason is a way of knowing that can give us certainty. But we have seen that this belief is open to serious doubt. For reason is only as certain as the premises on which it is based, and it is always possible that we have reasoned badly in arguing from premises to conclusions. We also raised various philosophical doubts about deduction and induction, but in practice it is difficult to see how we could do without these two ways of reasoning.

What seems to come out of this discussion is that reason, like other ways of knowing, is a double-edged tool. We need reason to develop consistent beliefs about the world, but we can sometimes become trapped in the 'prison of logic' and this can stifle our imagination and creativity. Furthermore, reason is not appropriate in every situation, and if someone is *too* rational they may simply come across as a cold and unfeeling automaton. In private life, for example, the best way to resolve a dispute with a loved one may not be by proving their inconsistency to them but by showing them empathy and understanding. In other words, reason needs to be balanced by emotion. We must now look at emotion and consider whether it, too, can contribute to our knowledge of the world.

Answers to selected questions

Uncritical inference test (page 152)

All of the statements are uncertain except (3), which is false, and (6), which is true. If you answered differently, you might want to go back to the story and look more closely at it.

Lateral thinking questions (pages 166–7)

1a The man has hiccups.

1b The man's parachute failed to open.

1c Anthony and Cleopatra are goldfish.

1d Friday is the name of the man's horse.

2. The boxers are women.

3. Turn switch 1 on for about five minutes and then turn it off. Turn switch 2 on and then go upstairs. The hot unlit bulb is controlled by switch 1, the lit bulb by switch 2, and the cold unlit bulb by switch 3.

4. Plant 3 trees equidistant from each other in an equilateral triangle. Then build a mound of the right height in the middle of the triangle and plant the fourth tree on top of it.

5. As the diagram below shows, if you extend one of the lines outside the square formed by the dots, the solution is easy.

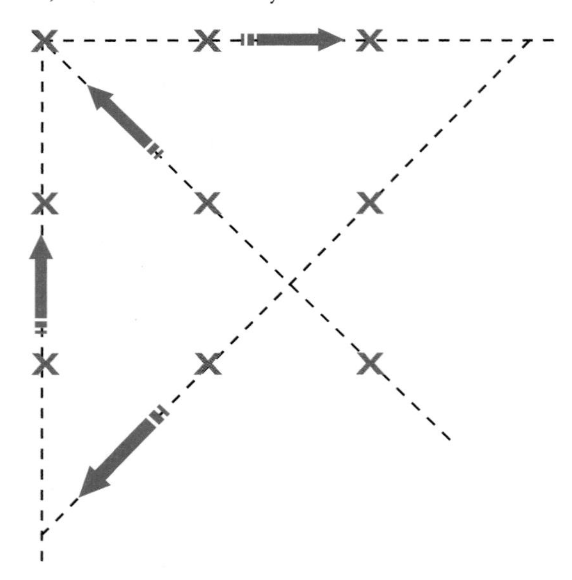

Figure 6.14

Key points

- Through reason we can acquire knowledge about the world that goes beyond the immediate evidence of our senses.
- According to rationalism, reason is a more important source of knowledge than experience, and we can discover important truths about reality by using pure reason.
- Deductive reasoning moves from the general to the particular, and inductive reasoning moves from the particular to the general.
- Pure logic is only concerned with the structure of arguments and the validity or invalidity of an argument is independent of the truth or falsity of its premises.
- When deductive reasoning is applied to the real world it is no more certain than the (inductively derived) premises on which it is based.
- Inductive reasoning sometimes leads to our making hasty generalisations which are then reinforced by our tendency to only notice things which confirm them.
- There are many other 'informal' fallacies that people sometimes commit when discussing things in everyday life.
- The main causes of bad reasoning are a combination of ignorance, laziness, pride and prejudice.
- Despite appearances, it is possible to doubt the certainty of even the basic laws of logic such as the law of identity.
- Although it is hard to see how we can justify our belief that the future will be relevantly similar to the past, this belief has obvious survival value.
- We sometimes get trapped in the prison of consistency and find it difficult to change our minds about things or look at them from a new perspective.

Key terms

belief bias
confirmation bias
deduction
enthymeme
fallacy
induction
lateral thinking
laws of thought
premises
quantifier
rationalisation
rationalism
rhetoric
syllogism
validity
Venn diagram

IB prescribed essay titles

1. 'Habit is stronger than reason.' To what extent is this true in two areas of knowledge? (November 2012)
2. Evaluate the strengths and weaknesses of reason as a way of knowing. (November 2008 / May 2009)

Further reading

Books

R. H. Thouless and C. R. Thouless, *Straight and Crooked Thinking* (Hodder and Stoughton, 2011). The new edition of this classic text usefully explores the most common reasoning errors and tricks that are used in argument to deceive people. The fallacies that are discussed are clearly explained and well illustrated.

Stuart Sutherland, *Irrationality: The Enemy Within* (Pinter & Martin, 2013). This book, which is written by a psychologist, explores the many ways in which our thinking can go wrong. Among the topics covered are conformity, misplaced consistency, ignoring evidence and false inference.

Online articles

Patricia Cohen, 'Reason Seen More as Weapon Than Path to Truth', *New York Times*, 14 June 2011.

Emily A. Schultz and Robert H. Lavenda, 'Logic and Cultural Relativism', in *Cultural Anthropology*, ed. Emily A. Schultz, Robert H. Lavenda and Roberta R. Dods (Oxford University Press, 2012).

The emotions

7

We think and name in one world, we live and feel in another.

Marcel Proust, 1871–1922

All emotions were abhorrent to his cold, precise but admirably balanced mind.

Sir Arthur Conan Doyle, 1859–1930 (about Sherlock Holmes)

The opinions that are held with passion are always those for which no good ground exists, indeed the passion is the measure of the holder's lack of rational conviction.

Bertrand Russell, 1872–1970

Man is a rational animal who always loses his temper when called upon to act in accordance with the dictates of reason.

Oscar Wilde, 1854–1900

Nothing great is accomplished in the world without passion.

Hegel, 1770–1831

Laws are only reached by non-logical methods. To make a law one has to have an intellectual love of the subject.

Albert Einstein, 1879–1955

Reason is always and everywhere the slave of the passions.

David Hume, 1711–76

Axioms in philosophy are not axioms until they are proved upon our pulses.

John Keats, 1795–1821

Deep thinking is attainable only by a man of deep feeling.

Samuel Taylor Coleridge, 1772–1834

What is moral is what you feel good after and what is immoral is what you feel bad after.

Ernest Hemingway, 1899–1962

Conquer your passions and you conquer the world.

Hindu proverb

Introduction

In Theory of Knowledge the emotions are treated as one of the eight ways of knowing. Since the emotions have traditionally been seen as more of an obstacle to knowledge than a source of it, this may initially seem surprising. There are some good reasons for the traditional suspicion of the emotions: an angry, frightened or infatuated person is unlikely to see clearly or reason well. That is why we usually advise people to 'be reasonable' rather than 'be emotional'. When we have recovered from an emotional outburst, we typically say things like 'I don't know what came over me', which suggests that we think reason *ought* to be kept under control. At the same time, our feelings matter to us a great deal, and we naturally consult them when we make important decisions. Indeed, some people believe that feelings are a better guide to the truth than reason. This view was popularised by romantic writers and poets in the early nineteenth century and it is still common today.

LQ – Reason: Are we driven more by reason or emotion?

ACTIVITY 7.1

1. 'You're being emotional' is usually taken as a criticism. Why? Could 'You're being rational' ever be seen as a criticism?
2. 'The mind is like a sailboat: emotions are the wind that fills the sails, and reason is the rudder which steers it.' What are the strengths and weaknesses of this analogy?

"That's right! No huffing and puffing for 30 minutes on a treadmill. We've developed a new stress test that is faster and more accurate."

Figure 7.1

The nature of the emotions

The word 'emotion' is derived from the Latin verb *movere* meaning 'to move'. We shall be using it in a broad sense to include such things as feelings, passions and moods.

An emotion usually consists of various internal feelings and external forms of behaviour, and it can vary in intensity from, say, mild irritation to blind anger. The word 'passion' is usually reserved for a strong emotion. You can, for example, be in a passionate rage, but you cannot be passionately irritated. A mood is more general and less intense than an emotional episode and it continues for a period of time. Emotions can dissolve into moods and they can also precipitate out of them. For example, getting angry with someone may put you in a bad mood all day and your behaviour may be punctuated by further outbursts of anger. At the most general level, emotions are connected with personality. When you describe someone's personality, you typically use words which are connected with emotions, such as cheerful, easy-going, irritable, timid, depressed.

Emotions can be usefully compared to sensations on the one hand and judgements on the other. They are similar to bodily sensations in that they involve feelings, but they differ from feelings such as toothache in that they are *directed towards* or *about* something. If, for example, you are angry, you are angry *with* someone or *about* something. Admittedly, you might sometimes feel happy for no reason, or be depressed about nothing in particular; but it could be argued that in such cases the object of your happiness or depression is life or the world in general. As regards our second comparison, emotions resemble judgements in that they are about something, but they differ from them in that they involve feelings. There is, for example, a difference between *thinking* that, say, a rabid dog is dangerous and the jolt of fear you experience when it lunges towards you. We might say that after this experience you have a deeper emotional understanding of the danger rather than a purely intellectual understanding of it.

RLS – Headline: 'Road Rage Incident Between BMW Driver and Bicyclist Caught on Video'. Is reason powerless to control hot emotions?

ACTIVITY 7.2

Which of the following words do you naturally associate with reason and which do you naturally associate with emotion?

a. Hot	**e.** Cool	**i.** Voluntary	**m.** Reflective
b. Folly	**f.** Powerful	**j.** Blind	**n.** Weak
c. Impulsive	**g.** Subjective	**k.** Wisdom	
d. Controlled	**h.** Objective	**l.** Instinctive	

Primary and secondary emotions

According to most psychologists there are six basic or **primary emotions** which are common to all cultures:

- happiness
- sadness
- fear
- anger
- surprise
- disgust.

KT – primary emotions: universal emotions which are usually said to comprise happiness, sadness, anger, fear, disgust and surprise

Each of these emotions is associated with a typical facial expression. For example, when you are happy your pupils dilate and the corners of your mouth lift in a smile, when you are surprised your eyes widen and your jaw drops open, and when you are disgusted you wrinkle your nose and raise your upper lip. When photographs of faces showing primary emotions are shown to people they can readily identify them no matter what country they come from. Moreover, children who are born blind and deaf make similar facial expressions in appropriate situations. This suggests that such emotions are inborn rather than learnt and that they are part of our biological inheritance. Our emotions also affect such things as heart-rate, breathing and perspiration. The adrenalin rush you get when you are angry or frightened by something is clearly designed to prepare your body for a 'fight or flight' response, and similar responses can be found in many other animals.

KT – secondary emotions: complex emotions which can be thought of as mixtures of primary emotions

In addition to primary emotions, we have a wide range of **secondary emotions** or 'social' emotions. Just as primary colours can be combined to form a wide range of secondary colours, so secondary emotions can be thought of as blends of primary emotions. For example, contempt can be thought of as a mixture of anger and disgust, and disappointment as a mixture of sadness and surprise. Commonly mentioned secondary emotions include: admiration, anxiety, awe, despair, embarrassment, envy, gratitude, guilt, jealousy, pity, pride, regret and shame.

Secondary emotions are shaped, in part at least, by language and culture. Without language, we would probably be unable to distinguish between anxiety, fear and terror, or between irritation, anger, and rage. Many secondary emotions also presuppose a degree of self-awareness. For example, feeling proud, or ashamed or embarrassed requires that you can see your behaviour through the eyes of another person. While there is no doubt that animals can experience primary emotions such as fear, since they are widely held to lack both language and self-awareness it seems unlikely that they are able to experience sophisticated secondary emotions. By contrast, our intelligence and imagination mean that we are not only aware of immediate threats, but are also able to anticipate and picture more distant dangers. You can, for example, be worried about your final exams, or the fact that you are going to die, or the eventual heat-death of the universe. Animals are lucky in that they do not have to worry about such things!

ACTIVITY 7.3

1. Study the six faces below and say which face goes with which of the six primary emotions.

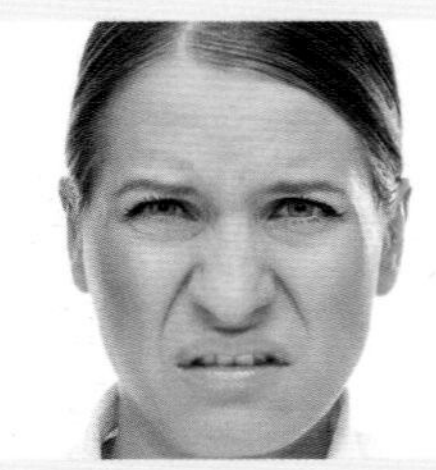

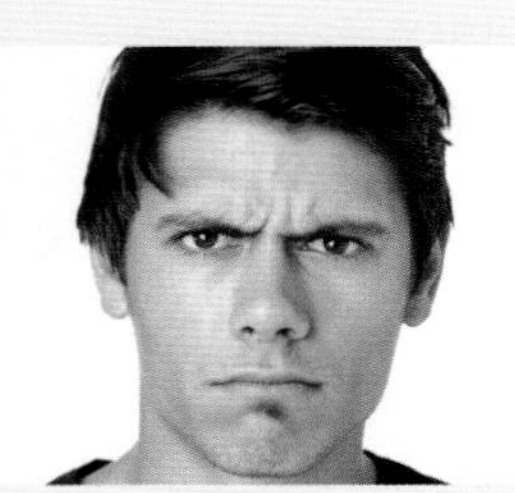

Figure 7.2

2. How are the emotions shown by human beings similar to those shown by dogs and how are they different?

The James–Lange theory

The fact that primary emotions have typical facial expressions associated with them suggests that there is a close connection between our emotions and our bodies. Indeed, according to the James–Lange theory (named after William James, 1842–1910, and Carl Lange, 1832–1900, the two psychologists who developed it) the emotions are essentially *physical* in nature, and bodily changes come before, and cause, emotional changes.

ACTIVITY 7.4

1. Imagine as clearly as you can the following situation. You are about to sit an exam and you are feeling very nervous. Your mouth is dry, you have a sinking feeling in the pit of your stomach, the palms of your hands are sweaty, and you want to go to the washroom. Now remove each of these physical symptoms one by one. What is left of your exam nerves?
2. Have you ever found yourself pretending to feel an emotion and then actually feeling it? What relevance does this have to our discussion?

If you went through the thought experiment in Question 1 above, you may have found that when you removed all the physical symptoms of nervousness, the nervousness itself disappeared. According to the James–Lange theory the same holds true for *all* of our emotions – if you remove the physical symptoms the corresponding emotion disappears.

Interestingly, the theory also suggests that if you mimic the appropriate physical symptoms you can generate the corresponding emotion. For example, if you smile you will feel happy, and if you scowl you will feel angry. You might like to test this idea out on yourself!

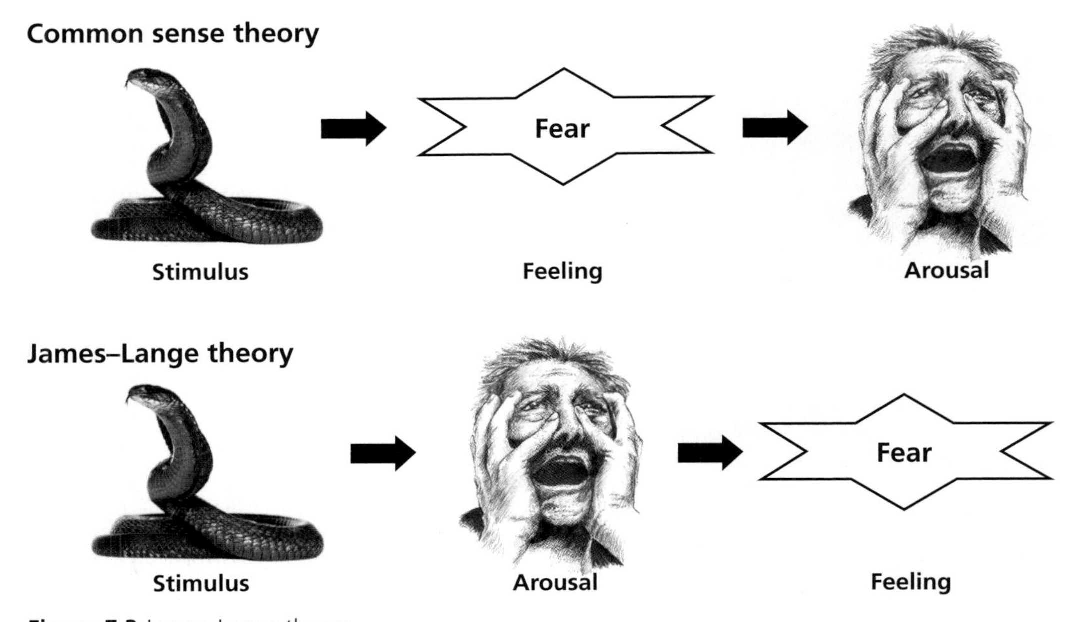

Figure 7.3 James–Lange theory

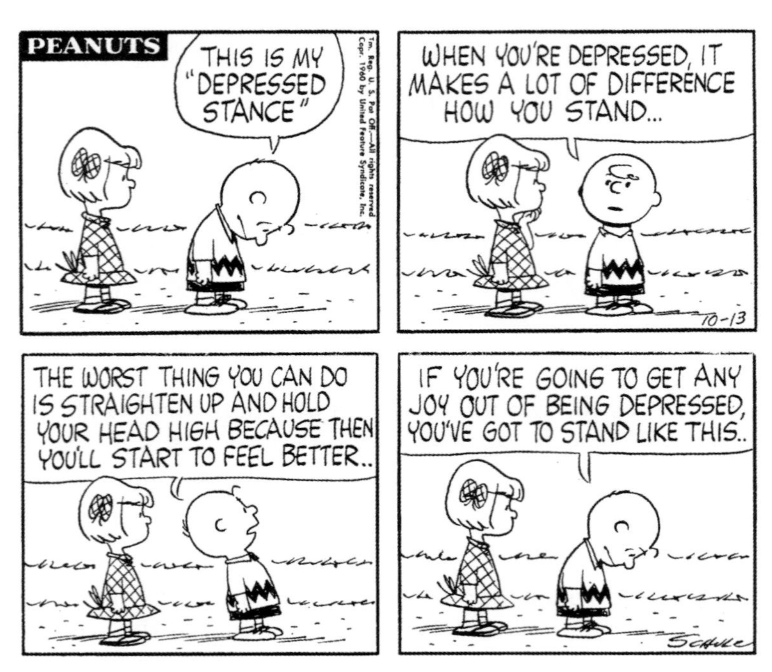

Figure 7.4

Emotional contagion

KT – emotional contagion: the tendency for emotions such as anger or fear to spread quickly through a group of people

The James–Lange theory also suggests a mechanism through which we can come to know something about other people's feelings. The idea is that when you talk to someone who is, say, feeling depressed, you unconsciously mimic some of the physical expressions of his mood. When he tells you his troubles, you might say something like 'Oh dear, I *am* sorry', and find yourself instinctively adopting his flat, depressed tone and hunched posture. As a result, you may pick up at least an echo of his depressed mood and this may help you to empathise with him. We shall explore empathy further in Chapter 9 (page 234).

Figure 7.5 Why do we laugh more in company than alone?

As the above implies, emotions are – in part at least – contagious and can quickly spread through a group. Studies show that if newborn babies hear other infants crying, they also become distressed and start crying themselves. If you find yourself in a seemingly dangerous situation, your fear is likely to be influenced by the fear of those around you. If you approach some friends who are laughing, you are likely to start laughing yourself before you know its cause. Furthermore, shared emotions tend to feed off and augment one another. That's why if you watch a comedy with friends you are likely to laugh much more than if you watch it alone. More ominously, waves of emotion can cascade through crowds of people and lead to outbreaks of mass hysteria or mindless aggression.

ACTIVITY 7.5

1. Have you ever noticed a class atmosphere or mood develop in a particular lesson at school? How helpful is the mechanism outlined above in explaining how this comes about?
2. 'If you can keep your head while those around you are losing theirs . . . you have probably misunderstood the situation!' To what extent is it rational to allow our emotions to be influenced by the emotions of those around us?
3. Do you think that crowds are more emotional and less rational than the individuals that make them up? Give specific examples to illustrate your answer.

The role of beliefs

Despite the attractions of the James–Lange theory, it can be criticised because it ignores the fact that our emotions have a mental as well as a physical aspect. Although our emotions are closely connected with our bodies, they can also be affected by our beliefs. This suggests that – in theory at least – a change in our beliefs can lead to a change in the corresponding emotion. For example, if you enter a badly lit cellar and see a snake in the corner, you will probably be frightened. But if, when you look more closely, you discover that it is not a snake but a coiled rope, your fear will vanish. Similarly, if you think someone has insulted you, you are likely to become angry; but if it turns out to be a misunderstanding, your anger will subside. In both cases, a change in your beliefs has led to a change in your emotions. There is, then, a two-way relationship between emotions and beliefs: not only do our emotions affect our beliefs – as we saw when discussing perception in Chapter 5 – but our beliefs also affect our emotions.

ACTIVITY 7.6

1. How do you think human emotions differ from the kinds of emotions an animal can feel?
2. Look at the two pictures. The first one, by the Norwegian expressionist painter Edvard Munch (1863–1944), is entitled *The Scream*. The second one is by a cartoonist. Why is the second picture funny? What has this got to do with our discussion?

Figure 7.6 Edvard Munch's famous painting *The Scream* (1893)

Figure 7.7 *The Screech*

Cultural factors

LQ – Cultural perspectives: How does the expression of emotions vary across cultures and how can this cause misunderstanding?

While our emotions may be rooted in our biology, they are also shaped by our culture. The evidence for this is that different cultures carve up the emotional landscape in different ways. Here are some examples of words for emotions in four languages for which there is no straightforward equivalent in English:

1. *Amae* (Japanese): the comfort one experiences in being completely dependent on another person.
2. *Litost* (Czech): the sudden awareness of the tragic sense of life and one's own misery.
3. *Abhiman* (Bengali): a mixture of anger and sorrow caused by the insensitivity of a loved one.
4. *Saudade* (Portuguese): a feeling of nostalgia and melancholic longing for something or someone absent.

There are also differences in the extent to which emotions are displayed in different cultures. For example, while Americans are more inclined to show their emotions, Japanese are more inclined to hide them. However, this does *not* mean that Japanese are less emotional than Americans. In one well-known experiment, Americans and Japanese subjects were shown a particularly unpleasant video-clip of nasal surgery. When the subjects thought they were unobserved, both groups showed expressions of disgust, but when they knew they were being observed the Japanese subjects smiled more and showed much less overt disgust than their American counterparts. This difference might be explained by the fact that American culture is more individualistic than Japanese culture. While Americans tend to think that showing one's emotions is a mark of honesty and authenticity, Japanese are more worried that emotional displays will disturb social relationships.

ACTIVITY 7.7

1. Give some examples of emotion words that are difficult to translate between any two languages with which you are familiar. What does this suggest to you about the extent to which emotions are shaped by culture?
2. What stereotypes are there about the extent to which different cultures display emotions? What truth, if any, is there in these stereotypes?

Emotions and the quest for knowledge

One key way in which the emotions are relevant to the search for knowledge is that they provide us with the energy to engage in intellectual activity. The ability to come up with new ideas in any area of knowledge undoubtedly requires a certain amount of genius, but it also needs a long apprenticeship and a great deal of persistence.

"It's an excellent proof, but it lacks warmth and feeling."

Figure 7.8

LQ – Mathematics: What role, if any, do the emotions play in the pursuit of mathematical knowledge?

LQ – Arts: Do the arts provoke emotions or purge them?

According to the so-called **ten-year rule**, proposed by the Swedish psychologist Anders Ericsson, raw talent must be supplemented by at least ten years (or ten thousand hours) of sustained effort to mature into greatness. The effortless grace we associate with intellectual, artistic, or sporting excellence is, in other words, the result of a great deal of hard work. So there would seem to be some truth in Thomas Edison's (1847–1931) famous estimate that 'Genius is one percent inspiration and ninety-nine percent perspiration'!

KT – ten-year rule: the claim that it takes at least ten years, or 10,000 hours, to achieve greatness in any field of endeavour

Since a great deal of day-to-day academic work is boring and repetitive you need to be well motivated to stick at it. A mathematician sharpens her pencils, works on a proof, tries a few approaches, gets nowhere, and finishes for the day. A biologist goes to the lab, gets the equipment out, does an experiment, it doesn't work, puts the equipment away again, and goes home. A writer sits down at his desk, produces a few hundred words, decides they are no good, throws them in the bin, and hopes for better inspiration tomorrow. To produce something worthwhile – if it ever happens – may require years of such fruitless labour. The mathematician Andrew Wiles (1953–) spent eight years trying to prove Fermat's Last Theorem – one of the great unsolved problems in mathematics – before making his crucial breakthrough in 1994. The Nobel-prize winning biologist Peter Medawar (1915–87) estimated that four-fifths of his time in science was wasted, adding glumly that 'nearly all scientific research leads nowhere'. The Chilean writer Isabel Allende suffered from writer's block for more than three years. What sustained all of these people in their work, and kept them going when things were going badly, was their *passion* for their subject. Without such passion, they would have achieved nothing.

Figure 7.9 What role does passion play in the quest for knowledge?

ACTIVITY 7.8

1. What do you think are the main qualities that make a person a good teacher? Would you include a word like 'passion' in your list? Give reasons.
2. What do you think is the relationship between liking a subject and being good at it? Do you like a subject if you are good at it, or are you good at a subject if you like it?
3. What are the pros and cons of holding a belief with passion? Give specific examples to illustrate your answer.

Emotions as an obstacle to knowledge

LQ – Natural and human sciences: How can emotional prejudices bias scientific research?

Since they are an integral part of our mental lives, our emotions are likely to have a significant influence on the way we see and think about the world. In this section we consider the traditional view that they are more of an obstacle to knowledge than a source of knowledge. We focus in particular on their ability to distort perception, twist reason and sabotage our best laid plans.

Distorted perception

Our perception of things can be distorted by strong emotions, and there is doubtless some truth in sayings like 'love is blind' and 'fear has many eyes'. Such emotional colouring can make you aware of some aspects of reality to the exclusion of others. If, for example, you are in love with someone you are likely to be blind to their faults; whereas if you loathe them you are likely to see *only* their faults. More generally, we can say that a happy person lives in a different world from an unhappy person. When you are in a good mood it is as if the world is smiling on you and anything is possible; but when you are in a bad mood, the smile turns to a frown and you feel that everything is against you. As if to justify our moods, our memories obligingly produce evidence to support them. Thus good moods tend to activate happy memories and bad moods sad ones.

ACTIVITY 7.9

1. To what extent do rival sports fans see and interpret what is happening on the pitch in accordance with their emotional prejudices? Give examples.
2. Analyse any speech given by a politician and explain how it appeals to the emotions of the listeners and tries to distort their perception.

Negativity bias

Four of the primary emotions mentioned earlier are negative (sadness, fear, anger, disgust) and only one is positive (happiness). As this suggests, our emotions are biased towards the negative and psychologists tell us that in general 'bad is stronger than good'. There are many examples of **negativity bias**. If you are typical, you are more upset by bad grades at school than you are pleased by good ones; you fear looking stupid more than you like looking smart; you dwell longer on criticism than you do on praise; you dislike losing one hundred dollars more than you like winning it; you react more strongly to negative words such as *war* and *vomit* than positive ones such as *peace* and *health*, and you are more sensitive to threats than you are to opportunities.

KT – negativity bias: the bias that leads us to focus more on negative things than positive things

There may be good evolutionary reasons for the prevalence of negative emotions. As discussed in Chapter 3 (see page 66), if you ignore something good, no great harm is done; if you ignore something bad you could die. So when we consider potential threats, it makes sense to err on the side of caution and over-react to them rather than under-react to them. There is an element of truth in the English expression 'Once bitten, twice shy': you only need to be bitten by a dog once to become permanently wary of it. As this suggests, we are quick to generalise from negative events, and a single bad experience can wipe out a whole series of good ones. The brilliant Italian soccer player Roberto Baggio scored more than three hundred goals in his professional career, but he is widely remembered for missing a penalty in the 1994 World Cup final, which handed the trophy to Brazil. In personal relationships, psychologists estimate that it takes at least five compliments to wipe out the effects of a single insult. Similarly, one moral transgression may be enough for us to revise our opinion of someone who has done many good deeds. Campaigning politicians seem to be instinctively aware of the power of negative emotions and they often spend more time denigrating their opponents and playing on people's fears than on building up their hopes.

Figure 7.10 Roberto Baggio misses a penalty in the 1994 World Cup final against Brazil. Are negative emotions always more powerful than positive ones?

ACTIVITY 7.10

1. Do your parents and/or teachers focus more on what you do wrong than on what you do right? To what extent might this give them a misleading impression of your character?
2. If someone offered you the opportunity to win $150 or lose $100 on the toss of a coin, would you be willing to make a bet? What do you think (a) most people would do; and (b) a rational person would do?
3. To what extent do politicians in your country engage in *negative campaigning* – that is, attacking their opponents rather than highlighting their own policies? How successful is this strategy?

The obvious problem with negativity bias is that it can distort our perception and cause us to have an unduly pessimistic view of the world. There is, however, an important exception to this bias. When it comes to assessing ourselves, we tend to suffer from positive rather than negative illusions. Research suggests that most people have an overly positive view of their own talents and abilities. They may, for example, believe that they have unusually good judgement, or unusually good social skills, or an unusually good sense of humour. It turns out that the people with the most accurate view of themselves are the clinically depressed. This view is aptly known as *depressive realism*.

ACTIVITY 7.11

1. We are often encouraged to think positively about things. What are the advantages and disadvantages of positive thinking?
2. Which is preferable: to have an unbiased view of reality and yet be depressed, or to be happily deluded? Give reasons.

Twisted reasoning

Emotions can also cloud our reason and there are many examples in everyday life of the way they can undermine our ability to think clearly. At some time or other, you have probably been in a 'rational discussion' with someone which degenerated into a slanging match. When our emotions are aroused, it is all too easy to stop listening to the person we are arguing with and to start trading insults rather than reasons. More generally, if you hold your beliefs with too much passion, this can prevent you being open-minded and all too easily lead to a 'my theory right or wrong' kind of attitude.

Rationalisation

When we are in the grip of strong emotions, we tend not to reason in an objective way but to rationalise our pre-existing prejudices. To clarify the difference between reasons and rationalisations, consider the following story by Aesop (sixth century BCE), the legendary writer of Greek fables.

A famished fox saw some clusters of ripe black grapes hanging from a trellised vine. She resorted to all her tricks to get at them, but wearied herself in vain, for she could not reach them. At last she turned away, hiding her disappointment and saying: 'The grapes are sour, and not ripe as I thought.'

This story suggests that if we have a particular emotional attitude about something we may manufacture bad reasons in order to justify it. According to psychologists, this kind of behaviour is quite common. We tend to rationalise when there is a conflict between two or more of our beliefs. For example, someone who eats junk food and is familiar with the evidence that it is bad for their health may try to explain away the evidence as in Figure 7.11.

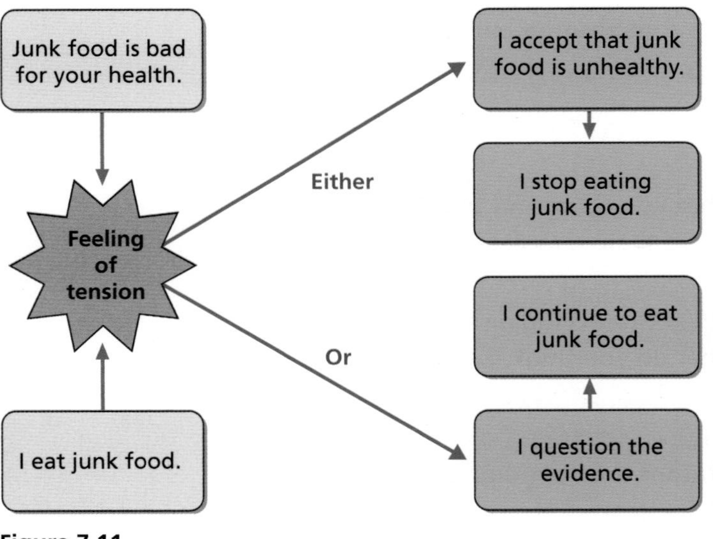

Figure 7.11

ACTIVITY 7.12

1. What is going on when someone who is losing badly at a game says that it is a 'stupid game'? Do you think they would say that if they were winning?
2. Are students who do badly on a test more or less likely to say that the test was unfair than students who do well on it? Give reasons.

At the limit, this tendency to rationalise can lead a person to develop an illusory but self-confirming belief system. Figure 7.12 shows how this can happen.

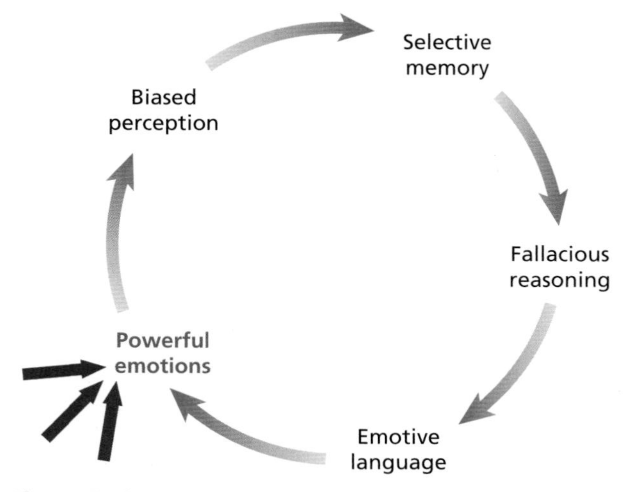

Figure 7.12

To illustrate, imagine that Henry has an emotional prejudice against immigrants. His prejudice will probably lead to the following:

1. *Biased perception.* He notices only lazy immigrants and overlooks hard-working ones.
2. *Selective memory.* He remembers other negative examples which confirm his prejudice.
3. *Fallacious reasoning.* He makes hasty generalisations from his own limited experience.
4. ***Emotive language***. He concludes that immigrants are 'bone idle' and 'don't know the meaning of hard work'.

KT – emotive language: highly charged language which is designed to arouse people's emotions

The above factors will reinforce the original prejudice and make it difficult for Henry to be objective. He can escape from such a vicious circle only if he is willing to question his prejudiced assumptions and actively consider other ways of looking at the situation.

The trouble is that fanatics – by definition – refuse to question their assumptions or consider evidence that runs contrary to their own distorted way of looking at the world. As the psychologist Leon Festinger (1919–90) observed:

> *A man with a conviction is a hard man to change. Tell him you disagree and he turns away. Show him facts or figures and he questions your sources. Appeal to logic and he fails to see your point. We have all experienced the futility of trying to change a strong conviction, especially if the convinced person has some investment in his belief. We are familiar with the variety of ingenious defenses with which people protect their convictions, managing to keep them unscathed through the most devastating attacks.*

Risk assessment

We typically judge risks by consulting our feelings rather than statistics. This may explain why many people are more frightened of sharks than power sockets, planes than cars, and terrorism than global warming. In each case, the evidence suggests that their assessment of the relative risks is wrong. All too often, it seems, we do not fear the right things. For example, the risk of dying in a plane crash is, per distance travelled, lower than any other means of transport. Mile for mile, it turns out that walking is one of the most dangerous means of transport, second only to travelling by motorcycle. In fact, more people die every year from drunk walking than they do from drunk driving – although you should be careful not to draw false conclusions from this observation!

There are a number of factors which can trigger the emotion of fear irrespective of whether it is justified. These include our evolutionary past, the unknown, control, immediacy and salience.

1. *Our evolutionary past.* Our emotions evolved in part to help us to cope with threats which existed in our past environment. Once upon a time, it doubtless made sense to fear spiders and snakes, but they are no longer a significant threat to most people living in urban environments. We may be 'hard-wired' to fear such things – which could explain why they are difficult to overcome – but in the modern world we would probably benefit more from a deep rooted fear of traffic.
2. *The unknown.* We are more frightened of unfamiliar risks, such as terrorism, radioactive waste, and anthrax than of everyday hazards such as sunbathing, slipping on ice, or catching influenza. You are probably familiar with the phrase 'war on terror', but there seems to be no corresponding 'war on flu'. In fact, far more people die of flu every year than die in terrorist attacks and some analysts argue that a global flu pandemic constitutes a greater threat to our security than global terrorism. (In this context, it is worth remembering that more people died in the 1918–19 flu pandemic than were killed in the whole of the First World War.)
3. *Control.* We usually fear things less when we feel that we are in control – for example, when we ski, or drive, or smoke. However, such controllable risks are often much greater than uncontrollable ones – not least because our control is often illusory. You may reassure yourself that you are a safe driver, but even if that is true you are forgetting about other drivers on the road, who may put your safety at risk. And many people may think they could break their tobacco addiction tomorrow, but, sadly, some people only quit *after* they have been diagnosed with lung cancer.
4. *Immediacy.* We tend to have a greater fear of immediate, abrupt threats than of more distant, gradual ones. If you take up smoking as a teenager, the risk of dying of cancer seems far off indeed. But imagine a world in which smoking is not bad for your health *except* that one cigarette in a hundred thousand is filled with dynamite rather than tobacco – and there is no way of knowing in advance which one is dangerous. So, occasionally, when someone lights a cigarette it blows their head off. Given the fear-inducing immediacy of the risk it would probably be easy to quit in such a world. In fact, smoking kills more people in the real world than it would in the one we have imagined.
5. *Salience.* Salience refers to the extent to which a risk sticks in your mind and is easy to recall. The news media play a key role here. Since they focus on dramatic, rare events such as terrorist attacks, child abductions and plane crashes we tend to recall and overestimate such risks at the expense of more mundane and less memorable ones.

ACTIVITY 7.13

1. In the light of the above discussion, explain why most people are more frightened of terrorism than of global warming.
2. Since you are much more likely to die in a car on the way to the airport than you are in a plane, would you agree that the fear of flying is an irrational fear? How would you explain it?
3. 'Since everyone is aware of the dangers, smokers are making a rational choice in deciding that the benefits of smoking outweigh the risks.' Do you agree or disagree? Give reasons.

Irrational behaviour

Our emotions can not only distort our perception and reasoning, but also lead us to make poor decisions. Many of our emotions are urgent and short-sighted and can easily blind us to the longer-term consequences of our actions. How often have you said something in a moment of anger that you immediately regretted? Or given in to temptation when it would have been better to exercise self-control? Aristotle (384–322 BCE) defined man as a rational animal, and economics is based on the assumption that we are all – producers and consumers alike – rational people. But the underlying reality may be more in line with Thomas Shelling's (1921–) amusing description of a smoker:

> *How should we conceptualize this rational consumer whom all of us know and who some of us are, who in self-disgust grinds his cigarettes down the disposal swearing that this time he means never again to risk orphaning his children with lung cancer and is on the street three hours later looking for a store that's still open to buy cigarettes; who eats a high-calorie lunch knowing that he will regret it, does regret it, cannot understand how he lost control, resolves to compensate with a low-calorie dinner, eats a high-calorie dinner knowing he will regret it, and does regret it; who sits glued to the TV knowing that again tomorrow he'll wake early in a cold sweat unprepared for that morning meeting on which so much of his career depends.*

As this suggests, we are all masters of acting against our own best interests and making resolutions that we break at the first sign of temptation. (Oscar Wilde joked, 'I can resist everything except temptation.') We will give further consideration to the weakness of the will when we look at ethics in Chapter 17.

ACTIVITY 7.14

1. 'What reason weaves, by passion is undone' (Alexander Pope, 1688–1744). Choose a character from a novel, play, or film to illustrate and analyse this quotation.
2. How might an economist respond to the charge that economics is based on the false assumption that we are rational agents?

Since turbulent emotions can distort our ability to think clearly and behave intelligently, you might think that the ideal situation would be one in which we did not have any emotions at all and could look at the world in a balanced and objective way. In ancient times, such a belief was held by a group of philosophers known as the **Stoics**, who emerged in Greece in the third century BCE. The Stoics advocated a state of mind called **apathy** – literally 'without passion' – in which the mind could mirror reality in a calm and untroubled way. However, it could be argued that such a state is neither achievable nor desirable. Admittedly, we might welcome losing negative emotions, but the trouble is that our emotions are interconnected. For example, loving someone brings with it the fear of losing them, and you can only rid yourself of the fear if you also rid yourself of the love. Most people would consider this too high a price to pay for tranquillity of mind.

KT – stoicism: a philosophy of life which advocates the control and subjugation of one's emotions

KT – apathy: a state of mind advocated by Stoic philosophers which literally means 'without passion'

ACTIVITY 7.15

1. What problems might there be in trying to be a good Stoic and striving to be apathetic?
2. Can you imagine a human life without emotions? If so, try to characterise what it might be like. If not, explain why not.
3. Have you ever felt so happy that it made you sad? What has this got to do with our discussion?
4. Under what emotional conditions do you think you are most likely to make an unbiased judgement about something: (a) a good mood; (b) a bad mood; (c) a neutral mood?

Emotions as a source of knowledge

Despite the Stoic ideal, it is difficult to imagine a meaningful human life without emotions. If you describe someone as being 'cold and unemotional', you do not literally mean that they do not have any emotions, but that they have, or show, few emotions *compared with the average person*. You might, for example, think that Mr Spock, the half-human, half-Vulcan character in the original *Star Trek* series, comes close to having no emotions. But Spock is not so much *lacking* in emotions as *in control* of his emotions. After all, he *cares* about what happens to the Starship Enterprise – and to care about something is to be emotionally engaged with it.

Some recent studies of brain-damaged patients in fact suggest that if you did not have any emotions then your life would quickly disintegrate. The psychologist Antonio Damasio (1944–) cites the case of a patient called Elliot who suffered damage to the emotional centres in his brain. Elliot appeared normal in many respects and performed just as well on IQ tests as he did before his accident.

Nevertheless, he became a 'rational fool' whose life fell apart because he had lost the ability to make decisions. Damasio speculates that emotions help us to make rational decisions about things by narrowing down our options so that we can choose between a manageable number of them. Since patients such as Elliot do not have any emotions to guide them, they try to decide what to do on the basis of reason alone and they end up experiencing a kind of paralysis.

ACTIVITY 7.16

1. Have you ever been in a situation where you had to choose between two equally attractive options? How did you come to a decision?
2. What role do you think is usually played by reason and emotion when people decide which universities to apply to? What role do you think each of these *should* play?
3. Peter has decided that he wants to marry Heloise. He came to his decision by weighing up all of Heloise's good points and bad points and comparing them with those of other potential life-partners. Heloise came out as the most rational choice. What can be said for and against this way of deciding whom you would like to marry? How would you feel if you were Heloise?

Damasio's research suggests that our emotions play a crucial role in enabling us to make decisions. Despite our earlier reservations, it could also be argued that, sometimes at least, they are a positive source of knowledge which contributes actively to our understanding of the world. To balance our earlier negative assessment, we will now consider the view that emotions can illuminate our perception, supplement our reason, and ground our values.

Emotional illumination

While it is tempting to dismiss emotions as subjective disturbances which distort our perception, some thinkers claim that they are analogous to the senses and enable us to discern important aspects of reality. Just as evolution has equipped us with senses to perceive objects, so, it could be argued, it has also furnished us with emotions to detect opportunities and threats. On this view, the world is as full of pleasant, depressing, frightening, annoying, disgusting and surprising things as it is of colours, sounds, tastes and smells. If our emotions are working correctly then we will experience, say, a feeling of fear when we encounter a fearful object in much the same way that we will experience a sensation of red when we look at a red object. In such cases, our emotions are not so much a projection on to reality as a reflection of it. At best, then, we do not call something fearful because we fear it; rather we fear it because it is fearful. In addition, our emotions can reveal and make salient aspects of reality that we might otherwise overlook. If a soldier is crawling through enemy lines his fear is likely to give him a heightened awareness of threats which will help him to see the reality of his situation. A relaxed soldier, blind to real dangers, would soon be a dead soldier.

We could also argue that our emotions give us a form of knowledge that is both immediate and profound. Think, for example, of the rush of joy you experience when you discover you have passed an exam, or the paralysing fear when you notice a poisonous snake slithering towards you, or the sickening disgust when you see maggots crawling over a piece of rotting meat. Without having to think or reason anything out, your emotions immediately alert you to the importance of these things. Moreover, it could be argued that they give us a deeper grasp of our situation than any purely intellectual awareness. So if you get top marks in an exam and you don't feel a sense of euphoria, then perhaps you have not really understood what has happened. The same could be said if a loved one dies and you feel no grief; or if a friend is racially abused and you feel no anger; or if you read about the victims of a devastating earthquake and you feel no pity.

ACTIVITY 7.17

1. 'If you are not horrified by genocide then you have not understood it.' Do you agree or disagree with this statement? Does it follow that the more horrified you are by genocide, the better you understand it? Could you be horrified by something and yet not really understand it at all?
2. What problems does the above raise for someone who is trying to write an 'objective' account of, say, the genocide in Rwanda in 1994?

In this context, it is interesting to mention a strange psychological condition known as *Capgras delusion*. Patients suffering from this delusion hold the extraordinary belief that someone close to them, such as a family member or friend, has been replaced by an identical-looking impostor. The psychologist Vilayanur Ramachandram has suggested that this condition is caused by a disconnect (resulting from brain damage) between the ability to recognise a significant other and the emotional feelings that usually accompany it. It is as if the patient is reasoning, 'This person looks like (say) my mother, but since she does not arouse any feeling of warmth and familiarity in me she must be an impostor.' There have even been cases of patients who believe that their dog or family home is an impostor. Thankfully, Capgras delusion is extremely rare, but it again suggests that emotions play a crucial role in helping us to make sense of the world.

Rational emotions

Although we tend to think of reason and emotion as two different things, in practice they are closely related to one another and it is difficult to make a clear distinction between them. Rather than think of reason and emotion as completely different *either–or* things, it may make more sense to say that there is a *more-or-less* continuum of mental activity running from the very rational to the very emotional. When you are engrossed in a mathematics problem you are at one end of the continuum, and when you lose your temper you are at the other end. Most of the time you are probably somewhere in the middle and have a complex mixture of thoughts and feelings floating around in your mind.

Figure 7.13 Reason–emotion continuum

Furthermore, it could be argued that our emotions can themselves be more or less rational. This view was held by the Greek philosopher Aristotle. In speaking of anger, he observed that: 'Anyone can be angry – that is easy. But to be angry with the right person to the right degree, at the right time, for the right purpose and in the right way – that is not easy.' What then distinguishes a rational from an irrational emotion? Two features suggest themselves. A rational emotion, we might say, is *appropriate* and *proportionate*.

1. *Appropriate.* An emotion is appropriate if it is *sensitive to the real nature of the situation.* Therefore, fear is rational if it is a response to something objectively fearful, something that any reasonable person would consider frightening. Conversely, an emotion is inappropriate if it is based on false beliefs that misconstrue the situation. Consider, for example, a racist whose pride derives from their assumption that other cultures are inferior. We would surely be justified in criticising such pride and might even describe it as a *false* emotion.
2. *Proportionate.* Not only should our emotions be appropriate, we should also have them to the right degree. To grieve at the death of the family pet might be appropriate, but if you lock yourself away and mourn for five years, then you have probably lost your sense of proportion. The same might be said of an infatuated lover who is compulsively obsessed with his girlfriend, or someone with clinical depression who ruminates endlessly on the futility of life.

Although our emotions often lead us to *overreact* to situations, it is worth emphasising that they can be deficient as well as excessive. To see this compare the following two imaginary scenarios:

1. Paul has arranged to meet Tom at 3:00 p.m. Tom arrives at 3:02 p.m. and apologises for being late. Rather than accept Tom's apology, Paul starts to scream and shout about Tom's lack of consideration and completely loses his self-control.
2. The hospital phones Judy with some terrible news. Her boyfriend has been assaulted by some hooligans and is lying unconscious in the intensive care unit. 'Oh dear', she says, 'that *is* annoying! I was hoping to play tennis this afternoon, but I suppose I had better come and visit him.'

The reactions of Paul and Judy in the above scenarios could both be described as irrational. Paul's problem is that he shows too much emotion, Judy's that she shows too little. If a friend arrives two minutes late for an appointment, you might reasonably show mild annoyance, but it would be inappropriate to lose your temper. On the other hand, if you *only* show mild annoyance on learning that a loved one has been assaulted, then there is surely something wrong with your emotional responses. For in this situation, you surely *ought* to feel shock and concern and anger. This suggests that showing too little emotion is as irrational as showing too much emotion. We need to find a balance between the two.

ACTIVITY 7.18

1. Since you got out of bed this morning, how much time have you spent *thinking* and how much time *feeling*? What does this suggest about the relationship between thinking and feeling?
2. Give some examples taken from the real world of emotional reactions that you consider to be (a) reasonable and (b) unreasonable. Explain why you think what you do.
3. 'While factual beliefs can be described as "true" or "false", emotions cannot.' Do you agree or disagree with this view?

Emotions as a source of values

LQ – Ethics: Is ethics more a matter of the heart than the head?

Some people claim that just as we can come to know facts through thinking, so we can come to know values through feeling. There is support for this view. After all, our emotions implicitly judge things as positive or negative, good or bad; and if we did not have any emotions then nothing would matter to us and we wouldn't care about anything. The fact that we *do* have emotions allegedly enables us to discern various moral qualities. For example, it could be argued that gratitude alerts us to kindness, anger to injustice, pity to suffering, guilt to wrong-doing, and disgust to perversion. Speaking metaphorically, we might say that in such cases we see with our heart rather than our head and discern the moral quality in question by having the relevant emotion.

KT – wisdom of repugnance: the claim that we can validly appeal to our feelings of disgust to justify our moral beliefs

Consider an emotion such as disgust. The American intellectual Leon Kass (1939–) has coined the phrase the **wisdom of repugnance** to suggest that disgust is not just a mindless bodily reaction to something unpleasant but conveys morally significant information which is 'beyond reason's power to articulate'. He says, for example, that human cloning is morally wrong, and that although we may be unable to give a reasoned argument against it, we should take seriously the shiver of revulsion we feel when we contemplate it. In Kass's view, then, our moral beliefs can sometimes be justified by feelings rather than reasons.

Figure 7.14 *"But, seriously . . ."*

ACTIVITY 7.19

1. What are typically seen as virtues and vices in your culture? How are they related to the emotions?
2. What role do emotions play in people's moral judgements? What role should they play?

Some doubts

Despite the above comments, we should be careful about blindly trusting emotions as a source of moral knowledge. To trust them on the grounds that they are natural would be to commit what we might call the **wise nature fallacy**. Just because something is natural does not mean that it is good. The untamed emotions of a 'wild child' who grew up entirely outside society would doubtless aid their survival, but they would be a poor guide to values.

KT – wise nature fallacy: the fallacious assumption that because something is natural it is therefore good

Even in civilised society our emotions can mislead us if they are *uninformed*, *egocentric*, or *unreliable*.

1. *Uninformed emotions.* Emotions can distort perception as often as they can illuminate it. Critics of Leon Kass claim that disgust is an especially poor guide to moral truth. At one time, for example, people considered interracial marriage to be disgusting; but this was surely an indication of the depth of their prejudice rather than the height of their wisdom.
2. *Egocentric emotions.* Our unreflective emotions are typically concerned with things that are beneficial or harmful to *us*. So, far from being a guide to universal values, they are often a reflection of our own self-serving interests. For example, we may feel angry when someone lies to us but happily lie to them; or we may feel sad about our own misfortune but indifferent to the misfortune of others.
3. *Unreliable emotions.* Our emotions are not entirely self-centred and we sometimes feel pity for the plight of others. The trouble is that such other-regarding emotions are unreliable. We may be moved by a harrowing account of a child in distress yet be untouched by a famine affecting hundreds of thousands of people; or we may feel pity today and be indifferent tomorrow. This suggests that how we happen to feel is a poor indicator of moral significance.

Considering the above points, those who insist that emotions can be a source of moral knowledge usually limit their claim to emotions that have been properly educated. Indeed, a great deal of informal education is implicitly or explicitly concerned with educating the emotions and building character. The philosopher Martha Nussbaum (1947–) has drawn particular attention to the role played by literature in this context. At its best, she claims, literature can help to awaken social emotions such as pity and gratitude and broaden their range. We shall explore this idea further when we discuss empathy in Chapter 9 (page 234).

ACTIVITY 7.20

1. To what extent should we try to model our emotional reactions on those of people we consider to be good?
2. Give some examples to show how novels and movies can educate our emotions. Can they ever corrupt them?

Emotional intelligence

KT – emotional intelligence: the ability to read and control or influence one's own and other people's emotions

Since our emotions look inward as well as outward, they can give us knowledge about ourselves as well as the world. The ability to understand our own and other people's emotions is part of what is known as **emotional intelligence**. This concept has deep historical roots, but it has been popularised in recent years by the American psychologist Daniel Goleman (1946–) who suggests that EQ may be more important for a happy and successful life than IQ.

ACTIVITY 7.21

1. Find and take a short online emotional intelligence test. What, if anything, did you learn about yourself?
2. What difficulties arise in trying to measure emotional intelligence (EQ)? What difficulties arise in trying to measure intellectual intelligence (IQ)?

Knowing our own emotions

LQ – Imagination: Why is it difficult to imagine and predict our own emotional behaviour?

We naturally think that since we experience our own emotions they are fully transparent to us. There is doubtless an element of truth in this view. After all, when we are feeling down we sometimes hide our emotions and 'put on a brave face' to the world. This suggests that we alone know our true feelings. Nevertheless, things are not as straightforward as they seem. Take, for example, an emotion such as love. Sometimes it is hard to disentangle what we really feel about someone and we might find it difficult to distinguish love from related feelings such as liking, infatuation, or lust. More generally, how we interpret our own emotional state may depend on context. There is, for example, evidence that if you are on a blind date and find yourself in a scary situation you may interpret your fear as attraction.

RLS – Headline: Film stars Richard Burton and Elizabeth Taylor married and divorced twice. To what extent can we know our own emotions?

We are particularly bad at predicting our own future emotional states. When you are calm and collected, it is hard to believe that hot emotions will lead you to behave foolishly. You might, for example, convince yourself that you won't get angry with an irritating friend or sibling only to find yourself losing your temper when you are in their company. Moreover, we tend to overestimate how happy or sad we would feel if fortune smiled on us or disaster struck. Despite what you might think, lottery winners are not permanently happy and paraplegics are not permanently depressed. In both cases, it seems, people adjust to their situation and in the long-run their overall level of happiness remains unchanged.

ACTIVITY 7.22

1. What role does observing your own behaviour play in discovering what you are feeling?
2. To what extent can writing about, or talking about, your feelings help you to clarify them? What does this suggest about the relation between language and emotion?
3. Could a friend of yours know better than you do whether or not you are really in love with someone? Give reasons.

Reading other people's emotions

'There's no art to find the mind's construction in the face', says a character in the play *Macbeth* by William Shakespeare (1564–1616). This suggests that other people are not 'open books' and that it is not always easy to read their emotions. We can get clues about what they are feeling from their facial expressions, their behaviour, and what they say; but we can never be entirely sure what is going on with their emotions. We may wonder whether someone is genuinely pleased to see us or just faking it, or whether their cheerful exterior hides a troubled mind.

Figure 7.15 How difficult is it to read someone's emotions?

Some people show their emotions more than others, and this may make them easier to read. But we should keep in mind that, as we saw earlier, rules governing emotional display vary between cultures. For example, in some Asian cultures children are taught to avoid looking their superiors in the eye. In Western culture, by contrast, you *should* look superiors in the eye, and a student who avoids a teacher's gaze may – often quite wrongly – be seen as deceitful and evasive. As this example suggests, there is plenty of scope here for cultural misunderstanding and confusion.

When we try to read someone's feelings, we do not look only at their face. To see this, consider the two pictures of the tennis star Serena Williams on the right. If you look only at the close-up, you might think that she is in intense pain, but when you pan out you see that her expression is in fact one of triumph rather than pain. As this example suggests, to understand someone's emotions we need to look at the overall context. Indeed, to grasp the complexities of what someone is feeling we probably need to know them well and be familiar with their personal story.

ACTIVITY 7.23

1. How easy do you find it to tell whether or not someone is attracted to you? What evidence do you look for? How sure can you be?
2. What truth, if any, is there in the stereotype that women are better at reading emotions than men?

Who is in control?

Another important element of emotional intelligence is emotional control. However, this assumes that we are able to control our emotions. In reality, we may know that an emotion is irrational and yet find it difficult to change it. For example, you may know that grass snakes are harmless, or that it is statistically safer to fly than to drive, but still be unable to contain your fear when you see a grass snake or are sitting in a plane. Many people also find it difficult to override unjustified feelings of disgust, as is shown by the following bizarre experiment. When subjects were invited to eat fudge that had been shaped to resemble dog poop, or drink apple juice poured out of a brand-new bed pan, the vast majority refused – even though such food and drink are usually desirable. Since it is difficult to switch off irrational emotions, we sometimes find it easier to adjust our beliefs to our emotions than bring our emotions into line with reason. We are back to the problem of rationalisation. When the object of our irrational fear and disgust concerns, say, a minority group, the consequences can be serious. Indeed, whether we are masters or slaves of our emotions has important implications not only for our understanding of what it means to be human, but also for the prospects for world peace.

ACTIVITY 7.24

1. To what extent do you think we are able to control our emotions? Which emotion is the most difficult to control?
2. What evidence is there that human beings are more in control of their emotions than they were, say, five hundred years ago?
3. 'Crimes of passion' are often judged less harshly than crimes committed in cold blood. How, if at all, can this difference be justified?

Conclusion

The discussion of the emotions in this chapter may have gone some way to convince you of their relevance to the search for knowledge. Not only do they provide the energy that fuels intellectual endeavour, but they also play a central role in our mental lives. At best, educated emotions reveal important features of the social world and contribute to our knowledge of values. At worst, unruly emotions are short-sighted and narrow-minded and can lead us to find bad reasons to justify our pre-existing prejudices. This suggests that, while we should listen to our emotions, we should listen with a critical ear and test them against other possible sources of knowledge, such as reason and sense perception, before accepting them.

Key points

- Emotions are feelings that are directed towards things that matter to us in the world.
- Emotions are relevant to the search for knowledge because they provide us with energy, affect our thinking and are sometimes used to justify our beliefs.
- Psychologists commonly distinguish six primary emotions which are said to be universal: happiness, sadness, fear, anger, disgust and surprise.
- While emotions are rooted in biology, different cultures describe and express them in different ways.
- The James–Lange theory says that emotions are essentially physical in nature, but they are also influenced by our beliefs.
- Our emotions are sometimes an obstacle to knowledge, and strong emotions can distort perception, twist reason and sabotage our plans.
- More positively, our emotions sometimes illuminate perception and draw our attention to important features of reality such as threats to our well-being.
- It might also be argued that knowledge based on emotions is more immediate and profound than purely intellectual knowledge.
- Rather than think of reason and emotion as opposites, it may be better to say that emotions can be more or less rational.
- Some people claim that emotions are a source of values; but since emotions can be uninformed, egocentric and unreliable, we should treat this claim with caution.
- Sometimes it is difficult to know both our own emotions and those of other people.
- There is an ongoing debate about the extent to which we are in control of our emotions and the extent to which they are in control of us.

Key terms

apathy
emotional contagion
emotional intelligence
emotive language
negativity bias
primary emotions
rationalisation
secondary emotions
stoicism
ten-year rule
wisdom of repugnance
wise nature fallacy

IB prescribed essay titles

1. Can we know when to trust our emotions in the pursuit of knowledge? Consider history and one other area of knowledge. (May 2013)
2. 'There can be no knowledge without emotion . . . until we have felt the force of the knowledge, it is not ours' (adapted from Arnold Bennett). Discuss this vision of the relationship between knowledge and emotion. (November 2008 / May 2009)

Further reading

Books

Antonio Damasio, *Descartes' Error* (Grosset/Putnam, 1994). In this fascinating book, Damasio, a neuroscientist, goes beyond the traditional either–or approach of reason versus emotion, and argues that, in order to make intelligent decisions, logical thinking must be grounded in, and supported by, emotions and feelings.

Dylan Evans, *Emotion: The Science of Sentiment* (Oxford University Press, 2001). A short, accessible exploration of the emotions which draws on scientific research and raises such intriguing questions as: 'Was love invented by European poets in the middle ages . . .? Will winning the lottery really make you happy? Is it possible to build robots that have feelings?'

Online articles

Steven Pinker, 'Fools for Love', excerpt from Pinker's book *How the Mind Works* (Penguin, 1997).

Sharon Begley, 'The Roots of Fear', *Newsweek*, 15 December 2007.

Intuition

8

Intuition is reason in a hurry.

Holbrook Jackson, 1874–1948

Intuition leads us astray because it's not very good at picking up flaws in the evidence.

Thomas Gilovich, 1954–

Truly successful decision making relies on a balance between deliberate and instinctive thinking.

Malcolm Gladwell, 1963–

The expert's snap judgment is the result of a deliberative process made unconscious through habituation.

Richard Posner, 1939–

Statistics and analysis almost always beat instinct and guessing.

Michael R. LeGault, 1959–

It is by logic that we prove, but by intuition that we discover.

Henri Poincaré, 1854–1912

The intuitive mind is a sacred gift and the rational mind is a faithful servant.

Albert Einstein, 1879–1955

When . . . philosophers run out of arguments, they appeal to intuition.

Timothy Williamson, 1955–

There can be as much value in the blink of an eye as in months of rational analysis.

Malcolm Gladwell, 1963–

Philosophy is the finding of bad reasons for what we believe on instinct.

F. H. Bradley, 1846–1924

The heart has its reason which reason does not understand.

Blaise Pascal, 1623–1662

8 Intuition

Introduction

Figure 8.1 Archimedes

The word 'intuition' is typically associated with the 'ah-hah' moment of insight when you suddenly see the solution to a problem. You are probably familiar with the story of Archimedes (c.287–212 BCE) who hit upon his famous principle while lying in the bath. So excited was he by his insight that he leapt out of his bath and ran naked down the street shouting 'Eureka! Eureka!' ('I've found it! I've found it!'). You may not have run naked down the street, but you have probably had your own moments of insight when the solution to a problem became suddenly clear to you. The change from not being able to solve a problem to suddenly seeing the answer is quite mysterious and no one is entirely sure how intuition works.

The focus of this chapter is on the extent to which intuition can be considered a reliable source of knowledge. The answer is likely to depend on the nature of the claim and the person making it. You might, for example, take seriously a mathematician's insight into a calculus problem, or a grandmaster's intuition about the best move in a game of chess, or a ski guide's sixth sense that an avalanche is imminent. Perhaps you also trust your first impressions when you meet people, or believe a friend who says they can tell when someone is lying, or go with your gut feeling when you make important decisions. However, you may doubt New Age thinkers who claim to have powers of intuition which enable them to 'eavesdrop on the mind of the universe'. Most people would be concerned if hospitals decided to use 'psychic healers' to cure patients, or the police appealed to 'psychic detectives' to solve crimes. Given the poor track record of alleged psychics such reservations would seem to be justified.

RLS – Headline: '"Psychic" tip-off sparks police hunt for mass grave in Texas'. Should police accept help from psychics when trying to solve crimes, or limit themselves to 'hard evidence'?

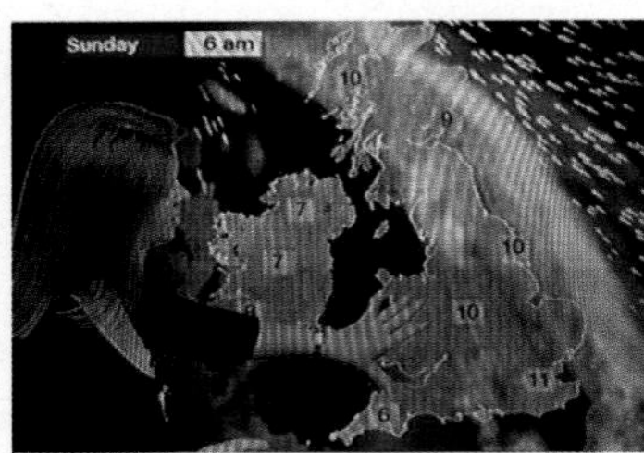

Weather forecaster

Financial adviser

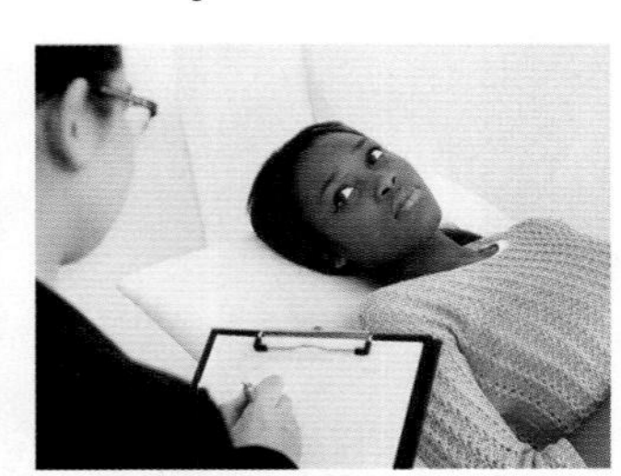

Psychiatrist

Philosopher

Politician

Psychic

Chess grandmaster

Figure 8.2 Whose intuitions would you trust?

In what follows, we begin by saying something about the nature of intuition. We then consider the reliability of our uneducated **folk intuitions** in different areas of knowledge and in the social world. This leads on to a discussion about the merits of expert intuition. A key problem with trusting our intuitions is that they are subject to various cognitive biases and we briefly highlight ten of them. We conclude by looking at the claim that all knowledge is ultimately based on 'core intuitions' which cannot be further justified.

KT – folk intuitions: our natural, uneducated intuitions about the way the world works, which often turn out to be false

What is intuition?

LQ – Human sciences: What can we learn from psychology about the reliability of intuition?

According to one definition, intuition is 'the ability to understand something instinctively, without the need for conscious reasoning'. The word is, however, somewhat vague and can be used to cover feelings of self-evidence, creative insights, gut feelings and instinctive responses.

ACTIVITY 8.1

1. What difference, if any, is there between saying 'My intuition is . . .' and saying 'My guess is . . .'?
2. Under what circumstances do people typically rely on their intuitions and gut feelings? How accurate do you think such feelings are?

RLS – Headline: 'I'm not a textbook player. I'm a gut player. I rely on my instincts' (George W. Bush, 1946–). What are the advantages and disadvantages of political leaders who go with their gut feelings over ones who take an analytic approach to decision making?

Since intuitions come to us directly without explicit step-by-step reasoning, it is natural to think of them as being more a matter of feeling than of thinking, connected with the heart (or gut) rather than the head. However, they are usually less 'hot' than emotions such as anger and typically come in a flash accompanied by a feeling of insight. We should, however, keep in mind that there are different kinds of intuitions. Some are more *emotional* – as when a person senses danger without being able to explain why; but others are more *intellectual* – as when the answer to a clue in a crossword puzzle pops into your head.

Preliminary comparison

We can get a preliminary sense of the nature of intuition by briefly comparing it with the seven other ways of knowing.

SENSE PERCEPTION	Intuition might be seen as a form of intellectual vision analogous to sense perception.
REASON	Intuition is direct rather than sequential and does not involve reasoning from premises to conclusions.
LANGUAGE	Intuitions seem to lie beyond language in that we are unable to explain how we arrived at them in words.
EMOTION	Intuitions might be classified as feelings, but some are more explicitly emotional than others.
IMAGINATION	Intuition is commonly associated with imaginative and creative individuals.
MEMORY	A well-stocked memory may help us to have good intuitions about a topic.
FAITH	It could be argued that our deepest intuitions are based on faith in that we cannot further justify them.

ACTIVITY 8.2

1. Compare and contrast intuition with one other way of knowing and assess their relative merits as sources of knowledge.
2. Is there any evidence to suggest that some cultures value intuition as a source of knowledge more than others?

Thinking fast

KT – automatic system: a fast, unconscious, intuitive and inflexible mode of thinking that governs many of our judgements and decisions

KT – reflective system: a slow, conscious, deliberative and flexible mode of thinking that can correct errors in the automatic system

KT – heuristic: a mental shortcut or 'rule of thumb' we use to make intuitive judgements and decisions

In recent years it has become popular to distinguish two different modes of thinking: automatic and reflective. The **automatic system** (roughly, intuition) is fast, unconscious, intuitive and inflexible. By contrast, the **reflective system** (roughly, reason) is slow, conscious, deliberative and flexible. While both systems have their place, the point is knowing when to use which system.

One of the main advantages intuition has over reason is its speed, and it has aptly been described as 'reason in a hurry'. In fact, the automatic system effortlessly takes care of hundreds of routine judgements and decisions we make every day. You buy a couple of items at the store and know without calculating that you should get change from 20 euros. You see 'at a glance' that someone is angry and should be avoided. You navigate your way effortlessly through a crowded shopping mall without bumping into anyone. We take such mundane skills for granted because they are so well rehearsed that they have become second nature. This is just as well: for if we tried to consciously reflect on everything that we do, we would experience analysis paralysis and be unable to function.

Our intuitive system typically makes use of 'fast and frugal' mental shortcuts and rules of thumb known as **heuristics**. Since we lack the time, information and ability to subject every judgement and decision to exhaustive analysis, our reliance on heuristics is often beneficial. Imagine, for example, making a gut decision to buy a popular new phone. Rather than carefully analyse the phone's technical specifications, you may simply rely on the heuristic 'If it's popular, then it's good quality.' Although it is not always reliable, this simple rule of thumb is often *good enough* for you to make a reasonable purchase. Indeed, research suggests that, when it comes to decision-making, *less is sometimes more* and we may do better to go with our gut feeling than accumulating mountains of information.

"From what I hear, the Atwood Intuition Tank is coming up with results faster than we are."

Figure 8.3

The need for reflection

The problem with quick, intuitive judgements is that speed is sometimes bought at the expense of accuracy. To see this, consider the following question: 'How many animals of each kind did Moses take on the ark?' You probably said 'Two'. Wrong! The guy with the ark was Noah, not Moses. Here's another example. Imagine you are on a quiz show and there is a $100 prize for the first person to correctly answer the following two questions:

1. What does S-H-O-P spell?
2. What do you do when you get to a green light?

Figure 8.4 Is intuition a reliable source of evidence?

If you reacted quickly, you probably answered *Stop* to the second question. The correct answer is, of course, *Go*; but your mind was primed – that is, misled – by the fact that 'stop' rhymes with 'shop' and it took the line of least resistance. As this shows, when we delegate thinking to the automatic system, we can easily get things wrong. That is why we also need the slower, more deliberative thinking associated with the reflective system.

Naive academic intuitions

We sometimes appeal to intuition to justify our knowledge claims in particular areas of knowledge, but research suggests that our naive 'folk intuitions' are poor guides to truth. Perhaps this is because they evolved to cope with the Stone-Age environment rather than with the modern world. At one time, it was believed that knowledge is simply organised common sense. But most psychologists would now say that we need to 'debug' – rather than blindly follow – our intuitions. Indeed, it could be argued that the aim of education is precisely to help us 'unlearn' our naive folk intuitions so that we can acquire an altogether more sophisticated and reliable understanding of the world.

To see why we should be cautious about trusting our naive academic intuitions, consider the following examples taken from different subject areas.

Physics

According to a common-sense belief that can be traced back to Aristotle (384–322 BCE), objects move only to the extent that they are given impetus or 'oomph', and if no force is applied to them they will grind to a halt. If something is going to move, you've got to push it, and if you stop pushing, it will stop moving. This reflects our everyday experience of the world, and for many centuries it struck people as intuitively obvious. However, this belief turns out to be false: according to Newton's first law of motion, 'Every object continues in its state of rest or uniform motion unless acted upon by a force.' Since you learnt this at school, you probably have no difficulty in accepting this law as true, but it is worth noticing that it is far from obvious and is in many respects counter-intuitive. After all, when did you last see an object continuing endlessly in a state of uniform motion?

There are many other examples of the gap between the physicists' description of the world and our common-sense description of it. For example, as we saw in Chapter 5 (p. 135), the desk I am sitting at strikes me as an obstinately solid object, but according to the physicists it consists mainly of empty space. And it gets worse. Many of the mainstream ideas of modern physics – such as quantum mechanics – are so contrary to our ordinary ways of thinking that even physicists struggle to make sense of them. At this level, our natural intuitions are not so much a guide to understanding as an obstacle to it. As an experienced physics professor once regretfully observed: 'With each freshman class, I must again face the fact that the human mind was not designed to study physics.'

Biology

Our uneducated folk intuitions about biology are as misleading as those we have about physics. Research shows that young children naturally believe that everything in nature has a purpose. They might, for example, say that the point of flowers is 'to make the world pretty', or that the point of bees is 'to give us honey'. A mere two hundred years ago biologists still took it as intuitively obvious that nature is purposive, and that since each species had its own unique essence one species could not evolve into another. Since Darwin, however, the consensus among biologists has been that nature works blindly and mechanistically with no goal in mind, and that species gradually evolve through random genetic variations that favour survival and reproduction. Nevertheless, the theory of evolution strikes many people as deeply counter-intuitive. Consider the intricate complexity of, say, the human eye. It is very difficult to resist thinking that since it *looks* designed it *has been* designed. Yet Darwinism insists that such complexity is the result of incremental chance variations over vast periods of time. Clearly, our intuitions in this area are a poor guide to truth. Indeed, as biologist Richard Dawkins (1941–) observes, it is almost as if 'the human brain is specifically designed to misunderstand Darwinism'.

Economics

Economics is another subject in which our folk intuitions can easily deceive us. Perhaps the best example concerns what is known as *zero-sum bias*. This is the widespread, seemingly self-evident, assumption that if one group gains in a social interaction then another group must be losing, with the balance of gains and losses summing to zero. If you take a bigger slice of the pie, then someone else will end up with a smaller slice. While this is obviously true in a static situation, it does not generalise to something dynamic like economics. Contrary to our zero-sum intuitions, economists insist that *trade* is a *positive-sum* game in which both sides unambiguously gain by trading with one another. To see this, imagine a simple two-person, two-product economy. You and I each bake bread and brew beer. But it happens that I am better than you at baking bread and you are better than me at brewing beer. So if I focus on the bread and you take care of the beer we can increase total production. If we then trade with each other we can both have more bread and more beer. This is a very simplified version of the economic argument for free trade. According to economists, the benefits of trade are undeniable, but many people do not believe this because they are misled by their naive intuitions.

Ethics

When it comes to ethics, we often trust our intuitive judgements about what is right and wrong; but such judgements sometimes lead us astray. This is partly because our moral intuitions evolved to cope with a *tribal* rather than a *global* community. For example, it strikes us as intuitively obvious that if you see a child drowning in the local village pond, you should help them. (Indeed, we would be shocked if you asked *why* you should help – you shouldn't need a reason.) At the same time, we are often deaf to the cries of strangers in distant lands who are in equally urgent need of help. This suggests that our naive intuitions do not give us a reliable moral compass and that they need to be refined by education and fortified by reason.

LQ – Ethics: Do professional philosophers have better intuitions about what is right and wrong than the average person?

We are also instinctively inclined to judge actions by their *consequences* rather than their *intentions*. Thus attempted murder is widely considered to be a less serious crime than successful murder. This may be a natural intuition, but it is, on reflection, an odd one. After all, since it was just *luck* that the victim didn't die, why should the assailant be rewarded with a lighter sentence? The reason, it seems, is that we intuitively hold people responsible for their luck. Some philosophers argue that we should reject such intuitions and judge actions by what the agent intended to do rather than by what actually happened.

The arts

Children often have naive intuitions about the nature of art. A poem should rhyme, a story should have a happy ending, a painting should represent something, and a piece of music should have a tune. Such intuitions can linger on into adult life and lead people to dismiss whole areas of modern art as 'rubbish'. The writer James Joyce (1882–1941), the painter Jackson Pollock (1912–56) and the composer Arnold Schoenberg (1874–1951) all defied conventional expectations, yet are considered to be great by the relevant experts. This suggests that our naive intuitions are not always the best guide to artistic merit.

LQ – Arts: How do creative people develop good intuitions and to what extent should they trust them?

As the above examples suggest, we would be unwise to put too much trust in our uneducated folk intuitions about different areas of knowledge. Indeed, it could be argued that intellectual history is largely the history of overturning such naive intuitions by appealing to evidence and argument.

ACTIVITY 8.3

Test the reliability of your intuitions about different subjects by answering the following questions:

1. Linda is thirty-one years old, single, outspoken, bright, and very much involved in social issues like disarmament and equal rights. Which of the following statements is more likely?
   a. 'Linda is a bank teller.'
   b. 'Linda is a bank teller and is active in the feminist movement.'
2. If an unbiased coin is tossed six times in a row, which of the following sequences is more likely?
   a. H-T-H-T-H-T.
   b. H-H-H-H-H-H
3. Take a soccer match with eleven players on each side and a referee. What are the odds of any two people on the field sharing the same birthday?
4. Briefly describe what will happen to the path of a ball after it is propelled through a spiral tube, as in Figure 8.5, and shot out of the top of it.

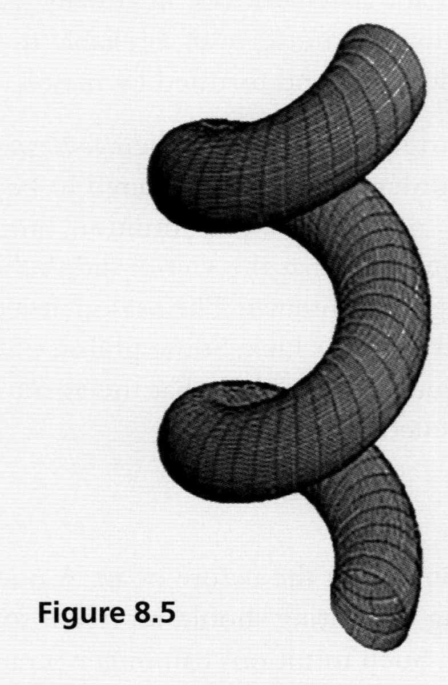

Figure 8.5

5. Imagine that you are standing on a large flat plain holding a bullet in your left hand and a loaded gun in your right hand. If you fire the gun horizontally and at the same instant drop the bullet from your left hand, which of the two bullets will hit the ground first?
6. You and a friend have just spent $10 each to go to the cinema and watch a film. After about half an hour you both realise that it is a really bad film. List some good reasons for staying until the end of the film, and then list some good reasons for leaving after half an hour.

[You will find the answers to the above questions at the end of this chapter.]

Social intuitions

One area in which we all like to think we are unusually skilled is in our ability to 'read' other people. We put a lot of trust in our social intuitions and pride ourselves on being good judges of character. (When did you last hear someone admit to being a *bad* judge of character?) In the case of people we know well, we are often good at picking up on subtle cues about their mood. However, when it comes to the accuracy of our first impressions, or our ability to size up an interviewee, or our sense of whether or not someone is lying, the evidence suggests that we are not nearly as good as we think.

ACTIVITY 8.4

1. If you are speaking to a friend on the phone, how good are you at sensing whether they are tired or upset simply from their tone of voice?
2. Can you tell if people have just been talking about you when you come in to a room? How?
3. Test your social intuitions by studying the two faces in Figure 8.6. One shows a genuine smile and one a false smile. Can you tell which is which?

Figure 8.6

4. What role does intuition play in judging whether someone accused of a crime is guilty or innocent? What role should it play?
5. What evidence is there that women generally have better social intuitions than men?

First impressions

According to psychologists, we form impressions of people within a few seconds of meeting them. There may be good evolutionary reasons for this; our ancestors' survival often depended on quickly determining whether a stranger was a friend or a foe. Fortunately, social encounters are now rarely a matter of life or death, but it is still important to get an accurate sense of whether someone is trustworthy and competent. There are, however, different opinions about whether or not our first impressions are reliable.

ACTIVITY 8.5

1. Which of these proverbs do you think is more accurate: (a) 'First impressions are last impressions'; (b) 'Never judge a book by its cover'? Do similar proverbs exist in other languages?
2. How quickly do you form an impression of a new teacher's effectiveness? How accurate do you think your first impression is?
3. Would you trust your first impression of someone from your own culture more than your first impression of someone from another culture? Give reasons.

You have probably come across stories about people with uncanny social intuitions. Consider, for example, the case of American Jackie Larsen who in April 2001 met a well-mannered stranger called Christopher Bono who told her that his car had broken down and asked for help. After a brief conversation with him, Larsen sensed that something was wrong and called the police. It turned out that Bono was on the run having murdered his mother. Larsen's 'sixth sense' may have been the result of **subliminal perception** – perception which operates below the level of conscious awareness.

KT – subliminal perception: perception that operates below the level of conscious awareness

While sensational anecdotes do not amount to scientific evidence, some studies support the idea that first impressions can be surprisingly accurate. In one experiment, students were asked to watch silent 30-second video clips of teachers they did not know and assess their effectiveness. Their ratings were very similar to those given by students who had been taught by the teachers for a whole semester. Some characteristics are easier to discern than others, and we seem particularly good at telling whether someone is an extrovert or introvert.

RLS – Headline: 'Amanda Knox: What's in a face? Amanda Knox was convicted of murder and her reputation sullied around the world, in large part because of her facial expressions and demeanour.' To what extent should we trust our first impressions?

Despite the above evidence, it is clear that first impressions can sometimes be spectacularly wrong – as people who have fallen victim to superficially charming fraudsters can testify. Think, too, of British Prime Minister Neville Chamberlain's (1869–1940) impression of Adolf Hitler when they met in 1938: 'In spite of the hardness and ruthlessness I thought I saw in his face, I got the impression that here was a man who could be relied upon when he gave his word.'

Figure 8.7 Amanda Knox

There are several reasons why we can get things so wrong. To start with, our impressions of character are often influenced by irrelevant factors such as physical appearance. There is a wealth of evidence to suggest that good-looking individuals are generally perceived as more intelligent, sociable and happy than other people. Appearance is also a good predictor of which candidate will win an election race – even though looks are unrelated to political competence. Since 1789 only five American presidents have been below average height – perhaps because people associate being tall with looking 'presidential'. Other crude stereotypes associated with such things as class, race and gender can also affect our judgement; but since they often operate unconsciously, we are less likely to be aware of them. Random order effects are another factor. You are, for example, likely to have a more positive impression of someone described as *intelligent, industrious, impulsive, critical, stubborn, envious* than someone described as *envious, stubborn, critical, impulsive, industrious, intelligent.* The two descriptions are, of course, identical – only the order is reversed. As this suggests, first impressions can easily become self-confirming prejudices – filters through which we judge the rest of someone's behaviour. It would seem, then, that the only reliable way of judging someone's character is actually going to the trouble of getting to know them.

Figure 8.8 Darcy and Elizabeth, the two main characters in *Pride and Prejudice*: How reliable are our first impressions?

ACTIVITY 8.6

1. Do you believe in love at first sight? To what extent does it confirm the power of our social intuitions?
2. Find out something about *speed dating*. Do you think it is a good way of finding a suitable partner?
3. Female musicians – especially those who play brass instruments – used to find it difficult to get jobs in orchestras. In the 1990s several well-known orchestras introduced a system of 'blind auditions'. The applicant played behind a screen so that the judges listening did not know their gender. As a result, there was a dramatic increase in women's success rate. What does this suggest about the difference between expert intuition and unconscious prejudice?
4. The original title of Jane Austen's famous novel *Pride and Prejudice* was *First Impressions*. What light does it – or any other novel you have studied – throw on the danger of such impressions?

Interviewer intuition

If you apply to university, you may find that in addition to submitting your academic transcripts you are also called for an interview. It is commonly thought that meeting a candidate in the flesh is the best way to get the measure of them and assess their potential. University admissions officers conduct many interviews every year and may pride themselves on their ability to choose the best candidates. However, studies suggest that impressions based on interviews are poor predictors of future performance and that hard evidence such as test scores and recommendations are much better guides. Part of the problem is that interviews are highly artificial situations. How someone behaves in an interview may not reflect their underlying ability or personality. They might interview well – perhaps because they seem confident – without being a particularly well-rounded student. Furthermore, interviewers rarely get good feedback about their decisions. If an admissions officer accepts a candidate who turns out well, they will probably see it as confirmation of their good social intuition. However, what they are unlikely to do is follow up on any of the candidates they did *not* accept to see if they turned out better. So while they may believe that they chose the best candidate, this may not in fact be true. If you happen to be called for an interview, it may be wise not to mention their unreliability!

Lie detectors

Figure 8.9

Another area in which our intuitions can lead us astray is in our ability to detect whether or not someone is lying. You may think that you are good at this – that it is written all over the person's face (see Figure 8.9). But countless experiments have shown that when most people try to distinguish true stories from false ones they do no better than chance. Apparently, even trained CIA agents are poor at spotting deception. Unfortunately – or perhaps fortunately – there are no set rules for detecting liars. Contrary to popular belief, they do not, for example, always avoid eye contact or fidget nervously. However, it turns out that a tiny elite of so-called *truth wizards* are good at picking up on the micro-expressions that flit, unnoticed by most people, across a person's face. As a result, their intuitions about whether or not someone is lying are way above average.

Expert intuitions

At this point, we should distinguish between *folk intuitions* and *expert intuitions*. As we have seen, our natural intuitions are not a particularly reliable source of knowledge, but it could be argued that we should take expert intuitions more seriously. Indeed, experts often seem to have almost magical insights into their specialist areas, which enable them to make good judgements and decisions. Consider the following examples:

- A mathematician who sees the solution to a problem before they have had time to reason it out.
- A historian who feels suspicious about a historical document and later confirms that it is a forgery.
- An artist who is guided by their intuitions and produces a great work of art. ('If I think, then everything is lost', said Paul Cézanne.)
- A chess grandmaster who rapidly surveys a chessboard and makes a brilliant move.
- A fire chief who senses that a burning building is about to collapse and evacuates their team.
- A senior doctor who can tell at a glance that someone is about to have a heart attack.

Figure 8.10 Sachin Tendulkar: What role does intuition play in expert know-how?

- A soccer player who seems to have a 'sixth sense' about exactly where to pass the ball.
- A chef who puts together a gourmet meal without mechanically following a recipe.
- An entrepreneur who has an instinctive eye for a promising money-making opportunity.

LQ – Memory: To what extent are our intuitions about what is likely or probable influenced by what we happen to remember?

As these examples suggest, intuition plays a key role in practical *know-how* as well as theoretical *know-that*. Indeed, in the real world, things may happen so fast that there is no time for conscious reflection. If a cricket ball is speeding towards you at 90 miles (140 kilometres) an hour, you have to rely on your intuitions – and hope they have been sufficiently sharpened by practice. That was certainly true of the great Indian cricketer Sachin Tendulkar: 'My subconscious mind', he said, 'knows exactly what to do – it's been trained to react for years.'

Although experts may be unable to explain how they arrive at their intuitions, there is nothing mystical about them. They require not only raw talent but also a vast mental database of background knowledge. Most psychologists think that they generally rely on *pattern recognition* and are the product of *unconscious information processing.* This may explain why it sometimes pays to 'sleep on a problem'. It also suggests that the more relevant information you have in your memory, the better your intuitions are likely to be.

"Sure technique counts, but at some point you've got to trust your criminal instincts."

Figure 8.11

Moral and aesthetic intuitions

Some people take the notion of expertise more seriously in the realm of facts than in the realm of values. Nevertheless, it makes sense to think that those who have thought long and hard about ethics and aesthetics may have better intuitions than the average person. Some philosophers have gone so far as to claim that moral intuition is a form of 'mental vision' analogous to sense perception that can be trained and developed. The philosopher G.E. Moore (1873–1958) held that if your 'moral sense' is working correctly you can see that something is morally good or bad in much the same way that you can see that something is yellow or green. It could, for example, be argued that you don't need to give any reason to justify your belief that child abuse is wrong – you can just *see* that it is wrong.

In a similar vein, the British art critic Clive Bell (1881–1964) claimed that in the arts some people have an intuitive sense of 'significant form' – lines and colours combined in certain ways – which enables them to distinguish great art from trivial art. Those who lack this sense are, he said, 'deaf men at a concert'. According to Bell, significant form is the quality common to artifacts as diverse as Mexican sculpture, a Persian bowl, Chinese carpets and the masterpieces of the French post-impressionist painter Paul Cézanne.

One obvious problem with the claim that we can appeal to intuition to justify our values is that people have conflicting intuitions. For example, intuitions differ about whether we are ever justified in sacrificing one person to save five. There also seems to be no objective standard to which we can appeal to arbitrate between competing intuitions. Nevertheless, in thinking about values we should at least take the intuitions of thoughtful people into account – for they might have seen things that we have overlooked.

Figure 8.12 *Lac D'Annecy* by Paul Cézanne: Do artists have an intuitive sense of 'significant form'?

ACTIVITY 8.7

1. If a man was stuck at the mouth of a pothole, would you be willing to kill him in order to save the five people trapped inside? What do your intuitions say? Does your reason agree?
2. Do you think that moral philosophers have better moral intuitions than the average person? Give reasons.
3. Do you think that critics' intuitions about art are anything more than expressions of taste?

Creative intuitions

We naturally associate creative intuitions with the arts, and they doubtless play a key role in the genesis of works of art. But they are equally important in the sciences. Indeed, many breakthroughs in intellectual history have come in flashes of creative insight. The case of Archimedes was mentioned at the beginning of this chapter, but there are many others. The person in question has usually spent months working doggedly on a problem without getting anywhere, only for the solution to hit them like a thunderbolt when they are idly daydreaming or taking a walk – or lying in the bath. (One eminent scientist even confessed to having his eureka moment of insight while in the toilet!) The French mathematician Henri Poincaré (1854–1912) described how he came to one of his great intuitions:

> *For fifteen days I strove to prove that there could not be any functions like those that I have since called Fuchsian functions. I was then very ignorant; every day I seated myself at my work table, stayed an hour or two, tried a great number of combinations and reached no results. One evening, contrary to my custom, I drank black coffee and could not sleep. Ideas rose in crowds; I felt them collide until pairs interlocked, so to speak, making a stable combination. By the next morning I had established the existence of a class of Fuchsian functions, those which come from the hypergeometric series; I only had to write out the results, which took but a few hours.*

Reflecting on his experience, Poincaré came to the conclusion that mathematical creativity is not a matter of mechanically following rules to generate endless combinations of symbols, but of having the insight to see which combinations are worth exploring. 'It is', Poincaré concluded, 'by logic that we prove, but by intuition that we discover.'

LQ – Mathematics: When should we base decisions on intuitions and when should we base them on the analysis of statistical data?

While new ideas may be *discovered* via intuition, it is worth emphasising that they still need to be *justified* using logic and/or empirical evidence. Poincaré still had to 'write out the results' to prove that his intuition was correct. Since history tends to celebrate the victors, we usually hear more about those whose intuitions turned out to be right than those whose intuitions turned out to be wrong.

ACTIVITY 8.8

1. Do you think it is possible to have a valuable insight in an area in which you have little background? Has this ever happened to you?
2. From your own experience, what do you think is the relationship between intuition, background knowledge and intellectual effort?
3. What relation, if any, is there between something being counter-intuitive and its being false?

Requirements for good intuitions

Although we may be in awe of experts' intuitions, it is important to keep in mind that experts are fallible and their intuitions may be more reliable in some areas of knowledge than in others. Research suggests that there are two key requirements for developing good intuitions:

1. *Experience* While intuition and experience are often seen as different sources of knowledge, the former in fact depends on the latter. If you have immersed yourself in a subject, you are likely to have better instincts about it than if you are relying on uninformed common-sense. As we saw in Chapter 7, it probably requires at least ten thousand hours of work to become a top expert in any area of endeavour, whether it is academic, sporting, or practical. In social life, too, we might speculate that what distinguishes individuals with good intuitions is that they have taken the time and shown unusual interest in other people.
2. *Feedback* To develop your intuitions, you need not only a wealth of relevant experience, but also clear and timely feedback. This can only be acquired in a regular and predictable environment. Mathematics is one such environment. If you have an intuition about how to solve a maths problem, you can quickly determine whether or not you are right. Similarly, you get immediate and unambiguous feedback when learning to ride a bicycle or ski: if you do something wrong you crash. If you practise enough in such environments, you can sharpen your intuitions so that they eventually become second nature. However, other environments may be so complex and unpredictable that it is difficult, if not impossible, to get reliable feedback from them. That may explain why the intuitions of, for example, political pundits are generally less reliable than those of astronomers.

LQ – Natural sciences: How reliable are the average person's intuitions about the nature of physical reality?

From the above points, it will be clear that intuition is not a shortcut to knowledge and that brilliant insights into things do not spring from nowhere. The apple that allegedly fell on Newton's head may have triggered a revolution in science, but only because Newton was steeped in physics and thought obsessively about it. If an apple fell on your head, there would probably be no eureka moment – just a bruised apple and a headache. Since intuition is the product of hard work and a great deal of experience, if you are going to have any worthwhile insights in a subject you will have to work hard for them!

Two dangers

In evaluating expert intuition, we should be particularly aware of the following two dangers:

1. *Overconfidence.* We tend to assume that experts who express their intuitions with great confidence must know what they are talking about, but in fact there is no correlation between confidence and truth. Sometimes overconfidence is the result of confusing luck with judgement. If, for example, a person makes a lot of money on the stock market, they might think they have expert financial intuitions; but they could simply be a *lucky fool* with no more financial judgement than someone who wins the lottery.
2. *Inconsistency.* Since we are only human, our intuitions can be influenced by all kinds of irrelevant factors such as weather, hunger, and tiredness – all of which can affect our mood and unconsciously influence our judgement. Research shows that even experts sometimes contradict themselves. For example, when doctors are asked to evaluate the same symptoms at different times, they sometimes make quite different diagnoses.

Intuitions versus algorithms

Some people predict that, in the information age, reliance on expert intuition will gradually be replaced – or at least complemented – by computer programs processing the relevant data using rules known as algorithms, (see Chapter 3, page 63). Indeed, this is already happening in areas as varied as medicine, crime detection and sports. There are, for example, computer programs which, when they are fed patients' medical histories, can predict health issues such as heart attacks more reliably than doctors. Similarly, the value of a sports star can often be more accurately assessed by analysing statistical data on their performance than by relying on the experience and intuitions of coaches. However, if we are not to become 'slaves to the machine', we should keep in mind that since computer programs are designed by people, they, too, are fallible. In practice, if your intuitions conflicted with a computer program, you might still be inclined to follow them.

ACTIVITY 8.9

1. Would you trust a computer dating service over a friend's intuition in deciding who to go on a blind date with? Give reasons.
2. Would you trust a website recommendation over that of a friend about a novel or piece of music you might enjoy? Give reasons.
3. In July 2002, two planes were getting dangerously close to each other in the skies over Switzerland. One pilot's computer system instructed him to ascend to avoid a collision, but an air-traffic controller, whose computer system was down, advised him to descend. The pilot chose to follow the air-traffic controller's intuition and, tragically, the two planes collided in midair leaving no survivors. Does this anecdote suggest that we should never trust our intuitions if they conflict with a computer program?

Cognitive biases

KT – cognitive bias: a bias rooted in the way we think which can easily distort our intuition

A major problem with our intuitions in both the academic and social realms is that they are prone to various biases which seem to be built into the structure of our minds. Cognitive biases are similar to logical fallacies in that both are concerned with ways in which our thinking can go wrong. Indeed, we might say that the former are to intuition what the latter are to reason. Strictly speaking, they differ in that while fallacies are *explicit* and concern erroneous ways of *arguing*, biases are *implicit* and concern erroneous ways of *seeing*. The dividing line between the two is, however, somewhat blurred – not least because we often use fallacious reasoning to justify our pre-existing biases.

Listed below are ten key biases which can distort our intuitions about the world. We have already encountered some of these in earlier chapters, but it is worth reminding ourselves of them.

Confirmation bias

A form of selective thinking, confirmation bias is the tendency to notice things which fit in with our beliefs and prejudices and to overlook things which do not. If, for example, you believe that vegetarianism is good for your health, you are likely to notice healthy vegetarians and fail to notice – or quickly forget – unhealthy ones. Since we actively look for information which confirms our prejudices and surround ourselves with people who share our outlook, we may end up thinking that our cherished beliefs are just *obvious*. If, as we suggested earlier, intuition is based on unconscious information processing, it is not surprising that a one-sided mental database usually results in distorted intuitions.

Affect heuristic

The affect heuristic refers to our tendency to take our gut feelings about something as an indication of its merits. (An *affect* is an instantaneous judgement of *liking* or *disliking*.) When someone asks us what we *think* about something, we often answer by consulting our *feelings*. For example, if you are uninformed about genetically modified crops, your feelings may determine your opinion about them. If you associate them with, say, *progress* you may feel good about them; whereas if you associate them with something *unnatural* you may feel bad about them. The problem is, of course, that our emotional reactions to complicated issues are a poor guide to their truth. To take another example, since climate change does not press our fear buttons in the same way that terrorism does, many people operate on the mistaken assumption that it is not a big problem.

Familiarity bias

Despite the well-known saying that 'familiarity breeds contempt', psychologists tell us that in fact the opposite is true and *familiarity breeds fondness*. We are naturally inclined to believe and like things we are accustomed to for no other reason than that we are accustomed to them. The clearest illustration of this bias is our tendency to assume that our own culture's way of looking at things is the right way. If we have comfortably inhabited a set of assumptions for long enough they come to strike us as intuitively obvious. Furthermore, studies show that the more often we hear something, the more likely we are to believe it, whether or not it is true. As propagandists have long known, repetition is the mother of belief and people often lack the time or energy to think critically and question what they hear. The corollary of our tendency to like and accept the familiar is that we often dislike and reject the unfamiliar. This may explain the instinctive suspicion many people have of new ideas. (See Chapter 3, page 47.)

Fluency heuristic

According to the fluency heuristic, if something is easy to process mentally, then we tend to believe it. Studies suggest that you are more likely to believe something expressed in a pithy slogan or rhyme than in more prosaic language. For example, people rate phrases like 'What sobriety conceals, alcohol reveals' and 'Woes unite foes' as more accurate than 'What sobriety conceals, alcohol unmasks' and 'Woes unite enemies'. Similarly, good stories – which are easy to process – often strike us as more plausible than dry statistics and abstract theories. We are often more attracted to beautiful falsehoods than to ugly truths. Indeed, it has even been suggested that intuitions about beauty may have delayed scientific progress. To take a well-known example, it took the astronomer Johannes Kepler (1571–1630) years of struggle to free himself from the intuitive but false belief that the planets orbit the sun in beautiful circles rather than 'ugly' ellipses.

Framing effect

The framing effect refers to our tendency to interpret information differently depending on the framework in which it is presented. Imagine, for example, that you are in hospital waiting for an operation. If you are told that it has a 90 per cent success rate, you will probably feel much more positive about it than if you are told that it has a 10 per cent failure rate. When people are told that a hamburger is 75 per cent fat-free they actually claim that it tastes better than when they are told that it contains 25 per cent fat. We rarely question the way in which information is presented to us, but, as these examples suggest, it can have a powerful influence on our gut reactions to things.

Hindsight bias

We suffer from hindsight bias when we are wise about something *after the event*. After something has happened, it often seems *obvious* that it was going to happen and we may have the feeling that we 'knew it all along'. However, it may not have been so obvious beforehand. Once a soccer team has won a game, or a political party has won an election, it is easy to explain why it was bound to happen. But we should not confuse our after-the-event feeling of inevitability with our before-the-event ability to foresee it. After the sudden and unexpected collapse of communism in Eastern Europe (1989–91), a spate of books appeared explaining why it was inevitable, but few such books appeared before these events.

Sunk cost bias

Sunk cost bias is the unthinking assumption that once you have invested time, money or effort in something you should stick with it. Imagine going to an expensive restaurant and ordering too much food. The temptation is to eat everything because you paid so much for it. So you end up not only wasting a lot of money, but also feeling sick. More seriously, sunk cost bias also explains why couples stay too long in unhealthy relationships, why scientists work too long on unpromising research projects, and why countries get mired in unwinnable wars. In each case, they instinctively feel, 'We have invested so much in this that we cannot walk away from it.' They can and they should.

Figure 8.13 Nelson Mandela: To what extent do our heroes benefit from the halo effect?

The halo effect

The halo effect is the bias of assuming that desirable traits and undesirable traits cluster together. Our natural default is, it seems, to see the world in terms of black and white heroes and villains. Nelson Mandela (1918–2013) was *all* good and Adolf Hitler (1889–1945) was *all* evil. The uncomfortable reality, however, is that even good people have flaws, and even evil people occasionally show kindness. As the psychologist Daniel Kahneman (1934–) observes: 'The statement "Hitler loved dogs and little children" is shocking no matter how many times you hear it, because any trace of kindness in someone so evil violates the expectations set up by the halo effect.' The halo effect helps to explain why a person's character is almost always more complicated than our first impressions suggest.

Just world bias

According to research, we seem to have a deep-rooted intuitive belief in *karma*, the Hindu idea that the world is a just place and that people get what they deserve. We *want* to believe that everyone reaps what they sow and that good people are rewarded and bad people punished. The trouble with the just world bias is that it can easily lead to a 'blame the victim' attitude. If bad things happen to people, rather than attributing it to *bad luck* we can easily find ourselves thinking that they somehow deserved it. At its most callous and disturbing, this can lead to the belief, for example, that the homeless are lazy and parents of abducted children are grossly irresponsible.

Blind spot bias

One of the most damaging biases we suffer from is *the bias that we have no biases.* Although we have no difficulty understanding cognitive illusions, we assume that they apply only to *other people. They* may be deluded, but *our* intuitions are unclouded by such biases and give us genuine insight into things. What strikes us as self-evident really is self-evident. Despite what we like to think, we are, of course, wrong – for we are just as fallible as the next person. Our blindness to our own cognitive shortcomings can result in a dangerous overconfidence and a reluctance to subject our own beliefs to critical scrutiny.

1. To what extent are our ideas about what is intuitively obvious shaped by our cultural background and feelings of familiarity?
2. To what extent do you think people blindly trust their intuitions and to what extent do you think they are willing to systematically test them?

Summary

The table below summarises the cognitive biases. While there is no foolproof way of avoiding them, if we can learn to recognise them and admit that we are prone to them, then we will have taken an important step in diminishing their hold over us.

TEN COGNITIVE BIASES:	SUMMARY
Confirmation bias	Noticing things which confirm your beliefs and prejudices and overlooking things which do not
Affect heuristic	Taking your gut feelings as an indication of the merits or demerits of something
Familiarity bias	Believing something simply because you are familiar with it
Fluency heuristic	Believing something because it is easy for your mind to process it
Framing effect	Interpreting information differently depending on the framework in which it is presented
Hindsight bias	Mistakenly thinking you knew something would happen, after it has happened
Sunk cost bias	Believing that if you have invested time, energy or money in something you should stick with it
The halo effect	Assuming that desirable and undesirable traits cluster together
Just world bias	Believing that people reap what they sow and get what they deserve
Blind spot bias	Believing that, unlike other people, you yourself have no biases

Core intuitions

We have expressed many reservations about the reliability of both folk and expert intuitions. Nevertheless, it could be argued that at the deepest level *all* knowledge is based on intuition. This is partly because reason and perception – which are perhaps the two most important ways of knowing – ultimately depend on it.

1. *Reason.* The laws of logic are the starting point for all our reasoning, but we cannot prove them in terms of any more fundamental laws. If asked to justify them, most people would say that they are intuitively obvious.
2. *Perception.* We cannot be sure on the evidence of our senses alone that life is not a dream – for any evidence we appeal to could itself be part of the dream. Yet it strikes us as intuitively obvious that the dream hypothesis is false and that what we are experiencing is reality.

A good way of seeing that our knowledge claims are ultimately based on intuition is to play the *Why?* game. Ask a friend to tell you one thing they claim to know, and then ask them why they believe it. When they answer, ask them why they believe *that*, and so on. The game is usually quite short. Your friend may be able to explain *A* in terms of *B*, and *B* in terms of *C*, and *C* in terms of *D* . . ., but sooner or later they will run out of reasons and tell you that their final knowledge claim is self-evident or intuitively obvious. We cannot, of course, take such intuitions for granted, but nor can we deny the important role they play in our thinking.

ACTIVITY 8.10

If someone asked you why you believe each of the following statements, what evidence, if any, could you give in support of them?

a. I exist.

b. Life is not a dream.

c. If something is a banana, then it is a banana.

d. 1 + 1 = 2.

e. Parallel lines never meet.

f. The laws of physics will not break down tomorrow.

g. My friends are not robots.

h. Innocent people should not be tortured for the fun of it.

i. All human beings are created equal.

j. Time has no beginning or end.

k. Nothing comes from nothing.

Conflicting intuitions

A major objection to the claim that our core intuitions are a reliable source of knowledge is that different people have conflicting intuitions. It would be nice to think that decent, open-minded, well-educated people could all agree about what is intuitively obvious. But we only have to look around us to see that this is not the case. Does the existence of the universe require an explanation? Could a machine think? Could a mind exist without a body? Is abortion wrong? Many people have strong intuitions about these things, but as often as not they disagree with one another. The problem, in short, is that what is obvious to you may not be obvious to me; and we can all too easily be blinded by our own sense of what is blindingly obvious!

Here are three general questions that might cast doubt on the value of taking core intuitions as a source of knowledge:

1. If something is intuitively obvious, must everyone agree about it? (Is there *anything* that everyone agrees about?)

2. Could you be wrong in thinking that something is intuitively obvious? (Might you one day come to realise that what you now think is intuitively obvious is in fact a deeply rooted prejudice?)

3. Whose intuitions should you trust? Are some people's intuitions better than others?

The upshot of this discussion is that we should be willing – at least occasionally – to subject even our most fundamental assumptions to critical scrutiny. For it is always possible that they are mistaken.

ACTIVITY 8.11

1. What is the difference between something being intuitively obvious and it being a deeply rooted prejudice?
2. Give some examples of things that once struck you as intuitively obvious which you no longer believe are true.

Conclusion

At the beginning of this chapter we saw that we rely on our intuitive automatic system to make hundreds of routine judgements and decisions every day, and that most of the time these are good enough. However, if we are seeking more accurate knowledge we need to tread carefully. After all, we do not trust our gut to tell us what to eat, so why should we trust it to tell us what to think? At worst, going with your intuitions can be an excuse for not thinking at all, and it can lead to the mindless idiocy of the cartoon character Homer Simpson. If, however, our intuitions are based on a stock of relevant experience they can be remarkably insightful. At the highest level, the creative intuitions of an Einstein or a Picasso can be the sparks that ignite revolutions in thought and change the way we look at the world.

Since we are fallible we must, however, test our intuitions against other sources of knowledge. If they are confirmed by reason, experience and other people's intuitions, then it makes sense to trust them. If they conflict with them, then we can either question the evidence or question our intuitions. Either way, we should at least have the humility to admit that just because something seems intuitively obvious to us it does not necessarily follow that it is true.

Answers to questions (page 204)

1a. It is more probable that Linda is a bank teller than that she is *both* a bank teller and an active feminist.

2. The probability of any two particular sequence of heads and tails is the same in each case – in this case $\frac{1}{2} \times \frac{1}{2} \times \frac{1}{2} \times \frac{1}{2} \times \frac{1}{2} \times \frac{1}{2} = \frac{1}{64}$

3. The simplest way to prove this surprising result is to begin by calculating not the thing we are looking for, but its complement – i.e. the probability of no one sharing a birthday. Imagine people entering a room one-by-one. When the second person enters the room, there are 364 possible days for him to have a birthday that differs from the first person. So the probability that he will have a different birthday from the first person is $\frac{364}{365}$. When the third person enters, there are 363 possibilities of him having a birthday different from both of the first two, so the probability that all three will have different birthdays is $\frac{364}{365} \times \frac{363}{365}$. When the fourth person enters, the probability of all four having different birthdays is $\frac{364}{365} \times \frac{363}{365} \times \frac{362}{365}$.

Continuing in this way, when 23 people are in the room, the probability of all of them having different birthdays is $\frac{364}{365} \times \frac{363}{365} \times \frac{362}{365} \times \ldots \times \frac{343}{365}$.

This works out to be 0.492. The above product first drops below 0.5 when you have 23 people. Thus, the probability that at least two of the 23 have the same birthday is 1 – 0.492 = 0.508.

4. If no other force were acting on the ball, it would continue in a straight line at the angle from which it emerged from the tube, but the force of gravity will bring it down to the ground.

5. The two bullets will reach the ground at the same time because a bullet's rate of fall is independent of its horizontal motion.

6. As a reason for staying, you should *not* list the fact that you have already spent $10 on the ticket. If that were your only reason for staying, then you would end up wasting not only your money but also your time. All that matters now is how best to use your time.

Key points

- Intuition can be defined as an immediate insight into something which does not require conscious reasoning.
- Our everyday intuitions are based on 'fast and frugal' heuristics which enable us to make quick judgements and decisions that are often good enough.
- The speed of our intuitive judgements is sometimes bought at the expense of accuracy.
- Our naive folk intuitions about many subjects are not very reliable, and it could be argued that one of the aims of education is to debug human intuition.
- We like to think we have good social intuitions, but our first impressions and our ability to tell whether or not someone is lying are not very accurate.
- The key to developing expert intuitions is experience combined with quick, clear feedback.
- Many intellectual breakthroughs have come about in a flash of creative intuition, but such intuitions presuppose a great deal of hard work.
- Given that expert intuitions are sometimes inconsistent, some people claim that computer programs are more reliable than human intuitions.
- We are prone to a range of cognitive biases which seem to be built into the structure of our minds.
- While there is a sense in which all knowledge is based on intuition, the problem remains that people have conflicting intuitions.

Key terms

automatic system
cognitive bias
folk intuitions
heuristic
reflective system
subliminal perception

IB prescribed essay titles

1. When should we discard explanations that are intuitively appealing? (May 2012)
2. Evaluate the role of intuition in different areas of knowledge. (November 2007/ May 2008)

Further reading

Books

Malcolm Gladwell, *Blink* (Allen Lane, 2005). An accessible and entertaining book, rich in anecdotes. Gladwell is something of a cheerleader for the power of intuition: 'There can be as much value in the blink of an eye as in months of rational analysis.' Worth reading, but with a critical eye.

Daniel Kahneman, *Thinking, Fast and Slow* (Allen Lane, 2011). Written by a highly influential psychologist, this book draws particular attention to the dangers of relying on intuition. Chapter 22, 'Expert Intuition: When Can We Trust It?', is particularly worth reading.

Online articles

Daniel Simons and Christopher F. Chabris, 'The Trouble with Intuition', *Chronicle of Higher Education*, 21 June 2010.

David G. Myers, 'The Powers and Perils of Intuition', *Psychology Today*, 1 November 2002.

Imagination

9

What is now proved was once only imagined.

William Blake, 1757–1827

You can't depend on your eyes when your imagination is out of focus.

Mark Twain, 1835–1910

Reality leaves a lot to the imagination.

John Lennon, 1940–80

Every great advance in science has issued from a new audacity of the imagination.

John Dewey, 1859–1952

Imagination is more important than knowledge. For knowledge is limited, whereas imagination embraces the entire world, stimulating progress, giving birth to evolution.

Albert Einstein, 1879–1955

Genius is seeing what everyone has seen, and thinking what no one has thought.

Albert Szent-Gyorgyi, 1893–1986

There's nothing like a dream to create the future. Utopia today, flesh and blood tomorrow.

Victor Hugo, 1802–85

Knowledge is a polite word for dead but not buried imagination.

E. E. Cummings, 1894–1962

There is an astonishing imagination in the mathematics of nature; and Archimedes had at least as much imagination as Homer.

Voltaire, 1694–1778

[Science is] a dialogue between two voices, the one imaginative and the other critical.

Peter Medawar, 1915–87

9

Imagination

Introduction

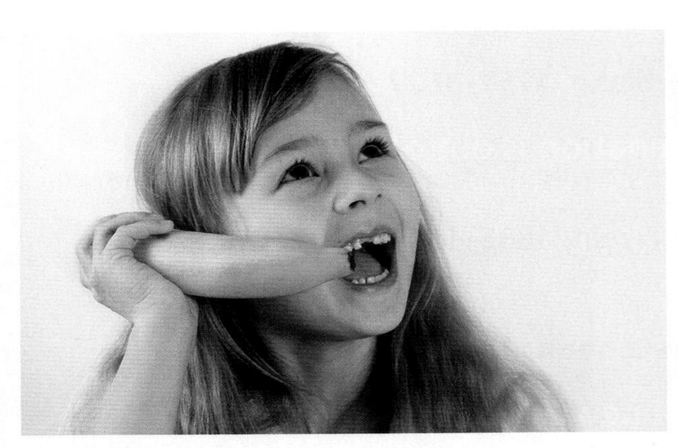

Figure 9.1 Why do children engage in fantasy?

Human beings are imagination junkies, and we spend vast amounts of our leisure time reading novels, watching movies, playing video games, imagining the consequences of various courses of action – and idly daydreaming about such things as winning the lottery! You might wonder why we invest so much time in, and derive such pleasure from, imagining things that, by definition, are not real. Perhaps it gives our species some kind of evolutionary advantage. In fact, imagination seems to be unique to human beings, and it is closely connected to other distinctively human attributes, such as language and freedom.

As always, our concern in this chapter is with the relationship between imagination and knowledge. Throughout history, the products of imagination have received a mixed reception. On the one hand, strict empiricists such as the philosopher John Locke (1632–1704) have been deeply suspicious of it and seen it leading at best to entertainment and at worst to escapist fantasy. Indeed, Locke advised parents who discovered a 'fanciful vein' in their children to 'stifle and suppress it'. On the other hand, romantic thinkers, such as the poet John Keats (1795–1821), celebrated the scope and power of the imagination. 'I am', said Keats, 'certain of nothing but the holiness of the heart's affections and the truth of the imagination.' There are problems and dangers with both of these extremes. In this chapter, we shall attempt to tread a thoughtful path between the puritanical dismissal of the imagination and the intoxicated celebration of it. Our main interest will be with the kind of imagination that is informed by critical thinking and judgement.

"Take a seat and I'll get right to the point. We're looking for someone with lots of imagination."

Figure 9.2

We begin with a brief definition of imagination and then distinguish three main types: fantasy, realistic imagination and creativity. This leads on to a discussion about the relationship between imagination and knowledge in which we suggest that imagination is not only an important source of knowledge, but also plays a role in its justification and constitution. Imagination in the form of empathy is particularly relevant to our knowledge of other people and we devote a section to this topic. This leads into a discussion about the relation between empathy and ethics. Since creativity is the furnace in which new ideas are forged, we then look at the 'mystery of creativity' and the extent to which it is possible to explain and assess it. Finally, we return to the traditional suspicion of the imagination and consider the extent to which such suspicion is justified.

Types of imagination

According to one common definition, imagination is the ability to form a representation of something which is not present to the senses. Although we naturally tend to associate imagination with imagery, the representation in question may or may not be a mental image. You can, for example, imagine Barack Obama sitting on a donkey eating an ice-cream in the sense of conjuring up a vivid mental image; but you can also imagine all kinds of possibilities – such as a world without war – without necessarily having *any* mental images. You simply entertain the relevant possibility. We shall use the word 'imagination' in this broad sense to cover both: mental *images* and the entertaining of *possibilities*. Much of our mental activity consists of imagining in this broad sense, and a great deal of what we call thinking consists in imaginatively exploring various possibilities.

What distinguishes imagination from neighbouring mental concepts such as perception and memory is *truth*. If you claim to see, or remember seeing, an apple on the table, then you are claiming that an apple is, or was, indeed on the table; but to imagine it is to make no such claim. Indeed, if a claim allegedly based on perception or memory turns out to be wrong, we simply downgrade it to imagination: 'I thought I saw it but I must have imagined it.' Of course, it is sometimes difficult to distinguish between the real and the imaginary. Traditionally, it was claimed that what distinguishes perception, memory, and imagination are different degrees of 'force and vivacity', with perception being the strongest; memory intermediate; and imagination the weakest. But this seems an unreliable criterion. Dreams and fantasies, for example, are sometimes more vivid than distant memories. At the limit, the clinically insane are unable to distinguish between external reality and the products of their own fevered imaginations. Given this, *coherence* may be a more useful criterion for distinguishing the real from the illusory. What convinces us that dreams are simply dreams is that they don't fit in with the rest of our waking lives.

LQ – Sense perception: How does imagination inform our everyday perception of the world?

As we mentioned in the introduction, three kinds of imagination can be distinguished: **fantasy**, **realistic imagination** and **creativity**.

KT – fantasy: an escapist form of imagination that is only distantly connected with the real world

KT – realistic imagination: imagination which is informed and guided by the relevant facts

KT – creativity: the ability to generate ideas or produce artefacts which are original, surprising and valuable

Fantasy

As we shall use the word, the distinguishing feature of fantasy is that it is not connected – or only distantly connected – with the real world. Dreams, reveries, hallucinations and whimsical speculations are all examples of fantasies. A common type of fantasy is what we might call *the dream of effortless achievement* in which we fantasise about *ends* without thinking about the concrete steps that must be taken in order to achieve them. This may be pleasurable, but, sadly, simply dreaming about, for example, getting straight 7s in your IB exams will do nothing to magically bring this about! Many advertisements implicitly or explicitly appeal to the dream of effortless achievement. Just buy this brand of cigarette/perfume/car and you will suddenly become irresistibly attractive!

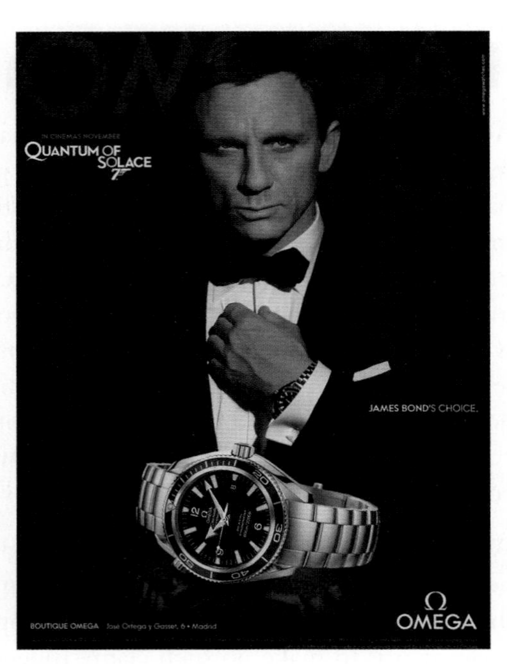

Figure 9.3 To what extent are advertisements selling us fantasies?

ACTIVITY 9.1

Select and analyse three examples of advertisements that are selling us fantasies. To what extent does it matter that such advertisements are misleading?

There is, of course, no clear dividing line between fantasy and more realistic forms of imagination, and the border between the two is blurred. For example, one generation's technological fantasy may become the next generation's genuine possibility. If one of our distant ancestors had imagined a mobile phone, it would have been dismissed as a fantasy; but it is, of course, a reality for us. In fiction, an author may begin with a fantasy premise and then rigorously – realistically – explore its consequences. A good example would be Franz Kafka's (1883–1924) famous novel *Metamorphosis* (1915) which begins with the line: 'As Gregor Samsa awoke one morning from uneasy dreams he found himself transformed in his bed into a gigantic insect'. The novel then explores, in an almost factual and dispassionate tone, the tragic consequences of this disturbing transformation. At best, fantasy can nourish the imagination and help to push back the borders of the possible; but at worst, it can lead to escapism and a refusal to engage with reality. The danger of fantasy will be explored further at the end of this chapter.

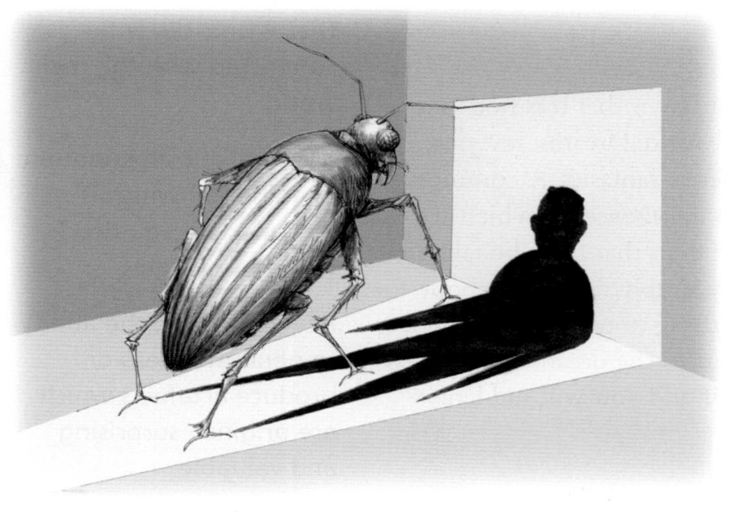

Figure 9.4 How can fantasy illuminate the human condition?

Realistic imagination

You might initially think that the phrase 'realistic imagination' is an oxymoron. After all, we usually contrast what is real with what is imaginary. Despite appearances, the phrase makes perfect sense. Indeed, most productive uses of imagination are realistic in the sense that they are *constrained by reality*. Consider inventions: when Alexander Graham Bell (1847–1922) invented the telephone, he didn't simply fantasise about talking to distant people; rather his imagination was constrained by what was practically possible. Similarly, Thomas Edison's (1847–1931) invention of the light-bulb was the result of a subtle interplay between imagination and reality. The same idea holds in other areas. When thinking about the past, you can try to imagine what it was like living at the time of the French Revolution, but if you picture yourself driving around Paris in 1789 in a red Ferrari then you have drifted into fantasy and your imagination is no longer disciplined by the facts. Similarly, when planning a trip, you may think of going by car or train, but if you also consider flying Icarus-like to your destination, then your imagination has ceased to be productive. The concept of realistic imagination even applies to fiction. We might, for example, criticise a novel for being *psychologically unrealistic* and argue that people would never behave in the way described by the author. In science fiction, a distinction is sometimes made between *hard* and *soft* science fiction which depends on whether or not the imagined world is *scientifically accurate*. Whatever their psychological insights and other merits, fantasy novels, such as the Harry Potter series, are often *scientifically unrealistic* – although that need not spoil our enjoyment of them!

RLS – Headline: 'Number of children reading for fun has fallen since 2005, study reveals'. How, if at all, can fiction contribute to our knowledge of the world?

ACTIVITY 9.2

1. Find some examples of imaginative science fiction writers who have successfully anticipated real-world technological developments. What does this suggest to you about the relation between science fiction and science fact?
2. To what extent are both the scientific and the literary imagination constrained by facts? How is the latter less constrained than the former?

Creativity

We naturally associate imagination with creativity, and calling someone 'imaginative' is often synonymous with calling them 'creative'. However, strictly speaking creativity is best thought of as a *subset* of imagination in the sense that while creativity requires imagination, one can imagine all kinds of things without being particularly creative. For example, I can imagine going on a cruise in the Mediterranean, but there is nothing particularly creative about this. What distinguishes creative imagination from run-of-the-mill imagination is *originality*. A creative idea is *novel* in the sense that it hasn't been thought of before, and it is often *surprising* in the sense that it could not have been predicted in advance. In fact, originality alone is not enough for us to call something creative. It must also have some kind of *value* – such as being interesting, beautiful, or fruitful. Yodelling with a bucket over your head while standing on one leg would doubtless be original, but most people would not consider it to be creative because it doesn't seem to have any *meaning* or *purpose*. It is also implicit in the word 'creative' that the value in question should be *positive*. If a sadist devised a new and exquisitely painful form of torture to inflict on other people, we would hardly wish to call such an idea creative.

Imagination and knowledge

Since knowledge is concerned with what *is* and imagination with what *is not*, it might at first sight seem as if imagination is the very antithesis of knowledge. Indeed, fantasies and wishful thinking can, at times, be detrimental to our sense of reality. Nevertheless, there are some subtle and intriguing connections between imagination and knowledge. In this section, we consider the idea that imagination is not only an important *source* of knowledge, but that it also plays a role in its *justification* and *constitution*.

ACTIVITY 9.3

What role does imagination play in the various IB subjects that you study? What role does it play in CAS (creativity, action, service)? Is it more relevant to some areas of knowledge than to others?

Imagination as a source of knowledge

As discussed in Chapter 2 (page 28), knowledge is concerned not so much with facts in themselves as with the underlying principles that make sense of the facts. To get a preliminary sense of the role played by imagination, we might say that if the facts are dots, then imagination helps us to think of ways of joining the dots together. While there is an obvious link between imagination and the arts, this analogy suggests that it plays an equally important role in the sciences (and, indeed, other areas of knowledge). This is because scientists need creative imagination if they are to make any sense of the data in front of them. Furthermore, there seems to be no purely logical process for generating imaginative ideas, and they are just as likely to emerge from 'irrational sources' in the sciences as in the arts. Consider, for example, dreams. According to Keith Richards of the Rolling Stones, the famous guitar riff in *I Can't Get No Satisfaction* came to him in a dream in Clearwater, Florida, when he was on tour with the band in 1965. One hundred years earlier, in 1865, the German chemist Friedrich August Kekulé (1829–96) was struggling to understand the structure of the benzene molecule when he had a vivid dream of a serpent biting its own tail, which led him to the crucial insight that benzene has a ring structure.

Sadly, many ideas seem more impressive in the depths of night than in the cold light of day, and it would be unwise to accept uncritically what comes to us in dreams. In the case of scientific ideas, we need to keep in mind the distinction between the *source* of an idea and its *justification*. According to the philosopher of science Karl

Popper (1902–94), the *source* of a scientific conjecture is – at least from a scientific point of view – irrelevant. All that matters is that it should be *testable*. While the relation between aesthetic ideas and reality is somewhat looser, they too must be subjected to critical scrutiny, and may be rejected by an artist if they do not work in practice or fit in with their overall vision.

Imagination and the justification of knowledge

While most people accept that imagination can be a *source* of knowledge, it is initially more difficult to see how it can play any role in the *justification* of knowledge. Nevertheless, it could be argued that there are at least three ways in which it can do this:

- as a surrogate for experience
- as a support for judgement
- as a guide to possibility.

We shall now consider each of these in turn.

1. Imagination as a surrogate for experience

Imagination can both *intensify* and *extend* our experience, and it could be argued that fiction serves both of these functions. As regards intensification, the writer and broadcaster Clive James once observed that 'Fiction is life with the dull bits left out.' Perhaps the concentrated nature of fiction means that it sometimes packs a bigger punch than actual experience in helping us to make sense of the world around us. For example, in an abstract way we all 'know' we are going to die; but reading Leo Tolstoy's (1828–1910) short novel *The Death of Ivan Ilyich* may give us a deeper understanding of what it really means to confront one's own demise. When it comes to the extension of experience, it has been pointed out that the average person's knowledge of what goes on in a police station, or a prison, or a hospital emergency ward, is derived not so much from personal experience, as from TV series, movies and novels. As we shall see when we discuss the relation between imagination and empathy, fiction can be a remarkably effective way of exposing us to situations of which we have no first-hand knowledge.

LQ – History: It is often said that a historian needs a good imagination. Why? How does a historian's imagination differ from that of a novelist?

Imagination can be a substitute for experience not only in the arts, but also in other areas of knowledge. Consider, for example, **thought experiments** which, as the name suggests, are experiments carried out in one's head rather than in the world. Such experiments are common in areas as diverse as physics, philosophy and history. One of the most famous thought experiments in physics derives from Galileo (1564–1642) who was seeking to refute the prevailing Aristotelian view that heavy objects fall faster than light ones. By this view, if a heavy cannon ball and light musket ball were dropped from a tower at the same time, the former would reach the ground before the latter. Galileo asks us to imagine that the experiment is repeated with the difference that the two balls are now joined by a string to form a composite object. Since the light musket ball supposedly moves slower than the heavy cannon ball, the former should act as a drag on the latter, ensuring that the composite object reaches the ground slower than an unattached cannon ball. But since the two balls

KT – thought experiment: an experiment carried out in one's imagination rather than in the world

LQ – Natural sciences: What role do thought experiments play in the development of new scientific ideas?

together are heavier than the cannon ball alone, the composite object should also hit the ground faster than an unattached cannon ball. We thus find ourselves caught in the contradiction that the composite object will fall both slower and faster than the cannon ball. The only way to resolve the contradiction is to reject the Aristotelian view in favour of the idea that all balls will fall at the same rate no matter what their weight.

This thought experiment was enough to convince Galileo that Aristotelian physics was irredeemably flawed; in this case he could have actually performed the experiment. But other experiments may be difficult, or impossible, to put into practice. For example, the political philosopher John Rawls (1921–2002) engaged in a very different kind of thought experiment in order to determine universal principles of justice that would apply to any society. Rawls asks us to imagine that we live behind a 'veil of ignorance' and know nothing about our talents or position in society. So we have no idea whether we are smart or dumb, beautiful or ugly, rich or poor, male or female, black or white; and we have no idea about our own beliefs, or tastes, or preferences. He then asks us to consider what laws we would implement if we found ourselves in this position. To cut a long story short, he concludes that, from behind the veil of ignorance, we would opt for a society in which basic human rights were respected, and in which inequalities were justified only if they benefited the worst-off members of society. The details of Rawls' view, and the extent to which his conclusions are justified, need not concern us here. What is interesting is that he seeks to construct his entire theory of justice on a thought experiment – that is, on imagination!

2. Imagination as a support for judgement

Imagination plays an important – and frequently overlooked – role in judgement. This role derives from the fact that judgement usually involves comparing the actual with the possible – and possibility lies in the realm of imagination.

Take, for example, explanations. In judging that a particular explanation is the best one, you need to compare it with other possible explanations; and the more alternatives you are able to imagine, the better your judgement is likely to be. In science, a chemist working with the same data as their colleagues may reject an 'obvious' explanation of the phenomena because they have the intellectual ability to envisage a range of different explanations and the judgement to be able to choose between them. Similarly, when you make a moral judgement about someone's behaviour, not only do you need to look at what they actually did, but you also need to imagine what they could have done. If someone does something bad, your judgement is likely to be harsher if you think there were better choices available to them, and more lenient if you think they really had no choice.

More generally, our attitude to reality is shaped by our beliefs about what is possible. For example, whether or not you feel happy is likely to be influenced not only by what you are doing right now, but also by the alternatives you imagine are open to you. Some people are never happy because they are troubled by the feeling that there is something better going on elsewhere. In the interconnected world of Facebook® and Twitter®, this phenomenon has acquired its own acronym: FOMO – fear of missing out.

When we judge the wisdom of future plans and possible courses of action, we again have recourse to imagination. In trying to decide what to do, we conjure up more or less plausible scenarios and try to think through their consequences. To be useful, this process must, of course, be well informed by background knowledge, but we can project such knowledge into the future only if it is animated by imagination.

ACTIVITY 9.4

1. Assess the roles played by background knowledge and imagination in trying to decide on a future career path.
2. In general, how reliable do you think that informed imagination is as a guide to the future?

At the most general level, imagination can be said to shape our conception of knowledge itself. Once we realise that the areas we have explored and the explanations we have found are not the only possible ones, we may conceive of knowledge in a more tentative and less dogmatic way. It requires a leap of imagination to see that the picture of the world held by future generations may be very different from – and perhaps more sophisticated than – our own; but if we can make that leap we may come to realise that our own words of knowledge are not the final word.

3. Imagination as a guide to possibility

Imagination is closely related to the concept of possibility, and the realm of the possible is itself a cognitive domain (of which the actual is a subset). You acquire knowledge when you discover that something is possible or impossible. Subjects such as philosophy, mathematics and logic are particularly concerned with mapping out this realm. The question that interests us here is how reliable imagination is as a guide to possibility.

LQ – Mathematics: Are mathematical entities, such as numbers, circles and straight lines, real or imaginary?

Two closely related claims are sometimes thought to be true: *if you can't imagine something, then it is impossible,* and *if you can imagine something, then it is possible.* Since imagination is both limited and fallible, we might be suspicious of both of these claims. In considering them, we should keep in mind that there are in fact two different kinds of possibility: *empirical* and *logical*. Something is **empirically possible** if it is consistent with the laws of nature; and it is **logically possible** if it is not self-contradictory. For example, while a flying elephant is empirically impossible, it is perfectly possible in a logical sense. A round square, by contrast, is impossible in the stronger logical sense of being self-contradictory.

KT – empirically possible: consistent with the laws of nature

KT – logically possible: can be described without involving a contradiction

The question of whether imaginability is a reliable guide to possibility may depend on who is doing the imagining. When someone says, 'I simply cannot imagine that X', this may tell us more about the limits of their imagination than the possibility of X. You may, for example, have heard someone say 'I simply cannot imagine how human beings could have evolved from apes.' This may be true for the speaker, but the vast majority of biologists in fact have no difficulty imagining this. Indeed, given the weight of supporting evidence, they think that it is not only possible, but also true. This example suggests that it sometimes makes sense to speak of *expert* imagination, and that there is a difference between what *you* can imagine (personal) and what can be imagined (shared). So while in theory it may be true that if something cannot be imagined then it is impossible, in practice the alleged impossibility can always be attributed to limited imagination.

Turning to the second claim, just because you can imagine something it clearly does not follow that it is empirically possible; but it does not even follow that it is logically possible. An argument or a story might seem perfectly imaginable, but it may turn out to be impossible because it harbours a hidden contradiction. We are not always good at spotting such contradictions – especially in the case of technical arguments. If you don't know much about geometry, you may think you can imagine a right-angled triangle in which the square of the hypotenuse does *not* equal the sum of the squares of the other two sides. But such a figure is, of course, impossible.

Even expert imagination may be unreliable. Some conjectures in mathematics seem perfectly imaginable, but may one day be proved to be false. An example here might be Goldbach's Conjecture that every even number is the sum of two prime numbers. The fact that the conjecture is imaginable does not prove that it is possible. In short, imagination is not demonstration.

Philosophers have occasionally tried to use arguments from conceivability to prove substantive truths. Most famously, René Descartes (1596–1650) claimed that since he could imagine the mind existing without a body, the mind can indeed exist without a body. If valid, this would appear to show that life after death is a real possibility. Not surprisingly, this argument is controversial. This is partly because, as we have seen, imagination may be a *useful* guide to the possible but it is far from being an *infallible* one.

Imagination and the constitution of knowledge

So far we have considered the role imagination can play as a *source of* and *justification for* knowledge. We now consider the more radical claim that it is an ingredient in our knowledge of reality itself. Since we usually contrast the real with the imaginary, this might sound contradictory; but the claim derives its plausibility from the fact that we *directly* experience – in the sense of perceive – only a tiny fraction of the world around us. This has led some philosophers to argue that imagination plays a key role in filling in the gaps and weaving these fragments of experience into a stable and coherent picture of reality.

You can get a sense of this claim at the micro level by considering the phenomenon of visual grouping discussed in Chapter 5 (see page 123). When you are presented with a series of blobs, your imagination naturally tries to make sense of them by filling in the blanks so that you see, for example, a dog. Another good example is the Kanizsa Triangle, shown in Figure 9.5, which is named after the Italian psychologist who devised it. When you look at this image, you can clearly see an inverted white equilateral triangle in front of a second triangle – but neither triangle is explicitly given. These examples illustrate the way in which imagination cooperates with perception to make sense of experience.

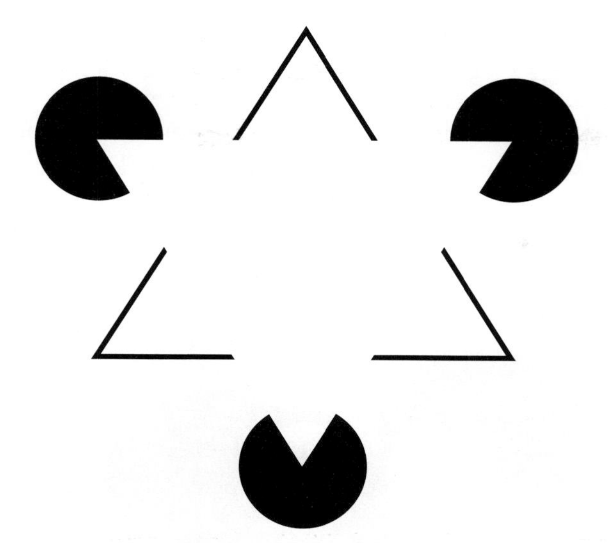

Figure 9.5

In the early twentieth century, a movement known as **Gestalt psychology** drew attention to the fact that we usually see things as a whole. (*Gestalt* is German for 'shape'.) For example, if you see a dog behind a picket fence, you do not see a collection of disconnected dog parts, but rather a dog behind a picket fence. What your imagination does is fill in the parts that are hidden behind the struts, and although you don't literally see those parts, they are implicit in your experience. In a similar way, imagination is constantly fleshing out our everyday experience of the world. For example, if you are walking down a street, strictly speaking you only see the fronts of the houses; but you experience them not as a Hollywood set but as houses with fronts and backs. Indeed, even when you are looking straight ahead and gazing into space, there is a strange sense in which you experience the objects behind your back. As these examples illustrate, your expectations about what you would see if you went to the other side of the picket fence, or the back of the houses, or turned around, are built into the fabric of perception. And such expectations are, of course, products of the imagination.

KT – Gestalt psychology: a school of psychology which suggests that, in trying to make sense of experience, we naturally tend to see things as a whole rather than in parts

Imagination plays an equally important role in constructing a coherent picture of the social and political world, and it fills in the blanks at the macro level in much the same way as it does at the micro level. Since no one can directly *see* large-scale events such as wars, famines or climate change, or broad groups such as socialists, Buddhists or Mexicans, we extrapolate from the sources available to us to form a mental conception of them. In this context, the news media play a particularly important role in shaping our perceptions. Our imagination works on the images and soundbites taken from television, the internet and newspapers, to build up a picture of, say, a civil war in Syria, or a recession in Spain, or a flood in Bangladesh. Even if you are directly involved in a major event, or are part of a particular social group, you personally experience only a small fragment of the underlying reality and you still have to rely on your imagination to form a broader picture of things. For example, if you happen to be Mexican, you may have considerable first-hand knowledge of Mexicans, but you have personally met only a tiny percentage of the Mexican population. Given this, there is a sense in which you belong to what the political scientist Benedict Anderson (1936–) has called an **imagined community**.

KT – imagined community: a community, such as a nation, which is based not on direct face-to-face interaction but on an image people hold in their minds – since they exist in reality, imagined communities are not the same as imaginary ones

Imagination, empathy and ethics

Our discussion about imagination and knowledge would hardly be complete without our saying something about empathy. This is the kind of imagination through which we gain knowledge of other people. In this section, we first consider the nature of empathy and ask how accurate it is as a source of knowledge. We then look at the relation between empathy and ethics and the extent to which fiction can play a role in developing ethical imagination.

Figure 9.6 Are human beings naturally empathic?

Empathy as a source of knowledge

Since we have no direct knowledge of other people's inner lives, we can know what it is like to be them only by imagination. The ability to imaginatively project yourself into another person's situation and understand what it is like from the inside is known as **empathy**. In everyday usage, 'empathy' is often used in a broad sense to include not only imagining what it is like to be someone, but also feeling **sympathy** or compassion for them. However, they are not the same thing. You can, for example, empathise with the plight of someone who has committed a crime, in the sense of imagining yourself in his situation, without feeling sympathy for him or condoning his behaviour.

KT – empathy: the ability to imagine another person's situation from their perspective

KT – sympathy: feeling concern and showing compassion for another person's situation

KT – autism: a condition characterised by difficulty in relating to other people, and by repetitive behaviour

Empathic accuracy

If empathy is a source of knowledge, we need to consider its accuracy. While it may be impossible to know exactly what someone else is thinking or feeling, there are clearly degrees of empathy. Our ability to empathise is determined in part by our personalities. At one extreme are those with an **autistic** cognitive style who find it very hard to relate to other people and tend to avoid social interactions. At the other extreme we find people who suffer from *extreme empathy* and experience other people's feelings so deeply that they are overwhelmed by them. Most of us lie between these two extremes somewhere in the middle of the empathy spectrum.

The psychologist Simon Baron-Cohen (1958–) has developed a test to measure people's empathy quotient, or EQ – a concept modelled on IQ. Here are some typical statements that respondents are asked to agree or disagree with:

1. I can easily tell if someone else wants to enter a conversation.

2. I find it difficult to explain to others things that I understand.

3. I find it hard to know what to do in a social situation.

4. People often tell me that I went too far in driving my point home in a discussion.

5. It doesn't bother me too much if I am late meeting a friend.

According to Baron-Cohen, humanities students have slightly higher EQs than science students, and females have slightly higher EQs than males. Such tests are, of course, open to criticism, not least because people's responses may reflect the image they want to project about themselves, rather than what they actually think and feel; but their accuracy is likely to increase with the size of the sample.

Egocentric bias

When we try to imagine other people in all their depth and complexity, and try to see things from their perspective, we sometimes find it hard to believe that they may have different tastes and preference to our own. If you hate blue cheese, fish, or Brussel sprouts you may find it difficult to imagine that anyone could like them: 'How could you possibly eat *that*!' This prejudice may explain why we sometimes buy people birthday gifts which reflect *our* preferences rather than *theirs*. Similarly, when it comes to controversial issues such as gun control, or gay marriage, or abortion, we struggle to understand how people of good will could disagree with us. Since we tend to think that the way we see things is the way they really are, we may be tempted to conclude that our opponents are either ignorant or evil. As these examples suggest, **egocentric bias** can be a major barrier to empathy. The greater the difference between ourselves and other people, the more difficult we find it to empathise with them. This may explain why we often understand minority groups or foreigners in terms of abstract statistics or superficial stereotypes which fail to do justice to the reality of their lives.

KT – egocentric bias: the tendency to look at everything from our own point of view and think that our beliefs and preferences are the correct ones

Figure 9.7 If we were more aware that chance determines the situation we are born in to, perhaps we would find it easier to empathise with distant strangers.

Other obstacles to empathy

Apart from egocentric bias, our ability to empathise with people can be eroded by such things as:

- beliefs and emotions
- social groups
- money
- power
- time pressure.

1. *Beliefs and emotions.* You might not feel much empathy for a homeless person if you believe they are lazy, or for a minority group if you have been indoctrinated into believing they are somehow inferior. If you are angry you won't even *try* seeing things from someone else's point of view, and your burning sense of indignation will effectively destroy your empathy.
2. *Social groups.* Evidence suggests that lonely people are more suspicious and less empathic than their more sociable peers. However, sociability also has a darker side. Sometimes members of *ingroups* can be thoughtlessly cruel to stigmatised *outgroups* – such as minorities, 'oddballs' and 'nerds' – and treat them as little more than objects of derision. You can find many examples of this phenomenon online in the form of cyber-bullying.
3. *Money and power.* Empathy can also be corrupted by money and power. Studies suggest that the rich are generally less empathic than the poor – perhaps because they can afford to pay little attention to other people. According to one study, people driving expensive cars are less likely to stop at pedestrian crossings than people driving cheap cars. Since politicians in many countries are very wealthy, one might question how much they are able to empathise with the people they claim to represent.
4. *Time pressure.* When we feel under time pressure we become less interested in other people and are more inclined to ignore their feelings and focus on our own business.

ACTIVITY 9.5

1. On a scale of 1 to 10, how empathic would you say that you are? In general, how accurate do you think self-assessments of empathy are?
2. When you imagine another person's situation, do you imagine *yourself* in their situation or *them* in their situation? Which is more important for empathy?
3. What are the advantages and disadvantages of doctors, psychiatrists and social workers empathically 'feeling the pain' of their patients?

The importance of empathy

Empathy plays an important role in many areas of life, both social and academic. In this section we briefly consider its relevance to communication, human sciences, and self-knowledge. Then in the following two sections we will look in detail at the role empathy plays in ethics and the extent to which it can be promoted by fiction.

LQ – Human sciences: Is empathy what distinguishes the method of the human sciences from that of the natural sciences?

Communication

To be able to write, speak or teach effectively you need to 'know your audience'. If you lack imagination and do not understand how they see things, you may adopt the wrong tone, or pitch your material at the wrong level. Some teachers suffer from what is known as the **curse of knowledge**: they know a great deal about their subject, but they are unable to explain it to their students because they have forgotten what it is like to be a novice. Writers of instruction manuals are also prone to the curse of knowledge. They may understand how a gadget works, but they are unable to think themselves into the mind of a person who has just bought it and is struggling to make it work.

KT – curse of knowledge: the difficulty that a very knowledgeable person may have in understanding the mind of a novice

ACTIVITY 9.6

1. What advice would you give a teacher about the dangers of the curse of knowledge and how to overcome them?
2. What role should communicative empathy play in the following: (a) writing a TOK essay / giving a TOK presentation; (b) recounting an experience to your friends?

Human sciences

Some people argue that empathy is central to the methodology of the human sciences (including history). An important goal of such areas of knowledge is, it is claimed, not only to *explain* things from the outside, but also to *understand* from the inside. From this viewpoint, these subjects are concerned not only with cause and effect, but also with meaning and significance, and in order to make sense of someone's behaviour you need to be able to get inside their skin and see the world through their eyes.

ACTIVITY 9.7

1. Is it possible to *know* what someone is feeling without being able to *feel* what they are feeling?
2. What problems arise in trying to empathise with someone from a very different culture or historical era?

Self-knowledge

Empathy can help us to understand not only other people but also ourselves. Indeed, to be self-conscious is to be aware of yourself as a possible object of perception by other people. To develop self-knowledge you need to be aware that others may see you quite differently from the way you see yourself. This requires being able to imagine how you look to them. For example, if you see yourself as a hero, but your friends and acquaintances consider you a coward, it is at least possible that their assessment is more objective than your own. This suggests that trying to imagine yourself from the outside is sometimes a more reliable guide to self-knowledge than eavesdropping yourself from the inside.

Empathy and ethics

Moral judgements

LQ – Ethics: Does imagining another person's situation make us more likely to help them?

KT – golden rule: the principle that you should 'do as you would be done by'

RLS – Headline: 'Cyberbullying on rise, warn charities'. Can imagination promote ethical behaviour?

The role played by empathy in our moral judgements can be summarised in the well-known Native American proverb 'Never judge a man until you've walked two moons in his moccasins'. In other words, before judging someone we should first try to imagine the situation from their point of view. However, *slow* judgement does not mean *no* judgement, and it is not always true – as another proverb claims – that 'to know all is to forgive all'. (Recall the example on page 234 of imagining yourself in a criminal's situation without condoning their behaviour.) Empathy can help us not only to make more humane judgements about other people, but also to regulate our own behaviour. According to the famous **golden rule** – variations of which can be found in most cultures – you should seek to 'do as you would be done by'. The idea behind this rule is that if we imagine ourselves in the place of the people affected by our behaviour, we will tend to do less bad and more good.

Moral motivation

As the above suggests, it is widely believed that empathy – imagining yourself in someone else's situation – leads naturally to sympathy – showing concern for them. However, it is important to be aware that this is a *hypothesis* rather than a self-evident *fact*. After all, you might be able to *imagine* what someone is feeling without *caring* about it. Even if you are distressed by another person's suffering, your concern may be self-directed rather than other-directed. For example, instead of being moved by

Figure 9.8

sympathy when you see a beggar in the street, or a charity advertisement depicting starving children, you might simply avert your gaze, harden your heart and keep your wallet closed. By looking the other way, you distance yourself from the source of your distress and no longer have to think about it.

Sometimes, we even take a perverse pleasure in other people's suffering. This phenomenon – which is known as ***schadenfreude*** – is more common than you might think. You can see it on display every week when sports fans take undisguised pleasure in the failures and defeats of their rivals. *Schadenfreude* is a particularly common response when we feel that someone has got their 'just deserts' and that they deserve their misfortune. In a species such as our own in which individuals are constantly competing for status, such ignoble sentiments may be as inevitable as they are regrettable. (The writer Gore Vidal once bleakly observed: 'Success is not enough: one's friends must also fail.') At the extreme, some disturbed individuals are completely deaf to the call of sympathy. Sadists, for example, take pleasure in other people's suffering; and it seems clear that what they lack is not so much imagination as common humanity.

KT – *schadenfreude*: taking pleasure in another person's misfortune

These examples suggest that empathy is not a *sufficient* condition for sympathy and does not *automatically* lead to concern for others. Nevertheless, it could still be argued that it is an *enabling* condition which helps to promote sympathy even if it does not guarantee it. Perhaps if we tried a little harder to imagine the plight of street beggars or suffering strangers our indifference would evaporate and we would be more moved to help them.

ACTIVITY 9.8

1. Do you think that empathy is a necessary or a sufficient condition for ethical behaviour, or both, or neither?
2. How, if at all, might trying to view things from the perspective of a criminal affect a person's attitude to prison reform?
3. How might empathy improve negotiations between rival political or social groups such as Israelis and Palestinians, or bosses and workers?
4. Do you think that TV news encourages sympathy for the plight of distant strangers, or does it simply encourage voyeurism and *schadenfreude*?
5. To what extent does showing compassion for animals depend on being able to imagine what it is like to be them?

The role of fiction

Some people – most notably the influential philosopher Martha Nussbaum (1947–) – believe that fiction is a particularly effective way of developing moral imagination. When you immerse yourself in a novel you see the world through the eyes of the characters and this can remind you that there are other perspectives on the world apart from your own. Stories have aptly been described as 'flight simulators for the brain'– the idea being that just as pilots can develop their professional skills in flight simulators, so we can develop our empathic skills by reading a lot of fiction. A great novel can convey, with a power and vitality that goes beyond any purely factual description, what it is like to be a woman in a conformist society struggling to break out of an oppressive marriage, or a prisoner coping with the numbing harshness of life in a Soviet-era labour camp, or a young black man trying to maintain his integrity in the face of a racist apartheid regime in South Africa. Such works enable us to imaginatively project ourselves into situations that lie beyond the frontiers of our own lives and to understand what they are like from the inside. This, it is claimed, is likely to make us more sympathetic to the plight of others in distant lands.

What are we to make of the knowledge claim that literature develops our empathy and arouses our sympathy? Since it is difficult – if not impossible – to conduct controlled experiments in this area, any evidence will by its very nature be ambiguous and inconclusive. Nevertheless, to support it we might point to studies which suggest that fiction readers score higher on empathy tests than those who read only non-fiction. We might also consider the influence of seminal novels such as Harriet Beecher Stowe's *Uncle Tom's Cabin* (1852) and E. M. Forster's *A Passage to India* (1924) which allegedly helped to change attitudes to Americans' treatment of slaves and to British imperialism in India. The historian Lynn Hunt (1945–) has even suggested that the 'invention' of human rights in the eighteenth century was fuelled by the rise of a novel-reading class. 'Novels', she says, 'made the point that all people are fundamentally similar because of their inner feelings.'

Such a grand claim for the power of fiction is not without its critics. To start with, it seems clear that not all fiction has positive effects. At its worst, fiction can simply perpetuate stereotypes, encourage *schadenfreude* and even fuel the flames of nationalism. So, presumably, the claim needs to be limited to 'good fiction' – whatever is meant by that. But even if such fiction is correlated with empathy, the direction of causation is unclear. Does fiction make people more empathic, or are empathic people more likely to be drawn to fiction? No one is sure. We might worry that rather than *stimulating* real-world empathy and compassion, our engagement with fiction becomes a *substitute* for it. Morally speaking, fictional worlds are also *frictionless* worlds, in the sense that you can effortlessly glide through them dispensing fantasy compassion which makes you feel good about yourself but which costs you nothing. One might wonder whether lavishing time and empathy on fictional characters really is the best way of helping real people in the flesh and blood world. Finally – and perhaps most ominously – we can find plenty of examples of cultured killers. Joseph Stalin (1878–1953) was well-read by any standard, as was Mao Zedong (1893–1976); but between them they were responsible for the deaths of millions of people.

Despite the above points, a moderate claim for the moral influence of literature might still be defended. Of course, no one is suggesting that all you need to do to make the world a better place is to read fiction. Fiction is just one tool we might use to achieve this. Furthermore, the link between fiction and compassion is a tendency rather than a strict law, and as such it can allow for exceptions like Stalin and Mao. Perhaps what really matters is not simply the length of one's reading list, but the extent to which it has been discussed and reflected on. Martha Nussbaum, for one, remains convinced that by engaging our imagination, expanding our horizons and developing our sympathy, literature can help to make us better world citizens.

ACTIVITY 9.9

1. Some law schools have compulsory literature courses for students. Why might this be a good idea?
2. Compare and contrast the effectiveness of (a) novels and (b) movies as media for developing our empathic imagination.
3. Do you think that any kind of novel can help to develop our sympathy or only certain kinds? Give reasons.
4. If a minority is discriminated against in a country do you think it is better to pass laws to protect them, or is it better to try to educate the moral imagination of the majority?

The mystery of creativity

Earlier in this chapter, we discussed how creative imagination can generate ideas which stimulate intellectual progress and help to push back the frontiers of knowledge. Since it involves the emergence of something new which did not previously exist, creativity is, however, a somewhat mysterious source of knowledge. Some people doubt that it is possible to have a *theory* of creativity on the grounds that theories are supposed to explain things and creative insights are by definition surprising and unpredictable. This has led some people to conclude that creativity is a 'gift' which is only bestowed on a few geniuses. Other people are more optimistic and insist that there is nothing inherently mysterious about creativity, and that rather than being the preserve of the few it is natural to everyone. In this section we focus on three related questions:

1 How, if at all, can creativity be explained?

2 Is genius a fact or a fiction?

3 How can we assess creativity?

Explaining creativity

One popular theory of creativity is the *combination theory*. According to this, creativity consists in taking existing ideas or elements and combining them in new ways. For example, if you take a horse and a pair of wings and stick them together, you get a flying horse (*Pegasus* in Greek mythology). You may recall a childhood game in which the heads, middles and bottom parts of animals are printed on cards which can then be joined together to produce 'crazy animals'. This is fairly low-level, mechanical creativity, and many combinations thrown up will be of little interest or value; but if in a particular field you have enough elements, a new combination can sometimes be illuminating. Indeed, we might say that so-called 'creative types' are those people who seem to have a 'nose' for discovering such combinations.

Figure 9.9

While there is much more to creativity than making mechanical combinations, it could be argued that *combination blurs imperceptibly into transformation*. When elements are combined in new configurations, there is a sense in which *we see them differently*. This is apparent in the case of *metaphor*, which forges a link between seemingly different things and implicitly compares them. To take a simple example: if you say 'Tom is a sly fox', you are suggesting an underlying similarity between Tom and foxes which changes our perception of him. Even a well-used metaphor can influence our perception, but a strikingly original one can shock us into seeing something with completely new eyes. For example, in his poem 'Seascape', the English poet Stephen Spender likens the sea to a harp. At first sight, this may not seem a very promising comparison, but Spender's genius is to show that it is – retrospectively – surprisingly apt. Given this example, we might argue that what distinguishes a good metaphor – or, more generally, a creative combination – from a bad one is that it is *surprising*, *appropriate* and *suggestive*, in the sense that it may lead us to think of further similarities between its elements.

ACTIVITY 9.10

1. Read Spender's poem 'Seascape' and – if you agree – explain in what ways it is surprising, appropriate and suggestive.
2. Find examples of metaphors which are: (a) surprising but not appropriate; (b) appropriate but not surprising; (c) surprising and appropriate.

While most creative individuals operate within an established form – such as a prevailing scientific framework or artistic style – a few giants not only make contributions *within* a field, but also bring about changes in perspective which *transform* the field. Such transformational creativity leads to a completely new way of looking at the phenomena in question and it can be found in every area of knowledge. Einstein's Theory of Relativity and Picasso's Cubism are good examples of transformational creativity. Both men questioned traditional assumptions, took a leap of imagination and 'changed the rules of the game'. Indeed, we might say that rather than creating *new moves within a game*, transformational creativity consists precisely in *inventing a new game*.

Figure 9.10

High-level creativity seems to benefit from a mixture of subject-specific expertise and interdisciplinarity. If you are familiar with other areas of knowledge, you may be able to make interesting and unusual connections with your own field. That, at least, was the view of the German physicist Werner Heisenberg (1901–76):

> *Fruitful developments frequently take place at those points where two different lines of thought meet. These lines may have roots in quite different parts of human culture, in different times or different environments, hence if they actually meet … new and interesting developments may follow.*

Interestingly, it seems that creative ideas also tend to arise in situations where there is a lot of cultural cross-fertilisation. At various times in their histories cities such as Athens (Greece), Cordoba (Spain), Florence (Italy) and New York (USA) have been important centres for creativity. There is also some evidence to suggest that meaningful exposure to another culture by, for example, living abroad, can contribute to a more creative mindset. The alleged reason is that such exposure makes us more aware that things are ambiguous and open to different interpretations.

The myth of genius

Although transformational creativity is commonly associated with *genius*, some people reject the very idea of genius as a myth. One reason for this is that, while genius doubtless requires talent, it is also built on a great deal of hard work. If you are to have any worthwhile creative insights you need to immerse yourself in your chosen field and achieve mastery of it, and (as we saw in Chapter 7 on page 179) it has been estimated that this usually takes at least 10,000 hours (or ten years). This suggests that there is some truth in Thomas Edison's (1847–1931) famous assessment that 'Genius is one percent inspiration and ninety-nine percent perspiration.'

Another reason for being suspicious of the idea of genius is that when we study the history of ideas it soon becomes apparent that creative individuals owe numerous intellectual debts to those who have gone before them – debts which they are sometimes unwilling to acknowledge. As the French fashion designer Coco Chanel allegedly observed: 'Only those with no memory insist on their originality.' This has led some to question the very notion of originality and claim that 'everything is a remix', and that allegedly 'new' ideas are simply variations on a few basic themes that recur throughout history. This seems too extreme. Admittedly, the glittering towers creative achievement are built on a common inheritance of ideas; but the fact remains that there are *degrees* of originality. Even after they acknowledge their cultural debts, some individuals continue to stand creatively taller than others. As is now well known, William Shakespeare 'stole' many of his plots from other people, but he indisputably added a tremendous amount of value to what he took. Similarly, Isaac Newton (1642–1727) may have been 'standing on the shoulders of giants', but his creative insights enabled him to see further than the rest of his contemporaries.

Having said that, it is worth nothing that the age of the 'creative hero' may be coming to an end. In the modern era, creative insights are more likely to be the product of teams rather than individuals working alone. This is particularly true in the sciences where almost everyone works in a laboratory in collaboration with other like-minded specialists. While the arts may be more individualistic than the sciences, even here artists, writers and musicians often collaborate and form movements, and the internet is likely to increase the number of such creative collaborations.

ACTIVITY 9.11

1. Do you think that creativity is more a matter of nature ('you're born with it'), or nurture ('it's a result of the way you're brought up')?
2. According to the ancient Greeks, memory is the mother of creativity. What do you think they meant by this and to what extent do you think it is true?
3. Name three individuals, one for each of the higher-level subjects that you study, whom you consider to be a genius. What role did creativity play in their achievements?
4. Do you think we will ever know, in the sense of being able to understand and explain, creativity, or will it always be a mystery?

Assessing creativity

There is no clear formula for determining whether or not something is creative, and no clear answer to the question 'How novel or valuable must an idea or artefact be in order to qualify?' Since values are partly a matter of opinion, it is perhaps not surprising that people sometimes disagree about whether or not something is really creative. Part of the problem is that when something is radically new, we may lack standards against which to judge it. In fact, research suggests that, while people endorse creativity in theory, they often reject it in practice. This may be because creative ideas are by definition new and so threaten the status quo. The resulting uncertainty can easily make people feel uncomfortable. So it is perhaps not surprising that some people's genius has gone unrecognised by their contemporaries.

In this context, the Dutch artist Vincent van Gogh is often mentioned, but there are doubtless other examples. However, it is also true that other people are hailed as geniuses during their lifetimes only to be rejected by subsequent generations. You have probably never heard of the composer Louis Spohr (1784–1859), who was once favourably compared to Ludwig van Beethoven (1770–1827), but is now all but forgotten.

Most of us will never come up with the kind of epoch-changing creative insights that are associated with an Einstein or Picasso, but we are all capable of more modest forms of creativity. There is plenty of scope for what might be called *personal* creativity – coming up with ideas that are new to *you*. Indeed, personal – albeit disciplined – creativity is one of the hallmarks of an outstanding, rather than a merely average, theory of knowledge essay or presentation.

LQ – The arts: Is creativity the main criterion for determining whether or not something is a great work of art?

ACTIVITY 9.12

1. Give an example of a creative insight – in the sense of an insight that was new to you – you have had in one of the subjects that you study. Try to explain how you came up with this insight.
2. How would you go about trying to assess an individual's creativity? Can creativity be measured?
3. There are computer programs which can create music, write poems and even invent jokes. To what extent do you think computers are capable of genuine creativity? What about animals?

Fantasy and distortion

Throughout this chapter, we have explored how a richly informed imagination constrained by facts plays an important role in fleshing out and pushing forward our knowledge of the world. However, imagination can sometimes degenerate into fantasy and impede rather than contribute to knowledge. As we come towards the end of this chapter, we should remind ourselves of the dangers of an undisciplined imagination, which can all too easily become prey to illusory patterns, seductive images, and imaginary fears.

Figure 9.11

Illusory patterns

Despite the fact that imagination is implicit in everyday perception, we sometimes project our private fantasies on to the objects around us and think we see patterns in things where no such patterns exist. Consider, for example, the ease with which we see faces in clouds, rocks and trees. This suggests that those who claim to have seen the face of Mother Teresa on a cinnamon bun (the so-called 'nun bun'), the face of Jesus on a tortilla, the Hindu god Ganesha in the shape of a potato, or the face of Satan in the smoke coming from the World Trade Center, may be reading more into the phenomena than they are reading out of them. Similarly, alleged sightings of UFOs, ghosts, the Loch Ness Monster, Bigfoot (a large ape-like creature said to inhabit the forests of north-west America) and Michael Jackson (whom some people think is still alive), would seem to owe more to fantasy than to fact. As these examples suggest, an overactive and unconstrained imagination can sometimes detract from, rather than contribute to, our knowledge of reality. At the limit, people suffering from mental illnesses, such as schizophrenia and paranoia, are unable to distinguish between fact and fantasy and find it difficult to function without help from society.

Seductive images

We live in a world full of seductive images which can have a powerful influence on the way we see things. Consider the images that people project of themselves (which can include using words as well as pictures). We are, of course, all concerned with our public image, and image management is probably as old as humanity itself. What is striking about the modern era is that this concern seems to have become an

Figure 9.12

obsession. While once only celebrities, politicians and corporations could afford to hire public relations consultants, the internet has led to the democratisation of perception management and it is now possible for ordinary people to spend several hours a day polishing their own Facebook® image. The result, some fear, is a growing divergence between how we imagine people to be and how they are in reality. This can have serious consequences in areas ranging from online dating, to university and job applications, to presidential elections.

At the level of the news media, images can illuminate and help us to make sense of reality, but they can manipulate and distort our conception of it. If, for example, a particular group is repeatedly associated with a particular trait, we are likely to end up imagining that *all members of the group are like that*. You only have to think of the way some news media have associated terrorism with Islam, or poverty with Africa, to see how our understanding of the world can be clouded by fantasy generalisations that have only a tenuous connection with reality. Images can also become a kind of shorthand – or even substitute – for the understanding of complex events – especially when they are endlessly repeated and accompanied by soundbites which do little more than serve as captions.

RLS – Headline: 'Senators call bin Laden film "grossly inaccurate"'. How can imagination distort historical truth?

At the extreme, we might fear that rather than *representing* reality, images are beginning to *replace* it. For example, when they go on holiday some people seem to be more interested in creating images than having experiences: travel becomes one long photo opportunity! The danger is that when they arrive home their actual experiences are replaced by a fictional reconstruction based on their photos of happy, smiling faces. Similarly, films can sometimes become a substitute for the reality on which they claim to be based. Thus we may come to understand the Holocaust through the movie *Schindler's List*, the 2004 tsunami in Thailand through *The Impossible*, and the assassination of Osama bin Laden in 2011 through *Zero Dark Thirty*. Whatever the merits of these movies, there are obvious dangers in the irresponsible mixing of fact and fantasy.

Imaginary fears

Our picture of the social and political world can also be distorted by bias and clouded by fantasy. Some critics claim that politicians and the news media contribute to this process by playing on our hopes and fears and painting imaginary futures that bear little relation to reality. Since it is such a powerful emotion, we are particularly susceptible to fear – whether it is fear of terrorism, or fear of global warming, or fear of being 'swamped' by immigrants – and we can all too easily scare ourselves by imagining worst-case scenarios. Since one person's timely warning may be another person's wild fantasy, the key question is, of course, the extent to which such fears are justified. Whatever your own view about the above issues, one thing seems clear: if our imagined futures are not to spiral into fantasies with no connection to reality, we must try to ensure that, wherever possible, they are based on the best available *evidence*.

ACTIVITY 9.13

1. 'The trouble with online dating is that people are usually disappointed when they meet one another in the flesh.' To what extent is it possible to accurately imagine someone if you have never met them?
2. To what extent are our perceptions of celebrities based on fact and to what extent are they based on fiction?
3. 'Candidates in presidential elections are more concerned with "looking presidential" than with explaining their policies to the electorate.' Why might someone say this, and what are the implications if it is true?
4. What role does imagination play in our perception of other cultures and how is this shaped by the media?

Conclusion

As this chapter has explained, imagination is a surprisingly powerful force which plays a key role in the production of knowledge. Indeed, it is an astonishing fact that everything in the social world – intellectual, organisational or technological – has its origin in the imagination. We have made progress as a species partly because throughout history some people have had the courage to ask 'What if?' and imagine alternatives to reality. Such people were not simply dreamers, and they understood the need to test their ideas against experience. For imagination is at its most powerful when it works in cooperation with, rather than in opposition to, reason. Since our continued progress will depend on imagination as much as reason, it is not surprising that many countries are actively seeking to give imagination a more central role in education.

Despite its value, we have seen that imagination also has a darker side and that we are sometimes tempted to substitute private fantasies for public facts. Here, too, education has a role to play, and it can help to ensure that exuberant imagination is balanced and guided by the more austere demands of critical thinking.

Key points

- Imagination is the ability to form a representation of something which is not present to the senses.
- Three kinds of imagination can be distinguished: fantasy, realistic imagination and creativity.
- Imagination is an important source of knowledge not only in the arts, but also in the sciences and in other areas of knowledge; but its products must pass critical scrutiny before they are accepted.
- Since it can help us to (1) understand things we have not experienced, (2) envisage alternative explanations and (3) explore what is possible, imagination is relevant to the justification of knowledge.
- Imagination also fills in the gaps in our everyday experience, and it therefore plays a role in the constitution of knowledge.
- Imagination in the form of empathy can give us knowledge of other minds; and, although we may question its accuracy, empathy plays an important role in the human sciences and in history.
- Some people claim that empathy leads naturally to sympathy and that fiction helps to develop our moral imagination.
- Creativity has its source in the combination of existing elements and ideas, but it can also lead to completely new ways of looking at things.
- One reason it is difficult to assess creativity is that people may have different views on the value of a new idea or artefact.
- While imagination has many benefits, we should not forget that it can also distort our picture of reality.

Key terms

autism
creativity
curse of knowledge
egocentric bias
empathy
empirically possible
fantasy
Gestalt psychology
golden rule
imagined community
logically possible
paradigm shift
realistic imagination
schadenfreude
sympathy
thought experiment

IB prescribed essay titles

1. 'Imagination is more important than knowledge. For knowledge is limited to all we now know and understand, while imagination embraces the entire world, and all there ever will be to know and understand.' (Albert Einstein) Do you agree? (November 2012)
2. Compare the roles played by reason and imagination in at least two areas of knowledge. (2007)

Further reading

Books

Jacob Bronowski, *The Origins of Knowledge and Imagination* (Yale University Press, 1979). In this fascinating and challenging series of essays, Bronowski argues persuasively that imagination plays a central role in the creation of knowledge in both the arts and the sciences.

Simon Baron-Cohen, *Zero Degrees of Empathy* (Penguin, 2012). A professor of psychology, Baron-Cohen explores conditions such as autism and psychopathy in order to cast light on the central role that empathy plays in our lives.

Online articles

Kathleen Taylor, 'Is Imagination More Important Than Knowledge?', *Times Higher Education Supplement*, 8 November 2002.

Paul Bloom, 'The Baby in the Well: The Case Against Empathy', *New Yorker*, 20 May 2013.

Memory

10

Memory is the mother of all wisdom.

Aeschylus, 525–455 BCE

Memory is the core of what we call reality . . . Almost every reality you 'know' at any given second is a mere ghost held in memory.

Howard Bloom, 1943–

What you remember defines who you are; when you forget your life you cease to be, even before your death.

Julian Barnes, 1946–

There is no perception which is not full of memories.

Henri Bergson, 1859–1941

The memory is sometimes so retentive, so serviceable, so obedient; at others, so bewildered and so weak; and at others again, so tyrannic, so beyond control!

Jane Austen, 1775–1817

Human memory is not like a computer which records things; it is part of the imaginative process, on the same terms as invention.

Alain Robbe-Grillet, 1922–2008

It isn't so astonishing the number of things I can remember, as the number of things I can remember that aren't so.

Mark Twain, 1835–1910

Creative people are at their most creative when writing their autobiographies.

Steven Pinker, 1954–

'I have done that,' says my memory. 'I cannot have done that' – says my pride, and remains adamant. At last – memory yields.

Friedrich Nietzsche, 1844–1900

Since the beginning of time, for us humans, forgetting has been the norm and remembering the exception.

Viktor Mayer–Schönberger, 1966–

Introduction

All our knowledge about the past is ultimately based on memory, and we often appeal to this way of knowing to justify our knowledge claims. At the personal level, memory is crucial to self-knowledge – for your sense of who you are consists in large part of your memory of what you have done. Academically, memory is closely associated with history, much of which is based on eye-witness recollections of events which may have happened long before they are put on record. In the practical sphere, the perceived accuracy of a witness's memory may determine whether someone is found innocent or guilty in a criminal trial. In fact, our entire stock of knowledge depends critically on memory. If you were to suffer *radical* amnesia and lost *all* of your memories, your knowledge, too, would evaporate.

The nature of memory

KT – personal memory: the internal recollection of the various events that make up our lives

KT – factual memory: our memory of meanings, facts and information

KT – practical memory: the remembered ability to know how to do something, such as playing the piano

Three different kinds of memory are commonly distinguished: **personal memory**, **factual memory** and **practical memory**.

Personal memory

Personal memory consists of your internal recollection of various events that make up your life, and it allows you to travel back in time and remember the *what*, *where*, and *when* of events 'from the inside'. This might include such things as falling off your bicycle when you were a child, your first day at school, or your holiday in Crete the summer before last. You may strengthen 'significant events' that you *want* to remember – graduations, weddings, holidays, etc. – with supports such as diary entries, photos and souvenirs; and you reinforce them when you reminisce with family and friends, or tell the 'story of your life' to an acquaintance. The rest of your memories are likely to be a mixture of unusual, emotional and completely random experiences that have impressed themselves on your mind. Personal memory gives you your sense of identity. If you suffered from amnesia and could remember nothing about your past then you would not know who you are.

Factual memory

Factual memory refers to the part of memory which is concerned with meanings, facts and ideas. For example, you may know that the word 'mercurial' means 'fickle', or that gold has atomic number 79, or that Riga is the capital of Latvia. Such memory is *undated* in that it is concerned only with the *content* of the knowledge and not with *when* it was acquired. You may not, for example, have any memories of *when* you learned the names of capital cities. Unlike personal memory, factual memory is typically abstract and lacking in emotional colour.

ACTIVITY 10.1

1. What kinds of memories do animals have? How are they similar to and how are they different from human memories?
2. What is your earliest memory? How confident are you that you remember the event itself rather than being told about the event?
3. Our earliest memories tend to coincide with the development of language. What does this suggest about the relation between language and memory?
4. Which of your memories would you say are central to your sense of who you are and which are peripheral?
5. 'The kinds of things you remember say a lot about the kind of person you are.' What does this mean, and to what extent do you think it is true?
6. What role do photos play in the preservation of personal memories? How can they distort such memories?

Practical memory

Practical memory consists of your memory of the various skills and habits you have acquired in your life, such as knowing how to type, or ski, or play the violin. Unlike personal and factual memory, practical memory is usually implicit in the sense that it is difficult or impossible to put into words. Sports psychologists use the phrase *muscle memory* to denote the ability to perform complex motor tasks without conscious awareness. If you can ride a bicycle, you can, for example, turn left without having to think about what you are doing. Some important practical memories – such as those associated with learning to walk and talk – are laid down before your earliest personal memories. Once established, they grow deep roots and become almost impossible to forget.

Memory and knowledge

The three types of memory discussed above map roughly on to the three kinds of knowledge discussed in Chapter 2: personal memory is related to knowledge by acquaintance, factual memory to knowledge by description, and practical memory to know-how. Indeed, an important part of what it means to *know* something is to be able to remember it. This is not, however, to say that memory is an *original source* of knowledge. For memory can only preserve knowledge that has been acquired from some other source. You can, for example, only remember your holiday by the sea last year if you actually went to the seaside and had various experiences there. Otherwise, you would not be *remembering* your holiday, but merely *imagining* it. To say that you *remember* something is to claim that what you are saying about the past is *true*.

"Remind me, again, what we're doing here?"

Figure 10.1

ACTIVITY 10.2

How do we know something is a genuine memory and not an imagined memory?

KT – short-term memory: our ability to hold small amounts – around seven bits – of information in our mind for a few seconds before forgetting them

We also associate memory with intelligence. We tend to admire people with good memories and consider them to be smart. There may be some justification in this. For example, there is evidence that people who do well on **short-term memory** tests also do well on tests of general intelligence. This is because if you are trying to make sense of an experience, or solve a mathematics problem, or grasp the meaning of a sentence, it helps if you can keep the various parts of the experience, or problem, or sentence, in your mind at the same time. Just as short-term memory plays a role in understanding, so long-term memory plays a role in critical thinking. If you are well-informed about many topics, this gives you the background knowledge that is necessary for good judgement.

LQ – Mathematics: How is having a good short-term memory related to mathematical ability?

ACTIVITY 10.3

1. What role does memory play in the various IB subjects that you study? Is having a good memory more likely to lead to success in some subjects than in others?
2. How does short-term memory contribute to your comprehension and enjoyment of a novel or movie in which there are many characters?
3. In what sense, if any, can you be said to know something if you have simply memorised the relevant information and are unable to apply your 'knowledge' to the real world?

The mechanics of memory

Figure 10.2 How does memory differ from a video camera?

A false picture

According to one popular view of memory – which we will call the *storehouse model* – memories are faithful copies of experiences which are stored in the mind and can be consulted as required. In a recent survey, more than 60 per cent of people who were asked agreed with the statement 'Human memory works like a video camera, accurately recording the events we see and hear so that we can review and inspect them later.' Despite its popularity, most psychologists reject the storehouse model and subscribe instead to the *reconstruction model*. As the name suggests, this holds that memories are not simply 'taken down from the shelf' when we need them, but are reconstructed every time we access them.

Three main memory processes are usually distinguished: *encoding*, *storage* and *retrieval*. These refer respectively to capturing, storing and accessing information.

ACTIVITY 10.4

To what extent would you say human memory is like a computer's memory and how would you say it is different?

Encoding and selective attention

To remember something, you first need to capture it and ensure that it leaves an enduring trace in your mind. Sometimes our inability to remember is simply due to distraction or lack of attention. Since there are many impressions flooding in to our senses all the time, we sometimes listen without hearing and look without seeing. Consider, for example, the common experience of meeting someone for the first time and forgetting their name within a few seconds of being introduced to them. You may simply be too busy thinking about the impression *you* are creating to focus sufficiently on *them*. You have doubtless experienced other short-term memory lapses, such as putting your hand up in class only for your mind to go blank when you are called on to reply, or going into the kitchen and forgetting what you went in there for. Even if you are repeatedly exposed to something, it may not find its way into your long-term memory if you fail to attend to it properly. You may, for example, have handled thousands of bank notes in your life, and yet still be unable to describe what is on the front and back of them.

Storage and decay

Even if you succeed in encoding information and impressing it onto your mind, there is no guarantee that it will remain perfectly preserved in your memory. On the contrary, if you do not revisit it or use it on a regular basis, it will quickly decay. Much of what you drum into your memory before an exam you forget soon after you have taken it. And while you may become proficient in another language, you will only retain your fluency if you practise regularly.

When you *do* remember something, what gets stored is usually a simplified sketch rather than a detailed copy of experience. As a result, our memories are usually simpler, more stereotypical, and more consistent than the events they claim to describe. Over time, our minds unconsciously smooth over the memories and make them more coherent, adding small details that seem to fit and rejecting anomalous ones that don't.

Retrieval and interference

Sometimes the problem with memory is neither encoding nor storage, but retrieval. Doubtless, you have sometimes had the *tip-of-the-tongue experience* and felt that you knew the answer to something, but could not quite find the words. If, for example, someone asks you what the capital of Colombia is, you may feel sure you know, and even remember that it begins with 'b' – and yet be unable to answer; but you immediately recognise 'Bogotá' as correct when someone else says it. Retrieval can benefit from hints and cues, and you may be able to *passively recognise* the answer when you see it even though you are unable to *actively produce* it. This explains why a person learning a second language may be able to read, say, a Spanish newspaper with relative ease, and yet struggle to string together a coherent sentence when actually required to speak the language!

ACTIVITY 10.5

1. In what sense, if any, can you be said to know something if you cannot remember it? What light does the 'tip-of-the-tongue experience' throw on this question?
2. Do you really know something if you can passively recognise the answer when you see it or hear it, but are unable to produce it when asked?
3. Does your mind ever go blank when you are under pressure? To what extent could such 'cognitive choking' explain why some people who are intelligent and hard-working do poorly in exams?

One powerful cue that can help retrieve information from memory is context. Research suggests that you are more likely to remember something if you revisit the environment where you had the original experience. If, for example, you have mislaid your door keys, it is a good strategy to retrace your steps to try to remember where you put them. Similarly, revisiting a childhood scene can reactivate powerful and long-dormant memories. The influence of context on memory justifies the widespread police practice of taking witnesses back to the scene of a crime, or staging a reconstruction of it using actors.

The reliability of memory

Having considered the mechanics of memory, we can see why it is less reliable than is commonly thought. Not only do we forget things, but we also misremember them.

MANKOFF

"Waiter, I'd like to order, unless I've eaten, in which case bring me the check."

Figure 10.3

Forgetting

We have all had cause to curse our memories, and forgetting things is one of life's great frustrations. Some memory lapses are trivial, but we also forget important appointments and anniversaries, or mislay valuable items. (The cellist Yo Yo Ma once famously 'forgot' a Stradivarius cello worth $2.5 million and left it in a New York taxi cab.) Although we tend to think of forgetting as a mental aberration, it seems to be the rule rather than the exception. As you are probably aware from revising for exams, most people struggle to remember abstract information such as mathematical formulae, technical scientific terms, dates in history and irregular verbs in foreign languages. Things are no better when it comes to our own experiences, and many of us have difficulty remembering what we had for lunch yesterday – let alone a week or a month ago. Indeed, most of the things we do seem to leave no permanent trace in memory. Perhaps you have had the experience of reading through an old diary and having no recollection of the day-to-day events it recounts. Think, too, of all the books and movies you have read and watched over the years about which you can now remember nothing! Nevertheless, it could be that even forgotten experiences leave a hidden trace and contribute to making us who we are today.

"Someday we'll look back at this time in our lives and be unable to remember it."

Figure 10.4

ACTIVITY 10.6

1. If you read and enjoy a novel and a few months later can't remember anything about it, in what way, if any, does it detract from the value of reading?
2. Most people wish they had better memories. What do you think would be the advantages and disadvantages of having a *perfect* memory?
3. Read Jorge Luis Borges' short story *Funes the Memorious.* What light does it shed on the value of forgetting?

Misremembering

In some ways, misremembering is more serious than not remembering at all, for it creates the *illusion* of knowledge. We may speak of 'unforgettable experiences' and claim to remember something 'as if it were yesterday', but the fact that different people can have very different memories of the same event should give us pause for thought. Admittedly, some information – such as poetry you have learned by heart – *can* be recalled with complete fidelity. This is because you make an effort to drum it into your head and can check your memory against the original text. By contrast, unless you have video evidence you cannot check your memory of past events against what actually happened. Moreover, when you tell your friends about something that happened to you, there are often no other witnesses present to challenge *your* version of events. In the absence of corrective feedback, it is not surprising that we often confidently *assume* that our memories are accurate; and it can come as a shock to discover that this is not always the case.

"Geez, can't you think of a better way to remember all of your passwords?"

Figure 10.5

RLS – Headline: 'Manhattan memory project: How 9/11 changed our brains'. Should we trust flashbulb memories?

ACTIVITY 10.7

If two people give different accounts of a past event, does it necessarily follow that one of them is lying, or could each of them simply have a different memory of the event?

Figure 10.6 How reliable are flashbulb memories?

Flashbulb memories

One group of memories that are commonly thought to be reliable are so-called 'flashbulb memories'. Our experiences of dramatic, emotionally charged events allegedly etch themselves onto our minds with such force that the resulting memories are unusually vivid, accurate and durable. A person might, for example, claim to remember exactly where they were, what they were doing, and how they reacted when they first heard about the assassinations of John F. Kennedy (1963) or of John Lennon (1980), or the terrorist attacks on the Twin Towers in New York (2001). Flashbulb memories are also associated with personal traumas, such as surviving a car accident, or a mugging, or an earthquake. The degree of personal involvement in such events may be an important factor in the strength of the corresponding memories.

Despite the mythology surrounding such memories, research suggests that they are not as accurate as is widely believed. When psychologists compared what a group of people said in surveys given to them shortly after 9/11 with their recollections one year and three years after the event, they found a marked deterioration in their memories, with up to 50 per cent of the details changing over time. Yet the participants' faith in their memories was undiminished. This suggests that what emotion bestows on memory is not accuracy but *confidence*.

Some memory biases

LQ – Emotion: Are our memories of the past always distorted by emotion?

Although autobiographies and personal recollections are an important source of knowledge, an individual's own accounts of their past cannot be taken entirely on trust. Among the biases and errors that might be mentioned are the following.

1. Egocentric bias

Egocentric bias refers to our tendency to attribute a more central role to ourselves in past events than is justified by the facts. Since we live our lives from the inside, our own experiences tend to be more vivid, immediate and hence memorable than those of other people. Given this, it is not surprising that we all tend to be the heroes of our own dramas. While you may remember being the life and soul of the party, or playing a decisive role in some famous sporting victory, it is worth keeping in mind that an impartial observer may see things differently. As we saw in our discussion of empathy in Chapter 8, egocentric bias is also a barrier to empathy (see page 235).

2. Narrative bias

Human beings are narrative animals and they like to tell a good story when they recall events. Narrative bias consists in imposing a structure on our memories and distorting them in order to fit a predetermined storyline. Sometimes we exaggerate and indulge in *poetic licence*; and if we repeat a story enough times we may end up believing our own exaggerations. In 2008, the American politician Hillary Clinton 'remembered' a 1996 visit to the war-torn former Yugoslavia, and she vividly described landing at Tuzla airport under sniper fire. However, when her memory was checked against TV footage of the event, it revealed a calm scene. While Clinton's account made a good story, it turned out to be false; but it is quite possible that she was not so much lying as misremembering. After all, how good is your memory of things that happened to you twelve years ago?

"They're not out of focus. They're just fuzzy memories."

Figure 10.7

3. Emotional bias

Our view of the past may be influenced by our current mood. When we are happy we tend to recall happy times, and when we are sad we tend to recall sad ones. Despite these variations, people are often **nostalgic** about the past and view it through rose-tinted spectacles. A pungent smell, an evocative song or a meeting with old friends may reawaken vivid memories of the 'good old days'. We seem to remember that the summers were longer, the grass was greener, and our friendships were deeper and more meaningful. What our memories conveniently edit out of this romanticised version of the past are the inevitable complications, disappointments and defeats that we also experienced.

KT – nostalgia: the tendency to see the past in an exaggeratedly positive light

ACTIVITY 10.8

1. What role do (a) music and (b) smells play in evoking memories of past times? Give some examples from your own experience and try to assess the accuracy of the resulting memories.
2. If a couple are involved in a bitter separation, to what extent do you think their current feelings colour their memory of their earlier life together?
3. If you had a video of your entire life to date, how much of a discrepancy do you think there would be between your memory and the reality?
4. How might an autobiography written by a politician be more accurate than a biography about them written by a historian? How might it be less accurate?
5. Do you think it is more important to have *accurate* memories of the past, or *happy* memories of the past? Give reasons.

4. Vividness bias

According to **vividness bias**, we are more likely to remember dramatic events than mundane ones. Since we tend to recall the *vividness* rather than the *frequency* of events, we often have a distorted sense of relative risks. That is why, as discussed in Chapter 7 (page 183), most people overestimate the probability of rare vivid threats, such as shark attacks, and underestimate the probability of common threats, such as power sockets.

KT – vividness bias: the bias that results from remembering vivid experiences and forgetting dull ones

5. Hindsight bias

KT – hindsight bias: the bias of being wise after the event and thinking that you knew something all along even though you didn't

As you may recall from our earlier discussion of cognitive biases (see page 215), **hindsight bias** refers to our tendency to be wise after the event – and adjust our memories accordingly. (We might call this the 'I knew it all along' bias.) Imagine, for example, discovering that an acquaintance is an only child, or a Scorpio, or has had plastic surgery. You might convince yourself that you had always suspected as much – even if you had not. Similarly, in the run-up to a presidential election your views about who will win may be equivocal; but after the result is announced, your selective memory may convince you that you correctly predicted the outcome: 'I just knew that Obama would win!' Social commentators and political pundits – who have a vested interest in being right – seem to have particularly compliant memories. After the fall of the Berlin Wall in 1989, and again after the banking crisis in 2008, many claimed that they had 'seen it coming'. However, they were strangely silent about these developments before they happened. As this suggests, there is a lot of truth in the observation that we are all very good at predicting the past!

ACTIVITY 10.9

1. How might selective memory contribute to someone being unduly optimistic about their chances of, for example, setting up a successful business or winning the lottery?
2. Using your own examples, explain how beliefs can contaminate memory. How might one try to prevent this happening?

6. Source amnesia

Source amnesia occurs when you misremember or completely forget the *source* of your knowledge. You may, for example, *think* you remember falling off your tricycle when you were three years old, when the real source of your memory is repeatedly being told about this incident by your parents. In the case of factual knowledge, source amnesia is the norm. This can be dangerous, as you may mistakenly think that you acquired information from a reputable source. For example, you might think that you read about the benefits of drinking red wine in a scientific journal when in fact it was hearsay passed on by friends. Source amnesia may be exploited by unscrupulous political leaders who have long known that if you repeat a memorable falsehood often enough many people will end up believing it!

ACTIVITY 10.10

To what extent does surfing the internet encourage source amnesia? What strategies might you use to try to combat it?

KT – unconscious plagiarism: unconsciously taking an idea, phrase or song from someone else while believing that you are its source

Source amnesia might also account for the phenomenon of **unconscious plagiarism**. This occurs when someone mistakenly believes that they came up with an idea, or turn of phrase or tune, when in reality they heard it somewhere else but have no memory of the source. A famous example of this concerns the ex-Beatle George

Harrison who was sued following claims that his 1970 single 'My Sweet Lord' plagiarised the Chiffons' 1962 hit 'He's So Fine', which was composed by Ronald Mack. In the ensuing legal battle, Harrison was ruled to have 'subconsciously copied' the earlier song.

ACTIVITY 10.11

How would you go about trying to determine whether an alleged case of plagiarism was deliberate or unconscious?

Eye-witness testimony

Eye-witness testimony plays a key role in academic studies such as history and in practical areas such as the criminal justice system. Since it is always given after the event, it is based as much on memory as on perception and for this reason its reliability is open to question. Unfortunately, the retrieval of memories can suffer from various kinds of interference which can retrospectively influence what we think we remember.

LQ – Sense perception: To what extent does memory inform our perceptions and expectations?

ACTIVITY 10.12

What criteria would you use to decide whether eye-witness testimony is a reliable source of evidence?

Four key sources of interference

1. Stereotyping

Your memory of people may be influenced by stereotypes related to things such as age, appearance, gender, ethnicity and occupation. For example, if you think of librarians as timid and introverted and athletes as loud and extroverted, you will tend to remember things that confirm these prejudices and forget things that don't. When eye-witness testimony is distorted by conscious or unconscious racial prejudice, stereotyping can have serious consequences. Indeed, it may help to explain why in many countries minorities account for a disproportionately large percentage of the prison population.

2. Misidentification

Another problem with eye-witness testimony is that witnesses can easily confuse a face they see in an identity parade with one they saw earlier at the scene of the crime. The confidence with which an eye-witness identifies a suspect is not a good predictor of accuracy. According to one study, confident witnesses tend to make more accurate identifications than unconfident ones, but they are still wrong about 30 per cent of the time. This suggests that, even if juries are impressed, the unsupported testimony of a single confident eye-witness does not meet the criterion of being 'beyond reasonable doubt'.

LQ – Imagination: How can we distinguish between memory and imagination?

"Well, I'm here to develop some false memories so I can forget about my own rotten past!"

Figure 10.8

3. Leading questions

The way that eye-witnesses are questioned can easily taint their memories and lead them to remember bogus details that were not in fact present at the scene of the crime. For example, if you ask someone to describe the scene of an accident, they are unlikely to mention a van if there wasn't one there. But if you ask, 'Did you see a van?', they may be tempted to say, 'Yes'; and the temptation increases if you replace 'an' with 'the' – 'Did you see *the* van?' – for this implies that a van *was* there and that they *should* have seen it.

4. Imagination inflation

According to a process known as imagination inflation, if you repeatedly imagine a past event, you can end up remembering something that never happened. The work of psychologist Elizabeth Loftus – one of the foremost experts on memory – suggests that it is easy to plant a false memory in someone's mind. In one well-known experiment, participants – all of whom had visited Disneyland™ as children – were exposed to a fake Disneyland advertisement featuring Bugs Bunny. When they were later asked if they remembered meeting Bugs Bunny at Disneyland and shaking his hand, more than a third said that they did. However, this is impossible: Bugs Bunny is a Warner Brothers creation and is not part of Disneyland!

KT – false memory syndrome: a deeply rooted false memory of an allegedly traumatic event which comes to dominate someone's personality

Loftus's research was motivated in part by a series of cases in the 1990s in which individuals, under the guidance of psychiatrists, claimed to have 'recovered' memories of being abused by their parents when they were children. Her work cast serious doubt on the credibility of some of these claims, not least because childhood memories are so easy to manipulate. While the topic remains controversial, it seems clear that at least some of these allegations were the result of what is known as **false memory syndrome**.

Figure 10.9 Bugs Bunny: can a false memory be planted in our minds?

ACTIVITY 10.13

1. Find out something about an alleged case of either (a) childhood abuse, or (b) alien abduction. What criteria would you use to try to judge whether the witness's memory of the events in question is reliable?
2. What special challenges arise when dealing with the eye-witness testimony of children? How, if at all, can such challenges be overcome?

Unreliable memories

Figure 10.10 Ronald Cotton and Bobby Poole: are our memories reliable?

The information in the previous section suggests that we would be unwise to uncritically accept the evidence of fallible eye-witnesses. Even in extreme and traumatic cases, there is room for doubt. Consider, for example, the case of Jennifer Thompson who was brutally raped at knifepoint in 1984 when she was an eighteen-year-old student in North Carolina. During her terrifying encounter, she concentrated on memorising the features on her attacker. Several weeks later, she picked out Ronald Cotton in an identity parade. Cotton was subsequently convicted of rape and sent to prison for life. The only problem was they got the wrong man. As Thompson ruefully observed, 'I was certain, but I was wrong.' As a result of her testimony, Cotton spent eleven years in prison for a crime he did not commit. He was finally released when DNA evidence proved that the actual rapist was a man called Bobby Poole. Amazingly, after Cotton was released, he and Thompson became friends and they wrote a book together about their ordeal called *Picking Cotton*.

We should also note that, since memory fades over time, people's recollections of distant events are usually less reliable than those of recent events. Together with the fact that supporting evidence tends to deteriorate or disappear, this explains why many countries put a limit on the length of time after a crime has been committed in which legal proceedings can be initiated. However, such *statutes of limitations* do not normally apply to the most serious crimes such as murder or genocide.

RLS – Headline: 'Spanish "memory law" reopens deep wounds of Franco era'. To what extent should a country dwell on dark episodes in its past?

Figure 10.11 Ronald Cotton and Jennifer Thompson

Despite its fallibility, it would be as foolish to reject all evidence based on memory as it would be to accept it. Admittedly, people often have different memories about the details of an event, but there is usually much more agreement about the basic facts of what happened. For example, while people's memories about the attack on the World Trade Center are certainly fallible, no one claims to remember that eight planes rather than four planes were hijacked, or that the White House was hit, or that the attacks took place in July rather than in September.

To summarise, here are four pieces of common-sense advice that are worth keeping in mind when assessing eye-witness testimony:

1. Consider the general reliability and honesty of the witnesses, and look at the coherence and plausibility of their stories.
2. Keep in mind that confidence is not a reliable indicator of truth and that memory is subject to the biases discussed above.
3. Look for areas of agreement between witnesses' memories. Such memories are more likely to be true when they confirm rather than contradict each other.
4. See how the subjective memories of witnesses stack up against 'hard evidence', such as contemporaneous reports, photographs, video footage and DNA traces.

ACTIVITY 10.14

1. What are the pros and cons of trying someone for war crimes they are alleged to have committed fifty years ago?
2. To what extent does being aware of the biases we have discussed help us to compensate for them and develop more accurate memories?

Memory and culture

LQ – Cultural perspectives: Do different cultures remember things in different ways?

Our discussion so far has focused on individual memory, but we should be aware that memory operates not only at the individual level, but also at the social level. Social memory is vital to the preservation and transmission of culture for it enables us to build on the achievements of our forebears so that we can cumulatively push back the frontiers of knowledge. A great deal of such knowledge is remembered and passed on in the form of language, but some techniques and practices may be passed on directly from master to apprentice. Moreover, it could be argued that the role of memory is different in oral, written and internet cultures.

Oral culture

In oral cultures, knowledge is limited to the collective memory of the group. This puts a serious limitation on the amount that can be known and it makes such knowledge very fragile. If the wisdom of the tribe is not committed to memory then it cannot be passed on to the next generation and will be permanently lost. Given this, oral societies tend to encode their knowledge in formulaic patterns, such

Figure 10.12 The epic 'hudhud' chants of the Ifugao people of the Philippines have been recited almost unchanged since the seventh century: how accurate is group memory in oral cultures?

as rhymes, proverbs and clichés, which are easy to memorise. They also tend to be cognitively conservative: for any experimentation or divergence from established ways of thinking puts the wisdom that has been accumulated over generations at risk. On the plus side, members of oral cultures are sometimes capable of prodigious feats of memory. Some scholars speculate that Homer's *Iliad* was originally an oral text which, despite being passed on by word of mouth from one storyteller to the next, was preserved with remarkable fidelity. Indeed, the story itself may have been composed centuries before it was first written down.

ACTIVITY 10.15

1. Take any proverbs and advertising jingles that you know and analyse the extent to which they are written in memorable language. What relevance does this have to our discussion?
2. 'Since it is easier to remember simple things than complex things, all thinking tends towards clichés and stereotypes.' Discuss.
3. What oral memories have been passed on from one generation to the next in your family, school or sports team? How would you go about trying to test the accuracy of such memories?
4. Imagine that we suddenly lost the ability to read and write and were unable to see words on paper as anything other than meaningless squiggles. How might schools function in such a situation?

Written culture

The emergence of writing in the third millennium BCE first made it possible to transfer memory to physical objects, such as clay tablets or rolls of papyrus. According to **great divide theories** the shift from oral to written culture, and the slow but steady rise of the latter, led to a fundamental change in the way people think. Since writing externalises ideas, supporters of this view claim that it leads to more abstract, detached, reflective patterns of thought. Moreover, once people are freed from the constraints imposed by memory, they may be more willing to speculate and question the traditions of the group. The invention of the printing press in the fifteenth century, which led to a dramatic increase in the number of books in circulation, encouraged the growth of written culture. But we should keep in mind that mass literacy – which is associated with the rise of compulsory education – is a relatively modern phenomenon. For most of human history, people's knowledge was limited to what they were personally able to remember.

KT – great divide theories: theories that claim that the shift from oral to written culture fundamentally changed the way people think

Internet culture

In our own era, it could be argued that digital technology is, once again, changing the way people think. As we saw in Chapter 3, since we can now access vast amounts of information at the touch of a button, we might wonder how much of it we should commit to our own memories and how much we can safely 'outsource' to computer memories – which are bigger, easier to access and less prone to corruption.

KT – Google effect (or Google amnesia): the tendency to forget information that can easily be found online

There is already evidence that the internet is affecting our memories. According to the so-called **Google effect**, we tend to forget information that can easily be found online. This may be a good thing, but since the brain operates on a 'use it or lose it' basis, some worry that it will weaken our overall ability to remember things. Others are more optimistic and see technology as a cognitive support which enhances rather than diminishes our faculties. For example, since mind-mapping programs make it easier for us to *organise* complex information, they may make it easier for us to *remember* it. If this is true, then the internet is leading not so much to a reduction as a reallocation of memory.

"David can't find anything without the Sat Nav these days."

Figure 10.13

One thing, however, is clear. The sheer quantity of information in the modern era means we have no choice but to store most of it in digital form. Unlike our ancestors who, relative to us, lived in a cognitively impoverished world, we can know – in the sense of have in mind – only a tiny fraction of all there is to know. The limits of human memory mean that, as individuals and societies, we have to make choices about what to preserve as 'living knowledge'. We can only guess which parts of contemporary culture will still be remembered and discussed in a thousand years' time.

ACTIVITY 10.16

1. Do you think that students today remember *fewer* things than students of previous generations, or do you think they simply remember *different* things?
2. 'The internet is no more of a threat to memory than writing is a threat to memory.' What can be said for and against this view?
3. 'The key thing we need to remember in the internet age is not information, but where to find information.' Do you agree or disagree?
4. What value, if any, is there in learning poetry by heart? Do you know a poem in a different way if you have committed it to memory rather than simply read it?
5. Which recent scientific, cultural or political developments do you think people in the year 2500 will remember, or ought to remember?

The ethics of memory

Since there is a difference between what we *actually* remember or forget, and what we *ought* to remember or forget, we conclude this chapter with a discussion about the ethics of memory.

Personal relationships

Shared memories are an ingredient in all personal relationships, and they play a particularly important role in cementing family ties and friendships. Such 'thick connections' carry obligations with them, in the sense that there are things we think friends and family *ought* to remember. For example, you would probably be upset if no one remembered your birthday, or if you were given the same gift two years running. Similarly, if you ever get married, you are likely to feel hurt if your partner forgets your wedding anniversary, for this implies that it – together with all that it symbolises – is not important to them. Most people also want to be remembered after they die – at least by their nearest and dearest – and they don't like the idea of being quickly forgotten.

LQ – Religion: To what extent do different religions encourage us to 'forgive and forget'?

While social relationships require the ability to remember, it could be argued that they also require the ability to forget. In past centuries, the chances were that a thoughtless insult uttered in a moment of anger would fade from memory and eventually be forgotten. However, in the internet age it is easy to retrieve an insulting email or text years after it was sent and relive the hurt in all its original intensity. There may be some wisdom in the advice that we should 'forgive and forget'; but it could be that in order to forgive you must first be able to forget, and in the brave new world of digital media this may become increasingly difficult.

Figure 10.14

LQ – Ethics: Is it always wrong to meddle with people's memories?

ACTIVITY 10.17

1. Would you feel more pleased if a friend remembered your birthday without being reminded by Facebook® or some other electronic device? What difference does it make?
2. A hundred years after your death, the chances are that no one will remember you. Is this a matter for concern or indifference?

Meddling with memory

"Sir, is the stuff we learn in this experiment supposed to go into our long or short term memory?"

Figure 10.15

Technological progress allied with our growing understanding of the brain is opening up the possibility that memory may one day be a matter of choice. Some people believe that we are on the verge of developing drugs that will enable us to eliminate specific unwanted memories. The benefits are obvious for people suffering from post-traumatic stress disorder, who are unable to rid themselves of traumatic memories. But where should we draw the line? What about erasing the memories of an embarrassing social *faux pas* you committed? If you split up with your partner, should you be able to erase your memory of them so that it is easier for you to move on? What would the implications of this be for personal identity? And what if a mad dictator started administering such drugs in order to rewrite not only history, but also individuals' memories? What if a memory pill enhanced your ability to *remember* things? Would it be legitimate to take such a pill in the run-up to your IB exams, or should it be treated in the same way that the International Olympic Committee treats performance-enhancing drugs? Such pills are still in the realm of speculation, but they raise many difficult ethical questions.

ACTIVITY 10.18

1. If you split up with your friend or partner, would you be tempted to digitally remove them from your holiday snapshots and group photos? (Some companies apparently offer this service!) Do you think there would be anything wrong in doing this?
2. If a pill were available that enabled you to erase some of your memories, what would be the pros and cons of taking such a pill?
3. If a pill was developed that could dramatically improve your memory in the run-up to the IB exams, should the IB allow you to use such a pill, or should they ban it?

The right to be forgotten

For most of human history, remembering was, as Viktor Mayer-Schönberger (1966–) observes, 'hard, time-consuming and costly' and forgetting was the easy option and therefore the norm. With the rapid advance of digital technology, this situation has been reversed. It is now so easy, quick and cheap to record, store and access information that remembering has rapidly become the new norm. In short, we have moved from a world of biological forgetting to one of digital remembering. This has many obvious advantages – indeed, it might seem like a dream come true. However, it also has troubling implications for our social relationships and it raises important questions about the right to be forgotten.

Before the digital revolution, if you did something stupid or embarrassing, more often than not it would quickly be forgotten. Now if someone captures your behaviour on video and posts it online, rather than fading away it may live on to haunt you forever. Sometimes people incriminate themselves by posting material online which they later regret, but it is important to be aware that every day a huge amount of data about you is collected without your knowledge. Every message you post and website you visit is potentially traceable. Some observers worry that if we know that everything we write online could potentially be found and used in evidence against us, we might engage in a form of self-censorship.

Figure 10.16

ACTIVITY 10.19

1. Do you ever worry that embarrassing photos or video clips that you feature in, which you or your friends have uploaded to the internet, will escape your control and live on to permanently haunt you?
2. Do you think that in the internet age people have 'the right to be forgotten' – that is, the right to demand that personal information about them be removed from websites and databases?

The politics of memory

Memory is a social as well as a personal phenomenon, and past events and national heroes are kept alive in historical memory through such reminders as monuments, memorials, museums, bank notes and street names. Many countries also set aside special days to commemorate national victories or tragedies, for example Bastille Day in France (14 July), Independence Day in the USA (4 July) and Hiroshima Day in Japan (6 August). Such events become part of a shared story which helps to forge a sense of national identity and define 'who we are as a people'. In this sense, historical memory plays a similar role in a country to the role personal memory does in an individual. However, 'historical memory' is not quite the same thing as history. History is an academic discipline which is based on evidence and argument; historical memory, by contrast, can easily blur into national mythology – which brings obvious dangers with it.

RLS – Headline: 'The woman who can remember everything'. What would be the advantages and disadvantages of having a perfect memory?

ACTIVITY 10.20

1. Give some examples from your own country of how national heroes and events are kept alive in historical memory. In what way, if any, does this contribute to a sense of national identity?
2. What role do the news media play in shaping our collective memory of events? How, if at all, can they distort such memories?

A key topic in the ethics of memory concerns how a country should come to terms with dark periods in its past, such as civil wars, human rights abuses and genocides. Among the countries that have had to confront this question in recent decades are Spain, Argentina, Cambodia, South Africa, Chile, Rwanda and Iraq. On the one hand, justice would seem to demand that the perpetrators of atrocities are brought to account and that we continue to remember the victims of such crimes. On the other hand, it could be argued that opening up old wounds does more harm than good and that if a country is to move forward it needs to put the past behind it. We may hope that keeping the memory of terrible events alive can bring about accountability and reconciliation – as well as serve as a salutary warning; but we may also fear that it will lead to instability and vengeance – and simply perpetuate a sense of grievance.

While we would need to look at the specific circumstances surrounding each situation, some philosophers argue that the real question is not so much *whether* we should remember as *how* we should remember. We should, at least, try to remember truthfully and in a way that transcends our partisan prejudices. Allowing that certain events should be remembered, we might also ask *who* should do the remembering and for *how long*. Hiroshima Day, mentioned above, is commemorated not only in Japan but also by anti-war and anti-nuclear activists around the world. In 2007, the United Nations designated 27 January as International Holocaust Remembrance Day. This was the day in 1945 when the Soviet army liberated Auschwitz–Birkenau, which was the largest Nazi death camp. Since the Holocaust was perhaps the worst – but, sadly, by no means the only – genocide in history, perhaps this date should be etched permanently on human memory.

ACTIVITY 10.21

1. How long into the future do you think the events of 11 September 2001 should be officially commemorated by the US government?
2. Do you think it is better for countries to face up to shameful incidents in their past, or is it better for them to put such incidents behind them? Illustrate your answer with specific examples.

Conclusion

One of the key points to learn from this chapter is that our memories are not as reliable as we like to think, and we have explored the problems that arise from our tendency to forget and misremember things. However, forgetting does have benefits as well as drawbacks. For example, we sometimes need to forget negative experiences in order to move on with our lives, and this may be good for our mental health and social relationships. Moreover, forgetting enables us to eliminate irrelevant or out-of-date information that is no longer useful. In fact, a perfect memory might be more of a curse than a blessing. If we never forgot anything, we might be so dazzled by the uniqueness of things that we would be unable to see the similarities between them. We would then be unable to generalise and we would experience a kind of mental gridlock. Forgetting details does, of course, lead to inaccuracies, but perhaps inaccuracy is the price we must pay for usefulness.

We have seen that even when people are very confident about what they claim to remember, they sometimes turn out to be wrong. Nevertheless, if we are to have *any* connection with the past, we have to believe that our memories do not *systematically* deceive us. To question your memory in its entirety and take seriously the possibility that it is a complete fiction amounts to questioning your sanity. Such radical scepticism can neither be lived nor justified.

As is often the case in Theory of Knowledge, we need to steer a middle course between blind trust and blanket scepticism. Our memories are likely to be flawed, but when it comes to knowledge of the past, they are the only thing that is available to us. We must hope that, in conjunction with other ways of knowing, they can help us to establish – or at least bring us closer to – the truth.

ACTIVITY 10.22

With reference to any novel or movie of your choice, discuss what light literature can throw on the nature of memory.

Key points

- Although memory is not an original source of knowledge, there is a sense in which all knowledge depends on it.
- Short-term memory plays a key role in understanding, and judgement benefits from a well-stocked long-term memory.
- The consensus view among psychologists is that, rather than being accurate and immutable, our memories are fallible and changeable.
- Since problems can arise with the encoding, storage and retrieval of memories, forgetting and misremembering are probably the norm rather than the exception.
- Personal memory seems to be unique to human beings and it is what gives us our sense of identity as individuals, but it can be distorted by various biases.
- Eye-witness testimony is notoriously unreliable, and witnesses may even claim to remember things that never happened.
- Factual memory can be affected by source amnesia and cognitive distortions such as vividness bias and hindsight bias.
- Practical memory is our memory of skills, and it could be argued that it is the foundation for all of our knowledge.
- In the internet era, so much information is instantly accessible online that we may wonder what is worth committing to memory.
- In discussing memory, we need to consider not only what we *do* remember, but also what we *ought to* remember.

Key terms

factual memory

false memory syndrome

Google effect

great divide theories

hindsight bias

nostalgia

personal memory

practical memory

short-term memory

unconscious plagiarism

vividness bias

Possible essay titles

1. Explore the knowledge issues raised by the fallibility of memory in two areas of knowledge.
2. 'All knowledge ultimately depends on memory.' Assess this claim. Does it follow that memory is the most important way of knowing?

Further reading

Books

Carol Tavris and Elliot Aronson, *Mistakes Were Made (But Not By Me)* (Pinter & Martin 2008). Chapter 3: 'Memory, the Self-Justifying Historian'. The title says it all. Tavris and Aronson, two well-known psychologists, dispassionately survey the evidence for the self-serving nature of many of our memories.

Viktor Mayer-Schönberger, *Delete: The Virtue of Forgetting in the Digital Age* (Princeton University Press, 2011). The author argues that the near-perfect digital memory of the modern era creates as many problems as it solves and that we need to rediscover the art of forgetting.

Online articles

William Saletan, 'The Memory Doctor', *Slate*, 4 June 2010.

Alexander Bloom, 'How the Web Affects Memory', *Harvard Magazine*, November–December 2011.

Faith

11

Reason is itself a matter of faith. It is an act of faith to assert that our thoughts have any relation to reality at all.

G. K. Chesterton, 1874–1936

Absolute faith corrupts as absolutely as absolute power.

Eric Hoffer, 1902–83

Science as a substitute for religion, and reason as a substitute for faith, have always fallen to pieces.

Miguel de Unamuno, 1864–1936

Reason's last step is the recognition that there are an infinite number of things which are beyond it. It is merely feeble if it does not go as far as to realise that.

Blaise Pascal, 1623–62

Faith: not wanting to know what is true.

Friedrich Nietzsche, 1844–1900

The light of faith makes us see what we believe.

St Thomas Aquinas, 1225–74

I have . . . found it necessary to deny knowledge in order to make room for faith.

Immanuel Kant, 1724–1804

No person is certain, apart from faith, whether he is awake or asleep...

Blaise Pascal, 1623–62

Religion is a culture of faith; science is a culture of doubt.

Richard Feynman, 1918–88

Doubt isn't the opposite of faith – it is an element of faith.

Paul Tillich, 1886–1965

It is wrong always, everywhere, and for anyone, to believe anything upon insufficient evidence.

W. K. Clifford, 1845–79

And all shall be well, and all manner of thing shall be well.

Dame Julian of Norwich, c.1342–1416

Introduction

Faith is a hot button concept. Some people think it is obvious that faith is an important source of knowledge; other people see it as equally obvious that it is not. Some people claim that faith complements and completes reason; other people insist that it contradicts and corrupts it. Some people embrace and respect beliefs that are based on faith; other people reject and ridicule them. One of the aims of this chapter is to diminish the heat surrounding this perplexing concept and shed light on the role it plays in our understanding of the world.

When people speak of faith they typically have in mind *religious* faith. Despite the close link between faith and religion, it is worth noting that one can reject faith as a source of knowledge while accepting religion as an area of knowledge. One could, for example, claim that belief in God is based on evidence and arguments rather than on faith. You should also take seriously the possibility that faith is relevant to areas of knowledge apart from religion.

This chapter begins with a preliminary look at the nature of faith. We then examine various theories which seek to justify faith as a source of knowledge and focus in particular on the relation between faith and reason. Whether or not you are religious, it could be argued that faith is inescapable in the sense that we all have faith in something. We evaluate this claim by looking at the role played by faith in the foundations of knowledge, the goals we pursue, and our relations with others. The chapter concludes with a discussion about the ethics of belief and the relation between faith and happiness.

ACTIVITY 11.1

1. To explore how we intuitively distinguish between reason and faith, consider the following statements. Which would you describe as matters of belief and which would you describe as matters of faith?
   a. 'I will complete my extended essay by the deadline.'
   b. 'There is no life after death.'
   c. 'São Paulo is the largest city in Brazil.'
   d. 'Love will triumph in the end.'
   e. 'Science will eventually solve the problems confronting humanity.'
   f. 'Democracy is the best system of government.'
   g. 'Human beings evolved from apes.'
   h. 'The BBC is a reliable source of information.'

i. 'The sun will rise tomorrow.'

j. 'Neil Armstrong was the first person on the moon.'

k. 'Intelligence is equally distributed between races.'

l. 'We can achieve enlightenment by following the teachings of Buddha.'

m. 'Human beings are capable of knowing the truth.'

n. 'Prayer works.'

o. 'Barcelona Football Club will win the Champions' League.'

2. What does the above exercise suggest to you about the difference between reason and faith?
3. Do other languages you are familiar with distinguish between 'belief' and 'faith', or do some use the same word for both concepts?
4. Does faith concern only religion, or is it also relevant to other areas of knowledge?

LQ – Language: Is it possible to give a neutral definition of faith that everyone can agree upon?

What is faith?

KT – atheism: the belief that God does not exist (some religions, such as Buddhism, are atheistic)

KT – worldview: an overarching theory about the nature of the universe and human beings' place in it

The word 'faith' is a contested concept which is difficult to define or characterise in a neutral way. A believer may understand it as a self-validating divine revelation, an **atheist** as an unjustified belief based on insufficient evidence. More generally, it is often used as a synonym for 'trust'. Rather than attempt to give a precise definition, we will distinguish three key elements of faith:

- a cognitive element
- an emotional element
- and an ethical element.

Cognitive element

Faith is commonly thought of as a subset of belief. You may, for example, have faith in the truth of various propositions, such as a religious creed, or ethical ideal, or political doctrine. Indeed, your faith may be so strong that you claim to know these things. However, while faith is a form of belief, many beliefs do not involve faith. I may believe that Donald Trump is arrogant, or that astrology is bunk or that house prices will rise, but such beliefs seem too trivial to merit the label 'faith'. We are more likely to use the word 'faith' to describe deeply held convictions. You might, for example, say, 'I have faith in the immortality of the soul', or 'I have faith that human beings are fundamentally good', or 'I have faith in democracy'. As this suggests, the word 'faith' is closely connected with a **worldview** – that is, a set of beliefs about the fundamental nature of reality and our place in it.

"Unfortunately, my holding on to tech. stocks was faith-based."

Figure 11.1

The relation between faith and evidence is controversial, but most people would agree that faith goes beyond evidence. Indeed, there seems to be a tension between the two which does not exist in the case of belief. If you believe something but are not sure, you can strengthen your belief by seeking further evidence. But if you seek evidence for something in which you have faith, there is a sense in which you *weaken* your faith. If you have faith in your partner's fidelity, you do not hire a private investigator to follow them. To do so is to show that you do not have faith in them at all. Somewhat paradoxically, this has led some people to claim that the weaker the evidence the greater – and more noble – the faith.

LQ – Emotion: What role does emotion play in faith?

Emotional element

Faith differs from many other beliefs in that it implies an emotional commitment. If you have faith in something, it is more likely to shape the pattern of your behaviour than if you merely believe in it. Moreover, you are likely to stick with it even when the going gets tough. You may, for example, keep faith in democracy even when you think that voters have elected the wrong person as president. At the limit, some people are even willing to die for their faith.

Since faith goes beyond the evidence, it involves risk and requires what is sometimes called a *leap of faith*. While faith lacks objective certainty, opinions differ about its subjective certainty. Some think of faith as an unwavering commitment; others say that doubt is a natural – and even welcome – element of faith.

Figure 11.2 Mother Teresa

ACTIVITY 11.2

1. Can you believe something intellectually without believing it emotionally? Can you believe something emotionally without believing it intellectually? Give examples.
2. Do emotions have a greater influence on religious beliefs than on non-religious beliefs? Should they?
3. Does faith imply certainty, or is doubt a key element of faith? If the former, how can we prevent faith being dogmatic? If the latter, how can we prevent it collapsing into mere belief?
4. Are there any beliefs you have for which you would be willing to die? Does the willingness to die for a belief have any bearing on its truth?

RLS – Headline: 'Mother Teresa's 40-year faith crisis'. Does faith require certainty or is it consistent with doubt?

Figure 11.3 Does 'faith' mean different things in different cultures?

Ethical element

Faith has an important ethical dimension and it carries with it the idea that things will work out for the best. Faith resembles hope in that it is usually oriented towards the future and is usually positive. For example, we might say we have faith that someone *will* recover from an illness, but not that they *won't* recover. However, while you can hope that something will happen without believing that it will happen, if you have faith that it will happen, you both hope and believe. We might therefore describe faith as *confident* hope.

Faith is also related to trust. Indeed, some people argue that faith is essentially a relationship of trust rather than a hypothesis about reality. Certainly, having faith *in* someone seems to be different from having faith *that* something is the case. You may, for example, have faith in your parents in the sense that you trust that they have your interests at heart, even when this is not readily apparent. However, faith *in* cannot be entirely divorced from faith *that*, if it is to have any meaningful content. Minimally, you cannot have faith *in* someone unless you believe *that* they exist; and if you have faith *in* your parents you probably have faith *that* they will be there when you really need them. Nevertheless, it may be difficult to capture such faith in a creed or a list of bullet points.

The evidentialist challenge

A key issue in any discussion of faith concerns the relation between faith and reason. While some people think that faith is rational and qualifies as a respectable source of knowledge, other people argue that it is irrational and is not a source of knowledge at all. As a reference point for our discussion, let us consider a position known as **evidentialism**. According to this view, if a belief is to count as rational, then it must be supported by adequate evidence. Moreover, the strength of a belief should be proportional to the strength of the evidence for it. The British philosopher–mathematician W. K. Clifford (1845–79), who popularised this view, held that: 'It is wrong always, everywhere, and for anyone to believe anything upon insufficient evidence.' In Clifford's view, evidentialism is the cornerstone not only of rationality but also of intellectual integrity.

KT – evidentialism: the idea that we should believe something only to the extent that there is evidence for it

Evidentialism may strike you as common sense. If, for example, you are trying to establish whether Oscar Pistorius intended to kill his girlfriend Reeva Steenkamp in the famous murder trial in 2013, it seems obvious that you should base your belief on the evidence. This is the normal procedure not only in criminal trials, but also in almost every area of knowledge – such as physics, economics, and history. Indeed, evidentialism really amounts to the view that we should *justify* our beliefs and it would therefore seem to be implicit in the standard definition of knowledge as justified true belief.

RLS – Headline: 'Faith healer sought medical help for own cancer'. Is it wrong to believe things on insufficient evidence?

Given our earlier description of faith, it is not surprising that most evidentialists reject faith as a possible source of knowledge. Their argument against it can be laid out as follows:

1. It is irrational to believe something on insufficient evidence.
2. Faith is belief based on insufficient evidence.
3. Therefore faith is irrational.

A group of thinkers known as the New Atheists gleefully endorse the above conclusion and are scathing about knowledge claims based on faith. For example, Christopher Hitchens (1949–2011) dismisses faith with the words: 'That which can be asserted without evidence can be dismissed without evidence.' In a similar vein, Richard Dawkins (1941–) argues that people only appeal to faith when they cannot find any evidence to support the things they want to believe in.

Some complications

Despite its intuitive appeal, evidentialism is not as straightforward as it seems. Among the critical questions we might ask are:

1. *What counts as evidence?* Different people may have different views about what counts as evidence. For example, some people count mystical feelings, miracles and sacred texts as preliminary evidence for the existence of God while others insist that we should limit ourselves to objective scientific evidence.
2. *How much evidence is sufficient?* Evidence is rarely conclusive and opinions may differ about what counts as sufficient evidence for a belief and at what point you should abandon a belief in the face of mounting counter-evidence.

Figure 11.4

3. *How should we interpret the evidence?* Evidence does not always speak for itself and it may be open to different interpretations. Just as different people may see one and the same picture as a duck or a rabbit, so a believer and a non-believer may interpret the evidence in different ways.

KT – burden of proof: the question of whether a knowledge claim should be rejected unless there is evidence for it, or accepted unless there is evidence against it, and who should provide that evidence

4. *Who has the burden of proof?* **Burden of proof** concerns the question of who has the obligation to produce evidence. As regards faith, the question is whether a believer should provide evidence for the truth of their belief, or a non-believer should provide evidence for its falsity. Different people have different opinions about this issue.

5. *Why accept evidentialism?* Although the evidentialist principle that the strength of a belief should be proportional to the evidence for it is intuitively appealing, we might ask why we should *always* adhere to it. Some people argue that in areas such as religion it is not appropriate and that faith is precisely a conviction that goes beyond the evidence.

With the above points in mind, a religious believer might make a preliminary response to the New Atheists' challenge to faith by insisting that there is evidence, such as divine revelation, to support faith. Furthermore, they might insist that it requires as much faith to deny the existence of God as it does to assert it.

ACTIVITY 11.3

1. 'It is always and everywhere wrong to believe things on insufficient evidence.' Do you agree or disagree with this statement? Give reasons.
2. If people disagree about what counts as evidence, is there any way the dispute can be resolved?
3. 'Extraordinary claims require extraordinary evidence' (Carl Sagan, 1934–96). How useful is this as a criterion for determining the burden of proof?

LQ – Reason: Is faith best described as rational, irrational or arational?

Defending religious faith: three options

Religious faith is typically faith in the truth of some kind of divine revelation which is directly based on personal experience or indirectly based on the authority of a religious text. There are at least three ways in which one might seek to defend such faith against the challenge of evidentialism:

1. *Compatibilism: faith is rational.* Compatibilism rejects premise 2 of the evidentialist argument against faith and holds that faith and reason are compatible with one another.
2. *Fideism: faith is irrational.* Fideism accepts the conclusion of the evidentialist argument against faith, but insists that faith is superior rather than inferior to reason.

3. *Separate domains: faith is arational.* The separate domains theory rejects premise 1 of the evidentialist argument against faith and claims that faith is neither rational nor irrational, but *beyond* reason.

ACTIVITY 11.4

1. Do you think that faith is rational or irrational? To what extent does your answer depend on the way you define reason?
2. If faith conflicts with reason, do you think it should be rejected as a source of knowledge?

Compatibilism: faith is rational

According to compatibilism, faith and reason are both God-given faculties and are compatible with one another. We briefly look at two versions of compatibilism:

1. the divine sense theory
2. the rational faith theory.

Divine sense theory

According to the *divine sense theory*, faith is an independent faculty which gives us knowledge in much the same way as sense perception gives us knowledge. Just as our eyes enable us to see that there is, say, an apple on the table, so, it is claimed, our divine sense enables us to sense the presence of God. According to this view, we sense God's presence as directly and immediately as we see the external world, and we do not need to give any further arguments to support either of these beliefs. Of course, some people are unaware of God, but this is easily explained. Just as you may not see the apple in front of you if your eyesight is defective, so you may not sense God if your divine sense is defective. This theory, then, claims that it is just as rational to base your belief in God on your divine sense as it is to base your belief in the external world on your sense perception.

ACTIVITY 11.5

'Just as a colour-blind person is unable to see red, so a person with a defective divine sense is unable to see God.' Assess the strengths and weaknesses of this analogy.

Possible criticisms

1. *The theory is based on a false analogy.* Critics of the divine sense theory claim that it commits the *fallacy* of false analogy (see page 157), and that there is a huge difference between sense perception and the alleged divine sense. In particular, no one questions the existence of sense perception – for if you consistently rejected it as a source of knowledge you would be unable to survive. By contrast, many people deny that we have a divine sense, and they seem to function perfectly well without it.

2. *The theory cannot explain the distribution of belief.* The divine sense theory seems unable to explain why the divine sense operates more strongly in some countries than in others. For example, according to a 2005 survey 95 per cent of people claim to believe in God in Turkey while only 23 per cent of people do in Sweden. This suggests that people's beliefs are shaped by their cultural background rather than by a universal divine sense.

3. *Postulating a divine sense seems arbitrary.* If we allow that a divine sense is needed to detect the existence of God, there is nothing to stop us postulating all kinds of other non-standard senses. We might, for example, suggest an alien sense for detecting extra-terrestrials, a voodoo sense for detecting evil spirits, and an astrological sense for detecting planetary influences. What seems to be lacking in the divine sense theory is independent evidence in support of its existence.

LQ – Cultural perspectives: How does the concept of faith differ in eastern and western religions?

ACTIVITY 11.6

Where do you think the burden of proof lies when it comes to evaluating the divine sense theory? Does it lie with the believer to show that we do have a divine sense, or with the sceptic to show that we do not? Give reasons.

Rational faith theory

According to the rational faith theory, what is grasped by faith can be supported by evidence and argument based on ordinary experience. For example, a person's faith in the existence of God may be derived from the authority of a sacred text and at the same time be supported by various philosophical arguments (we will explore some of these in Chapter 18). Just as you might claim to know the truth of Pythagoras' Theorem either by authority or by working it out yourself, so faith and reason can be thought of as two different ways of arriving at the truth. Any apparent conflict between them is due either to an improper appeal to faith or to unsound reasoning about the natural world. Interestingly, Pope John Paul ll (1920–2005) argued that faith and reason not only support one another but also keep one another in check: 'Faith without reason leads to superstition' – for example, believing in a lucky charm, or a personal ritual, or a false prophet. On the other hand, 'reason without faith leads to relativism' because, he claimed, we cannot be certain of anything on the basis of reason alone.

Possible criticisms

1. *Why is faith required at all?* If, as compatibilists claim, there are arguments in favour of religious belief, one might wonder why one needs to appeal to faith at all, for it would seem to drop out of the picture as irrelevant. In response, it could be argued that reason prepares the way for faith by providing arguments for the existence of God which at least make the idea of divine revelation plausible.

2. *Does reason support faith?* The rational faith theory depends crucially on the claim that faith is supported by reason, but atheists are unconvinced by the various arguments for the existence of God.

Fideism: faith is irrational

KT – fideism: the belief that faith is opposed and superior to reason

According to **fideism**, faith is opposed to, and superior to, reason and we must rely on the former rather than the latter in seeking religious truth. Faith does not give objective certainty but involves risk and requires us to make a 'leap of faith'. At the limit, fideists claim that religious beliefs can be justified by faith even if they seem absurd to reason. Since God is literally incomprehensible, he lies beyond reason, and our excessive confidence in reason is the result of our pride and our unwillingness to accept that we are finite beings with limited intellects.

Some fideists go further and argue that *all* of our beliefs are ultimately based on faith. We must, for example, have faith that our senses are not systematically deceiving us, and that whatever strikes us as obvious really is obvious. This would seem to establish the credibility of faith as a possible source of knowledge; and if it can be used as a basis for our fundamental beliefs about reality, then it can surely also be used as a basis for our fundamental religious beliefs.

Possible criticisms

1. *Fideism is too permissive.* A major problem with fideism is that it seems to be overly permissive and allow anyone to claim to know anything on the basis of faith. In practice, almost no one is willing to accept this, and the wilder claims of personal faith are usually kept in check by the discipline of a religious tradition. In the Catholic tradition, for example, visions of the Virgin Mary are only accepted as genuine if they correspond with the teachings of the Church.

2. *Faith in what?* Although fideism urges us to leave reason behind and make a leap of faith into religious belief, it appears to give us no guidance on the *direction* of the proposed leap. This is a problem in a world in which there are many different religions, for it seems to leave us with the question of whether I should have faith in, say, Islam, or Buddhism, or Christianity. It would seem that the only justification for choosing one rather than another is tradition, but for some people this seems unsatisfactorily arbitrary.

"Yes, but you were the defender of the wrong faith."

Figure 11.5

ACTIVITY 11.7

1. Can you have faith in something self-contradictory, or must the object of one's faith be minimally rational in the sense of conforming to the laws of logic?
2. To what extent does the fact that human reason is flawed and biased provide indirect support for fideism?
3. Do you think that religious faith is more a form of personal knowledge based on individual experience or shared knowledge based on tradition?
4. How do any religions with which you are familiar attempt to distinguish between divinely inspired and delusional faith?

Separate domains: faith is arational

One popular way of resolving the alleged conflict between faith and reason is to claim that each is appropriate to a different domain of enquiry and that both play a role in our attempt to understand reality. While reason is relevant to facts and theories about the natural world, faith deals with questions of ultimate meaning and moral values which lie beyond the reach of empirical enquiry. Scientific reason can shed light on the mechanics of the world, but it has no authority over ultimate questions such as 'What is the meaning of life?' or 'Why does anything exist?' Similarly, while religious faith may tell us about the meaning of life, it cannot tell us about how the world works.

According to this view, conflict only arises when one domain trespasses on the territory of the other. For example, when science pontificates about values by trying to conjure them out of evolutionary theory it falls into **scientism** – the dogmatic assumption that it alone can answer all meaningful questions. And when religion makes pronouncements about the natural world – for example, by trying to compute the age of the earth from dubious Biblical genealogies – it falls into **superstition**.

KT – scientism: the belief that knowledge can be achieved only through the use of the scientific method

KT – superstition: a form of false science based on an irrational belief in supernatural connections between things

One of the attractions of the separate domains theory is that it recognises there is no one method appropriate to all areas of knowledge. Just as we do not appeal to proof in history, or eye-witness testimony in mathematics, so perhaps we should not appeal to faith in science or empirical evidence in religion.

Possible criticisms

1. *Most religions make claims about the natural world.* The idea of separate domains may be appealing in theory, but in practice many religions make claims about the natural world which contradict science. For example, they may believe in the existence of miracles which are by definition 'unscientific', or they may reject the theory of evolution.
2. *Meaning and values need not be based on faith.* While we might agree that questions of meaning and value lie beyond the scope of scientific reason, it does not follow that they should be ceded to religion. We might instead appeal to philosophy to shed light on them. In practice, many people's values are based on their belief in human rights and the promotion of the general good and they seem to have no need for religion.

ACTIVITY 11.8

1. On the separate domains account, which of the following knowledge claims concern the natural world and which concern the realm of meaning and values?
   a. God created the world around 6,000 years ago.
   b. The soul is immortal.
   c. God is the source of all values.
   d. Sick people can be cured by prayer.
   e. Jesus rose from the dead.
   f. The Buddha achieved enlightenment.
   g. Hurricane Katrina was God's way of punishing a sinful nation.
   h. The Koran was dictated to the prophet Muhammad by the archangel Gabriel.
   i. God is love.
   j. The dead sometimes communicate with the living.
2. 'I suspect that alleged miracles provide the strongest reason many believers have for their faith' (Richard Dawkins). Is this the main reason why you, or people you know, are religious?
3. If science can tell us nothing about meaning and values, is our only alternative to look to religion for guidance?

Faith and interpretation

Some philosophers argue that, rather than seeing religion on the model of a scientific hypothesis, we should instead see it on the model of a literary interpretation. Just as people might have different and equally valid interpretations of, say, a poem, so, it is claimed, they might have diametrically opposed – but equally plausible – interpretations of reality as a whole. A religious person and an atheist 'see' the same facts, but they give different interpretations of them. The former sees the fingerprints of God on everything; the latter sees only a blind mechanical universe.

Generalising, we might claim that *all* **metaphysical questions** (questions concerning the nature of ultimate reality) are matters of interpretation which cannot be answered by any straightforward appeal to empirical evidence. The fact that equally intelligent and well-informed individuals have come to different conclusions about questions such as 'Does God exist?', 'Is the soul immortal?' and 'Do human beings have free will?' would appear to support this view. With this in mind, it could be argued that when it comes to such 'big questions' we are justified – indeed obliged – to appeal to faith to decide what to believe. This implies that it requires as much faith to answer such questions in the negative as in the affirmative and that *any* worldview – be it theistic or atheistic – is ultimately based on faith.

KT – metaphysical questions: questions about the nature of ultimate reality which cannot be solved by matters relating to observation and experience

Good and bad interpretations

Bad interpretations: an example

The idea that faith is primarily faith in an interpretation is an interesting one, but it raises the question of how, if at all, we can distinguish between good and bad interpretations. For not all interpretations that are nominally consistent with the evidence strike us as plausible. Consider the following example. In 1857 – two years before Charles Darwin published *On the Origin of Species* – a Christian called Philip Henry Gosse published a book in which he put forward the so-called 'Omphalos Hypothesis'. Gosse's aim was to reconcile the Biblical view that the earth is about 6,000 years old with the evidence from geology and the fossil record that it is hundreds of millions of years old. He did this by the simple expedient of claiming that God did create the universe 6,000 years ago but gave it the appearance of age by creating layers of rock that seem to be millions of years old and putting fossils in them. God allegedly did something similar when he created Adam with a navel; for this gave the illusion that Adam was born even though he was the first human being and so had no mother. ('Omphalos' is Greek for navel.) Why God would deceive us about the age of the earth Gosse does not tell us, but from a purely logical point of view his argument is entirely consistent with the evidence. Indeed no evidence could refute it. Had Gosse known about the evidence from cosmology which supports the view that the universe is 13.7 billion years old, he doubtless would have insisted that it was in fact created 6,000 years ago with the *appearance* of being 13.7 billion years old.

Although it is consistent with the evidence, something is clearly wrong with the Omphalos Hypothesis. After all, if we followed Gosse's logic we could, as one satirist has pointed out, establish a new religious sect called the Church of Last Thursday. According to Last Thursdayism, God created the universe last Thursday together with all the evidence which suggests that it is billions of years old. One could further imagine a heretical sect emerging from Last Thursdayism called Last Fridayism according to which God created the universe last Friday rather than last Thursday. These interpretations may be consistent with the evidence, but they strike us as bizarre and not to be taken seriously.

Some criteria for good interpretations

If we dismiss beliefs such as Last Thursdayism as irrational, we clearly need some way of distinguishing between reasonable and unreasonable interpretations. Among the most commonly mentioned criteria are the following:

- *Factual adequacy*: a good interpretation is consistent with the known facts and is able to account for them.
- *Internal consistency*: a good interpretation is internally consistent and does not contradict itself.
- *Theoretical fruitfulness*: a good interpretation suggests new insights about, and ways of looking at, the phenomena in question.
- *Simplicity*: a good interpretation explains the phenomena as simply as possible and avoids needless complications.
- *Comparative advantage*: a good interpretation will satisfy all of the above criteria better than any rivals in the field.

While the above criteria may be helpful, we still need judgement to apply them. For example, opinions may differ about what constitutes simplicity. Some people believe that the God hypothesis is the simplest overall explanation for the existence of the universe and such mysterious phenomena as consciousness, meaning and value; others think that it is an unnecessary complication which explains nothing and merely adds to the mystery. Given these conflicting views, we might charitably conclude that the evidence is ambiguous and open to different and equally reasonable interpretations.

What room for faith?

We might think that when the evidence for a belief is ambiguous, the best solution is to suspend judgement and remain **agnostic**. However, the American philosopher William James (1842–1910) argued that when it comes to religious questions we cannot simply sit on the fence and refuse to commit ourselves. This is because sitting on the fence amounts to deciding *not* to make a religious commitment. To put it paradoxically, we can say that not to decide is simply another way of deciding. So one way or another, we are obliged to make a leap of faith. Moreover, once we have made such a leap, we may see the world in an entirely different way and begin to notice evidence in support of our faith to which we were previously blind. This idea is common among religious thinkers around the world and you can find many versions of the claim that *we do not so much see in order to believe as believe in order to see.* The point, in short, is that faith may eventually generate its own justification.

KT – agnosticism: the belief that we cannot know whether or not God exists

This view of faith has been influential, but it depends crucially on the assumption that the religious and the non-religious interpretation of reality are equally plausible. Against this, believers and atheists might both insist that, far from being ambiguous, the evidence is in fact weighted in favour of their own view. Trying to find middle ground between these two positions might not be easy if, as was suggested above, the evidence for an interpretation is only apparent to those who already have faith in it. This may explain why so many conversations between believers and non-believers turn out to be 'dialogues of the deaf'.

ACTIVITY 11.9

1. Do you think the evidence for and against a religious interpretation of the world is equally balanced? If so, does this justify appealing to faith in deciding what to believe?
2. Do you agree or disagree that it requires as much faith to deny the existence of God as it does to assert the existence of God?

Is faith inescapable?

So far, the focus in this chapter has been mainly on *religious* faith; but some people claim that whether or not you are religious there is a sense in which faith is inescapable and that *everyone has faith in something*. This claim could be taken to mean that we all have one or more of the following:

1. *Faith in foundations*: faith in the philosophical, scientific or moral foundations on which all of our beliefs are based.
2. *Faith in ends*: faith in the ends we pursue, which gives meaning and purpose to our lives.
3. *Faith in others*: faith in other people, which is crucial for any kind of social or intellectual cooperation.

In this section, we consider each of these possibilities in turn.

Faith in foundations

Philosophical foundations

Some philosophers argue that there is a sense in which *all* of our beliefs are ultimately based on faith. We must, for example, have faith that our senses are not systematically deceiving us and that whatever may appear to us as obvious really is obvious. If we try to *prove* the reliability of sense perception and reason, we can only appeal to those faculties themselves; but we are then arguing in a circle and assuming what we are trying to prove. We cannot prove the reliability of perception by appealing to perception, or the reliability of reason by appealing to reason. So we must simply have faith that they are generally reliable. (This is not, of course, to deny that they may sometimes let us down.)

KT – infinite regress: a chain of reasoning in which statement A depends on statement B, statement B depends on statement C, and so on without end

KT – bedrock belief: a fundamental assumption on which all of our other beliefs are based

A similar problem arises if we claim that *all* beliefs should be based on evidence. If we push this claim to the limits, it leads to an **infinite regress**. For not only do we have to give evidence for our beliefs, but we have to give evidence for our evidence, and evidence for *that* evidence, and so on. In practice, if you keep asking someone 'How do you know?', they eventually run out of reasons and hit bedrock. Among the **bedrock beliefs** that we might claim are based on faith are the following:

1. *Belief in reality.* Since everything you experience is consistent with your being in a vast and extravagant dream, your belief that you are in touch with reality is based on faith.
2. *Belief in minds.* Since you do not have – and cannot have – any direct experience of other people's minds, your belief that they are not mindless androids is ultimately based on faith.
3. *Belief in the past.* Since it is logically possible that the world was created five minutes ago (together with what appear to be historical artefacts and fossils), your belief in the reality of the past is based on faith.

4. *Belief in the future.* Since it is abstractly possible that the laws of nature will break down tomorrow, your belief that you will be able to rely on, say, gravity in the future is based on faith.

While such bedrock beliefs cannot be further justified, they are very different from religious beliefs. After all, we have no choice but to believe in the existence of the external world and the existence of the past. Indeed, they are conditions of sanity and we would not take seriously anyone who denied them. By contrast, religious belief seems to be optional in that not everyone is religious. And, although some people think that atheists are misguided, there is no reason to think that they are insane. Given this, one might argue that bedrock beliefs which command universal assent are best described as 'core intuitions' (see Chapter 8, page 217) rather than as 'matters of faith'.

ACTIVITY 11.10

1. 'No person is certain, apart from faith, whether he is awake or asleep' (Blaise Pascal, 1623–62). Do you agree or disagree with Pascal?
2. According to the philosopher Alvin Plantinga (1932–), belief in God is just as rational or irrational as belief in other minds. What are the similarities and differences between believing that other people have minds and believing in God?
3. 'Reason is itself a matter of faith. It is an act of faith to assert that our thoughts have any relation to reality at all' (G. K. Chesterton, 1874–1936). What do you think of this claim?

Scientific foundations

While it is natural to think that science is based on reason (evidence and argument) and religion is based on faith, some people claim that science is as much based on faith as religion. In support of this view, they argue that there are two key articles of scientific faith:

- faith that the universe is orderly
- faith that we are capable of discerning that order.

If either of these assumptions were false, science would be impossible.

However, since science and religion seem to have very different attitudes to faith, talk of 'scientific faith' may be misleading. A non-believing scientist might say that, while religion is happy to celebrate appeals to faith, science seeks to minimise them. According to this view, science involves subjecting one's beliefs to critical enquiry and testing them against the evidence. Religion, by contrast, is static and protects itself from criticism by demanding faith and obedience. Given this, a scientist might conclude that our belief in laws of nature discoverable by human intelligence is best described as a 'pragmatic assumption' rather than an 'article of faith' and that it is justified by the fact that it works in practice.

LQ – Natural sciences: To what extent is the scientific worldview based on faith? How similar or different is this faith from religious faith?

A believer would doubtless question the alleged contrast between scientific and religious faith. They might point out that scientific beliefs are often held as dogmatically as religious beliefs, and that religious beliefs, too, are open to criticism and change and develop over time. As this suggests, the question of how similar scientific faith is to religious faith remains an open one.

ACTIVITY 11.11

1. Do you think the fundamental assumptions of science are as much based on faith as the fundamental assumptions of religion?
2. If key scientific beliefs can be justified on the grounds that they 'work in practice', could key religious beliefs be justified in the same way?
3. Do religious beliefs change and develop over time in response to criticism, or are they timeless truths which are immune from criticism?

Moral foundations

Some people believe that at the deepest level our moral values are based on faith. This is because they depend on two core beliefs that philosophers struggle to justify:

- belief in free will
- belief in the existence of objective values.

We have to believe that people are responsible for their actions and we have to believe that there are common standards of right and wrong by which they can be judged. If in some deep sense people cannot help what they do, then we surely have no right to praise and blame – or punish – them. (The 'free-will problem' will be explored further in the appendix to Chapter 14.) Similarly, if values are simply a matter of subjective taste, it is hard to see how we can condemn people whose 'tastes' are different from our own. As the philosopher – and champion of reason – Bertrand Russell (1872–1970) commented: 'I cannot see how to refute the arguments for the subjectivity of ethical values, but I find myself incapable of believing that all that is wrong with wanton cruelty is that I don't like it.'

Despite the above comments, some philosophers – including Russell – would see appeals to faith as unhelpful. They would say that the only way we can justify our beliefs in free will and objective values is by appealing to a mixture of intuition, argument and experience; and if we are unable to justify them by rational means, then, rather than appeal to faith, we should have the courage to give them up as illusions. Whether or not it is possible to live without such core beliefs in practice is a matter of continuing debate.

Faith in ends

Another version of the claim that 'everyone has faith in something' – which derives from the theologian Paul Tillich (1886–1965) – is that we all have faith in some ultimate end which gives meaning and purpose to our lives. The thought here hangs on the distinction between means and ends. Many of the things we do in life are means to some further end. For example, you may study hard at school not because you think it has intrinsic value, but as a means to going to university and hence getting a good job. Your ultimate end – which Tillich calls your 'ultimate concern' – is the thing which you think has value in itself and for the sake of which you do everything else. It is, in basic terms, 'what you think it's all about'.

Among the ends people might pursue are: art, country, family, freedom, God, justice, knowledge, love, money, nature, peace, pleasure, power, self-realisation, success and work. Such ends may be implicit in the way a person behaves or they may be made explicit. In the latter case, they sometimes take the form of a particular ideology or philosophy of life – often denoted by the suffix 'ism' – such as **theism**, humanism, nationalism, environmentalism or hedonism (which concern belief in God, humanity, country, nature, or pleasure, respectively). Tillich argued that, although our beliefs about what makes life meaningful may change over time, faith itself is inescapable. Admittedly, we may occasionally suffer bouts of meaninglessness; but if literally nothing mattered to us, we would have no reason to get out of bed in the morning and we would lapse into apathy.

KT – theism: the belief that God exists

ACTIVITY 11.12

1. What would you say is your ultimate end for the sake of which you do everything else? How would you seek to justify your pursuit of this end?
2. Do you think you can discover more about the nature of someone's ultimate concern by looking at what they say or by looking at what they do?
3. In what sense, if any, would you say that the ultimate ends in which you believe are a matter of faith?

Possible criticisms

The above argument may seem persuasive, but there are two possible criticisms we can make of it.

1. The idea of an 'ultimate concern' is a vague one, and it may be hard to specify. If, for example, someone 'lives for soccer', should we say that their ultimate concern is sport, or happiness or self-realisation? It is hard to say. If someone muddles through life without any clear idea of 'what it is all about', why should we assume that they *must* have an ultimate concern which can somehow be seen from the way they live their life? Well, maybe there are things for which they would be willing to sacrifice everything – even their life. But, then again, maybe not.
2. While it is clear that things matter to us, and some things matter greatly to us, it is less clear why we should see them as matters of faith. If, for example, you live for your family, or are obsessed with worldly success – or, indeed, with sport – you are surely not committed to saying that you have faith in their objective value, or that everyone else should pursue them. You might simply see them as personal preferences which loom large in your own life but need not do so in other people's lives.

The faith of idealists

KT – **humanism:** a worldview which rejects the supernatural and believes in human reason, scientific progress and moral improvement

Tillich might seem to be on stronger ground when it comes to idealists and those who subscribe to an 'ism'; for they are passionately committed to certain beliefs and ideals and seem to be confident of their eventual realisation – even in the face of counter-evidence. However, many secular idealists would insist that their outlook has nothing to do with faith. This would seem to be true of **humanism**, which rejects any appeal to religious belief and rests on the belief in human reason, scientific progress and moral improvement.

Figure 11.6 Is the widespread belief in democracy based on faith or reason?

Nevertheless, it might be argued that humanism is still based on faith – specifically faith in progress. According to the British philosopher John Gray (1948–), many people who do not consider themselves religious unthinkingly assume that history is progressive and that things have improved in the past and will continue to improve in the future. Gray sees this as a secular version of the religious belief that good will eventually triumph over evil; and he describes this widespread – and often unthinking – faith in progress as 'the Prozac of the thinking classes'.

Despite this dismissive assessment, humanists might respond that while they *hope* for progress they do not have *faith* in it or believe that it is in any sense inevitable. Hope is not prediction, and one can try to improve the world without having faith that one will succeed. (Admittedly, the conviction that you will succeed may help to motivate you.) More generally, although it may be true that one cannot live without hope, it does not necessarily follow that one cannot live without faith.

LQ – **History:** Is the widespread belief in progress – that is, that history has a direction – a matter of fact or a matter of faith?

ACTIVITY 11.13

1. What role, if any, do you think faith plays in one of the following ideologies: (a) capitalism, (b) socialism, (c) environmentalism?
2. Do you think that the following beliefs are based more on evidence and argument, or more on faith?
   a. 'Human beings are fundamentally good.'
   b. 'Progress is inevitable.'
   c. 'World peace is an achievable goal.'
3. Do you think that idealism is based more on hope or on faith – or does it vary from idealist to idealist?

Faith in others

A final version of the claim that 'everyone has faith in something' is that we could not survive if we did not have faith in other people. We could be said to demonstrate this every day of our lives: when we are ill, we have faith in the expertise of the doctors; when we travel by car, we have faith in the sanity of other drivers; when we read a textbook, we have faith in the knowledge and honesty of the author; and when we are in trouble we have faith in the support of our friends. As these examples suggest, 'faith' is being used here almost as a synonym for trust. Indeed, to say that you have faith in someone usually amounts to saying that you trust them.

Figure 11.7 Could we survive without trust?

Cognitive trust

As we saw in Chapter 3, the vast majority of our knowledge is shared knowledge which comes from other people, and the question 'What should I believe?' often comes down to the question 'Who should I trust?' If you personally know nothing about, say, quantum physics, or the causes of cancer, or the origins of the Cold War, you will probably just trust the experts. This has led some people to claim that faith is built in to the very fabric of shared knowledge.

While we could neither learn from others nor cooperate with them if we were universally suspicious, we should not rush to equate cognitive trust with faith. Since trust is sometimes disappointed, it surely needs to be *earned* and supported by evidence. Certainly, in the cognitive realm, academics are rightly suspicious of *blind* trust, and there are mechanisms in place – such as peer review and the demand that experiments be repeatable – to ensure that we are not obliged to simply accept someone's word without question. As Albert Einstein (1878–1955) wisely observed: 'A foolish faith in authority is the worst enemy of truth.'

Figure 11.8 Astrophysics made simple.

ACTIVITY 11.14

1. In general, do you think that people have too much faith in experts, or is their trust in them justified?
2. If we made contact with aliens who were benign and vastly more intelligent than us, would we be justified in taking their beliefs about the nature of the universe on faith?

Trust in personal relationships

When it comes to our personal relationships, we may consider it a virtue to have faith in someone without requiring evidence. But even here there are limits. We might initially admire someone who has faith in their friend in the face of incriminating evidence that they have cheated on them; but if the evidence continues to mount, such faith eventually becomes perverse or positively delusional. We might still insist that, at the deepest level, our trust in other people always goes beyond evidence and depends on faith. After all, as far as the evidence goes it is abstractly possible that everyone is constantly laughing at you behind your back (they are very careful and hide it well). However, unless you are suffering from paranoia, this probably does not strike you as a reasonable interpretation!

ACTIVITY 11.15

1. Do you think that trust should always be earned? Does this apply as much to friends and family as to anonymous strangers?
2. In the world of espionage, it may be hard to decide whether someone is a loyal agent, a double agent, or – indeed – a triple agent. What role should faith and reason play in deciding whether or not to trust a spy?

"If he's still missing by Friday, how about you and me having a little dinner together somewhere?"

Figure 11.9

The ethics of belief

To conclude this discussion of faith, we now consider three potentially degenerate forms of faith which concern respectively *how* we believe, *what* we believe and *why* we believe.

Dogmatic faith

Dogmatic faith is concerned with the *how* of belief and it is what we usually have in mind when we speak of 'blind faith'. Such faith is not restricted to religious fundamentalists, but also extends to political ideologues, scientific cranks, new age gurus and conspiracy theorists. The conviction that one is right irrespective of the evidence confuses the *feeling* of certainty with its reality, assuming that there is only one possible way of looking at things. This suggests a lack of humility and an unwillingness to accept that other people may have equally valid perspectives. Mahatma Gandhi (1869–1948) aptly described dogmatism as an 'arrogant caricature' of the truth and he saw it as the antithesis of the true spirit of religion. For a faith which systematically insulates itself from criticism is one that has no confidence in itself.

Dogmatists could be said to suffer from 'true believer syndrome'. As explained by the arch-sceptic James Randi (1928–): 'No amount of evidence, no matter how good it is or how much there is of it, is ever going to convince the true believer to the contrary.' An amusing example can be found in the 1979 Monty Python film *Life of Brian*, which parodies dogmatic faith. When Brian says to his followers, 'Will you please listen? I'm not the Messiah! Do you understand? Honestly!', a woman in the crowd shouts out, 'Only the true Messiah denies his divinity.' In real life, the Jehovah's Witnesses have frequently predicted the end of the world. The fact that none of their predictions have come true seems to have done nothing to shake their faith that *this time* they are right!

Figure 11.10 Why do dogmatists so rarely change their minds?

Figure 11.11

Is dogmatism dangerous?

If someone is convinced they are right, the danger is that they may try to impose their views on their 'less enlightened' contemporaries. When ordinary people put their faith in gurus and charismatic leaders who have a because-I-say-so theory of truth, they can quickly run into trouble. To take an extreme example, in 1978 Jim Jones, the leader of a cult called the People's Temple, who had established a settlement in Guyana, persuaded his followers to kill themselves and murder their children: 909 people, including Jones, died as a result. But the deaths caused by such religious extremists pale into insignificance when compared with those caused by twentieth-century political dictators. Hitler, Stalin and Mao all had dogmatic faith in their destructive ideologies, and according to some estimates they were between them responsible for the death of more than one hundred million people.

ACTIVITY 11.16

1. According to the philosopher Leszek Kolakowski (1927–2009), 'The certainty of a believer is not that of a mathematician.' What do you think he meant by that and do you think he was right?
2. Do you think that one can be personally certain of something (personal knowledge) which is not objectively certain (shared knowledge)?

Superstitious faith

RLS – Headline: 'Pope calls for conversion from witchcraft in Africa'. Is one person's faith another person's superstition?

Superstitious faith is concerned with the *what* of belief. Superstition can be defined as a form of false science based on the strong and irrational belief in supernatural connections between things. Since the word 'superstitious' has negative connotations, most people would resent having the label pinned on them; but we may be more superstitious than we like to think. We may laugh at the voodoo practice of sticking pins in dolls in order to harm other people, but most of us would be reluctant to throw darts at a photograph of a loved one despite the fact that it is only a photograph. We also tend to be wary of 'tempting fate' by, for example, boasting about how well things are going; and, even if we don't actually believe in it, we may find ourselves knocking on wood 'just to be on the safe side'.

Figure 11.12 Some footballers celebrate goals and victories with prayers. What role do faith and superstition play in sport?

While superstitions can help us to feel more confident and secure, most people would say that we are not intellectually justified in believing in them. Whether or not miracles should be classified as a superstition is a matter of dispute even among religious people. Some liberal theologians argue that we should seek to *demythologise* religion by interpreting miracles symbolically rather than literally. According to this view, religious symbols can be likened to art forms such as music and poetry in that they seek to communicate truths which are difficult to put into ordinary language. However, other believers take miracles literally and see them as being central to their faith. Miracles will be discussed further in Chapter 18 (see page 517).

LQ – Arts: Are the arts the best way of expressing things that lie beyond the limits of reason and are in the realm of faith?

ACTIVITY 11.17

1. How superstitious are you? Do you, for example, have any 'lucky objects' that you take with you into exams? Do you ever find yourself following superstitious practices even though you do not believe in them?
2. 'One tribe's faith is another tribe's superstition.' Do you agree or disagree with this statement? Which religious practices, if any, do you consider to be superstitious?
3. Do you think there is anything wrong with being superstitious? Are some superstitions more harmful than others? Are any beneficial?

Figure 11.13

Delusional faith

KT – wish fulfilment: believing that something is true for no other reason than that you want it to be true

Delusional faith is concerned with the *why* of belief and is closely connected with **wish fulfilment** – believing that something is true simply because you *want* it to be true. To illustrate wish fulfilment, consider a 1997 survey which asked Americans how likely they thought it was that various celebrities would go to heaven. A respectable 52 per cent thought that the then US president Bill Clinton would make it; Princess Diana fared better with 60 per cent; and, not surprisingly, the winner with 79 per cent was Mother Teresa. Respondents were then asked how likely they thought it was that they themselves would go to heaven. A whopping 87 per cent were confident that they were heaven-bound. This is a testament to our inherent egocentricity and it suggests that – in some cases at least – people will have faith in what they want to have faith in.

Positive thinking

Despite its dangers, wanting to believe that something is true or possible is sometimes beneficial and it can enable you to do things that would otherwise be beyond you. If you think positively and have faith that you can, for example, leap across a chasm, or write a novel – or an extended essay – then you are more likely to be able to do it than if you lack self-belief. When it comes to disease, there is even evidence to suggest that a positive attitude can aid your recovery. As these examples suggest, having faith can sometimes become a self-fulfilling prophecy.

KT – positive thinking: the idea that if you think positively about a goal, you are more likely to be successful

Academic research, too, can benefit from **positive thinking**. For example, a scientist may need to have faith in a hypothesis in order to be motivated to spend the time and energy looking for supporting evidence. The history of science is full of obstinate individuals whose 'unjustified' faith that they were right helped to push back the frontiers of knowledge. However, we should note that here faith is more an *engine of motivation* than a *criterion of justification*. Faith may impel a scientist to seek evidence for their hypothesis, but it does not in itself justify the hypothesis; and if the evidence does not materialise they should (eventually) change their mind. Without such intellectual flexibility, the inspired faith of the genius can all too easily degenerate into the obstructive faith of the crank.

Figure 11.14

Truth versus happiness

Some people propose that in thinking about the ethics of belief we distinguish between *intellectual* justification and *moral* justification. Consider a cancer patient who, against the evidence, is convinced that they will recover. Although their belief is not intellectually justified, one might claim that it is nevertheless morally justified. Those who advocate this view believe that the search for truth is sometimes secondary to more important considerations. If your faith makes you happy and you turn out to be wrong – well, at least you were happy! Others reject this way of thinking as dangerously permissive, and insist that if people base their beliefs on what makes them happy rather than on the evidence, then sooner or later their hopes will be ship-wrecked on the reef of unforgiving facts.

ACTIVITY 11.18

1. How would you go about trying to establish whether, on balance, appeals to faith as a source of knowledge have done more harm than good?
2. Do you think that some types of faith are good and other types of faith are bad? If so, what criteria would you use to distinguish between 'good faith' and 'bad faith'?
3. In what sense, if any, does someone have the *right* to hold unjustified beliefs? To what extent do you think that holding such beliefs has socially harmful consequences?

Conclusion

You may have found the discussion of faith in this chapter a challenging one, not least because the word itself is ambiguous and means different things to different people. This makes it hard to come to any general conclusion.

However, since no one thinks that faith should operate as a 'free pass' to justify *any* belief, we might agree that appeals to faith should at least be *informed* by reason. Indeed, this is essential if we wish to enter into a dialogue with people who do not share our worldview.

Since premature appeals to faith can quickly bring discussion to an end, a good rule of thumb might be: 'Keep the conversation going for as long as possible before appealing to faith.' Faith may well be an appropriate response to the mysteries of the universe, but it could be argued that in its highest form it consists not of confident assertions of belief but of practical activity that teeters on the brink of silence.

"Sorry, I'm travel and weather; philosophy's over there..."

Figure 11.15

Key points

- Faith as a possible source of knowledge evokes strong feelings. In particular, some people see it as corrupting reason while others see it as complementing it.
- Faith is difficult to define, but it is commonly thought to include cognitive, emotional and ethical elements and is closely connected with a person's worldview.
- According to evidentialists, it is wrong to believe things on insufficient evidence. This might suggest that we should reject faith as a source of knowledge.
- Some people claim that faith is rational because what is grasped by faith can also be supported by evidence and argument, or because we have a divine sense similar to sense perception. Both views are controversial.
- According to fideism, faith is opposed to, and superior to, reason. But it could be argued that when faith is not informed by reason it is dangerously permissive.
- Another theory is that reason and faith govern separate domains – the empirical world and the world of meaning and value, respectively. However, it is unclear whether this theory is descriptive or prescriptive.
- One might argue that faith is primarily a matter of interpretation. This raises the question of what distinguishes a reasonable interpretation from an unreasonable one.
- Faith may be inescapable either because reason cannot justify everything, or because we all have faith in an ultimate end, or because we could not survive without faith in other people.
- Among the forms of degenerate faith that might be distinguished are dogmatic faith, superstitious faith and delusional faith.
- While different people may mean different things by the word 'faith', it could be argued that at some level we need both faith and reason to make sense of the world.

Key terms

agnosticism
atheism
bedrock belief
burden of proof
evidentialism
fideism
humanism
infinite regress
metaphysical questions
positive thinking
scientism
superstition
theism
wish fulfilment
worldview

IB prescribed essay titles

1. Analyse the strengths and weaknesses of using faith as a basis for knowledge in religion and in one area of knowledge from the ToK diagram. (May 2012)
2. 'Every attempt to know the world rests on a set of assumptions that cannot be tested.' Examine this proposition in relation to two areas of knowledge. (November 2013)

Further reading

Books

Donald Crosby, *Faith and Reason: Their Role in Religious and Secular Life* (SUNY Press, 2012). This challenging but accessible book looks at the role played by faith not only in religion, but also in knowledge, science, and morality. It also considers secular forms of faith such as humanism and scientism.

Karen Armstrong, *The Case For God: What Religion Really Means* (Vintage, 2010). In this fascinating book, Karen Armstrong, a former nun, insists that the essence of religious faith is more a matter of practice than a matter of belief.

Online articles

Karen Armstrong, 'On Letting Go of the Desire to Know it All', *Huffington Post*, 12 September 2013.

Ed Yong, 'When in Doubt, Shout – Why Shaking Someone's Beliefs Turns Them into Stronger Advocates', *Discover Magazine* 'Not Exactly Rocket Science' blog, 19 October 2010.

Dialogue: On faith

Alex: One of the main things I've got out of my TOK course so far is that if we are going to avoid believing nonsense then we have got to justify our beliefs by appealing to evidence and argument. Do you agree with that?

Ethel: That sounds like a good rule of thumb for everyday life. I guess the reason we reject pseudo-sciences such as astrology and conspiracy theories such as the claim that Michael Jackson faked his own death is that the evidence for them doesn't stack up.

Alex: Exactly! I think we have an intellectual responsibility to base our beliefs on evidence and to refrain from believing things for which there is insufficient evidence.

Ethel: I agree with you up to a point. But I think it is important to keep in mind that we cannot justify *all* of our beliefs and that our most deeply rooted beliefs are actually based on faith.

Alex: Faith? And I was thinking we were in agreement! I believe in reason, and since faith is by definition irrational, it has no place in a reasonable person's worldview.

Ethel: Faith isn't irrational.

Alex: Of course it is. People only appeal to faith when they can no longer justify their beliefs with reasons. So it follows by definition that faith is irrational.

Ethel: Faith isn't so much *irrational* as *arational*. It doesn't contradict reason but simply goes beyond it. So in my view we can neither say that it is rational nor that it is irrational.

Alex: Look, if I ask someone, 'Why do you believe in astrology?' and they reply 'Faith!', surely they are being irrational and abdicating from their responsibility to give evidence for their beliefs?

Ethel: I am not suggesting that we can justify *any* belief by an appeal to faith. What I'm saying is that since we eventually run out of evidence all of our beliefs are *ultimately* based on faith.

Alex: My model for rationality is science, and I think that there is a huge difference between scientific reason and appeals to faith – which I associate with religion. While the former is open-minded and critical, the latter is close-minded and dogmatic. Science *requires* us to believe only what is supported by the evidence; religion *allows* us to believe whatever we want to believe. Given this, it seems to me that appealing to faith is intellectually irresponsible.

Ethel: What you fail to recognise is that at the deepest level science is also based on faith – namely, faith that the universe is orderly. We cannot rationally justify this belief because no matter how much order we have seen in the past, there is no guarantee that it will continue in the future. So our belief that the laws of physics will continue to hold in the future and that the sun will continue to rise each morning is ultimately a matter of faith.

Alex: I disagree with you. Our belief that the universe is orderly is not a matter of faith, but is simply part of what it means to be rational. Only a fool or a madman would keep sticking their hand in a fire on the grounds that 'Maybe it won't hurt this time'! Moreover, even if, for the sake of the argument, I accept your use of the word 'faith', it seems to me that there is a huge difference between scientific faith and religious faith. Scientists have faith in a *method* and are willing to subject their beliefs to critical scrutiny. Believers have faith in *dogmas* and are determined to protect their beliefs from such scrutiny.

Ethel: I think that your distinction is too black and white and that you are unjustifiably idealising science and demonising religion. Many scientists are dogmatically convinced that science has all the answers; and many theologians insist that doubt plays an important role in faith.

Alex: My impression is that religious people only appeal to faith because they lack evidence. If they actually found solid evidence for their beliefs, then I bet they would quickly abandon their talk of faith.

Ethel: While I agree that we should appeal to evidence in most areas of knowledge, when it comes to the big questions about life, the universe, and everything – questions that cannot be answered by science – we are entitled to appeal to faith. In fact, I think there is a sense in which *all* knowledge is ultimately based on faith. This is because we must trust our faculties and have faith that they are capable of discovering the truth.

Alex: I don't think that faith is a source of knowledge. As far as I am concerned there are only two fundamental sources – perception and reason. If you allow faith as a source of knowledge, it acts like a free pass that enables you to justify *anything* – voodoo, witchcraft, Zeus, Santa Claus, fairies – you name it!

Ethel: I think you need to dig a bit deeper here. You say that there are two main sources of knowledge, perception and reason, but how do you know they are reliable? How do you know that your senses are not systematically deceiving you? And how do you know that fallible human reason is capable of discerning the truth? In both cases, I would say the answer is faith. Without faith you cannot be sure that life is not a dream, for any evidence you give to show that you are in touch with reality could simply be part of the dream. And since you cannot without circularity justify reason by appealing to reason, your confidence in its power is also based on faith. So in the end it all comes down to faith.

Alex: It seems to me that you are using the word 'faith' in a very misleading way. As far as I am concerned, these are not articles of faith at all but *core intuitions*, or principles of sanity. After all, every sane person *knows* that life is not a dream and every sane person *knows* that they cannot keep contradicting themselves. If you ask me how they know, I would say that they simply *see* that these things are true; and if they can't then there's something wrong with them. That's why I call these kind of beliefs core intuitions.

Ethel: But you can't justify them in terms of either perception or reason, can you? You said earlier that these are the only two sources of knowledge.

Alex: OK, I'm willing to admit that there are perhaps *three* main sources of knowledge – perception, reason, and intuition. But I would still insist that the kind of intuition I am talking about is quite different from faith.

Ethel: Well, if you allow intuition as a source of knowledge, a believer might argue that religious faith is also a kind of intuition, and that if your religious intuition is working correctly, then you just *see* that God exists.

Alex: You are forgetting the fact that the intuitions of, say, Muslims and Christians may contradict one another. This suggests that religious intuitions are very different from core intuitions. While the former are local and consist of things we *want* to believe, they are probably false. The latter, by contrast, are universal and consist of things we *have* to believe, so they are probably true. In support of this, it's worth pointing out that from an evolutionary point of view, if our faculties were not generally reliable, we would not have survived.

Ethel: You are doubtless right to say that our faculties have helped us to survive, but if we are just intelligent apes what confidence can you have that our ape-like intelligence will deliver the truth in abstract realms such as mathematics, physics, and philosophy? After all, there is no reason to think that we were naturally selected to do calculus, or astrophysics, or epistemology, for these would have had no survival value to our remote ancestors living on the savannah in Africa.

Alex: Well, since trusting our faculties has given us a tremendous amount of knowledge which works in practice, this suggests that they are generally reliable.

Ethel: But that doesn't answer the kind of sceptical challenge I raised earlier. Since everything you experience is consistent with the whole of life being a dream, your conviction that it is not a dream is a matter of faith. And that's the point I want to emphasise – that knowledge depends ultimately on faith.

Alex: When religious people speak of faith, they normally have in mind not this kind of abstract, philosophical faith, but faith in particular doctrines, such as that Jesus rose from the dead, or that the Koran is the word of God, or that the soul is immortal. And they simply hide behind the word 'faith' to prevent people questioning or criticising their beliefs.

Ethel: You seem to think that faith is a peculiar form of belief which has a low degree of evidence. Many theologians would reject this view and say that religious faith is not so much a matter of believing specific doctrines as of trusting God. Having faith in God means having faith that He is fundamentally good. I don't think that is so different from the kind of faith that informs science. Wasn't it Einstein who said, 'God may be subtle, but he is not malicious'?

Alex: Yes, but Einstein was speaking metaphorically and he certainly didn't believe in the God of organised religion. I agree that science is based on the assumption that the universe is good in the sense of being orderly, but that is the only sense in which scientists think it is good. By contrast, believers also have faith that human beings are central to the scheme of things and that everything has been arranged according to some kind of divine plan. Scientists have no such faith and are happy to face up to our cosmic insignificance.

Ethel: I don't think that anyone – not even atheistic scientists – can live without hope. And since hope is by its nature something that goes beyond evidence, it can itself be regarded as a kind of faith.

Alex: I started this conversation, so perhaps I should finish it – and this seems to me like a good place to stop. I guess we just have to hope – or have faith – that conversations like this one can help us to get closer to the truth!

Ethel: I'll say yeah to that!

Part

3

AREAS OF KNOWLEDGE

Introduction

The Theory of Knowledge syllabus distinguishes eight areas of knowledge (AOKs): mathematics, natural sciences, human sciences, history, the arts, ethics, religion and indigenous knowledge. The last of these is somewhat anomolous and is best thought of as a *perspective* on knowledge rather than an area of knowledge with its own distinctive subject-matter. For this reason, we reserve our discussion of it until Part 4. The IB recommends that you study these eight areas of knowledge in detail.

While there may be different ways of dividing up the map of knowledge, it makes sense to group subjects together into areas such as natural sciences, human sciences and arts on the grounds of family resemblance. However, it is important to keep in mind that there are differences between subjects *within* each area of knowledge. For example, physics is different from biology, economics from anthropology, and visual arts from music. It is also worth noting that, although the roll-call of IB subjects may strike you as natural, the world does not arrive neatly divided into different subjects. Academic disciplines are not watertight compartments and at the borders, at least, they often flow into one another.

As we examine each area of knowledge, our focus will be on *second-order questions* about the nature of different subjects rather than first-order questions which can be answered within particular subjects. Among the questions we might ask are: What does it mean? What counts as evidence? How certain is it? How else can we look at it? What are the limitations? Why does it matter? How similar or different is it to/from other AOKs?

As the last of the above questions suggests, we are interested not only in how the various AOKs answer the question 'How do you know?' but also in how they are related to one another. It is sometimes claimed that there is a hierarchy of disciplines and that some subjects are more important or fundamental than others. (At school, you may have noticed that each of your teachers seems to think that *their* subject is the only one that really matters!) To illustrate such *subject imperialism*, consider the following quotations:

> 'Life is good for only two things, discovering mathematics and teaching mathematics' (Siméon Poisson, 1781–1840)
>
> 'Everything is either physics or stamp collecting' (Lord Rutherford, 1871–1937)
>
> 'The social sciences, as well as the humanities, are the last branches of biology' (E. O. Wilson, 1929–)
>
> 'Life only exists to make art possible' (Herbert von Karajan, 1908–89)

No prizes for guessing that these quotations come from a mathematician, a physicist, a biologist and a musician respectively!

The idea that all knowledge is in principle reducible to scientific knowledge has been particularly influential in recent times. Some people claim that one day we will be able to explain *everything* in terms of the basic laws of physics. This is, however, a highly contentious view, and we may suspect that reality is too complex to be explicable in terms of any one subject. It may be more productive to think of each area of knowledge as a map which highlights different features of reality and contributes something unique to our understanding of it.

So rather than think of the relation between different areas of knowledge as a *vertical* hierarchical one, we could perhaps think of it as a *horizontal* interactive one. We should be able to make interesting connections between any one area of knowledge and all of the others. For instance, with reference to the natural sciences we might ask: Why does mathematics play such a central role in the natural sciences? Can we study the human sciences in much the same way as we study the natural sciences? Why is it important for a scientist to know something about the history of their subject? What are the similarities between a scientific and an artistic approach to reality? What are the moral responsibilities of a scientist? Can the scientific view of the world be reconciled with the religious view of it? Similar comparative questions can be raised in every area of knowledge.

Knowledge frameworks

As we examine each area of knowledge, we can ask what role the various ways of knowing (WOKs) – language, sense perception, reason, emotion, intuition, imagination, memory and faith – play in its construction. But it is important to keep in mind that AOKs are not simply combinations of WOKs mixed in different proportions and that each area has its own distinctive structure.

The IB proposes what it calls a 'knowledge framework' to help structure your thinking about different AOKs and make comparisons between them. The suggested framework consists of the following five interrelated elements:

- scope, motivation and applications
- specific terminology and concepts
- methods used to produce knowledge
- key historical developments
- interaction with personal knowledge.

Scope and applications

An obvious starting point when we look at an AOK is to ask 'What is it and why is it useful?' We might, for example, characterise mathematics as 'the science of rigorous proof', or natural science as 'the study of the natural world based on observation and experiment', or history as 'the study of the past'. This may give us a preliminary idea of what is at stake in each case, but the precise nature of an AOK cannot be captured in a short definition. To really understand what a subject is all about, you need to immerse yourself in it, practise it and then step back and reflect on it!

A good way of gaining an understanding of what something *is* is to think about what it *is not*. To understand how statistics can be used to illuminate reality, you might consider how they can be abused. To grasp the nature of science, you could think about how it differs from pseudo-science. To shed light on what is involved in genuine historical research, you might look at someone in the grip of a conspiracy theory who has already decided what they believe. Similarly, you might think about the difference between genuine art and 'phoney' art, a moral principle and a personal preference, or a religion and a cult. Note, however, that in each of these cases, opinions differ about where we should draw the line.

Another useful strategy is to think about the limits of a subject. In this context, we can distinguish between *problems*, *mysteries* and *taboos*. A problem is a question we will sooner or later be able to answer; a mystery is one we will never be able to answer. For example, 'What is the cure for cancer?' is generally seen as a problem; 'What is the meaning of life?' is seen as a mystery. A taboo is something we should not investigate. There is, for example, a taboo on conducting experiments on human beings which cause physical or psychological damage. There may be other areas where we think it is better not to seek the truth.

Concepts and language

Every area of knowledge is structured by various key concepts which help to give it order and to define its scope. In mathematics, you should be familiar with concepts such as axiom, theorem, proof; in the natural and human sciences, controlled experiment, law, theory; in history, primary and secondary sources, bias; in the arts, form, content, style; in ethics, goodness, right, duty; and in religion, God, miracle, faith.

An area of knowledge may also be informed by various overarching metaphors which influence the way people think about a subject. As discussed in Chapter 4, metaphors invite us to see one thing in terms of another and they can be deeply rooted in the way we think. For example, people have sometimes thought of the universe as a clockwork mechanism, the mind as a computer, and God as a father. While such metaphors may be illuminating, they cannot simply be taken for granted and they should – at least occasionally – be challenged. So we should ask how the universe *differs* from a clock, how the mind *differs* from a computer; and how God *differs* from a father. We might then suggest more appropriate metaphors.

Our thinking in different areas of knowledge is also affected by various conventions, many of which are built into language. If we have grown up with certain conventions, they may strike us as natural. Indeed, some people claim that *all* knowledge is a matter of convention and that we are simply indoctrinated into the habit of our own tribe. But this seems implausible. After all, the law of gravity applies no matter what culture you belong to. Nevertheless, some things that seem natural *are* matters of convention – for example, the fact that we use base 10 in mathematics as opposed to, say, base 12. One of the challenges of TOK is to try to distinguish between what is natural and global and what is conventional and local.

Methodology

The various areas of knowledge are distinguished as much by the methods they employ as by their subject-matter. Mathematics proves things using strict deductive logic. Central to the scientific method is formulating hypotheses and testing them against reality. In humanities, such as history and the arts, we generally seek good interpretations rather than mathematical proofs or scientific verification. In ethics and religion, a common method consists in trying to bring intuitions and arguments into 'reflective equilibrium' by testing them against one another and adjusting them until they are consistent.

While all subjects seek to justify the knowledge claims they make on the basis of evidence and argument, they differ in the degree of certainty they require for something to count as knowledge. As the Greek philosopher Aristotle (384–322 BCE) observed:

> *It is the mark of an educated man to look for precision in each class of things just so far as the nature of the subject admits; it is evidently foolish to accept probable reasoning from a mathematician and to demand from a rhetorician scientific proofs.*

In learning the methodology of an area of knowledge, we also learn how to inoculate ourselves against typical reasoning errors. A good natural scientist will be alert to the danger of confirmation bias; a human scientist will be aware of how easy it is to confuse genuine causal connections with mere correlations; a historian will guard against hindsight bias – and so on.

Historical development

As a quick glance at the history of ideas reveals, knowledge is not static, but changes and develops over time. This simple observation reminds us of the fact that, rather than being a closed body of timeless truths, knowledge is an active, ongoing enterprise. Those who know nothing about the history of a subject tend to exaggerate its objectivity. Every generation has been dazzled by the idea that its way of looking at the world is the definitive truth. At the beginning of the twentieth century, there was a widespread feeling among physicists that the subject was basically finished and it was just a matter of tying up a few loose ends. That was just before Einstein put forward his revolutionary new ideas. A similar point can be made about other areas. Take a textbook in any subject written one hundred years ago and you will find that it is very different from the ones that are in use today!

As this suggests, we should expect future generations to have a different understanding of the world from our current understanding of it. Some parts of what we presently claim to know may stand the test of time, but others are likely to be rejected. Still others may be embedded in an altogether richer theory in much the same way that Newtonian physics is now seen as a special case of Einstein's theory of relativity. The former is still useful at a practical, everyday level, but we now know that it does not tell the whole story. This raises further interesting questions about intellectual progress. We might, for example, ask whether it is inevitable and whether it happens to the same degree in different areas of knowledge.

Links to personal knowledge

As discussed in Chapter 3, academic knowledge is a form of shared knowledge, but there is a dynamic interaction between the personal and the shared. On the one hand, individuals must sometimes be willing to question the prevailing orthodoxy in a subject in order to develop new ideas. On the other hand, we can only distinguish between private fantasy and genuine knowledge by testing our ideas against the opinions of the relevant intellectual community. As an IB student, your study of and reflection on the various areas of knowledge should help you to develop your own coherent picture of reality.

While the knowledge framework can be a useful organising device for thinking about and comparing the various areas of knowledge, you should not think of its elements as a shopping list to simply be ticked off as you go through each area of knowledge. As you explore the various AOKs in Part 3, these elements will be implicit rather than explicit in the discussion.

Mathematics

12

Mathematics is neither physical nor mental, it's social.

Reuben Hersh, 1927–

The useful combinations [in mathematics] are precisely the most beautiful.

Henri Poincaré, 1854–1912

Mathematics is the abstract key which turns the lock of the physical universe.

John Polkinghorne, 1930–

Everything that can be counted does not count. Everything that counts cannot be counted.

Albert Einstein, 1879–1955

The mark of a civilized man is the ability to look at a column of numbers and weep.

Bertrand Russell, 1872–1970

The advancement and perfection of mathematics are intimately connected with the prosperity of the state.

Napoleon Bonaparte, 1769–1821

In the pure mathematics we contemplate absolute truths which existed in the divine mind before the morning stars sang together, and which will continue to exist there when the last of their radiant host shall have fallen from heaven.

Edward Everett, 1794–1865

Instead of having 'answers' on a math test, they should just call them 'impressions', and if you got a different 'impression', so what, can't we all be brothers?

Jack Handey, 1949–

Mathematics began when it was discovered that a brace of pheasants and a couple of days have something in common: the number two.

Bertrand Russell, 1872–1970

Introduction

Mathematics is a subject that seems to charm and alarm people in equal measure. If someone asks you, 'What are you most certain of in the world?' you might reply '2 + 2 = 4'. Surely no one can doubt that! Mathematics seems to be an island of certainty in a vast ocean of doubt.

LQ – Language: How does mathematics resemble natural languages, such as English, and how does it differ from them?

LQ – Natural sciences: Is the book of nature written in the language of mathematics?

At the most general level, we might characterise mathematics as the search for abstract patterns, and such patterns turn up everywhere. When you think about it, there is something extraordinary about the fact that, for *anything* you care to name, if you take two of that thing and add two more of that thing you end up with four of that thing. Similarly, if you take any circle – no matter how big or small – and divide its circumference by its diameter, you *always* end up with the same number – π (roughly 3.14).

The fact that there seems to be an underlying order in things might explain why mathematics not only seems to give us certainty, but is also of enormous practical value. At the beginning of the scientific revolution, Galileo (1564–1642) said that the book of nature is written in the language of mathematics. If anything, mathematics is even more important now than it was in the seventeenth century, and mathematical literacy is a prerequisite for a successful career in almost any branch of science.

The certainty and usefulness of mathematics may help to explain its enduring appeal. The mathematician and philosopher Bertrand Russell (1872–1970) recalled how he began studying geometry at the age of eleven: 'This was one of the great events of my life, as dazzling as first love. I had not imagined that there was anything so delicious in the world.' Russell's description would be greeted with blank incomprehension by some people. For many, words such as 'love' and 'delicious' simply do not go with the word 'mathematics'. Mathematics may give some of us a reassuring feeling of certainty, but others find it threatening precisely because it leaves us with no place to hide. If you make a mistake in a maths problem you can be *shown* to be wrong. You can't say it's 'an interesting interpretation', or 'an original way of looking at it', or 'it all depends what you mean by . . .' You're just wrong!

"Maybe it's not a wrong answer – maybe it's just a different answer."

Figure 12.1

ACTIVITY 12.1

To what extent do you think our beliefs about the value of mathematics are determined by our ability in the subject?

Mathematical thinking also requires a kind of selective attention to things; you have to ignore context and operate at a purely abstract level. While some people find the resulting abstractions fascinating, others can find little meaning in them. The American novelist Philip Roth gives an amusing account of a father trying to sharpen the mind of his son, Nathan, by throwing maths problems at him:

> *'Marking Down', he [my father] would say, not unlike a . . . student announcing the title of a poem. 'A clothing dealer, trying to dispose of an overcoat cut in last year's style, marked it down from the original price of thirty dollars to twenty-four. Failing to make a sale, he reduced the price to nineteen dollars and twenty cents. Again he found no takers, so he tried another price reduction and this time sold it . . . All right, Nathan, what was the selling price if the last markdown was consistent with the others?' Or, 'Making a Chain.' 'A lumberjack has six sections of chain, each consisting of four links. If the cost of cutting open a link . . .' and so on.*
>
> *The next day . . . I would day dream in my bed about the clothing dealer and the lumberjack. To whom had the haberdasher finally sold the overcoat? Did the man who bought it realize it was cut in last year's style? If he wore it to a restaurant, would people laugh? And what did 'last year's style' look like anyway? 'Again he found no takers', I would say aloud, finding much to feel melancholy about in that idea. I still remember how charged for me was that word 'takers'. Could it have been the lumberjack with his six sections of chain who, in his rustic innocence, had bought the overcoat cut in last year's style? And why suddenly did he need an overcoat? Invited to a fancy ball? By whom? . . .*
>
> *My father . . . was disheartened to find me intrigued by fantasies and irrelevant details of geography and personality and intention, instead of the simple beauty of the arithmetic solution. He did not think that was intelligent of me and he was right.*

Figure 12.2 The Piraha tribe of north-west Brazil have no words for numbers.

The very success of mathematics has sometimes bred a kind of 'imperialism' which says that if you can't express something in mathematical symbols then it has no intellectual value. You might, however, feel that many important things in life escape the abstractions of a formal system. There are indigenous tribes in the world, such as the Piraha of north-west Brazil, who are free of the tyranny of numbers and have words only for 'one', 'two' and 'many'.

ACTIVITY 12.2

How different do you think your picture of the world would be if you had no words for numbers?

There is evidence that human beings – together with many animals – have an innate sense of number. This is hardly surprising, as some rudimentary ability to distinguish between more and less has obvious survival value. Our innate number sense has been greatly extended by the development of mathematical notation to which many cultures have contributed. For example, 1, 2, 3, 4, 5, 6, 7, 8 and 9 are known as Hindu-Arabic numerals since they originated in India and were spread by the Arabs. Similarly the concept of zero – which plays a crucial role in mathematics – comes from India. (It was also independently discovered by the Mayans of South America.)

LQ – Cultural perspectives: Is mathematics a universal language that is independent of any particular culture?

There are, of course, cultural differences in mathematical notation, and at various times different cultures have used different number bases. While base 10 may strike you as the most 'natural', it derives from the arbitrary biological fact that we have ten fingers. This in itself means nothing. You could just as easily say that base 5 is natural because it is the number of fingers we have on *one* hand; or base 20 because it is the number of digits on our hands and feet. Indeed, the Yuki people, an indigenous group from the west coast of America, used a base 8 system by counting the *spaces* between their fingers rather than the fingers themselves. Some mathematicians think that base 12 would be preferable to base 10 because it is an easier and more efficient way to calculate. (This is because 12 is a more divisible number than 10.) Despite these notational differences, most people would agree that mathematics itself is universal. After all, the value of π (the circumference of a circle divided by its diameter) is the same whatever your culture!

Figure 12.3 Children count with their fingers. Is base 10 natural or is it simply a matter of convention?

The mathematical paradigm

A good definition of mathematics is 'the science of rigorous proof'. Although some earlier cultures developed a 'cookbook mathematics' of useful recipes for solving practical problems, the idea of mathematics as the science of proof dates back only as far as the Greeks. The most famous of the Greek mathematicians was Euclid, who lived in Alexandria, Egypt, around 300 BCE. He was the first person to organise geometry into a rigorous body of knowledge, and his ideas have had an enduring influence on civilisation. The geometry you study in high school today is basically **Euclidean geometry**.

KT – Euclidean geometry: a system of geometry developed by the Greek mathematician Euclid (c300 BCE)

12 Mathematics

KT – formal system: a model of reasoning that consists of the key elements of axioms, deduction and theorems

KT – axiom: a starting point for reasoning that is accepted without proof

KT – deductive reasoning: reasoning from the general to the particular

KT – theorem: a statement that can be proved to be true on the basis of axioms or other already established theorems

The model of reasoning developed by Euclid is known as a **formal system**, and it has three key elements:

- **axioms**
- **deductive reasoning**
- **theorems**.

When you reason formally, you begin with *axioms*, use *deductive reasoning* and derive *theorems*. The theorems can then be used as a basis for reasoning further and deriving more complex theorems.

Axioms

The axioms of a system are its starting points or basic assumptions. At least until the nineteenth century, the axioms of mathematics were considered to be self-evident truths which provided firm foundations for mathematical knowledge. You might want to be awkward and insist that we prove our axioms. However, as discussed in Chapter 6, you can't prove everything. If you tried to, you would get caught in an *infinite regress* – an endless chain of reasoning – proving *A* in terms of *B*, and *B* in terms of *C* and so on for ever. We have to start somewhere, and there is surely no better place to start than with what seems to be obvious.

There are four traditional requirements for a set of axioms. They should be consistent, independent, simple and fruitful.

1. *Consistent.* If you can deduce both *p* and non-*p* from the same set of axioms they are not consistent. Inconsistency is bad news because, once you allow it into a system, you can prove literally anything.
2. *Independent.* For the sake of elegance, you should begin with the smallest possible number of axioms. You should not be able to deduce any one of the axioms from the others – for then it is a theorem rather than an axiom.
3. *Simple.* Since axioms are accepted without further proof, they should be as clear and simple as possible.
4. *Fruitful.* A good formal system should enable you to prove as many theorems as possible using the smallest number of axioms.

Starting with a few basic definitions – such as, a point is that which has no part, and a line has length but no breadth – Euclid postulated the following five axioms:

1. It shall be possible to draw a straight line joining any two points.
2. A finite straight line may be extended without limit in either direction.
3. It shall be possible to draw a circle with a given centre and through a given point.
4. All right angles are equal to one another.
5. There is just one straight line through a given point which is parallel to a given line.

Deductive reasoning

We discussed deductive reasoning in Chapter 6, and gave as one example of a syllogism:

All human beings are mortal. (1)

Socrates is a human being. (2)

Therefore Socrates is mortal. (3)

(1) and (2), we said, are the *premises* and (3) the *conclusion* of the argument; and if (1) and (2) are true then (3) is *necessarily* true. In mathematics, axioms are like premises and theorems are like conclusions.

Theorems

Using his five axioms and deductive reasoning, Euclid derived various simple theorems, such as:

1. Lines perpendicular to the same line are parallel.

2. Two straight lines do not enclose an area.

3. The sum of the angles of a triangle is 180 degrees.

4. The angles on a straight line sum to 180 degrees.

Such simple theorems can then be used to construct more complex proofs. Consider Figure 12.4. You are told that angle a plus angle c equals 180 degrees, and you are then asked to prove that angle b equals angle c.

Given $a + c = 180$
Prove $b = c$

$a°$ $b°$ $c°$

Figure 12.4

Here is a proof:

1.	$a + c = 180$	given
2. and	$a + b = 180$	angles on a straight line (theorem 4 above)
3. therefore	$a + c = a + b$	by substitution
4. therefore	$b = c$	QED

One of the attractive things about this proof is its generality. Whatever the size of angle a – be it 102 degrees or 172 degrees – if we know that angle a plus angle c equals 180 degrees, then angle b *must* equal angle c.

"I think you should be more explicit here in step two."

Figure 12.5

Proofs and conjectures

KT – conjecture: a hypothesis that appears to work but which has not yet been proved

We have seen that a formal system begins with axioms and uses deductive reasoning to prove theorems. To clarify what is meant by a 'proof' in the strict mathematical sense of the word, we can compare a proof with a **conjecture**. In a *proof* a theorem is shown to follow logically from the relevant axioms. A conjecture, by contrast, is a hypothesis that seems to work, but has not been shown to be *necessarily true*. To illustrate the difference between these two concepts consider the following proposition:

The sum of the first n odd numbers = n^2 (where n is any number).

If you are curious to know whether this is true, you might see what happens when you plug in the first odd number, then the first two odd numbers, then the first three odd numbers, and so on:

First	1	= 1	= 1^2	works
First two	1 + 3	= 4	= 2^2	works
First three	1 + 3 + 5	= 9	= 3^2	works
First four	1 + 3 + 5 + 7	= 16	= 4^2	works
First five	1 + 3 + 5 + 7 + 9	= 25	= 5^2	works

The proposition is true for every n we have tested. So can we say that we have *proved* that it is true – that it is true, full stop? No! All we have done is reason *inductively*. In Chapter 6 we said that induction involves reasoning from particular to general, and that, although it is a useful way of reasoning, it cannot give us certainty. No matter how many white swans you have seen, you cannot be sure that the next swan you see won't be black. Our claim about odd numbers works for the first five odd numbers; but that is no guarantee that it will work for the first 24 or 104 odd numbers. Relying on inductive reason we cannot be sure that at some point we won't encounter a metaphorical black swan.

To see the point, you might like to consider the following example. The question now is whether the following formula generates the sequence of square numbers (1, 4, 9, etc.) for any n.

$$n^2 + n \times (n - 1) \times (n - 2) \times (n - 3) \times (n - 4)$$

So let's test it:

When $n = 1$, we get: $1 + 1 \times (0) \times (-1) \times (-2) \times (-3) = 1$

When $n = 2$, we get: $4 + 2 \times (1) \times (0) \times (-1) \times (-2) = 4$

When $n = 3$, we get: $9 + 3 \times (2) \times (1) \times (0) \times (-1) = 9$

When $n = 4$, we get: $16 + 4 \times (3) \times (2) \times (1) \times (0) = 16$

Again, things seem to be working out. But now look at what happens, when $n = 5$:

When $n = 5$, we get: $25 + 5 \times (4) \times (3) \times (2) \times (1) = 145$

Shucks – a black swan! If you try it for 6, you get 756, and if you try it for 7, you get 2,569. In fact, beyond $n = 4$, the formula *never* generates the corresponding square number. (The example is in fact a contrived one. The formula was made in such a way that for numbers up to 4, one of the parts in brackets will sum to zero, thereby cancelling out everything to the right of the n^2. Beyond 4, this does not happen. Nevertheless, the example illustrates the danger of jumping to conclusions in mathematics.)

Now consider **Goldbach's Conjecture** – a famous mathematical conjecture according to which every even number is the sum of two primes. If you try it out, it seems to work:

KT – Goldbach's Conjecture: a famous mathematical conjecture which states that every even number is the sum of two primes

2 = 1 + 1	12 = 7 + 5
4 = 2 + 2	14 = 7 + 7
6 = 3 + 3	16 = 13 + 3
8 = 5 + 3	18 = 13 + 5
10 = 5 + 5	20 = 17 + 3

If you keep running through the even numbers into the hundreds, and the thousands and the tens of thousands, Goldbach's Conjecture still works. So how far do you have to go before you can say you have *proved* it? Mathematicians have used computers to help test the conjecture for all the even numbers up to 100,000,000,000,000 and they have not found any counter-examples. You might think that is a good enough proof. But it is still abstractly possible that the next number – say, 100,000,000,000,002 – will not be the sum of two primes.

Furthermore, it is worth keeping in mind that although 100,000,000,000,000 may seem like a big number, compared with infinity, it's peanuts. For even a very large number is infinitely far away from infinity. The philosopher Ludwig Wittgenstein (1889–1951) put it well when he said: 'Where the nonsense starts is with our habit of thinking of a large number as closer to infinity than a small one.' We may have tested Goldbach's Conjecture up to 100,000,000,000,000, but the ratio of tested to untested cases is still infinitesimal. (Imagine someone testing ten swans out of a total swan population of millions, and declaring on that basis that all swans are white.)

"*You want proof? I'll give you proof!*"

Figure 12.6

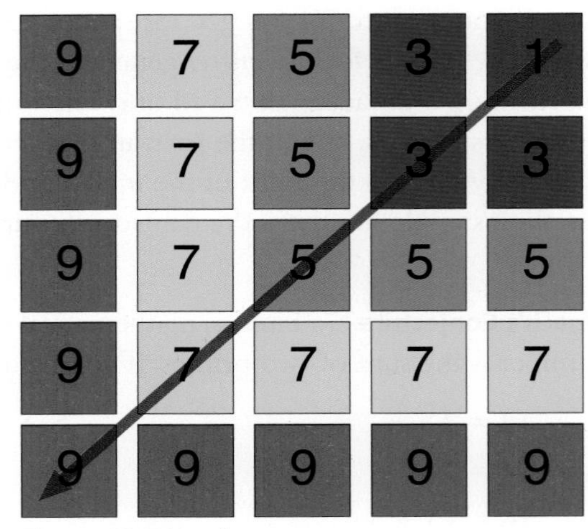

Figure 12.7 Number square

Most mathematicians believe that Goldbach's Conjecture is in fact true, but since no one has yet shown that it is necessarily true for any randomly chosen even number, it remains one of the great unproven conjectures in number theory.

In this context, it is worth mentioning that the proposition on page 318, 'The sum of the first n odd numbers = n^2' has in fact been proved. We will not give a formal proof here but you can get a visual sense of it from Figure 12.7. If you begin from the top right square and then add successive odd numbers of small squares, first 3 squares, then 5 squares, then 7 squares, then 9 squares etc. – you can see that each time they can be added to the previous square to make a larger one the side of which is equal to the number of odd numbers in the sequence.

Beauty, elegance and intuition

LQ – The arts: What is the role of beauty in mathematics?

Since any logical sequence of statements which leads to a theorem counts as a proof in mathematics, there may be many different proofs of a theorem. However, mathematicians generally seek proofs that are clear, economical and *elegant*. A particularly elegant proof might even be described as 'beautiful'. The great Hungarian mathematician Paul Erdos (1913–96) used to speak of 'the BOOK' in which God keeps the most beautiful proofs for theorems; and he once joked that, even if God does not exist, you cannot doubt the existence of 'the book'.

Although the average person may not associate mathematics with beauty, we can get a sense of what mathematicians mean by a 'beautiful' or 'elegant' solution by considering a couple of simple examples.

ACTIVITY 12.3

1. There are 1,024 people in a knock-out tennis tournament. What is the total number of games that must be played before a champion can be declared?
2. What is the sum of the integers from 1 to 100?

The tennis tournament problem seems fairly straightforward, and to solve it you might reason as follows. In the first round, there will be 512 games, in the second round, 256, in the third round, 128, in the fourth 64, in the fifth 32, and then 16, 8, 4, 2, plus the final. Summing these figures, you get 1,023. But there is another simpler way of solving the problem. If 1,024 people enter the tournament, there will only be one person who wins all of their games, and that is the eventual winner. All of the other 1,023 players will lose one and only one game – for as soon as you have lost a game, you are out of the competition. Since every game results in one winner and one loser, there is a one-to-one correspondence between losers and games played. Therefore, there must have been 1,023 games. This explanation may sound rather wordy when it is written out, but it is far more elegant and insightful than the standard way of solving the problem. While the first approach is, in effect, focusing on *winners* – there are 512 winners in the first round, 256 in the second round etc. – the insight of the second approach is to change perspective and focus instead on *losers*.

Turning to the second problem, the standard approach of grinding through the arithmetic will – if you avoid careless errors – give you the right solution: $1 + 2 = 3$, $3 + 3 = 6$, $6 + 4 = 10$, etc. However, there is, again, a more elegant way of solving the problem. If you write the numbers from 1 to 50 out from left to right, and then underneath the numbers from 51 to 100, but this time from right to left, you get the following:

1	2	3	4	5	...	46	47	48	49	50
100	99	98	97	96	...	55	54	53	52	51

When you lay the numbers out like this, you can see that if you sum each pair of numbers vertically, $1 + 100$, $2 + 99$, . . . , $49 + 52$, $50 + 51$, each pair sums to 101. How many pairs of numbers are there? 50! So the sum of the first 100 integers is $50 \times 101 = 5{,}050$. This may again be clumsy to explain in words, but with this insight you can solve the problem in seconds rather than minutes.

The other interesting thing about the insightful solutions to the above two problems is that they can be *generalised*. We can say that in any knock-out tennis tournament of n entrants the total number of games played will be $n - 1$. And we can say that the sum of the first n integers is $\frac{1}{2}n(n + 1)$.

ACTIVITY 12.4

Give a proof that the sum of the first n integers is $\frac{1}{2}n(n + 1)$.

What we can learn from this discussion is that creative imagination and intuition play a key role in mathematics. When the German mathematician David Hilbert (1862–1943) was told that one of his students had given up mathematics to become a novelist, he is said to have replied: 'It's just as well – he had no imagination.'

LQ – Intuition: How do we develop good mathematical intuitions and to what extent should we trust them?

Although some mathematicians, such as Henri Poincaré (1854–1912), stress the role played by intuition in creative mathematical work, it is important to keep in mind the distinction made in Chapter 8 between *natural intuitions* and *educated intuitions*.

ACTIVITY 12.5

If you tie a string tightly around the 'equator' of a football, and you then want to add enough string to make it go all the way round the ball one inch from its surface – as in the diagram – it turns out that you will need to add about 6 inches to your original piece of string.
Imagine that you tie a string going round the equator of the earth. (Assume the earth is a smooth sphere.) Again you decide you want the string to go round the earth one inch from its surface. How much will you need to add to the original length of string?

a. Make an intelligent guess about how much string you would need to add.

b. Calculate how much string you would need to add. (Hint π = circumference/diameter.)]

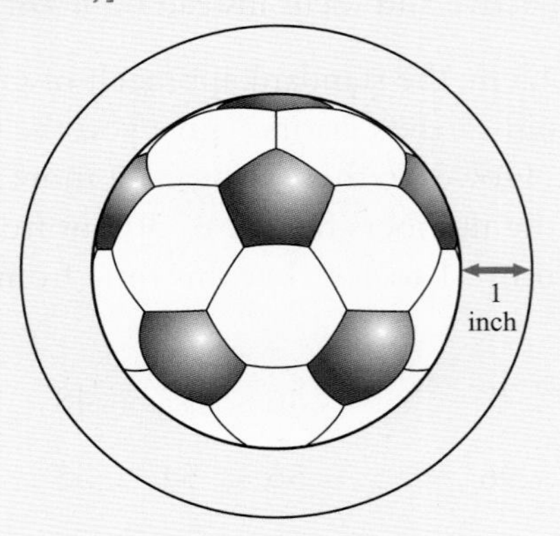

Figure 12.8

You will probably be surprised to discover that the answer for the earth is the same as the answer for the football – roughly 6 inches. This goes against most people's natural intuitions. But a mathematician with educated intuitions might not be surprised by the result. However, no matter how good a person's mathematical intuitions are, such intuitions will not be accepted by the mathematical community until they have been proved.

ACTIVITY 12.6

1. Do you think that mathematical insight can be taught, or would you say that it is something inborn and either you've got it or you haven't?
2. We sometimes use calculators and computers to help us solve mathematical problems. Does it follow that machines understand mathematics?

Figure 12.9

The social dimension and the role of technology

While a mathematically literate individual may have no difficulty in grasping a simple proof, the business of proving things has become more complicated as mathematics has progressed. Nowadays, proofs routinely run into hundreds of pages and they can only be understood by a small number of specialists who often work in teams to undertake the daunting task of verifying them. Outside their own specialist area, most mathematicians have to take the findings of their peers on trust. The mathematician Reuben Hersh (1927–) emphasises the social aspect of proof and argues that, in practice, 'The test of whether something is a proof is whether it convinces qualified judges.'

RLS – Headline: 'We need to base maths lessons on computers'. How can technology help us to extend mathematical knowledge?

Given the complexity of modern proofs, it is not surprising that mathematicians are increasingly making use of computers. In fact, they have always made use of technology, and calculating devices have a long history. For example, the abacus, which is still used in some countries, is thought to have been invented by the Chinese more than 2,000 years ago. Meanwhile, the Inca of South America used a series of knotted cords known as *quipu* to store vast amounts of numerical data. Computers are, of course, an altogether more radical and disruptive technology. According to one mathematician, 'The time when someone can do real, publishable mathematics completely without the aid of a computer is coming to a close.'

Computers are used not only to find interesting patterns in data, but also to help mathematicians prove things. While some practitioners welcome these developments, others are more ambivalent and express two main concerns:

- The first is that a computer program may contain unnoticed bugs which invalidate a proof. As this suggests, we should keep in mind that such programs are written by fallible human beings.
- The second concern is that we may end up outsourcing our understanding to machines and deferring to their authority. The point is that *knowing* the answer to something is not the same as *understanding* it – and it is surely the latter that we should seek.

What role computers should play in mathematics, and the extent to which we should trust the relentless logic of machines rather than the creative flashes of human intuition, will undoubtedly be a matter of continuing debate.

Figure 12.10 What role does technology play in mathematics?

Mathematics and certainty

After considering the nature of formal systems, we will now look in more detail at the nature of mathematical certainty.

KT – analytic proposition: a proposition that is true by definition

KT – synthetic proposition: a proposition that is not true by definition

KT – a priori knowledge: knowledge which can be justified independently of experience

KT – a posteriori knowledge: knowledge which can be justified only on the basis of experience

To do this, we will begin by making two distinctions. The first concerns the nature of propositions. An **analytic proposition** is one that is true by definition. We now add that a **synthetic proposition** is any proposition that is not analytic. So we can say that every proposition is either analytic or synthetic.

The second distinction concerns how we come to *know* that a proposition is true. A proposition is said to be knowable ***a priori*** if it can be known to be true independent of experience; and it is said to be knowable ***a posteriori*** if it cannot be known to be true independent of experience. As with the analytic–synthetic distinction, we can say that every true proposition can be known either *a priori* or *a posteriori*.

Combining the two pairs of distinctions, we can generate the following matrix:

		NATURE OF PROPOSITION	
		Analytic	Synthetic
HOW IS IT KNOWABLE?	*A priori*	1 ✓	4 ?
	A posteriori	2 ✗	3 ✓

Now let us try to explain what might fit into each of the four boxes:

Box 1 This concerns propositions that are true by definition and can be known independent of experience. Does anything go in this box? Yes! We can put all definitions in this box because they can all be known to be true independent of experience. Consider, for example, the question of how many, say, Bolivian bachelors are unmarried. I have never been to Bolivia and I know nothing about the profile of the average Bolivian bachelor, but I can say with complete confidence that every Bolivian bachelor is unmarried. Apart from a knowledge of the English language, I do not need any experience of the world to verify the truth of this proposition. It might, however, be described as a *trivial* truth. If you are told that all Bolivian bachelors are unmarried, you have learned nothing new about the world.

Box 2 For a proposition to go in box 2, it would have to be true by definition, but knowable only on the basis of experience. If a proposition is true by definition, then we can know that it is true independent of experience. So the idea of an analytic *a posteriori* proposition is self-contradictory and box 2 is empty.

Box 3 This concerns propositions that are not true by definition and that cannot be known to be true independent of experience. Does anything go in this box? Yes – our *empirical* knowledge of the world! For example, the proposition 'There are elephants in Africa' is not true by definition, and its truth can be established only on the basis of experience – *a posteriori*. Someone actually has to go to Africa and see that there are some elephants there.

Box 4 What would something that goes in box 4 look like? Well, it must be a *non-trivial* proposition – that is, one that is not true by definition – whose truth can be known independent of experience. Does anything go in this box? That is the big question!

The question is: in which box should we put mathematics? Given that box 2 is empty, there seem to be three options.

ACTIVITY 12.7

Read carefully the explanations for what kind of proposition should go in each box of the table. Decide in which of the available boxes you would put mathematics, and why.

Option 1: Mathematics as empirical

Some people, such as the philosopher John Stuart Mill (1806–72), have claimed that mathematics goes into box 3. According to Mill, mathematical truths are empirical generalisations based on a vast number of experiences that are no different in kind from scientific statements such as 'All metals expand when heated.' Mill said that the reason we feel more certain that $2 + 2 = 4$ than that all metals expand when heated is that we have seen so many more confirming instances of the former than of the latter, and this convinces us that $2 + 2 = 4$ must be true.

ACTIVITY 12.8

1. Imagine there are two hungry lions in a cage. You open the cage door and throw in two lambs. How many animals are in the cage when you return the next day? Does this do anything to convince you that 2 + 2 is not always equal to 4?
2. Can you imagine a world in which $2 + 2 = 5$? For example, what if every time you brought two pairs of objects close to one another, a fifth one popped into existence?
3. Does the fact that we usually teach children arithmetic by beginning with concrete objects, such as two apples and two apples, mean that arithmetic is an empirical subject?

Looking over the above questions, it is unlikely that the example of the lions and the lambs shakes your confidence in arithmetic. The fact that when you put two lions and two lambs together in a cage you do not end up with four animals but with two somewhat fatter lions tells you something about zoology, not arithmetic. The relevant arithmetical description of the situation would be $(2 + 2) - 2 = 2$.

Most people would deal with the second question in a similar way. There is clearly something weird about the physics of a world where a fifth object magically appears every time you bring two pairs of objects close to one another, and we would probably not allow this fact to stand against the truths of arithmetic. We might say that in this world $2 + 2 + 1 = 5$. (The inhabitants of such a strange world might never develop arithmetic – but that is another issue.) From this example it is clear that, while we can imagine a world in which the laws of physics are different, it seems to be impossible to imagine a world in which the laws of arithmetic are different.

What, if anything, can we infer from the fact that when we teach children arithmetic we usually begin with concrete objects? Let's take a closer look at the process. You show a child 2 apples and another 2 apples and ask, 'How many apples are there altogether?' She says '4'. You then do the same with oranges and bananas, and she comes up with the right answer each time. Then, at a certain point – and this is the crucial step – you ask the child, 'So what is $2 + 2$?', and you hope that she makes the *leap of abstraction* and says '4'. What the child has to grasp is that she is not simply learning interesting facts about fruit and vegetables. She has to catch on to the idea that $2n + 2n = 4n$ for any n – even if she is not yet capable of expressing it that way herself. Once the child has 'got it', she will know that if a person has 2 aardvarks and buys 2 more aardvarks, he will end up with 4 aardvarks – even if she has no idea what an aardvark is. So, while the child's knowledge undoubtedly begins with experience, it ends up going beyond experience.

ACTIVITY 12.9

Imagine that you try to teach a child arithmetic by beginning with concrete examples in the way described above. When you present them with various quantities of apples or oranges, they can do the relevant sums, but they never make the 'leap of abstraction'. They accept that 2 apples + 2 apples = 4 apples in this case, but they keep insisting that they cannot see why this should always be true. What, if anything, could you do to convince them of the general truth that $2 + 2 = 4$?

Option 2: Mathematics as analytic

A discussion of the above kind is enough to convince many people that mathematics is not empirical. We might conclude from this that it must therefore be analytic and fit in box 1 in the above diagram. According to this view, if you understand the meaning of the terms in the proposition $2 + 2 = 4$, you will see that it is true by definition. To say that $2 + 2 = 4$ is essentially the same as saying $(1 + 1) + (1 + 1) = (1 + 1 + 1 + 1)$. So when you solve a maths problem, you are simply unpacking a truth that is, in some sense, already contained in the statement of the problem. What is $2 + 2$? The answer is already there – you just need to take the wrapping off!

Despite its plausibility, there are some problems with the idea that the whole of mathematics simply consists of strings of definitional truths. To start with, if it is all just true by definition, you might wonder why mathematics is so hard. One response might be that it is difficult to keep in mind long chains of reasoning when you are trying to solve complex problems, and it is therefore easy to make an error. So perhaps a precondition for being good at mathematics is having a good short-term memory.

Another problem with the analytic claim is that mathematical truths do not seem to be trivially true in the way that 'All bachelors are unmarried men' is trivially true. Take, for example, the fact mentioned above that the sum of the first n odd numbers equals n^2. This seems more like an interesting *discovery* about numbers than something that is true by definition. The claim that mathematics is analytic seems even less plausible when we consider Goldbach's Conjecture, which has not yet been shown to be true or false. For if mathematics is analytic, we now find ourselves in the strange position of having to say that if it is true that every even number is the sum of two primes, then it is true by definition; and if it is false that every even number is the sum of two primes, then it is false by definition. This implies that we do not yet know the proper definition of terms such as 'even number' and 'prime number'. Against this, it would surely be better to say that we know what even numbers are, but have not yet discovered all of their properties, just as we might say that we know what gold is, but have not yet discovered all of its properties.

A final problem with the analytic claim is that, if we say that mathematical propositions are true by definition, we are left with the puzzling fact that they seem to fit the world so well.

Option 3: Mathematics as synthetic *a priori*

A third option is to say that mathematics is neither empirical nor analytic, but *synthetic* a priori *knowledge* and goes in box 4. The suggestion now is that mathematics gives us non-trivial, substantial knowledge about the most general features of reality, and that this knowledge can be known to be true independent of experience. If this is true, then it means that, on the basis of reason alone, human beings are able to discover truths about the nature of reality.

This is pretty much how people thought about mathematics from the time of Euclid until the nineteenth century. The system of geometry that Euclid devised seemed to combine two features that were greatly valued by those who sought the truth. First, it seemed to be absolutely certain that, if you begin with self-evident axioms and use deductive reason, you arrive at true theorems. Second, it seemed to give substantial knowledge about the nature of physical space. After all, we can use geometry to divide up areas of land, build pyramids and estimate the circumference of the earth.

Figure 12.11

Not surprisingly, Euclidean geometry was seen by many as a model for the whole of knowledge, and it became the dream of many philosophers to do for knowledge in general what Euclid had done for geometry in particular. Thus the French philosopher René Descartes (1596–1650) sought to establish a system of philosophy founded on the self-evident first principle, *Cogito, ergo sum* – 'I think, therefore I am.' (Another philosopher called Baruch Spinoza (1632–77) wrote a whole book on ethics in which he tried to prove various theorems from what he believed to be ethical axioms.) Descartes, who has been called the father of modern philosophy, famously observed:

> *To speak freely, I am convinced that it [mathematics] is a more powerful instrument of knowledge than any other that has been bequeathed to us by human agency, as being the source of all others.*

LQ – Ethics: Are basic ethical truths as certain as basic mathematical truths?

ACTIVITY 12.10

1. To what extent do you think the geometric paradigm can be applied to other areas of knowledge?
2. What are the dangers of trying to extend geometrical thinking to other areas of knowledge?

If we decide that mathematical knowledge is indeed *synthetic a priori*, we are faced with the question of how the human mind is able to discover truth about the world on the basis of reason alone. One answer is to say that God created a 'pre-established harmony' between the human mind and the universe. This may be fine if you believe in God, but it is less convincing if you do not. An alternative is to say that natural selection ensured that we evolved in such a way that our minds are in harmony with the environment. However, it is hard to see why mathematical ability would have given our remote ancestors an evolutionary advantage. A caveman didn't need calculus, and nature had no way of knowing that this would *eventually* turn out to be useful to the species. Perhaps, then, mathematical ability is a *by-product* of other abilities which do have survival value.

KT – empiricism: a school of thought which claims that all knowledge is ultimately based on sense perception

KT – formalism: (in mathematics) the belief that mathematical truths are true by definition

KT – Platonism: (in mathematics) the view that mathematical truths give us *a priori* insight into the structure of reality

We have now considered three different views about the status of mathematical knowledge, and we will put a label on each of them.

Empiricism (Option 1)	Box 3	Mathematical truths are empirical generalisations
Formalism (Option 2)	Box 1	Mathematical truths are true by definition
Platonism (Option 3)	Box 4	Mathematical truths give us *a priori* insight into the structure of reality. (This view can be traced back to Plato – hence the name.)

The empiricist view of mathematics has probably been the least popular of the three options, but you can find plenty of formalists and Platonists hiding in mathematics departments!

Discovered or invented?

A good way of highlighting the difference between Platonism and formalism is to consider the question, *Is mathematics discovered or invented?* While Platonists believe that mathematical entities are discovered and exist 'out there', formalists argue that they are invented and exist only 'in the mind'.

ACTIVITY 12.11

1. What is the difference between saying that something has been 'discovered' and saying that it has been 'invented'? What sorts of things do we usually say are discovered, and what sorts of things invented?
2. Do you think that intelligent aliens would come up with the same mathematics as us, or might they develop a completely different kind of mathematics?

At first sight, neither the 'discovered' nor the 'invented' options look very attractive. If mathematical entities exist 'out there', does that mean that if we travel far enough in a space ship, we will one day encounter pi? And if mathematics is all in the mind, does that mean that mathematicians are simply making it up as they go along?

If we think more deeply about this issue, we run into puzzling questions about the meaning of the word 'existence'. We want to say that mathematical objects exist because we are able to make objective discoveries about them. You can, for example, prove that a circle encloses the largest possible two-dimensional area for a given perimeter, and anyone who follows your proof will come to the same conclusion. However, it turns out that mathematical objects, such as circles, do not exist in the real world. Wait a minute! Aren't coins and car wheels circles, and can't you draw a circle on a piece of paper any time you feel like it? In a strict mathematical sense, the answer is 'no'.

To see this, we need to go back to the definition of a circle – 'the set of all points in a plane that are equidistant from a given point'. With that definition in mind, try drawing a circle. If you do it free-hand, your drawing will be far from perfect. You will get a better result if you use a pencil and compass; but if you look at it with a magnifying glass, you will see that the border is fuzzy and it is not a perfect circle. You cannot solve the problem by using a finer pencil because if you increase the power of your magnifying glass the same fuzziness will appear again. Extrapolating from this, you can see that it is in fact impossible to draw a mathematically perfect circle – or any other geometrical object. A line, for example, is defined as that which has length but no breadth – and that is clearly something you cannot draw on a piece of paper. In a similar way, it turns out that there are no exact measurements either. For example, there is no such thing as exactly 4 centimetres – only exactly 4 centimetres 'to a given number of significant places'. Such mathematical entities are *idealisations*; and, while you may get closer to the ideal, you will never be able to coincide with them.

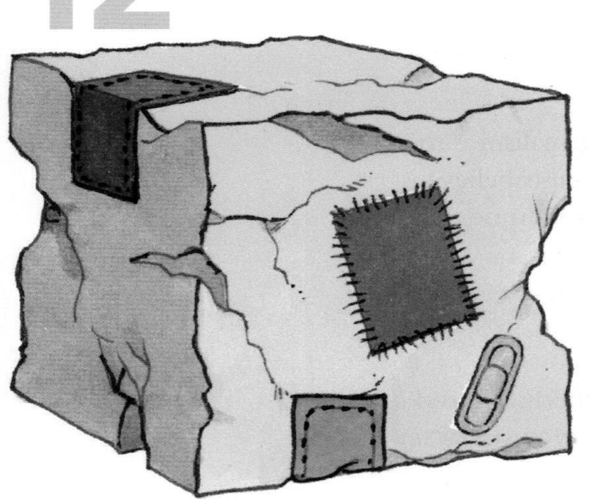

Figure 12.12 Platonism: physical reality is very different from mathematical perfection

The above discussion would seem to leave us with the following dilemma. On the one hand, since mathematical objects do not exist in the real world, they *must be mental fictions*. On the other hand, since we are capable of making discoveries about them, they *cannot be mental fictions*.

Plato's solution to the above dilemma was to say that mathematical objects exist 'out there', but not in the we-might-one-day-encounter-them-in-a-space-ship sense in which physical objects exist. Rather, they have their own unique way of existing; and although they cannot be perceived, they are just as real as physical objects. Indeed, Plato believed that they are *more real* than physical objects. How could anyone believe *that*?

Here is an updated Platonic argument. Consider the physical world. A physicist will tell you that the underlying reality of an everyday object, such as a table, is quite different from its appearance. Despite its apparent sturdiness and immobility, a table consists mainly of empty space in which atoms are whizzing around at great speed. Furthermore, tables and chairs – and human beings – come into being, exist briefly, and then return to dust. By contrast, mathematical objects have a clarity and immutability which – for Plato at least – gives them a superior existence. When you study Pythagoras' theorem at school, you are studying the same eternal truth that Pythagoras discovered more than two and a half thousand years ago; and it will be as true in a million years' time as it is now.

Plato's argument for the superior reality of mathematical over physical objects can be reduced to two key claims:

1. Mathematics is more certain than perception.
2. Mathematics is timelessly true.

ACTIVITY 12.12

1. 'In order for something to exist, it must be possible to observe it.' Do you agree or disagree with this statement? Give reasons.
2. Do you think that numbers have always existed? Did they exist at the time of the Big Bang? If they exist, where do you suppose they exist?
3. Do you think that the full expansion of pi, which goes on for ever, exists 'out there', and that we are gradually discovering more and more about it?

Criticisms of Platonism

While Platonism continues to be popular with some mathematicians, others dismiss it as 'pie in the sky' mysticism. Two main objections can be made against it:

1. Since the series of natural numbers is infinite, Platonism is committed to the view that there are literally an infinite number of abstract mathematical entities 'out there'. This seems hard to believe. If we abandon the idea that reality consists only of observable entities, we seem to be in danger of wandering off into mysticism.

2. If mathematical objects have some strange kind of ideal existence, then how can physically embodied beings such as ourselves get to know about them?

According to formalism, which sees the above objections as decisive, mathematics consists of nothing but man-made definitions, axioms and theorems. We might liken it to a game of chess. A certain position on a chessboard is like a theorem that follows from the 'axioms of chess'. Since no one would say that all possible chess moves exist 'out there' in a Platonic heaven, why should we be tempted to say this about mathematics?

Some philosophers have suggested that rather than think of mathematical entities as being either objective or subjective, we should think of them as having 'social existence'. Consider again the game of chess. In what sense does it exist? Does it still exist if no one is playing chess? What about if no one is thinking about chess? Would it still exist if we destroyed all the rule books on how to play chess? Most people would probably say that even if no one played chess for a year, there would still be certain statements about it that are true and others that are false. However, if the human race disappeared it wouldn't make much sense to say that the game of chess still existed.

ACTIVITY 12.13

Although Romeo and Juliet are fictional characters, it is true to say that Romeo loves Juliet and false to say that he hates Juliet. In what ways are mathematical objects similar to fictional characters and in what ways are they different?

Well, enough of these tricky questions about the meaning of existence. To develop our discussion about the nature of mathematics further, we must now look at the rise of alternative – 'non-Euclidean' – systems of geometry in the nineteenth century.

Non-Euclidean geometry and the problem of consistency

As we said earlier, Euclidean geometry was for many centuries seen as a model of knowledge because it seemed to be both certain and informative. There was, however, one small problem. The certainty of geometry was supposed to be guaranteed by the fact that one began with self-evident axioms and used deductive reason to derive theorems. However, one of Euclid's axioms, the axiom of parallels – which says that there is just one straight line through a given point which is parallel to a given line – struck people as being less self-evident than the other axioms. This doubt may have arisen from the fact that parallel lines are by definition lines that never meet even if you extend them to infinity – but who is to say what happens at infinity? Since mathematicians wished to get rid of all possible doubt, they expended a great deal of energy over the centuries in trying to demonstrate that the axiom of parallels was in fact a theorem. But no one succeeded in doing this!

Figure 12.13 Railtracks: Does it strike you as intuitively obvious that parallel lines never meet?

Riemannian geometry

In the nineteenth century, a mathematician called Georg Friedrich Bernard Riemann (1822–66) came up with the clever idea of replacing some of Euclid's axioms with their contraries. Most people thought that if you based a system of geometry on non-Euclidean axioms, the system would lead to a contradiction and so collapse. This would then show that Euclid's axioms were in fact the only possible ones. However, to people's amazement, no contradictions turned up in Riemann's system.

Riemann's axioms differed from Euclid's as follows:

A. Two points may determine more than one line (instead of axiom 1).

B. All lines are finite in length but endless – i.e. circles (instead of axiom 2).

C. There are no parallel lines (instead of axiom 5).

Among the theorems that can be deduced from these axioms are:

1. All perpendiculars to a straight line meet at one point.

2. Two straight lines enclose an area.

3. The sum of the angles of any triangle is greater than 180 degrees.

These theorems sound pretty strange. How can perpendiculars possibly meet at a point, or two straight lines enclose an area, or the angles of a triangle sum to more than 180 degrees? Fortunately, we can give intuitive sense to Riemannian geometry by imagining that space is like the surface of a sphere. Since we live on the surface of a sphere (more or less), this should not be too difficult to do!

The key to making sense of Riemann's system is to think about what a straight line will look like on the surface of a sphere. What is a straight line? The shortest distance between two points! Now, on the surface of a sphere, it can be shown that the shortest distance between two points is always an arc of a circle whose centre is the centre of the sphere. Such 'great circles' include not only all lines of longitude, but an endless number of other circles – as can be seen from Figure 12.14. (The only line of latitude that is a great circle is the equator.)

What this means is that, in Riemannian geometry, a straight line will appear curved when it is represented on a two-dimensional map. To illustrate this point, look at any airline flight map. Although the flight paths look curved, since airlines are in the business of making money, you can be sure that in reality they always take the shortest route to their destination.

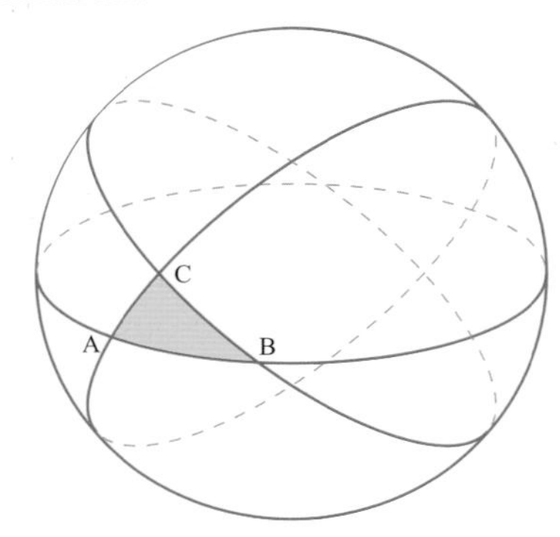

Figure 12.14 Riemannian geometry

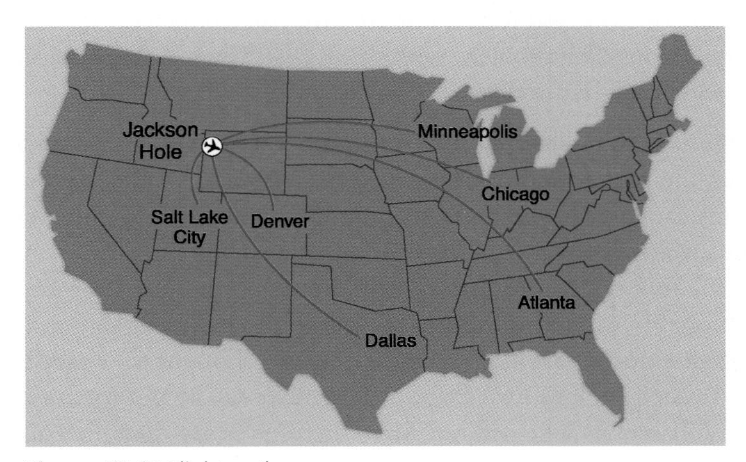

Figure 12.15 Flight paths

Once we have clarified the meaning of a straight line in Riemannian geometry, we can give a meaning to the three theorems mentioned above:

1. *All perpendiculars to a straight line meet at one point.* Lines of longitude are perpendicular to the equator, but they meet at the north pole.

2. *Two straight lines enclose an area.* Any two lines of longitude (straight lines) meet at both the north and south pole and so define an area (see Figure 12.14).

3. *The sum of the angles of any triangle is greater than 180 degrees.* This can be seen in Figure 12.14.

ACTIVITY 12.14

With our discussion of Riemannian geometry in mind, try to solve the following puzzle. A hunter leaves his house one morning and walks one mile due south. He then walks one mile due west and shoots a bear, before walking a mile due north back to his house. What colour is the bear?

The problem of consistency

Although Riemann did not find any contradictions in his system of geometry, some of his contemporaries were convinced that sooner or later a contradiction would be found and Riemann's system would collapse. After all, he had not *proved* that his system was free from contradiction. As a result of this, mathematicians became increasingly interested in the problem of consistency, and the question of how we can be sure that any given formal system is free from contradiction.

You might think that if no contradictions have been found in a formal system that has been studied by the mathematical community then that is good enough. After all, people have been using Euclidean geometry for thousands of years, and not a single contradiction has turned up. While this would be enough to convince most people, it is not mathematically compelling. For it is still only a *conjecture* and it does not *prove* that the system in question is free from contradiction.

Another approach might be to appeal to intuition. Surely, if you begin with things that are intuitively obvious and reason consistently, you can be confident you will not run into contradictions. The problem with this is that, as we saw in Chapter 8, our intuitions can sometimes let us down.

To illustrate, consider the following story of a barber who was in love with the king's daughter. When the king found out, he was very angry and wanted to put the barber to death. But his daughter begged him to spare the barber's life. Wishing to appear merciful while ensuring that the barber eventually died, the king came up with a cunning plan. He told the barber that he would not execute him if he obeyed one simple instruction. He was to go back to his village the following day and *shave all and only those inhabitants who do not shave themselves*. 'Wow', thought the barber, 'that's easy!' Overjoyed, he headed back to his village and the next day he got to work shaving all and only those inhabitants who did not shave themselves. By dusk, he had completed his task, and tired but happy he returned home. Opening the front door, he happened to glance in the mirror in the hallway. 'Ah', he thought, 'I've missed someone. I, too, am an inhabitant of this village; so the king's instruction also applies to me.' As the barber turned this over in his mind, it slowly dawned on him that he had been trapped. For according to the king's instruction, if he shaved himself, then he shouldn't shave himself, and if he didn't, then he should! The instruction which had sounded simple enough turned out to be impossible to fulfil, and the barber was duly executed. Given our interests, the moral of the tale is not 'Don't mess with kings' daughters' but 'Apparently clear instructions can sometimes be impossible to fulfil.' What this means in terms of mathematics is that intuition alone is no guarantee that a system is free from contradiction.

Gödel's incompleteness theorem

The concern with consistency continued into the twentieth century. Finally in 1931, a young Austrian mathematician called Kurt Gödel (1906–78) came up with an extraordinary proof, known as **Gödel's incompleteness theorem**, which shook the mathematical world to its foundations. What Gödel proved was that *it is impossible to prove that a formal mathematical system is free from contradiction.* We need to be a little careful here: Gödel did not prove that mathematics actually contains contradictions, but that we cannot be certain that it doesn't. What this means is that, at an abstract level, even mathematics is unable to give us certainty. For it is always possible that one day we will find a contradiction; and one small contradiction in a formal system would be enough to destroy the entire system. A mathematician friend of mine said that the first time he read Gödel's theorem it made him 'very sad'. Since as a matter of fact no contradictions have ever been discovered in the structure of mathematics, most mathematicians do not lose any sleep over Gödel's theorem, and they take a 'business as usual' approach to the subject. Nevertheless, there is a sense in which, after nearly two and a half thousand years, the last bastion of certainty has been breached by the turbulent waters of doubt.

KT – Gödel's incompleteness theorem: a theorem that suggests it is impossible to prove that a formal mathematical system is free from contradiction

Figure 12.16 Kurt Gödel

The story ends with not only the *certainty*, but also the *informative content*, of Euclidean geometry coming under fire. For if there are alternative systems of geometry, the question now arises: Which one provides the best description of physical reality? Although Euclidean geometry clearly works well enough at the 'local' level, it turns out that, according to Einstein's theory of relativity, the universe obeys the rules of Riemannian geometry, not Euclidean geometry. According to our best scientific theories, space is curved!

Applied mathematics

To complete our discussion of mathematics, we now turn to applied mathematics – mathematics that is used to model and solve problems in the real world. Our discussion in the last section has shown that we can no longer unquestioningly assume that human reason gives us insight into the structure of reality. For the main alleged example of such rational insight – Euclidean geometry – turned out to be a false description of reality. At the same time, mathematics is still amazingly useful, and it is hard to avoid Galileo's conviction that the book of nature is written in the language of mathematics.

LQ – Human sciences: How useful are mathematical models in the human sciences?

The Fibonacci series

In this context, we might mention the mathematical patterns based on the *Fibonacci series*, which can be found in nature. The series is named after the famous thirteenth-century Italian mathematician (but was also discovered independently by a sixth-century Indian poet called Virahanka). The series begins 1, 1 and then continues by adding the previous two terms of the series together: 2, 3, 5, 8, 13, 21, 34, 55, . . . This series has many interesting properties. Among them, if you take the ratios of adjacent numbers in the Fibonacci series – 3/2, 5/3, 8/5, 13/8, 21/13, etc. – they converge

RLS – Headline: 'US Election 2012: Statistician Nate Silver correctly predicts all 50 States'. How can statistics help us to make accurate predictions?

Figure 12.17 The Fibonacci series is widespread in nature

on what is known as the *golden ratio* (or 'golden mean') – roughly 1.618. Fibonacci numbers have been described as 'nature's favourite numbers', and patterns connected with them can be found in such things as the petals of flowers, the branching pattern in trees and the arrangement of seeds on the head of a sunflower. Such arrangements ensure that things fit together in an efficient way so that, for example, each petal on a flower gets maximum exposure to sunlight and moisture.

There are many extravagant claims made about the golden ratio and it can be hard to distinguish fact from fiction. One common assertion is that rectangular and spiral patterns based on it are particularly beautiful. This is, however, open to question. To test the claim, let us conduct a rectangle 'beauty competition'. Which of the rectangles in Figure 12.18 do you find most aesthetically pleasing? One of them is a 'golden rectangle' (find out which one on page X); but many people do not choose this as their favourite. This suggests that the claim is false. According to mathematician Keith Devlin, the rectangles we find most pleasing may simply be the result of habituation.

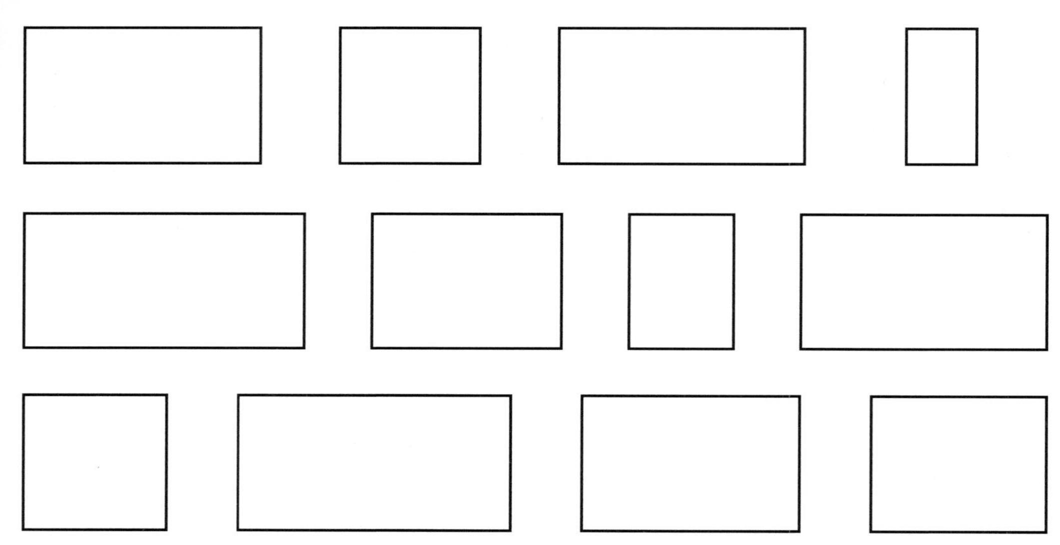

Figure 12.18 Which of these rectangles do you find most aesthetically pleasing? See page 338.

Why is maths so useful?

Despite the above reservations, there is no doubt that many of nature's patterns can be described in the language of mathematics. A particularly striking fact is that mathematical ideas which are developed as a purely intellectual exercise sometimes turn out to be applicable to the real world. For example, in the third century BCE, the Greeks became interested in the geometry of *ellipses*, and a mathematician called Apollonius of Perga (c262–c190 BCE) wrote eight weighty volumes about them. As fascinating as the topic was – at least to Apollonius – the knowledge he acquired was completely useless. If someone had asked him what the point of studying ellipses was, he might have quoted Euclid's crushing response to a student who asked a similar question: 'Give him a penny – he wants to profit from his learning!' The pursuit of such knowledge was considered to be an end in itself that did not need a practical justification. Yet the strange thing is that, when the seventeenth-century astronomer Johannes Kepler (1571–1630) was studying planetary motion, he discovered that, rather than being circular, as had previously been believed, the orbits of the planets round the sun are in fact elliptical. After being of merely academic interest for nearly two thousand years, Apollonius' work turned out to be of practical value!

Similarly, although Riemann developed non-Euclidean geometry as a purely intellectual exercise, thirty years later, Einstein concluded that space conforms to Riemannian rather than Euclidean geometry.

ACTIVITY 12.15

To what extent do you think governments should fund 'useless' research in pure mathematics?

How can we explain what one physicist has described as 'the unreasonable effectiveness of mathematics'? Here is what Einstein had to say on the subject:

> *How can it be that mathematics, being after all a product of human thought which is independent of experience, is so admirably appropriate to the objects of reality? Is human reason, then, without experience, merely by taking thought, able to fathom the properties of real things? In my opinion, the answer to the question is briefly this: – As far as the laws of mathematics refer to reality, they are not certain; and as far as they are certain, they do not refer to reality.*

RLS – Headline: 'Maths expert creates formula for "perfect" tennis serve'. To what extent can natural phenomena be explained in the language of mathematics?

This is an interesting way of looking at the connection between mathematics and the world. What Einstein is saying is that mathematical systems are *invented*, but it is a matter of *discovery* which of the various systems apply to reality. You can invent any formal system you like and prove theorems from axioms with complete certainty. However, once you ask which system applies to the world, you are faced with an *empirical* question which can only be answered on the basis of observation. Thus Einstein discovered that Riemannian geometry is a better description of physical space than Euclidean geometry.

You might ask why *any* purely invented system should have application to reality. A possible response is that some of the formal systems we invent are originally suggested to us by reality. For example, since geometry first arose in response to practical problems, and was then formalised by Euclid, it is perhaps not surprising that Euclidean geometry turned out to be a useful way of describing reality. In other words, the point is that, even if mathematics is a game, the rules for the most interesting or useful games may be suggested to us by reality.

Nevertheless, there are many unexpected connections in mathematics that are difficult to explain. For example, π – which, as we discussed earlier, is the circumference of any circle divided by its diameter – turns up in all kinds of seemingly unrelated places, such as the solution to *Buffon's needle problem*. This problem was posed by the French mathematician the Comte de Buffon (1707–78). Suppose you have a large sheet of paper ruled with parallel lines drawn at one unit intervals resting on a flat surface and you then throw a needle which is one unit long at random on to the paper. What is the probability that it will intersect one of the lines? Surprisingly, the answer to the problem turns out to be $2/\pi$.

Figure 12.19 Buffon's needle problem

At a deep level, then, there remains something mysterious about the 'unreasonable effectiveness of mathematics'. This is, I think, connected to the equally perplexing question of why there is order in the universe – in particular, order of the kind that can be uncovered by mathematical thinking. Perhaps all we can say is that if there wasn't any order we wouldn't be around to ask why not!

Conclusion

LQ – Religion: Does the belief some mathematicians have in 'an independent immaterial timeless world of mathematical truth' resemble a religion?

At the beginning of this chapter, we defined mathematics as 'the science of rigorous proof' and we discussed the commonly held view that it is an island of certainty in an ocean of doubt. There is something immensely appealing about the idea of demonstrating something in such a way that any rational person will come to the same conclusion, and it is not surprising that mathematics has often served as a model for knowledge.

Nevertheless, we have seen that even in this most rigorous of subjects there are limits to certainty. At an abstract level, Gödel showed that we can never prove that mathematics is free from contradiction; and although this is unlikely to keep mathematicians awake at night, it means that the dream of absolute certainty will never be realised. At a more practical level, we have seen that when mathematics is applied to the real world we usually have a choice of axioms and we can only decide which are the most useful by testing them against reality.

Although mathematics cannot give us absolute certainty, it continues to play a key role in a wide variety of subjects ranging from physics to economics, and there is something surprising and mysterious about its extraordinary usefulness. Nevertheless, it is important to keep in mind that we cannot capture everything in the abstract map of mathematics and, despite its value, there is no reason to believe that it is the only, or always the best, tool for making sense of reality.

About figure 12.8 (page 336): The rectangle second from right on the bottom row approximates to the golden ratio. You may not agree, but most people find this the most aesthetically pleasing rectangle.

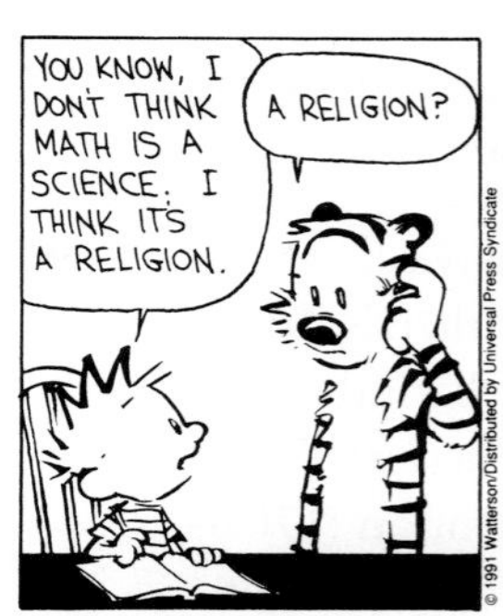

Figure 12.20

Key points

- Mathematics, which can be defined as 'the science of rigorous proof', begins with axioms and uses deductive reason to derive theorems.
- Although proof is the logical matter of deriving theorems from axioms, mathematicians consider some proofs to be more beautiful than others.
- According to three different views about the nature of mathematical truths, they are either: (1) empirical, (2) true by definition, or (3) rational insights into universal truths.
- While some people believe that mathematics is discovered, others claim that it is invented; but neither view seems to be entirely satisfactory.
- The development of non-Euclidean geometries in the nineteenth century raised the question of how we can be sure that a formal system is free from contradiction.
- Kurt Gödel proved that it is impossible to prove that a formal mathematical system is free from contradiction.
- Mathematicians and philosophers are still perplexed by the extraordinary usefulness of mathematics.

Key terms

a posteriori knowledge
a priori knowledge
analytic proposition
axiom
conjecture
deductive reasoning
empiricism
Euclidean geometry
formal system
formalism
Gödel's incompleteness theorem
Goldbach's Conjecture
Platonism
synthetic proposition
theorem

Knowledge framework focus

1. *Scope/applications*. Can everything be captured in the language of mathematics, or do some phenomena lie beyond its scope?
2. *Concepts/language*. Do mathematical concepts differ from everyday ones in that they can be precisely defined?

3. *Methodology.* How influential has the 'mathematical paradigm' been as a model for knowledge in general?
4. *Historical development.* How did the rise of non-Euclidean geometry change people's conception of mathematics? How is computer technology changing the nature of mathematics?
5. *Relation to personal knowledge.* Why are so many people frightened of mathematics?

IB prescribed essay titles

1. To what extent is truth different in mathematics, the arts and ethics? (November 2009 / May 2010)
2. Mathematicians have the concept of rigorous proof, which leads to knowing something with complete certainty. Consider the extent to which complete certainty might be achievable in mathematics and at least one other area of knowledge. (November 2007 / May 2008)

Further reading

Books

G. H. Hardy, *A Mathematician's Apology* (Cambridge University Press, 1994). In this short, readable book, G. H. Hardy seeks to justify his devotion to mathematics despite his insistence that '"real" mathematics is almost entirely "useless"'. The book contains many thought-provoking comments about the nature of mathematics and its relation to the arts and sciences. You don't have to be a mathematician to enjoy it.

Alex Bellos, *Alex's Adventures in Numberland* (Bloomsbury, 2011). Aimed at the 'reader with no mathematical knowledge', this book is a great romp through the history of mathematics and its applications to everyday life. Bellos does a great job of bringing the subject alive and highlighting its creativity and wonder.

Andrew Dilnot and Michael Blastland, *The Tiger That Isn't: Seeing Through a World of Numbers* (Profile Books, 2008). A useful and accessible account of how to make sense of statistics and avoid being misled by journalists and manipulated by politicians. As the authors show, when numbers are taken out of context they can be used to prove almost anything.

Online articles

Ian Stewart, 'Think Maths', *New Scientist*, 30 November 1986.

The natural sciences

13

Science may be described as the art of systematic oversimplification.

Karl Popper, 1902–94

When you cannot measure, your knowledge is meagre and unsatisfactory.

Lord Kelvin, 1824–1907

Science is a way of thinking more than it is a body of knowledge.

Carl Sagan, 1934–96

Don't believe the results of experiments until they're confirmed by theory.

Sir Arthur Eddington, 1882–1944

Science is a long history of learning how not to fool ourselves.

Richard Feynman, 1918–88

Science does not tell us how to live.

Leo Tolstoy, 1828–1910

Everything you've learned . . . as 'obvious' becomes less and less obvious as you begin to study the universe.

Buckminster Fuller, 1895–1983

The arrogance of scientists is not nearly so dangerous as the arrogance that comes from ignorance.

Lewis Wolpert, 1956–

Science is a way of describing reality; it is therefore limited by the limits of observation, and it asserts nothing which is outside observation.

Jacob Bronowski, 1908–74

Science is the only genuine permanent revolution in human affairs, since it is committed to challenging the findings of its forebears.

Daniel Bell, 1919–

Introduction

The story of the natural sciences is a story of remarkable achievements. The scientific revolution of the seventeenth century, which is associated with the names of such great scientists as Galileo Galilei (1564–1642), Isaac Newton (1642–1727) and Robert Boyle (1627–91), initiated a period of tremendous progress which shows no sign of coming to an end. In little more than three centuries, we have discovered the fundamental laws of physics, the 92 elements that make up the periodic table, and some of the secrets of life that are written into our DNA. Science has not only enabled us to split the atom, clone a sheep, and put men on the moon, it has also delivered all kinds of practical benefits such as cars, phones and computers.

KT – paradigm: a set of interrelated ideas for making sense of one or more aspects of reality

Perhaps not surprisingly, the extraordinary success of the natural sciences has led some people to see them as the dominant cognitive **paradigm** or model of knowledge. From time to time, there have been attempts to establish other areas of knowledge on a more scientific foundation that mimics the rigour and apparent certainty of subjects like physics. Some people have even argued that science is the *only* road to knowledge, and that if you cannot prove something scientifically then you don't really know it at all.

Figure 13.1 American astronaut Ed White doing the first American spacewalk in 1965: Are we impressed by science partly because of its success?

Despite the success of the natural sciences, we should be cautious about some of the more extravagant claims that are made on its behalf. For science is not infallible and despite its many strengths it also has its weaknesses and limitations. We often hear that *science has proved that* something or other is the case – as if scientific findings had the certainty of mathematical deductions. However, since science has a history and scientific beliefs change over time, we might wonder how far the natural sciences really do give us certainty. We also need to keep in mind that the natural sciences do not have a monopoly on the truth and that there may be other equally valid ways of making sense of the world.

ACTIVITY 13.1

Give some examples of things that were believed to be true by nineteenth-century scientists but which we now know to be false.

Recently, some critics of science have drawn attention to the dangers as well as the benefits of scientific knowledge, and there has been a reaction against 'science worship'. In some quarters, there is a feeling that science is 'out of control', and that scientists are 'playing God' and meddling with things they do not fully understand. Alarming predictions about nuclear war or the harmful effects of cloning may lead us to question whether in the long term the benefits of science outweigh the costs.

ACTIVITY 13.2

1. What connotations does the word 'science' have for you? Are they positive, negative or mixed?
2. How are scientists viewed in popular culture, such as novels and movies? Are they generally seen as heroes or as villains?

Our concern in this chapter is with the nature and status of scientific knowledge. We will begin by looking at why it is important to distinguish between science and non-science, and then go on to look at three different theories of how science works. Finally, we will come back to the question of science and values.

Science and pseudo-science

The natural sciences typically denote subjects like physics, chemistry and biology. Since the word 'science' is like a stamp of approval or guarantee of quality, advertisers sometimes appeal to the status of science to sell their products, and charlatans may describe dubious medicines and remedies as 'scientific' in order to deceive gullible people.

ACTIVITY 13.3

Find and analyse any two advertisements that use the language of science in order to market their products.

LQ – Language: What role do metaphors play in scientific thinking?

Among the huge number of things that have been described as 'scientific' by their proponents are the following.

- *Acupuncture* – the belief that by inserting needles into various parts of the body you can restore normal energy balance to relieve pain and cure various disorders.
- *Astrology* – the belief that our characters are determined by the celestial bodies (sun, moon, planets and stars) at the time of our birth.
- *Creationism* – the belief that the theory of evolution is false and that each species was uniquely created by God.
- *Crystology* – the belief that crystals have magical healing powers.
- *Feng shui* – the belief that the positioning and physical characteristics of your home can affect the balance and harmony of your life.

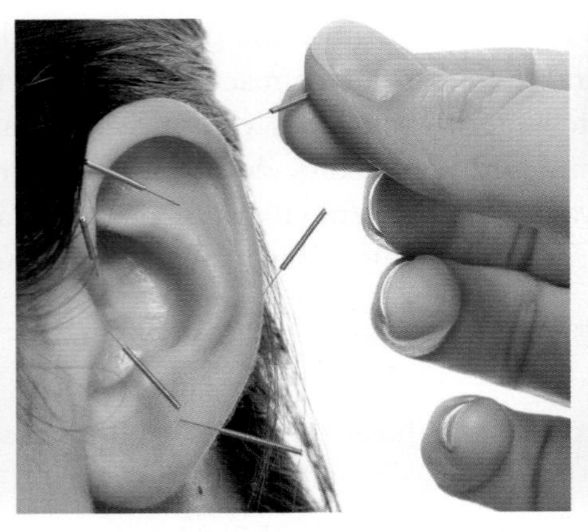

Figure 13.2 How would you go about trying to determine whether there is any truth in astrology, acupuncture or feng shui?

RLS – Headline: 'Homeopathy is "rubbish" and shouldn't be available on the NHS [British National Health Service], says Britain's top doctor'. What distinguishes science from pseudo-science?

- *Graphology* – the belief that by analysing a person's handwriting you can learn about their character.
- *Homeopathy* – the belief that an extremely small quantity of a substance that can cause certain symptoms in a healthy person can cure similar symptoms in an unhealthy person.
- *Phrenology* – the belief that the structure of a person's skull determines their character and mental ability.

We should perhaps be open-minded about some of the above beliefs and find out more about them before deciding whether or not there is any truth in them. For it could be argued that if they 'work' for people and, for example, help to alleviate pain, then, whether or not they are scientific, it would be foolish to condemn them. If millions of people claim to get relief from acupuncture, then even if we do not understand how it works, why not accept it as a useful tool in the medical armoury? Nevertheless, *if* acupuncture does work then it surely makes sense to try to find out *why* it works, and this will inevitably involve doing such things as formulating hypotheses and conducting **controlled experiments** to test them. If we are to understand what is going on, there does not seem to be any other way to proceed.

KT – controlled experiment: an experiment in which everything is held constant except for the variable under investigation

KT – pseudo-science: a set of beliefs which mimic the surface features of science without being genuinely scientific

While some people are willing to subject their beliefs to proper scientific tests, others are not. They simply *state* that their beliefs are scientific. But just because someone *says* that something is scientific does not mean that it *is* scientific. For example, a racist might claim that his theories are based on biological research, but we are not going to take *his* word for it. What we need are criteria for distinguishing genuine science from **pseudo-science** (fake science).

Of course, just because something is not a science does not mean that it is a pseudo-science. For example, literary criticism is not a science, but since it makes no claim to be scientific, it is not a pseudo-science either, and as a way of trying to make sense of a text it has its own validity. *What distinguishes a pseudo-science is that it claims the status of science while lacking its substance.*

Consider, for example, crystology – a set of beliefs about the magical power of crystals which claim to be scientific but have not been scientifically tested. Among

Figure 13.3

the claims made by advocates of crystology is that quartz crystals generate 'a field of positive crystalline energy'. Something called a 'bioelectric shield' – a kind of magic pendant – is said to be 'medically proven' and 'based on Nobel Prize-winning physics'. Among the alleged benefits of the shield are that it 'boosts your immune system and reduces stress while enhancing mental, emotional and physical performance'. You can buy such a shield for anything from $139 to over $1,000. Meanwhile, a 'certified Master of crystology' advertises a comprehensive healing session in which 'your aura will be cleansed and balanced', and any weaknesses or areas of the body under stress will be addressed through the practitioner's 'intuitive use of crystals'. The cost of a half-hour session is $90. Perhaps there is something in all this, but you would be wise to investigate these claims more thoroughly before parting with your money.

ACTIVITY 13.4

1. What is the difference between astronomy and astrology? Why is the former classified as a science and the latter not? Do you agree with this classification?
2. As a scientist, how would you go about trying to test the claims of astrology?
3. Do some research on the 'placebo effect' and give a short explanation of it. What is its relevance when we evaluate the claims of alternative medicine?

Figure 13.4

The difference between science and pseudo-science

KT – hypothesis: a tentative explanation for an observation or problem which, if it is to be scientific, is testable

The main difference between science and pseudo-science is that scientific **hypotheses** are *testable*, whereas pseudo-scientific ones are not. There are at least two ways in which pseudo-scientific hypotheses protect themselves from being testable:

1. *Vagueness.* If a statement is sufficiently vague, it will be impossible to verify or falsify it. A claim such as 'quartz crystals can restore the balance and energy of your life' is, as it stands, virtually meaningless. To turn it into a genuinely scientific claim would need some kind of criteria – preferably measurable ones – to determine the meaning of words like 'balance' and 'energy'. We might also want to know the time period within which these improvements are supposed to take place.
2. Ad hoc *exceptions.* A statement may be protected by various kinds of *ad hoc* exceptions. For example, if someone says 'All swans are white' and you show them a black one, they may qualify their statement by saying 'All swans are white except that mutation.' A good scientific hypothesis is one that is general in nature and does not keep making exceptions every time it meets counter-examples.

Given the above discussion, it seems reasonable to say that for a hypothesis to be a genuinely scientific statement it must be testable, and that it will be easier to test if the following are true:

1. It is clearly stated and makes precise rather than vague predictions.
2. It does not keep making *ad hoc* exceptions when it comes across counter-examples.

ACTIVITY 13.5

1. Which of the following statements make scientifically testable claims?
   a. In 2016 you may or may not win the lottery.
   b. It always rains on Tuesdays.
   c. We have all lived past lives, but most of us are too unenlightened to remember them.
   d. Real men don't cry.
   e. Unlike magnetic poles attract each other.
   f. Everyone is selfish.
   g. Acids turn litmus paper red.
   h. Something surprising will happen to you next week.
2. To what extent do you think astrology consists of genuinely testable propositions?

The scientific method

In trying to distinguish science from non-science, you might list all the subjects that count as science – such as physics, chemistry and biology – and then say that everything else is non-science. However, this is not very helpful because it does not explain *why* some things count as science and other things do not. A better approach might be to say that what distinguishes science from non-science is a distinctive *method*; science is therefore not so much a fixed body of knowledge as a way of thinking about the world.

ACTIVITY 13.6

1. Each of the elements below is relevant to the scientific method. Try to put them into the correct order and write a short description of how a scientist typically works.
   a. Experiment
   b. Induction
   c. Hypothesis
   d. Law
   e. Measurement
   f. Observation
   g. Repeatability
   h. Theory
2. How is each of the following similar to scientific activity and how is it different?
   a. Baking a cake by following a recipe.
   b. 'Experimenting' with ingredients and making your own recipe.
   c. Collecting and organising stamps from around the world.
   d. Repairing a car that has broken down.
   e. Heating a fixed volume of gas to see what happens to the pressure.
   f. Speculating on the origins of the universe.
   g. Studying human anatomy before making a sculpture.
   h. Doing detective work to solve a murder.
   i. Inventing the light bulb.
   j. Predicting rain because the clouds look threatening.
   k. Solving a crossword puzzle.
   l. Noticing that you always seem to need something just after you have thrown it away.

Inductivism

KT – inductivism: the traditional conception of the scientific method, using inductive methods of reasoning

The aim of science is not to reproduce reality, but to develop testable models which capture its essential features. According to the traditional approach, which is known as **inductivism**, there are five key steps in the scientific method:

1. observation
2. hypothesis
3. experiment
4. law
5. theory

You begin by observing and classifying the relevant data. You then look for a pattern in the data and formulate a hypothesis. You then make a prediction, which you test by an experiment. A good experiment should have the following features:

- *Controllability.* You vary only one factor at a time so that you can determine its effect. For example, you might vary the temperature of a gas while keeping its volume constant. This helps you to isolate the cause of the phenomenon that you are investigating.
- *Measurability.* You can measure the relevant variables. This adds precision and objectivity to your experiment.
- *Repeatability.* Your experiment can be repeated by other people who will be able to confirm your results. This ensures that your results have some kind of objectivity.

KT – law: a general statement confirmed by experimental evidence which describes some feature of reality

If your experimental results confirm your hypothesis, then you may have discovered a scientific **law**. If your results disconfirm your hypothesis, then you will need to go back and think again.

Finally, you may develop a theory which explains and unifies various laws in terms of some underlying principles. A good theory explains why the laws are the way they are and provides a focus for further research.

LQ – Mathematics: Why do scientists generally see numbers as 'the ultimate test of objectivity'?

Figure 13.5 Controlled experiments play a key role in the scientific method.

Figure 13.6 DNA: One of the most famous models in the history of science is James Watson and Francis Crick's double-helix model of the structure of DNA.

ACTIVITY 13.7

1. Scientists commonly make a distinction between *theorists* and *experimentalists*. What role does practical know-how play in science and how is it related to theoretical know-that?
2. How important do you think it is for IB students to do science practicals in order to understand the nature of science?

An example: the Copernican revolution

To illustrate the scientific method, consider the way our views have changed about the place of the earth in the universe. Since it does not look or feel as if we are moving, it is natural to think that the earth is stationary. So it is not surprising that the Greek astronomer Claudius Ptolemy (AD 85–165) developed a model of the universe with the earth at the centre of things and the sun and the planets going round it. Ptolemy's model not only reflected common sense, but also enabled people to make accurate predictions about the movements of the planets. The steps that led to the breakdown and eventual replacement of this model could be traced in the following simplified story:

Observation. As people made new and better observations, Ptolemy's model became increasingly complicated in order to accommodate them, so that, by the sixteenth century, it had become a 'disorderly monster'.

Hypothesis. This led Nicolaus Copernicus (1473–1543) to suggest a simpler and more elegant approach which put the sun at the centre of the solar system and had the planets revolve around it.

Prediction. In the Ptolemaic model, Venus orbits the earth and so always appears the same size; but Copernicus said that if Venus orbits the sun its apparent size should vary as its distance from the earth changes. To the naked eye Venus appears to be a constant size as predicted by the Ptolemaic model. But when Galileo (1564–1642) looked at it through a telescope in 1609, he discovered that its size does indeed vary as had been predicted by Copernicus.

Law. On the basis of the above observations and discoveries, Johannes Kepler (1571–1630) developed laws of planetary motion.

Theory. Finally, Isaac Newton (1642–1727) came up with the theory of gravity, which says that there is a force of attraction between objects whose strength is directly proportional to their masses and inversely proportional to the square of the distance between them. (That is, if you double the distance between two objects, the gravitational attraction between them will be ¼ of its original strength.) This was part of a more general theory that enabled Newton to explain a wide variety of phenomena such as why an apple falls from a tree, why people have weight, the movement of the tides, and the orbit of the planets. Newtonian physics also enabled later astronomers to make accurate predictions that led to the discovery of new planets such as Uranus in 1781 and Neptune in 1846.

We can draw the following points from this brief account:

- Scientific progress needs a background of careful observation. Kepler was able to develop his laws of planetary motion because another astronomer called Tycho Brahe (1546–1601) had made meticulous observations and discovered various **anomalies** in the orbits of the planets. (An anomaly is an observation that seems to contradict a generally accepted theory.)

KT – anomaly: an observation that seems to contradict a generally accepted theory

- Technology can extend our powers of observation, thereby making it easier to test new ideas. Galileo was only able to detect the change in the apparent size of Venus by using the newly invented telescope.
- Models play a key role in scientific explanations. Copernicus's heliocentric model was originally presented as a useful calculating device for predicting the movements of the planets, but eventually came to be seen as an accurate description of physical reality.
- Developing new scientific ideas requires imagination. Part of Copernicus's genius was that, while he saw what everyone else saw when he looked up at the night sky, he came up with a different way of interpreting it. (In fact, as early as the third century BCE a Greek astronomer called Aristarchus had suggested that the earth goes round the sun, but the idea didn't catch on.)
- Scientific ideas are usually explained in the language of mathematics. Newton's law of gravity not only fitted the observational data, but could also be expressed in precise equations.
- Many scientific discoveries are *counter-intuitive* and go against untutored common sense. We now take it as obvious that the earth rotates on its axis and orbits the sun but, when you think about it, it is difficult to believe that the earth is spinning at 1,000 miles an hour and travelling round the sun at about 67,000 miles an hour!

ACTIVITY 13.8

Try explaining the following to someone who doesn't know much about physics.

a. If the earth is round, why don't people fall off the bottom?

b. If the earth is moving round the sun and rotating on its axis, how come it doesn't feel like we are moving?

c. Since birds fly far slower than the earth rotates, how come they don't get left behind when they fly in the direction of the rotation (west to east)?

Our discussion so far might suggest that there is a straightforward procedure for generating scientific truth from raw observations, and that all you have to do is follow the scientific method. But things are not that simple. In the next section we will explore the various stages of the scientific method again, and see that each step is more complicated than it first appears.

Problems with observation

Science is based on observation but, as we saw in Chapter 5, observation is not as straightforward as it first seems. In what follows, we shall briefly consider problems of relevance, expectations, expert seeing and the observer effect.

Relevance

ACTIVITY 13.9

Imagine that you are interested in finding out why some students catch a cold in the winter term and other students do not. Which of the following factors might you look at in comparing the two groups, and which would you consider irrelevant?

a. Diet

b. Colour of underwear

c. Exercise

d. Middle name

e. Domestic heating

f. Movies watched

g. Warmth of clothing

Quite reasonably, you probably said that (a), (c), (e) and (g) are relevant, and (b), (d) and (f) are irrelevant. How, after all, could the colour of your underwear, or your middle name, or the movies you have watched, affect whether or not you catch a cold?

The important point from this example is that we always begin with some idea of what is and what is not relevant to the problem. If we did not, we would drown in a flood of observations. However, the selective nature of perception means it is always possible we have overlooked a factor that later turns out to be relevant. For example, when you do an experiment in chemistry you do not normally count how many people are in the room. However, this will affect the temperature of the room, and in a sensitive experiment that might affect the speed of the chemical reaction.

Expectations

Another problem with observation is that *our expectations can influence what we see.* When the planet Mercury was found to be deviating from the orbit predicted by Newton's laws, some nineteenth-century astronomers suggested that the anomaly was caused by an undiscovered planet called Vulcan. So confident were they in their belief that several astronomers then claimed that they had observed Vulcan. But it turned out that Vulcan does not exist. The correct explanation for the deviation of Mercury had to wait for Einstein's theory of relativity.

Expert seeing

The use of *scientific equipment* such as microscopes and telescopes to make observations causes further complications. We may laugh when we hear that some of Galileo's contemporaries refused to look through his telescope, preferring to rely on the authority of the Church rather than the evidence of their senses. But it is worth pointing out that the telescope Galileo used to discover the phases of Venus and the moons of Jupiter was a fairly crude instrument. Some of Galileo's drawings of the moon are quite inaccurate and include some craters and mountains that do not in fact exist. From your own experience in the science lab, you are probably aware that it takes quite a lot of practice to learn how to see through a microscope.

The observer effect

A final problem with observation is that *the act of observation can sometimes affect what we observe.* To take a simple example, imagine that you want to know exactly how hot a cup of tea is. You put a thermometer in the tea and read off the temperature. The problem is that, instead of measuring the temperature of the tea, you are now measuring the temperature of the tea-with-the-thermometer-in-it. The very act of putting the thermometer in the tea has changed its temperature. Of course, for most practical purposes this does not make a significant difference. If you are in bed with a fever and the doctor comes and tells you that you have a temperature of 102 °F, it would be pedantic to point out that she has in fact taken the temperature of you *plus* the thermometer. However, the effect of the observer on the observed plays an important role in a branch of physics known as quantum physics. We shall also have more to say about the observer effect when we discuss the human sciences in the next chapter.

While our discussion has focused on the fallibility of perception, it is important not to exaggerate the problem. The great strength of science is that it is a communal and self-correcting enterprise. Sooner or later the errors of one individual are likely to be corrected by someone else.

ACTIVITY 13.10

'An uneducated child and a trained astronomer, both relying on the naked eye and 20/20 vision, will literally see a different sky.' What do you understand by this quotation?

Testing hypotheses

Testing hypotheses is also less straightforward than the naive account of the scientific method implies. Among the complications are: confirmation bias, background assumptions and the fact that many different hypotheses are consistent with a given set of data.

Confirmation bias

We have already come across confirmation bias several times in this book (see pages 14, 151 and 214). As you may remember, it refers to the fact that people tend to look for evidence that confirms their beliefs and overlook evidence that goes against them. If, for example, you believe that Virgos are particularly shy individuals, you will notice every time you come across a shy Virgo. But if you only observe confirming instances of your hypothesis this does not show that it is true. You also need to look for evidence that might falsify it.

ACTIVITY 13.11

In the above example, as well as looking at Virgos who are shy, what else might you look at that could falsify your hypothesis?

The two other key things you should look out for are:

a. Virgos who are not shy

b. people of other star signs who are also shy.

When all the evidence is in, it may turn out that, despite your initial belief, there is no relationship between a person's star sign and whether or not they are shy.

A good scientist will be aware of the danger of confirmation bias and actively seek to combat it. In one of his notebooks Charles Darwin (1809–82) stated that 'I followed a golden rule, namely that whenever a new observation or thought came across me, which was opposed to my general results, I make a memorandum of it without fail and at once; for I had found by experience that such facts and thoughts were far more apt to escape from the memory than favourable ones.' This is a tribute to Darwin's intellectual integrity.

One common form of confirmation bias is for a scientist to dismiss results they don't expect as 'experimental error'. Imagine, for example, that you do an experiment and get the results shown in Figure 13.7. You would probably be tempted to ignore observation X_4.

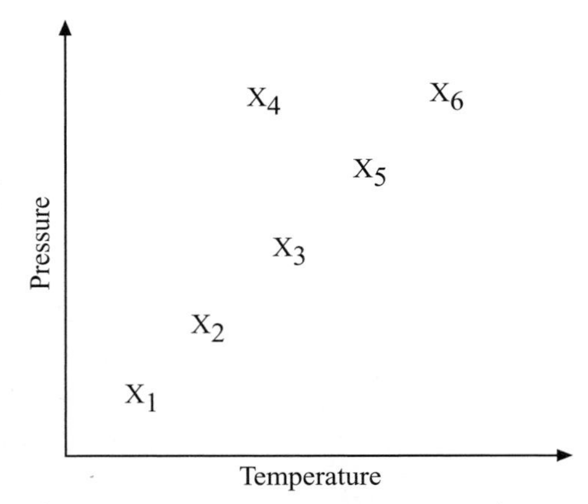

Figure 13.7 Pressure–temperature graph

ACTIVITY 13.12

In Figure 13.7, to what extent do you think you would be justified in dismissing observation X_4 as experimental error?

It might seem reasonable to assume that X_4 is a result of human error, but it would be wise to take more observations to be on the safe side. In practice, however, it is difficult to say where 'trimming' one's results to exclude experimental error ends and 'cooking the books' begins. Scientists naturally want to show their results in the best possible light, and they often have strong expectations about the way an experiment should turn out. When the notebooks of one famous physicist were examined, the following comments were found alongside his experimental observations:

'Very low. Something wrong.'

'This is almost exactly right and the best one I have ever had!!!'

'Agreement poor.'

To take another example, Gregor Mendel's (1822–84) work on the hereditary traits of peas laid the foundations for modern genetics. But according to some modern geneticists, his results are just too good to be believable, and he has been accused of only reporting results that favoured his case. The following is an amusing account of Mendel's method:

In the beginning, there was Mendel, thinking his lonely thoughts alone. And he said: 'Let there be peas,' and there were peas, and it was good. And he put the peas in the garden, saying unto them, 'Increase and multiply, segregate and assort yourselves independently,' and they did, and it was good. And now it came to pass that when Mendel gathered up his peas, he divided them into round and wrinkled and called the round dominant and the wrinkled recessive, and it was good. But now Mendel saw that there were 450 round peas and 102 wrinkled ones; this was not good. For the law stateth that there should be only three round for every wrinkled. And Mendel said unto himself, 'Gott in Himmel, an enemy has done this; he has sown bad peas in my garden under the cover of night.' And Mendel smote the table in righteous wrath, saying, 'Depart from me, you cursed and evil peas, into the outer darkness where Thou shalt be devoured by the rats and mice,' and lo, it was done, and there remained 300 round peas and 100 wrinkled peas, and it was good. It was very, very good. And Mendel published.

Background assumptions

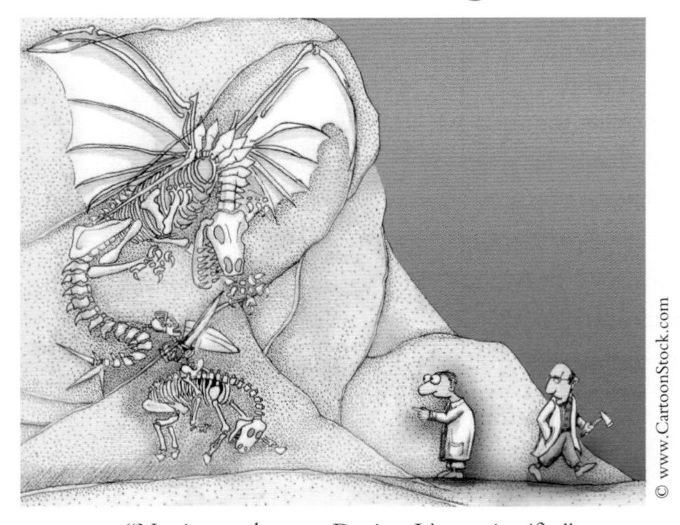

"No, ignore that one Davies. It's unscientific."

Figure 13.8

Whenever we test a hypothesis, we make various background assumptions, any one of which could turn out to be false. For example, at the time of Copernicus, it was generally agreed that the fixed stars are relatively close to the earth. Given this, it follows that if the earth is orbiting the sun the position of nearby stars relative to more distant stars ought to change as the earth moves round the sun. Such a change of relative position is known as a *parallax*. (An analogy may help here. Hold a pencil out in front of you so that it exactly covers a distant object, such as a tree. If you now close each of your eyes in turn, the position of the pencil relative to the tree will appear to change. In a similar way, the relative position of the stars should change if the earth is moving.) The problem was that no one was able to observe the required parallax; and neither Copernicus nor Galileo had an answer to this criticism. Finally it turned out that the assumption that the fixed stars are relatively close to the earth was wrong, and in the nineteenth century the stellar parallax was finally observed.

Many different hypotheses are consistent with a given set of data

Since it is possible to come up with many different hypotheses that are consistent with a given set of observations, it is in practice impossible to *prove* that any particular hypothesis is true. For example, in our discussion of astronomy above, we saw that Galileo observed that the relative size of Venus changes as predicted by Copernicus's heliocentric theory. While this observation is inconsistent with Ptolemy's model, it is in fact consistent with another model according to which the sun orbits the earth and the other planets orbit the sun.

In fact, there are an endless number of different hypotheses consistent with a given set of observations. This can easily be shown by considering the graphs in Figure 13.9. Imagine you are investigating the relationship between the temperature and pressure of a gas. You make some observations, X_1, X_2 and X_3. On the basis of your observations, you formulate a hypothesis H1, and make a prediction P. Your prediction is confirmed. Does this conclusively confirm hypothesis H1? No! For your observations are also consistent with another hypothesis H2.

To decide between hypotheses H1 and H2 you might make some further observations, Y_1, Y_2 and Y_3 as in Figure 13.9b. These new observations would seem to confirm H1 and eliminate H2.

But once again H1 is not conclusively confirmed. For we might now make another hypothesis H3 which is also consistent with our observations (Figure 13.9c). Further observations might eliminate H3 and confirm H1, but you could then make another hypothesis H4 and so on. Extrapolating from this, you can see that, no matter how many observations you make confirming H1, there will always be other hypotheses that are also consistent with the data.

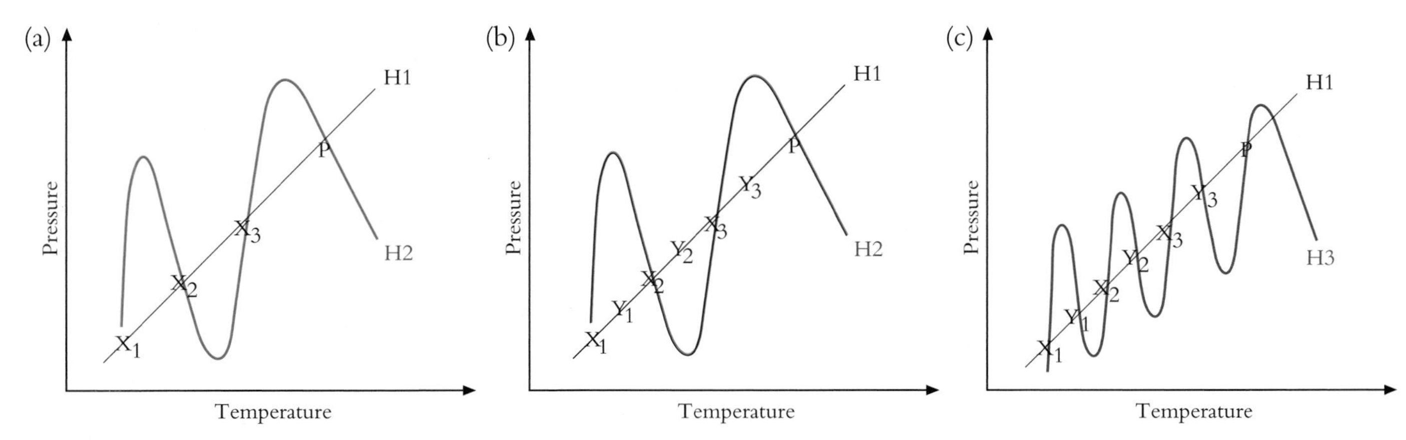

Figure 13.9 Temperature–pressure graphs. (a) Temperature–pressure graph showing hypotheses H1 and H2 (b) Temperature–pressure graph with extra observation (c) Temperature–pressure graph with new hypothesis H3

Figure 13.10 *"Oh, if only it were so simple."*

The principle of simplicity

Having said that, hypotheses such as H3 do seem absurd, and it is hard to avoid thinking that H1 is the more natural hypothesis. In fact, scientists usually appeal to a **principle of simplicity** which says that, given two competing theories which make exactly the same predictions, the simpler theory is to be preferred. This justifies our preference for H1 over H2 or H3. However, if you asked a scientist to justify their belief in the principle of simplicity, they would probably shrug their shoulders and say that's just what they believe. The principle reflects a deep belief in the orderliness and comprehensibility of nature, but no further justification can be given for it. Since simplicity is also related to concepts such as 'beauty' and 'elegance', we can say that in practice aesthetic considerations are likely to play a role in a scientist's choice of hypothesis.

KT – principle of simplicity: a rule which says that if we have two competing hypotheses which make the same predictions we should prefer the simpler one

But we must be careful. For our aesthetic prejudices can sometimes lead us astray. Copernicus was convinced that the planets must orbit the sun in circles because he thought that a circle is a perfect figure. However, it turned out that planetary orbits are elliptical rather than circular. The moral of the tale is that nature's aesthetic may not be the same as our own, and beautiful theories are sometimes ruined by ugly facts!

The problem of induction

A final problem with the naive picture of the scientific method concerns induction. As we saw in Chapter 6, inductive reasoning goes from the particular to the general, and it plays a central role in the way that scientists think. Take, for example, our belief that all metals expand when heated. How did we come by this belief? Not by reason, or intuition, or divine revelation, but by observation. As far as we know, every time a piece of metal has been heated, it has expanded, and there are no recorded cases of metals not expanding when heated. So it seems reasonable to conclude that this is a law of nature. What's the problem?

Although it is unlikely to keep you awake at night, the problem is that when we reason inductively we are moving from the observed to the unobserved. For example, when we reason that since metal A and metal B and metal C, etc. expand when heated, then *all* metals expand when heated, we are making a generalisation from things we have observed to things we have not observed.

Practical problems

At a practical level, the problem of induction raises the question of how many observations we should make before we are entitled to make a generalisation. We saw in Chapter 6 that we have a tendency to jump to conclusions on the basis of insufficient evidence, and we looked at various criteria for distinguishing reasonable generalisations from unreasonable ones. However, there is no hard and fast rule about how many observations you should make before you are entitled to generalise. All we can say is the more observations you make that support your hypothesis the more confident you will feel about it.

The trouble is that even well-confirmed generalisations sometimes let us down. Up until the eighteenth century, it was commonly believed by Europeans that all swans are white. There were innumerable confirming instances of this belief and no disconfirming instances. Then some black swans were discovered in Australia. More dramatically, for two and a half centuries, experiment after experiment seemed to confirm the truth of Newtonian physics. Nevertheless, Einstein showed that there is a deep sense in which Newton's laws are not the best description of physical reality. What this appears to show is that even very well-confirmed hypotheses can sometimes turn out to be wrong.

When you start to think about it, our confidence in scientific knowledge is quite breathtaking. On the basis of a few observations that we have made on planet Earth, we claim to have discovered laws of physics that apply to *all* times and *all* places – billions of years ago and billions of light-years away. Yet we have observed only a minute fraction of the universe. (As we mentioned in Chapter 1, astronomers estimate that there are ten times more stars in the night sky than grains of sand in the world's deserts and beaches!)

Given the above, you might argue that scientists should show greater humility and make less ambitious claims. For example, instead of saying 'all metals expand when heated', perhaps we should restrict ourselves to the more modest assertion that 'all *observed* metals expand when heated'. This may show admirable humility, but the fact is that deep down most physicists believe that they really are discovering the fundamental laws in accordance with which the universe operates.

Theoretical problems

The problem of induction applies not only at the practical level, but also at the theoretical level. For science is supposed to be an **empirical** discipline which makes no claims beyond what has been observed. Indeed, the claim that it is grounded in observation is supposed to be what distinguishes genuine science from pseudo-science. So we seem to be faced with a dilemma. On the one hand, we could take

KT – empirical: something which can be verified by observation the alleged empiricism of science seriously, and refuse to make any claims that go beyond what has actually been observed. There would, however, be a very high price to pay for this. For it would mean that we would have to abandon any talk of discovering laws of nature that apply in all times and all places. On the other hand, we could defend the right of scientists to reason from the particular to the general, and abandon the claim that science is a strictly empirical discipline. Again, this seems to be a high price to pay. Another approach is to simply not worry about the problem too much and just get on with the business of doing science!

THE SCIENTIFIC METHOD: SUMMARY OF PROBLEMS	
Observation	1. Selectivity
	2. Expectations
	3. Expert seeing
	4. The observer effect
Hypothesis	5. Confirmation bias
	6. Background assumptions
	7. Under-determination
Law	8. Problem of induction

ACTIVITY 13.13

Write a short paragraph to explain each of the problems with the scientific method in your own words.

Falsification

Figure 13.11 Karl Popper

One person who took the problem of induction seriously and tried to resolve the dilemma was a philosopher called Karl Popper (1902–94). Popper's interest in the problem grew out of his concern to distinguish genuine science, such as Einstein's theory of relativity, from what he saw as pseudo-science, such as Marxism and psychoanalysis.

As a young man, Popper had been impressed by the ability of theories put forward by people such as Karl Marx (1818–83), Sigmund Freud (1856–1939) and Alfred Adler (1870–1937) to explain *everything*. Adler, for example, believed that human beings are dominated by feelings of inferiority. 'To be human', he said, 'means to feel inferior.' He then used this insight to explain more or less the entire range of human behaviour. As impressive as this seems, Popper came to the conclusion that what looked like a strength of the theory – its ability to explain everything – was in fact a weakness.

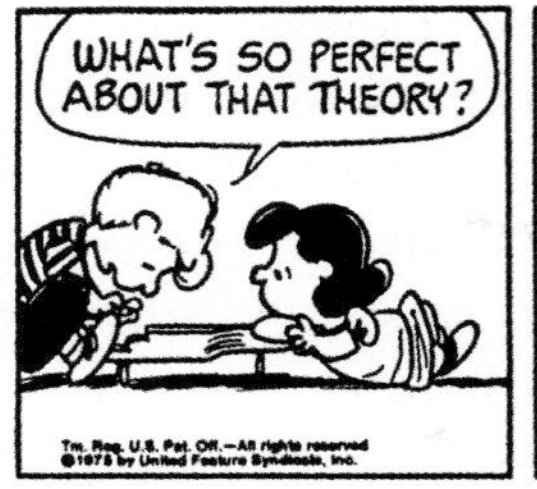

Figure 13.12

Imagine, for example, that a man is walking along the bank of a fast-flowing river when he sees a child fall in. He has two choices: either he jumps in and tries to rescue the child or he does not. Suppose that he jumps in and tries to rescue the child. 'Ah', says Adler, 'this is exactly what my theory predicted. The man was clearly trying to overcome his feeling of inferiority by demonstrating his bravery.' Now suppose that the man does not jump into the river. 'Just as I thought', says Adler. 'This man is clearly suffering from an inferiority complex which he is unable to overcome.'

The above may be a caricature of Adler's beliefs, but it draws attention to the fact that from a scientific point of view *a theory that explains everything explains nothing*. According to Popper, a genuinely scientific theory differs from the one considered above in that it puts itself at risk. For example, Einstein's general theory of relativity led to certain predictions being made which were famously tested and confirmed in 1919. Had the relevant observations not confirmed Einstein's theory, scientists would have rejected it.

LQ – Imagination: How important is imagination in developing scientific hypotheses?

Conjectures and refutations

KT – conjectures and refutations: the approach to science advocated by Karl Popper, according to which scientists should come up with imaginative hypotheses which are open to falsification

The scientific method advocated by Popper is based on **conjectures and refutations**. A conjecture is basically an imaginative hypothesis and, in his discussion of conjectures, Popper emphasises the fact that there is no mechanical way of coming up with good hypotheses on the basis of the observational data. What is frequently required is a leap of imagination that enables you to look at the data in a different way. This is essentially what Copernicus did when he first put forward the idea that the earth goes round the sun rather than vice versa. As we saw when discussing intuition in Chapter 8, scientists often have their best ideas in a flash of intuition. For example, Newton is said to have come up with the idea of universal gravity when he saw an apple fall from a tree, and Mendeleyev's idea for the periodic table came to him in a dream. However, you are only likely to have such intuitions if you have the right background knowledge and have put in the necessary work. When Newton was asked how he had discovered the law of gravity, he replied, 'By thinking on it continually.' And Mendeleyev made a set of cards with the names of the elements written on them, and played around with them endlessly before he finally made his great breakthrough.

The most important thing about genuinely *scientific* conjectures is that they are *testable*. This brings us to the concept of 'refutations' and Popper's attempt to solve the problem of induction. In thinking about this problem, Popper was struck by the asymmetry between confirmation and falsification. Consider again our standard example, 'All metals expand when heated.' We cannot be sure that the law is true no matter how many confirming observations we have made; for it is always possible that the next metal we test will *not* expand when heated. But we only need to find one metal which does *not* expand when heated to be sure that it is *false* that all metals expand when heated. In other words, while confirmation is tentative and cannot prove that a law is true, refutation is decisive: we need only one counter-example to prove that a law is false.

The conclusion Popper drew from this is that scientists should not waste their time trying to prove that their hypotheses are true; for the problem of induction shows that this is impossible. Rather, they should spend their time trying to prove that their hypotheses are *false*. Despite its strangeness, Popper's ingenious approach is in many ways attractive. He believed that a properly scientific approach to a subject should explore the shortcomings of currently accepted theories. What he disliked above all was any form of scientific dogmatism which blindly accepted the prevailing orthodoxy. For if science is to progress then people must question and criticise the current state of scientific knowledge.

There is, of course, no virtue in going around falsifying *absurd* hypotheses, such as 'an apple a day makes you good at calculus', or 'people who wear jeans are less likely to have car accidents'. The point is rather to look closely at apparently well-confirmed hypotheses in order to discover their shortcomings.

Take, for example, the scientific law that water boils at 100°C. If you mindlessly boil pan after pan of water, you will never conclusively prove that this law is true and you will not make any meaningful contribution to science. A better strategy would be to look for situations in which water does *not* boil at 100°C. If you adopt this approach, you might discover that, at high altitudes, water boils at less than 100°C. The challenge is then to find an explanation for why water boils at a lower temperature at a higher altitude. And you are then in a position to test new ideas and make real scientific progress.

According to Popper, any theory that resists our best efforts to falsify it should be *provisionally accepted* as the best we have for the time being. But he insists that it cannot be said to be true in any *absolute* sense; for it is always possible that in the future it will be replaced by a better theory. That, after all, is what happened to Newtonian physics!

Criticisms of Popper

Despite the attractions of Popper's philosophy of science, it is itself open to criticism.

KT – falsificationism: the belief attributed to Karl Popper that science progresses by falsifying rather than verifying scientific hypotheses

Falsification is conclusive in theory but not in practice

Falsificationism turns on the idea that, although confirmation is provisional, falsification is decisive. While this is true in theory, it turns out that in practice falsification is no more conclusive than verification. Imagine, for example, that you do an experiment in the physics laboratory that contradicts one of Newton's laws of motion. Do you announce that you have just disproved Newton? Probably not!

The most reasonable conclusion is that you have messed up the experiment. What this example suggests is that, while in theory a single counter-example is enough to overturn a law of nature, in practice it is not. When there is a conflict between hypothesis and observation we have a choice: we can either reject the hypothesis, or we can reject the observation.

LQ – History: Why is it important for scientists to know something about the history of science?

There are in fact many examples in the history of science where scientists have refused to abandon their theories in the face of observational evidence which appeared to contradict them. Here are three such examples.

- ***Physics.*** Newton's theory of gravity implied that, given the attractive forces between the stars, the universe should collapse in a gigantic cosmic crunch. Newton saw that this was a serious problem, but rather than abandon his theory, he somewhat desperately concluded that God must be counteracting gravity and keeping the stars in their places.
- ***Chemistry.*** When Dimitri Mendeleyev (1834–1907) came up with the periodic table by arranging elements according to their atomic weights, the weights of some elements did not quite fit his model. Mendeleyev did not abandon this theory but concluded that the anomalous weights must be due to experimental error.
- ***Biology.*** Charles Darwin's theory of evolution required that the earth be hundreds of millions of years old to allow enough time for species to evolve. But according to the calculations of the leading physicist of the day, Lord Kelvin (1824–1907), the earth was no more than 100 million years old. Kelvin's figure was based on the best knowledge available at the time. Darwin found it 'preposterously inadequate', and he stuck with his theory.

With hindsight, we can say that Newton, Mendeleyev and Darwin were right to stick with their theories in the face of observations that seemed to contradict them. The universe does not collapse in on itself because the speed at which the stars are moving away from each other counteracts gravity. The anomalous weights of some of Mendeleyev's elements were due to the presence of various isotopes. And Kelvin's way of calculating the age of the earth was eventually shown to be wrong.

Figure 13.13 *"Always the last place you look!"*

Auxiliary hypotheses can rescue a falsified theory

What these examples show is that we should not always reject a promising theory as soon as we come across counter-evidence. For the counter-evidence may turn out to be experimental error, or our background assumptions may turn out to be wrong. Of course, if the experimental evidence consistently goes against a theory, then we should eventually abandon it; but a well-established theory may survive a long time in the face of counter-evidence that no one is able to explain away. Consider, for example, the following story told by the philosopher of science Imre Lakatos (1922–74):

> *The story is about an imaginary case of planetary misbehaviour. A physicist of the pre-Einsteinian era takes Newton's mechanics and his law of gravitation (N), the accepted initial conditions, I, and calculates, with their help, the path of a newly discovered small planet, p. But the planet deviates from the calculated path. Does our Newtonian physicist consider that the deviation was forbidden by Newton's theory and therefore that, once established, it refutes the theory N? No. He suggests that there must have been a hitherto unknown planet p1 which perturbs the path of p. He calculates the mass, orbit, etc. of this hypothetical planet and then asks an experimental astronomer to test his hypothesis. The planet p1 is so small that even the biggest available telescopes cannot possibly observe it: the experimental astronomer applies for a research grant to build a yet bigger one. In three years' time the new telescope is ready. Were the unknown planet p1 to be discovered, it would be hailed as a new victory for Newtonian science. But it is not. Does our scientist abandon Newton's theory and his idea of the perturbing planet? No. He suggests that a cloud of cosmic dust hides the planet from us. He calculates the location and properties of this cloud and asks for a research grant to send up a satellite to test his calculations. Were the satellite's instruments (possibly new ones, based on a little-tested theory) to record the existence of the conjectural cloud, the result would be hailed as an outstanding victory for Newtonian science. But the cloud is not found. Does our scientist abandon Newton's theory, together with the idea of the perturbing planet and the idea of the cloud which hides it? No. He suggests that there is some magnetic field in that region of the universe which disturbed the instruments of the satellite. A new satellite is sent up. Were the magnetic field to be found, Newtonians would celebrate a sensational victory. But it is not. Is this regarded as a refutation of Newtonian science? No. Either yet another ingenious auxiliary hypothesis is proposed or . . . the whole story is buried in the dusty volumes of periodicals and the story never mentioned again.*

As this story suggests, there is in fact no such thing as a perfect theory, and you will find anomalies and unresolved problems in every area of science. If a theory is well established and generally successful, then practitioners in the field tend to assume that, with time, outstanding problems will be resolved. For example, when it was discovered that the planet Uranus was not behaving as predicted by Newton's laws, scientists did not abandon Newtonian physics but argued that there must be some unknown planet affecting it. In this case, they rejected neither the observation nor the theory, but made an *auxiliary hypothesis* – the existence of an unknown planet – to explain their observations. This led to the discovery of Neptune in 1846. However, when they tried to explain the misbehaviour of Mercury in the same way by postulating the existence of a planet called Vulcan, they turned out to be wrong. This time Mercury's behaviour could not be explained within the Newtonian paradigm, and this eventually led to a scientific revolution and the replacement of Newtonian physics by the theory of relativity.

The rationalist strand in scientific thinking

When there is a conflict between observation and hypothesis, there are in fact three options:

- reject the hypothesis
- reject the observation
- accept both the hypothesis and the observation and make an auxiliary hypothesis.

LQ – Reason: Is there a logic of scientific discovery?

What our discussion shows is that there is both a **rationalist** and an empiricist strand in scientific thinking. You may remember that a rationalist is someone who sees reason as the main source of knowledge and an empiricist is someone who sees experience as the main source of knowledge. When prediction and observation conflict with one another, a rationalist is more likely to stick with a beautiful theory, and an empiricist is more likely to stick with the observational evidence. Many great scientists have had rationalist sympathies in the sense that they have been unwilling to abandon a promising theory in the light of contrary evidence. Einstein was once asked how he would have reacted if his general theory had not been confirmed by experiment. He replied: 'Then I would feel sorry for the good Lord. The theory is correct.'

KT – rationalism: the belief that reason rather than experience is the most important source of knowledge

The power of science derives from the fact that it combines reason in the form of mathematics with experience in the form of observational data. The rationalist part of science is the belief that there is order 'out there', and that this order can be captured in scientific theories. The empiricist part is that if a theory is to survive and flourish then it must be consistent with the observational facts.

What comes out of our discussion of Popper is that scientific theories cannot be conclusively verified or falsified. They cannot be conclusively verified because of the problem of induction; and they cannot be conclusively falsified because, when an observation contradicts a theory, it is always open to us to reject the observation rather than the theory. Strictly speaking then, the concept of *proof* is only relevant to mathematics and logic, and we cannot speak of science *proving* things in any absolute sense. In science, as in every other area of knowledge that applies to the world, we have to make do with something less than certainty.

Science and society

We have seen that neither inductivism nor falsificationism can give us an adequate account of the nature of science. A third perspective is provided by the historian and philosopher of science Thomas Kuhn (1922–96) who is best known for having introduced the concept of a *paradigm* to the philosophy of science. In its technical sense, the word "paradigm" was first used to describe an overarching scientific theory which is used to make sense of some aspect of reality; but we can usefully speak of paradigms in other areas of knowledge as well. Three important scientific paradigms you are likely to have come across at school are Newtonian mechanics in physics, atomic theory in chemistry, and evolutionary theory in biology.

Figure 13.14 Thomas Kuhn

Normal science

While Popper argued that scientists should constantly be questioning their assumptions, Kuhn drew attention to the fact that during periods of what he calls 'normal science' the vast majority of scientists are busy solving problems within a paradigm while taking the paradigm itself for granted. To take an example mentioned earlier, the irregularity in the orbit of Uranus did not lead scientists to seriously question Newtonian mechanics; rather they tried to solve the problem within the framework of Newtonian mechanics. Popper might condemn such an uncritical approach, but the fact is that, if you are going to get anything done, you cannot endlessly question your assumptions. While great scientists such as Newton, Dalton and Darwin were architects who established new paradigms, most scientists are bricklayers patiently filling in the details and extending the body of scientific knowledge.

Scientific revolutions

Despite his emphasis on the stability of 'normal science', Kuhn argued that, far from progressing smoothly over time, the history of science is punctuated by revolutions. A *scientific revolution* takes place when scientists become dissatisfied with the prevailing paradigm, and put forward a completely new way of looking at things. If their ideas triumph, the new paradigm will replace the old one and inaugurate another period of normal science. The shift from the geocentric to the heliocentric model of the universe is the classic example of a scientific revolution. Other examples are the replacement of Aristotelian physics by Newtonian mechanics in the seventeenth century, and the replacement of Newtonian mechanics by Einstein's theory of relativity in the early twentieth century.

While we tend to think of science progressing along the lines of Figure 13.15a, according to Kuhn the reality is more like Figure 13.15b.

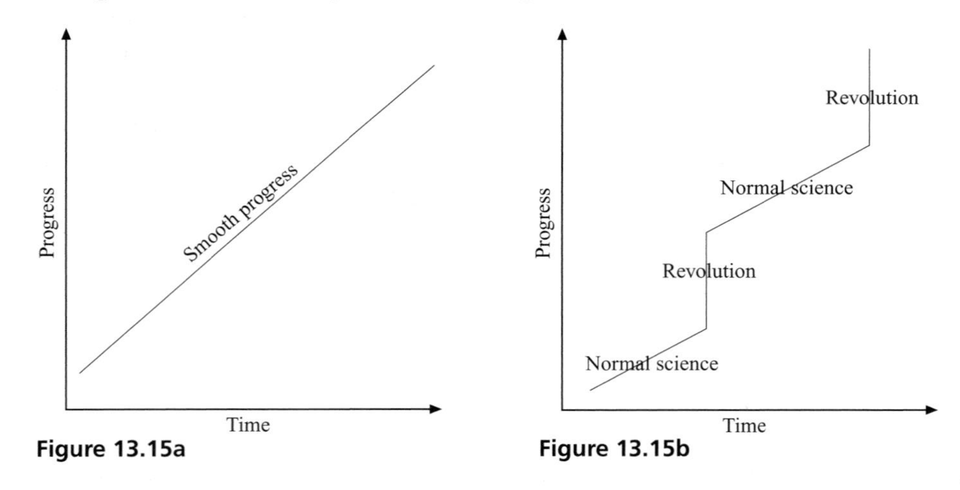

Figure 13.15a **Figure 13.15b**

ACTIVITY 13.14

Do you think Figure 13.15a or b more accurately reflects the way in which a subject with which you are familiar progresses over time?

We said earlier that there is no such thing as a perfect theory in science and that at any given time there are all kinds of problems and puzzles that have not yet been solved. During periods of normal science, there is widespread confidence that such problems can be solved by the existing paradigm. However, if over time the number of unresolved problems reaches a critical mass, some people may begin to question the paradigm itself. If a new paradigm provides a better explanation of things a scientific revolution is likely to occur. But not everyone will be converted to the new way of thinking, and during periods of scientific crisis there are likely to be violent arguments between those who adhere to the old paradigm and those who advocate the new one. Often, the new ideas triumph only after older, more conservative, scientists have died and a new generation has grown up that is familiar with the new way of thinking.

ACTIVITY 13.15

1. What truth, if any, do you think there is in the idea that older people are more conservative and suspicious of new ideas than younger people?
2. Find out how old some of the key figures in the history of science were when they came up with the ideas for which they later became famous. What conclusions, if any, can you draw from your enquiry?

How rational is science?

According to Kuhn, the progress of science is not as rational as is sometimes thought. During periods of scientific crisis there may be no definite point at which we can say it is irrational or unscientific to adhere to an old paradigm rather than convert to a new one. This follows from the point made earlier that in practice a theory can never be conclusively verified or falsified. For we can always dismiss observations that seem to falsify the old paradigm as experimental error or explain them away by making various auxiliary hypotheses. (Recall Lakatos's story of planetary misbehaviour.) Since there may be no purely rational way of choosing between competing theories, Kuhn likened switching from one paradigm to another to a religious conversion which may be influenced by a range of non-scientific factors such as personal ambition and social pressure.

LQ – Faith: How similar is a scientist's 'faith in the order of the universe' to religious faith?

There is doubtless an element of truth in Kuhn's view. We may like to think that scientists are motivated purely by love of truth, but that only tells part of the story. A brief glance at the history of science suggests that other more questionable motives, such as ambition, vanity and envy, also play a role. The vicious **priority disputes** that punctuate the history of science would seem to bear out the wry observation of the French biologist Charles Nicolle (1866–1936) that 'Without ambition and without vanity no one would enter a profession so contrary to our natural appetites.' The fact is that scientists are as concerned as the next person with their social status and public recognition. The astronomer Edwin Hubble (1889–1953) was so anxious to get the Nobel Prize that he even employed a public relations expert to help him secure it. Sadly for Hubble, there is no Nobel Prize for astronomy and his efforts were in vain.

KT – priority dispute: a dispute about who was first to discover a particular law or come up with a particular theory

The social context also plays a role in the development of science and it may determine a scientist's choice of problems and the questions he or she is willing to investigate. A great deal of scientific research is connected with the military's desire for power and big business's desire for profit, and this has undoubtedly influenced the direction it has taken in recent decades. Ambitious scientists may be attracted to areas in which there is a plentiful supply of money to fund research; and they may shy away from politically sensitive areas, preferring to work in less controversial ones. Moreover, if they seek promotion, they will also be under pressure to conform to the beliefs and values of the scientific community.

Figure 13.16

KT – peer review: the evalution of research by other qualified experts

RLS – Headline: 'The Hubble space telescope has cost US taxpayers some $10 billion in the quarter century since the project was approved'. How can we justify the money spent on scientific research?

Peer review and replication

As the above discussion suggests, science is a social endeavour and as such it is fallible. Two traditional safeguards against error and fraud are **peer review** and replication. Ideally, qualified experts should endorse a research group's work and should be able to reproduce their results. Recently, some investigators have expressed doubts about the efficacy of these safeguards. As scientific research becomes more complex and expensive to conduct, scientists may lack the time and motivation to check one another's work with sufficient attention. Several recent studies found that peer reviewers failed to spot basic errors in deliberately flawed research they were asked to assess. Furthermore, replication is costly and unglamorous, and ambitious scientists may be more interested in pursuing their own research than in trying to confirm other people's experiments. (As someone once observed, 'Nobody has ever won a Nobel Prize by agreeing.') The result of this is that a lot of published scientific research may eventually turn out to be false. This is clearly a cause for concern. Nevertheless, we might hope that in the long run poor research will be exposed and rejected.

Assessment of Kuhn's position

We have now looked at three key elements in Kuhn's theory of science, which can be summarised as follows:

1. During periods of normal science, most scientists do not question the paradigm in which they are operating and focus instead on solving problems.
2. The history of science suggests that, rather than progressing smoothly, science goes through a series of revolutionary jumps.
3. During periods of scientific crisis, there is no purely rational way of deciding between rival paradigms.

To determine how convincing Kuhn's ideas are, let us look more closely at each of the above points.

Normal science

There is probably some truth in Kuhn's claim that during periods of normal science most scientists work within the dominant paradigm without seriously questioning it. The question, however, is whether or not it is a good thing. Admittedly, if scientists are to make any progress they cannot be endlessly questioning their assumptions, but if they *never* do this, their beliefs may end up freezing into dogmatism. That, at least, was Popper's view:

> *In my view the 'normal' scientist, as Kuhn describes him, is a person one ought to be sorry for . . . The 'normal' scientist . . . has been taught badly. I believe . . . that all teaching on the University level (and if possible below) should be training and encouragement in critical thinking. The 'normal' scientist, as described by Kuhn, . . . has been taught in a dogmatic spirit: he is a victim of indoctrination. He has learned a technique which can be applied without asking for the reason why . . . He is, as Kuhn puts it, content to solve 'puzzles'. The choice of this term seems to indicate that Kuhn wishes to stress that it is not a really fundamental problem which the 'normal' scientist is prepared to tackle: it is rather, a routine problem, a problem of applying what one has learned . . . The success of the 'normal' scientist consists, entirely, in showing that the ruling theory can be properly and satisfactorily applied in order to reach a solution of the puzzle in question.*

ACTIVITY 13.16

To what extent are you encouraged to question your assumptions in your science classes at school? Can questioning your assumptions sometimes be counter-productive?

Scientific revolutions

We also need to be careful with Kuhn's account of the history of science in terms of revolutions. For it is sometimes taken to imply that *all* of our current scientific beliefs will one day be swept away in a new revolution. However, the fact that science is punctuated by periods of intellectual upheaval does not necessarily mean that when one paradigm replaces another the old one vanishes without trace. In fact, the history of science suggests that scientific knowledge is broadly cumulative and that, over time, scientific knowledge is getting closer to the truth.

Take, for example, physics. Despite the fact that Newtonian mechanics was replaced by Einstein's theory of relativity, the former is still valid across a vast range of phenomena, and is in fact a special case of the latter. This suggests that, rather than being straightforwardly right or wrong, we would do better to think of theories as being more or less inclusive. Despite its limitations, Aristotle's physics provided a reasonable description of many everyday phenomena. It was replaced by Newtonian physics, which is more rigorous and can account for a far wider range of phenomena. But if we wish to explain the motion of electrons inside an atom or the nature of a gravitational field near a black hole then we must turn to the theory of relativity.

We can illustrate the idea of inclusiveness with the following analogy. If you are laying the foundations of a house, you can treat the earth as if it were flat and make your calculations in accordance with plane geometry. However, if you are dealing with a much larger area, then you will need to take into account the curvature of the earth. Here, plane geometry turns out to be a special case of the geometry that is appropriate to the surface of a sphere. In much the same way, physicists see Newtonian mechanics as a useful approximation that can be incorporated into the more general theory of relativity.

Given what we have said, it seems reasonable to suppose that science will continue to progress in a cumulative way in the future. Admittedly, some of our well-tested theories may eventually turn out to be false; but it is difficult to imagine future scientists rejecting our belief that the earth goes round the sun or that water consists of two atoms of hydrogen and one of oxygen. They may, however, discover that such beliefs are approximations to richer and more inclusive theories, the details of which we cannot at present imagine.

Choosing between rival paradigms

Kuhn claims that during periods of scientific crisis there is no purely rational way of deciding between rival paradigms, and that a scientist's beliefs will be influenced by the society in which she lives.

As we saw earlier, there is doubtless some truth in this claim. At this point, however, we should distinguish between the *origin* of a belief and its *justification*. For the origin of a belief is not of any great relevance to science. All that matters is that the belief should be *testable*. If it is confirmed by experiment, then we provisionally accept it; if it fails then we reject it.

KT – relativism: the belief that there is no absolute truth and that what people believe to be true depends on their culture

Since different paradigms interpret the world in fundamentally different ways and we can never conclusively prove which one is true, some have taken Kuhn's ideas to be a form of **relativism**. However, the fact that there are no conclusive proofs does not mean that scientific knowledge is relative, but simply that – as in every area of knowledge – it depends on *judgement*. We need judgement to decide such things as which factors should be observed and which can be safely ignored, which hypotheses make good sense of the data and which are too outlandish to be useful, which anomalies to take seriously and which to dismiss as experimental error. Such judgements are of course fallible, and they may turn out to be wrong, but this does not make them any less rational. When astronomers speculated that the irregular orbit of Mercury was due to an undiscovered planet, Vulcan, they were wrong; but given the previous successes of Newtonian mechanics, it was a perfectly rational hypothesis. The point, in short, is that just because reason is fallible, it does not follow that it has no value.

One of the great strengths of science is that in the long run it tends to be self-correcting. The fact that scientists work in communities may put pressure on them to conform to the prevailing orthodoxy; but their natural competitiveness will ensure that they check up on one another's results. Moreover, the history of science suggests that good ideas are eventually accepted; and it appears that the time it takes for such ideas to win acceptance is getting shorter. While Copernicus's theory took more than a hundred years to win general acceptance, Einstein's theory was accepted by physicists in less than fifteen years.

Just as good ideas win acceptance, so crackpot theories are weeded out. Despite the support of an oppressive dictatorship, the Soviet biologist Trofim Lysenko, who denounced genetics as 'reactionary and decadent', could not make his wheat grow. Similarly, when in 1989 two scientists, Stanley Pons and Martin Fleischmann, claimed they had produced a nuclear reaction called 'cold fusion' – thereby raising the prospect of a source of energy that would be 'too cheap to meter' – no one else was able to replicate their results and they were quickly discredited.

What comes out of this discussion is that, although there is no straightforward criterion for choosing between rival paradigms, some theories begin to look increasingly plausible and others increasingly implausible as evidence accumulates over time. Beyond a certain point, we are probably justified in dismissing a discredited theory as irrational. Almost no one now takes seriously the claims of the Flat Earth Society. Some ideas have had their day!

Science, truth and values

We have come a long way in our discussion of scientific knowledge and it is time to take stock. Despite the high regard in which science is held, we have seen that there can be no absolute proof in science and that we can neither conclusively verify nor conclusively falsify a hypothesis. But this does not mean that we should embrace relativism. If a scientific theory accounts for the known evidence, is internally consistent and works in practice, then we should – for the time being at least – accept it as true. Admittedly, it may be replaced by a better theory in the future; but it seems reasonable to think that as one theory follows another we can at least get closer to the truth.

At the same time we should maintain a critical attitude to our scientific beliefs and be willing to question our assumptions. Given our tendency to notice only things that confirm our beliefs, there is, at the psychological level, something to be said for actively seeking evidence that falsifies them. This is one of the advantages of Popper's approach to science.

A theory of everything?

Some people believe that the ultimate goal of science is to discover a theory that is so general that we have a complete understanding of nature. Yet it seems unlikely that the map of science will ever be able to reproduce the territory of reality. The American physicist Richard Feynman (1918–88) once observed that understanding nature is like understanding chess. In both cases, to understand means to know 'the rules of the game'. To learn the rules of chess is a relatively straightforward matter but, even if you know them all, it is impossible to predict the course of any particular game. (It has been estimated that there are 10^{120} possible moves in chess – an unimaginably large number!) When it comes to nature, we are dealing with a game that is a great deal more complicated than chess. Not only is it very difficult to discover the rules of the scientific game, but – as with chess – even if we succeed in doing this, our understanding remains general rather than specific. You may be armed with all the rules, but you will never get anywhere near knowing all of the ways in which atoms can combine with one another. So a 'complete' understanding of the rules of nature will still leave plenty of room for surprises!

Perhaps in the case of nature we will never even know all the rules of the game. Science operates on the assumption that by isolating key variables we can discover the truth. When we do experiments we assume that some factors are relevant and that others can safely be ignored. Up until now this has been a successful strategy. Yet the history of science suggests that as science advances we have to take more and more factors into account that were previously dismissed as irrelevant. Perhaps, as we delve into the complexities of nature, we will eventually find that at the deepest level *everything* is connected to everything else. Since we are finite creatures, we will never be able to grasp the totality of connections, and at that point we will have reached the limits of science.

ACTIVITY 13.17

If you drop a stone into a pond, ripples spread out from the point of impact. The ripples gradually diminish in size, but at what point do the effects of your action end? What has this got to do with the discussion above?

Science and scientism

The success of science and technology has sometimes led people to make extravagant claims about the scope of scientific knowledge. According to the view known as **scientism**, science is the only way we can make sense of reality and discover the truth. A typical representative of this view was the philosopher Rudolf Carnap (1891–1970): 'When we say that scientific knowledge is unlimited, we mean that there is no answer in principle unattainable by science.' What Carnap is, in effect, saying is that science is capable of finding all the answers to all the questions, and if something is non-science then it is little different from nonsense.

KT – scientism: the belief that science is the only way we can make sense of reality and discover the truth

There is a big difference between such dogmatic scientism and the more modest conception of science we have looked at in this chapter. We can be proud of what science has achieved; but it is important to keep in mind that it is a fallible human enterprise which may get us closer to the truth but can never give us certainty. Whatever Carnap may have thought, it seems clear that science does not have all the answers, and there are many perplexing questions that lie beyond its scope.

LQ – Ethics: What are the moral responsibilities of scientists?

Science and ethics

Some people worry that science promotes a materialistic picture of the universe which undermines values and robs life of its meaning. This may be a common concern, but it could be argued that, rather than *undermining* values, science actually *presupposes* them. There are, after all, things that we think a good scientist *ought* to do.

For example, they *ought* to be honest and care about the truth, and they *ought* to be open-minded and follow the evidence wherever it leads. This suggests that without ethics there could be no science.

Figure 13.17 An anti-GM foods rally in the USA

Science's pursuit of truth may, however, conflict with other values. The physicist Enrico Fermi (1901–54) once observed: 'I was put on Earth to make certain discoveries, and what the political leaders do with them is not my business.' Since science operates in a social context, this view may strike you as too simplistic. Indeed, Fermi himself seems not to have believed it and he was strongly opposed to the development of the hydrogen bomb in the period after the Second World War. As this example reminds us, scientific knowledge brings dangers as well as benefits, and it would be irresponsible for a scientist to pursue their research oblivious of its possible consequences.

While science itself has no privileged insight into values, scientific research can shed light on the dangers associated with such things as global warming, nuclear energy and genetically modified food, and this can help us to make informed decisions. The problem is that many people no longer trust science; they think that it has been corrupted by political and business interests. As a social endeavour, science doubtless has its flaws, but if we wish to inform ourselves about the nature of physical reality or make informed decisions about the safety of technology, there seems to be no alternative to trusting the scientific consensus.

RLS – Headline:
'The environmental movement professes a deep attachment to science in areas such as climate change but rejects it when it comes to genetically modified crops.' To what extent should we trust the scientific consensus about controversial issues?

Conclusion

The scientific spirit, which is opposed to the uncritical acceptance of dogma, has been largely responsible for the enormous growth of knowledge over the last three centuries, and science is widely seen as one of humanity's great success stories. Our pride in science should, however, be tempered by a degree of humility, and it is worth keeping in mind Bertrand Russell's comment that 'Science tells us what we can know, but what we can know is little, and if we forget how much we cannot know we become insensitive to many things of great importance.' It is striking that some of the world's greatest scientists have been aware of the limited nature of their achievements and the extent of their ignorance. Towards the end of his life, Albert Einstein observed that 'All science, measured against reality, is primitive and childlike.' And yet he still believed that it is 'the most precious thing we have'.

Key points

- The success of the natural sciences has led some people to see them as the most important form of knowledge.
- The main difference between science and pseudo-science is that scientific hypotheses can be tested and pseudo-scientific ones cannot.
- According to the traditional picture of the scientific method, science consists of five key steps: observation, hypothesis, experiment, law, theory.
- Among the problems that arise in applying the scientific method are that observation is selective, and that you are more likely to notice things that confirm your hypothesis than those that contradict it.
- Since scientific laws are based on a limited number of observations, we can never be sure that they are true.
- According to Karl Popper, science should be based on the method of conjectures and refutations, and scientists should try to falsify hypotheses rather than verify them.
- In practice, a hypothesis can no more be conclusively falsified than it can be conclusively verified.
- Thomas Kuhn drew attention to the role played by paradigms in science and argued that the history of science is punctuated by revolutionary jumps or 'paradigm shifts'.
- Although scientific beliefs change over time, it could be argued that each new theory is closer to the truth than the previous one.
- Despite the success of the natural sciences, they cannot give us absolute certainty and there are many perplexing questions that lie beyond their scope.

Key terms

anomaly
conjectures and refutations
controlled experiment
empirical
empiricism
falsificationism
hypothesis
inductivism
law
paradigm
peer review
principle of simplicity
priority dispute
pseudo-science
rationalism
relativism
scientism

Knowledge framework focus

1. *Scope/applications.* Are the natural sciences the model for all other forms of knowledge?
2. *Concepts/language.* Why are so many scientific laws written in the language of mathematics?
3. *Methodology.* Is there an agreed scientific method that we can use to generate new discoveries?
4. *Historical development.* Is scientific progress smooth, or is it punctuated by periods of turmoil and revolution?
5. *Relation to personal knowledge.* Why are some people suspicious of scientific findings, and to what extent are they justified?

IB prescribed essay titles

1. 'In what ways may disagreement aid the pursuit of knowledge in the natural and human sciences?' (May 2013)
2. 'The ultimate protection against research error and bias is supposed to come from the way scientists constantly re-test each other's results.' To what extent would you agree with this claim in the natural sciences and the human sciences? (November 2012)

Further reading

Books

A. C. Chalmers, *What Is This Thing Called Science?* (Open University Press, 2013). This book gives a good overview of the main ideas about the nature of science. You might not want to read it from cover to cover, but there are useful chapters on traditional inductivism, Popper's falsificationism and Kuhn's paradigms.

Richard P. Feynman, *'Surely You're Joking Mr. Feynman!'* (W. W. Norton, 1997), especially pp. 338–46, 'Cargo Cult Science'. Richard Feynman was one of the great physicists of the twentieth century. In this chapter he considers the difference between science and pseudo-science in his own inimitable and entertaining style.

Online articles

Richard Dawkins, 'Crystalline Truth and Crystal Balls', in *A Devil's Chaplain* (Weidenfeld & Nicolson, 2003).

Hilary Lawson, 'The Fallacy of Scientific Objectivity', *The Listener*, 29 February 1986.

The human sciences

14

I am more interested in how a man lives than how a star dies.

Sherwin Nuland, 1930–

In every science man speaks only of himself.

Oswald Spengler, 1880–1936

We make our surroundings and then they make us.

Winston Churchill, 1874–1965

Life is heredity plus environment.

Luther Burbank, 1849–1926

If the brain were simple enough to understand, we would be too simple to understand it.

Anon

The only possible conclusion the social sciences can draw is: some do, some don't.

Ernest Rutherford, 1871–1937

An economist is an expert who will know tomorrow why the things he predicted yesterday did happen today.

Laurence J. Peter, 1919–88

It is quite possible – overwhelmingly probable, one might guess – that we will always learn more about human life and human personality from novels than from scientific psychology.

Noam Chomsky, 1928–

Human behaviour makes most sense when it is explained in terms of beliefs and desires, not in terms of volts and grams.

Steven Pinker, 1954–

In carefully controlled laboratory conditions animals do what they damned well please.

The Harvard law of animal behaviour

Know then thyself, presume not God to scan / The proper study of mankind is man.

Alexander Pope, 1688–1744

Introduction

Since human beings have been able to reflect about themselves and their place in the scheme of things, they have been struck by their own complex and mysterious nature. The human sciences are an attempt to reduce the mystery by studying human behaviour in a systematic way. Under the heading 'human science' are subjects such as psychology, economics, anthropology and sociology. Despite the obvious differences between these subjects, they are all based on observation and seek to discover laws and theories about human nature.

We may, however, wonder to what extent human beings can be studied in a purely scientific way. At one level we are simply animals composed of atoms and molecules. According to the theory of evolution, we have descended from the apes, with whom we share 99 per cent of our genes, and we are made up of the same basic ingredients as all other living things – 63 per cent hydrogen, 25.5 per cent oxygen, 9.5 per cent carbon, 1.5 per cent nitrogen, and 0.5 per cent of a few other elements.

But most people would reject the idea that we are 'just animals', or 'nothing but a bunch of chemicals', and would draw attention to the differences between us and the rest of the natural world. One of our most important distinguishing characteristics – from which all others could be said to flow – is that we are *self-conscious* animals. Many other animals are conscious, but unlike us it seems that they are not aware of themselves. Some evidence for this is provided by the so-called **mirror test**. Although you recognise yourself in a mirror, a dog will bark at its own image without ever realising that it is barking at itself. (Some animals, such as chimpanzees, bottlenose dolphins, Asian elephants and even magpies have passed the mirror test, and this suggests that they may have the glimmerings of self-consciousness.)

KT – mirror test: a test that gauges self-awareness by seeing if a human infant or non-human animal recognises itself in a mirror

Among the other features associated with self-consciousness that seem to be unique to us are language, reason, free-will and creativity. Some people also believe that we

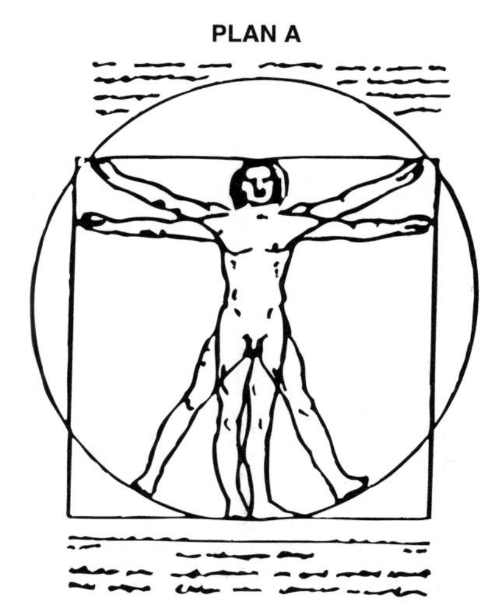

Figure 14.1

Figure 14.2 The mirror test: while young children and monkeys pass the mirror test, dogs do not.

LQ – Reason: What are the pros and cons of assuming that human beings are rational animals?

have an animating spirit or soul which cannot be explained in terms of material processes. Whatever your opinion about this, there are likely to be special challenges in studying human beings in a scientific way.

In this chapter, we will look at four key aspects of the scientific method – observation, measurement, experiments and laws – and consider what special problems arise when these steps are applied to the study of human beings. This will lead on to a more general discussion of the similarities and differences between the natural and human sciences.

ACTIVITY 14.1

1. List as many features as you can that distinguish human beings from other animals.
2. To what extent do these features make it difficult to study human beings in a scientific way?

Observation

Perhaps the most important characteristic of science is that it is based on observation. One problem in the human sciences is that, although you can observe other people's behaviour, you cannot directly observe their minds. You may be able to make an educated guess about what they are thinking, but you can never be entirely sure that you are right.

LQ – Language: Can questionnaires be written in neutral language?

One way to find out what people think is, of course, to ask them. Since most people are reasonably honest, we can learn a lot from questionnaires, opinion polls and interviews. At the same time, since people generally want to see themselves in a good light, we cannot always take what they say at face value. There is evidence from psychology to suggest that we tend to overestimate our strengths and underestimate our weaknesses. For example, in one well-known survey of a million US high-school seniors, *all of them* ranked themselves as above average in terms of their ability to get on with other people! Since people care about what others think of them, they may also be unwilling to admit holding unpopular opinions. This may explain why extreme political parties often do better in general elections than in opinion polls.

ACTIVITY 14.2

1. Complete a copy of the following short questionnaire as honestly as possible. Then collate the results for the class as a whole. How would you interpret the results and what conclusions would you draw from them?

	BELOW AVERAGE	AVERAGE	ABOVE AVERAGE
a. How much do you worry about what other people think of you?			
b. To what extent do you see yourself as a considerate person?			
c. Do you have a good sense of humour?			
d. How open are you to new ideas?			
e. How worried are you about environmental problems?			

2. In some countries it is forbidden to publish opinion polls in the week running up to a general election. Do you think this is a good policy, or a denial of free speech?

Loaded questions

Another problem with asking people what they think is that it is not easy to frame questions in an unbiased way. A **loaded question**, which contains a hidden assumption, may encourage people to answer one way rather than another. Consider, for example, the following 1980 US poll in which a similar question was worded in two different ways:

KT – loaded question: a question which is biased because it contains a built-in assumption

	IN FAVOUR	OPPOSED
1. Do you think there should be an amendment to the Constitution prohibiting abortions, or shouldn't there be such an amendment?	29%	67%
2. Do you believe there should be an amendment to the Constitution protecting the life of the unborn child, or shouldn't there be such an amendment?	50%	34%

ACTIVITY 14.3

1. Which of the above questions do you think is loaded? Give reasons.
2. Take a controversial topic – such as abortion, or capital punishment – and try to design an unbiased questionnaire to discover people's opinions about it.

This example suggests that if you ask questions with sufficient skill and cunning, you may be able to get people to give you the answer you want. An amusing example of this can be found in an episode of an old British comedy series *Yes, Prime Minister.*

Two bureaucrats, Sir Humphrey Appleby and Bernard Woolley, are discussing an opinion poll which shows that 67 per cent of people are in favour of reintroducing National Service (compulsory military service). Sir Humphrey asks Bernard to commission another opinion poll which will give them the opposite result. When Bernard asks how this can be done, Sir Humphrey demonstrates how two different lines of questioning can lead a person to give a different answer to the same question.

Line One
'Mr Woolley, are you worried about the rise in crime among teenagers?'
'Yes'
'Do you think there is lack of discipline and vigorous training in our Comprehensive Schools?'
'Yes'
'Do you think young people welcome some structure and leadership in their lives?'
'Yes'
'Do they respond to a challenge?'
'Yes'
'Might you be in favour of reintroducing National Service?'
'Yes'

Line Two
'Mr Woolley, are you worried about the danger of war?'
'Yes'
'Are you unhappy about the growth of armaments?'
'Yes'
'Do you think there's a danger in giving young people guns and teaching them how to kill?'
'Yes'
'Do you think it's wrong to force people to take up arms against their will?'
'Yes'
'Would you oppose the reintroduction of National Service?'
'Yes'

"How would you like me to answer that question? As a member of my ethnic group, educational class, income group, or religious category?"
Figure 14.3

A final point we can make about questionnaires is that there is often a difference between what people say they would do in a hypothetical situation and what they actually do in reality. You might, for example, say that you would be willing to buy a product at a certain price, but have second thoughts about it when you actually have to part with your money. More dramatically, you might imagine that if you were trapped in a burning building, you would selflessly help other people to escape before leaving yourself. We are all heroes in our dreams, but if this happened in reality, you might be the first to run for safety!

The observer effect

KT – observer effect: the tendency of people to behave differently when they are being observed

Another problem with observation in the human sciences is the so-called **observer effect**. If a geologist is studying rocks they are indifferent to his presence; but if a psychologist is observing people they may become nervous or embarrassed by his attention and this may lead them to change their behaviour.

Figure 14.4

Imagine, for example, learning that a television crew were coming to your school tomorrow to film a typical TOK class for a documentary to be shown on national television. How would this affect your behaviour? You might dress differently, try to look interested in class and speak with unusual eloquence. Or you might be so anxious not to make a fool of yourself that you were not able to contribute at all. Either way, the presence of the TV cameras will ensure that the class is not a typical one.

LQ – Sense perception: To what extent does observing human beings affect their behaviour?

ACTIVITY 14.4

1. What ways, if any, are there of getting round the 'observer effect'?
2. Reality TV has become popular in many countries, with series like *Big Brother*, *Survivor* and *Star Academy*. What, if anything, do we learn about human nature from such programmes?

There are at least two ways in which a human scientist can try to get round the observer effect. The first is *habituation*. If a television crew came and filmed your TOK class for a whole term, you would probably get used to the presence of the cameras and eventually ignore them. Anthropologists use a similar strategy when they **go native** and live with a tribe for an extended period of time. The hope is that the people they are studying will eventually get used to them and behave normally in their presence.

KT – go native: adopting the attitudes and behaviour of a foreign group with whom one has lived for an extended period

Another solution to the observer effect is to use hidden cameras. If you don't know that you are being observed, then it won't affect your behaviour. But this raises ethical questions about whether or not it is acceptable to film people without their knowledge.

A variant of the observer effect concerns the way in which a prediction can affect the outcome of what is predicted. A classical example of this can be found in the Greek tragedy *Oedipus Rex*. When Oedipus was born, a prophecy was made that he would kill his father and marry his mother. When his father, the king of Thebes, learned of

© www.CartoonStock.com

"It would seem that grooming one another is very important in maintaining social order."

Figure 14.5

this he was horrified and abandoned the new-born child in the mountains, hoping that he would die so that the prophecy would not come true. But Oedipus was rescued by a shepherd and eventually adopted by the king and queen of Corinth. He grew up believing that they were his real parents. Then, as a young man, he learned of the prophecy about himself and fled from home in terror. On the road, he got into an argument with a stranger and killed him. He then turned up in Thebes where he eventually married the recently widowed queen. Without realising it, Oedipus had killed his father and married his mother. When at the end of the play, he discovered the truth, he was not a happy man. Sophocles' tragedy derives its power from the fact that in the very act of trying to escape the prophecy Oedipus brought it down on himself. If only he had stayed in Corinth, everything would have been fine!

The effects of predictions on human behaviour are not usually as dramatic as in *Oedipus Rex*, but they can still have serious consequences. Here are three examples taken from different human sciences.

LQ – Ethics: How do ethical factors limit experiments in the human sciences?

1. Psychology

In a well-known psychology experiment, school children were randomly allocated to one of two groups labelled 'bright' and 'less bright'. Although there was no initial difference between the two groups, the children labelled 'bright' made greater academic progress in the following year than the students labelled 'less bright'. This suggests that teachers' expectations affected how well the students did and helped to produce the differences between the two groups.

ACTIVITY 14.5

1. To what extent do you think your teachers' expectations about your abilities affect how well you do at school?
2. Would it be better if teachers had no expectations about you? To what extent is that possible?
3. Do you think that primary-school teachers should divide children into good readers and not-so-good readers? What would be the pros and cons of doing this?
4. To what extent can your own expectations about yourself affect your academic performance?

2. Economics

If you follow the stock market, you are probably aware that people's expectations can affect share prices. In a *bull market*, when most people expect prices to rise, a rational investor will buy stocks now, hoping to sell them later at a higher price thereby making a profit. If everyone behaves like that, the demand for stocks will increase and cause prices to rise. Conversely, in a *bear market* when most people expect prices to fall, a rational investor will sell stocks now, hoping to buy them back later at a lower price. But if everyone does that, the increased supply of stocks will push prices down. So if everyone expects prices to rise they will rise, and if everyone expects prices to fall they will fall.

ACTIVITY 14.6

1. Do you think the behaviour of stock markets is governed more by reason or more by emotion?
2. Do you think that it is possible to predict with accuracy where the stock market will be in twelve months' time? Give reasons.

3. Anthropology

According to anthropologist Wade Davis, when a sorcerer in an aborigine tribe points at an individual and casts a death spell over him, 'the individual invariably sickens and almost always dies'. One explanation for such cases of 'voodoo death' is that the individual has been conditioned since childhood to believe in the power of the sorcerer's spell. So when the sorcerer curses him, he in effect loses the will to live. He may, for example, retire to his shelter and refuse to eat until he wastes away and dies. The individual's belief that he is going to die seems to be an important factor in his eventual death.

ACTIVITY 14.7

1. Have you ever been caught breaking a taboo and said something like 'I feel so ashamed I could die'?
2. Do you think that mental states, such as happiness or depression, can affect our physical well-being?
3. Try to find some information about alleged cases of 'voodoo death'. Do you believe they really happen? If so, how would you account for them?

A final point to notice about predictions is that they can be self-negating as well as self-fulfilling. For example, if I predict that you are going to break your leg playing soccer this afternoon, you will have a strong incentive not to play, thereby falsifying my prediction. In this case, the very act of making the prediction helps to ensure that it does *not* come true.

ACTIVITY 14.8

According to a phenomenon known as psychological **reactance**, if a person is inclined to do X, and you then tell him to do X, he becomes more likely not to do X. This may explain why some teenage anti-smoking campaigns have the perverse effect of encouraging teenagers to smoke. With this in mind, how would you try to organise an effective anti-smoking campaign?

KT – reactance: the tendency of people to react against advice, rules and regulations perceived as a threat to their freedom

Measurement

LQ – Mathematics: To what extent can we measure human phenomena?

While measurement plays an important role in the sciences by adding precision to our knowledge, it is generally more difficult to measure things in the human sciences than in the natural sciences. Consider, for example, consciousness. If you were asked *how many* thoughts you have had today, it is doubtful that you could answer this question. Part of the problem is that we have no units for measuring thoughts and determining where one ends and another begins, for they simply melt into one another. Furthermore, if you try to count your thoughts, the very process of counting will interfere with what you are trying to count. So, rather than think of consciousness as a series of discrete thoughts, it may make more sense to follow the American psychologist William James (1842–1910) and think of it as a continuous **stream of consciousness**.

KT – stream of consciousness: the idea that consciousness consists of a continuous flow rather than a series of discrete thoughts and feelings

KT – behaviourism: a school of thought which says that the subject-matter of psychology should be overt behaviour rather than hidden thoughts and feelings

While consciousness played a key role in William James' conception of psychology, some twentieth-century psychologists dismissed it as unscientific on the grounds that it can be neither objectively observed nor precisely measured. This gave rise to a school of psychology known as **behaviourism**, which redefined the subject as the scientific study, not of consciousness, but of *behaviour*. Despite the difficulties involved in trying to study consciousness, there are many variables in the human sciences that *can* be measured with relative ease: for example, population, income and the rate of inflation. Furthermore, as the American scientist Jared Diamond has argued in an article entitled 'Soft Sciences are often Harder than Hard Sciences', human scientists have developed a variety of sophisticated techniques for translating what look like qualitative concepts into measurable ones.

ACTIVITY 14.9

1. When you try to make sense of other people, do you pay more attention to what they say or to what they do?
2. Do you agree that since consciousness cannot be objectively observed, it should not be part of psychology?
3. Would you be willing to reject talk of electrons in physics and genes in biology on the grounds that they cannot be directly observed?

RLS – Headline: 'Denmark the world's happiest country'. What special challenges arise in attempting to measure phenomena in the human sciences?

Who really won the Centennial Olympics?

When we apply numbers to things it sometimes creates a spurious sense of objectivity. After the 1996 Olympic Games in Atlanta, an article appeared in a Canadian newspaper headed 'Who really won the Centennial Olympics?' You might think that we can find the answer simply by consulting the official rankings.

RANK	COUNTRY	MEDALS TOTAL
1	USA	101
2	Germany	65
3	Russia	63
4	China	50
11	Canada	22

The above table shows some of the results, ranking the countries in terms of the total number of medals won. The USA came first with 101 medals, and Canada eleventh with 22. However, you might point out that simply knowing the *number* of medals each country got does not give us enough information to decide who really won the Olympics. We also need to know the *colour* of the medals. If the USA had 101 bronze and Germany 65 gold, there would be a strong case for saying that Germany, not the USA, had won the Olympics. Here, then, is the breakdown of medals won:

COUNTRY	GOLD	SILVER	BRONZE	MEDALS WON
USA	44	32	25	101
Germany	20	18	27	65
Russia	26	21	16	63
China	16	22	12	50
Canada	3	11	8	22

We now have to decide how to *interpret* these figures. Consider Germany and Russia: Germany won two more medals in *total* than Russia, but Russia won six more *gold* medals than Germany. So who did the best? Well, the standard Olympic convention is to award 3 points for a gold, 2 for a silver and 1 for a bronze. Following that convention we get the following results:

RANK	COUNTRY	GOLD	SILVER	BRONZE	POINTS
1	USA	44	32	25	221
2	Russia	26	21	16	136
3	Germany	20	18	27	123
4	China	16	22	12	104
11	Canada	3	11	8	39

The only change at the top is that Russia and Germany change places. Canada stays in eleventh place.

But what if we now take into account the *population* of each country? After all, the USA has a much larger population base than Canada from which to choose its athletes. (At the time of the Atlanta Olympics, the figures were 255 million as against

28 million.) This dramatically changes the picture. If we now look at points per million we get the following result:

RANK	COUNTRY	POINTS PER MILLION PEOPLE
1	Tonga	20
2	Bahamas	6.6
3	Cuba	4.6
25	Canada	1.3
37	USA	0.9

If we look at the results in this way, some island nations rise to the top of the table. Cuba's results are now more than 5 times better than those of the USA, and Canada's results are 1.5 times better than the USA's.

But we don't have to stop there. We might think of more ways of refining the ranking.

- Since children and seniors do not form part of the pool of potential athletes, we should perhaps take into account age distribution, and look not at points per million people, but points per million people of eligible age – say between 16 and 60.
- We might consider comparative wealth on the grounds that athletes from wealthy countries have better training facilities than their poorer counterparts.
- We might want to compensate for the fact that the USA had 'home advantage' – for it is well known that a team playing at home tends to do better than one playing away from home.

We now risk getting lost in a welter of rankings established in accordance with different criteria. It is beginning to look as if there is never a clear answer to the question 'Who won the Olympics?' Perhaps we should simply abandon the obsession with ranking countries. That, however, is easier said than done!

ACTIVITY 14.10

1. Do you think it is possible to answer the question 'Which country won the Olympics?' Does it matter?
2. 'You can no more say that a gold medal is worth three bronzes than that an apple is worth two oranges.' What do you think of this criticism of Olympic rankings?
3. What effect do you think doing well in the Olympics, or winning the World Cup, might have on a country's economy?
4. What value, in general, is there in ranking things? Have you ever looked at university rankings? How seriously do you take them? How seriously should you take them?

One point that comes out of the above discussion is that we run into problems when we try to measure different things – such as gold, silver and bronze medals – on a common scale. People are often accused of 'comparing apples and oranges' when they try to do this. However, an economist might argue that we can in fact compare different things on a common scale by looking at how much people are willing to pay for them. Whether or not it is in practice possible to put a price on everything, is something for you to decide!

ACTIVITY 14.11

1. How would you go about trying to put a monetary value on a human life?
2. Can you think of situations in which society puts a monetary value on human life? How do you feel about trying to weigh a life in terms of money?
3. Which of the following is easy to measure and which is not? How would you go about trying to measure it?
   - a. Weight
   - b. Brand loyalty
   - c. Temperature
   - d. Social class
   - e. Inflation
   - f. Intelligence
   - g. Happiness
   - h. Reading ability
   - i. Progress
   - j. Age
4. What truth do you think there is in the following poem?

   Economists have come to feel
   What can't be measured isn't real.
   The truth is always an amount
   Count numbers only numbers count.
   (Robert Chambers)

Figure 14.6 Can intelligence be measured?

"Do you have 'Intelligence for Idiots'?"

Figure 14.7

RLS – Headline: 'Exam grades "more nature than nurture"'. Why is it so difficult to determine the roles played by nature and nurture in traits such as intelligence?

Experiments

KT – nature–nurture debate: the debate about whether we are influenced more by our biological nature (genetic inheritance) or our cultural nurture (environmental experiences)

We typically associate the word 'science' with a person in a white coat doing experiments in a laboratory. Ideally, experiments should play as big a role in the human sciences as they do in the natural sciences; but in practice this is not usually the case. There are at least three reasons for this.

1. Human scientists are often trying to make sense of complex real-world situations in which it is simply impossible to run controlled experiments.
2. The artificiality of some of the experiments that can be conducted may distort the behaviour of the participants.
3. There are ethical reasons for not conducting experiments that have a negative effect on the people who participate in them.

Figure 14.8 Elyse Schein and Paula Bernstein are identical twins who were separated at birth and adopted by different families. They discovered each other after 35 years apart. What light can such cases shed on the **nature–nurture debate**?

Faced with the above difficulties, what are human scientists to do? One solution is to wait for nature to provide the appropriate experimental conditions. We can, for example, learn something about how a normal brain functions by looking at people who have suffered brain damage; and we can gain some insight into the roles played by genes and the environment by studying identical twins who have been separated at birth and brought up in different families. In the case of economics, economic history can provide us with a bank of – admittedly not very well-controlled – experimental data.

Human scientists do not just sit around waiting for natural experiments to arise. They also devise ingenious experiments of their own. Suppose you want to know how a baby sees the world. Does it see it as a 'blooming, banging confusion' as the psychologist William James (1842–1910) thought, or is there more of a structure to its experience? We cannot, of course, ask the baby since it has not yet learnt to speak. So it might seem that all we can do is *speculate*. That is what people thought until two psychologists, Elizabeth Spelke and Renée Baillargeon, pointed out that babies tend to stare at surprising things longer than at unsurprising ones. This key insight was like opening a window onto the developing mind. There was now a way of testing babies' expectations and getting some idea of how they see the world. The resulting experimental evidence suggests that, before they are six months old, babies have figured out that objects consist of parts that move together, are aware of the difference between living and non-living things, and can even do simple arithmetic!

ACTIVITY 14.12

1. How accurate do you think 'stare time' is as a way of measuring a baby's expectations? What if a baby looks at something for two seconds, looks away for three, and then looks back again for another two?
2. Do you think there is any danger that psychologists see what they want to see in these kinds of experiment?

Two famous experiments

The Milgram experiment

One of the best-known experiments in the history of psychology took place at Yale University (USA) in 1963. Stanley Milgram was interested in the extent to which people are willing to obey orders. He advertised for volunteers to participate in an experiment allegedly to 'test the effects of punishment on learning'. When a volunteer arrived he was told that he was to play the role of 'teacher', and another 'volunteer' – in reality an actor – was to play the role of 'learner'. The learner was strapped to a chair and electrodes were put on his wrists. The teacher was then taken to an adjoining room and asked to give the learner a simple memory test. Every time the learner answered incorrectly, the teacher was to give the learner a successively higher electric shock by flicking a switch on a generator. Each switch was clearly labelled with voltage levels ranging from 15 to 450 volts, and verbal descriptions such as 'slight shock', 'strong shock', 'intense shock', 'danger', and finally 'XXX'. Although the teacher could not see the learner, he was able to hear his responses. Once the voltage reached 120V, the learner began to complain; at 150 volts he demanded that the experiment be stopped; at 270V he started screaming; and after 330V there was an ominous silence. Whenever the teacher hesitated to administer a shock, a scientist standing behind him insisted that it was very important that he continue with the experiment. In reality, of course, the learner did not receive any shocks, but the 'teacher' was not aware of this at the time.

ACTIVITY 14.13

1. Given your knowledge of human nature, what percentage of 100 volunteers do you think would continue administering electric shocks up to 450 volts?
2. If you had been a volunteer in this experiment, what do you think you would have done?

The result of the experiment was that almost two-thirds of the volunteers continued to give electric shocks up to 450 volts. Many expressed concern about what they were doing, and had to be reassured that they would not be held responsible for the fate of the learner; but it did not seem to occur to them to refuse to comply. Only one-third of the volunteers refused to continue to the end.

The Milgram experiment raises some disturbing questions about human nature. Why were so many of the volunteers willing to obey white-coated authority figures and give what they thought were lethal shocks to complete strangers? One crumb of comfort was that if, instead of working alone, the volunteer was paired with two other teachers (who were again actors), and the other teachers rebelled, then only 10% of the volunteers were willing to continue giving shocks up to 450 volts.

Changing perspective, we might question the ethics, not of the participants, but of the experiment. After all, the volunteers were misled about what they were getting involved in, were made to feel uncomfortable during the experiment, and may have suffered a permanent loss of self-esteem once the experiment was over. You are probably not going to feel great about yourself if you discover that you are the kind of person willing to administer a lethal electric shock to a stranger! On the other hand, it could be argued that the knowledge gained from the experiment outweighs any moral qualms we might have about the way it was carried out.

ACTIVITY 14.14

1. What difference do you think it would have made if the original advertisement asking for volunteers for the Milgram experiment had mentioned electric shocks? What conclusion would you draw from this?
2. Design your own ethical code of conduct for the running of experiments in the human sciences. What three or four key points would you include and why?

The Stanford prison experiment

A second famous experiment designed by psychologist Philip Zimbardo took place at Stanford University in 1971. The aim of the experiment was to see how 'the power of the situation' can influence the behaviour of ordinary people. The basement of the psychology department was made to look like a prison and twenty-four student volunteers were recruited and divided randomly into guards and prisoners. The guards were given complete control over the prisoners. The experiment was supposed to last two weeks but it had to be abandoned after six days because some of the guards were behaving sadistically and the prisoners were becoming psychologically traumatised. Zimbardo took the experiment to show that the situation is more important than character traits in determining how people behave. When news emerged of prisoner abuse by American guards in Abu Ghraib prison in Iraq in 2004, Zimbardo said he was horrified but not surprised. As he memorably put it, 'You can't be a sweet cucumber in a vinegar barrel.' Zimbardo's work can be seen as an extension of Milgram's in that it suggests that people can do terrible things not only when they are told to by authority figures but also when they find themselves in a toxic environment.

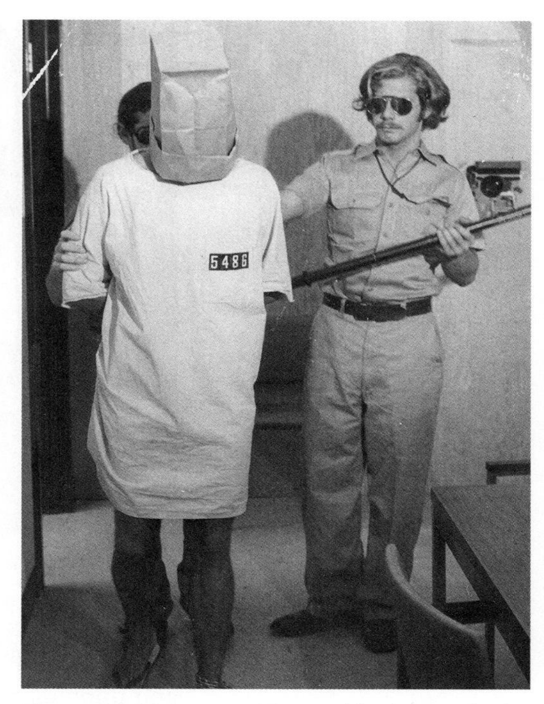

Figure 14.9 Prisoner with guard in the Stanford prison experiment. What conclusions can we draw from this experiment?

Together with the Milgram experiment, the Stanford prison experiment is often cited as an example of unethical research. One might try to justify it on the grounds that the insight it gives us into human nature was worth the suffering that it caused. Whatever your thoughts on that, one might also question the alleged findings of the experiment on the following grounds.

1. *Selection bias.* To find participants for his study, Zimbardo made an advertisement which explicitly mentioned an experiment about 'prison life'. Such an experiment may have appealed to atypical – and possibly aggressive – individuals who were not representative of the general population.
2. *Experimenter expectations.* At the start of the experiment, Zimbardo briefed the guards on how to behave, and it could be argued that the guards were simply doing what he encouraged them to do.
3. *Ambiguous results.* Although some guards did engage in sadistic behaviour, others did not; so it could be argued that the overall results of the experiment suggest that a bad situation does not turn everyone into a sadist.

Arguments about the significance of the Stanford prison experiment, together with the question of whether behaviour is influenced more by character traits or the situation, continue to this day. As this brief discussion suggests, experiments in the human sciences are sometimes inconclusive and open to a variety of different interpretations.

Laws

While observation, measurement and experimentation are important parts of the scientific method, the main goal of science is to develop laws and theories to explain the phenomena that it studies. The human sciences are faced with a number of challenges when it comes to formulating such laws.

Making predictions

Another problem for the human sciences is that our belief in human free-will would seem to conflict with the idea that there are law-like regularities in human

Figure 14.10 Ukrainian anti-government protesters (2014). To what extent is it possible to predict the behaviour of crowds?

behaviour. How, after all, could we ever reduce the behaviour of inconsistent, wilful and unpredictable human beings to a neat set of laws? Isaac Newton (1642–1727) was doubtful, and famously observed: 'I can calculate the motions of heavenly bodies, but not the madness of crowds.'

Despite Newton's comment, a great deal of human behaviour does in fact seem to be fairly predictable. If people lack food, they are unhappy; if the price of lemons goes up, people buy fewer lemons; and if someone drops their tray in the school dining hall, everyone cheers! We make literally thousands of generalisations about human beings every day, and if they were completely unpredictable no one would ever get into a car and venture onto the road.

ACTIVITY 14.15

1. To what extent do you find the behaviour of your friends and family predictable? Do you ever find that when your parents are giving you advice you are able to finish many of their sentences for them?
2. What makes a person an interesting person? Would you prefer to have predictable friends, or unpredictable friends, or some combination of the two?
3. State three generalisations about human behaviour that you think are true of all human beings.

KT – law of large numbers: a statistical principle which says that random variations tend to cancel out when a population is large enough

The law of large numbers

Although individual behaviour may be unpredictable, we can make surprisingly accurate short-term predictions about such things as the number of births, marriages and deaths in a country. The explanation for this derives from the **law of large numbers**, which says that in a large population *random variations tend to cancel out.*

For example, there are all kinds of social customs and expectations which affect the number of people who get married in a particular time period. In general we can say that confirmed bachelors are unlikely to get married, and engaged couples are likely to get married. However, random factors are also at work and occasionally confirmed bachelors fall in love and marry, and engaged couples fall out of love and do not. If we are dealing with a large enough population, then the number of unexpected marriages is likely to be cancelled out by the number of unexpected non-marriages.

ACTIVITY 14.16

Briefly explain how the law of large numbers enables insurance companies to offer cover against risks such as car accidents, house fires and death.

Since the law of large numbers enables us to predict group rather than individual behaviour, many laws in the human sciences are *probabilistic* in nature. Although we cannot predict with any certainty whether or not John Smith will get married this year, we may be able to predict the probability of this happening.

You might think that such probabilistic laws are inferior to the universal laws that are typically associated with the natural sciences. But in fact the laws governing the behaviour of atoms and genes are also of a probabilistic kind, and a physicist can no more predict the behaviour of an individual gas molecule than a human scientist can predict the behaviour of a man in a crowd.

Trends and laws

Despite the law of large numbers, the human sciences do not have a very good record of prediction. There is, for example, no consensus among demographers about the size of world population in fifty years' time; economic forecasters seem to get it wrong as often as they get it right; and almost no one predicted the collapse of communism in the 1980s. A well-known example of a prediction that turned out to be way off the mark was the one made by the population economist Paul Ehrlich in 1973. Ehrlich was very pessimistic about the state of the planet and he predicted that, by 1990, 65 million Americans would be starving to death. Ironically, that turned out to be the number of Americans who were overweight in 1990!

To understand why the predictions of human scientists sometimes turn out to be wrong, we need to explain the difference between a *trend* and a *law*. Critics argue that too often human scientists have simply uncovered trends rather than genuine laws. A trend shows the direction in which a variable is moving, but since it gives no explanation for the movement it is not very reliable. That is why 'betting on a trend' is a dangerous game. A horse may have won its last three races, and a company may have made profits for the last three years, but this alone does not mean that the horse will win its next race or the company will make a profit next year. If we know something about the horse's breeding and physical condition, or the company's financial background and investment strategy, we are likely to make better predictions than if we simply bet on a trend.

A good example of the danger of betting on a trend is the *Phillips curve* in economics. In the 1960s, an economist called A. W. Phillips gathered data on the relationship between inflation and unemployment in the UK from 1861 until 1967. The data appeared to suggest a stable relationship between the two, as illustrated in Figure 14.11.

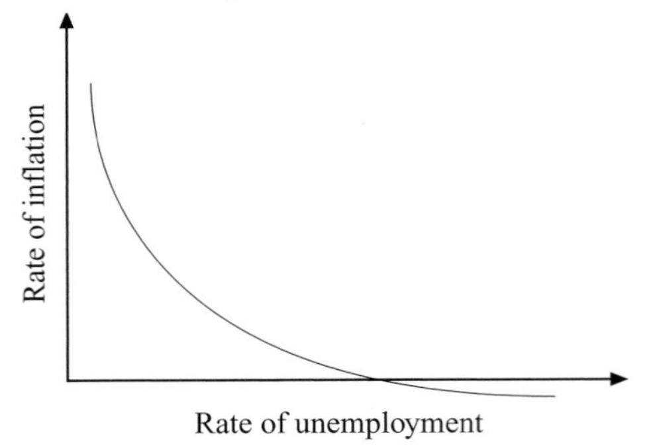

Figure 14.11 A Phillips curve

Many governments understood the curve to show that there was a trade-off between inflation and unemployment, and that lower unemployment could be bought at the cost of higher inflation, and vice versa. Unfortunately, when they tried to reduce unemployment by allowing inflation to rise, the Phillips curve broke down, and for much of the 1970s many countries experienced both rising inflation *and* rising unemployment.

What this example shows is that just because two things are *correlated* it does not follow that the first is the cause of the second. To think that it does is to commit the **fallacy of *post hoc ergo propter hoc*** (see also Chapter 6, page 153). A correlation between two variables, *A* and *B*, could mean that *A* causes *B*, or that *B* causes *A*, or that *A* and *B* are both caused by some other factor, *C*.

KT – fallacy of *post hoc ergo propter hoc*: the fallacy of confusing a mere correlation with a causal connection

ACTIVITY 14.17

1. How might you explain each of the following correlations?
   a. Children with low self-esteem tend to do badly at school.
   b. People who watch violent movies tend to be violent in real life.
   c. As a country develops economically, birth rates tend to go down.
   d. Children brought up by talkative parents tend to be talkative themselves.
   e. Married people tend to be happier than unmarried people.
2. According to economist Steve Levitt, 'Economists . . . have more or less given up on the idea of macroeconomic forecasting.' Why is it so difficult to make accurate predictions in economics and what implications, if any, does this have for economics' alleged status as a science?

RLS – Headline: 'Facebook causes depression new study says'. Why is it so difficult to distinguish genuine from spurious causal connections in the human sciences?

The complexity of real-world situations

Another reason why it might be difficult to uncover laws in the human sciences is the complexity of the situations they deal with. In the real world, it is often difficult to untangle a complicated web of causal relationships to determine which one is decisive.

Imagine, for example, that one night a man is driving along a country lane and crashes into a wall. He is lucky to escape unhurt, but his car is a write-off. What caused the crash? Here is some background information.

- The accident happened on a sharp bend on an unlit road.
- There was ice on the road.
- The man was speeding.
- He had drunk two pints of beer earlier in the evening.
- He was known to enjoy driving fast.
- He had just broken up with his girlfriend.

Given this information, it may be impossible to determine the *one* thing that caused the crash. Rather than search for a single cause, it might make more sense to say that it resulted from a *combination* of things. Perhaps if any one of the above facts had been different, the accident would never have happened. What this suggests is that it may be impossible to come up with a simple law of car accidents of the form 'If *X*, then there will be a car accident.'

If it is difficult to determine the cause of a small-scale event like a car accident, then it is a great deal more difficult to determine the cause of such complex phenomena as teenage depression, crime or inflation. And if we cannot say what the cause of an event was, then it will be hard to predict what will happen when similar events happen in the future. So it is perhaps not surprising that economists sometimes get their forecasts wrong!

Summary: the role of laws in the human sciences

We have seen that, although individuals may be unpredictable, the law of large numbers means that we can sometimes make accurate predictions about the behaviour of a large population. However, some of these predictions are based on trends rather than laws, and we should be careful not to confuse a correlation with a causal connection. In practice, the complexity of real-world situations means that it is difficult to unearth simple laws of the 'If . . ., then . . .' variety. Nevertheless, subjects such as economics still have many tried and tested laws, such as the law of demand and the law of diminishing returns.

The relation with natural sciences

When we consider the relationship between the various sciences, it is commonly thought that there is a continuum of subjects running from the 'hard' natural sciences to the 'soft' human sciences. This reflects the fact that the human sciences have generally been held in lower esteem than their natural science cousins. They seem to lack the explanatory power of Newtonian mechanics, the atomic theory of gases, or molecular biology. Human scientists themselves have sometimes envied the

LQ – Natural sciences: Can we study human beings in the same way that we study other natural phenomena?

mathematical rigour, immutable laws and cumulative nature of the natural sciences; and some people might even agree with Ernest Rutherford's (1871–1937) dismissive observation that 'The only possible conclusion the social sciences can draw is: some do, some don't.'

ACTIVITY 14.18

Do you think there is a hierarchy of sciences? If so, try to order the various sciences according to any criteria of your choice. If not, explain why not.

Subjects such as psychology, economics and anthropology are undoubtedly a great deal more valuable than uninformed common sense in helping us to make sense of the human condition. Nevertheless, there is a suspicion in some quarters that they still lack the well-established paradigms that characterise the natural sciences. Consider, for example, the following comparison between biology and psychology by the neuroscientists V. S. Ramachandran and J. J. Smythies:

> *Anyone interested in the history of ideas would be puzzled by the following striking differences between advances in biology and advances in psychology. The progress of biology has been characterized by landmark discoveries, each of which resulted in a breakthrough in understanding – the discoveries of cells, Mendel's law of heredity, chromosomes, mutations, DNA and the genetic code. Psychology, on the other hand, has been characterized by an embarrassingly long sequence of 'theories,' each really nothing more than a passing fad that rarely outlived the person who proposed it.*

Reductionism

KT – reductionism: the belief that some subjects can be explained in terms of other more fundamental ones

Some thinkers hold out the hope that, as our knowledge in areas such as neuroscience and genetics grows, it will eventually be possible to establish the human sciences on firmer foundations. Since it seeks to explain some subjects in terms of other, more fundamental, ones, such a position is known as **reductionism**. A reductionist might, for example, argue that one day we will be able to understand economics in terms of psychology, and psychology in terms of neuroscience. At the limit, a reductionist might argue that everything is ultimately a matter of atoms whizzing around in space in accordance with the laws of physics (see Figure 14.12).

Since science is supposed to explain complex phenomena in terms of simpler underlying principles, reductionism might seem to be an attractive position. A subject such as physics has, after all, been amazingly successful in explaining a wide variety of phenomena in terms of a small number of underlying laws. A good example of the success of this approach was the reduction of thermodynamics to mechanics, which enabled scientists to explain heat in terms of the motion of molecules. Perhaps in a similar way we will one day be able to explain mental phenomena in terms of underlying physical ones.

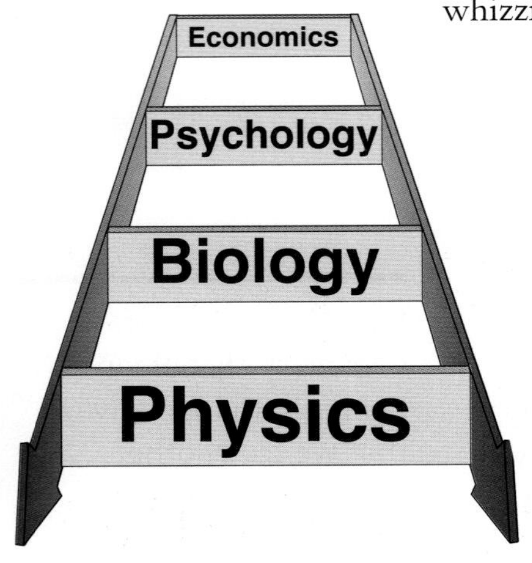

Figure 14.12 Reductionism

The reductive fallacy

When we try to explain complex things in terms of simpler underlying ones, there is, however, a danger that we commit the **reductive fallacy**. This is the fallacy of saying that just because *A* is composed of *B* it follows that *A* is *nothing but B*. Here are some examples of such 'nothing-butism':

> A cathedral is nothing but a heap of stones.
>
> A violin sonata is nothing but a sequence of vibrating strings.
>
> A human being is nothing but a bunch of chemicals.

KT – reductive fallacy: the fallacy of saying that just because *A* is composed of *B*, it follows that *A* is nothing but *B*

At one level, it is true that we are 'just a bunch of chemicals'; and it is humbling to discover that there is no secret ingredient in the recipe for a human being, and that we are made of the same basic stuff as cats, cucumbers and chrysanthemums. Nevertheless, there is all the difference in the world between so much hydrogen, oxygen and carbon measured out in a chemistry laboratory and a living human being. We may know the ingredients that make up a human being, but we are still very far from understanding the recipe!

There are, in fact, good reasons for doubting that the reductionist programme can succeed. For it has been pointed out that when simple things are combined together the resulting properties cannot always be predicted in advance from their constituent elements. This is as true in the physical world as in the human world. For example, if you combine hydrogen with oxygen, the property of wetness emerges from two non-wet elements. Similarly, when you combine sodium, one of the most unstable elements, with chlorine, one of the most toxic, you end up with salt – a stable compound which tastes good on food!

Since we cannot even reduce chemistry to physics, it seems unlikely that we will ever be able to explain the human sciences in terms of physics. In any case, the resulting knowledge would probably not be very useful. Trying to understand the laws of supply and demand at the level of atoms and molecules would be like trying to learn a computer program by analysing the flow of electrons through the electrical circuits. If you want to know what determines the price of fish, you would do better to read a book on economics than one on atomic physics!

Holism

The reductionist idea that the best way to understand something is to break it up into parts seems particularly inappropriate when it comes to the study of living things. For, as the writer Douglas Adams observed, 'If you try to take a cat apart to see how it works, the first thing you have on your hands is a non-working cat.' This might suggest that we can only make sense of some things by looking at them as a whole. Such a view is known as **holism**, and its central claim is that *the whole is greater than the sum of the parts* – that the whole contains properties that cannot in principle be discovered through an analysis of the parts.

KT – holism: the belief that the best way to understand some things is by looking at them as a whole rather than by analysing them into separate parts

When applied to the human sciences, holism means that you cannot understand a group only in terms of the individuals that make it up, or an action independent of the context in which it takes place. Thus economists distinguish between macro-

Figure 14.13 To what extent is it possible for an anthropologist to understand how other people see the world?

economics – which studies the economy as a whole – and micro-economics – which studies the behaviour of individual economic agents – on the grounds that you cannot understand a complex economy simply by analysing the behaviour of individual economic agents. Anthropologists insist that you should immerse yourself in a culture before trying to make sense of its individual practices. At a more mundane level, you may have noticed that a class at school can have an atmosphere which cannot always be explained in terms of the people in it.

ACTIVITY 14.19

1. Do you think that a group can have a 'character' that is distinct from the individuals that make it up?
2. A football team may consist of eleven great players and yet do badly in the league. How would you explain this?
3. What do you understand by 'team spirit'? Is 'team spirit' the sum of the 'spirit' of each individual on the team? If not, where does it come from?

At the heart of the argument between holism and reductionism is the question of the relation between wholes and parts. Rather than make an *either–or* choice between these two positions and say that you must understand the whole in terms of its parts, or the parts in terms of the whole, perhaps it would be better to think in terms of there being two-way traffic between parts and wholes. Take, for example, the relation between individuals and society. Although society is influenced by the individuals that make it up, it is also true that individuals are affected by the society they live in. To ask which comes first may make no more sense than asking whether the chicken comes before the egg or the egg before the chicken.

The *Verstehen* position

One reason for doubting that we will ever be able to reduce the human sciences to the natural sciences is that human sciences typically explain things in terms of *meanings* and *purposes* rather than mechanical causes and effects. To illustrate the difference between these kinds of explanation, imagine that a group of Martian scientists land on planet Earth on a busy road near some traffic lights. They notice that when the lights turn red the traffic stops and when the lights turn green it moves again. After observing the traffic for several hours, they conclude that red light causes a temporary malfunction in car engines. Unfortunately, they have come up with the wrong *kind* of explanation. What causes the traffic to behave as it does is the existence of a social *rule* which says that a red light *means* stop and a green light *means* go. If the Martians analyse the situation in terms of physics they will never figure out what is happening – for you cannot conjure social rules out of atoms and molecules.

According to what is known as the ***Verstehen* position** – *Verstehen* is German for 'understanding' – the main aim of the human sciences is to understand the meaning of various social practices *from the inside* as they are understood by the agents themselves. The common sense of this is that, if you want to figure out what a group of people are up to, you cannot simply observe their physical movements, but must try to get 'inside their heads' and understand how *they* see the situation. If you are unable to do this, then you are likely to misunderstand what is happening. For example, a Martian anthropologist who knows nothing about sports might misinterpret a cricket match as a religious ritual in which a bowler tries to kill a batsman with a speeding projectile.

KT – *Verstehen* position: the belief that the main aim of the human sciences is to understand the meaning of various social practices as they are understood by the agents themselves

ACTIVITY 14.20

Imagine that you are such a Martian anthropologist with no understanding of human practices. Try to think up bizarre explanations for some of the following rituals:

- **a.** Eating at McDonald's
- **b.** Taking an IB exam
- **c.** Attending a birthday party
- **d.** Checking in at an airport
- **e.** Shopping at a supermarket
- **f.** Working out in a gym
- **g.** Going to the hairdressers

Since many explanations in the human sciences are in terms of meaning rather than mechanism, it is perhaps not surprising that the human sciences have few universal laws to their credit. For the meaning of an action depends on the *context* in which it takes place, and it is therefore difficult to generalise. For example, if a man is writing his name on a piece of paper, he could be writing a cheque, giving an autograph, or signing a death warrant. Since the consequences of the same physical action are completely different in each case, you cannot make a universal law of the form, 'If a person writes his name, then . . .'

ACTIVITY 14.21

Think of as many different explanations as you can for each of the following actions:

a. A woman picks up a glass of wine.
b. A man goes out with an umbrella.
c. A woman walks into a room, walks round, and walks out again.
d. A man gets a gun out.
e. A woman waves her hand.

LQ – The arts: Do we learn more about human nature from psychology or from literature?

While the *Verstehen* approach to making sense of human behaviour is illuminating, we should not get carried away with it. Just because a lot of human behaviour can only be understood in context, we should not, for example, conclude that there are *no* universals in the human sciences. On the contrary, anthropologists have found many traits that seem to be common to all cultures – including gossiping, joking and taking an interest in sex!

We should also be cautious about taking people's self-descriptions at face value, for the consequences of their actions sometimes bear little relation to their intentions. In the case of economics, Adam Smith (1723–90) famously argued that, although individuals tend to seek their own gain, they are led by an 'invisible hand' to promote the general good. For example, an entrepreneur's desire for profit may result in our ending up with cheap high-quality goods and services. This suggests that, as well as trying to understand people's behaviour from the inside, social scientists should also look at the *unintended consequences* of their actions. When it comes to studying something as complicated as a human being, there is no reason why we should limit ourselves to a single approach. Truth has many eyes!

Alleged weaknesses

The problem of bias

One common accusation against the human sciences is that they are more prone to bias – and therefore less scientific – than their natural science cousins. We are, after all, more likely to begin with prejudices about the nature of individuals and societies than we are about the nature of atoms and molecules. This means that we may find it difficult to be genuinely open-minded about controversial topics such as gender differences or taxation policy. In this situation, the danger is that we simply look for evidence that confirms our pre-existing prejudices while overlooking evidence that contradicts them.

Since we naturally form emotional attachments with other people, a related problem is that a human scientist may over-identify with the people she is studying. When, for example, an anthropologist 'goes native' and lives with a tribe, her insider's understanding of the culture may be bought at the expense of her ability to be objective.

At this point, it is worth recalling that bias can also be a serious problem in the natural as well as the human sciences. (Recall our discussion of confirmation bias in Chapter 13 on page 353.) A physicist, for example, may be so committed to her own favourite theory that she obstinately refuses to abandon it in the light of contrary evidence. Or her research into the safety of nuclear energy may be tainted by the fact that it is funded by big commercial businesses. Since natural scientists are only human, they will sometimes be swayed by emotion as well as reason, and there are plenty of controversies in physics, chemistry and biology that are as bitter and partisan as anything that can be found in the human sciences.

Whatever the subject-matter, a good antidote to bias is to make it a matter of principle to actively look for evidence that would count *against* your hypothesis. For example, if you think that younger siblings are more rebellious than older ones, you should not only trawl for evidence that confirms your hypothesis, but also look for examples of rebellious older siblings and conformist younger ones.

At a practical level, experiments should be repeatable, and researchers should be able to check one another's results. However, since there is a skill to conducting experiments well and since results are sometimes ambiguous and open to interpretation, replication is rarely a straightforward matter. For example, some researchers have been unable to reproduce a classic social priming experiment which showed that people walk more slowly after they have been exposed to age-related words. Whether this is because the original experiment was flawed or because the replication was poorly executed is a matter of continuing debate. The fact that replication is difficult can open the door to outright fraud. When fellow researchers were unable to reproduce the experimental results of a Dutch psychologist called Diederik Stapel, they assumed it was because they lacked his skill; but it turned out that Stapel had fabricated his data. The fact that Stapel was eventually found out is perhaps reassuring, and it suggests that obviously biased or fraudulent research is eventually exposed and discredited. Indeed, it could be argued that one of the great strengths of science is that in the long run it tends to be self-correcting – and there is no reason to think that this is any less true of the human sciences than of the natural sciences.

ACTIVITY 14.22

1. Who do you think would be the best judge of a child's character?
   a. their parents
   b. their teachers
   c. a professional psychologist

   Give reasons.
2. Give some specific examples of bias that you have come across in the natural sciences and human sciences that you have studied.
3. Explain what is meant by 'falsificationism', and how it can help to reduce the danger of bias in scientific research. (You may wish to refer back to Chapter 13, page 358, to remind yourself about falsificationism.)

Poor predictive record

We saw in our discussion of laws and trends that the human sciences have been less successful than the natural sciences in making accurate predictions. In seeking to explain this fact, three points can be made in their defence:

1. The human sciences usually deal with extremely complex situations in which it is not possible to run controlled experiments. Indeed, it could be argued that when critics contrast the success of the natural sciences with the lack of success of the human sciences they are not comparing like with like. For it is a great deal more difficult to make accurate predictions in the real world than in the controlled conditions of the physics laboratory. You may, for example, know a lot of physics, but still be unable to predict where a leaf blown off a tree on a windy autumn day will land. Changing the analogy, we might say that trying to predict human behaviour is a bit like trying to predict the course of a water molecule going over Niagara Falls. While there is nothing difficult about it in theory, in practice there are simply too many variables for us to be able to make accurate predictions.
2. Some of the predictions made by social scientists are valuable, not because they accurately describe the future, but because they give us an incentive to change it. If, for example, economists in Ruritania predict that unemployment is likely to rise by 20 per cent in the next two years unless something is done, then the Ruritanian government will have a strong incentive to change its policies and try to ensure that the prediction is falsified.
3. Advocates of the *Verstehen* position might argue that the purpose of the human sciences is not so much to explain and predict as to describe and understand.

ACTIVITY 14.23

Do you think that weather forecasting is generally more or less reliable than economic forecasting?

Figure 14.14

The above points might help to explain the human sciences' poor record of prediction. But a critic might give a less flattering explanation and argue that the human sciences' lack of success shows that they are at a pre-paradigm stage in their development and await a Newton to establish them on a proper scientific foundation.

Hasty generalisations

A final alleged weakness of the human sciences is that they are prone to the fallacy of hasty generalisation – jumping to conclusions on the basis of a small, unrepresentative sample. We saw above that the Stanford prison experiment could be criticised for this reason. More generally, researchers have drawn attention to the fact that the vast majority of experiments in the behavioural sciences are conducted on so-called 'WEIRD' people – where WEIRD is an acronym for Western, Educated, Industrialised, Rich, Democracies. This is relevant because there is a growing body of evidence that weird people are not representative of humanity as a whole. Indeed, cross-cultural studies suggest that there are significant cultural differences in the way people see and think about the world.

Consider, for example, 'the ultimatum game' – much loved by psychology and economics researchers. The game involves two players, one of whom is randomly designated as 'deal-maker' and the other as 'responder', and a sum of money, say $100. The deal-maker proposes how the money should be divided between them and the responder can either accept or reject the offer. If the responder accepts the offer, the money is divided according to the proposal; if he rejects the offer, neither player gets anything. When this game is played in Western societies, the deal-maker typically proposes a 50–50 split and the responder typically accepts it. If the deal-maker proposes a split which is perceived as unfair – say 85–15 – the responder usually 'punishes' the deal-maker by refusing the offer, and neither player gets anything. This might be taken to show that we have a deep and innate sense of unfairness. However, it turns out that different cultures behave quite differently in the ultimatum game. For example, when Machiguenga people from the Amazon basin play the game, responders almost always accept an offer, no matter how low, on the grounds that it is crazy to reject free money. By contrast, in cultures with a strong gift-giving tradition, such as the Gnau of highland Papua New Guinea, responders sometimes reject generous offers of over 60 per cent. This is because they do not like the idea of being under an obligation to the deal-maker. As this example shows, we should be cautious before concluding that a particular form of behaviour is universal. Doubtless we have much in common, but there are also significant differences in the ways that people from different cultures behave.

Figure 14.15 The ultimatum game

ACTIVITY 14.24

Look at the table below. In seeking to defend the human sciences, how would you respond to each of the problems mentioned?

HUMAN SCIENCES: SUMMARY OF PROBLEMS		
Observation	1.	We cannot directly observe other people's minds.
	2.	Questionnaires may be misleading or biased.
	3.	Observing people may affect the way they behave.
Measurement	4.	Social phenomena are difficult to measure.
Hypothesis	5.	The act of prediction may affect the behaviour predicted.
Experiments	6.	Human sciences study complex social situations in which it is difficult to run controlled experiments.
	7.	Various moral considerations limit our willingness to experiment.
Laws	8.	There is a tendency to generalise from unrepresentative samples.
	9.	Human sciences are not very good at predicting things.
	10.	Human sciences usually uncover trends rather than laws.
	11.	Human science laws are probabilistic in nature.

Conclusion

We might conclude our discussion of the human sciences by saying that they are neither as flawed as their critics believe nor as successful as their defenders hope. Since they deal with complex phenomena, it is perhaps not surprising that they seem to lack the explanatory power of the natural sciences. Nevertheless, we can learn a great deal more about human beings by studying subjects such as psychology, economics and anthropology than we can by relying on uninformed common sense.

Any discussion about the human sciences inevitably raises some big questions about our place in the scheme of things. How, for example, are minds related to bodies? Could a machine think? Do we have free-will? Could a mind exist without a body? Perhaps scientific research will cast light on these questions, but it may be that in this area there are mysteries that will always lie beyond our understanding.

Key points

- Since human beings seem to be different from other natural phenomena, we may wonder to what extent they can be studied in a purely scientific way.
- Among the problems that arise in trying to get information about other people are: that it is difficult to frame questions in a neutral way; and that observing people may affect the way they behave.
- Some important phenomena in the human sciences are difficult to measure, and this can make it difficult to study them scientifically.
- Social scientists have devised many ingenious experiments, but ethical considerations limit our ability to conduct experiments on human beings.
- Although a great deal of human behaviour is predictable, it is unclear how far it can be reduced to law-like regularities.
- Since we typically explain human behaviour in terms of its meaning and purpose, we may never be able to reduce the human sciences to the natural sciences.
- Since they deal with controversial topics, the human sciences are more prone to bias than the natural sciences, but the extent of the problem should not be exaggerated.
- A question that continues to perplex both scientists and philosophers is how the mental is related to the physical.

Key terms

behaviourism

fallacy of *post hoc ergo propter hoc*

go native

holism

law of large numbers

loaded question

mirror test

nature–nurture debate

observer effect

reactance

reductionism

reductive fallacy

stream of consciousness

Verstehen position

Knowledge framework focus

1. *Scope/applications.* Is the goal of human sciences primarily to predict human behaviour or to understand it?
2. *Concepts/language.* To what extent can human phenomena be expressed in mathematical language? What problems arise with biased language?
3. *Methodology.* What special challenges arise in applying the scientific method to the human sciences?
4. *Historical development.* Are the human sciences still at an early 'pre-paradigm' stage in their development?
5. *Relation to personal knowledge.* How can we reconcile the scientific worldview with the belief in human dignity and free-will?

IB prescribed essay titles

1. 'Knowledge gives us a sense of who we are.' To what extent is this true in the human sciences and one other area of knowledge? (November 2013)
2. What is it about theories in the human sciences and natural sciences that makes them convincing? (May 2012)

Further reading

Books

Reuben Abel, *Man is the Measure* (Simon & Schuster, 1997), Chapter 11: 'The Social Sciences'. This chapter is a good introductory account of the social sciences. A large part of it is taken up with an excellent discussion of the *Verstehen* position.

Steven Pinker, *The Blank Slate* (Penguin, 2002), Chapter 17: 'Violence'. Pinker argues that many human traits, such as violence, are more the result of genetic inheritance than environmental conditioning. He writes with such verve and style that, whatever your own beliefs, this chapter should engage your interest.

Online articles

Jared Diamond, 'Soft Sciences are often Harder than Hard Sciences', *Discover*, August 1987.

John Horgan, 'Is "Social Science" an Oxymoron? Will That Ever Change?', *Scientific American Blog*, 4 April 2013.

Appendix to Chapter 14: The free-will problem

Introduction

One of the issues that we touched on in our discussion of the human sciences was the problem of free-will. This concerns the question of how we can reconcile the belief that human beings have free-will with our scientific picture of the world. Since it raises questions about both our place in the universe and the nature of knowledge, we will explore this problem in more detail.

At first sight, the existence of free-will seems to be a self-evident and unproblematic fact. In our everyday negotiations with the world, we constantly experience ourselves making choices about our actions. To take a simple example, suppose at lunch-time you are faced with a choice between a pizza and a hamburger – both of which you like – and that you choose the pizza. There is nothing that *compelled* you to choose the pizza, and you could just as easily have taken the hamburger if you had wanted to. So in making your choice you surely exercised free-will. There seem to be countless equally simple and compelling everyday demonstrations of free-will. Right now, you can, for example, either raise your hand or not raise it, and nothing is forcing you to choose one way or the other.

Our belief in free-will is not only based on our own experience, but is also deeply embedded in the way we think about other people; and it is hard to imagine how social life could function without it. Every time you praise or criticise someone's actions, you are implicitly assuming that they are free and that they could have done otherwise. Indeed, the whole of ethics is based on the assumption that we have free-will. It would, after all, be unreasonable to pass judgement on someone for doing something that they couldn't help doing and about which they had no choice. That is why we do not hold insane people criminally responsible for their actions. The existence of free-will, then, is central to our conception of what it is to be a responsible human being, and to deny its existence would seem to rob us of our dignity and reduce us to the status of biological machines.

Determinism

Despite such troubling consequences, some scientists and philosophers have nevertheless denied that human beings have free-will and have adopted a position known as determinism. According to this, the universe operates in accordance with the causal principle that every event has a cause. Since this principle is said to apply to human actions as well as the natural world, determinists believe that our actions can ultimately be traced back to factors beyond our control, thereby robbing us of our free-will.

Figure 14A.1

The determinist position would seem to be supported by scientific developments in areas such as genetics which confirm the common-sense observation that we inherit many of our personality traits from our parents. Admittedly social scientists may argue about whether our characters are determined more by 'nature' in the form of our genetic inheritance, or 'nurture' in the form of the environment in which we grow up; but, whatever the proportions, neither of these alternatives seems to leave much room for free-will. After all, you chose neither your genes nor the environment in which you grew up.

ACTIVITY 14A.1

1. How different do you think your personality would have been if you had been adopted at birth and brought up in a different culture?
2. Some controversial research has been done which suggests that there are striking similarities between identical twins who were separated at birth and brought up by different families.
   a. Find out something about this research and some of the criticisms that have been made of it.
   b. What would you conclude from this research about the roles played by nature and nurture in determining our characters?
3. How far do you think our behaviour is determined by unconscious motives? How might one go about testing such a hypothesis?
4. To what extent do you think the behaviour of the following individuals is predictable?
   a. Your parents   b. Your friends   c. You

Further support for determinism would seem to come from our knowledge of the brain. A determinist might point to the fact that our mental activities are correlated with various brain states, and that our brains are subject to the laws of physics and chemistry. As far as neuroscience is concerned, when you do something, such as raise your arm, the cause of your action is the various neurons firing in your brain. This pattern of neuronal activity is in turn caused by the previous material state of your brain, which is in turn caused by an earlier state, and so on in a backward chain. Looked at in this way, it seems that the real causes of our actions are to be found at the level of physics and chemistry, and the feeling that they flow from our freely made decisions is merely a beguiling illusion.

Perhaps the most comprehensive case for determinism can be made at the level of atoms moving around in space in accordance with the laws of physics. As the French mathematician Pierre Laplace (1749–1827) famously expressed it:

> *We ought to regard the present state of the universe as the effect of its antecedent state and as the cause of the state that is to follow. An intelligence knowing all the forces acting in nature at a given instant, as well as the momentary positions of all things in the universe, would be able to comprehend in one single formula the motions of the largest bodies as well as of the lightest atoms in the world, provided that its intellect were sufficiently powerful to subject all data to analysis; to it nothing would be uncertain, the future as well as the past would be present to its eyes.*

According to Laplace, then, every event in the universe has been rigorously determined by the preceding one, and it is – in principle at least – possible to predict the entire future history of the universe. In this bleak and uncompromising picture of things, there seems to be no room for human free-will.

How does determinism threaten free-will?

To respond to the threat that determinism poses to our belief in free-will, we should begin by clearing up two common misconceptions which may help to reduce the gap between the two positions.

On the one hand, a believer in free-will is not saying that we are free to do anything we like, and would readily admit that we are limited in various ways by our nature and environment. Indeed, one of life's great frustrations is to bump up against our own limitations. You may desperately want to be a concert pianist, but if you have a tin ear and a poor sense of timing, then, sadly, you are never going to make it. Since we are not endlessly talented, it is clear that we all have a restricted list of options in the banquet of life. Nevertheless, a believer in free-will insists that we do *still* have options, and that, at least sometimes, we are capable of exercising them and making genuinely free decisions.

On the other hand, a determinist is not saying that the future is determined irrespective of what you do. For that would be to adopt fatalism, and determinism is not the same as fatalism. According to fatalism, your destiny is written in the stars and there is nothing that *you* can do to change the future. However, it is clear that what you do *does* affect the future. If, for example, you work hard, then you are more likely to pass your exams than if you do nothing. Admittedly, there are no guarantees, but what you do will certainly change the balance of probabilities. So much for fatalism. Coming back to determinism, a good way to think of it is as steering between fatalism and free-will. Against fatalism, it says that the choices you make do affect the future; but, against free-will, it says that you have no control over your choices.

To summarise, we can say that a believer in free-will will accept that much of our behaviour is determined by factors beyond our control; and a determinist will accept that the choices we make do affect our future. Yet a seemingly unbridgeable gap remains between these two positions. For a believer in free-will will continue to insist that there is some space for genuinely free decisions: something which a determinist will continue to deny.

Faced with the free-will problem, there are at least three possible responses we could make:

1. We could reject the claim that every event has a cause and argue that this leaves room for free-will.
2. We could accept determinism, but insist that free-will and determinism are compatible with each other
3. We could accept determinism and conclude that, no matter how unpalatable it might be, human free-will is an illusion.

Does every event have a cause?

With the first of the above options in mind, let us begin by asking what evidence there is for the claim that every event has a cause. You might say that it is an *empirical* claim which is supported by the fact that, as science has developed, we have discovered the causes of more and more events. Extrapolating from this, it seems reasonable to suppose that if we look hard enough we can always find the cause of an event. We may not know the exact cause of AIDS, but nobody doubts that there is a cause, and most people believe that we will eventually discover it.

You may doubt that we would allow anything – in the physical world, at least – to count against our belief that every event has a cause. Imagine, for example, that your table lamp suddenly stops working. You check the bulb, the fuse and the electricity supply, but are unable to find the cause of the problem. You call an electrician, but he is no more successful than you. Do you conclude that you have discovered an uncaused event and that there was no reason why your lamp stopped working? No, you will conclude that you hired an incompetent electrician! Even if you never solve the problem, you will probably still insist that *something* must have caused your lamp to stop working.

ACTIVITY 14A.2

If you were unable to find the cause of an event, would you ever be willing to conclude that it did not have a cause?

This suggests that the belief that every event has a cause is not so much an empirical one that can be verified or falsified by evidence, as a metaphysical one about the nature of ultimate reality. What makes it attractive is the underlying belief that the universe is an orderly place in which things don't happen randomly or for no reason. Indeed, without some such belief, science – which is essentially a search for causes – would be impossible.

Subatomic randomness

There is, however, an area of science where the causal principle that every event has a cause does not seem to hold. For the world of subatomic particles is governed by Heisenberg's uncertainty principle which says that it is impossible to know both the position and velocity of subatomic particles with complete certainty. It would seem to follow that – at this level, at least – events are governed by pure chance.

The indeterminacy that can be found at the subatomic level might seem to loosen the vice-like grip of the causal principle, and provide a physical basis for our belief in free-will.

There is, however, reason to think that what is happening at the subatomic level is irrelevant to the free-will problem. For even if random events sometimes occur, mere randomness is not what the believer in free-will is looking for. Imagine, for example, that you are holding a gun and that a random event in your brain causes various neurons to fire which results in your finger squeezing the trigger. You would be as surprised as anyone else by what had happened and could hardly be held responsible for it. *So free-will is not the same as random will*; and in rejecting determinism we are not saying that our actions are uncaused, but rather that they are caused by our wills. In any case, Heisenberg's uncertainty principle applies only to the subatomic level, and when it comes to anything bigger – which is everything that is of interest to us – physicists are agreed that the law of cause and effect still holds sway.

Capturing a free action

Despite this previous discussion, a believer in free-will might argue that, no matter what physics says, we should not be bullied into denying the plain facts of experience. For our immediate experience of freedom surely *proves* that the causal principle is false.

There may be something in this; but to find and describe a moment of free choice turns out to be harder than you might think. For a start, we seem to spend quite a lot of each day on 'automatic pilot', going through well-rehearsed routines that do not involve much conscious thought. When, for example, the alarm goes off in the morning, it is unlikely that you consciously decide on each step of your morning routine: getting out of bed, going in the shower, brushing your teeth, putting your clothes on, and so on. For it would simply be too exhausting if you had to agonise over each of these micro-decisions every day. A more accurate picture of what happens might be to say that you simply get out of bed and initiate 'plan A' – your tried and tested routine for getting ready for school.

Nevertheless, our days are punctuated by various mundane decisions, such as what to wear or what to have for lunch. Let's go back to an earlier example, and take a closer look at your lunch-time choice between pizza and hamburger. How exactly does the choice get made? Well, if you are someone who loves pizzas and hates hamburger, you do not really have a choice and you will take the pizza. So let us assume that you love pizzas and hamburger and haven't had either of them for a long time. How do you decide which one to take? The strange thing is that there seems to be a kind of emptiness at the moment of decision. Do you make some kind of mental grunt and choose the pizza, or do you dither for a moment and then simply find yourself taking it? It is very difficult to say exactly what does happen. Things do not get any easier to describe when it comes to important decisions.

ACTIVITY 14A.3

1. Describe as accurately as you can what happens when you make a free decision, such as getting out of bed when the alarm goes off rather than snoozing for another twenty minutes.
2. How much of what you do every day would you say is determined by routine and habit, and how much by your conscious decisions?
3. When do you feel most free?
   a. When you fulfil your desires
   b. When you overcome your desires
   c. When, on a whim, you suddenly decide to do something
   d. When you do something creative
   e. Some other situation

Suppose you have a choice between two university offers and must decide which one to take. If university A ranks much higher than university B in terms of all your preferences, then there is again a sense in which you have no choice: you are bound to choose A. But what if it is finely balanced and you prefer A in some ways and B in others? If you still can't make up your mind after agonising over it and discussing it with your friends and family, you will probably 'sleep on it' and hope that the decision comes to you. So, once again, it seems that either the odds are stacked in favour of one particular option, in which case you are not really making a choice; or the two options are finely balanced, in which case it is very difficult to say just how you do make a choice.

Despite the difficulties involved in capturing and describing a freely chosen action, we do generally consider ourselves as active beings who are the authors of their actions. So, even if it is impossible to explain how free-will works, we surely cannot doubt that it exists.

Is the feeling of freedom an illusion?

However, a determinist is unlikely to be satisfied with this admission of ignorance. He may want to know exactly how a free decision affects what is going on in our brains. Does it somehow cause an atom or subatomic particle to swerve from its original course? If so, how can this be made consistent with the laws of physics? You might, once again, want to appeal to the uncertainty principle, but it is far from clear how this can help us to solve the problem.

Furthermore, it might be pointed out that just because you *feel* free doesn't mean that you *are* free – for the feeling could simply be an illusion. That, at least, is what the philosopher Baruch Spinoza (1632–77) thought: 'Men think themselves free because they are conscious of their actions, but ignorant of their causes.' If falling stones were conscious, said Spinoza, they would probably believe that they were falling of their own free-will. So perhaps we are simply puppets that are unaware of the strings of physical causation that are pulling us.

ACTIVITY 14A.4

1. If every morning someone delivered in a sealed envelope some precise predictions about what you would do during the day, and every evening you opened the envelope and found that they were all true, would this convince you that you did not have any free-will?
2. If the future is determined for the kinds of reasons that Laplace gave (see page 407), but we are never in practice able to predict it, why, if at all, should we be worried?

At this point in our discussion, we seem to reach an impasse. If you are more convinced that the universe is orderly than that human beings have free-will, you are likely to insist that every event has a cause; and if you are more convinced that human beings have free-will than that the universe is orderly, you are likely to deny that every event has a cause.

Is free-will compatible with determinism?

One way of trying to get beyond this impasse is to take the second of the responses to the problem of free-will (see page 408) and argue that free-will and determinism are compatible with one another. This view is known as compatibilism and it has proved popular with some philosophers.

Is freedom simply a matter of doing what you want?

While compatibilists believe that every event has a cause, they insist that this still leaves room for free-will. To be free, they say, is simply to be able to do what you want, and so long as you are not compelled or hindered by someone else, you are surely free. Such a common-sense view of freedom is quite consistent with determinism. Indeed, compatibilists argue that free-will is possible only to the extent that determinism is true. For, as we saw above, if your actions were uncaused they could not be said to be yours at all. This looks like a neat solution to the free-will problem, for it seems to give us human free-will *and* an orderly and rule-governed universe.

ACTIVITY 14A.5

1. If an animal does what it likes, can it be called free? How does its freedom differ from that of a human being?
2. To what extent do you think the free-will debate is simply an argument about the meaning of the word 'freedom'?

Can we control our desires?

The trouble with the compatibilist solution to the free-will problem is that it depends on a superficial analysis of the word 'freedom'. To understand this, consider a smoker who feels like a cigarette and smokes one. Since he is doing what he wants without any external hindrance, a compatibilist would say that he is acting freely. But suppose our smoker is trying to quit smoking, and that when he desires a cigarette he has at the same time a higher-order desire *not* to desire a cigarette. Although at one level he is doing what he wants, at another level it is tempting to say that he is a *victim* of his desires. This description becomes more and more appropriate as we move up the scale of addictive habits. At the limit, I doubt that anyone would describe a heroin addict as free; and it might therefore be better to think of an addict as sick rather than criminal.

ACTIVITY 14A.6

1. At what point on the road from non-addiction to addiction would you say that free-will ends and compulsion begins?
2. To what extent do you think we should hold drug addicts responsible for their behaviour?

In response to the above, you might point out that most of our desires are not in fact addictive, and that there is a clear difference between being in the grip of an addiction and making ordinary choices. While there may be some truth in this, the smoker example is not so easily dismissed. For it raises not only the question of where ordinary behaviour ends and addiction begins, but also the deeper question of the extent to which we are able to control or change our desires. Compatibilism says that you are free when you can do what you desire; but if your desires are themselves beyond your control, there would seem to be a deeper sense in which you are not free even when you are doing what you want.

ACTIVITY 14A.7

1. What distinguishes addictive behaviour from ordinary behaviour?
2. Which of the following might be described as addictive?
   - a. Coffee
   - b. Hamburgers
   - c. Marijuana
   - d. Work
   - e. Shopping
   - f. Love
   - g. Crime
   - h. Extreme sports
3. To what extent do you think we are able to change our desires? Could you, for example, decide to:
   - a. like cheese, if you have always hated it
   - b. find someone interesting, if you have always found them boring
   - c. work hard, if you have always been lazy
   - d. show more concern for others, if you have always been selfish?

To common sense, this talk of being 'victims' of our desires is at best misleading and at worst false. Such language may be appropriate to a smoker who is unable to quit, but the fact is that we are quite happy with many of our desires and have no wish to change them. If I enjoy listening to music and eating cheese and pickle sandwiches, why should I think of myself as a *victim* of these desires? The response may be, 'because' you are unable to change them. The fact that you are happy with your desires does not mean you are free. A prisoner may be happy if he does not want to leave his cell, but he is still a prisoner.

But surely this talk of our being imprisoned by our desires is again misleading. For while a prisoner cannot decide to leave prison, we can – in some cases at least – change our desires. After all, some people quit smoking. This suggests that if you really want to give up smoking – or change yourself in some other way – then you can. Perhaps it is simply a matter of positive thinking, about which we read so much in self-help manuals.

Could you have done otherwise?

This brings us to the heart of the matter. Any freedom worth having surely requires not simply that you can do what you want, but more radically that *you could do otherwise*. Let us go back to our smoker who wants to give up smoking and zoom in on a moment of temptation. He feels like a cigarette, briefly tries to resist, and then gives in and reaches for the packet. Could he have resisted the temptation to have a cigarette? One response is to say that he could *if he had chosen to*. But that simply transforms the question into, 'Could he have chosen otherwise?' You might be tempted to say 'yes' on the grounds that if he had shown more will power then he could have chosen to resist. However, I think that determinism is committed to saying that if you replayed the videotape it would come out the same way every time. Admittedly, our smoker could have resisted temptation if he had shown more will power; but the point is that, being the kind of person that he was, in the situation that he was in, he just did not have the necessary self-control.

For a determinist, then, although your decisions may be determined by your character, your character itself has been determined by factors beyond your control. The upshot is that, given the kind of person that you are, you cannot help making the kinds of decisions that you do. Indeed, we sometimes excuse our behaviour by saying 'I can't help it – that's just the way I am', and we are all aware how difficult it is to change aspects of ourselves that we dislike. Just think of those broken New Year resolutions!

ACTIVITY 14A.8

To what extent do you think you can change your character, and to what extent do you think you just have to live with it?

The upshot of our discussion would seem to be that determinism is incompatible with free-will in the sense that, although you can do what you want, you can never do otherwise than you do, and your wants and your will power are ultimately determined by factors beyond your control. This does not mean that determinism is true, but it does suggest that compatibilism is false. So in trying to solve the free-will problem, we seem to be back at square one!

Is free-will an illusion?

As a final approach to the free-will problem, we might be bold and say that determinism is true and human free-will is an illusion. However, this implies that there is no such thing as moral responsibility or rationality, and many people would say that this is too high a price to pay for accepting determinism.

Does determinism undermine ethics?

Some philosophers have argued that the implications of determinism for ethics are not in fact as serious as they look. Admittedly, we will have to abandon the idea that people deserve to be praised and blamed, or rewarded and punished for their actions. For, in a deterministic world, good people cannot help being good, and bad people cannot help being bad. Given this, you might think that we should close the courts and empty the prisons. After all, criminals are not responsible for the rotten genes and bad neighbourhoods that shaped their behaviour. However, a determinist would say that we are still justified in locking up criminals in order to:

1. protect society
2. modify their future behaviour.

Without wishing to offend human dignity, we might make an analogy with the way we treat dogs. We do not hold dogs responsible for their actions, but we still lock up mad dogs in order to protect people, and punish bad ones in order to reform them.

Here we have touched on two different theories of punishment:

1. the retribution theory, which justifies punishing criminals on the grounds that they deserve it

Figure 14A.2

2. the reform theory, which justifies punishing them only if it will change their behaviour.

While the former is retrospective and looks to the past, the latter is prospective and looks to the future. And while the former is inconsistent with determinism, the latter is perfectly consistent with it.

A determinist might argue that, even if we have free-will, the only civilised reason for punishing people – apart from protecting society – is to reform them. To punish someone if it is not going to improve their behaviour – merely 'because they deserve it' – seems like vindictiveness. As critics of capital punishment say, executing someone for murder 'won't bring the victim back'. According to this view, punishment is best seen as a form of education, and to punish for any reason other than reform (or protection) is itself a crime.

"Great news, Phil! The governor has determined that you don't have a high enough I.Q. to merit execution."

Figure 14A.3

ACTIVITY 14A.9

1. Imagine a criminal contemplating a crime and thinking to himself: 'If I am caught, they will say that it's not my fault, that I couldn't help it. As a result, I will probably get off lightly. So I might as well do it.' Is this a good argument against the reform theory of punishment?
2. Do you think that punishment should be based more on reason, or emotion, or a combination of the two?
3. At what age would you say that a person becomes criminally responsible? Justify your view.
4. Do you think we should punish someone for a crime they committed fifty years ago? Does it depend on the nature of the crime? Give reasons for and against.
5. What is the difference between evil and insanity? Are mass murderers necessarily insane?
6. What difference do you think it would make if we thought of criminals as ill rather than bad, and spoke in terms of cure rather than punishment? Is this a better or worse way of looking at things?
7. To what extent do you think it is true that 'to know all is to forgive all'?

Despite its attractions, the reform theory of punishment is not without its critics. Two common objections to it are that it weakens the deterrence effect of punishment, and that it is hard to know where reform ends and brainwashing begins. More could be said about both of these points, and no doubt there are responses that could be made to them. However, we will not pursue this discussion further here. For, even if we allow that determinism is consistent with some forms of punishment, there is another, more serious, problem facing the theory.

Does determinism undermine rationality?

The main problem is that determinism does not seem to leave any room for the possibility of rationality. For reasoning implies that we are free to believe something or not to believe it; and it typically involves such things as weighing up evidence, considering implications, and making judgements. But if determinism is true, none of these factors plays any role in shaping our beliefs, which – like everything else – are determined by our characters and the surrounding environment. I, being the kind of person that I am, simply cannot help believing the kinds of things that I do; and you, being the kind of person that you are, cannot help believing the kinds of things that you do. It follows that trying rationally to prove that determinism is true is self-defeating in the same way that trying rationally to prove that you don't exist is self-defeating. In both cases, if the argument is convincing, then it undermines itself. What comes out of this is not that determinism is false, but that if it is true then you cannot rationally believe that it is true (or false), because in a deterministic world you cannot rationally believe anything.

More radically, one might argue that if determinism is true, then there is not even any room for language. For if we are not free to think about what we are saying and reflect on what we are hearing, then there would seem to be no difference between the talking of human beings and the singing of birds or the noises barking of dogs.

ACTIVITY 14A.10

1. To what extent do you think that people's beliefs are shaped by:
   a. their characters
   b. their environment?
2. Where do your thoughts come from? Does it make more sense to say that you think your thoughts or that your thoughts think you?

Conclusion

We have explored three ways of trying to resolve the conflict between our everyday belief that human beings have free-will and the scientific belief that we live in a law-governed and deterministic universe. But we have not been able to solve the problem. While there are some good arguments in favour of determinism, in practice it would be almost impossible for us to abandon our belief in free-will. Some people take human free-will to show that we are fundamentally different from the rest of the natural world and have some kind of spiritual dimension. However, the free-will problem is as much of a problem for someone who believes in God as it is for an atheist. For, as we shall see in Chapter 18, if God is all-knowing, then He presumably knows our future as well as our past. This, again, suggests that our future is in some sense already determined.

So there is, it seems, no easy way of avoiding the free-will problem. Perhaps the only conclusion we can draw from our discussion is that there are limits to knowledge and that some things lie beyond human understanding.

History

15

The past is never dead. It's not even past.

William Faulkner, 1897–1962

The past is another country. They do things differently there.

L. P. Hartley, 1895–1972

Who controls the past controls the future, who controls the present controls the past.

George Orwell, 1903–50

What is history but a fable agreed upon?

Napoleon Bonaparte, 1769–1821

History will be kind to me, for I intend to write it.

Winston Churchill, 1874–1965

No man ever yet tried to write down the entire truth of any action in which he was engaged.

T. E. Lawrence, 1888–1935

History abhors determinism, but cannot tolerate chance.

Bernard de Voto, 1897–1955

History is but the register of human crimes and misfortunes.

Voltaire, 1694–1778

History is a kind of experiment, albeit an imperfectly controlled one.

Steven Pinker, 1954–

The history of the world is but the biography of great men.

Thomas Carlyle, 1795–1881

The only thing we learn from history is that we learn nothing from history.

G. W. F. Hegel, 1770–1831

History: An account, mostly false, of events mostly unimportant, which are brought about by rulers, mostly knaves, and soldiers, mostly fools.

Ambrose Bierce, 1842–1914

Introduction

Imagine waking up one morning to discover that you have lost your memory. After a few minutes of blind panic, you begin to examine the room you find yourself in. You discover a scribbled note which says 'Meet George, Piccadilly Circus, 9.30.' You glance at the clock. It is 8.00 a.m. Since you don't want to tell anyone about your predicament, you give yourself an hour and a half to work out who you are from the contents of what is clearly *your* bedroom and make it to Piccadilly Circus to meet George – whoever he is . . .

ACTIVITY 15.1

If you found yourself in the above situation, to what extent do you think you would be able to reconstruct your identity by examining the objects in your room? What problems would you experience in trying to do this, and how similar are they to those facing a historian?

The thought of losing your memory is a frightening one not only because memories are precious in themselves, but also because your sense of who you are and where you are going is bound up with what you have done. Without the compass of memory to guide you, you would be adrift in a meaningless ocean of time with no sense of identity or direction.

One interesting approach to thinking about history is to begin with our own micro-histories. To a greater or lesser extent, we all try to make sense of the past by weaving the various episodes of our lives into a meaningful narrative. This raises a number of interesting questions.

ACTIVITY 15.2

1. Why should you care about your past? What dangers are there in being obsessed with your past, and what dangers are there in ignoring it?
2. Given the points discussed in Chapter 10, how reliable do you think memory is as a guide to the past?
3. If you keep a diary, what determines what you choose to include and what you choose to omit?
4. Would you be more inclined to trust an autobiography, or a biography about the same person written by a historian?
5. To what extent do you think that people learn from their mistakes, and to what extent do you think they keep making the same mistakes?

There are some interesting parallels between the above questions and those that arise when we consider history as an academic subject. In thinking about the latter, a good place to start is with the question of what we mean by history. Why, after all, do we normally think of history as the catalogue of 'great events' and assume that the details of our own micro-histories have nothing to do with it?

What is history?

In answering the question 'What is history?', we might begin by saying that it is the study of the past. This may be a reasonable first approximation, but the answer is in fact more complicated than that.

Evidence

To start with, since we can know the past only to the extent that we have *evidence* for it, it would be more accurate to say that history is not so much the study of the past as of the *present traces* of the past.

In trying to reconstruct the past on the basis of the evidence, one of two problems may arise: *too little* evidence, or *too much* evidence. When we study the distant past, the problem is usually that of too little evidence. A real danger in such a situation is that we misinterpret the evidence that exists, and jump to conclusions that are not justified by it. Imagine, for example, that after our civilisation has vanished, a Martian archaeologist unearths exhibit A in Figure 15.1. If he knows nothing about our culture and its practices, he might interpret his find as a 'ceremonial collar' and reconstruct it as in Figure 15.2.

RLS – Headline: 'Library of Congress (USA) to archive every tweet ever made'. How useful will social media archives be to future historians?

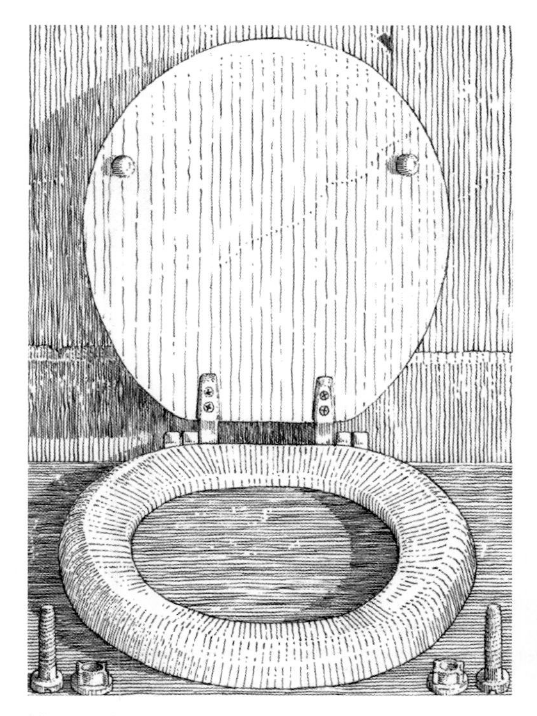

Figure 15.1

Figure 15.2

The problem of lack of evidence is a real one, and it is sometimes surprising to discover that our knowledge claims about the past are less well justified than we might have imagined. For example, our knowledge of the wars between Persia and Greece in the fifth century BCE is based on a single, quite unreliable, source – the Greek historian Herodotus (*c.*485–420 BCE).

When it comes to modern history, we are usually faced with the opposite problem: that there is too much evidence. If you tried to write a definitive history of the world for a single year – say, the year 2000 – you would be overwhelmed by a tidal wave of evidence from newspapers, TV and the internet.

Significance

This brings us to a second qualification we need to make about the nature of history. History is not a record of *everything* that happened in the past, but is concerned with only the *significant* events in the past. For example, while the assassination of John F. Kennedy on 22 November 1963 is a historically significant event, the fact that you had cereal for breakfast on 9 February last year is probably not.

ACTIVITY 15.3

Using any criteria of your choice, rate the historical significance of the following events.

a. The publication of Charles Darwin's *The Origin of Species* in 1859.
b. Your last TOK class.
c. The assassination of Mahatma Gandhi in 1948.
d. The 1930 soccer World Cup Final – which was won by Uruguay.
e. The birth of Bill Gates in 1955.
f. Former US president Bill Clinton's affair with Monica Lewinsky.
g. The terrorist attacks on the World Trade Center and the Pentagon in 2001.

Once we start talking about 'significant events' we run into the problem of how to decide whether or not an event is significant. While you might think that significance – like beauty – is in the eye of the beholder, there are various *criteria* we might appeal to in order to decide whether or not an event is historically significant. For example, you can look at how many people are affected by the event, and the extent to which they are affected. While a dramatic event, such as political assassination, is likely to affect many people in a significant way, the same cannot be said of a TOK class.

Figure 15.3 Soldiers prepare to go 'over the top' at the battle of the Somme during the First World War in 1916. What makes an event historically significant?

So is there any way in which a TOK class might become at least a footnote in history? Here are a couple of possibilities:

- Your teacher makes a chance remark in a TOK class that inspires you to enter politics, and you eventually become world president. Years later when you write your memoirs, you observe: 'During that fateful TOK class in February 2014, I first felt the hand of destiny on me and knew that I must enter politics.'
- A series of nuclear wars at the end of the twenty-first century devastates the planet. Many centuries pass before civilisation re-establishes itself. As luck has it, one of the few things that survive from the early twenty-first century are your TOK notes. Future historians pore over them and try to get an idea of what life was like at the beginning of the twenty-first century.

Explaining the past

In going beyond our preliminary characterisation of history as the study of the past, we have mentioned *evidence* and *significance*. A third important feature of history is that it is concerned not simply with describing the past, but also with *explaining and understanding* it. After all, history is more than just a catalogue of important dates and events; and although a historian may need to devote considerable energy to establishing *what* happened, this is usually a prelude to trying to understand *why* it happened. Historians might typically be trying to understand such things as the collapse of the Roman Empire, or the causes of the First World War, or the rise of Fascism.

Why study history?

Since history does not seem to have the immediate practical value of science, you might wonder why we should bother studying it. The car maker Henry Ford (1863–1947) dismissed history as 'more or less bunk', and in an age obsessed with progress, it is sometimes seen as 'yesterday's news' with no relevance to the present. There are, however, some good reasons for studying the past.

We can justify history on the grounds that it:

1. gives us a sense of identity

2. is a defence against propaganda

3. enriches our understanding of human nature.

ACTIVITY 15.4

'The study of history is so important that it should be a compulsory IB subject.' Think of as many arguments as you can for and against this claim.

History gives us a sense of identity

According to a well-known saying, a country without a history is like a person without a memory. At the beginning of this chapter, you were asked to imagine waking up one morning to discover that you had lost your memory. As we saw, if that were to happen, you would lose not only your sense of who you are but also your sense of direction. What is true of an individual is also true of a country. If as a community you don't know where you have come from, it will be impossible for you to make any sense of the present or what you should do in the future.

To extend the analogy between a person and a country, it could be said that, just as you can know a person only if you know something about their history, so you can know a country only if you know something about *its* history. If you are to have informed opinions about current affairs, and your judgements about other countries are to go beyond mere prejudice, then a knowledge of history is indispensable. For example, anyone trying to make sense of the Middle East situation needs to have a good knowledge of the history of the region.

ACTIVITY 15.5

1. How important do you think it is for our political leaders to have a good knowledge of history?
2. Do you think that some countries are more obsessed with their history than others? What dangers, if any, are there in:
   a. ignoring the past
   b. being obsessed with the past?

History is a defence against propaganda

Since most governments take a great interest in the way history is taught in schools, it is easy for national pride to dictate a one-sided interpretation of the past which highlights a country's achievements and overlooks its mistakes. At worst, history can be exploited by a corrupt regime to legitimise its rule, justify territorial expansion and whitewash past crimes. One of the best-known examples of the abuse of history is from the Stalinist era in the former Soviet Union. As well as liquidating his political opponents, Stalin (1879–1953) also sought to erase them from the historical record.

In the first of these photographs (Figure 15.4), which was taken on the second anniversary of the October Revolution in 1919, Trotsky (1879–1940) can be seen centre-stage, standing to Lenin's left. After Trotsky fell from grace and fled into exile, he and other 'undesirables' were erased from the photograph (Figure 15.5) to leave a rather lonely-looking Lenin in the middle of the picture.

Such blatant abuses of history are rare, but governments may try to 'spin' the historical record to serve their interests in more subtle ways. A politician standing for re-election might trumpet the achievements of her first term in office while

Figure 15.4

Figure 15.5

showing a remarkable blindness to her policy failures and errors of judgement. When in later life politicians come to write their memoirs, they are generally keen to paint themselves in as good a light as possible. (There is doubtless some truth in the observation that people are at their most creative when they write their autobiographies!)

History can also be used to challenge some of the myths we have about the past. Consider the following words allegedly spoken by American Indian Chief Seattle (1786–1866) in 1854 when the US government sought to buy some of his land:

> *How can you buy or sell the sky? The land? The idea is strange to us . . . Every part of this earth is sacred to my people. Every shining pine needle, every sandy shore, every mist in the dark woods, every meadow, every humming insect. All are holy in the memory and experience of my people . . . Will you teach your children what we have taught our children? That the earth is our mother? What befalls the earth befalls all the sons of earth. This we know: the earth does not belong to man, man belongs to the earth. All things are connected like the blood that unites us all. Man does not weave the web of life, he is merely a strand in it. Whatever he does to the web, he does to himself.*

These fine words have sometimes been used to support the idea that before the arrival of the Europeans native Americans were living in peace and harmony with nature. However, historical research reveals that no one knows what Chief Seattle said on the day in question, and that the above speech was in fact written for an ABC television drama in 1971 by someone called Ted Perry!

ACTIVITY 15.6

What do you understand by George Orwell's observation, 'Who controls the past controls the future, who controls the present controls the past'? To what extent do you think it is true?

History enriches our understanding of human nature

History enriches our understanding of human nature by showing us what human beings have thought and done in a wide variety of circumstances. While subjects such as psychology, sociology and economics seek to explain things in terms of general principles, history focuses on the concrete and particular and reminds us that human behaviour can never be fully explained in terms of neat and tidy models.

ACTIVITY 15.7

Read the following quotation from the German philosopher Immanuel Kant (1724–1804):

'One cannot avoid a certain feeling of disgust, when one observes the actions of man displayed on the great stage of the world. Wisdom is manifested by individuals here and there; but the web of human history as a whole appears to be woven from folly and childish vanity, often, too, from puerile wickedness and love of destruction: with the result that at the end one is puzzled to know what idea to form of our species which prides itself so much on its advantages.'

From your own study of history, to what extent do you think that Kant's pessimistic assessment of human beings is justified? Are there any grounds for taking a more optimistic view?

Whether the historical record should make us feel optimistic or pessimistic about human nature is open to question. We should, however, be careful with the phrase 'History shows . . .' when it is used by someone who is trying to prove that something or other is an enduring feature of the human condition. It has, for example, been said that history shows that war is inevitable, or that different races are unable to live together in harmony. The problem with such beliefs is that they can easily become **self-realising expectations**; for if you think that something cannot be changed, you won't even bother *trying* to change it. However, the historical record can sometimes be a source of hope rather than despair; for it suggests that the future does not have to be like the past, and that it is possible to change things. The last 200 years have seen many historically unprecedented changes, such as the abolition of slavery, the emancipation of women, and the birth of the United Nations. Such changes would never have come about if people had seen themselves as the victims of history. Perhaps, then, if we focused our energies on putting an end to war we really could bring about a more peaceful world.

KT – self-realising expectations: beliefs which if held help to bring about their own fulfilment

How can the past be known?

History is concerned with the past, and one obvious problem with trying to know the past is that it no longer exists. Like fleeting shadows, things that happened long ago sometimes have an air of unreality about them, and we may find it hard to believe they really happened. At a sceptical extreme, it is abstractly possible that God created the universe five seconds ago together with apparent memories, fossils and copies of yesterday's newspapers. Since any evidence you give to the contrary – such as Stonehenge, the Rosetta stone, or the Elgin marbles – might itself have been created five seconds ago, it is impossible to falsify this belief. However, it is difficult to see why God should engage in such an elaborate deception. When it comes to it, no sane person seriously doubts the existence of the past any more than they seriously doubt the existence of the external world.

"It may seem dull to you now, Harry, but at one time, everything in that book was breaking news."

Figure 15.6

At the opposite extreme from scepticism, it could be argued that, since the past no longer exists, it cannot be changed and is therefore completely objective. In this vein, the historian G. R. Elton (1921–94) provocatively argued that:

> *In a very real sense the study of history is concerned with a subject matter more objective and independent than that of the natural sciences. Just because historical matter is in the past, is gone . . . its objective reality is guaranteed; it is beyond being altered for any purpose whatsoever.*

ACTIVITY 15.8

Compare Elton's claim that history is objective with Samuel Butler's (1835–1902) wry comment: 'Though God cannot alter the past, historians can.' Which of these views do you think is closer to the truth?

While you would probably agree that the past cannot be changed, when it comes to the question of whether or not history is objective, we should make a distinction between the past and our *knowledge* of the past. Elton's argument may show that the past is objective, but it says nothing about our knowledge of the past. Such knowledge is problematic because we can know the past only by reconstructing it on the basis of evidence that exists in the present. Since memory is fallible, evidence ambiguous and prejudice common, we might have serious doubts about the claim that historical knowledge is more objective than scientific knowledge.

LQ – Human sciences: How does history differ from other human sciences?

Despite these doubts, objectivity surely remains an important ideal in history. For if we abandon it, we have no way of distinguishing between history on the one hand and propaganda and fiction on the other. The real question is to what extent a trained historian can approach the ideal of objectivity, and this requires that we look in more detail at the nature of historical evidence.

KT – primary source: a document, recording or physical object produced at the time under study

KT – secondary source: a second-hand account, such as a history textbook, of a historical event

Primary sources

Historians commonly distinguish between **primary sources** and **secondary sources**. Roughly speaking, a primary source is one that is written by someone who was there at the time, while a secondary source is a later, second-hand account of what happened. For example, Julius Caesar's (100–44 BCE) *The Conquest of Gaul* is a primary source because it is Caesar's own account of the wars he fought. By contrast Edward Gibbon's (1737–94) *The Decline and Fall of the Roman Empire* is a secondary source because it is a much later reconstruction of the fate of the Roman Empire.

LQ – Perception: How reliable is eye-witness testimony as a primary source?

Some accounts of what happened in the past are based only on secondary sources. For example, if you write an essay about the causes of the French Revolution, your bibliography may list a range of history books but no original documents. But it is obvious that if such sources are to have any authority they must ultimately be grounded in primary sources – the first-hand accounts of individuals who witnessed the events in question. For this reason, primary sources are often described as the 'bedrock of history'.

Given our discussion of ways of knowing in Part 2, you might wonder how firm this bedrock is. For there are reasons for thinking that primary sources cannot be taken at face value and that they are, in a sense, already contaminated.

ACTIVITY 15.9

How can different ways of knowing, such as language, perception, reason and emotion, distort the production of a primary source such as a diary?

Fallible eye-witness

Imagine that several diarists are witness to the same historical events. We would probably end up with as many different accounts as there are writers. Since no two individuals see things in the same way, their perceptions and memories are likely to be shaped by such things as their interests, expectations and cultural background. The role played by emotion and prejudice in what we see and remember may explain why rival soccer fans and warring countries often give such different accounts of the same events. Further biases may creep in when pen is put to paper. For a diarist must decide not only what to write down, but also how to describe what he has seen, and how to shape the stream of events into a coherent narrative. While some events may be exaggerated or described in emotional language, others may be played down or completely ignored.

Social bias

Another problem with primary sources is that they sometimes reflect the interests of one particular social group rather than society as a whole, and this may give us a distorted picture of events. For example, we tend to think that medieval Europe was a very religious place; but this may simply reflect the fact that the chroniclers of the time were mainly religious people who considered it important to record everything related to religion. If, as is usually the case, the people with the power also control the pens and the printing presses, it is not surprising that primary sources have often reflected their interests and activities at the expense of other social groups. Since the illiterate usually pass through history without a trace, we will probably never know much about how Greek slaves, or feudal peasants, or Aztec warriors saw the world. Although their stories may be irredeemably lost, it is important to be aware of the blank pages in history.

ACTIVITY 15.10

1. If you were to make a time capsule to be opened in five thousand years' time, what things would you put in it to give future historians as objective a picture as possible of life in the early twenty-first century?
2. How useful is **oral history** – recording or transcribing the memories of ordinary people or minority groups – in giving a voice to those who are usually not heard in history?

KT – oral history: historical information obtained using tape or video recordings of interviews with people who have first-hand knowledge of past events

Figure 15.7 Can oral history help to give us a more balanced view of the past?

Deliberate manipulation

A more disturbing problem arises when primary sources are deliberately manipulated by governments and other interest groups to change the 'facts' of history. (Recall Figure 15.5 on page 423, the photo in which Trotsky has been airbrushed out.) Writing in 1944, the English writer George Orwell made the following observation:

LQ – Memory: How reliable is oral history?

> *Up to a fairly recent date, the major events recorded in the history books probably happened. It is probably true that the battle of Hastings was fought in 1066, that Columbus discovered America, that Henry VIII had six wives, and so on. A certain degree of truthfulness was possible so long as it was admitted that a fact may be true even if you don't like it. Even as late as the last war it was possible for the Encyclopedia Britannica, for instance, to compile its articles on the various campaigns partly from German sources. Some of the facts – the casualty figures, for instance – were regarded as neutral and in substance accepted by everybody. No such thing would be possible now. A Nazi and a non-Nazi version of the present war would have no resemblance to one another, and which of them finally gets into the history books will be decided not by evidential methods but on the battlefield . . .*
>
> *During part of 1941 and 1942, when the Luftwaffe was busy in Russia, the German radio regaled its home audiences with stories of devastating air raids on London. Now, we are aware that those raids did not happen. But what use would our knowledge be if the Germans conquered Britain? For the purposes of a future historian, did those raids happen, or didn't they? The answer is: If Hitler survives, they happened, and if he falls they didn't happen.*

Orwell's point is that if the Nazis had won the Second World War then the basic 'facts' would have been what the propaganda ministry said they were, and all kinds of lies would have made their way into the history books and so become 'truths'. Fortunately, the Nazis did not win; and in an open society freedom of speech helps to ensure that there are some limits on a government's ability to manipulate the truth. Doubtless, we are still the victims of a great deal of 'spin' and misinformation; but behind the propaganda fog one hopes that it is still possible to discern at least an outline of the truth.

ACTIVITY 15.11

According to a well-known adage, 'history is written by the victors'. How different do you think it would be if it were written by the losers instead?

So what are we to say about the value of primary sources? Despite their limitations, if they are properly used we should not be overly sceptical about their value. There are, after all, ways of distinguishing a more reliable from a less reliable source. To start with, we can ask questions such as:

Who wrote it?

What was their motive in writing?

How long after the event was it written?

In addition, we can compare different primary sources to see how far they agree with one another. For example, if Israeli and Palestinian eye-witnesses agree about something, then it is likely to be true. Finally, we can look at documents of a legal and administrative nature which are less likely to be biased than such things as letters and diaries. So although it would be naive to accept primary sources at face value, some of them are reliable, and in the end they are all that we have to distinguish truth from fiction.

The fact that historians frequently disagree with one another should not blind us to the truth that there are a vast number of basic historical facts that everyone agrees about. No one seriously doubts that Julius Caesar crossed the Rubicon in 49 BCE, or that the atomic bomb was dropped on Hiroshima in 1945, or that Nelson Mandela was released from prison in 1990. There is, however, far less agreement about the meaning and significance of such facts.

Writing history

LQ – The arts: How is history similar to fiction and how is it different?

As we said earlier, history is more than a catalogue of past events, and the main job of the historian is to *explain* and *interpret* the past. The starting point of historical investigation is often a question or problem which reflects contemporary preoccupations. Such preoccupations may give the historian an interest in the causes of war, or the growth of democracy, or the status of women. Our current worries about the environment have led to a growing interest in the role played by environmental factors in the rise and fall of civilisations.

History is a selection of a selection

When it comes to writing history, the historian will usually have to make a selection from the available evidence – for, as we saw earlier, it is usually impossible to deal with in its entirety. Since primary sources are themselves a selective interpretation of events, this effectively means that history is a selection of a selection, and so is twice removed from what actually happened.

The fact that our knowledge of the past is filtered first through the eyes of those who witnessed it, and then through the eyes of the historian who wrote about it can make it difficult to establish the truth. However, as we have seen, it is by no means a hopeless task. For if a historian is aware of the bias in her primary sources, she may be able to compensate for it. Moreover, when it comes to secondary sources, an exhaustive survey of all the available evidence would be as undesirable as it is impossible. Imagine trying to read a history of the cultural revolution in China which included literally all of the evidence. Not only would the book be absurdly large, but you would end up drowning in a sea of detail. This may explain Lytton Strachey's (1880–1932) paradoxical observation that 'Ignorance is the first requisite of the historian, ignorance which simplifies and clarifies, which selects and omits.'

The advantages of hindsight

One of the advantages a historian has over the people whose behaviour he describes is *hindsight*. Unlike them, *he* knows how things turned out. An event which seemed insignificant at the time might later turn out to be of great importance, and vice versa. At the end of the day on which the Bastille fell, Louis XVI is said to have written in his diary the single word '*Rien*' – 'Nothing'; but we now see this event as heralding the beginning of the French Revolution.

Furthermore, certain ways of describing events may not be available to people at the time, but only retrospectively. For example, we can say 'The author of *War and Peace* was born in 1828', but that was not a description available to Tolstoy's mother at the time of his birth. Similarly, we can talk about the First World War, but since people in the 1920s did not know there would be another one they called it the Great War. (Sadly, their description of the First World War as 'the war to end all wars' now sounds very hollow.)

The division of history into various periods is similarly influenced by hindsight. In European history, we commonly speak of eras such as 'the Dark Ages', 'the Renaissance' and 'the Enlightenment'. But, of course, no one drew the curtains one morning in fourteen hundred and something and said 'Hey people, it's the Renaissance!' Such terms are retrospective ways of trying to capture the spirit of a particular historical era.

Figure 15.8 In 2008, the Australian prime minister Kevin Rudd apologised for the systematic dispossession and mistreatment of the indigenous population of Australia. To what extent can the current generation in a country be held responsible for the misdeeds of their predecessors?

ACTIVITY 15.12

1. What description do you think future historians will use to sum up the age in which we are living?
2. According to the historian G. M. Trevelyan (1876–1962), 'Unlike dates, periods are not facts. They are retrospective conceptions that we form about past events, useful to focus discussion, but very often leading historical thought astray.' How can dividing history into periods be useful and how can it be misleading?

LQ – Ethics: Should historians make moral judgements about the past?

The writing of history is also influenced by the era in which it is written. The passage of time is constantly adding new pages to the book of history, and this means that what has gone before will be reassessed by each new generation in the light of subsequent experience. Since we judge events partly in the light of their consequences, this suggests that we may be too close to recent events to understand their significance. We can, for example, only speculate about how future historians will look back on the invasion of Iraq in 2003. As an event recedes into the past, it is usually easier to see it in its historical context, but we may never be able to come to a definitive interpretation. When the Chinese premier Chou En Lai (1898–1976) was asked what he thought the impact of the French Revolution was, he famously replied: 'It is too soon to tell.' This may have been said in jest, but it reminds us of the fact that, until the story of humanity comes to an end, there can be no last word in history.

Since each generation interprets the past in the light of its own experience, we might agree with E. H. Carr's characterisation of history as 'an unending dialogue between the present and the past'. This suggests that when you read Gibbon's *The Decline and Fall of the Roman Empire* you may learn as much about the values and prejudices of eighteenth-century England as about the events Gibbon purports to describe.

ACTIVITY 15.13

Do you think you should study current events in history – say, things that have happened in the last five years – on the grounds that they are relevant to your experience, or do you think they should be excluded on the grounds that they are too close for you to see them objectively?

The disadvantages of hindsight

Despite the advantages of hindsight in helping us to determine the significance of things, it can also distort our understanding of the past. When you are living through events they seem genuinely open and you are not sure how they will turn out; but when you look back on them, it is hard to avoid the feeling that they were inevitable and could not have happened any other way. This can easily lead to **hindsight bias**. After a catastrophe, it is easy to believe that any fool could have seen what would happen, and that if you had been in the situation in question you would not have made the same mistake.

KT – hindsight bias: mistakenly thinking, after something has happened, that you had known it would happen

To give an example, in March 1980, US president Jimmy Carter sought to rescue seventy Americans who were being held hostage in Tehran, Iran. The mission was aborted when a sandstorm disabled half the helicopters being used in the operation. Afterwards, many journalists said that the rescue attempt had been 'doomed from the start', but they said this only after they knew that it had failed. If there had been no sandstorm and the hostages had been successfully rescued, the same journalists might have been praising Carter for his vision, courage and daring.

The fact is that we are all good at being wise after the event. When we look back at the Second World War, it is hard to avoid thinking that Hitler was bound to lose; but that was hardly a foregone conclusion in 1940 when Britain was on the verge of collapse and the United States had not yet entered the war. Similarly, many commentators now see the collapse of communism in Eastern Europe as inevitable, but almost no one was predicting its fall in the 1970s. If we are to get into the minds of historical actors and see situations as they themselves saw them, then we must try to avoid such hindsight bias.

Our discussion suggests that hindsight can be both a benefit and a drawback to the historian. On the plus side, it enables us to see the significance of events in the light of their consequences; on the minus side, it may lead to our being wise after the event and failing to appreciate how open and uncertain the past was to the people living through it.

The problem of bias

We should now go back to the problem of bias – which we mentioned in our discussion of primary sources – and address the widespread perception that history is more prone to bias than the natural sciences. There are at least three reasons why someone might think that this is the case:

1. *Topic choice bias.* A historian's choice of topic may be influenced by current preoccupations; and the questions that he asks – or fails to ask – are likely to influence the answers that he finds.
2. *Confirmation bias.* A historian might be tempted to appeal only to evidence that supports his own case and to ignore any counter-evidence. (As we have seen in Chapters 13 and 14, this is also a problem in the natural and human sciences.)
3. *National bias.* Since people come to history with a range of pre-existing cultural and political prejudices, they may find it difficult to deal objectively with sensitive issues that touch on things like national pride. Questions such as 'To what extent were ordinary Germans aware of the Holocaust?' or 'Was the British bombing of Dresden a war crime?' or 'Why did the United States drop the atomic bomb on Hiroshima?' may be hard to answer without strong emotions colouring our interpretation of the facts. Faced with such questions, the danger is that we begin with our prejudices and then search for the evidence to support them. At worst, history may then become little more than the finding of bad reasons for what we believe through prejudice.

RLS – Headline: 'Japanese school textbooks accused of rewriting wartime history'. To what extent is history biased by national prejudices? Can it ever be objective?

Figure15.9 How does people's national background influence their perspective on history?

Although we should not underestimate the danger of bias in history, something can be said in response to each of these points.

Topic choice bias. Although a historian's choice of topic may be influenced by the society he grows up in, this does not necessarily mean that the topic, once chosen, cannot be studied objectively. This is not so different from the situation in the natural sciences. For example, during the Second World War, some US physicists were doing atomic research as part of the Manhattan Project to develop the atomic bomb. The direction of research was clearly determined by social priorities, but the research itself was objective in the sense that it was conducted in accordance with the scientific method. With respect to both science and history, it could therefore be said that, while there may be an element of bias in a historian's *choice* of topic, this will not necessarily affect their *treatment* of it.

Confirmation bias. Although history is selective, and a bad historian may be tempted to simply find the facts she is looking for, a good historian is likely to do the opposite and actively seek out evidence that goes against her hypothesis. As a matter of fact, as the historian Keith Windschuttle (1942–) has observed, it is a common experience among historians to find that the evidence 'forces them, often reluctantly, to change the position they originally intended to take'.

LQ – Cultural perspectives: Could there be a single historical narrative of the world on which all nations could agree?

National bias. When it comes to the third point, it must be admitted that there is a serious danger of national bias infecting history. However, if rival historians of different nationalities and with different background assumptions and prejudices are able to critique one another's work, then at least the more obvious errors and biases should be rooted out.

A pluralistic approach

KT – cubist history: history which explores the past from a variety of perspectives

There is, of course, no easy solution to the problem of bias, for we can never entirely escape from our own prejudices and achieve a god's-eye view of history. Since history has often been used to promote the interests of dominant nations and powerful elites it is not surprising that some people are suspicious of the 'official' version of the truth. And in an increasingly multi-cultural world, one might argue that textbooks should reflect the experiences not only of elites, but also of groups such as women, the poor and ethnic minorities. Indeed, rather than speak of *history* in the singular, it might be better to think in terms of *histories*. The ideal might then be a kind of **cubist history** which, like a painting by Picasso, explores the past from a variety of perspectives.

Such a pluralistic approach to history does not mean that we have to abandon the ideal of historical truth, or say that there are as many truths as there are people writing history. For within each approach to history there are likely to be better and worse reconstructions of the past. For example, while some women's histories may be more propagandist and emotional, others are likely to be more accurate and objective. Thus we can embrace a pluralistic approach to history without succumbing to relativism.

While there are many different perspectives in history, it is necessary to keep hold of some notion of historical truth. For on a basic level, it is surely the case that event X either did or did not happen. And although it is often difficult to discover the truth, this does not mean that there is no truth to discover. For example, we surely owe it to the victims of the genocides that have punctuated world history to bear witness to the fact that these things really happened.

Theories of history

In discussing the nature of history earlier in this chapter, we found that it is not simply concerned with *describing* the past, but also with *explaining* it. We usually explain something in terms of the causes that brought it about; but since history deals with complex situations, it is often difficult to isolate *the* unique cause of an event.

ACTIVITY 15.14

1. At the battle of Waterloo in 1815 Napoleon Bonaparte was defeated by the British commander, the Duke of Wellington. Which of the following factors do you think a historian might take into account in explaining Napoleon's defeat?
   a. There was a communications breakdown between Napoleon's generals.
   b. Napoleon's parents did not die in infancy.
   c. At Waterloo, Napoleon was suffering from chronic haemorrhoids which made it difficult for him to mount a horse.
   d. The wet weather led Napoleon to postpone his attack on Wellington.
   e. Napoleon underestimated Wellington's abilities as a general.
   f. Newton's laws of motion determined the flight of the artillery shells.
   g. The French troops didn't have any nails to put Wellington's captured artillery pieces out of action.
   h. During the battle Marshall Ney had five horses shot from underneath him and this caused him to make errors of judgement.
2. Do you think it would be possible to isolate one of the above factors and see it as decisive in explaining Napoleon's defeat?

In considering the above factors, you probably dismissed **b** and **f** as irrelevant to the historian. Admittedly, if Napoleon's parents had died in infancy, Napoleon would not have been around to lose at Waterloo; and if the laws of motion had been different, the artillery would not have worked as expected. But neither of these factors explains Napoleon's defeat because the existence of Napoleon and Newton's laws of motion were as necessary to victory as to defeat.

What we are looking for when we seek to explain Napoleon's defeat is *the factor that made the difference*. At this point, however, it is worth pointing out that there is rarely one single cause of an event – especially a complex event such as a battle. Indeed, we might agree with the historian H. A. L. Fisher (1856–1940) when he observed: 'The human universe is so enormously complicated that to speak of *the* cause of any event is an absurdity.' Rather than there being a unique cause of Napoleon's defeat, it is more likely that it resulted from a combination of factors, such as bad communications, the weather and (possibly) haemorrhoids!

In considering the engine of historical change, we might think in terms of a range of causal factors from the more general to the more specific. Such factors might include:

- geographical conditions
- individual motives
- social and economic conditions
- chance occurrences.

Some historians who are interested in the broad sweep of history have argued that the history of civilisations ultimately depends on such geographical factors as situation, climate and soil. For example, a country with access to the sea and good natural harbours is likely to develop in a quite different way from a land-locked mountainous country. In a fascinating book called *Guns, Germs and Steel*, the American academic Jared Diamond has argued that the main reason why some cultures have been historically more successful than others has more to do with differences in geography than with differences in the natural abilities of different races. This is an attractive thesis for anyone interested in promoting international understanding (although we should keep in mind that the attractiveness of a thesis does not in itself make it true).

ACTIVITY 15.15

To what extent do you think that your country's history has been influenced by its geography?

The 'great person' theory of history

KT – 'great person' theory of history: the belief that history is driven by great individuals

As the name suggests, the **'great person' theory of history** holds that the course of history is mainly determined by great individuals. For example, the historian A. J. P. Taylor (1906–90) claimed that 'The history of modern Europe can be written in terms of three titans: Napoleon, Bismarck and Lenin.' What this theory implies is that if one or other great individual had not existed, then the course of history would have been different. Winston Churchill (1874–1965), who wrote history as well as making it, was sympathetic to this view. His grandson Nicholas Soames tells the story of how, when he was six years old, he once crept in to Churchill's study and asked in awe 'Grandpapa, is it true you are the greatest man in the world?' 'Yes,' replied Churchill, 'Now bugger off!'

ACTIVITY 15.16

1. If you could travel back in time and interview one character from history, who would it be and why? What questions would you want to ask them?
2. The psychologist Nicholas Humphrey has argued that if Newton had not existed someone else would have discovered the law of gravity, whereas if Shakespeare had not existed no one would have come up with *Hamlet*. Do you think that great historical figures are more like Newton or Shakespeare?

RLS – Headline: 'Nelson Mandela changed the course of history' (*The Guardian*, 5 December 2013). To what extent is history made by great individuals rather than impersonal economic forces?

Collingwood on empathy

If the focus of historical research is on individuals, then we need to get beyond the outside of events, and think ourselves into the minds of the agents. According to the historian R. G. Collingwood (1889–1943), with whom this idea is particularly associated:

> *When a historian asks 'Why did Brutus stab Caesar?' he means 'What did Brutus think which made him decide to stab Caesar?' The cause of the event, for him, means the thought in the mind of the person by whose agency the event came about: and this is not something other than the event, it is the inside of the event itself . . . All history is the history of thought.*

What Collingwood meant by his observation that 'all history is the history of thought' is that we can understand people's actions only by delving into their minds and trying to make sense of their motives. Collingwood drew particular attention to the importance of **empathy** in trying to understand a situation in the same way that a historical agent would have understood it. Some people have gone further and used ideas from psychoanalysis to shed light on the motivations of historical characters.

KT – empathy: the ability to imagine and understand another person's situation

Despite its merits, a number of criticisms can be made of Collingwood's approach to history. To start with, although the ability to empathise may be a useful tool of the historian's trade, it clearly has its limits. For most people would find it difficult to empathise with some of the monsters of history, such as Genghis Khan, Ivan the Terrible, or Adolf Hitler. Furthermore, in trying to explain historical events, it is not clear why we should limit ourselves to the agent's perception of the situation. As we saw earlier, one of the advantages that a historian has over the people he studies is hindsight, and his retrospective vantage point may enable him to find a significance in events that was not apparent to people at the time.

LQ – Imagination: What role should empathy play in a historian's work?

ACTIVITY 15.17

1. To what extent do you think one can and should try to empathise with Hitler in order to understand his actions?
2. Give two examples from history of actions which had consequences that could not have been imagined by the agent.
3. When he was a young man, Hitler once sought a job as a stage designer. Armed with a letter of introduction, he went to the Vienna Court Opera to see the set director, Alfred Roller, three times, but each time he lacked the courage to knock on the door. According to the historian Frederick Spotts, 'If Hitler had been taken up by Roller, he would have been very happily engaged as a stage designer. It would have been heaven for him.' How different do you think twentieth-century history would have been if Hitler had summoned up the courage to knock on Roller's door?

How important are individuals?

A more fundamental criticism of the 'great person' approach is that it exaggerates the role played by individuals in the process of historical change. In his novel *War and Peace*, the Russian writer Leo Tolstoy (1828–1910) speculates on the nature of history and argues that, far from being in control of events, Napoleon was the passive instrument of much deeper historical currents:

> *Although in that year, 1812, Napoleon believed more than ever that to shed or not to shed the blood of his peoples depended entirely on his will (as Alexander said in his last letter to him), yet then, and more than at any time, he was in bondage to those laws which forced him, while to himself he seemed to be acting freely, to do what was bound to be his share in the common edifice of humanity, in history.*

KT – economic determinism: the belief that history is driven by economic factors

Figure 15.10 Karl Marx

Economic determinism

At the other extreme from the 'great person' view of history is a theory known as **economic determinism**. This theory claims that history is determined by economic factors, and its most famous exponent was Karl Marx (1818–83). Marx claimed to have discovered the laws of historical change which operate with 'iron necessity', and from which the future course of history can be predicted; and he claimed to have done for history what Isaac Newton (1642–1727) did for physics almost two centuries earlier. According to Marx, it is not great individuals but rather technological and economic factors that are the engines of historical change. For changes in technology determine how society is organised, and this in turn determines how individuals think. An industrial economy, for example, will need to be organised in a very different way from a peasant economy, and this will affect how people think about such things as time, work and money. So rather than focusing on the actions of great men, we might do better to study the effects of key inventions such as the printing press, the steam engine and the computer.

ACTIVITY 15.18

1. Which invention do you think has had the most decisive impact on history in the last two thousand years, and why?
2. Do you agree or disagree with Marx's claim that technology plays a bigger role in shaping the future than the actions of individuals?
3. We can predict the behaviour of a gas with a great deal of accuracy even though the behaviour of an individual molecule is unpredictable. Do you think that, in a similar way, we can make accurate predictions about society even though individual behaviour is unpredictable?

Marx's emphasis on economics as the engine of historical change has been very influential, but most people now reject his deterministic approach to history. The idea that one can predict the future from a study of history seems intuitively implausible, and Marx's own predictions about where revolutions would occur have not in fact come true.

The philosopher Karl Popper (1902–94) went further in his criticism of Marx, saying that the belief in the predictability of the future is not merely implausible, but *incoherent*. The essence of Popper's argument is that if you could perfectly predict the future then you would be able to predict such things as future scientific discoveries; but if you could predict the details of such discoveries, you would then have discovered them now and not in the future – and that contradicts the original supposition.

The role of chance

Some people have concluded that there is no meaning in history and that it is governed by chance. This idea was dramatised by the French philosopher Blaise Pascal (1623–62) when he observed: 'Had Cleopatra's nose been shorter, the whole history of the world would have been different.' For if Cleopatra's nose had been shorter Mark Antony might have found her less attractive and not fallen in love with her. If Mark Antony had not fallen in love with Cleopatra, he might not have fallen out with Octavian (the future emperor Augustus). If Mark Antony and Octavian had not fallen out, Rome might have remained a republic rather than becoming an empire. If Rome had remained a republic it might have been able to resist the barbarian invasions of the fourth and fifth centuries. If Rome had resisted the barbarian invasions it might never have fallen, and Europeans and North Africans might still be living under the Roman dispensation!

Figure 15.11 If Cleopatra's nose had been shorter, would the course of history have been different?

Most people would agree that unpredictable events do play an important role in history. For example, if Hitler had died in a car accident in 1930, the subsequent history of Europe – and, indeed, the world – would probably have been quite different. Nevertheless, it seems too extreme to say that history is an entirely random process. So perhaps we should adopt a compromise position and say that history is driven by a mixture of great people, technological factors and chance events. We may not be able to find any fixed patterns, but a good historian can still help us to make sense of the past by distinguishing its main strands and weaving them into a meaningful narrative.

Conclusion

Despite the fact that the past no longer exists, history seeks to reconstruct it on the basis of evidence that can be found in the present. In this chapter we have seen that scepticism about the past is no more justified than any other form of scepticism and that it is possible to establish a bedrock of generally agreed historical facts. There is, however, much less agreement about the meaning and significance of these facts. For there are many different interpretations of the past, and trying to determine which one is the best is a matter of judgement rather than proof. But if history is not to collapse into fiction, we must take seriously the idea that there is some kind of truth about the past and that a good historian can at least help us to get closer to this truth.

Why study history? To understand the present! Do we learn from history? The jury is still out! You have probably heard it said that we should study the past to learn from our mistakes. But, since history never repeats itself, there are no simple lessons that we can take from the past and mechanically apply to the present. What the study of history can perhaps give us is something altogether more elusive: good judgement about human affairs. If that is the case, then we might agree with the historian Jacob Burckhardt (1818–97) that it does not 'make us more clever the next time, but wiser for all time'.

"Those who don't study history are doomed to repeat it. Yet those who do study history are doomed to stand by helplessly while everyone else repeats it."

Figure 15.12

Key points

- History seeks to study and explain the significant events of the past on the basis of currently existing evidence.
- The study of history can be justified on the grounds that it contributes to our sense of identity, is a defence against propaganda, and enriches our understanding of human nature.
- History is based on primary sources, but since they are a selective interpretation of events, they cannot always be taken at face value.
- Since historians usually make a selection from the available evidence, there is a sense in which history books are twice removed from what actually happened.
- In seeking to explain the past, a historian has the advantage of hindsight, but this can sometimes result in hindsight bias.
- Although it is impossible to achieve a completely objective, God's eye view of history, we can perhaps get closer to the truth by exploring the past from a variety of perspectives.
- Since history deals with complex situations, historical events rarely have a single cause but are usually the result of a combination of factors.
- Two contrasting theories of history are the 'great person' theory, which says that history is determined by great individuals, and economic determinism, which says that it is determined by economic factors.
- We can understand both the past and ourselves better if we study history than if we choose to ignore it.

Key terms

cubist history

economic determinism

empathy

'great person' theory of history

hindsight bias

oral history

primary source

secondary source

self-realising expectations

Knowledge framework focus

1. *Scope/applications.* What is history and why should we study it?
2. *Concepts/language*. Can history be written in neutral, unbiased language? To what extent is it distorted by the desire to tell a good story?
3. *Methodology.* How is a historian's method similar to and how is it different from that of a scientist?
4. *Historical development.* What does it mean to say that each generation interprets history in the light of its own preoccupations and experience, and how much truth is there in this claim?
5. *Relation to personal knowledge*. What is the relation between the personal histories of individuals and the histories of the societies in which they live?

IB prescribed essay titles

1. 'Our knowledge is only a collection of scraps and fragments that we put together into a pleasing design, and often the discovery of one new fragment would cause us to alter utterly the whole design' (Morris Bishop). To what extent is this true in history and one other area of knowledge? (November 2013)
2. Using history and at least one other area of knowledge, examine the claim that it is possible to attain knowledge despite problems of bias and selection. (May 2012)

Further reading

Books

Barbara Tuchman, *Practising History* (Papermac, 1989). This book consists of a series of insightful essays on the nature and value of history. Try 'When does history happen?' or 'The historian as artist'.

Niall Ferguson (ed.), *Virtual History* (Penguin, 2011). This book consists of nine speculative essays on what might have happened if historical episodes had turned out differently, such as 'What if Germany had invaded Britain in May 1940?' and 'What if Communism had not collapsed?' Read any one of these essays and it will soon have you thinking about the nature of historical explanations.

Online articles

Gareth Cook, 'Why did Japan Surrender?', *Boston Globe*, 7 August 2011.

The arts

16

Art is what you can get away with.

Andy Warhol, 1928–87

Life imitates art more than art imitates life.

Oscar Wilde, 1854–1900

Art is meant to disturb, science reassures.

Georges Braque, 1882–1963

The essential function of art is moral.

D. H. Lawrence, 1885–1930

Art is not a copy of the real world; one of the damn things is quite enough.

Virginia Woolf, 1882–1941

Lying, the telling of beautiful untrue things, is the proper aim of art.

Oscar Wilde, 1854–1900

An artist is always out of step with the time. He has to be.

Orson Welles, 1915–85

Art is a human activity, whose purpose is the transmission of the highest and best feelings to which men have attained.

Leo Tolstoy, 1828–1910

God is really only another artist. He invented the giraffe, the elephant and the cat. He has no real style. He just goes on trying other things.

Pablo Picasso, 1881–1973

The art of seeing nature is a thing almost as much to be acquired as the art of reading the Egyptian hieroglyphs.

John Constable, 1776–1837

Art is a lie that makes us realize the truth – at least the truth that is given us to understand.

Pablo Picasso, 1881–1973

Introduction

Imagine waking up one day to discover that the Martians have landed on Earth. Fortunately, they are benign, curious and highly intelligent – and they are keen to learn about human civilisation. You begin by telling them something about our mathematical and scientific theories, and they quickly grasp what you are talking about. You then show them some of our technological and engineering achievements – skyscrapers, planes and computers – and they are quite impressed. Your brief account of human history also interests them. You then take them to an art gallery. They are completely baffled. 'But what is this stuff for?' they ask. You mumble something about art illuminating the human condition. 'This stuff illuminates the human condition?' they ask in genuine surprise as you stroll through the modern art section. You then take them to a concert to listen to Bach's *St Matthew Passion*, but for all the pleasure it gives them you might as well take them to listen to the roar of traffic on a busy intersection. They simply cannot see the difference between music and noise. Finally, you get them to read a selection of plays, novels and poems. When they ask if Tolstoy's novel *War and Peace* is true, you explain to them that literature is concerned not with fact but with fiction. The Martians quickly lose interest in this stuff called literature, and cannot see why anyone is interested in heaps of words that contain nothing but falsehoods. 'If you want to understand human beings', they say, 'why not simply study history, psychology and anthropology?'

ACTIVITY 16.1

How would you go about trying to explain to the Martians the difference between art and non-art? And how would you try to convince them of the value of art?

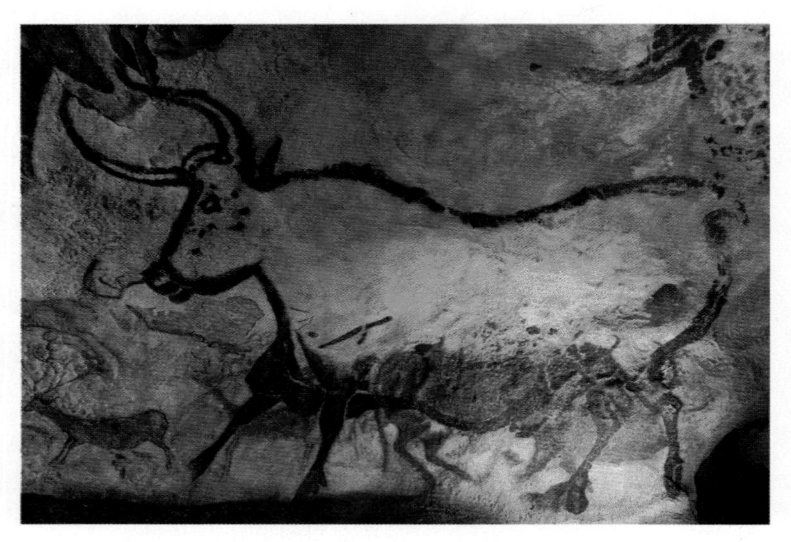

Figure 16.1 Lascaux bull. Are the arts common to all cultures?

The desire to create objects which are aesthetically pleasing rather than of practical value seems to exist in all cultures. More than twenty thousand years ago, our ancestors were daubing the walls of caves in Lascaux, France, with images of animals; and the irrepressible urge to paint, sing, dance, act and beautify one's surroundings has continued up to the present time. The Martians might be mystified about why we engage in such apparently pointless activities, but the aesthetic urge is deeply rooted in the human psyche, and – along with language, tool-making and self-awareness – seems to distinguish human beings from other animals. Indeed, many people think that being a creative artist is the highest and most satisfying form of human life.

We will consider four main questions in this chapter, all of which are connected with the relationship between art and knowledge:

1. What is art?

2. Are aesthetic judgements objective or subjective?

3. How do the arts contribute to our knowledge of the world?

4. What are the similarities and differences between the arts and the sciences?

Although many of the examples in this chapter come from the visual arts, you should keep in mind that the arts include not only painting and sculpture, but also such things as dance, film, literature, music and theatre. You will therefore need to decide whether the points made about a particular art form apply to the arts in general.

What is art?

Since the arts have traditionally claimed a right to our thoughtful attention, we need to spend some time exploring their nature and value. Hence the question 'What is art?' In thinking about this question, the real focus of our interest is on what distinguishes worthwhile art from junk. At a practical level, this is an important question because we have limited amounts of time and money and we have to decide what to spend them on. We don't want to waste our time on junk and we don't want governments to waste our money buying junk for our national collections, or supporting its production.

RLS – Headline: 'Call that art? No, they're just simple light fittings, say the experts from the EU'. Why is it difficult to define art – and why does it matter?

Most people would agree that for something to be a 'work of art', it must be man-made. A sunset may be beautiful and Mount Everest awe-inspiring, but neither would be called a work of art. Beyond this, opinions differ about what makes something art. We will explore three possible criteria:

1. the intentions of the artist

2. the quality of the work

3. the response of spectators.

ACTIVITY 16.2

Which of the following would you classify as art? Give reasons for your choice.

1. Pottery
2. Manufactured pots and pans
3. Ballet
4. Gymnastics
5. Soccer
6. Mount Everest
7. A holiday snap-shot of Mount Everest
8. A painting of Mount Everest
9. A beautiful face
10. A rock that happens to resemble a face
11. A child's drawing of a face
12. An artist's drawing of a face done in the naive style of a child
13. A caricature
14. Opera
15. Rap music
16. A piece of music generated by a computer
17. Bird song
18. The *Mona Lisa*
19. A copy of the *Mona Lisa* with a moustache and beard added
20. *Hamlet*
21. A TV soap opera
22. A nursery rhyme
23. A joke
24. A person dripping paint randomly on a canvas
25. A monkey dripping paint randomly on a canvas
26. Flower arranging
27. Flowers growing in a field
28. A bucket and mop left in an art gallery by a cleaner
29. A bucket and mop exhibited in an art gallery by an artist
30. A meal made by a famous chef
31. Tattoos
32. Video games

Figure 16.2 Tattooing has been practised in traditional cultures, but it is particularly associated with Polynesia, from where the word tattoo derived. Is a tattoo art?

Intentions of the artist

According to the intention criterion, something is a work of art if it is made by someone with the intention of evoking an **aesthetic** response in the audience. We naturally think of an artist as wanting to communicate something to us, and communication is a deliberate, intentional activity. A sunset may evoke various emotions in us, but it is not a work of art because it does not *intend* to have any effect on us. Similarly, if some ants crawling around on a patch of sand happen to trace out what looks like a portrait of Barack Obama, we would not say they had produced a work of art. This is because the portrait is the result of random activity rather than conscious design.

KT – aesthetics: the branch of philosophy which studies beauty and the arts

If something is to count as a work of art, then it should not be made with a practical end in mind, but simply with the intention of pleasing or provoking people. You would not describe a manufacturer of pots and pans as an artist because his intention is to produce kitchen utensils rather than works of art. Admittedly, many functional objects also have an aesthetic element built into them, and we may prefer attractive and elegant pots and pans to ugly and awkward ones. Nevertheless, there exists a special class of objects that are made with a specifically aesthetic intention, and these are the ones that we properly call works of art.

We can say, then, that works of art differ from natural objects in that they are made with an intention, and they differ from everyday objects in that they are made with the specific intention to please or to provoke a response rather than for some practical end.

LQ – Religion: How is artistic creation similar to and different from divine creation?

ACTIVITY 16.3

1. Oscar Wilde (1854–1900) once said that 'All art is quite useless.' What do you think he meant by this? Do you agree with him?
2. Do you consider cookery to be an art? How is it similar to other art forms, and how does it differ from them?

Criticisms of the intention criterion

Despite the appeal of the intention criterion, some critics have doubted that simply intending something to be art is enough to magically transform it into art. For example, if I take my desk with papers and a half-drunk cup of coffee on it, put it in an art gallery with a glass case around it, and call it *Teacher's Work Desk – VIII*, is it magically transformed into a work of art simply because I intend it to be so?

The artist Tracey Emin did something not so different with a work called *My Bed*, which was exhibited at the Turner Prize exhibition in London in 1999, and which consists of an unmade bed with packets of condoms and a bottle of vodka next to it. (When Emin's work was first exhibited, two art students caused a stir by staging a semi-naked pillow fight on it with the intention, they said, of making it 'more interesting'. They claimed that what they did was itself a work of art, which they called *Two Naked Men Jump Into Tracey's Bed*. Some years ago, a canny Scotsman called Fife Robertson came up with a name for this kind of thing: he called it PHony ART, or 'phart' for short. It is worth noting that Emin's work was eventually bought by the collector Charles Saatchi for £150,000.)

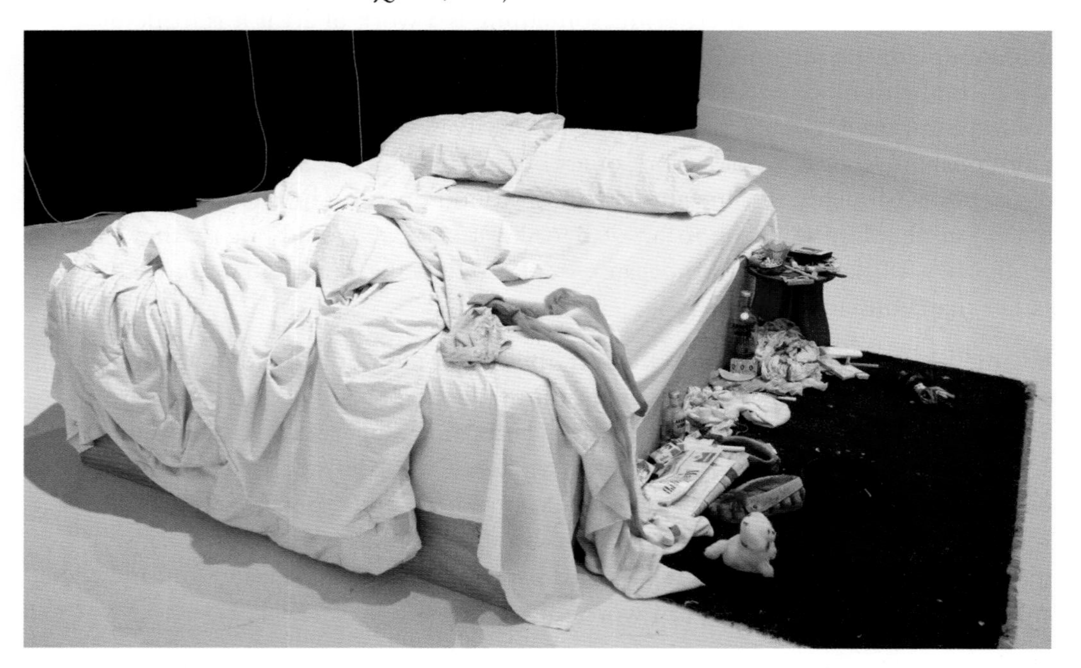

Figure 16.3 Tracey Emin: *My Bed*

ACTIVITY 16.4

Imagine that Tracey Emin's work *My Bed* comes up for sale again. Would you be happy for your tax money to be used to buy the work for your local art gallery?

In his book *The Culture of Complaint*, the art critic Robert Hughes gives the following amusing example of what can happen when art is judged merely by the intentions of the creator with no regard to its quality:

In Holland . . . the government set up a fund to buy work by artists almost irrespective of how good it was. All that mattered was that they should be alive and Dutch. About 8000 Dutch artists are represented in that collection. None of it is shown and as everyone in Holland except the artists involved now admits, about 98 per cent of it is rubbish. The artists think it's all junk except their own work. The storage, air-conditioning and maintenance expenses are now so high that they have to get rid of the stuff. But they can't. Nobody wants it. You can't give it away. They tried giving it to public institutions, like lunatic asylums and hospitals. But even the lunatic asylums insisted on standards – they wanted to pick and choose. So there it all sits, democratic, non-hierarchical, non-elitist, non-sexist, unsalable and, to the great regret of the Dutch government, only partially bio-degradable.

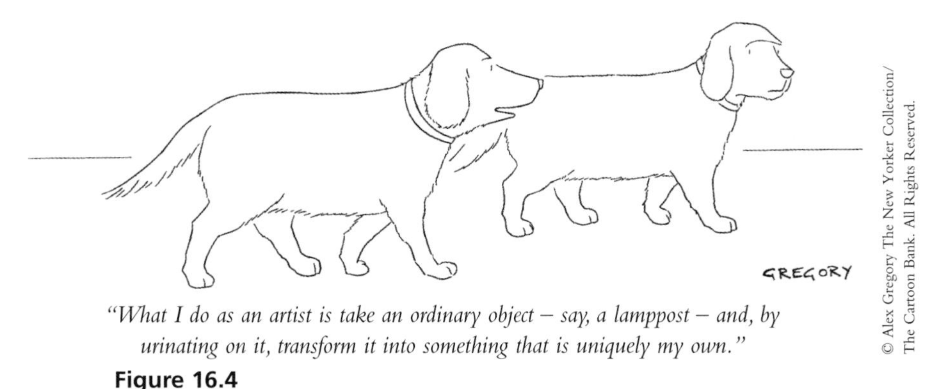

Figure 16.4

Taken together, these two criticisms of the intentions criterion suggest that the intentions of the creator are neither a necessary nor a sufficient condition for something to be a work of art. They are not necessary because something that was not originally intended as art may now be treated as such; and they are not sufficient because something that is intended as art might simply be junk.

Quality of the work

The second criterion for distinguishing art from non-art is the intrinsic quality of the work. This criterion is closely connected with the idea of *skill*. We generally expect an artist to have a high level of technical competence, and feel that an artist should be able to make a good likeness, a musician a pleasing melody, and a poet a well-crafted rhyme. In short, we feel that a work of art should not be something that a person with no talent or training in the arts could have made.

The belief that a work of art should have some kind of intrinsic quality has often been associated with the idea of beauty. Traditionally, it was believed that beautiful art is produced by painting beautiful objects, or by *revealing* the beauty in everyday objects. But, since we can speak of beauty with respect to the *form* of a work of art as well as its *content*, perhaps we should say that a great work of art is a perfect marriage of form and content.

Figure 16.5 Wall tiles from the Alhambra, Granada, Spain. Islamic art emphasises form over content and makes great use of mathematically precise geometrical patterns.

- The *content* of a work of art is what it depicts – such as a face, a landscape, or a bowl of fruit.
- The *form* of a work of art concerns the way it is put together, and such things as unity, order, rhythm, balance, proportion, harmony and symmetry are relevant to it.

In fact, a great deal of modern art may seem less concerned to produce beautiful things which please the senses than to shock or challenge the viewer. However, you might still feel that if a work of art is to be worthy of our interest it should have some kind of quality which reflects the skill of its creator.

ACTIVITY 16.5

1. According to one definition, 'beauty is the proper conformity of the parts to one another and to the whole'. Do you agree with this definition, or can you suggest a better one?
2. Do you think there are universal standards of beauty, or do you think they vary from country to country?
3. Do you think art can reveal the beauty in something that has not previously been seen as beautiful?
4. Compare the following two dictionary definitions of music, the first from 1911, the second from 1974. What do these suggest to you about the changing role of beauty in the arts?
   a. 'Art of combining sounds with a view to beauty of form and expression of emotion.'
   b. 'The science or art of ordering tones or sounds in succession, in combination, and in temporal relationship.'
5. Can something be a great work of art and yet be disturbing or ugly or disgusting?

Criticisms of the quality criterion

Despite the appeal of the quality criterion, it is open to criticism. A work of art may, for example, have a great deal of technical competence but lack originality. There are plenty of competent but unoriginal artists turning out impressionist pictures for calendars and greeting cards. Such art is known as **kitsch** – from the German *verkitschen etwas* meaning to 'knock something off'. Kitsch is basically any form of clichéd art. The USA's 'most popular painting' – see page 456 – is an example of kitsch, as is the music you hear in shopping malls, or the soap operas you see on television.

KT – kitsch: derivative, clichéd art

The problem of *forgeries* is also relevant here. Perhaps the most famous forger of paintings was the Dutch artist Han Van Meegeren (1889–1947), who painted some fake Vermeers in the 1930s that fooled the art world and were widely accepted as genuine. (Vermeer was a seventeenth-century Dutch painter.) Even after Van Meegeren's hoax was exposed, some art critics continued to insist that the paintings were genuine! The best-known of Van Meegeren's 'Vermeers', called *The Disciples at Emmaus*, is shown in Figure 16.6.

Figure 16.6 Van Meegeren: *The Disciples at Emmaus.* Can a forgery be art?

ACTIVITY 16.6

1. What do you think of the painting in Figure 16.6? If it is any good, why should its value depend on who painted it?
2. Why is an exact copy of a painting worth far less than the original? Can this difference be justified, or is it simply an irrational prejudice?

The other side of this argument is that a work of art can sometimes show originality, and yet require little technical skill. Consider the bull's head by Pablo Picasso (1881–1973). The head is made of an old bicycle saddle and a rusty pair of handlebars, and a small child probably *could* have put it together. Yet for Picasso to see beyond the everyday function of these objects is considered an astonishing insight and is, in a way, similar to a great writer making a strikingly original metaphor.

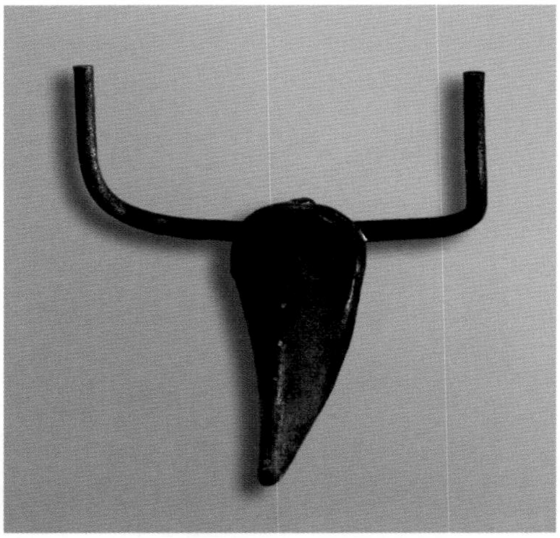

Figure 16.7 Picasso's *Bull's Head*. Does the fact that you could have done this yourself diminish its aesthetic value?

To summarise, we can say that quality and skill seem to be neither a necessary nor a sufficient condition for something to be a work of art. It is not necessary because works such as Picasso's *Bull's Head* are original but do not require much skill; and it is not sufficient because kitsch and forgeries may require skill but are hardly interesting works of art.

Response of spectators

The third criterion for distinguishing between art and non-art is the response of spectators. It might be said that, just as a joke requires someone to laugh at it, so a work of art requires an appreciative spectator in order to complete it. Writers want to be read, painters want exhibitions, and performers crave an audience.

"I like his earlier work better, particularly the ones I said I didn't like at the time."

Figure 16.8

One of the key questions in thinking about this criterion is *which* spectators we should appeal to. Since 'the general public' usually prefer the familiar to the strange and content to form, they have often been hostile to new artistic movements, and many artists have had little time for their opinions. The poet Percy Bysshe Shelley (1792–1822) once observed that 'Time reverses the judgement of the foolish crowd', and there seems to be some truth in this. The 1913 world première of Igor Stravinsky's music for the ballet *The Rite of Spring* in Paris was booed off stage by the audience, and Picasso's *Les Demoiselles d'Avignon* (1907) met with shock and outrage from his contemporaries. Both works are now considered to be part of the **canon** of great works of art.

KT – canon: the collection of works of art considered by scholars to be the most important and influential

At the same time, we must keep in mind that some artists may have a vested interest in dismissing the opinions of the 'uninformed' public – for the public have the annoying habit of pointing out the absurdities of the more extreme fringes of modern art. An artist may comfort himself with the thought that many new works of art now accepted as great art were originally dismissed as 'rubbish' by the public; but perhaps some of the things the public dismiss as rubbish really are rubbish!

"I know more about art than you do, so I'll tell you what to like."

Figure 16.9

At this point, we might appeal to expert opinion to help us to decide which works of art are genuinely worthwhile. Some people think it makes no sense to speak about 'expert opinion' in the arts on the grounds that you cannot argue about matters of taste. But good critics can help you to decide which of the millions of art works available are worth your time and attention; and they can also help you to see things in a work of art that you might otherwise have overlooked. Indeed, just as a psychoanalyst may reveal things about a person that they are not consciously aware of, so a good critic may understand the meaning of a work of art better than the artist who made the work. Admittedly, experts sometimes disagree in their judgements, but their arguments are usually much more sophisticated than the 'I like it' / 'I don't like it' disagreements of those who do not have any background knowledge.

ACTIVITY 16.7

Do you think that the idea of expert opinion is more problematic in the arts than in the sciences? Give reasons.

Other ideas about the nature of art

Given the difficulties with the above criteria, a simple answer to the question 'what is art?' might be 'art is what is found in an art gallery or treated by experts as a work of art'.

Is everything art?

In the early twentieth century, the French artist Marcel Duchamp (1887–1968) began exhibiting what he called 'readymades'. As the name suggests, these were simply objects taken out of their everyday context, renamed, and put in an art gallery. Perhaps the most famous of Duchamp's readymades was his work called *The Fountain*, which was a white porcelain urinal with the pseudonym 'R Mutt' daubed on it.

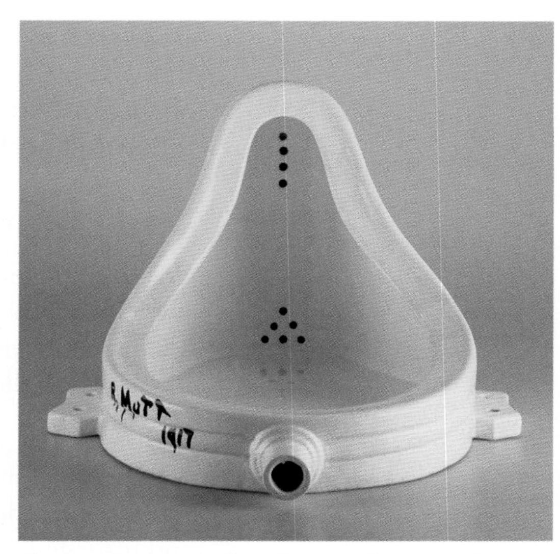

Figure 16.10 Marcel Duchamp: *The Fountain*

By suggesting that everyday objects might have aesthetic value, Duchamp can be seen as raising the question of where art ends and non-art begins. Taking our cue from Duchamp, we might be tempted to say that if we just opened our eyes we would see that *everything* is art. But if we say that *everything* is art, then the word 'art' is in danger of losing its meaning because it no longer distinguishes some things from other things. Just as 'high' only means something relative to 'not-high', so 'art' only means something relative to 'not-art'.

Instead of saying that everything is art we could perhaps rescue the above idea by saying that *everything can be looked at from an aesthetic point of view.* When something is put in an art gallery, that is precisely the way we are invited to look at it. Thus, while an unmade bed in a hotel room is unlikely to engage your aesthetic interest, if you put a glass case round it and put it in an art gallery, you will stop looking at it as a purely functional object, and this might set in motion the wheels of thought and feeling . . . But then again it might not! After all, just because something is in an art gallery does not necessarily mean that it is worthy of our interest.

Inexhaustibility

Perhaps the distinguishing feature of a great work of art is that it is *inexhaustible* in the sense that every time you come back to it you discover new things in it. A related idea is that great works of art stand the test of time and speak across generations and cultures. There is, for example, something extraordinary about the fact that Sophocles' play *Oedipus Rex* can move us with the same power and intensity that it moved Athenian audiences two and a half thousand years ago. Indeed, it could be argued that the sorting effects of time act as a kind of *ideal spectator*, helping us to distinguish enduring art from art which is merely fashionable.

ACTIVITY 16.8

Which pieces of music produced in the last ten years do you think will still be admired and listened to in a hundred years' time? Give reasons.

Judging art

Sophocles' play *Oedipus Rex* is generally considered to be part of the canon of great works of world literature, and it is widely studied in schools and colleges. You are probably familiar with other canonical works of art such as pieces by Mozart and Beethoven in music, Shakespeare and Goethe in literature, and Leonardo and Picasso in the visual arts. The question we will now consider is how far our judgements about what distinguishes good art from bad are objective and how far they are influenced by the culture we grow up in and our personal tastes.

The paradox of aesthetic judgement

We might begin by observing that there is something paradoxical about aesthetic judgement. On the one hand, we take seriously the idea that there are *standards* of aesthetic judgement and that some judgements are better than others; on the other hand, we say that 'beauty is in the eye of the beholder' and 'there is no accounting for tastes'.

The first half of the paradox – that there are standards of judgement – is what justifies a teacher grading a piece of creative writing, or a composition, or a painting, and it suggests that there are criteria for distinguishing good art from bad art. But the second half seems to be equally compelling; for it would appear that you cannot *argue* about tastes in the arts any more than you can argue about tastes in food. Either you like something or you don't like it. If I hate oysters and love burgers, you cannot tell me I am wrong, so why should you do this if I say that I hate Shakespeare and love J. K. Rowling (the author of the *Harry Potter* books)?

ACTIVITY 16.9

1. With reference to food and drink, does it make sense to speak of someone 'educating' their palate, and learning to appreciate, say, good wine?
2. 'Andy Murray is one of the best tennis players in the world.' Is this a fact or an opinion? How is it similar to and how is it different from the kinds of judgements we make in the arts?
3. 'It's a great work of art, but I don't like it.' How, if at all, can someone say this with consistency?

With reference to culinary tastes, it is worth pointing out that although we have some basic likes and dislikes that are permanent features of our make-up – perhaps you cannot imagine *ever* liking oysters – it may still make sense to speak of 'educating' our culinary tastes. You may, for example, learn to appreciate the 'vocabulary' of Thai cuisine, such as the subtle blend of peppers, coconut and lemon grass in a green curry. If we can learn to educate our culinary tastes, then perhaps we can also learn to educate our aesthetic tastes.

Should aesthetic judgements be disinterested?

According to the philosopher Immanuel Kant (1724–1804), there is a big difference between judgements of taste and aesthetic judgements. For, unlike judgements of taste, aesthetic judgements make a universal claim and have a sense of 'ought' built into them. You can see this if you compare the following two statements:

1. 'I like this painting.'

2. 'This painting is beautiful.'

If I say I like the painting and you say you *don't* like it, these two statements can happily coexist with one another. But if I say that the painting is beautiful and you say that it is *not* beautiful, then we are contradicting one another. To say that something is beautiful implies that other people *ought* to find it beautiful. Kant put it well when he said that in our aesthetic judgements we are 'suitors for agreement'.

According to Kant, what distinguishes aesthetic judgements from personal tastes is that they are **disinterested**. If you see a picture of a Banana Split on a dessert menu, you are *interested* in the sense that it is likely to fuel your desire for ice-cream rather than evoke an aesthetic response. Similarly, if you like a play because you are in love with the actress, or a piece of music because it reminds you of 'a happy time in your life', or Cézanne's *Still Life with Apples* because you are hungry, you are in each case *interested.* There is nothing wrong with such responses, but they are not *aesthetic* responses.

KT – disinterested: free from bias and self-interest, which may help us to make objective aesthetic judgements

The point is that if you are going to judge a work of art on its merits you should not bring your biography with you. I imagine that Mary Todd Lincoln hated the play *Our American Cousin* because her husband, Abraham Lincoln, was assassinated during a performance of it. But the tragedy of Lincoln's assassination has no bearing on the literary merits or demerits of the play. When Kant says that we should look at a work of art disinterestedly, he does not mean that we should be *uninterested* in it, but rather that we should try to go beyond our individual tastes and preferences so that we can appreciate it from a more universal standpoint.

There is an interesting parallel here between aesthetic judgements and judgements about sports. A soccer fan, for example, is *interested* if he refuses in principle to recognise the beauty of a rival team's playing style. He is *disinterested* if he is able to rise above his own prejudices and appreciate their style – even though he does not like them. We also take seriously the idea that there are standards in sports. For example, if you say 'Pelé was one of the best footballers of all time', it could be argued that it is more of a *fact* than an opinion. You may not be interested in Pelé, or in soccer; but the fact is that he is considered a great player by people who know about these things.

Since we take seriously the idea of standards in sports, then perhaps we should also do so in the case of the arts. Admittedly, the arts differ from sports in that they do not have any clear rules for determining winners and losers. But if someone thinks that Shakespeare is a useless writer they are surely at least as wrong as if they think that Pelé was a bad footballer. This is not to say that everyone should *like* Shakespeare; but you can acknowledge that he is a great writer even if you find that he is not to your taste.

Are there universal standards in art?

Psychological factors

Since all human beings share the same basic perceptual equipment, you might expect to find some similarities in our aesthetic judgements. Consider, for example, the two paintings in Figures 16.11 and 16.12 – the first by J. M. Turner (1775–1851) and the second by David Bomberg (1900–57).

Figure 16.11 Turner: *The Lake, Petworth: Sunset, a Stag Drinking*

Figure 16.12 Bomberg: *The Mud Bath*

ACTIVITY 16.10

Write down five to ten adjectives that come to mind when you look at the first painting. Now do the same for the second painting. Compare your list with someone else's. How similar are your lists? What, if anything, does this suggest to you about the nature of aesthetic judgement?

Think about the adjectives you came up with to describe these paintings. You may have used words like 'peaceful' and 'serene' for the first, and 'disturbing' and 'aggressive' for the second. It is unlikely that you described the first painting as 'disturbing' and the second as 'peaceful'. Why do most people find the Turner peaceful and the Bomberg disturbing? The fact that the former consists mainly of horizontals and the latter mainly of diagonals is surely relevant; and it could be argued that since we are subject to the pull of gravity, we naturally tend to find the former peaceful and the latter disturbing. There is, of course, a great deal more to paintings than the juxtaposition of lines, but this is a significant element we can analyse in considering the effect they have on us.

ACTIVITY 16.11

Find some more examples of paintings in which either horizontals or diagonals predominate and consider the extent to which the former are generally 'peaceful' and the latter generally 'disturbing'.

Komar and Melamid

Further evidence for the idea that some aesthetic judgements are universal comes from two Russian artists, Vitaly Komar and Alexander Melamid, who set out to discover what kinds of painting people find most attractive. To their surprise, they found a striking similarity in the most popular paintings across a wide range of cultures. What these paintings had in common was that they depicted landscapes in which the viewer can see without being seen. Some people have argued that our preference for such landscapes is rooted in our biological past, and it is not hard to see why they might appeal to a human animal struggling to survive in a hostile world.

Other research by Komar and Melamid indicates that there is a similar universality in people's musical tastes. We might speculate that the metronome of the human pulse is the biological basis for our sense of rhythm in music.

Rather than attribute the similarity of people's aesthetic tastes to biology, some commentators argue that it derives from the fact that we live in a world that is dominated by American culture. Since we are increasingly exposed to the same kind of image on posters, the same kind of music in shopping malls, and the same kind of movie in cinemas, it is perhaps not surprising that, despite our cultural differences, we end up with broadly similar tastes.

Courtesy Ronald Feldman Fine Arts, New York

Figure 16.13 Komar and Melamid: The USA's Most Wanted painting from their People's Choice series, 1994–7. Can the value of a work of art be determined by popular vote?

ACTIVITY 16.12

1. Do you think the world is becoming culturally more homogeneous? To what extent do you think that your own cultural tradition is under threat?
2. To what extent do you think there are universal standards of what makes a face beautiful, and to what extent do you think it varies from culture to culture?

LQ – Cultural perspectives: Are aesthetic values universal or do they vary from culture to culture?

Cultural differences

At this point we might ask how similar the aesthetic tastes of different cultures really are. To some extent, it is simply a matter of perspective: some people are more inclined to see the similarities between things, and others are more inclined to see the differences between them. We may decide that there are universal elements running through all cultures; but this should not blind us to the differences between them. You can get an idea of such differences by looking at two paintings of Derwentwater in England (Figure 16.14a, b), the first done by an English painter, the second by a Chinese painter. Although they show the same scene, they are strikingly different in style.

The difference between Chinese opera and European opera is even more striking, and those accustomed to one tradition may – initially at least – find it very difficult to make sense of what is going on in the other. In the same way, someone raised on baseball may find it difficult to make sense of cricket. However, in the case of both sports and the arts, we may be able to learn a new vocabulary and gradually come to appreciate the subtleties of a sporting or artistic tradition that is different from our own.

(a)

(b)

Figure 16.14 Two paintings of Derwentwater

ACTIVITY 16.13

How much can we learn about the way a culture sees the world by studying the art that it produces?

Art and knowledge

Since works of art do not have any practical function like other man-made objects, you might think that their only purpose is to give pleasure. Doubtless, works of art *do* frequently give us pleasure, but many people would say that they also contribute to our knowledge of the world. To explore this idea further, let us consider three popular theories about the nature of art:

1. art as imitation

2. art as communication

3. art as education.

Art as imitation

KT – mimetic: from *mimesis*, the Greek word for 'imitation', associated with the idea that art should copy reality

Perhaps the best-known theory of art is the imitation or copy theory, which says that the purpose of art is to copy reality. (This is also known as the **mimetic** theory of art.) Many great artists, such as Michelangelo (1475–1564) and Auguste Rodin (1840–1917), have subscribed to some version of this theory, which derives its plausibility from the fact that we naturally expect a portrait to be a good likeness of its sitter, or a novel to be true to life. Since it requires great skill to paint well or to describe something accurately in words, the arts have for much of their history been driven by the desire to achieve a perfect likeness.

The development of perspective in the fifteenth century was a major step forward in the pursuit of this goal in the visual arts. But the invention of the camera in the nineteenth put the whole tradition in question. Why try to copy the world by daubing paint on a canvas when a perfect image can be produced at the click of a button? This led to revolutionary changes in the visual arts which spilled over into the other arts and led people to start questioning traditional assumptions in other areas such as music and literature. The copy theory had, in any case, never seemed satisfactory when applied to music. What, after all, could a Mozart piano concerto, or a Beethoven symphony, be a copy of?

You might even have doubts about the copy theory when applied to photography. For although photos are in a sense copies of reality, some capture a landscape or a person's likeness better than others. A good likeness, we might say, is one that, out of the thousands of possible images, captures 'the essential you'. While holiday snapshots are simply meant to remind us of 'happy times' and do not have much to do with art, a skilled photographer with a good eye is clearly doing a great deal more than pressing a button and taking a copy of the world.

ACTIVITY 16.14

1. According to a well-known saying, 'The camera never lies.' Do you agree or disagree with this?
2. Do you think that some photos of you capture your likeness better than others? How is this possible?
3. Does a colour photograph capture nature more accurately than a black and white one?
4. Give some arguments for and against the claim that photography is an art.

Before rejecting the copy theory, we should perhaps analyse in more detail what it means to copy something. You might think that to copy something is simply to reproduce what you see and that there is no more to be said. But in reality things are not as simple as that; for as we saw in Chapter 5, seeing does not passively mirror reality, but has an element of interpretation built into it. This point opens the way to a more sophisticated version of the copy theory in which we think of art not as a slavish reproduction, but as a *creative reinterpretation* of reality.

According to this more sophisticated view, great art helps us to see the world with new eyes by drawing attention to previously unnoticed features of reality. This is perhaps what the Swiss painter Paul Klee (1878–1940) meant when he observed, 'Art does not reproduce the visible; rather, it makes visible.' For example, an artist may reveal the beauty of an everyday object, or the play of light on a lily pond, or the geometric forms underlying the human body, which we have never noticed before, but which we *now recognise for the first time*. When reading a novel, you may have had the experience of reading a passage and thinking to yourself, 'That is exactly what I have always felt' – and yet you were never previously aware of it!

LQ – History: How much can we learn about the past by studying the history of art?

The idea here, then, is that the arts can subtly influence the way in which we experience the world. Some people have suggested that we see faces differently after Rembrandt's self-portraits, think about love differently after Shakespeare's *Romeo and Juliet*, and feel differently about the seasons after Vivaldi's *The Four Seasons*. Although these may not be your aesthetic points of reference, you might ask yourself how much the images you see, and the films you watch, and the music you listen to affect the way you see things.

ACTIVITY 16.15

1. Oscar Wilde once said that 'Life imitates art far more than art imitates life.' What do you think he meant by this?
2. When Picasso was told that his portrait of Gertrude Stein didn't look like her, he said, 'Never mind, it will!' What do you think he meant by this?
3. The poet Wallace Stevens (1879–1955) once said: 'Reality is a cliché from which we escape by metaphor.' What do you think he meant by this?

Figure 16.15 Picasso: *Gertrude Stein*

KT – avant-garde: innovative ideas considered to be at the forefront of new developments and techniques in the arts

While new movements in the arts *challenge* our understanding of reality, they can in time lose their shock value and simply become part of the way in which a culture sees the world. Thus what is **avant-garde** art to one generation may be normal to the next and kitsch to the third. Rather than challenge and provoke, kitsch is designed to soothe and reassure people. Against kitsch, it could be argued that the real job of art is to question traditional ways of looking at things and give us new ways of experiencing the world. Since many people prefer the comfortable to the challenging, it is perhaps not surprising that many great artists who struck out in new directions were not recognised by their contemporaries.

ACTIVITY 16.16

1. To what extent can Thomas Kuhn's talk of *paradigms* (see Chapter 13, page 363) be applied to the arts?
2. Do you think that people turn to the arts more to be challenged or more to be comforted?
3. Give some examples of great artists who were not recognised by their contemporaries. Give some examples of great artists who *were* recognised by their contemporaries. What conclusions would you draw from this?

Art as communication

RLS – Headline: 'Why dictators love kitsch: Kim Jong Il – Clinton photo op spotlights a style that has long glorified tyrants'. What is the relation between art and propaganda?

A second way of thinking about art is as a means of communication. It seems natural to think of an artist as trying to communicate a message to a spectator. Indeed, we sometimes speak of 'the language of art'; but it is, of course, quite different from ordinary language. If you try to explain a poem in prose, the real meaning of the poem will escape you. Similarly, the sense of triumphant joy in the last movement of Beethoven's Ninth Symphony goes beyond anything that can be expressed in words.

The analogy between art and language suggests that, just as you need to understand the grammar and vocabulary of a language to know what a native speaker means, so you may need to understand the grammar and vocabulary of art in order to know what an artist means. So perhaps before dismissing, say, classical music or modern art, we need to make an effort to learn the language. We are then in a better position to decide whether what is being communicated is worthwhile or not.

ACTIVITY 16.17

To what extent do you think you can understand or appreciate a work of art if you know nothing about the context?

We might think of the art-as-communication theory as having two dimensions to it:

- a horizontal one which enables us to explore the breadth of human experience
- and a vertical one which enables us to explore its depth.

With respect to breadth, literature, in particular, can be a remarkably effective way of imaginatively projecting ourselves into situations that lie beyond the frontiers of our own lives, and in this way it enables us vicariously to broaden the scope of our experience. As the Russian novelist Alexander Solzhenitsyn (1918–2008) put it:

> *Art can amplify man's short time on this earth by enabling him to receive from another the whole range of someone else's lifelong experiences with all their problems, colours and flavours. Art recreates in flesh experiences that have been lived by other men, and enables people to absorb them as if they were their own.*

LQ – Emotion: Is art the language of the emotions?

With respect to depth, the arts seem to be particularly concerned with communicating emotions. According to philosopher R. G. Collingwood (1889–1943), 'The artist proper is a person who, grappling with the problem of expressing a certain emotion, says, "I want to get this clear".' Many people instinctively turn to the arts if they feel something deeply enough. Part of the reason for this may be that ordinary language seems to be unable to capture the uniqueness and complexity of our deepest emotions. When you are in love with someone, the words 'I love you' somehow fail to do justice to your feelings – for that is what everyone says. So you may reach for a poem or a piece of music to try to make sense of the depth and intensity and uniqueness of your feelings.

ACTIVITY 16.18

1. How is music similar to a language and how is it different from a language?
2. Are there things that can be expressed in music, but not in language? Are there things that can be expressed in language but not in music?
3. Why do you think so much pop music has love as its theme? To what extent does such music help you to understand your own emotions?

Art as education

LQ – Ethics: What evidence is there that the arts civilise people?

According to a third theory of the arts, the arts have a moral and educative role. The connection between the arts and ethics is said to derive from the fact that they provoke emotions that influence our behaviour. They also shape our attitudes by offering us a range of role-models. For the ancient Greeks, Homer's *Iliad* played a key role in a young man's moral education. We now have Hollywood and Bollywood, and we might speculate about the extent to which the movies we watch influence our attitudes about good and bad, and right and wrong. At a more general level, it could be said that great art challenges us to question our assumptions by giving us a different perspective on things. Almost all works of art raise some kind of question about how we ought to see things, or think about things, or live our lives. So, in this broad sense, we might describe art as a moral provocation.

Thinking more about the relationship between art and ethics, we might say that the arts broaden our awareness, develop our empathy, and sharpen our intuitions. In discussing art as communication, we saw that literature can be said to give us a sense of the variety of possible lives that can be lived, and so help to give us a broader conception of what it means to be human. The awareness that there are other equally valid perspectives on the world may make us more willing to question and reflect on our own values and move beyond the inevitable limitations of our own culture towards a more universal perspective on things.

As we saw in chapter 9 (p.240), literature can also develop our ability to empathise with other people by enabling us to imaginatively project ourselves into situations that lie beyond the frontiers of our own experience. By communicating the inside of another person's experience to us, a great novel or play can move and inspire us in a way that a purely factual description or an abstract book on ethics cannot. For example, you may have no direct experience of what it was like to be a poor American tenant farmer in the Great Depression of the 1930s, but by reading John Steinbeck's novel The Grapes of Wrath, you can get a vivid sense - from the inside - of what life was like and the kinds of challenges that people faced.

ACTIVITY 16.19

What can a war poem tell you about the First World War that a purely factual account cannot?

We might also think of works of literature as thought experiments which give us a space in which to test and sharpen our moral intuitions. Since good literature presents us with moral problems in all their real-life messiness and ambiguity, it encourages us to go beyond simplistic black-and-white ways of thinking about ethics. This may explain why in recent years some universities have introduced compulsory literature courses for their law students.

Despite the above points, some people insist that a work of art should be judged purely on its aesthetic rather than its ethical merits. When an artist starts to preach and tries to teach moral lessons through their art, there is a danger that they will end up being both a bad artist and a bad preacher.

Plato versus Aristotle

While the arts are sometimes described as 'the language of the emotions', some people are suspicious of them precisely because they appeal to emotion rather than reason. This view can be traced back to Plato (428–348 BCE) who held that, by inflaming the emotions, art weakens our ability to lead rational lives. He therefore banished artists from the ideal society which he described in his famous work *The Republic*.

Plato's younger contemporary and pupil, Aristotle (384–322 BCE), had a different view of the relation between art and emotion. According to him, art does not *incite* emotion as much as *purge*, or *cleanse* us of it. This cleansing effect is known as **catharsis**. A good example would be someone who goes to watch a 'tear jerker' at the movies and feels better after 'a good cry'. Given the number of violent and pornographic movies that are readily available, the dispute between Plato and Aristotle is of great contemporary relevance.

KT – catharsis: the release of emotional tension that is brought about by reading, viewing or listening to a work of art

ACTIVITY 16.20

1. Why do you think some people watch movies that they know in advance will terrify them, or make them cry?
2. Do you think that watching violent movies makes people more or less likely to be violent?
3. When, if ever, do you think that a work of art should be censored?

RLS – Headline: 'Goldfish in a blender? Marco Evaristti calls it art'. Should there be moral limits on art?

Whatever your view of the effect of the arts on our emotions, there are reasons for doubting that they have a civilising influence on people. Some people have argued that even morally uplifting art stimulates sentimentality rather than action. You may weep at scenes of injustice in a movie, thereby convincing yourself that you are a caring individual, and yet be blind to injustice in the real world. The point about imaginary – as opposed to real – injustice is that it requires only an imaginary response. At worst, literature can make us feel good about ourselves in a way which costs us nothing and becomes a substitute for, rather than provocation to, action.

More disturbingly, the historical record suggests that the arts have done little to inoculate people against barbarism. The twentieth century has thrown up plenty of literate tyrants, such as Hitler, Lenin, Stalin and Mao, but their interest in the arts did nothing to stop them organising the slaughter of human beings on an industrial scale. Perhaps the problem with such tyrants was, as the Russian poet Joseph Brodsky (1940–96) noted with chilling understatement, that their hit lists were longer than their reading lists.

In the absence of clear evidence one way or the other, the belief that the arts can civilise us may come down to a matter of faith, although we would probably all like to believe that it is true!

ACTIVITY 16.21

1. Analyse a moral dilemma in a novel with which you are familiar. How, if at all, has it affected the way you think about ethics?
2. Do you think that teachers of art and literature have greater moral sensitivity than teachers of physics and chemistry? What implications does this have for our discussion about the relation between the arts and ethics?
3. To what extent do you think artists ought to engage with the political issues of the day?

Science, art and truth

Whatever the relationship between the arts and knowledge, there seems to be a big difference between the contribution made by the arts to our understanding of the world and that made by the sciences. Indeed, these two areas of knowledge have often been separated by a gulf of mutual incomprehension. On the one hand, some artists accuse the sciences of robbing the world of its mystery. The English writer D. H. Lawrence (1885–1930) said, 'Knowledge has killed the sun making it a ball of gas with spots.' On the other hand, the arts have sometimes been dismissed by the scientifically-minded as little more than a frivolous diversion.

LQ – Natural and human sciences: Does knowledge that we get from the arts complement scientific knowledge?

ACTIVITY 16.22

1. How are scientists and artists portrayed in any of the Hollywood movies with which you are familiar?
2. If cutbacks in your school's education budget required that you cut either a science subject or an arts subject from the school curriculum, which would you cut and why?

Reason, imagination and beauty

Despite the obvious differences between the arts and the sciences, there are also some interesting similarities between them. At the deepest level, we might say that both are trying to make sense of the world by looking for patterns in things. The difference is that in science the patterns are expressed in mathematics and logic, and in the arts they are expressed in more allusive and intuitive forms.

ACTIVITY 16.23

What would you say are the main similarities and differences between the arts and the sciences? The following words may help to stimulate your thinking:

beauty	creation	discovery	emotion	fact	fiction
general	inside	outside	particular	reason	

Furthermore, although science appeals more to reason, and the arts more to imagination, reason and imagination play an important role in both areas of knowledge. On the one hand, an artist needs to impose some kind of rational control on their creative insights if they are to be of lasting value. If, for example, you are writing a love poem, you can't simply write down your feelings – you need to impose some kind of form on them. On the other hand, a scientist needs to have a good imagination if she is to come up with new ways of looking at things.

Interestingly, many great scientists have appealed to the beauty of their ideas in order to justify them. For example, Albert Einstein (1879–1955) once observed that the theory of relativity was too beautiful to be false. After the theory was confirmed by astronomers during a solar eclipse in 1919, Einstein was asked what he would have done if the results had contradicted rather than confirmed his theory. He replied: 'Then I would feel sorry for the good Lord. The theory is correct.' Such a reference to beauty is, at first sight, puzzling; but it makes sense once we realise that beauty and order are closely related concepts, and that a scientist's appeal to beauty is usually a reflection of his conviction that the universe is orderly.

The Einstein story shows that aesthetic considerations play a role in convincing scientists of the truth of their theories. However, two important points should be kept in mind. First, the kind of beauty scientists are thinking about is often of a mathematical nature and cannot be appreciated unless you have a training in mathematics. Second, beauty is no guarantee of truth. If Einstein's theory of relativity had been repeatedly contradicted by experimental results, he would eventually have had to abandon it and think again. For it is always possible that the universe operates with an aesthetic that is quite different from our own.

Discovered or invented?

One important difference between science and art would seem to be that while scientific laws are *discovered*, works of art are *invented*. But, as usual, things are not quite as simple as they appear. Many great artists have felt that their work is as much one of discovery as of invention – that the form is somehow already out there waiting to be unpacked. 'The pages are still blank', said the novelist Vladimir Nabokov (1899–1977), 'but there is a miraculous feeling of the words being there, written in invisible ink and clamoring to become visible.' This idea is nicely illustrated by Michelangelo's (1475–1564) famous unfinished sculptures known as *The Prisoners*. When we look at these figures, it is hard to avoid the feeling that they are already in the marble and are simply waiting to be released with the help of the sculptor's chisel.

Just as some people have argued that art is as much discovery as invention, so others have argued that science is as much invention as discovery. To support this idea, they point out that even if a scientific law is useful and illuminating, it may eventually turn out to be false. That, after all, was the fate of Newtonian physics. So rather than think of scientific laws as eternal truths, we should perhaps see them as *useful fictions* which help us to make sense of reality.

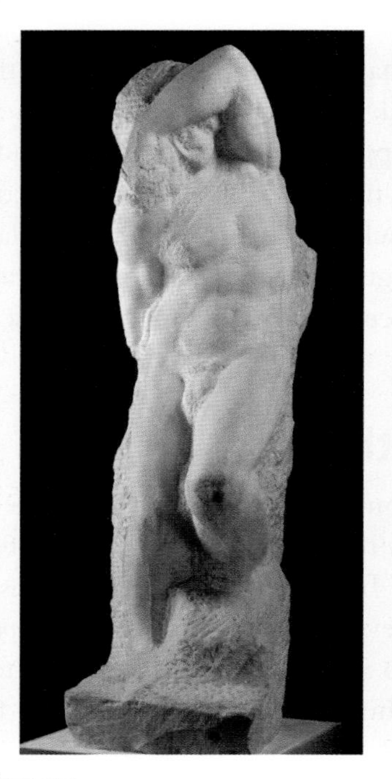

Figure 16.16 Michelangelo: *The Prisoners*

Nevertheless, it may still make sense to say that science is more discovered than invented, and that art is more invented than discovered. To see why, imagine the following situation. A building is on fire and the last surviving copy of Darwin's *The Origin of Species* is in one room and the last surviving copy of Shakespeare's *Hamlet* is in the other room. Ignoring the danger to yourself, you leap into the building, but you only have time to rescue one of the books. Which should you rescue?

There is an argument for saying that you should go for *Hamlet* rather than *The Origin of Species*. Why? Because if Darwin's manuscript goes up in smoke, then sooner or later someone else will come up with the theory of evolution. (In fact, Alfred Russel Wallace, 1823–1913, came up with the theory around the same time as Darwin.) But if Shakespeare's manuscript meets a similar fate, no one else is going to write *Hamlet*. The play as we know it will be lost for ever.

What this example suggests is not that works of art are more precious than works of science, but that there is an impersonal aspect to scientific discoveries that is lacking in the case of the arts. It is this which justifies our using the word 'discovery' more in the case of the former than in that of the latter.

Science and art as complements

Another way of thinking about the relation between the sciences and the arts is to say that they are complementary ways of making sense of the world and that for a balanced outlook we need both. Following this line of thought, it could be argued that while science looks at things from the outside, art looks at them from the inside. Einstein once said that science does not give the taste of the soup. What I think he meant by this is that while science can tell you what soup is made of and why it is good for you, it has nothing to say about what it feels like to drink soup on a cold day.

Admittedly, soup is not a major theme in the arts, but they do deal with other complex experiences. Think again of an emotion such as love. While science may be able to tell you what happens to your hormones and heart-beat when you fall in love, it is to the arts that many people instinctively turn to make sense of the *experience* of love. We are back to the idea of art as the language of the emotions. With this in mind, it could be argued that at the most general level the arts help to remind us that subjective experience is as much a part of the scheme of things as objective measurable facts.

The arts and truth

LQ – Perception: To what extent do the arts enable us to see the world with new eyes?

What, then, can we say about the relationship between the arts and truth? At the literal level, the Martians at the beginning of this chapter would seem to be right in saying that works of art are by definition untrue because they deal with fiction rather than fact. But at a deeper level we might speak of the *paradox of fiction* – the fact that fiction is sometimes able to reveal deep truths about the human condition. While it may seem strange that we human beings often turn to fiction in search of the truth, it also seems to be true!

ACTIVITY 16.24

1. What can science tell us about the nature of love that the arts cannot; and what can the arts tell us about the nature of love that science cannot?
2. Take any work of art, piece of music, or novel, of your choice and explain how it has given you a deeper understanding of some aspect of the human condition.
3. According to Noam Chomsky (1930–), 'It is quite possible – overwhelmingly probable, one might guess – that we will always learn more about human life and human personality from novels than from scientific psychology.' What is your opinion about this?

We have drawn attention to the fact that the arts can help make sense of our experience of the world. Yet the kind of truth we find in them does seem to be different from that found in the sciences. If two scientific theories contradict one another, and one of them is true, then we must conclude that the other one is false. But when it comes to the arts, we may feel that two quite different works can be equally revealing of the truth. This suggests that when we look at a work of art, it may be more illuminating to ask, not 'Is it true?' but 'What has the artist seen?' Understood in this way, the arts might be said to contribute richness and depth to our experience of the world.

ACTIVITY 16.25

1. Do you think it makes sense to say that some works of art are 'truer' than others? Illustrate your answer with examples of your choice.
2. Do you think we can speak of artistic progress in the way we usually speak of scientific progress? What does this suggest to you about the similarities or differences between art and science?

Conclusion

We began this chapter with the story of Martians who have no understanding or appreciation of the arts. For human beings, however, a life without the arts is difficult to imagine and it would surely be a cold, grey, drab affair. (A single day without music would be more than some people could bear!) Since we derive great pleasure from the arts, that in itself is enough to justify them. But, as we have seen in this chapter, they can also be said to contribute to our knowledge of the world. Typically, great works of art make the familiar strange or make the strange familiar. At their best they can perhaps help us to recognise truths we were previously unaware of and reignite our sense of wonder at the world.

Key points

- Art of one form or another can be found in all cultures, and the desire to make aesthetically pleasing objects seems to be universal.
- Among the criteria for distinguishing art from non-art are the intentions of the artist, the quality of the work, and the response of spectators.
- It could be argued that great art stands the test of time and is inexhaustible in the sense that it constantly reveals new things to us.
- Although it is often said that beauty is in the eye of the beholder, we take seriously the idea that there are standards for judging art.
- According to Immanuel Kant, aesthetic judgements differ from personal tastes in that they are disinterested.
- The copy theory of art says that the purpose of art is to copy reality; but it could be argued that art is not so much a slavish reproduction of reality as a creative reinterpretation of it.
- A second theory sees art as a means of communication which enables us to imaginatively project ourselves into new situations and communicate emotions that lie beyond everyday language.
- According to a third theory, the arts have an educative role and at their best broaden our awareness, develop our empathy and sharpen our moral intuitions.
- Despite the obvious differences between the arts and sciences, reason and emotion play an important role in both of these areas of knowledge.

Key terms

aesthetics

avant-garde

canon

catharsis

disinterested

kitsch

mimetic

Knowledge framework focus

1. *Scope/applications.* What distinguishes art from non-art? Can *anything* be art? Can *everything* be art?
2. *Concepts/language.* Do you need to learn the 'language' of a particular art form before you are able to understand and evaluate it?
3. *Methodology.* To what extent should artistic creativity be constrained by a specific style and to what extent should the only rule be 'Anything goes'?
4. *Historical development.* How have artistic styles changed over history? Why do we commonly speak of scientific progress, but not of artistic progress?
5. *Relation to personal knowledge.* Are the arts the most personal form of knowledge – more of an 'I' than a 'we'?

IB prescribed essay titles

1. 'In the natural sciences progress can be made, but in the arts this is not possible.' To what extent do you agree? (November 2013)
2. 'Art is a lie that brings us nearer to the truth' (Pablo Picasso). Evaluate this claim in relation to a specific art form (for example, visual arts, literature, theatre). (November 2010 / May 2011)

Further reading

Books

Donald Palmer, *Does the Center Hold?* (Mayfield, 1991), Chapter 10: 'But is it art?'. This chapter gives a clear and readable account of some major theories of art, including those of Plato, Aristotle, Freud, Marx and Wittgenstein.

Ernst Gombrich, *Art and Illusion* (Phaidon, 1960). This classic book by a famous art critic explores the psychology underlying the visual arts. Gombrich likens the visual arts to a language and he explores the way in which artistic styles and conventions influence the way we see the world.

Online articles

Steven Pinker, 'How Much Art Can the Brain Take?' Adapted from *How the Mind Works* (Penguin, 1999).

Lewis Wolpert, 'Which Side Are You On?', *The Observer,* 10 March 2002.

Patricia Cohen, 'A Textbook Example of Ranking Artworks', *New York Times,* 4 August 2008.

Ethics

17

Broken promises don't upset me. I just think, 'Why did they believe me?'

Jack Handey, 1949–

These are my principles and if you don't like them – I have others.

Groucho Marx, 1890–1977

Whenever I'm caught between two evils, I take the one I've never tried.

Mae West, 1892–1980

I am human and therefore indifferent to nothing done by humans.

Terence, 186–159 BCE

Everything has been figured out, except how to live.

Jean-Paul Sartre, 1905–80

Happiness is for idiots.

Charles de Gaulle, 1890–1970

Happiness is good health and a bad memory.

Ingrid Bergman, 1915–82

I cannot see how to refute the arguments for the subjectivity of ethical values, but I find myself incapable of believing that all that is wrong with wanton cruelty is that I don't like it.

Bertrand Russell, 1872–1970

There is no duty we so much underrate as the duty of being happy.

Robert Louis Stevenson, 1850–94

Man's brain lives in the twentieth century; the heart of most men still lives in the Stone Age.

Erich Fromm, 1900–80

Introduction

One of the ways in which dogs have an easier time than humans is that they never have to worry about ethics. We, by contrast, have to think for much of the time about what is right and wrong; good and bad. This is because, unlike dogs, we are capable of asking the question 'What should I do?' We are not constantly troubled by this question, and much of our behaviour is guided by habit and custom, but from time to time we have to consider our options and think seriously about the best course of action. Should you keep your promise to help a friend when you are behind with your school work and need to revise for tomorrow's exam? Is it OK to make illegal copies of music? What should you do to help protect the environment? What should you do with your life?

We are also confronted by controversial social questions which force us to think about our values:

- Is abortion ever justified?
- Should drugs be legalised?
- Are there limits to free speech?
- Is there such a thing as a just war?

The problem with questions such as these is that they do not always have a straightforward answer. This may lead us to wonder how, if at all, we can justify our moral judgements and whether it makes sense to talk about 'moral knowledge'.

In this chapter, we will begin by looking at the nature and limitations of moral reasoning. We will then look at two threats to ethics – relativism and self-interest theory. The first claims that there is no such thing as moral knowledge, the second that, even if there is, we are incapable of acting on it. We will suggest that these threats are not as serious as they may appear, and then go on to look at three different theories of ethics:

- religious ethics
- duty ethics
- utilitarianism.

While none of these theories is entirely satisfactory, they are nevertheless useful tools for helping us to think about and make sense of our values.

Moral reasoning

Those who are sceptical about the possibility of moral knowledge claim that moral values and judgements are simply matters of *taste*. This implies that statements like 'abortion is acceptable' / 'abortion is unacceptable' are on a par with statements like 'I like spinach' / 'I don't like spinach'. But the very making of the comparison suggests that this is not right. For we take values more seriously than tastes, and, while there is no arguing about tastes, we expect people to justify their value-judgements and support them with reasons.

A simple model

When we argue about ethics, we typically appeal to a commonly agreed moral principle and then try to show that a particular action falls under it. Consider, for example, the following argument:

> Cheating on a test is wrong.
>
> Tom cheated on the test.
>
> Therefore what Tom did was wrong.

Given that cheating on a test is wrong, then if Tom cheated on the test, it follows that what he did was wrong. This is the way we reason about many moral issues – although, in practice, we usually take the underlying principles for granted.

ACTIVITY 17.1

What moral principle is being assumed in each of the following arguments?

a. Paula shouldn't have kept the money she found – it doesn't belong to her.

b. James was caught bullying his classmates, so he deserves to be punished.

c. Jenkins should be released from prison – he didn't receive a fair trial.

d. Danny is malicious – he's been spreading false rumours about everyone.

e. The president accepted bribes, therefore he should be thrown out of office.

f. Simon shouldn't have told that joke – it wasn't funny, it was racist.

When we argue about ethical questions, there are two things we often look at: whether people are being consistent in their judgements, and whether the alleged facts on which those judgements are based are true.

Figure 17.1 Do different cultures have different views about what counts as cheating? What does the IB's academic honesty policy say about this?

Figure 17.2

Consistency

We expect people to be consistent in their moral judgements, just as we expect them to be consistent in their judgements in other areas of knowledge. If, for example, you think it is wrong for Tom to cheat on a test, then it is surely as wrong for Dick and Harriet to cheat on a test. The belief that people should be consistent in their judgements is closely connected with the belief that they should be *impartial*. If Tom, Dick and Harriet are all caught cheating on a test, then, other things being equal, we expect them to receive a similar punishment.

LQ – Reason: How important is consistency in moral reasoning?

Trying to decide whether or not someone is being consistent is complicated by the fact that they might not only apply moral rules inconsistently, but also hold inconsistent principles.

ACTIVITY 17.2

To what extent do you think the following individuals are morally inconsistent?

a. An anti-abortionist who supports the death penalty.

b. A vegetarian who buys leather shoes.

c. A socialist who educates his children at a private school.

d. A politician who advocates family values and has an extra-marital affair.

e. An environmental activist who drives an SUV (sports utility vehicle).

f. Someone who thinks stealing is wrong but makes illegal copies of music and computer software.

Facts

All kinds of facts are likely to be relevant to our moral judgements, and many arguments that initially look like disputes about values turn out to be disputes about facts. For example, if we are arguing about whether or not John behaved badly at the party on Saturday night, our disagreement may turn on the question of whether or not John punched Ken. Similarly, if we are arguing about the pros and cons of capital punishment, our disagreement may turn on the question of whether or not it is an effective deterrent. In both cases, we can – in principle at least – settle our dispute by looking at the empirical evidence. This is not to say that all moral disagreements can be settled in this way. For there may be cases where we agree on all the facts but make different value-judgements. For example, we may both agree that capital punishment is an effective deterrent, and yet you might be in favour of it because you think it is good for society and I might be against it because I think that all life, including that of a criminal, is sacred.

ACTIVITY 17.3

What facts, if any, are relevant in assessing the following value-judgements?

a. Child labour should be outlawed.

b. Cannabis should be legalised.

c. Genetically modified food should be banned.

d. Rich countries should give more financial aid to poor countries.

Disagreements about moral principles

We began this section by setting up a simple model of moral reasoning: *moral principle – fact – value-judgement*. Our discussion has suggested that many arguments can be settled by looking at the background facts and at whether people are being consistent in their judgements. If we agree that cheating is wrong, and there is factual evidence to establish that Tom was cheating, then Tom himself may be willing to admit that what he did was wrong.

"We've got to draw the line on unethical behaviour and then get as close to that line as possible."

Figure 17.3

If we all share the same underlying moral principles, there is likely to be plenty of scope for moral reasoning. But what if we don't? What if Tom thinks there is nothing wrong with cheating? What if the president thinks it is OK to take bribes? What if Simon approves of racism? What if someone has a whole set of values that are diametrically opposed to our own? How, if at all, can we convince them that they are wrong? Perhaps we can't! Perhaps our values have no ultimate justification. Perhaps our moral rules are no more universal than the grammatical rules of the language we speak!

Moral relativism

According to **moral relativism** our values are determined by the society we grow up in, and there are no universal values. Moral values are simply customs or conventions that vary from culture to culture. ('Ethics' and 'morality' are both derived from words that originally meant 'custom'.) Just as people drive on the left in some countries and on the right in others, so some cultures eat pork while others prohibit it; some are monogamous while others are polygamous; and some bury their dead while others cremate them.

KT – moral relativism: the belief that there are no universal values but that our values are determined by the society in which we grow up

Arguments for moral relativism

There are two main arguments for moral relativism: the diversity argument and the lack of foundations argument.

The diversity argument

According to the diversity argument, the sheer variety of moral practices suggests that there are no objective moral values. The dietary, marriage and burial practices mentioned above might not seem to reflect any very serious differences in values. But you don't have to look very hard to find examples of more unsettling practices. According to anthropologists, there are, or have been, cultures which have permitted such things as: keeping slaves; female genital mutilation; killing adulterers; burning widows on the funeral pyres of their dead husbands; slaughtering prisoners by ripping the hearts out of their bodies; killing unproductive members of society; and cannibalism.

The sheer diversity of such practices has been enough to convince some people of the truth of moral relativism. Of course, given the way we have been brought up, we are likely to find such practices barbaric; but since we must assume that the people engaging in them saw nothing wrong with them, it is tempting to conclude that morality, like beauty, is in the eye of the beholder.

ACTIVITY 17.4

1. Do you think there is a difference between moral values and customs or conventions?
2. Which of the following would you say are morally wrong and which would you say are simply matters of convention?
   a. You should not burn your country's flag.
   b. A man should not go to work wearing a dress.
   c. You should not persecute minority groups.
   d. A woman should not have more than one husband.
   e. You should not torture the innocent.
   f. You should not have sex with an animal.

g. You should not use dead people for dog food.
h. You should not execute adulterers.
i. You should not execute murderers.
j. You should not eat meat.

3. To what extent do you think you can predict someone's moral beliefs from a knowledge of their cultural background?

LQ – Mathematics: Do moral truths exist in the same way as mathematical truths?

The lack of foundations argument

The second argument for relativism is that moral values are somehow ungrounded or lacking foundation. There does not seem to be an independent 'moral reality' against which we can test our values to see if they are true or false, and this suggests they are simply the result of the way we have been brought up and conditioned by society.

We usually settle disputes in other areas of knowledge by appealing to perception or reason, but neither of these appeals seems to work when we are arguing about values. We cannot appeal to perception because we cannot see values in the way that we can see shapes and sizes and colours: and we cannot appeal to reason because there does not seem to be any logical way of getting from an *is* statement to an *ought* statement. Consider, for example, the following argument:

Some people in the world are starving.
I have more food than I need.
Therefore, I *ought* to give some of my food to the starving.

This argument may be emotionally appealing, but the conclusion does not follow from the premises. Indeed, from a purely logical point of view, it is no better than saying:

Some people in the world are starving.
I have more food than I need.
Therefore, lucky me!

The Scottish philosopher David Hume (1711–76) dramatised the gap between an 'is' and an 'ought' by observing that, ''tis not contrary to reason to prefer the destruction of the whole world to the scratching of my finger'. This may sound like an extreme example, but it could be argued that most people worry more about their own minor problems than they do about world poverty.

We saw earlier that, *given* certain moral principles, we can use reason to derive a particular moral judgement (e.g. *given* that people with more food than they need ought to give some of it to the starving, and I have more food than I need, then it follows that I *ought* to give some of it to the starving). However, if we cannot justify these principles themselves, then it might seem that we have no choice but to accept moral relativism.

Does relativism imply tolerance?

One of the things that attracts some people to moral relativism is that it seems to encourage a tolerant 'live and let live' attitude to other cultures. Since different cultures have different beliefs, it would surely be arrogant to assume that *our own* culture's values are right and everyone else's are wrong. Such a dogmatic attitude can easily lead to **cultural imperialism** – that is, to one culture imposing *its* values on other cultures. (History suggests that conquering nations have routinely given the defeated the choice between conversion and death.) Surely it is more reasonable to say that we have our values and they have theirs, and we have no more right to condemn their values than they have to condemn ours.

KT – cultural imperialism: a powerful foreign culture imposing its values on a weaker indigenous culture

Despite the value of tolerance as an antidote to cultural imperialism, we cannot in fact conjure tolerance out of moral relativism. To see why not, imagine that you come across a culture – let us call them the Thugs – imposing their values on another culture. As a good relativist, you argue with them and insist that they have no right to impose their values on other people. But what if they reply, 'In our culture it is OK to impose our values on other people, and you have no right to impose your value that you-shouldn't-impose-your-values-on-other-people on us!' What the Thugs are, in effect, saying is that while tolerance may be a value in *your* culture, it is not a value in *their* culture. As a consistent relativist, you are obliged to say that their intolerant values are no worse than your tolerant values. If, on the other hand, you want to insist that *everyone* should be tolerant, you are implicitly saying that there is at least one universal value – namely, tolerance – and you cannot then call yourself a relativist. What comes out of this example is that *the belief in universal tolerance is not consistent with moral relativism.*

Once moral relativism is separated from the belief in tolerance, it becomes a much less attractive position. A well-known – and some would say compelling – objection to it is that it seems to leave us with no way of answering the committed Nazi who says that in *his* value system genocide is acceptable. The he's-got-his-values-and-I've-got-mine-and-who-am-I-to-say-he's-wrong response seems completely inappropriate in this case. For we surely want to say that the Nazi really *is* wrong – as wrong as anyone could be about anything.

ACTIVITY 17.5

1. Imagine that you arrive in a 'democratic' country in which adult women have the vote but men have no political power. When you interview them, the men tell you that they are quite happy with the situation, that public life is for women, and a man's place is in the home. To what extent would you accept the situation, and to what extent would you try to 're-educate' the men and make them see the extent to which they have been indoctrinated?
2. Which of the following 'cultural practices' should we tolerate and which should we seek to have banned?

a. Punishing adultery by stoning to death
b. Punishing murder by lethal injection
c. Female genital mutilation
d. Infanticide
e. Imprisoning suspected terrorists without trial
f. Discriminating against minority groups

3. Read 'Relative values: a dialogue' at the end of this chapter (on page 505) and answer the following questions.
   a. According to Jack, our moral beliefs are simply the result of the way in which we have been brought up. Could the same be said about all of our beliefs?
   b. Assess the exchange between Jill and Jack concerning relative values. Who do you think gets the better of this exchange?
   c. If Jack is a relativist, then he must accept Jill's belief that values are objective as 'true for her'. To what extent does this weaken his own position?

Arguments against moral relativism

There are two ways of responding to the threat posed by moral relativism. First, it could be argued that, despite appearances, there are in fact some core values that have been accepted by all cultures. Since human beings have broadly similar needs and are confronted by broadly similar problems, it is plausible to think that they will come up with similar rules to regulate communal life. Perhaps not surprisingly, there is evidence to suggest that every society has rules of some kind to limit violence, protect property and promote honesty. In fact, it is difficult to imagine how a society could survive and flourish if it inflicted needless suffering on its members, encouraged theft and honoured deception.

LQ – History: Does history show that we have made moral progress?

But the worrying fact is that, for much of history, people have had no moral concern for outsiders who do not belong to their community and they have sometimes treated them with the kind of indifference we might treat lobsters. For example, the Wari tribe of the Amazon considered anyone who was not a member of the tribe as 'edible'; the Spanish Conquistadors managed to convince themselves that the people they encountered in the New World were sub-human – and then proceeded to butcher them with a clear conscience.

There are clearly some dark and disturbing chapters in the moral history of the human species. But if it is true that all communities have regulated themselves by some recognisably moral values, then it could be argued that their treatment of outsiders was in some sense a *factual error* which they could, in principle at least, be reasoned out of. The Wari were wrong to think that outsiders were nothing but a potential meal; and the Conquistadors were wrong to think that American Indians were not fully human. The optimistic interpretation of our moral history is that we have gradually expanded the moral circle from the tribe, to the nation, to the race, and to the whole of mankind, as we have come to recognise our common humanity.

ACTIVITY 17.6

1. Compare and contrast the moral codes of some of the world's great religions. How much overlap is there between them?
2. Which five values would you say have the best claim to be universal and why?
3. We have clearly made scientific progress over the last three hundred years. Does it also make sense to speak of moral progress? Give reasons.

A second possible response to moral relativism is to say that we can in fact justify our values. For it could be argued that some core values – such as the belief that it is wrong to inflict needless suffering on other people – are intuitively obvious, and that scepticism about such values is no more justified than any other form of scepticism. Admittedly, we cannot prove that our basic moral intuitions are true; but if you can't just see that, for example, random torture is wrong, there is probably nothing to be done to convince you. Fortunately, the vast majority of people believe that the statement 'random torture is wrong' is at least as obvious as 2 + 2 = 4.

We should, however, be careful about appealing to intuition as a *general* way of justifying our moral beliefs. For when it comes to detailed questions of right and wrong, there is no consensus about what is intuitively obvious. (You cannot, for example, resolve the abortion debate by appealing to intuition.) Nevertheless, if we could at least agree on a small number of core intuitions, these would establish boundary conditions that any viable theory of ethics must satisfy.

ACTIVITY 17.7

1. Just as a person who cannot distinguish red and green is said to be colour blind, can we say that a person who cannot distinguish right and wrong is morally blind?
2. To what extent can immorality be seen as a form of mental illness? Do you, for example, think that serial killers are best described as 'bad' or 'mad'?

Self-interest theory

Having done something to diffuse moral relativism, we will now consider another idea that threatens to undermine our values. According to **self-interest theory**, human beings are always and everywhere selfish. Since selfish behaviour is usually seen as the opposite of moral behaviour, this theory suggests that, even if there are objective moral values, we are incapable of living up to them. We will consider four arguments for self-interest theory:

- the definitional argument
- the evolutionary argument
- the hidden benefits argument
- the fear of punishment argument.

We will also look at criticisms of each of these arguments.

KT – self-interest theory: the claim that human beings are universally selfish

Figure 17.4 A volunteer helping an elderly person. To what extent are we capable of genuine altruism?

The definitional argument

According to the definitional argument it is true by definition – that is, *necessarily* true – that everyone is selfish. The idea behind this argument is very simple: you are being selfish when you do what you want to do, and you always end up doing what you most want to do – otherwise you wouldn't do it.

You might object that we often find ourselves doing things that we don't want to do; but, according to self-interest theory, this is not true. Imagine that one afternoon you have a choice between playing tennis – which you enjoy – and visiting a lonely elderly lady – which you feel obliged to do, but do not enjoy. What do you do? We would normally say that if you decide to play tennis you are being selfish, and if you decide to visit the elderly lady, you are being *un*selfish or **altruistic**. However, according to the definitional argument, even if you visit the elderly lady, there is a sense in which you are *still* being selfish. For once we take into account the fact that you will feel *guilty* if you don't visit the elderly lady, overall you would rather visit her than play tennis.

KT – altruism: selfless behaviour in which we put other people's welfare before our own

This simple, but apparently powerful, argument seems to mean that genuine altruism is not merely difficult, but *impossible*. To see this, compare Donald Trump – the American property developer – with Mother Teresa – the Catholic nun who devoted her life to helping the poor. At first sight, the contrast between these two people could not be greater; for while Donald Trump spends his time making money, Mother Teresa spent hers helping the poor. However, according to self-interest theory they are both doing what they want but merely have different tastes. Donald Trump gets his buzz out of making money, while Mother Teresa got hers out of helping the poor; and while Donald Trump would probably hate doing what Mother Teresa did, Mother Teresa would have hated doing what Donald Trump does. Since both of them are doing what they most like doing, we seem forced to conclude that they are both equally selfish!

RLS – Headline: 'Man is rescued by stranger on subway tracks'. Is altruism more a matter of reason or emotion?

Criticisms of the definitional argument

The problem with the definitional argument is that it effectively robs the word 'selfish' of its meaning. For if people are selfish no matter what they do, then it can no longer be a criticism to describe someone as selfish. Since no evidence is allowed to stand against it, what initially looked like an interesting empirical claim collapses into an empty truism!

The Mother Teresa-Donald Trump example shows how counter-intuitive the definitional argument is. Even if we admit that people always do what they most want to do, common sense suggests that we should distinguish between **self-regarding desires** and **other-regarding desires** and use the word 'selfish' to describe only the former. We usually praise someone if they do nice things for other people, but not if they do nice things for themselves. If I buy myself an ice-cream, you are

KT – self-regarding desires: desires which are focused on the self

KT – other-regarding desires: desires which are focused on other people unlikely to think well of me, but if I buy *you* an ice-cream you might. The fact that I may get pleasure from buying you something does not mean that my action is selfish, but simply that I get pleasure from your pleasure. What could be nicer than a world in which everyone got pleasure from helping other people?

The evolutionary argument

The second argument for self-interest theory takes its inspiration from the theory of evolution, and claims that human beings are naturally selfish creatures who are programmed to pursue their own interests. To succeed in the struggle for survival and get our genes into the next generation, we inevitably spend a huge amount of time looking after 'number one', and other people's interests usually concern us only to the extent that they affect our own. According to this view, the reason capitalism is a more successful political system than socialism is that it taps into our natural self-interest and competitiveness.

Criticisms of the evolutionary argument

The problem with this argument is that there is plenty of evidence to suggest that empathy and altruism are as much a part of our biological inheritance as selfishness. In one intriguing experiment, monkeys refused to pull a lever that would give them food if pulling it also gave an electric shock to one of their companions. They were, in other words, willing to sacrifice food to avoid causing pain to another monkey. With regard to our own species, empathy – which is the emotional basis for altruism – has been observed in babies as young as one year. For example, if a baby sees its mother crying, it may try to console her by giving her a security blanket, or a favourite toy. This suggests that empathy may be a natural part of our make-up. The bottom line is that traits such as empathy and helpfulness pay in evolutionary terms. As the biologist Edward O. Wilson observes: 'Cooperative individuals generally survive longer and leave more offspring.'

LQ – Emotion: Is ethics more a matter of the head or of the heart?

The hidden benefits argument

The third argument for self-interest theory is that we get various hidden benefits – such as gratitude, praise and a positive image of ourselves – from being kind to other people. Furthermore, if we help other people when they are in trouble, then we can ask for their help when we need it. Admittedly, we sometimes help other people who will never be able to 'repay the debt', and we may do socially useful things such as donate blood. Such activities not only make us feel good about ourselves, but also enhance our reputation as 'good people' and this, too, can be socially advantageous.

ACTIVITY 17.8

1. If you went out of your way to help someone in trouble, would it bother you if they showed no gratitude?
2. If you helped a friend when she had a problem, would you be annoyed if she refused to help you when you had a problem?
3. If you gave a lot of money to charity, would you rather your friends knew what you had done, or would you rather they did not know?

Figure 17.5 What motivates people to give money to beggars?

Consider, for example, a mother's love for her child, which is sometimes held up as the highest example of altruism. A supporter of self-interest theory might argue that, since a mother loves only *her* children and not *all* children, such love is still self-interested. Many parents are competitive on behalf of their offspring and are anxious for them to do better than other people's children. Such natural competitiveness turned into murderous rivalry in 1991 when a Texas 'cheerleader Mom' plotted the murder of her daughter's rival for a place on the cheerleader team! Fortunately, most parents do not go quite so far in trying to further their children's prospects!

What, then, of a hero who lays down his life for his friends or a martyr who sacrifices it for a noble cause? Well, even heroes and martyrs could be said to get some kind of satisfaction from their sacrifice. They may, for example, think of the posthumous fame they will achieve, or the rewards that await them in heaven. Perhaps as a young child, you occasionally thought to yourself, 'I wish I was dead! . . . And then they'd be sorry!' You may then have imagined your parents weeping at your grave, and saying: 'If only we had been kinder to our son when he was alive!' Such are the consolations of martyrdom!

Criticisms of the hidden benefits argument

The problem with the hidden benefits argument is that, although we do often help other people expecting that they will at some point return the favour, there are some situations in which this cannot be our motive. Consider the everyday example of someone leaving a tip in a restaurant they will never visit again. From a self-interested point of view, this is hardly rational behaviour; but people do it all the time – from, it seems, a sense of fairness. You may, of course, feel good about yourself if you leave a tip, but this hardly justifies calling it selfish.

There are other more dramatic examples of altruism. During the Second World War, the people of Chambon in France risked their lives to hide Jews fleeing from

Nazi persecution. Similarly, a German Czech called Oskar Schindler took huge personal risks to save the lives of hundreds of Jews. Again, these people doubtless got satisfaction from what they did; but perhaps what really matters is not so much their motives – which are often obscure – as their actions. As one survivor rescued by Schindler observed: 'I don't know what his motives were . . . But I don't give a damn. What's important is that he saved our lives.'

The existence of 'ordinary heroes' who have other-regarding rather than self-regarding desires, and who are sometimes willing to take great personal risks to help other people, effectively takes the sting out of self-interest theory. As philosopher David Hume observed:

> *I esteem the man whose self-love, by whatever means, is so directed as to give him a concern for others, and render him serviceable to society; as I hate or despise him who has no regard to anything beyond his own gratifications and enjoyments.*

The fear of punishment argument

The fourth argument for self-interest theory says that the main thing that keeps us in line and prevents our doing wrong is fear of punishment. When people are thinking of doing something wrong, they usually ask themselves, 'What if I get caught?' The fear of a fine, imprisonment or even death is enough to deter most people. In situations where law and order break down and there is no longer any fear of getting caught, things can quickly revert to the law of the jungle. Imagine, for example, that the police and security guards in your town went on strike for a day, or a week, or a month. What do you think would happen? Past evidence suggests there would be chaos. Here is a brief description of what happened during a one-day strike by the Montreal police back in 1969:

Figure 17.6 Rioting in London, 2011. How do people behave when law and order break down?

At 8:00 AM on October 17, 1969 . . . the Montreal police went on strike. By 11:20 AM the first bank was robbed. By noon most downtown stores had closed because of looting. Within a few more hours, taxi drivers burned down the garage of a limousine service that had competed with them for airport customers, a rooftop sniper killed a provincial police officer, rioters broke into several hotels and restaurants, and a doctor slew a burglar in his suburban home. By the end of the day, six banks had been robbed, a hundred shops had been looted, twelve fires had been set, forty carloads of storefront glass had been broken, and three million dollars in property damage had been inflicted, before city authorities had to call in the army . . . to restore order.

Criticisms of the fear of punishment argument

Although law enforcement plays an important role in maintaining social order, there is no reason to think that *all* good behaviour is motivated by fear. We cannot really explain the behaviour of people like Mother Teresa in this way. A cynic might argue that religious people are motivated primarily by the fear of being punished in the afterlife. But God would probably take a dim view of people who did good simply to avoid punishment. In fact, most of the world's great religions – at least in their more sophisticated form – teach that virtue is its own reward.

In one of his dialogues, the Greek philosopher Plato (428–348 BCE) wrote about a fabled ring called the *ring of Gyges*, which enabled its bearer to become invisible at will. If you found such a ring, you might be tempted to transgress; but there are surely things you would still be unwilling to do. It is likely that most people would not want to harm the weak, deprive the needy, persecute the oppressed, corrupt the innocent, betray their friends, or dishonour their families – even if there was no danger of being caught. And that is surely enough to suggest that not *all* good behaviour is motivated simply by fear of punishment.

ACTIVITY 17.9

1. If you discovered the ring of Gyges, how, if at all, would it affect your behaviour?
2. If the perfect crime existed, would you be tempted to commit it? (Imagine you could break into the computer of a major bank, shave a few cents off each customer's account, and end up with millions of dollars for yourself. No one will ever notice what has happened, let alone be able to trace the crime to you.)

How selfish are we?

We might conclude from this discussion that, although we often pursue our own interests at the expense of other people, we are not *always* selfish and we *are* in fact capable of genuine altruism. However, this still leaves plenty of room for disagreement about the *extent* of altruism. According to one economist, 'the average human being is about 95 percent selfish in the narrow sense of the term'; but people who have experienced the kindness of strangers at first hand may well have a more positive view of human nature.

ACTIVITY 17.10

1. Do you think it makes more sense to say that people are basically good and corrupted by society, or that people are basically bad and must be kept in line by society?
2. Do you think society works best when each individual pursues his own best interest, or do you think this is a recipe for disaster?

Theories of ethics

The discussion in the last two sections has done something to neutralise the threats posed by moral relativism and self-interest theory. While it may be that *some* values are relative and that people are *often* selfish, we do not have to conclude that *all* values are relative or that people are *always* selfish. This leaves space for the idea that there is such a thing as *moral knowledge* and that people are capable of acting on this knowledge. We should now perhaps look for a more systematic and coherent approach to ethics which enables us to make sense of our various moral beliefs and intuitions. In what follows, we will briefly consider religious ethics, and then look in more detail at duty ethics and utilitarianism.

Religious ethics

LQ – Religion: How have religions shaped people's moral beliefs?

Perhaps the simplest approach to ethics would be to find an authoritative rule book which told us what moral principles to follow. Some people believe that such books are to be found in religion. The world's great religions have been, and continue to be, important sources of moral insight and guidance to millions of people. However, they do not settle all the questions, or free us from the responsibility of thinking about ethics. We still have to decide which sacred texts to follow and how to interpret and apply their rules. The Christian Bible, for example, says that if anyone works on the Sabbath they should be put to death (Exodus 35:2). It is unlikely that any religious people would take this injunction seriously today, and they would probably point out that religious ideas change and develop over time. If we reject what some people have called the 'idolatry of literalism', this leads to the idea that we should follow the *spirit* rather than the letter of a moral code.

The Greek philosopher Plato argued that we cannot derive ethics from religion. In one of his dialogues, he raised the following tantalising question: Is something good because God says it is good, or does God say that it is good because it *is* good? On the one hand, if something is good simply because God says it is good, then if God suddenly decided that murder was good, it would be good. Most people would reject this conclusion. On the other hand, if God says that something is good because it *is* good, then it seems that values are independent of God and we do not need to appeal to Him in order to justify them. This suggests that, rather than deriving our values from religion, we already have values by which we decide whether to accept or reject what religion tells us to do. Since a religion-based ethics is, in any case, not going to satisfy atheists, we will need to look at other ways of justifying our moral values.

Figure 17.7

ACTIVITY 17.11

1. According to the New Testament in the Christian Bible, 'it is easier for a camel to go through the eye of a needle than for a rich man to enter the kingdom of God' (Matthew 19:24). How do you think this statement should be interpreted?
2. Fasting is one of the 'five pillars' of Islam. Can a person still be a good Muslim if they do not fast during the holy month of Ramadan?
3. Since the Pope condemns birth control, can a person still be a good Catholic if they practise birth control?
4. Can religious texts give us moral guidance on the use of genetic engineering and other technologies that were unheard of when such texts were written?
5. The Russian novelist Fyodor Dostoevsky said that, 'if God is dead, everything is permitted'. What do you think he meant by this? Do you agree or disagree with him?

LQ – Natural sciences: Are scientists responsible for how their discoveries are used?

Duty ethics

According to some philosophers, ethics is fundamentally a matter of doing your duty and fulfilling your obligations. Since the word 'duty' has sometimes been associated with mindlessly obeying orders, this idea has not always had a good press. But we do take seriously the idea that people have duties. You would, for example, probably agree that a teacher has a duty to help you pass your exams and a doctor has a duty to try to cure you. Most people would prefer to talk about their **rights** rather than their duties. But it is worth noting that *rights* and *duties are two different sides of the same coin*. If, for example, you have a duty not to steal, there must be a corresponding right to property; and if you have a right to life, there must be a corresponding duty not to kill.

KT – rights: moral principles which lay down what people are free to do or entitled to expect from other people

ACTIVITY 17.12

1. Imagine that you and a group of space colonists have just arrived on a fertile and uninhabited planet and decide to make a ten-point declaration of rights. What rights would you include in your declaration? How would you justify your choice?
2. What difference do you think it would make if we replaced the UN Declaration of Human Rights with a UN Declaration of Human Duties?
3. If everyone has the right to life, who exactly has a duty to keep alive the thousands of people who starve to death every day? Do you?

KT – duty ethics: the belief that ethics is fundamentally a matter of doing your duty and fulfilling your obligations

If **duty ethics** is to be viable, we will, of course, need to know what our duties are. One idea might be to consult a table of commandments which list all the thou-shalt-nots. But which table should we consult and how can the duties it imposes on us be *justified*? Perhaps we can appeal to intuition; but the problem is that people may have conflicting intuitions. Some people, for example, believe that we have a duty not to commit adultery; others do not. So if our list of duties is not to be arbitrary, we need to find a more compelling criterion for determining what they are.

According to the philosopher Immanuel Kant (1724–1804) our duties are not arbitrary and we can determine what they are in an objective way by appealing to *reason*. Since Kant's approach to ethics has been so influential, we will devote the rest of this section to an exploration of his ideas.

Kant's approach to ethics

Kant argued that the way to decide if something is your duty is to see whether or not you can consistently generalise it. Imagine that you are wondering whether or not it is OK to jump the lunch queue because you can't be bothered to wait in line. According to Kant, you should ask yourself what would happen if everyone did that. The answer is, of course, that there would be chaos. Indeed, if everyone jumped the queue, there would be no queue left to jump! So if you try to generalise the rule, 'Jump the queue whenever you feel like it', you end up with a contradiction. Therefore, it is your duty *not* to jump the queue whenever you feel like it.

Kant used a similar line of reasoning to argue that we should keep our promises and refrain from such things as stealing, murder and suicide. Consider promising; imagine that you wish to break a promise because it is inconvenient to keep it. Using the generalisation test, you should ask yourself, 'What would happen if everyone broke their promises when they felt like it?' The result is again a contradiction. If you say to someone, 'I promise to do X unless I change my mind', then you have not made a promise at all. To promise to do X is to commit yourself to doing it even if it becomes inconvenient. That is *supposed* to be why people make marriage vows. After all, there would be little point in making a vow such as, 'For richer and for poorer, in sickness and in health – unless someone better turns up'! Since you cannot consistently generalise the rule 'Break your promises whenever you feel like it', it is your duty *not* to break your promises.

ACTIVITY 17.13

1. Using the examples of queue-jumping and marriage vows as a model, construct arguments to show what our duty is with regard to each of the following:
   a. Stealing
   b. Cheating on tests
   c. Polluting the environment
   d. Voting in elections
   e. Suicide
   f. Writing honest references for university applications
2. How convincing are these arguments?

RLS – Headline: 'Campaign to legalise assisted suicide in South Africa'. What light can moral theories throw on the question of whether assisted suicide is ever justified?

Figure 17.8

KT – special pleading: making an exception in your own case that you would not find acceptable if it came from someone else

KT – egoism: putting your own interests before those of other people

The reason Kant attached so much importance to the idea of consistency may have been because he was aware of the extent to which we engage in **special pleading** and make excuses to justify our own behaviour that we would not find acceptable if they came from someone else. Our natural **egoism** encourages us to think that while rules should *generally* be respected, we are special and they do not apply to *us*. Consider, for example, how some people casually lie to their friends without thinking anything of it, and yet are outraged if they discover that their friends have done the same thing to them. To counter this tendency, the great Muslim mystic Al-Ghazali (1058–1111) gave the following advice:

> *If you want to know the foulness of lying for yourself, consider the lying of someone else and how you shun it and despise the man who lies and regard his communication as foul. Do the same with regard to all your own vices, for you do not realize the foulness of your vices from your own case, but from someone else's.*

Figure 17.9

At the heart of Kant's approach to ethics is the idea that we should each adopt a dual conception of ourselves as not only *me* but also *one among others*. For reason demands that we should at least *try* to be impartial and look at things objectively without making exceptions in our own case. This idea lies behind the so-called **golden rule**, 'Do as you would be done by', versions of which can be found in all of the world's great religions.

KT – golden rule: the rule found in many cultures which says that you should do as you would be done by

KT – veil of ignorance: a thought experiment in which the morality of an issue is decided by imagining that our places in society are redistributed and we do not know what position we will be assigned

A good way of trying to be objective is to imagine various situations through what philosophers have called a **veil of ignorance**. Imagine, for example, that person *X* does action *p* to person *Y*, and that you are either person *X* or person *Y*, but you do not know which one. How do you feel about the action? Do you think it is acceptable or unacceptable? (A good way of getting two children to share a cake fairly is to suggest that one of them cut the cake and the other one choose which half to take.) This method – which is really a generalisation of Al-Ghazali's advice – can be an effective way of getting us to think more objectively about ethics.

Value and dignity

Kant uses the dual conception of the self to argue not only that no individual should be given preferential treatment, but also that no individual should be discriminated against. For example, he claimed that it is never right to sacrifice one individual's life for the greater good. To explain why not, we can simply reverse the dual conception of the self. For an individual is not only *one among others* but also a *me*, and his life is the only one that he has. Therefore, he should never be treated as a mere means to some further end. In this respect, there is a crucial difference between objects and persons, which Kant marks by saying that, while the former have *value*, only the latter have *dignity*. To see the difference between value and dignity, compare the following two situations.

1. A friend borrows your laptop computer and accidentally drops it. The computer is broken beyond repair and you are furious. Being a decent fellow, your friend immediately goes out and buys you an identical computer to replace the one he broke. Assuming that he also replaces the software and copies the files that were on your old machine, you will probably conclude that no great harm has been done. You no longer have your original computer, but you have a replacement that is in every respect as good as the one that was broken.

2. You are in hospital dying of an incurable disease. Your parents come to visit you every day and weep at your bedside. They are devastated by the thought of your impending death. But you are incredibly brave and do what you can to comfort them. One day they arrive looking a great deal more cheerful. 'We have some good news for you', they say. 'The doctor tells us that although you are going to die, we can clone you, so that after your death we will be able to replace you. Although your clone won't actually be you, he will look like you and in many ways behave like you. We can give him your bedroom and your old toys. Isn't it wonderful news?' Think about how you would feel if you heard this speech. How dare they imagine that they can replace *you*! You are a unique individual and, unlike a broken computer, you cannot simply be replaced by someone genetically identical to you.

According to Kant, if something has value it can be replaced by something else of equal value, but if it has dignity it is irreplaceable. Since individuals have dignity rather than merely value, it is never right to sacrifice their lives for the greater good.

The importance of motives

Another key aspect of Kant's ethics is that the moral value of an action is determined by the *motive* for which it is done rather than the *consequences* that follow from it. Many of our everyday moral judgements seem to reflect this principle. If you are trying to be helpful but things turn out badly, we do not usually blame you – after all, you meant well. On the other hand, if you intend to harm someone, but your efforts are not successful, we will still think of you as a bad person. In practice, we tend to blame someone more for serious accidents than for minor ones; you are likely to be more annoyed if someone drops ten plates than if they break one plate – especially if they are *your* plates. Kant would say that is an immature way of thinking, and insist that all that really matters is the motive for your action.

Kant not only focused on motives but also insisted that to be truly moral our actions should be motivated by *reason* rather than *feeling*. He had a low opinion of feelings because he thought that they are too unreliable to justify our values. If you only do good things when you *feel* like it, what happens if you feel like helping someone today but not tomorrow, or helping person A but not person B? Kant sought to avoid this problem by basing values on reason rather than feeling, and insisting that reason tells us we have certain duties regardless of what we may feel. We can in fact distinguish at least three different motives for doing good:

1. you expect something in return

2. sympathy

3. duty.

According to Kant, your action has moral value only if you act on motive 3. You might agree that if you help someone only if you expect something in return, then although this might make pragmatic sense, it does not deserve moral praise. However, it is harder to understand why Kant thinks that being motivated by sympathy has no moral value. I think Kant would say that to the extent that someone is a *naturally* friendly and sympathetic person they do not deserve any praise for it. After all, they

Figure 17.10

can't *help* being like that, any more than someone who is naturally anti-social can help being the way they are. Somewhat paradoxically, this suggests that a naturally anti-social person deserves more moral praise for being kind and friendly than a naturally sociable person!

ACTIVITY 17.14

1. If a cat jumps into a pram and attacks a baby, who deserves more praise for removing it: someone who likes cats, or someone who is frightened of cats?
2. Who deserves more praise: a person who helps another person because they like them, or a person who helps another person even though they don't like them?
3. How does Kant's view differ from the view attributed to Hume in our discussion of self-interest theory?

Criticisms of Kant

Despite its positive features, Kant's approach to ethics can be criticised on a number of grounds.

Rule worship

To start, some critics have pointed out that it leads to **moral absolutism**. This is the belief that certain moral principles should *always* be followed irrespective of context. To see the problem, consider the ethics of lying. Using the universalisability test, Kant said that you cannot consistently will that people lie whenever they feel like it, because if they did, language would no longer be an effective means of communication. Kant concluded that it is *always* wrong to lie. This is, however, counter-intuitive. Imagine that an axe-wielding maniac rushes into your school screaming that he is going to kill your teacher – who promptly hides in the cupboard. The maniac bursts into your classroom and demands to know where

KT – moral absolutism: the belief that there are universal moral principles which should always be followed irrespective of the context or their consequences the teacher is. Reasoning that you should never lie, you calmly reply 'He's hiding in the cupboard!' Something has clearly gone wrong here, and no one is going to congratulate you for telling the truth. For in this situation you surely *ought* to lie to save the life of your teacher. Kant might say that you can avoid lying by refusing to answer the maniac's question. However, if *you* were the person in the cupboard, you would probably think it was fine to lie and send the maniac off in the wrong direction!

KT – rule worship: blindly following moral rules irrespective of whether or not they are appropriate

The problem with Kant's approach to ethics, then, is that it seems to lead to **rule worship** – that is, to blindly following a moral rule without regard to the consequences. Many people would say that rather than mechanically applying moral principles irrespective of the context, we should try to be sensitive to the details of a situation and make a *judgement* about when it is appropriate to make an exception to a generally agreed principle.

ACTIVITY 17.15

Which of the following is a special case that justifies breaking a generally accepted rule?

1 a. You should respect the highway code, but it's OK to drive through a red light if you are late for work.
  b. You should respect the highway code, but it's OK to drive through a red light if you are taking a critically ill person to hospital.

2 a. You should keep your word, but it is OK to break a social engagement if something more interesting comes up.
  b. You should keep your word, but it is OK to break a social engagement if you have just contracted an infectious disease.

3 a. You should pay your taxes, but it is OK not to pay them if you are short of money this year.
  b. You should pay your taxes, but it is OK not to pay them if they are being spent on a nuclear arms programme.

4 a. Murder is wrong, but it would have been OK to assassinate Hitler in 1942.
  b. Murder is wrong, but it would be OK to kill someone who was planning a terrorist attack.

Conflicts of duty

A related problem is that Kant's ethics leaves us no way of resolving conflicts of duty. Consider, for example, the following dilemmas:

- If a person has been unfaithful to their partner, should they confess and make their partner unhappy, or say nothing and deceive them?
- If your grandmother and a world-famous doctor are trapped in a burning building and you only have time to rescue one of them, should you save your grandmother because she is a family member, or the doctor because of the good she can do for society?

- If your brother is dying of a rare disease and your family cannot afford to buy the drugs that will cure him, are you justified in stealing the drugs?
- If a terrorist group takes a civilian hostage and threatens to kill them unless the government releases five convicted terrorists, should the government give in to their demands?

It is difficult to see how Kant's approach can help us to resolve these kinds of dilemma, for it seems to give us no criterion in accordance with which our duties can be ranked.

ACTIVITY 17.16

1. Explain which two moral principles are in conflict in each of the above dilemmas.
2. Take one of the above dilemmas and give as many arguments as you can for resolving it one way and then as many arguments as you can for resolving it the other way.

Moral coldness

A final problem with Kant's approach to ethics is that it seems to be too focused on reason at the expense of feelings. Allowing that we should try to be consistent in our moral judgements, what outrages most people about, say, war criminals, is not their *inconsistency* but their *inhumanity*. Kant is unable to accommodate this common-sense intuition because he refuses to give any place to feelings in his moral philosophy. As discussed on page 490, he rejected feelings on the grounds that they are unreliable; but, in practice, appeals to reason might be equally ineffective. For just as you cannot appeal to people's sympathy if they have none, so you cannot appeal to their reason if they don't mind being called irrational. (It is, for example, hard to imagine a hardened torturer being bothered by such an accusation.) Furthermore, taking feelings out of moral consideration seems to lead to a cold and heartless ethics. Many people would say that it is better for a husband to help his wife because he *loves* her and *wants* to help her than because it is his *duty* to help her.

We might even reverse Kant's position and argue that feelings are what connect us with other people, and reason is what isolates us. When you see someone in distress, your natural impulse is to help them, but once reason kicks in you might start weighing costs and benefits. In reflecting on what motivated him, one of the inhabitants of Chambon who helped the Jews during the Second World War said: 'The hand of compassion was faster than the calculus of reason.' What he may have meant was that if he had stopped and thought too much about what he was doing, he would probably never have done it. This suggests that reason has its limits and that we would sometimes do better to follow our hearts.

ACTIVITY 17.17

1. 'The advantage of following moral rules is that it helps to avoid special pleading; the disadvantage is that it leads to rule worship.' What role do you think rules should play in moral reasoning?
2. What relevance do the following two quotations from the Irish playwright George Bernard Shaw (1856–1950) have to our discussion of Kant's moral philosophy? Do you agree or disagree with them?
   a. 'Don't do unto others as you would have them do to you – their tastes might be different.'
   b. 'When a stupid man is doing something he is ashamed of, he always declares that it is his duty.'
3. 'What if everyone did that?' 'But they don't!' To what extent does this response undermine Kant's approach to ethics?

Utilitarianism

KT – utilitarianism: the belief that ethics can ultimately be reduced to the principle that we should maximise happiness

Utilitarianism is a deceptively simple theory of ethics, which says that there is one and only one supreme moral principle – that we should seek *the greatest happiness of the greatest number.* This slogan can be reduced to two words: *Maximise happiness!*

LQ – The arts: To what extent should the arts have a moral function?

The theory of utilitarianism was developed in the late eighteenth and early nineteenth century by Jeremy Bentham (1748–1832) and John Stuart Mill (1806–73), who wanted to establish ethics on a scientific foundation. Just as Newton had explained natural phenomena in terms of the principle of gravity, so Bentham and Mill tried to explain ethical phenomena in terms of the principle of utility. According to this principle, the only thing that is good in itself is happiness, and *actions are right in so far as they tend to increase happiness and wrong in so far as they tend to decrease it.* If we ask 'What is happiness?', Bentham tells us that it is the sum of pleasures, and that a happy life is one that maximises feelings of pleasure and minimises feelings of pain.

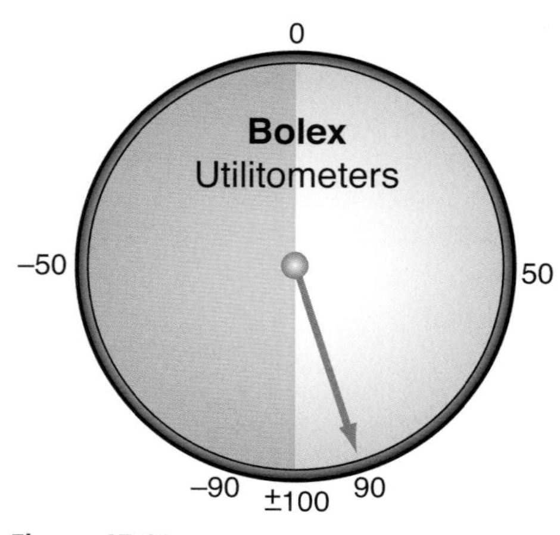

Figure 17.11

To get a sense of how utilitarianism might work in practice, imagine that you are living at the beginning of the twenty-second century. While people still wear wristwatches on their left arms, on their right arms they now wear something called a *utilitometer.* This has a needle and a dial going from 0 to +100 on half of its face and from 0 to −100 on the other half. The details of how a utilitometer works need not concern us, but it plugs into your central nervous system and measures your pleasure. If, for example, you are at a party and want to know how good you are feeling, you can consult your utilitometer: 'Wow! Plus 92 – ecstasy.' If you are bored in class on a Friday afternoon, you can determine just how bad things are: 'Minus 70 – seriously dull.'

Your utilitometer also has a little button on the right which you can press to find your total net happiness for the day (sum of pleasures minus sum of displeasures). At the end of each day, it automatically sends this figure to a central computer which calculates the total for the whole country – the *gross national happiness* (GNH). We can now say that utilitarianism comes down to the claim that a higher GNH means a morally better world and a lower GNH means a morally worse world.

RLS – Headline: 'Cash-strapped Britons are selling kidneys to pay mortgages and clear debts'. Assess the arguments for and against allowing people to do what they like with their own bodies.

Arguments in favour of utilitarianism

As a moral theory, utilitarianism has a number of attractive features:

1. Utilitarianism is a simple and coherent theory which is able to explain all of our beliefs about right and wrong in terms of the greatest happiness principle. This gives us a simple way of solving moral dilemmas which are such a problem in duty ethics. If you are faced with a conflict of duties, all you need to do is see which course of action has the greatest effect on GNH.
2. Utilitarianism is a democratic theory because each individual is considered to be the best judge of what makes him or her happy, and every individual's happiness is taken into account in determining GNH.
3. Utilitarianism is a rational theory because it encourages us to take into account not only the short-term but also the long-term consequences of our actions. For example, although smoking gives some people short-term pleasure, a utilitarian might argue that you shouldn't smoke because in the long term it is likely to give you more pain than pleasure.
4. Finally, it could be argued that utilitarianism is an egalitarian theory because it can, for example, justify redistributing money from the rich to the poor. Since a dollar means more to a poor person than to a rich person, a progressive system of taxation which takes some money from the rich and gives it to the poor will increase GNH.

ACTIVITY 17.18

1. How might a utilitarian try to justify or criticise the following actions?
   a. Eating ice-cream every day
   b. Wearing seat-belts in cars
   c. Forcing a reluctant child to learn the piano
   d. Voluntary euthanasia
2. How do you think a utilitarian would try to resolve the various moral dilemmas on pages 492–3? What problems arise in trying to use the greatest happiness principle to resolve them?
3. Take any moral dilemma from a novel or play that you have studied and explain how a utilitarian and a Kantian would analyse it.
4. When calculating GNH, do you think the happiness and suffering of animals as well as human beings should be included in the calculation?

Practical objections to utilitarianism

Despite the theoretical attractions of utilitarianism, it is not so easy to put into practice. To start with, how do we measure happiness? Although Bentham defines happiness as the sum of pleasures, it is difficult to see how different pleasures can be measured on a common scale. Imagine, for example, that someone gets pleasure from eating ice-cream, listening to opera, and spending time with their friends. How can we attach numbers to such pleasures and compare them with one another? 20 scoops of ice-cream = ½ an hour of opera = 1 afternoon spent with friends? An economist might say that we can measure different pleasures by seeing how much people are willing to pay for them. But is it really possible to put a price, or a 'happiness value', on such things as health, or love or friendship?

Furthermore, we might question the idea that a constant stream of pleasures makes for a happy life. You only have to think of the lives of some of the idle rich to see that someone can have a great deal of pleasure and yet still be bored and unhappy. Although we all want to be happy, the strange fact is that most of us are unable to say what it is that we really want; and it sometimes seems as if, the more we actively pursue happiness, the more difficult it is to find.

ACTIVITY 17.19

1. What do you think is the relationship between pleasure and happiness? Is happiness just the sum of pleasures, or can you have many pleasures and still be unhappy?
2. What connection, if any, do you think there is between money and happiness?
3. Which of the following two situations would you prefer? A world in which you earn $50,000 a year and all your friends earn $25,000, or a world in which you earn $100,000 a year and all your friends earn $250,000? What does this suggest to you about the nature of happiness?
4. 'I thought I was happy at the time, but now I realise that I was wrong.' Do you think that we are always the best judges of whether or not we are happy? Could the men in the 'democratic' country described in Question 1 on page 477 be wrong in thinking they are happy?
5. According to Bertrand Russell (1872–1970), 'To be without some of the things you want is an indispensable part of happiness.' What do you think he meant by this? Do you agree with him?

A final practical problem concerns how we can predict the consequences of our actions. Imagine that a married woman falls passionately in love with a colleague at work and is wondering whether or not to leave her husband. What should she do? In theory, utilitarianism gives a straightforward solution to the problem. The woman should compare the consequences of staying with her husband with the consequences of leaving him and do whatever maximises the happiness of the people involved. The trouble is that, in practice, it is very difficult to know what the consequences of our actions will be. A utilitarian might say that we usually have some idea of the consequences of our actions, but they may still be difficult to predict in any detail. To take an extreme example, in a short story by Roald Dahl, called *Genesis and Catastrophe*, a doctor saves a mother and child in a difficult birth. The story ends with the doctor saying 'You'll be all right now, Mrs Hitler.'

"It's a new anti-depressant–instead of swallowing it, you throw it at anyone who appears to be having a good time."

Figure 17.12

Theoretical objections to utilitarianism

As well as practical objections, utilitarianism is also open to a number of theoretical objections. Three common criticisms are:

- that pleasure or happiness is not always a good thing
- that actions should be judged by their motives rather than their consequences
- that utilitarianism is incompatible with the belief that we have moral obligations and individual rights.

Bad pleasures

As we have seen, utilitarianism is based on the assumption that the only things that are good in themselves are pleasure and happiness. But you might argue that there are in fact many bad pleasures – such as *malicious pleasures* and *empty pleasures*.

a. *Malicious pleasures* are pleasures that are derived from the suffering of other people. Imagine, for example, that a sadist meets a masochist (someone who wants to be hurt) and obligingly beats him up. On utilitarian principles, the world has become a better place because GNH has gone up. But many people would argue that, far from the world becoming a better place, the world has in fact become a worse place, and that any well-adjusted human being ought not to get pleasure from sado-masochism.

To take another example: imagine a mugger who assaults someone in the street and gets a buzz out of doing it. A utilitarian would no doubt say that the mugger's action is wrong because it has a negative effect on GNH. However, he would seem committed to saying that the more pleasure the mugger gets from his action the less serious his crime because the smaller its negative effect on GNH. Against this, many people would say that the fact that a criminal enjoys his crime and gets pleasure from it makes it worse not better.

b. *Empty pleasures* are pleasures that do not help us to develop our potential, or flourish as human beings. While pleasures such as shopping or eating chocolate may have their place, a critic would say that a life devoted exclusively to their pursuit is unworthy of a human being.

In the novel *Brave New World*, the writer Aldous Huxley (1894–1963) imagined a world where people are genetically engineered and conditioned to be happy and where a drug called 'soma' is freely available so that everyone can live on a permanent 'high'. If you are familiar with this novel you might agree that what

Figure 17.13 Is consumerism the route to happiness?

Huxley describes is not so much a perfect world, or utopia, as a perfectly awful world, or dystopia. A world of happy junkies does not seem like the best of all possible worlds.

ACTIVITY 17.20

1. What problems does the idea that some pleasures are better than others create for utilitarianism? How might a utilitarian try to respond to these problems?
2. Do you think that there are other things apart from pleasure and happiness that are good in themselves?

"I think the dosage needs adjusting. I'm not nearly as happy as the people in the ads."

Figure 17.14

Judging actions

According to utilitarianism, the rightness or wrongness of an action depends on its consequences: an action is right if it increases happiness and wrong if it decreases it. But, as we saw in our discussion of Kant's ethics, it could be argued that actions should be judged by their motives rather than their consequences, and that we should praise a well-intentioned bungler whose clumsy efforts accidentally reduce general happiness, and condemn a malicious person whose evil intentions accidentally increase it.

ACTIVITY 17.21

1. Most legal systems punish attempted murder less severely than actual murder. Do you think this is right? What would a Kantian say? What would a utilitarian say?
2. What good utilitarian reasons might there be for generally praising people who have good motives and condemning people who have bad motives?

Obligations and rights

A final criticism of utilitarianism is that it does not seem to leave any room for respecting moral obligations or human rights. When we discussed Kant's ethics we saw that it can be seen as too inflexible in its approach, but critics of utilitarianism argue that it suffers from the opposite weakness and is too unprincipled. For example, while Kant said you should *never* lie, utilitarianism would seem to justify lying to people whenever it makes them happy. However, many people would feel uncomfortable with the idea of shamelessly flattering or systematically deceiving someone just to make them happy.

ACTIVITY 17.22

1. Imagine that you are at a dinner party and the food is awful. Your host asks you if you are enjoying your meal. What would you reply?
2. If someone asks you what you think of them, how honest would you be in your response? How honest *should* you be?

Furthermore, since utilitarianism is only concerned with maximising happiness, it does not seem to pay sufficient attention to individuals' rights. To see the problem, imagine that Thomas, who is an orphan with no family and few friends, is in hospital for a minor eye operation, and that the man in the bed on his left is dying of kidney failure, and the man in the bed on his right is dying of heart failure.

ACTIVITY 17.23

1. What do you think a utilitarian would say you should do in this situation, and what difficulties does this create for utilitarianism?
2. What response, if any, could a utilitarian give to these difficulties?

Here is another example. Jones is a malicious individual who devotes his time to making life as difficult as possible for everyone in your community. You are a good utilitarian and one day you decide that it is time to do something to increase happiness. You hide behind the door and when Jones comes in you hit him on the head with a baseball bat and throw his unconscious body in the river. Goodbye Jones, hello happiness!

What is troubling about each of the above examples is that utilitarianism seems to justify sacrificing an individual to increase general happiness. A utilitarian doctor pillages a healthy body for 'spare parts'; and a community kills an individual whom everyone hates. In reality, of course, the doctor and the community would probably feel *guilty* about killing someone, and such feelings might reduce general happiness. Nevertheless, on purely utilitarian grounds, such guilt would seem to be irrational. If you are sure that you have done the right thing, why feel bad about it?

Despite appearances, a utilitarian is not obliged to say that the above killings are justified. In practice, there may be good utilitarian reasons why it is a bad idea to kill innocent people. If you live in a society where people who go into hospital with minor ailments are sometimes killed and used for spare parts, you will probably keep postponing that cataract operation! And if in your community unpopular people are sometimes killed, you may begin to worry if you get the impression that people don't like you any more. The point in both cases is that killing innocent people is likely to create an atmosphere of *fear* and this is likely to have a negative effect on GNH. In practice, then, there are probably good utilitarian reasons for protecting people's rights.

The place of rules

The above way of thinking has led some people to adopt a position known as *rule utilitarianism*. According to this we should judge the rightness or wrongness of an action not by whether it promotes general happiness but by whether it conforms to a rule that promotes general happiness. Since it is impossible to calculate the consequences of each individual action, rule utilitarianism says that in practice it makes more sense to let our actions be guided by rules which experience has shown tend to promote happiness. So in the case of making a promise, the question is no longer 'What will the effect on the general happiness be if I break this particular promise?' but rather 'What will the effect on general happiness be if we abandon the rule that people should keep their promises?' On this approach, it is not difficult to see that the world will generally be a happier place if we have rules against such things as lying, theft and murder, and we are likely to end up with the kinds of rules that can be found in many moral codes.

"But on the positive side, money can't buy happiness – so who cares?"

Figure 17.15

This emphasis on rules pushes utilitarianism closer to duty ethics – with the advantage that the rules can be more flexible than allowed by Kant. For example, rather than say 'Never tell lies', we could instead adopt the rule 'Never tell lies unless you can save a great deal of suffering by doing so'. This rule is admittedly rather vague, but it enables us to deal with the axe-wielding murderer example considered earlier (page 491), and is more in keeping with the way we normally think about ethics. Rule utilitarianism might therefore seem to be a good compromise between rule worship on the one hand and unprincipled behaviour on the other. However, we might still wonder why on a particular occasion we should follow a rule if we can increase GNH by breaking it. But perhaps this just shows that we must sometimes weigh the negative effects on happiness of following a rule against the dangers of weakening respect for the rule. There is, it seems, no substitute for good judgement!

ACTIVITY 17.24

1. Imagine that you are the sole heir to your great-uncle's fortune of $5 million. On his deathbed, he makes you swear to use the money to establish a butterfly farm. After his death, and without telling anyone, you decide to ignore your promise and give the money to an AIDS charity. Is your action right or wrong?
2. People sometimes talk about 'the ends justifying the means'. When, if ever, do you think that this is true?
3. What light can the moral theories we have looked at in this chapter shed on the questions we raised at the beginning?
   a. Is abortion ever justified?
   b. Should drugs be legalised?
   c. Are there limits to free speech?
   d. Is there such a thing as a just war?

Conclusion

Since we are, during the course of our lives, bound to be confronted by all kinds of moral dilemma, there is a sense in which ethics is inescapable; and, since we can never be sure that we are doing the right thing, there is a sense in which ethics is insoluble. Such dilemmas are typically the stuff of novels and films. For example, in a film called *The Bridges of Madison County*, an unfulfilled Iowa housewife meets the man of her dreams while her husband is out of town. He asks her to go away with him, but in the end she refuses. Did she make the right decision or not? What would a Kantian say? What would a utilitarian say? How much use are such theories in practice? Perhaps they do help to illuminate things; but in the end we cannot pass on the moral responsibility, and no matter how thick our rule book is, in the end we have to make our own decisions about what to do. The fact that we can never be sure that we have done the right thing, or that we are painfully aware that we could have done better, is perhaps part of the tragedy of the human condition.

Key points

- When we argue about ethics we typically appeal to various moral principles, but we might wonder how these principles can be justified.
- According to moral relativism, our values are determined by the society we grow up in, but it could be argued that some core values are universal.
- Some people claim that human beings are always and everywhere selfish, but since this robs the word 'selfish' of its meaning, it makes more sense to say that we are sometimes capable of altruism.
- We might try to derive moral values from religion, but Plato put forward an argument against this, and such an approach is in any case not going to satisfy an atheist.
- According to Immanuel Kant, ethics is a matter of doing your duty, and the test of whether something is your duty is whether or not it can be consistently generalised.
- Despite its attractions, Kant's approach to ethics is too absolutist and leaves us with no way of resolving moral dilemmas.
- According to utilitarianism, happiness is the only thing that is good in itself and we should seek 'the greatest happiness of the greatest number'.
- Two objections to utilitarianism are that some pleasures seem to be bad, and that the greatest happiness principle is inconsistent with our belief in human rights and moral obligations.
- Some form of rule utilitarianism might be a good compromise between the extremes of duty ethics on the one hand and act utilitarianism on the other.
- In ethics, as in other areas of knowledge, there is in the end no substitute for good judgement.

Key terms

altruism
cultural imperialism
duty ethics
egoism
empathy
golden rule
moral absolutism
moral relativism
other-regarding desires
rights
rule worship
self-interest theory
self-regarding desires
special pleading
utilitarianism
value-judgements
veil of ignorance

Knowledge framework focus

1. *Scope/applications.* Do some people exaggerate the objectivity of scientific facts and the subjectivity of moral values? Are moral values built into the very quest for knowledge?
2. *Concepts/language.* Is the prescriptive 'ought' of moral discourse fundamentally different from the descriptive 'is' of factual discourse?
3. *Methodology.* What role do intuition, empirical evidence, rational argument, emotion and imagination play in the search for moral knowledge? Is there any agreed method for solving moral disagreements?
4. *Historical development.* How has the way we seek to justify our moral beliefs changed over time? Is there any evidence that we have higher moral standards than our ancestors?
5. *Relation to personal knowledge.* Can there be a general answer to the question 'How should I live?' Do some moral codes, such as utilitarianism, demand too much of us as individuals?

IB prescribed essay titles

1. 'Through different methods of justification, we can reach conclusions in ethics that are as well-supported as those provided in mathematics.' To what extent would you agree? (May 2012)
2. 'Moral wisdom seems to be as little connected to knowledge of ethical theory as playing good tennis is to knowledge of physics' (Emrys Westacott). To what extent should our actions be guided by our theories in ethics and elsewhere? (November 2008 / May 2009)

Further reading

Books

Simon Blackburn, *Being Good* (Oxford University Press, 2001). This is an excellent short introduction to ethics. After considering various sceptical threats to ethics, Blackburn insists that it still makes sense to speak of moral knowledge. There are short, clear discussions of a wide range of topics including relativism, egoism, utilitarianism and human rights.

Matt Ridley, *The Origins of Virtue* (Penguin, 1997). This engaging and provocative book asks why naturally competitive human beings cooperate with one another. A zoologist by training, Ridley takes an interdisciplinary approach to his subject and brings insights from anthropology, biology, economics and history to bear on his thesis that it pays to cooperate.

Online articles

Paul Bloom, 'How Do Morals Change?', *Nature*, 25 March 2010.

Steven Pinker, 'The Moral Instinct', *New York Times Magazine*, 13 January 2008.

Dialogue: Relative values

In the following dialogue by Richard van de Lagemaat, two characters, Jack and Jill, argue about whether or not there are any objective moral values.

Jill: We've been talking about whether values are subjective or objective. I believe that certain basic values are objective.

Jack: Certain values may be objective *for you*, but you cannot say that they are objective, period.

Jill: I don't see why not.

Jack: Well, name me some objective values.

Jill: How about: Murder is wrong!

Jack: Well, murder may be wrong for you, but what about people for whom it is OK? What about cannibalistic societies? What about war? What about capital punishment?

Jill: OK. What about: Terrorism is wrong! The random killing of innocent civilians is wrong!

Jack: But one person's terrorist is another person's freedom fighter.

Jill: Let's stop talking in the abstract. Look, take the Oklahoma City bombing in 1995. Timothy McVeigh bombs a government building in downtown Oklahoma City, killing 168 people and injuring 400 others. 19 of the victims are children. What McVeigh did was wrong.

Jack: Wrong *for you.*

Jill: No, just wrong. I don't know what you mean by all this 'for you' stuff. Are you saying that the statement 'I believe that murder is wrong' is equivalent to the statement 'Murder is wrong for me'?

Jack: Pretty much.

Jill: OK, that's an interesting way of putting it. But note that when I say 'I believe that murder is wrong', what I actually believe is not that murder-is-wrong-for-me, but that murder-is-wrong-period – i.e. that murder is wrong irrespective of what I or anyone else happens to believe. And that's what I mean when I say that what McVeigh did was wrong, and that certain basic values are objective.

Jack: But McVeigh presumably thought that what he was doing was right.

Jill: Well, he was wrong to think that what he was doing was right.

Jack: But you have no right to say that what he was doing was wrong absolutely. You're not God. All you can say is that from your point of view it was wrong.

Jill: If you're telling me that I have no right to say that what McVeigh did was wrong absolutely, then you have no right to say that I have no right to say that!

Jack: Now you're just trying to be clever. Look, I don't like what McVeigh did, but that's just my personal feeling.

Jill: But there must be more to it than personal feelings. After all, we incarcerate murderers and terrorists. What if at his trial McVeigh's defence was that as far as he was concerned, what he did was OK. So he thinks he did the right thing in blowing up the government building in Oklahoma City, and the jury thinks he did the wrong thing. If there's no way of arbitrating between these two views, then we surely have no right to lock McVeigh up.

Jack: Well, we have to protect society.

Jill: So it's right to protect the innocent?

Jack: Yes. Right *for us*.

Jill: What you appear to be saying is that there is no real difference between morality and tastes, that we just *happen* to feel that what McVeigh did was wrong and that we just *happen* to feel that innocent people should be protected.

Jack: Yes, that's pretty much what I think.

Jill: But that's absurd. We don't just *happen* to have the moral beliefs that we have. They are the reflective product of an entire cultural tradition. I don't just wake up one day and suddenly feel that murder and terrorism are wrong.

Jack: We have the beliefs that we have because of the way in which we've been brought up. If we'd all grown up in a society that approved of acts of terrorism, then we probably wouldn't object to what McVeigh did.

Jill: I'm not sure I can imagine that kind of society.

Jack: Try thinking about how countries act in times of war. That should give you a reasonable approximation.

Jill: Well, I believe that there are such things as war crimes, and I also believe that if a society seriously approved of random acts of terrorism, then it would be a sick society.

Jack: But if you grew up in such a society you wouldn't think the way you do now.

Jill: Maybe not, but then I'd be horribly deluded. If I had grown up in a society that believed that the earth was flat, then I would believe that the earth was flat. But that would do nothing to show that the earth *is* flat.

Jack: That just shows that there is a difference between scientific facts and moral values. We can, after all, prove that the earth is round. But you can't *prove* that murder is wrong.

Jill: I agree that there is *some* difference between science and morality, but that doesn't mean that all our values are merely subjective. Let me take the most extreme case that I can think of: random torture – torturing other people just because one feels like it. That is absolutely wrong.

Jack: My point is that you cannot prove that it's wrong. It's just your personal feeling that it's wrong – a feeling with which I happen to agree. After all, there may be some people in the world who see nothing wrong with random torture.

Jill: I agree with you. I can't prove that random torture is wrong, but that is simply because it is self-evident. It doesn't need any further proof. You can't *prove* that 2 + 2 = 4, but that doesn't mean that it's just your personal feeling that it's true. And the fact that there may be a few rationally challenged people in the world who don't believe that 2 + 2 = 4 is irrelevant to the truth of the matter. It simply shows that when it comes to mathematics some people are morons. In the same way, I also believe that some people are ethical morons.

Jack: That's not a good analogy. I *can* prove that 2 + 2 = 4. I get two apples and another two apples and then make you count them.

Jill: In that case, I can prove that random torture is wrong. I take you some place where innocent people are being tortured and make you watch.

Jack: But that doesn't prove that it's wrong. It simply 'proves' that you have a feeling of revulsion when you see innocent people being tortured.

Jill: Well, you haven't proved that 2 + 2 = 4. All that you have proved – assuming that your eyes are not deceiving you and that you are not dreaming – is that *in this particular case* 2 + 2 = 4. You have done nothing to prove the general truth that two plus two is always equal to four.

Jack: You're making a very good debating point, but only by appealing to the topsy-turvy world of philosophy, which, as everyone knows, has no relation to the real world. However, for the sake of the argument, I shall let that pass. Given what you have just said, it seems to me that you are now implicitly admitting that there are no absolute moral values. For if nothing – not even arithmetic – is certain, then there can be no absolutes in any area, least of all in morality.

Jill: Absolutely not! You clearly aren't getting my point. I'm not arguing for radical scepticism – I'm simply saying that *by your standards* we can't be certain of anything.

Jack: But we can't, can we? I mean, you can't even prove that the whole of your life isn't just some weird dream and that we are all simply figments of your imagination.

Jill: That kind of blanket scepticism just isn't interesting and does nothing to illuminate experience.

Jack: Maybe not. But you can't disprove it, can you?

Jill: It depends what you mean by *proof*. If your model for proof is mathematics, then I cannot disprove that life isn't a dream. The fact, however, remains that it isn't a dream.

Jack: But how do you know?

Jill: It's intuitively obvious that life isn't a dream; just as it is intuitively obvious that 2 + 2 = 4 and intuitively obvious that random torture is wrong. I'm not interested in arguing about some kind of blanket idiot scepticism. My claim is that there are a few basic moral insights which are as certain as anything is certain.

Jack: But who are you to say that your basic moral insights are the correct ones? And how come there has been so little agreement about what these insights are?

Jill: Actually, I think there has been quite a lot of agreement. But in any case I am not claiming that my beliefs are *necessarily* true. That, indeed, would be to claim the status of God. The possibility of error is built into all our beliefs; but, in the absence of error, if you have a belief about something, then you believe that it is true independent of the fact that you happen to believe it.

Jack: If, as you say, the possibility of error is always present, that surely means that you can never be certain about anything. It follows that you can say only that something is true *for you* – which is exactly what I have been arguing all along.

Jill: You seem to think that if we cannot achieve certainty, then any opinion is as good as any other – and that is a big mistake. It is a dangerous and misguided democratic prejudice to believe that all moral beliefs are of equal value, and such a belief flies in the face of common sense.

Jack: So, according to you, some beliefs are inherently better than others! Hmm, that's the kind of arrogance that led to Western imperialism. That's how the Europeans thought when they arrived in Africa and the Americas and forcibly converted the indigenous peoples to Christianity. That's the kind of arrogance that rides roughshod over other cultures and thinks it has nothing to learn from them.

Jill: It's hardly appropriate for you to adopt that condemnatory tone. After all, you are the one who is a relativist – not me.

Jack: What do you mean?

Jill: Well, your position commits you to saying that what the European imperialists did was right for them, and that there is no higher standard according to which we can judge and condemn them. Of course, what they did was wrong for the indigenous people, but the Europeans were the ones with the guns, so they triumphed. Since, in your view, there is no truth of the matter and hence nothing to argue about, moral disagreement amounts to nothing more than a power struggle. Might is right.

Jack: No, you're the one who's in error. You believe in moral absolutes and that commits you to saying that some cultures are better than others, in the sense that some cultures are closer to the absolute moral truth. That's cultural racism.

Jill: You, on the other hand, are saying that, independent of the evidence, all cultures' ethical beliefs are of equal value. Now, that may, at first glance, sound open-minded and tolerant, but in reality it is the result of some very confused thinking. Consider a culture based on Nazi values. You would surely agree that it is in some sense worse than a culture based on the principles of human rights and tolerance?

Jack: You use the word tolerance, but your own position is a very intolerant one, and your reference to Nazism is simply muddying the waters. We can, I'm sure, both agree that Nazism is loathsome and odious; but with respect to our disagreement, this leads us nowhere. What I object to in your position is the presumptuous belief that, in a multi-cultural world, we have the right to dismiss some belief systems without a second thought. Do you honestly think that we have nothing to learn from other cultures?

Jill: That is not what I meant at all. Such an automatic and thoughtless dismissal of an alien way of life would, I agree, be quite unacceptable. What I would advocate is thoughtful dialogue between cultures; but I would want to keep in play the idea that at the end of this process we might come to the conclusion that some cultures are in some respects better than others.

Jack: But that would be a conversation of condescension. In any such conversation you would be bound to believe from the start that your own views were better than those of your interlocutor. You wouldn't truly believe that you had anything to learn from them.

Jill: On the contrary, it is you who is committed to saying that we have nothing to learn from other cultures.

Jack: I don't see how.

Jill: Well, if you know from the start that all cultures and all opinions are of equal value, then no one has anything to learn from anyone at all. Conversation – *all* conversation – then ceases to have any kind of educative function and it becomes nothing more than a way of passing the time.

Jack: Well, this has been an interesting conversation, and it has indeed passed the time; but you've done nothing to convince me of the falsity of relativism.

Jill: All I can say is that relativism may be true for you, but it is certainly not true for me!

Religion

18

I believe in God, only I spell it Nature.

Frank Lloyd Wright, 1867–1939

Religion is as much a human universal as language.

Talcott Parsons, 1902–79

To live at all is miracle enough.

Mervyn Peake, 1911–68

Some piously record 'In the beginning God', but I say 'In the beginning hydrogen'.

Harlow Shapley, 1885–1972

You must abandon your reason, know nothing of it, annihilate it completely, or you will never enter heaven.

Martin Luther, 1483–1546

The Tao that can be talked about is not the Eternal Tao. The name that can be named is not the Eternal Name.

Lao Tzu, c.600 BCE

When men cease to believe in God, they don't then believe in nothing – they believe in anything.

G. K. Chesterton, 1874–1936

A religion which declares war on reason will not in the long run be able to hold out against it.

Immanuel Kant, 1724–1804

What is it: is man only a blunder of God's, or God only a blunder of man's?

Friedrich Nietzsche, 1844–1900

Men never do evil so completely and cheerfully as when they do it from religious conviction.

Blaise Pascal, 1623–62

The religious geniuses of all ages have been distinguished by the kind of religious feeling, which knows no dogma.

Albert Einstein, 1879–1955

Introduction

We devote a great deal of time and energy to our material needs, but when we have finally satisfied them, we are still troubled by questions about the meaning and purpose of our lives. Since we naturally ask questions like 'What is the meaning of life?', 'Why do innocent people suffer?' and 'Is death the end?', we might describe human beings as 'religious animals'. For many people turn to religion in seeking the answers to such questions, and some kind of religious dimension has been found in every culture that has been studied by anthropologists. The trouble is that different religions give different answers to these questions, and some people are not satisfied with any of the answers that are on offer.

RLS – Headline: 'Scientology case has judges debating the meaning of religion'. What difficulties are involved in trying to distinguish religion from non-religion? Why might it matter?

Since many cultures have organised their understanding of the world around their religious beliefs, our exploration of the various areas of knowledge would be incomplete if we did not include a discussion of religion. Having said that, it remains an open question whether it makes sense to speak of 'knowledge' in relation to religion. Much of the discussion in this chapter will focus on the extent to which it is possible for human reason to penetrate the mysteries of religion. Perhaps we should take our cue from Thomas Jefferson (1743–1826) who advised that we 'Question with boldness even the existence of God; because if there be one, he must more approve of the homage of reason than that of blindfolded fear.' Although it is no easy matter to discuss our deepest convictions in an objective and dispassionate way, it could be argued that as 'global citizens' we have an obligation to ask how our own beliefs relate to those of people from different cultures and backgrounds.

LQ – Cultural perspectives: What does the fact that religion can be found in every culture suggest about the truth of religious beliefs?

Figure 18.1 Aymara Indian religious leaders perform a traditional new year ritual in Bolivia

18 Religion

Figure 18.2

ACTIVITY 18.1

Suggest ways in which a person's religious beliefs may affect their understanding of the following areas of knowledge:

a. science
b. history
c. the arts
d. ethics

LQ – Ethics: Are values based on religion?

Some preliminary distinctions

We begin by distinguishing three broad views about religion: theism, pantheism and atheism. (*Theos* is Greek for 'God', *pan* for 'all', and *a* for 'not'.)

1. **Theism.** A theist believes that the universe is governed by an eternal, all-powerful, all-knowing, all-loving creator God (Judaism, Christianity and Islam are examples of theistic religions).
2. **Pantheism.** A pantheist believes that God is everything and everything is part of God, and that reality is spiritual in nature and the everyday world is an illusion (Hinduism, Taoism and Buddhism are examples of pantheistic religions).
3. **Atheism.** An atheist denies the existence of a creator God and believes that the universe is material in nature and has no spiritual dimension.

Figure 18.3 The Buddha: Buddhism denies the existence of an eternal creator God

Theists, pantheists and atheists have strikingly different beliefs about the meaning of life, the universe and everything. Since these beliefs are

metaphysical in nature, we cannot determine whether they are true or false on the basis of experience alone. Given this, it is perhaps not surprising that some people have adopted a fourth position, known as **agnosticism**, which neither asserts nor denies the existence of God or some higher reality, but keeps an open – albeit sceptical – mind about these things. You might dismiss agnostics as people who 'sit on the fence', unable to commit themselves; or you might welcome their admission of ignorance about some of the deeper questions that confront us.

KT – metaphysical: relating to the area of philosophy that explores the nature of ultimate reality

KT – agnosticism: a position which neither asserts nor denies the existence of God or some higher reality, but remains sceptically open-minded

The nature of God

Since we have only a single chapter in which to consider religion, we will focus mainly on theistic religions and spend some time looking at various arguments for and against the existence of God. To start with, it is necessary say something about the meaning of the word 'God', for we need to know what it is that people are claiming when they say 'I believe in God' or 'I do not believe in God'. However, in trying to describe God in human language, there is a danger that we either reduce Him to something less than God or run into insoluble paradoxes.

The danger of anthropomorphism

Since we are human beings, it is natural to think of God in human terms by, for example, speaking of Him as a father or thinking of His love as similar to human love. The tendency to picture God in this way is known as **anthropomorphism** (literally 'in the form of man') and it is particularly apparent in the religion of the ancient Greeks where the gods are portrayed as glorified human beings. This led the philosopher Xenophanes (*c.*580–478 BCE) to say that if oxen, horses or lions could draw they would give their gods the same bodily shapes as themselves. Some atheist philosophers argue that, rather than God creating man in His own image, as the Christian Bible claims, man created God in *his* own image and that we continue to project human qualities onto Him.

KT – anthropomorphism: attributing human characteristics to something non-human – in this case, God

Figure 18.4 Michelangelo: *The Creation of Adam*

However, many people would claim that we have outgrown such childish ways of thinking about God. Michelangelo may have painted Him as an old man with a beard (see Figure 18.4) but we do not take such images seriously. And, although religious people continue to speak of God as a father, they would say that they are simply making an *analogy* between God and human beings and a father and his children. Indeed, it could be argued that all religious language is based on analogy. Even when you say 'God *exists*', you are not using the word 'exists' in its normal sense. After all, if you take off in a spaceship, you might one day find another planet or star that is believed to exist, but you will never find God, no matter how far you travel.

ACTIVITY 18.2

1. Do you think of God as a 'he' or a 'she' or an 'it'? What difference, if any, do these different words make to the way you think about God?
2. Do you think that God exists – or is supposed to exist – as a thing, or a force, or in an entirely different way?

The God of the philosophers

Some philosophers argue that the best way to avoid the taint of anthropomorphism is to describe God in abstract language. According to the so-called *God of the philosophers*, God is the eternal, all-powerful (**omnipotent**), all-knowing (**omniscient**), all-loving (**omniamorous**) creator of the universe. This may strike you as a very cold and impersonal definition, but it does seem to capture the key elements of what most people mean by the word 'God'. The problem is that, when we look at this definition more closely, we run into all kinds of paradoxes. Here are four:

1. **The paradox of omnipotence.** Consider the question 'Could God create a being that he could not subsequently control?' If He couldn't, then there is at least one thing He can't do and therefore He is not omnipotent; and if He could, then as soon as He creates such a being He ceases to be omnipotent. This suggests that the idea of an omnipotent being is self-contradictory.
2. **The paradox of change.** This paradox arises when we ask how a God who is perfect can intervene in human history as He has traditionally been thought to do. The problem is that being perfect is like being at the top of a mountain in the sense that if you move at all you can only go in one direction: down. So it seems that, if God takes any action, He will inevitably become imperfect, which contradicts our assumption that He is a perfect being.
3. **The paradox of suffering.** This troubling paradox arises from the twin assumptions that 'God is all-loving and does not want us to suffer' and that 'God is all-powerful and is able to prevent us from suffering'. Why then is there so much suffering in the world? We will discuss the problem of suffering in more detail later in this chapter (see page 525).

4. **The paradox of free-will.** If God is all-knowing, then He knows not only the past and the present, but also the future. This means that He knows not only everything we have done in the past, but also everything we will do in the future. This would seem to make human free-will an illusion and reduce us to nothing more than characters in a divinely predetermined script.

LQ – Language: Does religious experience lie beyond language?

A believer might be undisturbed by the above paradoxes and simply argue that human reason is unable to comprehend the infinite. Since we are finite beings, it could be argued that we can no more understand God than a worm can understand a human being. Faced with the difficulty of talking about God without running into paradoxes, some mystics have claimed that the highest religious truths lie beyond language and are to be found only in silence.

Is religious language meaningless?

At this point, an atheist may become impatient and insist that if religion cannot tell us anything about the nature of God, then believers are not really saying anything when they claim that God exists. This was the line taken by a group of philosophers, known as the **logical positivists**, who were active in the middle of the twentieth century. They argued that a statement is genuinely meaningful only if it can be empirically verified or falsified. Since they thought that religious statements do not satisfy this requirement they concluded that they are meaningless. If we accept this position, then so-called religious statements are *not even false* and they have no more significance than the sound of the wind on a stormy night or the baying of a dog at the moon.

KT – logical positivism: the view of a group of twentieth-century philosophers who claimed that a statement is genuinely meaningful only if it can be empirically verified or falsified

Fortunately, we are not obliged to accept the logical positivists' theory of meaning and most philosophers are unconvinced by the arguments put forward to support it. At a common-sense level, we might agree that religious language is sometimes difficult to understand, but still insist that we have some idea what people are talking about when they discuss the existence of God.

Furthermore, although 'God exists' is a metaphysical rather than an empirical proposition, there may be evidence that is at least *relevant* to determining its truth or falsity. Indeed, if it turns out that there is life after death, we will presumably be able to verify the truth of religious propositions in the next life, even if we are unable to do so in this one. (On the other hand, if death really is the end, we will never be able to *falsify* religious propositions. So if atheists are right, they will never have the satisfaction of being able to say, 'I told you so!')

Figure 18.5 "*You're kidding! You count S.A.T.s?*"

ACTIVITY 18.3

1. Which, if any, of the following would convince you that God exists?
   a. A world littered with pieces of granite stamped with the words 'Made by God'.
   b. Scientific evidence that people who pray are more likely to survive heart surgery than people who do not.
   c. A thousand people at an atheist convention having a religious experience which makes them believe in God.
   d. An earthquake which destroys a city, killing all of the atheists but none of the believers.
   e. Surviving completely unharmed in a plane crash in which everyone else is killed.
   f. A declaration by the world's 500 most intelligent people saying that they believe in God.
2. What evidence, if any, would convince you that God does not exist?

Figure 18.6 FIRST CONTACT

The argument from religious experience

LQ – Perception:
How should alleged religious experiences be interpreted?

In the previous section we saw how difficulties arise when we try to define God, and some theologians have pointed out that there is a big difference between the so-called 'God of the philosophers' and the 'God of Abraham, Isaac and Jacob'. Since the biblical patriarchs claimed to be directly acquainted with God, they would have felt no more need to define Him than we feel the need to define our mother or father. This draws attention to the fact that all religions are founded on a bedrock of intense personal experiences. Indeed, if no one had ever claimed to have had a religious experience, religion might not exist.

Despite their importance, religious experiences are, of course, very different from everyday experiences, and they are difficult, if not impossible, to verify. This has led sceptics to try to give natural or scientific explanations of such experiences. Therefore, when a mystic claims that God spoke to him in a dream, a sceptic might say that this is no different from saying that the mystic dreamt that God spoke to him. A sceptic might also point out that, since mystics frequently deprive themselves of food and sleep for long periods of time, it is not surprising that they have strange experiences. As the philosopher Bertrand Russell (1872–1970) wryly observed: 'From a scientific point of view, we can make no distinction between the man who eats little and sees heaven and the man who drinks much and sees snakes.' More recently, neuroscientists have observed that epileptic seizures can result in intense religious experiences, and this has led some people to speculate that people such as St Paul and Joan of Arc may have been epileptics. A Canadian neuroscientist called Michael Persinger has even claimed that by stimulating the temporal lobes of the brain he can artificially induce religious experiences in people.

How should we respond to natural explanations for alleged religious phenomena? A religious person might begin by pointing out that *to explain something is not necessarily to explain it away*. Since we are primarily material beings, it is perhaps not surprising that religious experiences can be correlated with various states of the brain, but it does not necessarily follow that they are illusions. After all, your experience of colour is also correlated with various states of the brain, but you would probably not conclude that colours are therefore unreal. Nor does the claim that epileptics are particularly prone to religious experiences prove anything one way or another. For it is possible that God has chosen to communicate to humanity primarily through such people. Perhaps, as the neuroscientist V. S. Ramachandran says:

> *God has vouchsafed for us 'normal' people only occasional glimpses of a deeper truth … but these patients [epileptics] enjoy the unique privilege of gazing directly into God's eyes every time they have a seizure. Who is to say whether such experiences are 'genuine' (whatever that might mean) or 'pathological'?*

There is, however, still the question of how religious experiences should be interpreted. The fact that people tend to interpret them in terms of their own cultural traditions – Buddhists do not have visions of the Virgin Mary, and Catholics do not have visions of the Buddha – suggests that they cannot simply be taken at face value. Moreover, since no one accepts *all* such experiences as valid, there is also the question of how to distinguish revelations from delusions. For example, David Koresh (1959–93), the leader of an American religious cult called the Branch Davidians, claimed that he was the reincarnation of Jesus Christ; but most orthodox Christians would dismiss such a claim as blasphemy.

Miracles

As part of our discussion of religious experience, we should also say something about miracles. A miracle can be defined as an extraordinary event which is brought about by God's intervention in the natural order of things.

If, for example, you survived a plane crash that killed everyone else on board, you might say 'It was a miracle that I survived.' This is because there was an extremely low probability that anyone would survive. However, it is worth noting that extremely unlikely events happen surprisingly often if you look at a large enough population. For example, in a country of 300 million people, you should expect 300 chances-in-a-million to happen every day! So we should occasionally expect someone to survive a tragedy against the odds.

Perhaps we should adopt a more robust definition of a miracle and say that it is not merely an extremely unusual event, but one that contravenes the laws of nature. Think, for example, of biblical miracles such as the parting of the Red Sea, the turning of water into wine, or the raising of Lazarus. Such events, if they could be verified, would seem to provide compelling evidence for the existence of God. What are we to make of them?

Hume's argument against miracles

The Scottish philosopher David Hume (1711–76) was in no doubt about what we should think. He denied the existence of miracles and argued that it is never rational to believe in them because the weight of evidence must always be against them. Imagine a workman telling you that while he was working on a tenth-floor scaffolding yesterday he accidentally dropped a large brick. Since the street below was crowded with people, the brick could easily have killed someone. However, instead of falling to the ground, the brick miraculously stopped midway through its fall and then floated upwards into the heavens. Should you believe the workman? Hume says that you should not. Since there is a uniform body of evidence to show that when bricks are dropped they fall to the ground, it is surely more likely that the workman is deluded or lying than that the law of gravity has been broken. According to Hume, the same line of argument can be used against any alleged miracle. In short, it is always more likely that the witnesses to an alleged miracle are mistaken than that the laws of nature should suddenly stop working.

ACTIVITY 18.4

1. What, if anything, would convince you that a miracle had occurred? To what extent would you take into account the following factors?
   a. The nature of the alleged miracle
   b. The number of witnesses
   c. The reliability of the witnesses
   d. How long ago it happened
2. Do you think that Hume's argument against miracles would carry any conviction with someone who claimed to have witnessed a miracle themselves?
3. We sometimes speak of 'the miracle of birth'. Is this just a metaphor, or do you think there is a sense in which birth really is a miracle?

4. G. K. Chesterton (1874–1936) once asked: 'Do you know why a pumpkin goes on being a pumpkin? If you don't, then you can't know whether sooner or later it won't turn into a coach?' What do you think Chesterton is getting at here?
5. Look back at our discussion of the problem of induction in Chapter 13 (page 356). If we take the problem seriously, does it make belief in miracles more or less reasonable?

Does Hume's argument prove too much?

Hume's argument against miracles might be said to prove too much; for it implies that it is irrational to believe not only in miracles, but also in *any* observations that do not fit in with our current understanding of the world. However, in our discussion of natural science in Chapter 13, we saw that anomalous observations – ones that do not fit in with current ways of thinking – can play an important role in helping to bring about scientific revolutions. When nineteenth-century astronomers found that Mercury was deviating from the path predicted by Newton's laws of motion, Hume would presumably have said that they should reject the observation on the grounds that it was more likely that they were mistaken than that Newton's laws were wrong. But if they had done that, Einstein might never have come up with the theory of relativity. The problem, then, is that if we adopted Hume's approach, not only would miracles be outlawed but scientific progress would also grind to a halt.

This suggests that we should not simply dismiss unusual or extraordinary events out of hand, but be willing to take them seriously. At the same time, we should keep in mind Carl Sagan's (1934–96) point that 'extraordinary claims require extraordinary evidence' (see Chapter 1, page 15). Even if we accept that an event contradicts the laws of nature, we are not obliged to say that it is a miracle. For it might simply show the limitations of our current understanding of the world. As science progresses, what seems miraculous to one generation may be normal to the next. After all, a great deal of modern technology would seem miraculous to someone living two thousand years ago. This suggests that whether or not something is interpreted as a miracle depends, in part at least, on the state of scientific knowledge and our understanding of how the universe normally works.

We have said that a miracle is something that contradicts the laws of nature, but perhaps we should understand the word 'miracle' in a broader sense. For it could be argued that the underlying order and harmony of the universe – which makes the discovery of laws of nature possible – is itself a miracle. Some scientists claim to experience a feeling of wonder and awe bordering on the religious when they survey the universe. But, sadly, most people are so habituated to the world that they have lost whatever sense of wonder they might once have had. The result, in the words of a Jewish Sabbath prayer, is that 'Days pass, years vanish, and we walk sightless among miracles.'

The idea that everything is a miracle is in some ways an attractive one; but whether or not the word 'miracle' has at this point become so broad as to lose its meaning is something for you to decide.

The argument from design

KT – argument from design: an argument which says that the order and harmony of the universe is evidence for the existence of an intelligent creator

According to the **argument from design**, the order and harmony of the universe could not have come about by chance, but must have been made by an intelligent creator. The eighteenth-century theologian William Paley (1743–1805) made a famous analogy between a watch and a watchmaker on the one hand and God and the world on the other. If you discovered an old watch on a beach, opened up the back and saw the intricate mechanism that drives it, you would naturally conclude that it had been made by a skilled watchmaker. Similarly, when you look at the order and harmony of the natural world, you can see the fingerprints of an intelligent designer on everything. As evidence, a biologist might point to the exquisite design of the eye, and a physicist to the majestic harmony of the heavens. According to Isaac Newton (1642–1727): 'This most beautiful system of the sun, planets and comets, could only proceed from the counsel and dominion of an intelligent and powerful Being.' The evidence from biology and physics was enough to convince most eighteenth-century scientists that the universe had indeed been designed.

"Sorry – He's changed His mind again. Stripes on the zebra, spots on the giraffe, no stars on the lion and make the elephant bigger and the amoebae smaller."

Figure 18.7

ACTIVITY 18.5

1. How does the 'hypothesis' of a divine creator to explain the order and harmony of the universe resemble a scientific hypothesis?
2. How good is the analogy of the watch and the watchmaker? How does the universe resemble a watch and how does it differ from it?

Hume's criticisms of the argument from design

There were, however, dissenting voices, and once again David Hume was foremost among the critics. According to Hume:

1. Paley's analogy is a poor one because there is in fact little resemblance between the world and a machine.
2. The most the argument from design can prove is the existence of an *architect* god – not a creator god. After all, a watchmaker does not create his parts out of nothing, but fashions them out of pre-existing material.

3. If we look at the universe objectively, it is far from clear that it was designed by an omnipotent and benevolent God. Indeed, for all we know, says Hume, the world 'is very faulty and imperfect, compared to a superior standard, and was only the first rude essay of some infant deity who afterwards abandoned it, ashamed of his lame performance'. As an anonymous wit once said, 'Don't worry, God is alive and well and now working on a less ambitious project.'

Does the theory of evolution make design unnecessary?

The theory of evolution would seem to cast further doubt on the argument from design. For it gives us a way of explaining the complexity and harmony of nature without having to appeal to a designer God. According to biologists, such complex and apparently well-designed features as a human eye or a bird's wing have developed through random changes over long periods of time. And the so-called 'balance of nature' can be explained by the fact that species evolved to fit in with their environment. As the scientist Paul Davies (1946–) summarises it:

> *Darwin's theory of evolution demonstrated decisively that complex organization efficiently adapted to the environment could arise as a result of random mutations and natural selection. No designer is needed to produce an eye or a wing.*

Since everything we see around us can be explained in terms of natural processes, it would seem, echoing Paley, that nature itself is the watchmaker – but, unlike God, a blind rather than prescient watchmaker.

Physics and the new argument from design

Recently, a new version of the argument has emerged which focuses more on physics than biology, and the laws underlying the universe rather than the things within it. Some physicists have drawn attention to the mysterious fact that the universe is not only orderly, but orderly in such a way that it can be understood by human beings. To the religiously inclined, this suggests that there is some kind of rational plan behind the universe.

The mystery deepens when we ask ourselves why the laws of physics are the way they are. For it almost looks as if some of the key values, such as the speed of light, the force of gravity and the charge carried by electrons, have been fine-tuned to guarantee the emergence of life in the universe. Take, for example, gravity, which determines how much things are attracted to each other. If it was any stronger, things would be crushed together; and if it was any weaker, they would fly apart. The other laws are equally fine-tuned, and if their values had been even slightly different, then life would never have appeared in the universe. Yet scientists have no explanation for these astonishing coincidences. How, then, should we interpret them? According to Paul Davies,

> *If it is the case that the existence of life requires the laws of physics and the initial conditions of the universe to be fine-tuned to high precision, and that fine-tuning does in fact obtain, then the suggestion of design seems compelling.*

A different possibility, which is taken seriously by some physicists, and which avoids invoking a creator God, is that we inhabit a 'multiverse', and our universe is only one of an infinite number of universes. Since every conceivable value for the laws of physics is explored in one universe or another, the values that hold in our universe were bound to turn up somewhere. So the multiverse hypothesis explains the coincidence of fine-tuning, but only if we accept the idea of an infinite number of universes. This hypothesis is, of course, highly speculative, and, on our current understanding at least, there is no way we could prove the existence of these other universes.

We seem to be left with a choice between two metaphysical hypotheses: a universe designed by an intelligent creator, or an infinity of universes. If you do not like either of these options, you might say that the laws of nature are simply hard facts about the universe that we will never be able to explain. Yet hard facts sit uncomfortably with the human intellect, and it is hard for us to resist the temptation to make sense of things.

ACTIVITY 18.6

Read the following piece by Douglas Adams (1952–2001). How does it affect your view of the argument from design?

'Imagine a puddle waking up one morning and thinking, "This is an interesting world I find myself in – an interesting hole I find myself in – fits me rather neatly, doesn't it? In fact it fits me staggeringly well, must have been made to have me in it!" This is such a powerful idea that as the sun rises in the sky and the air heats up and as, gradually, the puddle gets smaller and smaller, it's still frantically hanging on to the notion that everything's going to be alright, because this world was meant to have him in it, was built to have him in it; so the moment he disappears catches him rather by surprise. I think this may be something we need to be on the watch out for.'

The cosmological argument

KT – cosmological argument: an argument which see the very existence of the universe as strong evidence for the existence of a creator God

The **cosmological argument** for the existence of God is based not on the order of the universe but on the fact that it exists at all. Science can trace the history of the universe all the way back to the Big Bang fifteen billion years ago, but that is as far as it can go. It is unable to answer the ultimate question, 'What caused the Big Bang?' Yet there must be an explanation. After all, the universe could not have sprung into existence out of nothing. Nothing can come from nothing. So the only possible explanation is that the universe was created by God. God, we might say, lit the fuse that set off the Big Bang.

ACTIVITY 18.7

How convincing do you find the cosmological argument? What criticisms, if any, would you make of it?

Some alternatives

Figure 18.8 The Hindu God of Creation, Brahma

Many arguments for the existence of God come down to the feeling that 'there must be something'. This may explain the popularity of the cosmological argument. But the question remains: do we really need a creator God to explain the existence of the universe? At least two other alternatives have been suggested:

The universe has always existed

Although cosmologists believe that the universe originated in the Big Bang, some are willing to entertain as a speculative possibility the idea that the Big Bang is itself the result of a Big Crunch, and that the universe has been expanding and contracting for ever in an endless series of cycles. Interestingly, a similar idea can be found in Hindu philosophy, which traditionally had a much better grasp of the vast extent of cosmic time than the West. (The basic cycle in Hinduism is known as a 'day of Brahma' and lasts 4,200 million years. This is very different from Archbishop Ussher, a seventeenth-century Irish cleric, who calculated that the world was created on the evening of 22 October 4004 BCE!)

ACTIVITY 18.8

Do you think it makes sense to say that the universe is eternal and goes back infinitely far in time?

The Big Bang was the uncaused first cause

A second alternative to a creator God is to deny that everything has a cause and to argue that the Big Bang was an uncaused event – the ultimate brute fact. Perhaps the universe was born by chance. The idea of something coming from nothing is, admittedly, as difficult to understand as the idea that the universe is eternal; for we tend naturally to believe that everything has a cause and that nothing can come into existence out of pure nothingness. But perhaps our belief in the causal principle is simply a metaphysical prejudice, perhaps it is simply wrong to think that every event has a cause.

To many people the idea that God created the universe makes more sense than the idea that it has always existed or that it appeared by chance. But this solution invites the question that children sometimes ask: 'And who made God?' The answer is, of course, that God is the *uncreated* creator and requires no cause; but this answer contradicts our initial assumption that everything has a cause. For we are now saying that everything *except God* has a cause. As the philosopher Arthur Schopenhauer (1788–1860) observed, supporters of the cosmological argument treat the causal principle like a hired cab which they dismiss when they have reached their destination. So we seem to be faced with the following dilemma: either everything

"This is a little embarrassing to admit, but everything that happens happens for no real reason."

Figure 18.9

has a cause, in which case God must have a cause; or it is not the case that everything has a cause, in which case the universe could have come into existence by chance. Neither of these options leads ultimately to an uncreated creator.

ACTIVITY 18.9

1. When you create something new, such as a piece of music, a novel or a painting, the whole is greater than the sum of the parts. Does this show that something can come from nothing? What has this got to do with our discussion?
2. Imagine finding a sandcastle on the beach. When you ask someone who made it, they reply 'The Unknown Builder'. How does this differ from saying 'I don't know'? What has this got to do with our discussion?
3. What distinguishes a good explanation from a bad explanation? Do you think the claim that God created the universe is a good explanation or a bad one? Give reasons.

Perhaps one reason that a believer finds the idea of a creator God a satisfying explanation is not so much that it solves the problem of where the universe came from as that it guarantees that the universe has a meaning and that our lives have significance. Most people would rather believe that we are part of a divine plan than that we are simply a cosmic accident in a meaningless universe. However, an atheist might say that it is a category mistake to ascribe meaning to the universe in the same way that it is a category mistake to ascribe weight to a dream. If that is the case, then it makes no more sense to say that the universe is meaningless than that it is meaningful – just as it makes no more sense to say that dreams are light than that they are heavy. From this viewpoint, meaning is not so much something we discover in the universe as something we create in our lives. At this point in the argument we reach an impasse, with a believer asserting, and a non-believer denying, that the universe must have some kind of deeper meaning.

Whether or not you believe in God, the existence of the universe remains a highly puzzling fact. If you are a believer, you might wonder why God bothered creating the universe. Was He lonely, or bored, or somehow incomplete? If you are not a believer, you might wonder why the universe goes to all the bother of existing, why anything at all exists rather than nothing. This is surely a mystery that will always lie beyond the reach of science.

ACTIVITY 18.10

1. Can you imagine anyone ever coming up with a compelling answer to the question of why the universe exists? Why, or why not?
2. Do you think it is worth spending time thinking about questions to which there are no definite answers? Give reasons for your answer.

The problem of suffering

KT – problem of suffering: the problem of how we can reconcile the belief in an all-powerful and all-loving God with the existence of suffering

We now need to consider one of the main arguments against the existence of God – the problem of suffering. As we saw earlier, the problem arises from the fact that God is supposed to be not only all-powerful, but also all-loving. For it would seem that if He is all-powerful, He is able to prevent our suffering; and if He is all-loving, He does not want us to suffer. So why is there so much suffering in the world? We seem forced to conclude either that God is not all-powerful and that suffering is the result of circumstances beyond His control, or that He is not all-loving and that He doesn't care about our plight. Perhaps God created the universe, but it didn't turn out the way He had planned; or perhaps He created it and then lost interest in it. Neither of these options is very attractive. If God is an incompetent bungler, or a heartless dictator, then He hardly seems worthy of worship.

The free-will defence

KT – free-will defence: an argument which attributes the existence of evil in the world not to God but to human free-will

One standard response to the problem of suffering is known as the **free-will defence**. This says that God gave human beings free-will, and that we have misused our freedom to inflict suffering on one another. If you look at the raw statistics, there would seem to be support for this argument. Take war, for example. Since 1500, an estimated 142 million people have died in more than 600 wars around the world. During the same period, there have been at least 36 genocides, leading one commentator to bleakly observe that 'Genocide is as human as art and prayer.' Now consider poverty. Thousands of people starve to death every day; yet the United States and Europe spend more money on pet food every year than it would take to feed the one billion undernourished people on the planet. With these uncomfortable facts in mind, we clearly have a lot to answer for in terms of our contribution to world suffering.

Does the free-will defence 'let God off the hook' when it comes to responsibility for suffering? Some critics have argued that it does not. We might, for example, ask why God could not have made the universe with slightly different laws of physics so that we could not develop weapons of mass destruction. Indeed, why could He not have made us in such a way that we are free, yet always freely choose to do what is good? Well, perhaps always 'freely' choosing to do what is good is no different from not being free at all. A believer might argue that, if we are to have genuine freedom, then the freedom to sin must be a real option.

However, even if the free-will defence resolves one paradox, it seems to do so only at the expense of creating another. For if the problem of suffering is explained by the fact that human beings have free-will, we might now ask how we can reconcile human free-will with divine omniscience. The problem is that, if God knows everything, then He must know our future as well as our past – indeed, He must have known our entire life stories from the beginning of time. This would seem to reduce us to little more than characters in a divine novel, or computer simulation. However, in response to this it could be said that, since God does not *force* us to make the choices that we make, divine foreknowledge is perfectly compatible with human free-will. Whether or not the two really are compatible is something that different people have different intuitions about.

Natural suffering

RLS – Headline: 'Tsunami sufferers question faith'. Do natural disasters count as evidence against the existence of God?

Another problem with the free-will defence is that it only addresses the suffering which is brought about by human beings. What are we to say about all of the 'natural' suffering in the world? The argument from design suggests that God's goodness can be seen in His creation; but you might well disagree with that. For while some religious believers see the beauty and harmony of nature, we could just as easily point to its ugliness and cruelty. Think, for example, of such things as earthquakes, tornadoes, sharks, scorpions, cancer and malaria. Such examples of nature's cruelty would seem to be difficult to reconcile with the existence of a benevolent creator.

One possible response to the existence of natural suffering is to argue that, despite appearances, we live in *the best of all possible worlds*. The key idea here is that the world comes as a 'package deal', and it would be impossible to have a perfectly good world without any suffering, just as it would be impossible to have a mountain without a valley. Advocates of this view generally argue that the best possible world is not necessarily the happiest, but the one that brings the most opportunity for growth and development. With this in mind, it could be argued that the apparent cruelty of nature contributes to the greater good and that 'good cometh out of evil'. This was an argument made by the philosopher Immanuel Kant (1724–1804). He claimed that the reason God created mosquitoes was 'to urge . . . primitive men to drain the marshes and bring light into the dense forests that shut out the air, and, by so doing . . . to render their abodes more sanitary'.

This line of argument is connected with the idea that suffering has an educative value. When parents punish their children, they sometimes speak of being 'cruel to be kind'; and sports coaches are fond of the expression, 'No pain, no gain'. So perhaps natural suffering helps us to grow and develop as individuals. Despite the havoc caused by such things as earthquakes, forest fires and tsunamis, one might point out that they sometimes bring out the best in people, and give rise to acts of heroism, self-sacrifice and simple generosity. They may also give survivors a new sense of perspective and help them to see that what really matters in life are not material possessions, but personal relationships.

ACTIVITY 18.11

1. Give some examples of the apparent goodness and kindness of nature.
2. Give some examples of where the apparent cruelty of nature turns out to be beneficial.
3. Do you think that on balance nature is more cruel than kind, or more kind than cruel?

All Things Bright and Beautiful	**All Things Dull and Ugly**
All things bright and beautiful, All creatures great and small, All things wise and wonderful, The Lord God made them all. Each little flower that opens, Each little bird that sings – He made their glowing colours, He made their tiny wings.	All things dull and ugly, All creatures short and squat, All things rude and nasty, The Lord God made the lot. Each little snake that poisons, Each little wasp that stings, He made their brutish venom, He made their horrid wings.
From a hymn by Cecil Frances Alexander	A parody of the Alexander hymn from Monty Python

There are two main problems with the above defence of suffering. First, it is far from clear that the alleged benefits of natural suffering outweigh the costs in terms of death and destruction. Second, even if they do, this does not explain the *distribution* of suffering. If good people prospered and only bad people were struck down, we might claim to see the working of divine justice in the distribution of suffering. But it seems that the good suffer as much as the bad, the innocent as much as the guilty. The suffering of little children seems particularly difficult to reconcile with the belief in an all-loving God. For it is hard to see how anything could justify the death of thousands of innocent children in an earthquake or a tsunami.

ACTIVITY 18.12

1. Given that God is omnipotent, do you think that He could have created the world with less suffering in it?
2. To what extent do natural disasters bring out the best in people, and to what extent do they bring out the worst in people?
3. In the novel *The Brothers Karamazov,* by Fyodor Dostoevsky, one of the characters, Ivan, gives his brother, Alyosha, the following challenge:

   '"Imagine that you are creating a fabric of human destiny with the object of making men happy in the end, giving them peace and rest at last, but that it was essential and inevitable to torture to death only one tiny creature – that baby beating its breast with its fist, for instance – and to found the edifice on its unavenged tears, would you consent to be the architect on those conditions? Tell me and tell me the truth."

   "No, I wouldn't consent", said Alyosha softly.'

   Do you agree or disagree with Alyosha's response to Ivan's challenge? Give reasons.
4. To what extent could it be argued that so-called 'natural disasters' are the result of our interfering with the balance of nature, and are therefore our responsibility?

While an atheist sees the existence of natural suffering as evidence against the existence of God, a believer might say that it is foolish to try to comprehend the will of God in any detail. For religion is based more on faith than reason – in this case, faith that there is a divine plan and that everything is for the best.

Reason versus faith

We have looked at various arguments for and against the existence of God, but we have not arrived at any definite conclusion. This is hardly surprising – since certainty cannot be found in any other area of knowledge, we should not expect to find it in an area as difficult and controversial as religion. Indeed, since human understanding is limited and cannot comprehend the infinite, many believers would say that it is absurd to try to prove the existence of God. If God wished, then presumably He could reveal Himself in a way that left us in no doubt about His existence; but then we would have no choice about what to believe. So perhaps the lack of proof gives us the freedom to decide for ourselves and the lack of knowledge leaves room for faith.

At this point, should say something about the relation between faith and reason. We have already said a great deal about the nature of faith in Chapter 11, but here we will briefly revisit the issue in this context. If you want to explore the topic in more detail, you should refer back to the earlier chapter.

Is faith rational?

The word 'faith' is difficult to define in a neutral way. On the positive side, St Paul defined it as 'the conviction of things hoped for and the assurance of things not seen'. On the negative side, Sigmund Freud (1856–1939) dismissed it as 'the believing of propositions upon insufficient evidence'.

KT – wish fulfilment: believing that something is true simply because you want it to be true

As Freud's definition of faith suggests, most atheists would say that, while scientific belief is rational, religious faith is irrational and amounts to little more than **wish fulfilment**. Since you are keen to believe that something is true, you convince yourself, on the basis of little or no evidence, that it really is true.

An atheist might point out that, as our scientific knowledge of the universe has expanded, the role played by God has contracted. While primitive people explained thunder and lightning as the anger of the gods, we can now explain them in terms of build-up of electricity in the atmosphere; and while people once attributed complex organs such as eyes and wings to a designer God, we can now explain them in terms of Darwin's theory of evolution. Extrapolating from this, an atheist might argue we will eventually be able to explain everything that is worth knowing in terms of science, and that religion, which Freud saw as a childish form of escapism, will eventually wither away.

Despite Freud's belief that faith and reason are opposed to one another, many religious traditions emphasise the rationality of faith. For example, in Islam, the prophet Muhammad said that 'God has not created anything better than reason'; and, in Christianity, the philosopher Thomas Aquinas (1225–74) argued that reason and faith are complementary ways of seeking the truth. As we have seen, there are several rational arguments for the existence of God, and even though none of them is conclusive, taken together they might be said to provide a rational foundation for faith.

Thomas Aquinas claimed that once we have acquired faith we look at the world differently, and begin to see God's fingerprints on everything. This is perhaps what he meant when he said: 'The light of faith makes us see what we believe.' We might then think of religious faith as a kind of **paradigm** through which we interpret our experience and make sense of the world. However, this argument cuts both ways: perhaps if you commit yourself to atheism, you will see signs of God's non-existence wherever you look!

KT – paradigm: a set of interrelated ideas for making sense of one or more aspects of reality

Science and religion

When it comes to the relation between science and religion, most religious believers would claim that they are quite consistent with one another. After all, many famous scientists have believed in God, and seem to have had no difficulty in reconciling their scientific beliefs with their religious beliefs. One way of trying to do this is to say that while science is concerned with the *how* of the universe, religion is concerned with its *why*, and that problems arise only when religion gets involved with *how* questions, or science with *why* questions. If religion tries to answer scientific questions by, for example, insisting that the sun goes round the earth, or that each species is uniquely created by God, then it will find itself having to retreat before the forward march of science. (The Catholic Church belatedly acquitted Galileo of heresy in 1993; and it finally accepted evolution 'as an effectively proven fact' in 1996.) If science tries to answer religious questions by pontificating about ultimate reality or human destiny, then it effectively ceases to be science and becomes a kind of religion.

LQ – Natural sciences: Do science and religion contradict one another?

A religious apologist might also point out that there is a sense in which not only religion but also science is based on faith. For a scientist must have faith that the universe is orderly, and that human beings are capable of discovering that order. (Since we can never be certain of anything, it could, indeed, be argued that there is an element of faith built into *all* knowledge claims.) However, an atheist might argue that the faith of a scientist is quite different from that of a religious person, and that while our belief in an orderly universe is confirmed by experience every day, we may struggle to find consistent signs of God's love for us.

ACTIVITY 18.13

1. How is the faith of a scientist similar to the faith of a religious believer? How is it different?
2. Do you think that having faith in something necessarily means that one is religious?

Pascal's wager

The philosopher Blaise Pascal (1623–62) argued that a rational person ought to bet on the existence of God. The argument runs as follows: since we do not know whether or not God exists, let us assume that the odds are 50/50. Now consider the gains and losses of betting on God's existence or non-existence. If you bet that God exists and you are right, you hit the jackpot – heaven: if you are wrong – well, you haven't really lost anything. If you bet that God does not exist and you are right, you win nothing: but if you are wrong, it's bad news – hell. Given this distribution of potential gains and losses, Pascal concluded that a rational gambler ought to bet on the existence of God.

	GOD EXISTS	GOD DOES NOT EXIST
You bet that God exists	You win everything	You lose nothing
You bet that God does not exist	You lose everything	You win nothing

KT – Pascal's wager: the claim made by the philosopher Blaise Pascal that, bearing in mind the potential rewards and punishments, it pays to bet on the existence of God

Despite its ingenuity, most people have been unconvinced by **Pascal's wager** and there are many arguments against it. In fairness to Pascal, he saw his wager as being only the first step in pushing a wavering atheist towards religion. His idea seems to have been that religion is ultimately a matter of *practice*, and that if you begin leading a religious life you will end up genuinely believing in God.

ACTIVITY 18.14

1. Do you think it is possible to bring yourself to believe in God if you have not previously believed in Him?
2. Assuming that God exists, how do you think He would feel about someone who cynically gambles on His existence as a kind of insurance policy?
3. Would you agree that you lose nothing if you bet that God exists and it turns out that He does not?
4. If you don't believe in God, but have led a good life, do you think that you would still lose everything and go to hell if it turns out that God exists?
5. Since there are many different religions in the world, does Pascal's wager apply to all of them? Does this mean that you should subscribe to every religion?

Is faith irrational?

Some religious believers have taken a different approach to the relation between faith and reason and have argued that faith is indeed irrational, but that faith without evidence is superior to faith based on evidence. When in the Christian tradition the apostle Thomas refused to believe that Jesus had risen from the dead until he had the evidence of his own eyes, Jesus then said to him: 'Because you have seen me, you have believed; blessed are those who have not seen and yet have believed.'

"We're thinking maybe it's time you started getting some religious instruction. There's Catholic, Protestant, and Jewish – any of those sound good to you?"

Figure 18.10

One way of trying to make sense of this appeal to the irrationality of faith is by seeing that there are limits to reason. Pascal once said that reason's last and greatest step is to recognise that there are many things that lie beyond it. His point was that reason can take us only so far, and that when it comes to our 'core intuitions' about the nature of reality – such as our belief that life is not a dream – we have no choice but to appeal to faith.

So rather than say that faith is as rational as our other beliefs, we might say that faith is indeed irrational but so are our other core beliefs. In this situation, what is required is not so much a proof as a decision – a *leap of faith*.

The varieties of religion

For much of this chapter the discussion has suggested there is some one thing called religion; but there are, of course, many different religions in the world. The five biggest in terms of numbers of adherents are: Christianity (2,100 million), Islam (1,500 million), Hinduism (900 million), Chinese traditional religion (394 million) and Buddhism (376 million). Other major world religions include Confucianism, Shintoism, Taoism, Judaism, Jainism, Sikhism and the Baha'i faith. The question that we will now consider is how these different religions are related to one another.

"You picked the wrong religion, period. I'm not going to argue about it."

Figure 18.11

If we take what different religions say at face value, then they clearly contradict one another. For there are many different views about such things as the nature of God, what happens when you die, and which prophets and holy books contain the truth.

ACTIVITY 18.15

Compare and contrast the beliefs of two different religions about the following topics:

a. How the universe came into existence
b. The existence of suffering
c. What happens when you die

Responses to the contradictions between religions

There are three possible ways of responding to the fact that different religions contradict one another.

1 One religion is true and all the rest are false

This approach has the attraction of simplicity, but it raises the question of how we should determine which religion is true and which are false. The problem is complicated by the fact that within each religion there are many different sects, each claiming that *it* is the sole guardian of the truth. For example, in North America, there are more than a thousand different Christian groups, many of which believe that they alone are the one true Church.

ACTIVITY 18.16

1. What reasons, if any, are there for believing that some religions are superior to others?
2. If one religion was found to be true and all the rest are false, what do you think the consequences will be for good people who happen to have followed the wrong religion?

LQ – Human sciences: What can psychology tell us about the nature of religious belief?

2 All religions are false

The second option, favoured by atheists, is to take the variety of religious beliefs as evidence for their all being false. Several related points can be made here.

a. Since any evidence in support of one religion counts as evidence *against* every other religion, and since every religion puts forward evidence in support of its own doctrines, the balance of evidence and counter-evidence for any particular religion would seem to cancel out.

b. We cannot appeal to the passion of the faithful to decide between different religions because the faithful of different religions hold their beliefs with equal passion.

c. The fact that, in practice, the vast majority of religious people follow the beliefs of the community they grow up in might suggest that they are simply culturally conditioned beliefs.

ACTIVITY 18.17

1. To what extent do you think your religious beliefs, if any, have been affected by the society you grew up in?
2. If a religious person's beliefs are the result of indoctrination, could the same be said about an atheist's beliefs?

3 All religions point towards the same underlying truth

A third possible response to the fact that different religions contradict one another is to argue that, despite superficial differences, they are all pointing towards the same underlying truth. An analogy that is sometimes used to illustrate this idea is that of the blind men and the elephant. One blind man holds the elephant's leg and thinks that an elephant is like a big tree; a second grabs its trunk and insists that it is like a large snake; a third touches its side and concludes it is like a huge wall. While each of the blind men is convinced that he is right and the others are wrong, they are, of course, all touching the same elephant. Perhaps in a similar way, different religions have captured different aspects of the same underlying truth.

RLS – Headline: 'Malaysia court rules non-Muslims cannot use "Allah"'. Although they use different languages, do all religions point to the same underlying truth?

ACTIVITY 18.18

How good do you think the analogy of the blind men and the elephant is? What are its main strengths and weaknesses?

This option, which is sometimes known as **religious pluralism**, is an attractive one for at least three reasons. First, it takes seriously the religious beliefs of millions of people. Second, while admitting that the world's religions are culturally conditioned, it nevertheless holds that they are genuine responses to the same underlying religious truth. Third, if widely embraced, it might do something to reduce religious conflicts in the world. However, as noted elsewhere, the mere attractiveness of an option does not guarantee that it is true.

KT – religious pluralism: the belief that different religions have captured different aspects of the same underlying truth

Figure 18.12 The distribution of world religions

Figure 18.13 Mystical practices can be found in all religions. In Islam's Sufi tradition, the Whirling Dervishes are renowned for dancing themselves into trance-like states.

Despite the analogy of the blind men and the elephant, the biggest obstacle to religious pluralism remains the fact that different religions appear to contradict one another. One way of trying to get round this problem is to argue that many religious statements are not literally true, but only metaphorically true. The Bible, for example, says that God created the world in seven days, but many Christians are comfortable with the idea that this is not literally true.

The idea that some religious statements should be interpreted metaphorically rather than literally is an interesting one, but it solves one problem only by creating another. For the question now is: which statements should we interpret literally and which metaphorically? A Christian, for example, might be happy to take the idea that God created the world in seven days metaphorically, but what about the virgin birth or the resurrection?

As attractive as religious pluralism is, it is hard to avoid the conclusion that the explicit beliefs of different religions contradict one another. And yet the similarities that can be found in the mystical experiences of people from many different traditions continue to nourish the belief that, at the deepest level, all religions point towards the same underlying truth.

Pantheism

There are many people who do not subscribe to any organised religion, and yet experience a sense of wonder when they contemplate starry skies, or stormy seas or snow-covered mountains. Since such feelings engender a sense of being part of something greater than ourselves, they, too, might loosely be described as religious.

Perhaps not surprisingly, **pantheism** – the belief that God and nature are one – seems to be particularly popular among scientists. For example, although Einstein (1879–1955) explicitly denied that he believed in a God 'who concerns himself with the fate and actions of human beings', he often spoke of his sense of awe in contemplating the universe, and he once wrote to a colleague: 'I have found no better expression than "religious" for confidence in the rational nature of reality, insofar as it is accessible to human reason.'

KT – pantheism: the belief that God and the universe are one

Such a 'nature religion' seems to be very different from theistic religions which speak of a creator God, and an immortal soul, and heaven and hell, and miracles and prayer. So perhaps it is misleading to use the word 'religion' to cover both sets of beliefs. Indeed, since pantheism claims that God and nature are one, we might be tempted to agree with Schopenhauer (1788–1860) that it is simply a polite form of atheism. For it is difficult to see the difference between saying that everything is God and nothing is God. There does, however, seem to be at least difference in *flavour* between pantheism's reverence for nature and some cruder forms of atheistic materialism which lack any sense of wonder at the world and see nature as merely something to be exploited for human ends.

ACTIVITY 18.19

1. Do some online research and read the Pantheist Credo drawn up by the World Pantheist Movement. Which points in the Credo do you agree with and which do you disagree with?
2. What arguments can be made for and against Schopenhauer's claim that pantheism is simply a polite form of atheism?

Conclusion

Our discussion in this chapter has raised many of the big questions about the meaning and purpose of life. While some people turn to religion to find the answers to these questions, others believe that religion raises more questions than it answers. If anything has come out of our discussion, it is that there are no easy options in this area. Perhaps religious believers and atheists can at least agree that – in this life at least – we will never have the answers to the deepest mysteries. And perhaps if we can learn to hold even our deepest beliefs with a degree of humility, then we will be less likely to kill one another in the name of things we do not fully understand.

Key points

- Religions are concerned with questions of meaning and purpose which trouble all human beings.
- If we try to define God, we are in danger of falling into anthropomorphism or running into paradoxes, but this does not mean that religious language is meaningless.
- All religions are founded on a bedrock of intense personal experiences, but opinions differ about how such experiences should be interpreted.
- The argument from design sees the order and harmony of the universe as evidence for the existence of God, but critics argue that there are natural explanations for it.
- The cosmological argument says that, since everything has a cause, the universe must have been created by God; but we might then ask 'Who created God?'
- Some see the existence of suffering as incompatible with an all-powerful and all-loving God; but it could be argued that much of the suffering in the world is a consequence of human free-will.
- Faith plays an important role in religion, but people have different views about what faith is and whether or not it is rational.
- The fact that there are many different religions in the world raises the question of whether they all contradict one another or whether they all point towards the same underlying truth.
- Some people are attracted by the pantheistic belief that God and nature are one; but critics argue that pantheism is simply a polite form of atheism.
- Since we will never have the answers to the deepest mysteries, it may be wise to hold our religious beliefs with a degree of humility.

Key terms

agnosticism
anthropomorphism
argument from design
atheism
cosmological argument
free-will defence
logical positivism
metaphysical
omniamorous
omnipotent
omniscient
pantheism
paradigm
paradox of omnipotence
paradox of suffering
Pascal's wager
problem of suffering
religious pluralism
wish fulfilment

Knowledge framework focus

1. *Scope/applications.* Are religious questions about the meaning and purpose of life by definition the most important questions we can ask?
2. *Concepts/language*. Should religious language be interpreted metaphorically rather than literally? Do the highest religious truths lie beyond language?
3. *Methodology*. Can religious truths be based on rational argument, or are knowledge claims in this area based more on faith, revelation and authority?
4. *Historical development.* Are alleged religious truths timeless, or do they change and develop over time in response to changing historical circumstances?
5. *Relation to personal knowledge.* Should we understand religions more in terms of personal beliefs or social practices?

IB prescribed essay titles

1. Can the scientific view of the world be reconciled with the religious view of the world? (November 1995 / May 1996)
2. Analyse the strengths and weaknesses of using faith as a basis for knowledge in religion and in one area of knowledge from the TOK diagram. (May 2012)

Further reading

Books

Richard H. Popkin and Avrum Stroll, *Philosophy Made Simple* (Heinemann, 1986), Chapter 4: 'Philosophy of religion'. This chapter gives a very clear and easy-to-follow account of some of the main arguments for and against the existence of God.

Todd C. Moody, *Does God Exist?* (Hackett Publishing, 1996). This short and accessible book explores the question of the existence of God through a series of dialogues. It is worth reading a couple of them to get a sense of how arguments and counter-arguments can be developed in this area.

Online articles

Julian Baggini, 'Give Me a Reasonable Believer Over an Uncompromising Atheist any Day', *The Guardian*, 15 March 2012.

John Gray, 'Can Religion Tell Us More Than Science?', *BBC*, 16 September 2011.

Ian Sample, 'Tests of Faith', *The Guardian*, 24 February 2005.

Part
4

THE BIG PICTURE

Cultural perspectives on knowledge

19

We must educate people who can operate as world citizens with sensitivity and understanding.

Martha C. Nussbaum, 1947–

[History] shows that there are no pure races or pure cultures; all owe something to the others.

Jacques Barzun, 1907–2012

A wise person learns from everyone.

Ancient rabbinic saying

Human cognition is not everywhere the same.

Richard Nisbett, 1941–

Seek knowledge even unto China.

Islamic Hadith

I am human: nothing human is alien to me.

Terence, d. 159 BCE

The core of intercultural awareness is learning to separate observation from interpretation.

Geert Hofstede, 1928–

I want all the cultures of all lands to be blown about my house as freely as possible. But I refuse to be blown off my feet by any.

Mahatma Gandhi, 1869–1948

We gaze continually at the world and it grows dull in our perceptions. Yet seen from another's vantage point, as if new, it may still take our breath away.

Alan Moore, 1953–

The point of conversation isn't consensus, it's understanding.

Kwame Anthony Appiah, 1954–

Although we are in different boats you in your boat and we in our canoe we share the same river of life.

Chief Oren Lyons, 1930–

Introduction

One of the things that makes human beings unique is that in addition to our biological inheritance, we are also shaped by **culture**. Culture consists of those beliefs and practices that are passed on from one generation to another and it is closely connected with language. If we think of the brains and bodies we are born with as the hardware, we might say that culture is the software which formats our minds and inclines us to think and behave in one way rather than another. This suggests that the answer to the central TOK question 'How do you know?' may depend in part on who *you* are and the culture you belong to.

KT – culture: the beliefs and practices which are passed on from one generation to another

While we often identify cultures with countries and speak of, say, Japanese culture, French culture, or Argentinian culture, there are many more cultures in the world than there are countries. An estimated 350 million people belong to **indigenous cultures** – that is, cultures which have deep historical links with a particular geographical territory. Historically, indigenous groups have varied in size and complexity ranging from *bands* of nomadic hunter-gatherers made up of one or more extended families to *chiefdoms* consisting of thousands, or even tens of thousands, of individuals living under a hereditary chief. We might also describe as 'indigenous' various peasant communities around the world and the descendants of people who belonged to once-mighty empires such as the Inca empire of South America or the Mali empire of West Africa.

KT – indigenous culture: a minority culture which has deep historical links with a particular geographical territory

In this chapter we will look at how cultural perspectives – including indigenous ones – influence what we claim to know about the world. We begin by saying something about **globalisation** and the threat it poses to cultural diversity. We then focus on three main questions:

KT – globalisation: the process by which the world is becoming politically, economically and culturally integrated

1. How does culture influence the way people think about the world?

2. To what extent can we *understand* other cultures?

3. What, if anything, can we learn from other cultures?

As an IB student, you are doubtless to celebrate cultural diversity. Nevertheless, there are difficult questions lurking beneath the surface, such as: Are all cultural perspectives equally valid? Do we have the right to judge other cultures? What are the limits of acceptable diversity? As usual, there are no simple answers to these questions, and you will need to think them over and draw your own conclusions.

The advance of globalisation

The backdrop to any contemporary discussion about cultural perspectives on knowledge is globalisation. This refers to the process by which the world is becoming politically, economically, and culturally integrated. While some welcome globalisation as a force for enlightenment and prosperity, others see it as a steamroller which is threatening diversity and leading to an increasingly homogeneous world. One indication of the threat to cultural diversity is the speed at which languages are dying out. Some linguists predict that more than half of the 6,000 or so languages in existence will disappear in the next 100 years, and there are only 600 languages with enough speakers to be considered safe. When a language dies, so too does a unique way of looking at the world, built up over countless generations.

ACTIVITY 19.1

1. Most people are more aware of and concerned about the loss of biological diversity than the loss of cultural diversity. Why do you think this is and to what extent do you think it is justified?
2. What difficulties are there in estimating the number of languages in existence and the rate at which they are likely to disappear?
3. How can the widespread use of an official language, such as English or Spanish, affect indigenous cultures in a country?

Figure 19.1 Are multinational companies such as McDonald's undermining local cultures?

Globalisation is also affecting cultures with robust languages. Superficially, it is apparent in the spread of multinational brands, such as Coca-Cola™, McDonald's™, and Nike™. Such brands can, of course, coexist with local cultures, and you will not lose your cultural identity simply because you consume foreign goods. Nevertheless, cultural exports, such as education, movies, and music can gradually influence the way people think, and result in what some have called the 'colonisation of the mind'. This may be a loaded expression, but the information we use and the categories that are available to us for making sense of the world are likely to influence our understanding of reality.

To illustrate the problem, consider Wikipedia, which is the main source for information in many parts of the world. According to the Oxford Internet Institute, the range of cultural information it contains is hugely biased. When researchers analysed a 2010 dataset of Wikipedia articles written in any language which had been tagged for geographical location, they found that 84 per cent of them concerned Europe and North America, and only 1 per cent were related to China – which accounts for around 20 per cent of the world's population. Furthermore, there were more articles written about the barren and uninhabited continent of Antarctica than any country in Africa. Indeed, there are more articles about the fictional realm of *Middle-earth* (of *Lord of the Rings* fame) than many African countries. Since Africa has a population of over one billion people and an extraordinarily rich diversity of cultures, this is a cause for concern. We may hope that in the future such information inequalities are rectified as new Wikipedia editors from under-represented countries fill in the gaps in cultural knowledge; but the unequal distribution of power and influence in the world may mean that these informational inequalities will remain.

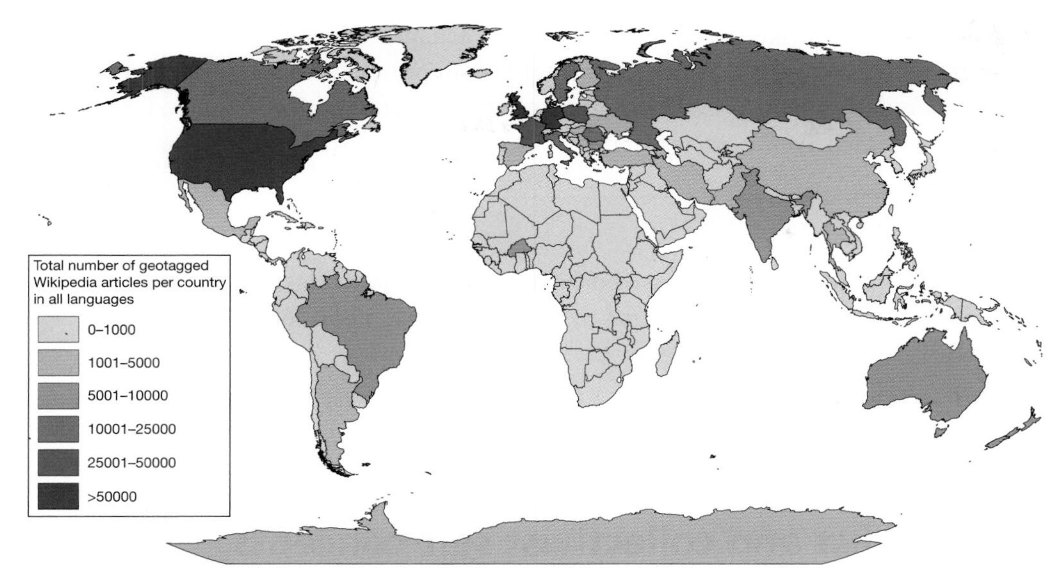

Figure 19.2 Geotagged map of the world

At a deeper level, we might worry that globalisation is forcing us all to think in the same way. This might, of course, be a good thing. Perhaps the spread of universal reason will enable us to overcome ignorance and superstition. To some, this may seem like **cultural imperialism**. For who is to say that our way of justifying beliefs is the only way? What if the various ways of knowing we use to support our beliefs are themselves culturally biased? What if different cultures perceive the world in different ways, or have different standards of reason, or find different things intuitively compelling? This is a possibility that we should take seriously and we will consider it further in the next section.

KT – cultural imperialism: the imposition by a dominant culture of its beliefs and values on a minority culture

ACTIVITY 19.2

1. Some people claim that the IB in general, and TOK in particular, is 'too western' in its approach and outlook. What do you think this means and to what extent do you think it is true?
2. Do you think that, on balance, the internet is leading to greater cultural diversity or greater cultural uniformity?

Culture and cognition

Human beings are all descended from a relatively small group of people who lived in Africa until around 55,000 years ago and then went on to colonise the entire planet. Given this it is clear that from a biological point of view we are all basically the same. Since we share the same cognitive hardware (brains, sense organs, etc.), it might seem reasonable to suppose that all human beings think in basically the same way. Until recently, this was the default assumption of most psychologists. However, there is a growing body of research which suggests that there are bigger differences in the way people from different cultures think than was previously believed. Such differences may have been overlooked because, as we saw in Chapter 14, generalisations about human nature have often been based on highly unrepresentative samples of so-called WEIRD people – where WEIRD is an acronym for people from Western, Educated, Industrialised, Rich Democracies.

ACTIVITY 19.3

1. If Martian anthropologists arrived on Earth and began to study us, do you think they would be more struck by the similarities between our cultures or the differences between them?
2. How can studying other cultures help to make us aware of assumptions we take for granted in our own culture?

Individualist and collectivist self-concepts

According to one widely held theory, the way in which people think is closely related to their concept of the self. Some cultures have a more *individualist* self-concept, others a more *collectivist* one. While individualist cultures value 'me-centred' independence and self-expression, collectivist cultures value 'we-centred' interdependence and social harmony. In the former, people are keenly aware of their own uniqueness and they value being true to themselves; in the latter, people have a more social concept of themselves and are keen to fit in. (Compare the American proverb 'The squeaky wheel gets the grease' with the Chinese saying 'The loudest duck gets shot'.) While individualist cultures think of the self in terms of fixed personality traits – such as 'smart', 'kind', 'open-minded' – collectivist cultures have a more fluid conception of the self which varies according to the situation. In Japanese, for example, there are many different words for 'I' depending on the context and your relationship to the listener. The map below, based on the work of the Dutch social psychologist Geert Hofstede (1928–), shows where different cultures around the world appear on an individualist – collectivist continuum.

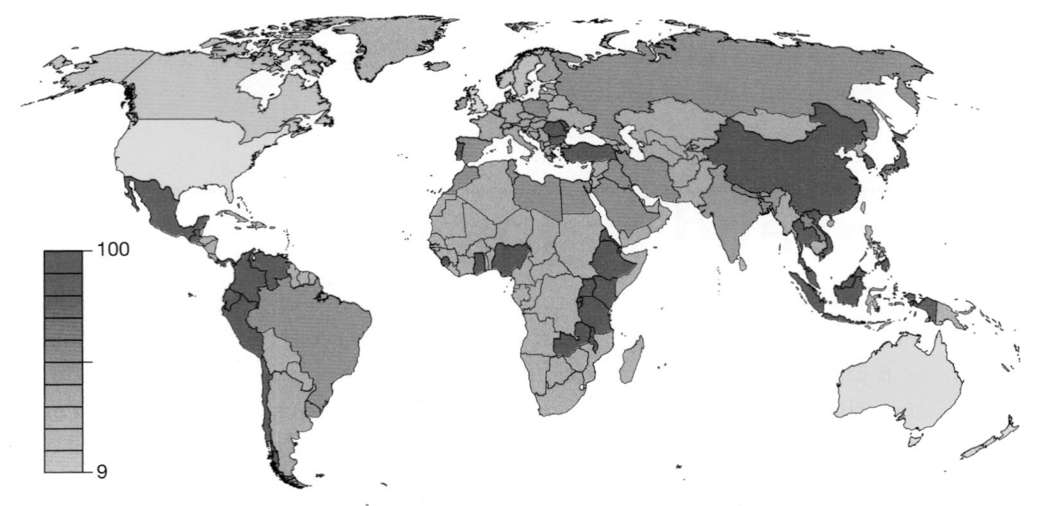

Figure 19.3 World map showing the degree of individualism (yellow) or collectivism (red). Grey represents countries for which no data were available.

ACTIVITY 19.4

1. How might one go about trying to measure the extent to which a culture is individualist or collectivist?
2. To what extent do you think your character is fixed and to what extent do you think it varies with the people you interact with?
3. What are the pros and cons of having a collectivist as opposed to an individualist conception of the self?

Analytic and holistic thinking

These contrasting concepts of the self appear to serve as a model for the way people think in general. Individualism is associated with **analytic thinking**, and collectivism is associated with **holistic thinking**. Analytic thinking is the tendency to break things into their *individual* parts and examine their elements. Holistic thinking, by contrast, is the tendency to look at things *collectively* and see them as one integrated whole. While the former seeks explanations at the level of *objects and their properties* and is related to *explicit reasoning*, the latter focuses more on *contexts and relationships* and is related to *intuitive judgement*.

KT – analytic thinking: the tendency to break things into their individual parts and examine their elements

KT – holistic thinking: the tendency to look at things as one integrated whole rather than as individual parts

Psychologists have devised various tests to see where individuals lie on an analysis–holism scale. Subjects are given statements such as the following and asked how strongly they agree or disagree with them:

1. Everything in the universe is somehow related to everything else.
2. It is more desirable to take the middle ground than to go to extremes.
3. It is more important to pay attention to the whole than to its parts.
4. Any phenomenon has numerous causes and consequences, although some of them are not known.
5. When I hear two sides of an argument, I often agree with both.
6. When one's opinions conflict with another's opinions, it is more important to find a point of compromise than to debate who is right/wrong.

As you may have guessed, if you strongly agree with each of the above statements you lie at the holistic end of the scale; and if you strongly disagree with each of them, you lie at the analytic end of the scale.

Two main groups of academics have been at the forefront of research into the effects of culture on cognition: psychologists and anthropologists. In what follows, we look at some of the alleged differences between western, eastern and traditional indigenous cultures. However, two brief words of warning are appropriate. First, this analysis is at a very general level, and labels such as 'western', 'eastern' and 'indigenous' cover a wide variety of cultures whose differences may be as important as their similarities. Second, the extent to which culture influences cognition is a matter of continuing debate.

East and west: the geography of thought

In his influential book *The Geography of Thought,* the psychologist Richard E. Nisbett (1941–) analyses the difference between ways of thinking in some Asian and western countries. (His research is based mainly on comparisions between Chinese, Japanese and Korean subjects on the one hand, and American subjects on the other.) As you can see from the map in Figure 19.3, the former typically have a collectivist/holistic mindset and the latter typically have an individualist/analytic one. According to Nisbett, the difference between these two mindsets impacts on the way people talk, see and think about the world.

Language

If language reflects the way a culture sees the world, we might (as a rough approximation) say that for the west the world consists of *stable things* while for the east it consists of *changing processes*. If we compare, say, English and Chinese, the difference is apparent. English values clarity – you should say what you mean – and the subject–verb–object structure of its grammar gives prominence to things. Indeed, it even *invents* things in order to ensure that every sentence has a subject. For example, in the sentence '*It* is raining' there is, of course, no *it* doing the raining – there is just the process: *raining*. Similarly in the sentence, 'The lightning flashed': there is no lightning that *does* the flashing – there is just the flashing. In Chinese, by contrast, many words function as both verbs and nouns, so it is easier to think of the things denoted by them as processes. (If we take seriously the idea that everything is changing all the time, then there is a sense in which all nouns are simply 'slow verbs'.) In general, Chinese is more ambiguous than English and the meanings of words tends to vary with context. This mirrors the idea that to understand something we need to look at the overall situation.

ACTIVITY 19.5

1. Do you think it is more accurate to say that the world consists of things, or that the world consists of processes?
2. Referring back to the Sapir–Whorf hypothesis (see Chapter 4, page 98), to what extent do you think language influences how we see the world?

Perception

Since we all have the same sense organs, we might think that we all see the world in the same way; but there are significant cultural differences in what we perceive and remember. These differences are thought by some psychologists to stem from differences in social perception. As discussed earlier in this section, research indicates that westerners tend to focus on individuals, while many Asians are more sensitive to the broader social context. For example, when American and Japanese subjects were shown the cartoon in Figure 19.4, the Americans judged the central figure to be happier

Figure 19.4 To what extent are our judgements of people's emotions influenced by the surrounding context?

Figure 19.5 How much does culture influence perception?

than their Japanese counterparts did. While the Americans tended to focus on the central figure in isolation, the Japanese were influenced by the context of the sad faces in the background and qualified their judgements accordingly.

In another well-known study called the Michigan Fish Test, American and Japanese subjects were briefly shown the image in Figure 19.5 and then asked to describe what they had seen. The Americans typically focused on the salient object and said 'There was what looked like a trout swimming to the left.' The Japanese, by contrast, tended to start with the context, observing 'There was a lake or pond.' When the picture was altered, the Japanese were better at noticing changes in the background, while the Americans were better at recognising that it was the same fish in a different environment. Such differences in perceptual processing are likely to influence not only what people remember, but also the kinds of narratives – agent-centred or context-centred – they construct about the world.

ACTIVITY 19.6

How do you think the way different cultures perceive the world influences the kind of art they typically produce?

Reason

There is evidence to suggest that people from different cultures have different default reasoning styles, and that this may influence how they classify things. Consider, for example, the following question: 'Which is the odd one out: monkey, panda, banana?' When American and Chinese subjects were asked this question, there was a marked tendency for the former to say 'banana' and the latter to say 'panda'. This is because westerners are inclined to think in terms of categories: monkeys and pandas are animals, so banana is the odd one. Asians, by contrast, tend to think in terms of relations: monkeys eat bananas, so panda is the odd one out. While our own way of classifying things may strike us as 'obvious', both approaches are equally valid.

When it comes to logic, some people take it as axiomatic that A = A, while others are more aware that A may change with time and context. Westerners often take a black-and-white, either–or, right-or-wrong approach, whereas people from Asian cultures tend to have a more shades-of-grey, both-and, truth-on-both-sides style which makes them more willing to accept apparent contradictions. To illustrate, consider the following results from cross-cultural studies:

- When Americans were asked to explain the conflict between a mother and daughter, they tended to think that one person was right and the other wrong, whereas Chinese subjects tended to explain the conflict in terms of mutual misunderstanding.
- When subjects were given a graph which showed accelerating economic growth and asked to make a prediction, American subjects were more likely to think that the growth would continue, Chinese subjects that it would reverse.
- When subjects were asked to rate various proverbs, American subjects particularly liked unambiguous ones, such as 'Half a loaf is better than none', while Chinese subjects preferred seemingly contradictory ones, such as 'Too humble is half proud'.

Convergence

The above generalisations are based on research by cultural psychologists, and they seem to hold true even though labels such as 'Asian' and 'western' cover many different cultural traditions. Nevertheless, it is important to emphasise that they indicate trends and tendencies rather than exceptionless laws. So it is easy to find counter-examples. Indeed, there is evidence to suggest that with globalisation these two styles of thinking may be converging and interpenetrating. For example, in Asia there is a strong emphasis on developing critical thinking skills; while in the West, there is great interest in Buddhism and other kinds of eastern philosophy. Rather than being locked into one or other of these two ways of thinking, some psychologists think that we can learn to switch between them as the situation demands. Therefore, perhaps analytic and holistic thinking should be seen as equally useful tools that can be used in different contexts to help us make sense of the world.

ACTIVITY 19.7

1. How is your own culture's way of thinking similar to and different from the ones discussed above?
2. Why is it important to understand how different cultures see and think about the world when trying to resolve international disputes?

Indigenous perspectives on knowledge

Indigenous communities do not appear on the map of individualist and collectivist cultures shown in Figure 19.3 (page 544); but they generally fall at the collectivist end of the continuum. This has led some scholars to say that the real cultural divide is not between the west and the east, but between the west and the rest. With the advance of globalisation, many traditional communities are disappearing, but there are still some which have been largely unaffected by formal education and the global market.

Such cultures do not make any clear-cut distinction between the physical and the spiritual world, and human beings are seen as an integral part of nature – active participants rather than passive observers. We will now consider three interrelated aspects of their thinking styles: oral communication, perceptual acuity and concrete thinking.

Oral communication

Traditional indigenous societies are oral rather than written cultures. The absence of writing means that the total amount of knowledge available is limited to the collective memory of the group. Nevertheless, group members often have prodigious memories, and explicit knowledge is usually communicated via stories which are passed down (and creatively reinterpreted) from one generation to another. One reason why tribal elders are usually held in high regard is that they have long memories. This makes them a potential source of knowledge about rare – and possibly dangerous – events that younger members of the tribe may never have experienced. A great deal of knowledge that is important for survival is, however, implicit and is acquired by imitation and practice.

Figure 19.6 To what extent are older people in your culture seen as a source of wisdom?

The memories of people from indigenous cultures are also closely connected with the land, and there is some truth in the observation that for Amazonian Indians, for example, the forest is their library. (Recall the point made on page 256 that memories are more easily triggered in the place where we acquire them.) Therefore, if they lose their land, there is a sense in which they also lose their memory. In this context, it is worth noting the 'songlines' of the Aborigines of Australia. As the name suggests, these are pathways, often extending over hundreds of kilometres of barren terrain, which knowledgeable travellers can navigate by repeating songs that describe various geographical features and landmarks.

ACTIVITY 19.8

1. Is there any reason to think that oral history is more subjective and biased than written history?
2. To what extent are the elderly seen as a source of wisdom in your culture? To what extent *are* they a source of wisdom?
3. Compare and contrast the effects on memory of: (a) a person from an indigenous culture losing their land; (b) an IB student losing their computer and access to the internet.
4. How does the knowledge of an aborigine following a songline differ from the knowledge of a driver using a satellite navigation device?

As we explored in our discussion of memory in Chapter 10, some scholars claim that there are significant differences in the thinking styles of people in oral and written cultures. While the spoken word quickly fades away, writing is more permanent, and this makes it easier to keep track of ideas, reflect on them and monitor their consistency. This in turn is said to lead to a more abstract style of thinking. If you imagine trying to compose a theory of knowledge essay in your head without the help of writing, you will see the extent to which abstract thinking depends on writing.

Nevertheless, purely oral languages are as sophisticated as any others, and they contain a wealth of subtle distinctions. Consider, for example, the language of the Tuyuca, a small tribe who straddle the borders of Brazil and Colombia. It contains a feature known as evidentiality which, in effect, obliges you to answer the question 'How do you know?' every time you make an assertion. To take an example given by the linguist David Crystal, in Tuyuca you cannot just say 'He played soccer'; you must support your claim with one of five kinds of evidence:

Visual	*diiga apé-wi* 'I saw him play soccer'
Non-visual	*diiga apé-ti* 'I heard the soccer game and him, but I didn't see it or him'
Apparent	*diiga apé-yi* 'I have seen evidence that he played soccer – such as his clothes in the changing room – but I did not see him play'
Second-hand	*diiga apé-yigi* 'I obtained the information that he played soccer from someone else'
Assumed	*diiga apé-hiyi* 'It is reasonable to assume that he played soccer'

If you were a native Tuyuca speaker, perhaps thinking in a TOK way would be second nature to you!

ACTIVITY 19.9

1. The United Nations organisation UNICEF (United Nations Children's Fund) has long campaigned for universal access to education. Should schooling in reading and writing be compulsory (a) in your own country? (b) throughout the world?
2. If a strange virus destroyed our ability to read and write, do you think it would still make sense to have schools? What might a purely oral curriculum look like?
3. To what extent do technologies such as writing and the internet affect the way in which people think?

Perceptual acuity

While the academic knowledge of written cultures is more *extensive* than that of oral cultures, some people claim that the 'lived' knowledge of oral cultures is more *intensive* than that of written cultures. The quantity of knowledge available in modern societies clearly dwarfs anything that can be found in traditional ones (partly because of the sheer number of people contributing to it), but some people claim that indigenous people are more aware of the sights, sounds, textures, tastes and smells in their environment than literate people are. We might speculate that as literacy is educated into us, perceptual acuity is educated out, and that when we perceive the world through abstract categories we overlook the unique particularity of things. The problem may be greater in technological societies where we are often so distracted by our gadgets that we fail to see what is in front of us.

ACTIVITY 19.10

1. Compare and contrast the knowledge of an average US citizen with that of an average Amazonian indian. Who do you think has the *broader* knowledge and who do you think has the *deeper* knowledge?
2. How much of what you learn at school is directly relevant to your life? How much of what someone from an indigenous culture learns is directly relevant to their life? Illustrate your answer with specific examples.
3. If there was a catastrophic and permanent worldwide failure in electrical supply, how useful do you think your practical knowledge would be relative to someone from an indigenous culture?

It has often been observed that indigenous people have a remarkably detailed knowledge of local plants and animals. Consider, for example, anthropologist Robert Bradford Fox's (1918–85) description of the Negrito people of the Philippines:

> *Most Negrito men can with ease enumerate the . . . names of at least four hundred and fifty plants, seventy-five birds, most of the snakes, fish, insects, and animals, and of even twenty species of ants . . . and the botanical knowledge of the mananambal, the medicine men and women, who use plants constantly in their practice, is truly astounding.*

RLS – Headline: 'Ecuador mixes folk and modern medicine'. How can we test the effectiveness of traditional medical practices?

Furthermore, the Negrito 'employ nearly one hundred terms in describing the parts or characteristics of plants', and they are curious about everything in their environment – even if it is of no practical value.

Many modern drugs are based on traditional herbal cures that were originally discovered by indigenous peoples. For example, quinine, which is found naturally in the bark of the cinchona tree, was long used by the Quecha people of Peru and Bolivia to treat fevers. Later, it became the first effective treatment for malaria – which still kills an estimated three million people a year. Similarly, artemisinin, which comes from the sweet wormwood plant, has been known to traditional Chinese medicine for thousands of years. It, too, is a potent anti-malarial drug and may also be useful in the treatment of cancer. Many other drugs in everyday use are also derived from natural products. Such knowledge has been developed over many centuries through careful observation, classification, and trial-and-error experimentation. If we define science as 'a systematic approach to acquiring knowledge of the natural world', then we might call this 'indigenous science'.

ACTIVITY 19.11

1. How is indigenous knowledge of plant-based medicines similar to scientific knowledge and how is it different?
2. Why, if at all, does it *matter* whether or not we describe indigenous peoples' knowledge of their environment as 'scientific'?
3. 'There is no such thing as "alternative medicine" – just medicine that works and medicine that doesn't.' Discuss.

RLS – Headline: 'Monsanto to face biopiracy charges in India'. Under what circumstances can a group or organisation justifiably claim to own knowledge?

As the above examples suggest, there is a wealth of useful local knowledge hidden in the indigenous cultures of the world, and **ethnobotanists** are scrambling to document it before it disappears. More ominously, some pharmaceutical companies are engaging in what is known as **biopiracy** and are patenting and exploiting such knowledge for profit without compensating – or even recognising – the communities that developed it.

KT – ethnobotanist: a scientist who studies indigenous peoples' knowledge of local plants

KT – biopiracy: the commercial use of indigenous knowledge without permission, recognition or compensation of the relevant communities

Concrete thinking

The uncompromising empiricism of traditional indigenous people may explain why they tend to be suspicious of abstract thinking. When the Russian psychologist Alexander Luria (1902–77) tried to test the reasoning skills of a nomadic people in central Asia, they refused to cooperate. For example, Luria gave one man the following information: 'All bears in the North are white, and a friend who lives in the North has sent me a letter saying that he had seen a bear.' He then asked the man what the colour of the bear was. The answer may be obvious to us, but the man replied: 'How should I know? Ask your friend who saw the bear.' Another man explained, 'We always speak only of what we see; we don't talk about what we haven't seen.' Of course, the nomads were perfectly able to use their knowledge to solve practical problems in their everyday lives. Their refusal to engage with formal logic does not imply a lack of intelligence, but merely shows that people in different cultures direct their intelligence in different ways.

While 'educated' people often see abstract thinking as a sign of sophistication, the French anthropologist Claude Lévi-Strauss (1908–2009) insisted that concrete and abstract thinking are simply reflections of different needs and interests. Consider the Piraha people of north-west Brazil whose language (as discussed in Chapter 12, on page 314) only has words for 'one', 'two' and 'many'. The reason for this limited vocabulary is simply that they have no use for numbers in their culture. So, not surprisingly, they have shown no interest in learning basic arithmetic when attempts have been made to teach them. As an IB student, abstract and quantitative reasoning may be second nature to you, but this is simply because it is 'on the syllabus' and it has been drilled into you from an early age.

If you are interested in your immediate environment, then concrete reasoning embedded in local knowledge may serve you better than abstract reasoning. As an analogy, imagine an outsider planning a route through the jungle using a map. Their proposed route might initially seem more direct than the longer one proposed by local people. However, the outsider may be unaware that part of the route shown on the map always floods at this time of the year and is therefore impassable. What appears rational from the abstract perspective of the outsider may not make sense to an insider with detailed knowledge of the local terrain.

ACTIVITY 19.12

1. What reason, if any, is there to pursue knowledge if it is of no practical value to you?
2. What problems might arise in giving standard IQ tests to indigenous people? How, if at all, might such problems be overcome?

Glocal knowledge

While some anthropologists think that there is a basic continuity between traditional thought and modern scientific thought, others consider that the two patterns of thinking are completely different. On the one hand, all cultures look for regularities in their surroundings and seek to explain them. On the other hand, there are significant differences in the *kinds* of explanations that are given. A widespread assumption in indigenous cultures is that everything has a cause and that there is no such thing as an accident. This may sound reasonable enough, but it often leads to magical thinking. For example, if a rotten branch falls off a tree and kills someone as they walk by, the Azande of central Africa will conclude that what would seem to us to be an accident was in fact the work of a sorcerer. While *we* would doubtless reject such an explanation, there is no reason to think that the average so-called 'educated' person's understanding of the world is superior to that of indigenous people. For example, *we* may attribute rainfall to physical causes and *they* may attribute rainfall to the gods, but most of us would struggle to explain why we are right and they are wrong. At the level of *justification*, the majority of people simply believe what everyone else in their community believes.

ACTIVITY 19.13

Do you think that the average person in your own culture is more or less superstitious than people in traditional indigenous cultures? Give reasons.

At a practical level, we do not need to choose between the abstract scientific knowledge associated with modern societies and the concrete ecological knowledge associated with traditional ones. We can instead think of them as two complementary maps drawn to different scales – a very abstract map of the world outlining its general features and a very fine-grained map of a small district showing specific details. To make sense of the world, we surely need both. Given this, we might advocate what is known as **glocal** knowledge – that is, global scientific knowledge which is nevertheless sensitive to local conditions.

KT – glocal: a combination of the global and the local; glocal knowledge arises when general principles are applied to and take account of specific local conditions

Can we understand other cultures?

Since we tend to see other cultures through the lens of our own beliefs and values, it is difficult to get an accurate picture of them. According to the philosopher Martha Nussbaum, there are two key vices we need to avoid.

Chauvinism

KT – chauvinism: the unthinking assumption that your culture is superior to others; roughly synonymous with 'ethnocentrism' and closely associated with 'cultural imperialism'

Chauvinism is the unthinking assumption that your own culture is superior to others. This attitude is often associated with western imperialism, but it seems to be universal. In the fifth century BCE the Greek historian Herodotus observed: 'If anyone, no matter who, were given the opportunity of choosing from amongst all the nations in the world the set of beliefs which he thought best, he would inevitably – after careful considerations of their relative merits – choose that of his own country.' Chauvinism can be found not only in western, eastern, and Islamic cultures, but also in indigenous cultures. For example the Piraha of Brazil call foreign languages 'crooked head' and consider them to be vastly inferior to their own. Another Amazon tribe, the Suruwaha, consider themselves to be the perfect race. Of course, some people do question and criticise – and even reject – their own culture; but the historical record suggests that this is a relatively rare and largely recent phenomenon.

When people are completely immersed in their own culture, it is hardly surprising if they assume that *its* way of looking at things is the *only* way. When we have nothing to compare our local conventions with, they are likely to strike us as natural and universal. (Remember our discussion in Chapter 3, on page 57, of how dividing a day into twelve hours seems natural simply because we are habituated to it.) It requires a considerable effort to free ourselves from this narrow-minded straitjacket, and it is probably not possible without at least some exposure to other cultures.

From a psychological point of view, chauvinism can be seen as a form of egoism: you embrace your own culture, unthinkingly assume it is superior, and refuse to tolerate any criticism of it for no other reason than that it is *your* culture. However, while you may be justifiably proud of the culture in which you were raised, this should not blind you to the fact that it is likely to have weaknesses as well as strengths. While you may bask in the reflected glory of your culture's achievements, it is worth remembering that you did not *personally* create the customs and traditions of which you are so proud. You are simply their lucky inheritor.

Romanticism

Romanticism is the belief that *other* cultures – and not one's own – are the source of wisdom and virtue. This view can lead people to uncritically embrace everything that is alien and seemingly exotic. For example, westerners sometimes identify India with gurus, meditation and spiritual enlightenment. While there is much to be admired in that country's powerful mystical traditions, we should guard against what the Indian film-maker Satyajit Ray (1921–92) called 'the false exotic'. For other-worldly mysticism can coexist with this-worldly materialism, and people can be as occupied with making money as they are with meditating!

Must you belong to a culture to understand it?

Some people claim that you can only really understand a culture if you belong to it. This is because outsiders will inevitably view it through the filter of their own – often invisible – cultural assumptions. Consider, for example, the categories that have been used in this book to divide up the map of knowledge, such as science, the arts and religion. Although they may strike *us* as natural, many cultures have, as we have seen, a more integrated conception of knowledge. *We* may classify the botanical knowledge of indigenous people as 'science', or aboriginal cave paintings as 'art', or Confucianism, Buddhism and Voodoo as 'religions'; but we are likely to misunderstand such phenomena if we ignore their cultural context. Similarly, if we assume that indigenous communities think in terms of 'conservation' or 'sustainability', we may, once again, be looking at their practices through the lens of our own concerns.

Figure 19.7 Does art play a different role in traditional cultures compared with modern cultures?

Anthropologists may seek to overcome the problem of cultural bias by immersing themselves in other cultures for extended periods of time in an effort to understand them 'from the inside'; but they are not chameleons and they can never fully 'go native' and forget their own cultural background. Someone who was born and raised in Tokyo will never be able to see the world in quite the same way as someone who has spent their entire life in a traditional community. Nevertheless, we should not exaggerate the problem; for there are surely *degrees* of understanding, and it seems reasonable to think that descriptions of cultures can be more or less accurate, empathic and insightful.

ACTIVITY 19.14

1. Do you agree or disagree with the claim that in order to *truly* understand a culture you must belong to it?
2. If you live abroad, what challenges are there in understanding the host culture in which you live?
3. To what extent do you think a European can understand another European culture better than a non-European can?
4. To what extent do you think a person from an indigenous culture can understand another indigenous culture better than a non-indigenous person can?

The belief that you must belong to a culture in order to fully understand it raises the question of whether everyone in a culture is equally qualified to speak about it, or

"I'm already seeing an anthropologist."

Figure 19.8

whether some people have greater expertise about their own culture than others. In practice, politicians are often the *de facto* spokespersons for the cultures they claim to represent; but they may reflect the interests of the rich and powerful rather than the culture as a whole. So when the prime minister of Singapore speaks of 'Asian values' or the president of the United States of 'American values', they are not necessarily describing values agreed on by everyone in their respective societies.

It could, in fact, be argued that outsiders are sometimes better placed than insiders to understand certain aspects of a culture. When you inhabit a culture, you may be so thoroughly immersed in its way of looking at things, that, like the proverbial fish in water, you are unaware of them. Just as friends can sometimes improve your self-knowledge by, for example, pointing out mannerisms you are unaware of, so outsiders may help insiders to become aware of hidden assumptions that, to their surprise, are not universal. (It can, for example, come as a shock to discover that not all cultures have the same concept of the self.) As this suggests, our understanding of a culture (our own included) is likely to benefit from dialogue with people who have different perspectives – both internal and external – on it.

ACTIVITY 19.15

1. Do all members of a culture understand it equally well, or do some people understand it better than others?
2. How, if at all, can an informed and sympathetic outsider contribute to a culture's understanding of itself?
3. 'There are likely to be as many descriptions of a culture as there are backgrounds of the people making them.' Why might someone say this, and to what extent is it true?
4. What oddities about your own culture have you learnt through your interaction with people from different cultures?
5. 'The skills required to understand another culture are no different from those required to understand another historical era.' Discuss.

Understanding indigenous cultures

One problem which arises in trying to understand other cultures is that evidence is often ambiguous and open to competing interpretations. This is especially true in the case of traditional indigenous cultures. Such cultures are sometimes thought to give us insight into our 'true nature'. If you think that human beings are naturally good and have been corrupted by civilisation, you may be keen to stress the positive aspects of tribal societies; but if you think human beings are naturally bad and are held in check by civilisation, you may prefer to focus on their negative traits. Since we have a tendency to find what we are looking for, different experts may come to quite different conclusions. Consider, for example, the popular image of indigenous people as egalitarian, peace-loving conservationists. While some people are sympathetic to this view, others are critical of it.

Figure 19.9 What can studying traditional ways of life tell us about human nature?

Egalitarian or hierarchical?

There are different kinds of indigenous cultures and some are more egalitarian than others. Among nomadic hunter-gatherers, such as the !Kung bushmen of the Kalahari desert or the Hadza of Tanzania, there are no chiefs or hierarchies, almost everything is shared among the group, and generosity and humility are important social virtues. Since nomads cannot own more than they can carry, they tend not to accumulate sufficient wealth for it to be a source of inequality. Nevertheless, all societies make some distinction between people according to their age, gender and skill. In settled communities, such differences can become entrenched. For example, in many New Guinea societies, a distinction is made between 'big men', 'ordinary men', 'rubbish men' according to their ability to reciprocate gifts and meet other social obligations. And among the hereditary chiefdoms of the Pacific Northwest in Canada, there are clear differences in wealth and status.

Peaceful or violent?

Sadly, there are no human societies in the world that are oases of peace and harmony. Murder can be found in all societies, and war can be found in almost all of them. The interesting question is how violent traditional societies are relative to state societies. According to Jared Diamond, the evidence is clear: you are ten times more likely to die a violent death in the former than in the latter. This view is disputed by *Survival International*, an organisation dedicated to protecting the rights of indigenous communities. They claim that Diamond's argument depends on selective use of data and focuses disproportionately on tribes with a reputation for violence such as the Yanomamo in Venezuela. Moreover, they suggest that a lot of tribal violence is due not to the absence of 'civilisation', but to its presence in the form of exploitative states which corrupt the social fabric of indigenous groups.

Figure 19.10 The Yanomamo people of Venezuela have been described by anthropologist Napoleon Chagnon as a 'fierce people' who are very prone to violence. However, other anthropologists dispute this claim. How can we decide who is right?

Cultural perspectives on knowledge

Conservationists or exploiters?

Human beings have always actively shaped their environment in order to meet their needs. While some people have a romantic picture of the sustainable practices of indigenous groups, others are more sceptical. There is evidence to support both views. On the one hand, traditional communities have intimate knowledge of their local environment and have found many ways to live sustainably within the carrying capacity of their habitat. Resource use is often governed by strong **taboos** and traditions which can help to protect important species. For example, the Itza-Maya people of Mexico believe that the ramon tree is sacred and that anyone who harms it will be punished by the forest spirits. The tree, in fact, plays a key role in the local ecosystem, and research suggests that the taboo against harming it helps to maintain a sustainable environment. On the other hand, the historical record suggests that some indigenous groups have over-exploited local resources. For example, the Maori of New Zealand hunted the flightless Moa bird to extinction; and Pacific islanders exterminated many species of birds long before the arrival of Europeans. One might also mention the fate of Easter Island where the inhabitants allegedly destroyed their environment by cutting down all the palm trees in order to build their famous statues.

KT – taboo: a sacred value that is not questioned

Figure 19.11 How sure can we be about what happened on Easter Island?

ACTIVITY 19.16

1. Why is it so difficult to establish the truth about the nature of traditional indigenous communities?
2. What light, if any, can studying such communities throw on our understanding of human nature?

As the information in this section suggests, there may not be any simple answers to the above questions – not least because there are many different kinds of indigenous cultures and only a few of them have been studied in any detail. Since anthropologists themselves disagree about how the relevant evidence should be interpreted, we should look carefully at both sides of any debate before drawing (tentative) conclusions.

What can we learn from other cultures?

According to a 2001 United Nations declaration, 'cultural diversity is as necessary for humankind as biodiversity is for nature'. Among other things, it says that such diversity is 'a source of exchange, creativity and innovation'. There seems to be some truth in this claim. The exchange of ideas between cultures is as old as humanity itself, and almost all indigenous groups have traded goods and ideas with their neighbours. Research suggests that, rather than being the achievement of a single culture, key inventions such as the stone axe, the alphabet and numerals resulted from the contributions of many different cultures. During the course of history, cross-cultural fertilisation seems to have been the norm rather than the exception. As we learnt in our discussion of creativity in Chapter 9, cities standing at the crossroads between cultures have often been important centres of creativity.

While the degree of interaction between cultures may vary, the above suggests that there is no such thing as a *pure* culture. Although cultural traditions embody the inherited wisdom of different peoples, they are *living* traditions which change and develop over time – often as a result of contact with other cultures. If you trace any tradition back far enough, you will find that it started life as an innovation. Sometimes things taken from the outside are quickly integrated into a culture. Consider, for example, the 'traditional' attire of Herero women in Namibia. Their dress is based on that worn by nineteenth-century German missionaries; but they replaced the dour colours of the missionaries' clothes with their own exuberant range and made them distinctly their own (see Figure 19.12). What is true of material things is equally true of ideas. As the great Mughal emperor of India, Akbar the Great (1542–1605), observed: 'If traditionalism were proper, the prophets would merely have followed their own elders (and not come with new messages).'

Figure 19.12 Is there such a thing as 'authentic' culture?

Cultural cross-fertilisation

To illustrate the value of cultural exchange, we will now consider a few examples taken from different areas of knowledge.

Science

In the West, modern medicine is often said to have begun with English physician Edward Jenner's (1749–1823) discovery of the smallpox vaccination. However, Jenner built on the work of Islamic medics who were already familiar with the principle of inoculation. Indeed, for many centuries Islamic medicine was the most advanced in the world. The first public hospital was opened in Baghdad in the ninth century; and a book called *Canon of Medicine*, written by the Islamic scholar Avicenna (980–1037), has been described as the single most useful guide for practical medicine until the modern era.

Figure 19.13 Niels Bohr's coat of arms

To take a quite different example, two of the greatest physicists of the twentieth century, Werner Heisenberg (1901–76) and Niels Bohr (1885–1962), both went on lecture tours to Asia and were influenced by the ideas they encountered there. Heisenberg had many conversations with the Indian poet and polymath Rabindranath Tagore (1861–1941) and subsequently reflected: 'After these conversations . . . some of the ideas that had seemed so crazy suddenly made much more sense.' Bohr was sufficiently impressed by the Taoist ideas he encountered in China that when he was knighted in 1947 he integrated the *taijitu* yin and yang symbol into his coat of arms together with the motto 'Opposites are complementary'.

ACTIVITY 19.17

1. What role has cross-cultural fertilisation played in the development of mathematical ideas? (You might refer back to the information on page 315.)
2. To what extent is scientific knowledge universal and to what extent is it shaped by the culture from which it emerges?

The arts

When it comes to the arts, there are numerous examples of cross-cultural fertilisation. One of the best-known is the influence of African art on Pablo Picasso (1881–1973). Picasso's interest was awakened after he visited an exhibition of African art at the Ethnographic Museum in Paris in 1907. The effect on his work was dramatic and immediate – as can be seen if you compare the Dan mask from west Africa with his painting *Mother and Child* (1907) (Figure 19.14). In the same year Picasso produced his famous *Les Demoiselles d'Avignon* – which is widely seen as one of the most important paintings of the twentieth century. If you search for this painting on the internet, you will again see that the African influence is readily apparent. Paris was also where the French composer Claude Debussy (1862–1918) first heard traditional Balinese gamelan music when he visited the Universal Exposition of 1889. Gamelan is said to have made a profound impact on the composer and affected his mature style.

Figure 19.14 West African Dan mask and Picasso's *Mother and Child*, 1907

ACTIVITY 19.18

Give some examples of your own of how the arts have been enriched by exchanges between cultures.

Politics

Some scholars claim that Native American forms of political organisation had an influence on the US Constitution. They point to the Iroquois confederation of six tribes governed by a Great Council which sought to avoid the concentration of power in any single individual's hands; and to the fact that the Iroquois were a fiercely independent people who were horrified by the European idea of social classes. Both of these ideas play an important role in American political culture. While the Iroquois probably had no *direct* influence on the Constitution, the author Charles C. Mann argues that they may have had an *indirect* influence and that the founding fathers 'were pervaded by Indian images of liberty'.

ACTIVITY 19.19

1. Why is it difficult to establish the influence, if any, of the Iroquois on the framers of the US Constitution?
2. How might people's political and emotional prejudices distort their interpretation of the evidence about this issue?

Judging cultures

As well as giving practical arguments for cultural diversity, one might seek to justify it on moral grounds. Since a person's culture is intimately connected with their sense of identity, it is widely held that everyone has a *right* to their own culture. This is a compelling point. Among other things, it implies that indigenous cultures should not be forced to assimilate to surrounding majority cultures and that they should be allowed to determine their own futures. Since the traditional way of life of indigenous people is under threat in many parts of the world, there is clearly an urgent need to protect their rights.

Given the dangers of ethnocentrism, we might understandably insist that we have no right to judge other people's ways of life. After all, who are *we* to say that *we* are right and *they* are wrong? Such a view goes hand-in-hand with relativism which, as discussed in Chapter 17, is the belief that truth is relative to the culture in which you live.

RLS – Headline: 'Ghanaians ban "spirit child" killing'. How can we determine the limits on acceptable cultural diversity? What practices in your own culture have or should be prohibited?

Despite its appeal, non-judgementalism is a difficult position to maintain in practice. Indeed, it could be argued that it is both impossible and undesirable. It is impossible because by advocating it, you are yourself making a judgement - namely, that non-judgementalism is preferable to judgementalism! It is undesirable because it implies that we have nothing to learn from one another. For if we take non-judgementalism seriously, then not only do we have no right to *criticise* other cultures, but we also have no right to *praise* them – for that, too, is to make a judgement. Furthermore, it implies that other cultures have no right to criticise or praise *our* culture.

The good thought behind non-judgementalism is that people are often far too quick to make negative judgements about other cultures on the basis of minimal knowledge and reflection. We should, of course, reject such narrow-minded or uninformed assessments. However, what follows from this is not that we should make *no* judgements, but that we should make *slow* judgements – *not only about other cultures, but also about our own*. Such judgements should be well informed, empathic, and sensitive to the situation. In addition, we should be willing to question our own *standards* for making judgements and be open to the idea that we may need to modify them. Having reflected on the beliefs and practices of another culture, we may conclude that they are neither better nor worse than our own, but equally valid. After all, there is no reason to think that there is only *one* correct way of making sense of the world or organising society.

ACTIVITY 19.20

1. According to a well-known saying, 'Travel broadens the mind'. Do you agree or disagree with this statement? To what extent does it depend on *how* you travel?
2. Name some practices found in other cultures from which you think your own culture could learn.
3. Name some practices found in other cultures that you think are wrong and should be prohibited.
4. If every culture is equally worthy of respect, does it follow by analogy that every historical epoch is equally worthy of respect?

What price diversity?

In practice, our commitment to cultural diversity may conflict with other things that we value, such as freedom, truth and progress.

1. *Diversity versus freedom.* Although generally positive about diversity, we might feel ambivalent about traditions that do not respect individual freedom. We may, for example, be justifiably concerned about discrimination against people on the basis of gender or race. This suggests that people have the right to abandon traditions if they find them oppressive. Consider, for example, the Karen 'long neck' women of northern Thailand (Figure 19.15). While tourists may flock to see them and find their neck rings 'exotic', some of the women themselves say they would like to abandon the custom.

Figure 19.15 Should we always try to preserve cultural traditions?

ACTIVITY 19.21

1. In 1947 the American Anthropological Association refused to endorse drafts of what became the Universal Declaration of Human Rights on the grounds that it was an ethnocentric document. Why do you think they said this, and to what extent do you think they were justified?
2. Should young people in indigenous cultures be actively encouraged to maintain their traditional way of life if they are reluctant to do so?

2. *Diversity versus truth.* During the course of history, human beings have held a vast number of different beliefs about the world. Some of these beliefs may strike us as profound and insightful, others as superstitious and misguided. In the interests of cultural preservation, it would probably be good to try to document all such beliefs. However, it is less clear whether we should encourage people to continue living in what we consider to be false belief systems; and we may struggle to find the right balance between showing respect for traditions – our own and other people's – and being willing to question them.

ACTIVITY 19.22

1. Is diversity always preferable to uniformity? If so, to what extent should diversity *within* cultures also be encouraged?
2. To what extent should we seek to preserve diverse opinions if we think that some of them are false?

RLS – Headline: 'Peru struggles to keep outsiders away from uncontacted Amazon tribe'. What difficulties arise in trying to compare the benefit of a traditional way of life with that of a modern way of life?

3. *Diversity versus progress.* Some supporters of economic development argue that traditional societies need to integrate themselves into the modern world in order to benefit from 'progress'. This raises difficult questions about the meaning and value of progress, but they could be said to include the ability of people to live longer, healthier, more meaningful lives. While we might question whether economic development and the acquisition of material goods give meaning to our lives, access to modern medicine can certainly help to increase life expectancy by reducing infant mortality and combating curable diseases.

ACTIVITY 19.23

1. The anthropologist Marshall Sahlins once described hunter-gatherers as the 'original affluent society' on the grounds that they have limited desires which they can satisfy without having to work too hard. What evidence is there for and against this view?
2. What challenges arise in trying to determine whether people living in traditional societies are happier than people living in modern nation states?
3. In a notably sympathetic pamphlet called 'Remarks Concerning the Savages of North America', the American polymath Benjamin Franklin (1706–90) recounted the following anecdote. At a 1744 treaty between the government of Virginia and the Six Nations of the Iroquois Confederation, the Iroquois were invited to send six of their sons to William and Mary College to be 'instructed in all the learning of the white people'. After due reflection, the Iroquois declined the offer with the following words:

> We know that you highly esteem the kind of learning taught in those colleges, and that the maintenance of our young men, while with you, would be very expensive to you. We are convinced, therefore, that you mean to do us good by your proposal, and we thank you heartily. But you, who are wise, must know that different nations have different conceptions of things; and you will therefore not take it amiss, if our ideas of this kind of education happen not to be the same with yours. We have had some experience of it. Several of our young people were formerly brought up at the colleges of the Northern Provinces. They were instructed in all your sciences; but when they came back to us, they were bad runners, ignorant of every means of living in the woods, unable to bear either cold or hunger, knew neither how to build a cabin, take a deer, or kill an enemy, spoke our language imperfectly; were therefore neither fit for hunters, warriors, or counselors; they were totally good for nothing. We are, however, not the less obliged by your kind offer, though we decline accepting it; and to show our grateful sense of it, if the gentlemen of Virginia will send us a dozen of their sons, we will take great care of their education, instruct them in all we know, and make men of them.

Write a reply to the Iroquois explaining why you would or would not be willing to send 'a dozen of your sons' to be educated in their ways.

Globalisation and diversity

In addition to the possible conflicts discussed above, the promotion of cultural diversity can lead to a seeming paradox. For it could be argued that the more we encourage cultures to be open to one another, the more they lose their distinctive features with the result that in the end there is less diversity. This takes us back to our initial discussion of globalisation. At one level, it might seem that globalisation is making cultures more homogeneous; but we might question how deeply this goes. As we said earlier, drinking Coca-Cola and eating McDonalds will not in themselves destroy your cultural identity. Moreover, it could be argued that, even if globalisation is reducing diversity *between* cultures, it is increasing diversity *within* them. For at the individual level, more people have more access to ways of thinking other than their own than ever before. (To what extent they are taking advantage of this opportunity is, of course, another matter.)

As this suggests, globalisation may have pros as well as cons. On the one hand, we may fear that it is promoting mindless consumerism and the exploitation of nature on an industrial scale. On the other hand, we may hope that it is giving us more choice about how to live our lives and helping to promote enlightened values that are shared by almost everyone. This hope was perhaps what led to the development of specifically *international* approaches to education – such as the International Baccalaureate.

We should, however, resist the temptation of thinking that there is only one correct way of seeing the world. Indeed, one of the key benefits of being exposed to other cultures is that it reminds us that our own culture's map of reality is only one among many, and that there may be other beliefs and practices which are equally valid. As a result, we may become aware of assumptions in our way of thinking that we had previously overlooked and realise that things we thought were natural and universal are in fact conventional and local.

If, as seems reasonable, we accept that no one culture has a monopoly on truth or virtue, then we must take seriously the idea that we have something to learn from one another. Indeed, we might think of the various cultures of the world as natural experiments in solving common human problems, such as how to satisfy our basic needs, live harmoniously together, make sense of the world, and find meaning in life. While some solutions clearly work better than others, we should be open to the idea that there may be many equally illuminating answers to these questions. The spirit of openness is nicely captured in the observation of the British historian Theodore Zeldin (1933–): 'Our education cannot be complete until we have had conversations with every continent, and every civilization.' This may be ambitious, but it is surely a worthy ideal.

Conclusion

The staggering variety of beliefs that human beings have had at different times and in different places shows how strongly culture influences the way we think. Nevertheless, we should not come to a one-sided conclusion. For it could be argued that beneath the kaleidoscope of cultural diversity there are underlying similarities between us. Indeed, the fact that we are capable of understanding one another *at any level* suggests that we all have a great deal in common. We do, after all, share a common biology and we are all born with the same cognitive equipment for making sense of the world. Moreover, we are all confronted by the same physical reality.

While there may be differences between us, these differences lie within certain well-defined limits. In the end, whether we are more inclined to emphasise similarities or differences may be a matter of temperament. Either way, our encounter with other cultures can help to enrich our understanding of what the Ghanaian philosopher Kwame Anthony Appiah reminds us is 'the one race to which we all belong'.

Key points

- We live in an increasingly globalised world in which cultural diversity is under threat and languages are disappearing at an alarming rate.
- Despite our common biology, the culture we grow up in influences not only *what* we think but also *how* we think.
- Research suggests that Asians have a more holistic and westerners a more analytic thinking style.This influences the way each group perceives the world and reasons about it.
- The thinking style of people in traditional indigenous cultures is based on oral traditions and tends to be concrete and local rather than abstract and general.
- While our approach to other cultures may be distorted by chauvinism and romanticism, cultural understanding can be enhanced by dialogue between insiders and outsiders.
- Cultures have always exchanged ideas with one another and, historically, cross-cultural fertilisation has been a tremendous stimulus to the growth of knowledge.
- To learn from other cultures, we should not only be informed and empathic, but also be willing to judge the pros and cons of their beliefs and practices relative to our own.
- Our commitment to cultural diversity may conflict with other things we value, such as freedom, truth, and progress; and it is difficult to know how to resolve such conflicts.
- One might claim that, although globalisation is reducing diversity between cultures, it is increasing diversity within cultures.
- Perhaps the most important thing we can learn from other cultures is that our own way of looking at the world is only one of many alternatives.

Key terms

analytic thinking
biopiracy
chauvinism
cultural imperialism
culture
ethnobotanist
globalisation
glocal
'go native'
holistic thinking
indigenous culture
taboo

Knowledge framework focus

1. *Scope/applications.* Why is it important to expose oneself to the ways of thinking of other cultures?
2. *Concepts/language.* How do a culture's language and conventions influence the way it sees the world?
3. *Methodology.* Do cultures have different methods for determining what counts as knowledge?
4. *Historical development.* How do cultures change and develop through their interaction with one another?
5. *Relation to personal knowledge.* To what extent is your picture of the world shaped by your cultural background?

Possible essay titles

1. How much does culture influence the way people perceive the world and reason about it? What does this suggest to you about the objectivity of these two ways of knowing?
2. Are some areas of knowledge more universal and less relative to culture than others? Discuss with reference to the natural sciences and one other area of knowledge.

Further reading

Books

Richard E. Nisbett, *The Geography of Thought* (Free Press, 2003). On the basis of evidence from numerous psychology experiments, Nisbett claims that there are significant differences in the thinking styles of westerners and Asians. While the former have ' tunnel vision', the latter 'view the world through a wide-angled lens'.

Jared Diamond, *The World Until Yesterday* (Penguin, 2013). In this fascinating book, Diamond explores what we can learn from traditional societies and he tries to offer a balanced account. 'There are', he says, 'horrible things that we want to avoid, but there are wonderful things that we should emulate.'

Online articles

Sharon Begley, 'East Versus West: One Sees Big Picture, Other Is Focused', *Wall Street Journal*, 28 March 2003.

Kenan Malik, 'Who Owns Knowledge?' *Index on Censorship*, Autumn 2007.

David Weisman, 'Buddhism and the Brain: Many of Buddhism's Core Tenets Significantly Overlap with Findings from Modern Neurology and Neuroscience', *Seed Magazine*, 9 March 2011.

Truth and wisdom

20

There are no whole truths: all truths are half-truths.

Alfred North Whitehead, 1861–1947

All truth is a species of revelation.

Samuel Taylor Coleridge, 1772–1834

Truth is what stands the test of time.

Albert Einstein, 1879–1955

Knowledge is an unending adventure at the edge of uncertainty.

Jacob Bronowski, 1908–74

Keep the company of those who seek the truth, and run away from those who have found it.

Václav Havel, 1936–

When we believe with every fibre of our being that we have reached the truth, we must know that we believe, and not believe that we know.

Jules Lequier, 1814–62

What is truth but to live for an idea?... It is a question of discovering a truth which is truth for me, of finding the idea for which I am willing to live and die.

Søren Kierkegaard, 1813–55

Men stumble over the truth from time to time, but most pick themselves up and hurry off as if nothing had happened.

Winston Churchill, 1874–1965

There are many kinds of eyes . . . and consequently there are many kinds of 'truths', and consequently there is no truth.

Friedrich Nietzsche, 1844–1900

We may be learned with another man's learning, but we can only be wise with wisdom of our own.

Michel de Montaigne, 1533–92

Introduction

In reading this book you have been engaged in an investigation into the nature and limits of knowledge, there is a sense in which truth, like a ghost, has haunted the pages of this book. We cannot understand the nature of knowledge without some reference to the truth; and yet when we turn to examine it directly it seems to vanish before our eyes. The question 'What is truth?' looks innocent enough, but we can easily tie ourselves up in knots in trying to answer it. This chapter begins by looking at three different theories of truth:

- the correspondence theory
- the coherence theory
- the pragmatic theory.

Although none of these is entirely satisfactory, each of them seems to capture a fragment of the 'truth about truth'. We will then ask how, if at all, we can know the truth, and whether it makes sense to say that we are getting closer to the truth. Perhaps we can steer between the extremes of dogmatism – the belief that you possess the absolute truth – and relativism – the belief that there is no such truth to possess – by adopting what we might call a 'cubist' theory of truth. The thought here is that although absolute truth may lie beyond our grasp, we still need to keep hold of some concept of truth if we are to distinguish between reality and fantasy. There is, after all, a difference between *wishing* that something were true and its actually being true.

LQ – Ethics: Is truth more important than happiness?

The habit of truth may help to discipline our thinking and encourage us to be objective, but difficult questions remain about whether we should seek the truth at any price. Should we, for example, pursue the truth if it makes people unhappy, or if it can be exploited by the unscrupulous for evil and destructive ends? Since we live in a world of rapid technological growth, such questions are of obvious relevance.

As we hurtle towards the future, we will need to think carefully about how to use the knowledge we possess and the extent to which we should pursue it further. With this in mind, it is perhaps appropriate that this chapter concludes with a discussion about the nature and value of wisdom.

Correspondence theory

According to the **correspondence theory of truth**, a statement is true if it corresponds to a fact. For example, the statement 'Grass is green' is true if, and only if, grass is green; and the statement 'The sky is blue' is true if, and only if, the sky is blue.

KT – correspondence theory of truth: the theory that a statement is true if it corresponds to a fact

At first sight, this 'theory' may strike you as trivial. For it appears to be saying nothing more than that a statement is true if, and only if, it is true. Didn't we already know that? However, one of the strengths of the correspondence theory is that it insists that truth depends on how things are in the world, and that a statement is true not because an authority said it was true, or because you happen to feel that it is true, but because it corresponds to something in reality. This belief was a powerful impetus behind the scientific revolution of the seventeenth century which helped to bring about the modern way of looking at the world.

Criticisms

1 Problems with facts

The correspondence theory says that a statement is true if it corresponds to a fact, but we might ask what it means for a fact to exist. The more you think about this question, the more puzzling it becomes. You may feel comfortable about the existence of particular facts, such as 'Paris is the capital of France': but do you want to say that general facts, such as 'All metals expand when heated', or negative facts, such as 'There are no donkeys on Mars' also exist? If so, *where* do they exist? Does a catalogue of all true facts exist 'out there' or in the mind of God? What about the fundamental laws of physics? Do they exist in addition to the phenomena they describe? Did they exist before the Big Bang? Philosophers spend a lot of time puzzling over these kinds of questions.

2 Correspondence is never perfect

Since there is a gap between language and the world, correspondence can never be perfect. To see the point, look back at Figure 1.3 in Chapter 1, 'The Treason of Images' (on page 6). What does the picture show? A pipe! So why did Magritte write underneath it '*Ceci n'est pas une pipe*' ('This is not a pipe')? Well, because it is not really a pipe, but only a picture of a pipe. You can't smoke the picture! As we saw in Chapter 4, what is true of pictures is equally true of language. You can describe something in as much detail as you like, but the truth described can never match up to the truth experienced, and the map of true propositions can never capture the underlying richness of the world.

With this in mind, perhaps we should abandon the idea that truth is an all-or-nothing concept – either a statement corresponds to reality or it does not – and think instead of there being *degrees of truth*. For, although there can never be a perfect correspondence, some statements, pictures and maps are surely more accurate than others. If they are accurate enough for the purposes we have in mind, we might reasonably call them 'true'.

3 Truth cannot be determined in isolation

A final criticism of the correspondence theory is that it is not possible to determine the truth or falsity of a proposition in isolation from other propositions. You might say, 'Surely I can test the truth of a proposition such as "There is a snake in the cellar" by simply going down to the cellar and looking?' But it is always possible that your eyes are deceiving you. As we found in our discussion of sense perception in Chapter 5, the only way of determining whether or not something is an illusion is to determine how what you think you see fits in with other things that you believe to be true.

ACTIVITY 20.1

How, if at all, might the following propositions be said to correspond to facts about reality? What problems are there with them?

a. The cat is on the mat.

b. All metals expand when heated.

c. Elephants do not have wings.

d. Archduke Franz Ferdinand of Austria was assassinated in August 1914.

e. Random torture is wrong.

f. The *Mona Lisa* is a beautiful painting.

Coherence theory

According to the **coherence theory of truth**, a proposition is true if it fits in with our overall set of beliefs. In contrast to the correspondence theory, the focus here is not so much on *going and looking* as on *sitting and thinking*. Such an approach is particularly appropriate in the case of knowledge by testimony. In a criminal trial, for example, there is no question of checking up on what the various witnesses say by literally 'going and looking' – for the events to which they relate are in the past. All we can do is to see how coherent the evidence is, and whether or not it all points in the same direction. If at the end of a trial you are willing to say that the accused is guilty, then you presumably think the evidence is compelling enough to establish the truth.

KT – coherence theory of truth: the theory that a proposition is true if it fits in with our overall set of beliefs

Coherence also plays a role in establishing the truth of empirical propositions. If, for example, someone claims to have seen a shark in Lake Geneva, you might reason that this has to be false because sharks live in salt water and Lake Geneva is a freshwater lake. As this example shows, coherence is particularly effective as a negative test of truth and means that we don't have to waste time checking up on every wild belief we come across. If, for example, someone told me that Elvis Presley is alive and well and living in Scunthorpe, I would reject this claim on the grounds that there is documentary evidence to show that he died in August. Elvis may live on in the hearts of many, but he is not living on in Scunthorpe.

LQ – Reason: How important are coherence and consistency for truth?

Criticisms

1 Coherence is not sufficient for truth

Although coherence may be a good negative test of truth, it does not seem to be such a good positive test. More formally, we can say that, while coherence may be a necessary condition for truth, it does not seem to be a *sufficient* one. For example, although a work of fiction may be coherent, that does not make it true. Shakespeare's play *Richard III*, loosely based on the English king of that name, makes perfect sense, but it is not the historical truth. The same can be said of Oliver Stone's movie *JFK* about the assassination of President Kennedy in 1963.

2 Coherence cannot exclude crazy beliefs

By using a bit of ingenuity, it is possible to make even the most outlandish theory seem coherent. You could, for example, make the flat earth theory consistent with the fact that the Apollo astronauts saw that the earth was round by simply claiming that the space missions were faked in a Hollywood studio. In fact, this is precisely what the International Flat Earth Research Society does!

ACTIVITY 20.2

Devise absurd but coherent explanations for each of the following.

a. The movement of the sun across the sky
b. Insomnia
c. The price of stocks and shares
d. The assassination of US President John F. Kennedy
e. Global warming
f. The variety of species on the planet

3 Coherence can lead to complacency

The coherence theory can lead to a kind of intellectual complacency which leads you to reject anything that does not fit in with your way of looking at things. However, just because something does not fit in with your way of looking at things does not mean that it is false – for it may be *your* way of looking that needs to be changed. If, for example, a racist comes across evidence which contradicts his prejudice that immigrants are lazy, he should not – as the coherence theory appears to suggest – reject the evidence; rather he should change his worldview. The point is that, painful as it may be, we sometimes need to question our assumptions and change our way of looking at the world.

ACTIVITY 20.3

How might the discussion in Chapter 13, of the role played by anomalies in bringing about scientific revolutions, count against the coherence theory of truth?

Pragmatic theory

KT – pragmatic theory of truth: the theory that a proposition is true if it is useful or works in practice

According to the **pragmatic theory of truth**, a proposition is true if it is *useful* or *works in practice*. This theory takes a down-to-earth approach to truth and might seem to cut through a lot of nonsense. Rather than worry about whether insubstantial negative facts exist or how to deal with coherent fictions, all that is required to determine if an idea is true is to put it to work in the world. Pragmatists often speak of the 'cash value' of a statement. What interests them is the difference that a statement's being true or false makes in practice. You might think of this as an engineer's approach to truth: if the bridge does not fall down, then the principles on which it was built must be true!

Since people are often convinced of the truth of something if it works in practice, the pragmatic theory would seem to be on the right track. While scientists have enabled us to put men on the moon, build computers and cure diseases, astrologers, witch-doctors and faith-healers have been much less successful in helping us to achieve our goals. According to William James (1842–1910), one of the founders of the pragmatic theory, 'an idea is true so long as to believe it is profitable to our lives'. With reference to religious belief, James argued that 'if the hypothesis of God works satisfactorily in the widest sense of the word, it is true'.

RLS – Headline: 'Scientists can't read your mind with brain scans (yet)'. Should scientists pursue the truth without worrying about the use to which their discoveries might be put?

ACTIVITY 20.4

1. How would you try to test whether the 'hypothesis of God' works in practice? What do you think it would mean for such a belief to work?
2. What would (a) the correspondence theory, and (b) the coherence theory say must be the case for the proposition 'God exists' to be true?

Criticisms

1 A statement can be useful but not true and true but not useful

There are many examples of statements that are useful but not true:

- There are all kinds of 'rules of thumb' in mathematics and science which are useful but not true. For example, Newton's laws of motion are useful for making day-to-day calculations, but since they only approximate to Einstein's theory of relativity a physicist will tell you that they are not strictly true.
- It is often socially useful to hold beliefs that match those of other people. If, for example, you had grown up in Nazi Germany it would have been 'useful' to have racist beliefs. But the fact that such beliefs might have been good for your 'career' would not justify our calling them true!
- On a personal level, there are many statements that would be useful to believe, in the sense that they would make us happy, but which are not true. My belief that I am a deeply misunderstood genius may make me happy, but the sad reality might be that I am just deluded!

Looking at it the other way, there are also many examples of statements that we want to say are true but which are not useful.

- At an abstract level, a great deal of mathematics seems to be useless in the sense that it has no practical application. (The mathematician G. H. Hardy, 1877–1947, proudly boasted that he had 'never done anything useful'.)
- More prosaically, there are literally millions of trivial facts which do not seem to do any useful work. For example, how useful is it to know that Sweden came 10th in the 1965 Eurovision Song Contest with a song called 'Absent Friends', or

that British footballer David Beckham's father-in-law is called Tony Adams? Such gobbets of useless information are of value only for trivia quizzes and game shows – but they are still true!

- There are also many 'inconvenient truths' about ourselves and other people which may not be very helpful to believe, but which are nevertheless true.

ACTIVITY 20.5

1. Classify each of the following beliefs according to whether you think they are:
   - true and useful
   - true but not useful
   - useful but not true
   - not useful and not true. What does this suggest about the pragmatic theory of truth?

   a. John Lennon's first girlfriend was called Thelma Pickles.
   b. If a French noun ends with the suffix '-ion', then it is feminine.
   c. I am a very sociable person with a good sense of humour.
   d. John Smith has exactly 113,574 hairs on his head.
   e. After we are dead we will soon be forgotten.
   f. You should never talk to strangers.
   g. 2 + 2 = 4.
   h. Santa Claus is watching you to see if you are good or bad.
   i. Human beings have free-will.
   j. If you take cocaine your teeth will drop out.
   k. I am surrounded by people who love and care for me.
   l. We are fighting a just war and have God on our side.
   m. We were all put on the earth for a reason and each of us has a special talent that makes us unique.
   n. Anyone can be successful if they work hard enough.
2. Imagine you are an astronomer and that you have just discovered that a meteorite will hit the earth in twelve hours' time, destroying all life as we know it. How useful is this truth? Would you announce it to the world or keep this information to yourself?

2 The pragmatic theory implies that two contradictory beliefs could both be true

For example, while a Buddhist believes that the Buddha is the highest source of spiritual authority, a Christian believes that role is played by Jesus. Since these beliefs contradict one another they cannot both be true, but if they make their respective adherents happy, a pragmatist seems committed to saying that they are *both* true.

3 'Useful' and 'works in practice' are too vague to give us a workable theory of truth

A final criticism of the pragmatic theory is that it is not clear what it means to say that something is 'useful' or 'works in practice'. Perhaps a belief is useful if it gives us a feeling of power or security, or makes us feel happy. But then, as in Criticism 1, many statements we naturally want to call true do not seem to be useful in this sense.

You might try to defend the pragmatic theory by pointing out that a statement which is useful in the short term might not be useful in the long term. If, for example, you have an exaggerated belief in your own abilities, it might be good for your self-esteem in the short term but it will not ultimately help you to cope with reality. The most useful thing in the long term is surely to have a realistic grasp of your own strengths and weaknesses.

The trouble with adopting this broader sense of 'useful' is that it seems to rob the pragmatic theory of its value. We said that a statement is useful if it enables us to cope with reality; but if we then ask what kinds of statement enable us to cope with reality, we naturally want to say 'statements that are true'. This is surely an example of **circular reasoning** – explaining A in terms of B, and B in terms of C, and C in terms of A. The pragmatic theory now seems to come down to little more than sticking the label 'useful' on statements that we have decided for independent reasons are true, and 'not useful' on ones that we have decided are false.

KT – circular reasoning: the fallacy of assuming the truth of what you are supposed to be proving

The common-sense conclusion, which fits the way we naturally think, is that it is not usefulness that makes a statement true, but truth that makes a statement useful. In other words, *usefulness is not a criterion of truth as the pragmatic theory claims, but a consequence of it.*

ACTIVITY 20.6

1. Give some examples of statements that might be useful in the short term, but not in the long term.
2. Do you think that someone could inhabit a comfortable illusion for their whole life without ever being let down by it? What are the implications of this for our discussion?
3. What are the benefits and drawbacks of modern technology? What do you think a Buddhist monk would say about its usefulness? What, if anything, does this imply about the truth of the scientific theories on which technology is based?
4. When a religious person says 'God exists' do you think they are saying any more than 'It is useful to believe that God exists'? If so, what?

1. A statement is true if it is useful

2. A statement is useful if it enables you to cope with reality

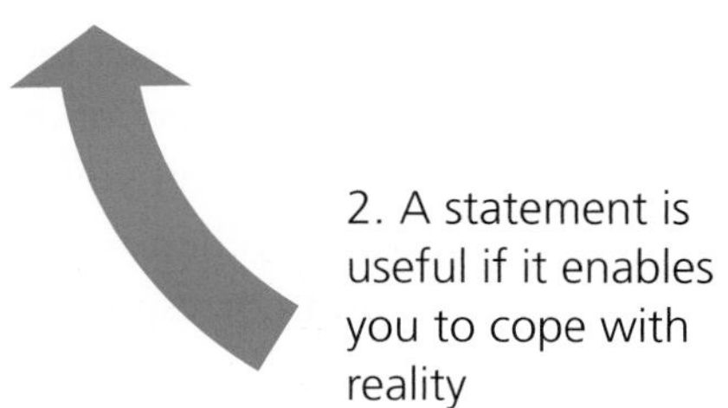

3. A statement enables you to cope with reality if it is true

Figure 20.1 Circular reasoning

Summary of theories

We have now examined three different theories of truth and have discovered that, despite their attractions, they each have various weaknesses. These can be summarised in the table below.

THEORY	CRITICISMS
Correspondence A proposition is true if it corresponds to a fact.	**1** The correspondence theory requires the existence of all kinds of insubstantial facts to which true statements are supposed to correspond. **2** Since there is a gap between language and the world, correspondence can never be perfect. **3** We cannot determine the truth or falsity of a proposition in isolation from other propositions.
Coherence A proposition is true if it fits in with our overall set of beliefs.	**1** Coherence is not sufficient for truth. A fairy-tale may be perfectly coherent, but it is still a fairy-tale. **2** With a little ingenuity, any crazy belief can be made to appear coherent. **3** A knowledge claim that does not fit in with your way of thinking might still be true.
Pragmatic A proposition is true if it is useful or works in practice.	**1** A proposition can be true but not useful, and useful but not true. **2** The pragmatic theory implies that two contradictory beliefs could both be true. **3** The words 'useful' and 'works in practice' are too vague to get us very far.

Perhaps we should try to combine the above theories to make a three-part test of truth. We might then say that a theory is true if it reflects the facts, is coherent, and works in practice by, for example, enabling us to make good predictions!

Can we know the truth?

The three-part test of truth suggested at the end of the last section may be an effective way of distinguishing between truth and falsity in everyday life; but at a deeper level you might still have doubts about whether we can actually know the truth. When we think about truth, it is hard to avoid the idea that a true proposition must correspond to reality. The problem is that, since we can never escape from our own distinctively human way of looking at things, we can in practice never compare our picture of reality with reality itself to see if our picture is true. The point in short is that *our picture of the world is always an interpretation and we can never be sure that our interpretation is true.*

The limitations of our knowledge tools

The idea that we are in some sense trapped inside our own interpretation of reality would seem to be supported by our discussion, in Part 2, of the eight ways of knowing. As we saw, these knowledge tools play an important role in helping us to construct a workable map of reality, but it could be argued that they also limit our ability to know the truth. Consider, for example, the following points:

- *Language*. Since the map is not the territory, there will always be aspects of reality that lie beyond our best attempts to describe them.
- *Perception*. If our senses had evolved differently, we would have a very different experience of reality.
- *Reason*. Just as a rat cannot solve a differential equation, so there may be truths about the universe that lie beyond our intellectual abilities.
- *Emotion*. The fact that you passionately believe something does not guarantee that it is true.
- *Intuition*. Just because something strikes you as obvious does not mean it is true. After all, people often have different intuitions.
- *Imagination*. While imagination may be an important source of new ideas, there is no guarantee that such ideas are true.
- *Memory*. Our memories are notoriously fallible and just because we claim to remember something does not mean it really happened.
- *Faith*. Having faith that something is true is not self-validating and it is always possible that you are simply deluding yourself.

Perhaps if intelligent aliens exist in some far-away galaxy they will have a very different picture of reality from our own, and understand some of the deeper truths of the universe that lie beyond our more limited grasp!

LQ – Sense perception: How far can our senses be trusted to give us the truth?

LQ – Language: Does language hide the truth more than reveal it?

ACTIVITY 20.7

What does the following passage by Albert Einstein (1879–1955) imply about our ability to discover the truth?

'In our endeavour to understand reality we are somewhat like a man trying to understand the mechanism of a closed watch. He sees the face and the moving hands, even hears its ticking, but he has no way of opening the case. If he is ingenious he may form some picture of a mechanism which could be responsible for all the things he observes, but he may never be quite sure his picture is the only one which could explain his observations. He will never be able to compare his picture with the real mechanism and he cannot even imagine the possibility of the meaning of such a comparison.'

Are we getting closer to the truth?

KT – problem of induction: are we justified in using our experience of things in the past to form the basis of our beliefs of how things will be in the future?

Despite the above comments, you might insist that knowledge progresses over time, and that we are at least getting *closer* to the truth. Perhaps! But the success of the quest for knowledge in the past is no guarantee that it will continue to be successful in the future. Indeed, if we take the **problem of induction** seriously, perhaps the laws of nature will inexplicably break down one day and the world dissolve into chaos. Admittedly, these laws have worked well enough up until now, but how can we be sure that they will continue to do so in the future? Perhaps the 'great truths' we have discovered will turn out to be nothing more than local anomalies in the tangled fabric of the universe!

What confidence can we then have that our way of looking at things is the right one? If you are religious, you may say that 'God made man in his own image' and designed us so that if we use our faculties correctly we can discover the truth. However, you would probably agree that there is still a gulf between the truth as grasped by us and the truth as it is known to God. If you are not religious, you might argue that since we have evolved to cope with reality, our faculties are likely to be generally trustworthy – for otherwise we would not have survived. However, the father of evolutionary theory, Charles Darwin (1809–82), was not so sure about this, and once mournfully confessed: 'With me the horrid doubt always arises whether the convictions of man's mind, which has been developed from the mind of the lower animals, are of any value or at all trustworthy.'

LQ – Religion: Does religious truth lie beyond human understanding?

The upshot of our discussion seems to be that at the most fundamental level there is an unbridgeable gap between our picture of reality and reality itself. This might suggest that while we can continue to talk about truth in an ordinary, everyday sense – truth with a small 't' – we may need to abandon the belief that we can ever achieve *the* Truth.

Beyond dogmatism and relativism

Perhaps it is a good thing if we abandon the search for absolute truth; for it brings with it the danger that if you think you are in possession of such a truth, you seek to impose it on other people. You only have to glance at history to see the damage done by various kinds of **dogmatism**. The world might be a better place if people held their beliefs with a degree of humility.

KT – dogmatism: the unthinking conviction that one is in possession of the truth without subjecting one's beliefs to critical examination or considering other points of view

ACTIVITY 20.8

1. Give some examples from history of the damage done by dogmatists and fanatics who are convinced that they are in possession of the truth.
2. Do you think the conviction that one has discovered the truth is always harmful, or can it sometimes be beneficial?
3. What practical difference would it make if we abandoned our belief in 'the truth' and concluded that truth is relative?

Figure 20.2

The lure of relativism

Since we do not have an absolute 'God's-eye' view of the universe and can only know the universe as it is for us, you might think that our only choice is to embrace **relativism** and say that truth is relative. There is *my* truth, and there is *your* truth, and there is *Mervyn the Martian's* – but there is no absolute truth. We should, however, be careful here. To say that we can never know the truth is not the same as saying that no such truth exists. You might say that a truth that can never be known has no practical value, but that does not make it any less true. If a man is murdered and all the evidence is destroyed in a fire, we may never know who killed him, but there is still a truth of the matter.

KT – relativism: The belief that truth is relative to the culture in which you live.

You may still find relativism an attractive position on the grounds that it encourages a tolerant 'live and let live' attitude, which is appropriate in a multi-cultural world. But, as discussed in Chapter 1, relativism is also open to the objection that it is self-contradictory. The statement 'There is no truth' seems to refute itself as soon as you ask if it is true. If it is true, then there is at least one truth; and if it is false then it is *not* the case that there is no truth. A sophisticated relativist might try to avoid this problem by suggesting that we should simply abandon all talk of truth. But the concept of 'truth' seems to play too important a role in our thinking for us to be able to dispense with it completely.

Whether or not relativism encourages tolerance is debatable; but it may be that in practice the drawbacks of embracing it outweigh the benefits. For if you abandon the belief that the truth is 'out there' independent of us, you no longer have any objective grounds for evaluating beliefs and distinguishing wishful thinking from 'facts'. If your beliefs are no longer disciplined by the truth, they are likely to end up being determined by nothing more than *prejudice*, *persuasion* or *power*. The danger is that you will then believe something simply because it fits in with your prejudices, because someone has *persuaded* you to believe it, or because you have been *bullied* or *indoctrinated* into believing it. This is clearly not a desirable state of affairs.

"Do you swear to tell the truth, the whole truth, and nothing but the truth, and not in some sneaky relativistic way?"

Figure 20.3

Arguments against relativism

1. The fact that we cannot know something to be true does not mean there is no truth to be known.
2. Statements such as 'There is no truth' are self-refuting.
3. Relativism reduces truth to such things as personal preferences, persuasion and power.

Degrees of truth

If we reject both dogmatism and relativism, and distrust not only those who claim to have found the truth, but also those who say that there is no truth, you might wonder what options are left to us. One possibility is to think of truth as an *ideal*, which – like all ideals – is unattainable, but which nevertheless gives direction to the quest for knowledge and which we can be nearer to or further away from.

ACTIVITY 20.9

1. In the US justice system you must swear to tell 'the truth, the whole truth, and nothing but the truth'. To what extent do you think it is possible to do this? How would you rephrase the demand to make it more realistic?
2. What does it mean to call something a 'half-truth'? Give some examples of statements that you consider to be half-truths.
3. What difference do you think it would make if, instead of thinking of a statement as 'true' or 'false', we thought of it as having a truth-value between 0 and 10?
4. The poet T. S. Eliot (1888–1965) once said that if a person takes hold of a truth too hard it transforms itself into a falsehood. What do you think he meant by this?

What, then, does it mean to say that something is nearer to the truth than something else? Well, it is surely nearer the truth to say that a Labrador is a 'dog' than to say that it is an 'animal'; and it is nearer the truth to say that the earth is round than to say that it is flat; and Einstein's theory of relativity is nearer the truth than Newtonian mechanics. Admittedly, our current 'truths' may be replaced in the future by other truths, but at least until now it has made sense to think of each revolution in thought as bringing us closer to the truth.

The cubist theory of truth

Another way to understand 'nearness to truth' is to say that you are nearer to the truth about something the more perspectives you have on it. Imagine, for example, that you are trying to find out what someone – let us call him Henry – is 'really like'. His mother describes him in one way, his brother in another, his teachers in a third, and his friends in a fourth. While there may be some overlap between these perspectives, each one captures only some aspects of Henry, and, in a sense, gives us only *half-truths* but not the *whole truth* about him. (This may explain why if a child gets into trouble at school his surprised parents say 'But he's never like that at home!') According to what we might call the **cubist theory of truth**, we get closer to the truth about Henry the more perspectives we have on him.

The cubist theory of truth should not be confused with relativism, and it is worth emphasising that, just because the truth varies with your perspective, this does not mean that there is no truth at all. To see that the latter is an error, imagine four people are looking at Mount Everest, and one is standing to the north, one to the south, one to the east, and one to the west; the fact that they have different perspectives on the mountain and describe it in different ways does not mean that truth is relative. For there can be more and less accurate descriptions of Mount Everest as seen from north, south, east and west, and there is a sense in which they all point to the same underlying truth.

Figure 20.4 Juan Gris, *Portrait of Picasso*, 1912. Perhaps we get closer to the truth the more perspectives we have on something or someone.

One of the attractions of this way of thinking about truth is that it seems to avoid the errors of both dogmatism and relativism. *The error of dogmatism is to mistake a half-truth for the whole truth; and the error of relativism is to think that, since the truth varies with your perspective, there is no truth at all.* The theory also enables us to go beyond an 'I am right and you are wrong' approach to truth; for it suggests that when we come across someone with a different view from our own, it might be more illuminating to ask not 'Is she right or is she wrong?', but rather 'What has she seen?' and 'How does her perspective enrich my understanding of the truth?'

KT – cubist theory of truth: the belief that the more perspectives you have on something, the closer you get to the truth about it

What price truth?

During the course of this book, we have generally assumed that seeking the truth is a 'good thing'. At the beginning of the western tradition, Aristotle (384–322 BCE) claimed that human beings naturally desire to know the truth, and Socrates (470?–399 BCE) famously identified knowledge with happiness and virtue. As we come to the end of our enquiry, we should perhaps examine these optimistic pronouncements and ask whether the costs of the quest for knowledge and truth sometimes outweigh the benefits.

ACTIVITY 20.10

Many traditions have myths about the dangers of curiosity and wanting to know too much. Give two examples and explain what relevance, if any, they have for us today.

LQ – Human sciences: Do human beings have privileged access to the truth?

Do we naturally seek the truth?

The idea that we naturally seek the truth might seem to be supported by the observation that children are naturally curious and are constantly asking 'why?'. However, it is worth pointing out that children are not only naturally curious but also naturally *credulous*. This trait seems to persist into adult life; for, despite the enormous growth of knowledge in the last hundred years, we do not seem to be any less superstitious than our ancestors.

There is a wealth of evidence to suggest that people often engage in wishful thinking and believe what they want to believe rather than what is justified by the evidence. Some people are reluctant to disturb their peace of mind by questioning their fundamental assumptions and prefer to inhabit their own comfortable illusions rather than face up to harsh and unsettling truths. To protect their beliefs, they may use a variety of *defence mechanisms*, such as **selective attention** (seeing what they want to see), **rationalisation** (manufacturing bad reasons to justify their prejudices) and **communal reinforcement** (mixing exclusively with people who hold similar beliefs).

Sadly, there is no reason to believe that if we are confronted with the truth it will make us happy, and there would seem to be something in the well-known saying that 'ignorance is bliss'. Perhaps there are things about ourselves, and other people, and the world we live in that it would be better not to know. We might, for example, be happier if we never discovered that we are not as smart as we like to think, or that our friends gossip about us behind our backs, or that there is untold suffering in the world.

Nevertheless, it is probably not a good idea to disengage completely from reality and retreat into a fool's paradise. For, if we are to adapt successfully to the world, we need accurate feedback, and the longer we harbour comforting illusions, the more difficult it will be to make the necessary adjustments. Zak may dream of being the next Einstein, but at some point he may have to face up to his low grades in physics and maths and rethink his career plans. The truth may not make us happy in the short term, but perhaps confronting it is the best strategy for avoiding unpleasant surprises in the long term.

Figure 20.5

ACTIVITY 20.11

1. To what extent do you agree or disagree with the following quotations?
   a. 'There is nothing I would not rather know than not know' (Samuel Johnson, 1709–84).
   b. 'For in much wisdom is much grief and he who increases knowledge increases sorrow' (The Bible).
   c. 'Mankind cannot bear too much reality' (T. S. Eliot, 1888–1965).
2. If there was a completely objective way of measuring intelligence on a scale of 1 to 100, would you want to know your score? Would there be any disadvantages in knowing it?
3. Imagine a parallel world identical to this one except that each individual is born with a 'sell by' date stamped on their thigh which accurately states the day they will die. Would you prefer to live in our world or the parallel world? Why?
4. To what extent should you tell other people the truth if you know that it will hurt them?
5. Imagine that a manufacturer develops a portable lie-detector which can be integrated into your mobile phone and is 100% accurate. Whenever someone you are talking to face-to-face or by phone tells you a lie, the lie-detector beeps. What would be the pros and cons of such a machine being generally available?
6. What do you think a utilitarian would say about the extent to which we should pursue the truth?

Ought we to seek the truth?

Since the task of any area of knowledge is surely to tell us what *is* the case rather than what we would *like* to be the case, some people insist that we should seek the truth whether or not it makes us happy, and that the truth has value simply because it is the truth. Some of the great thinkers of the past – such as Socrates, Copernicus or Darwin – were willing to follow the truth wherever it led; they seem to have believed that truth is more important than happiness.

There are nevertheless two problems with the belief that the search for truth has some kind of intrinsic value. First, knowledge does not come free, and the time and money we invest in it could be spent on other things. Some people have, for example, questioned how we can justify spending vast amounts of money on space exploration when millions of people in the world lack basic necessities such as food, clean drinking water and shelter.

A second problem is that, even if we think that knowledge has intrinsic value, we also need to take account of the fact that it is a double-edged commodity which can be used for both good and bad ends. For example, nuclear physics can be used to develop a cheap and safe source of energy or to make bombs of huge destructive power; and genetic engineering can be used to eradicate hereditary disease or to breed the 'master race'. Similarly, the human sciences can be used to alleviate the suffering of the mentally ill or to manipulate and control people's behaviour. History can be used to promote truth and reconciliation or to keep alive past grievances and fan the flames of hatred. The arts can be used to illuminate the human condition and extend the bonds of empathy or to celebrate gratuitous violence.

RLS – Headline: 'Spaniards want truth on Franco crimes'. Should we always pursue the truth about the past, or is it sometimes better to forget so that society can move forward?

Perhaps the greatest danger in the unregulated pursuit of knowledge lies in science and its foster-child, technology. If there was a moment in history when the search for truth lost its innocence, it was surely 8:15 a.m. on 6 August 1945 when a B-29 bomber called the *Enola Gay* dropped an atomic bomb on Hiroshima. We are now condemned to live with the fact that we are in possession of knowledge that could be used to bring about our own destruction.

LQ – Natural sciences: Is the scientific method the best way of trying to find the truth?

Some people have argued that knowledge in itself is always a good thing and that we should distinguish between the *possession* of knowledge and the *use* to which it is put. This might suggest the following neat division of labour: the responsibility of scientists and academics is to seek knowledge, and the responsibility of politicians – who are (or claim to be) the representatives of the people – is to decide how such knowledge should be used.

The problem with this argument is that, in practice, it is difficult to distinguish between the possession and the use of knowledge; for once the genie of knowledge is out of the bottle, it may be difficult to control. Some new technologies, such as *genetic engineering* and *nanotechnology* (building tiny machines from the bottom up, molecule by molecule), which do not require large facilities and can be developed in small laboratories using knowledge that is readily available, may be impossible to regulate. That is why some observers see them as a greater long-term threat to our survival than nuclear weapons.

At the same time we should not forget the potential benefits of new technologies that could, for example, lead to the elimination of genetically inherited diseases, and thereby improving the quality of life for millions of people. According to James Watson (1928–), one of the co-discoverers of DNA, 'you should never put off doing something useful for fear of evil that may never arrive', for 'we can react rationally only to real (as opposed to hypothetical) risks'. Ideally, we should perhaps do a cost–benefit analysis before deciding whether or not to adopt a new technology, but in practice this may be difficult to do – not least because the relevant costs and benefits are very difficult to estimate.

Figure 20.6

ACTIVITY 20.12

1. Make a list of the potential benefits and drawbacks of any technology of your choice. Do you think that on balance the benefits outweigh the drawbacks, or vice versa?
2. How seriously should we take the claim that technological developments may make it easier for future terrorists to commit massively destructive acts?
3. Do some research into something called the 'precautionary principle'. What are the pros and cons of using this principle to guide scientific research?
4. According to the science fiction writer Brian Aldiss, 'Man has the power to invent but not control.' Do you think that it is possible to control scientific research in areas such as genetics?

Wisdom

The poet T. S. Eliot once lamented 'Where is the wisdom we have lost in knowledge? / Where is the knowledge we have lost in information?' We discussed the difference between knowledge and information in Part 1 of this book, and it is perhaps appropriate to conclude by thinking about the difference between wisdom and knowledge. We will briefly consider five key features of wisdom:

- good judgement
- breadth of vision
- self-knowledge
- responsibility
- intellectual humility.

"I think I've acquired some wisdom over the years, but there doesn't seem to be much demand for it."

Figure 20.7

ACTIVITY 20.13

Who would you describe as a wise person? What characteristics do they possess which make them wise?

Good judgement

Human beings are fallible creatures, and you will have learnt from your TOK course that the dream of certainty is an impossible dream. But just because we cannot achieve certainty, it does not follow that any opinion is as good as any other. We are surely right to take more seriously opinions that are informed, coherent and insightful than those which are not; and we are surely justified in saying that we *know* something if we have enough evidence for it. If we ask 'how much evidence is enough evidence?', there is no definite answer and we can only say that it is a matter of judgement.

RLS – Headline: 'Kerchers may never know truth about murder'. In criminal trials, what are the main challenges in trying to establish that something is true 'beyond reasonable doubt'?

Since every situation that confronts us is unique, we must also use our judgement when we apply knowledge to the world. The relevance of good judgement in areas such as history, ethics and the arts is clear, but it also plays a role in something as seemingly objective as measurement. For example, to say that 'X is exactly 5 cm long' is based on the judgement that it has been measured to the appropriate number of decimal places for the task at hand.

"I'm on the verge of a major breakthrough, but I'm also at that point where chemistry leaves off and physics begins, so I'll have to drop the whole thing."

Figure 20.8

How can we develop good judgement? Sadly, it is not something that can be learnt from books but only from experience and practical engagement with the world. This may be why we tend to associate wisdom with old people rather than young people. In fact, it is not experience itself that matters, but *reflection on experience* and the ability to learn from it. That is why you can be old without being wise!

Breadth of vision

Wisdom requires not only good judgement, but also breadth of vision. We live in an increasingly specialised world in which there are said to be more than 8,000 definable fields of knowledge. Such an intellectual division of labour has doubtless helped to fuel the explosive growth of knowledge over the last hundred years, but it has also resulted in a fragmented picture of reality. In order to succeed in the modern world, you need to specialise, but if you are *too* specialised, you may end up becoming what the Germans call a *Fachidiot* – a person who is very brilliant in a narrow area but who has no real understanding of the world.

To understand the world, it makes sense to take it apart and examine the pieces. This is why we divide knowledge into different subjects. But the world does not arrive in neat packages labelled 'physics', 'biology', 'economics', 'ethics', etc.; and at some point we have to put the separate pieces together again. That is why we put so much emphasis in TOK on comparing and contrasting knowledge claims in different subjects. The ideal is surely to have both depth and breadth, to have specialists with a sense of the whole.

This is of more than theoretical interest. If we are to solve some of the urgent problems that confront us in the modern world – such as the destruction of the natural environment, or poverty, or the spread of infectious diseases – we will need an interdisciplinary approach that goes beyond the narrow vision of a *Fachidiot* and integrates the perspectives of many different subjects.

Self-knowledge

A third ingredient of wisdom is self-knowledge. Among other things, the quest for self-knowledge encourages us to question our beliefs and motives and to become aware of our underlying prejudices. As you will have learnt in our discussion of paradigms (page 363), our prejudices can be likened to a pair of tinted glasses that colour the way we see and think about the world. Just as we look through *but rarely see* the glasses that are on the end of our nose, so the underlying prejudices through which we make sense of reality usually remain invisible to us.

We like to think that we are rational beings, but we sometimes find it easier to comfortably inhabit our prejudices than to question them. There is perhaps an element of vanity in this, and it seems that we are often attached to our beliefs for no better reason than that they are *ours*. So perhaps what is needed – at least occasionally – is the courage to question our convictions and to ask ourselves *why* we believe what we believe and how far our beliefs are justified by the evidence. If we can develop self-knowledge and become aware of some of the prejudices that underlie our beliefs, then we have taken a step towards overcoming them and moving towards a more inclusive picture of the world.

Responsibility

A wise person is aware of the relation between knowledge and values. Since the search for knowledge is as much a communal as an individual enterprise, there is a sense in which values are built into it from the beginning. You may be attracted by the heroic image of the lonely thinker struggling with the truth, but the reality is that almost any statement you accept as true requires that you are willing to believe a great many people. You cannot conduct every biology experiment yourself, or personally check all the documentary evidence on which a book on the Second World War is based; so you have to trust that the biologists are not faking their results and the historians are not making it up as they go along. Indeed, if you had not trusted other people, you could never have learnt language in the first place and so would be unable to express your doubt. Trust, then, is the glue that holds the enterprise of knowledge together, and doubt only makes sense in a broader context of trust.

LQ – Mathematics: Are mathematical truths timeless and universal?

If knowledge is based on trust, then each of us must exercise responsibility in our knowledge claims. There are certain things we *ought* to do before we say that we know something. For example, we *ought* to look at the evidence, we *ought* to be consistent and we *ought* to be open to criticism. We are accustomed to making a clear distinction between facts and values, but perhaps, at a deep level, facts depend on values. How, after all, can there be knowledge without such **intellectual virtues** as honesty, perseverance, courage, humility and tolerance?

KT – intellectual virtues: virtues that are required for the pursuit of knowledge

As discussed in the last section, we must exercise responsibility not only in the *production* of knowledge but also in its *use*. You can be clever if you know many things, but you can be wise only if you have also thought about the use to which knowledge should be put. Perhaps one of the problems in the modern era is that we have plenty of clever people with know-how, but few wise ones with what might be called know-why.

Figure 20.9 The Dalai Lama. Who exemplifies wisdom?

Intellectual humility

The last aspect of wisdom is intellectual humility. Since we are not gods but finite beings with limited minds we can never achieve absolute knowledge. Such knowledge lies beyond our reach because we interpret the world through *our* senses and *our* reason and *our* concepts – and these can never give us the whole picture. We can perhaps be proud of our achievements and confident that we are making progress, but it seems that as our knowledge expands so does our ignorance and that every answer breeds new questions. In view of this, it is unlikely that we will ever know all there is to know about even a single grain of sand. At the limit, some of the big questions about life and the universe may lie permanently beyond our grasp – mysteries to be contemplated rather than problems to be solved.

Some of the great minds of the past have been profoundly aware of the limits of knowledge. Socrates famously observed that all he knew was that he knew nothing, and Isaac Newton (1642–1727) compared himself to 'a little boy playing on the sea-shore, and diverting myself in now and then finding a smoother pebble or a prettier shell than ordinary, while the great ocean of truth lay all undiscovered before me'. Such learned ignorance – achieved after a lifetime of thought – is very different from the empty ignorance of short-circuiting the search for knowledge by abandoning it at the first step.

The intellectual humility of a Socrates or a Newton is, perhaps, connected with a sense of wonder. (That may be why dogmatists, who think they already have all the answers, never seem to experience it.) Wonder is common among children who come to the world with new eyes and see everything as a miracle; but as we grow older we tend to get habituated to the mystery of things and can end up finding the world dull and uninteresting – *boring*. Perhaps it is the inability to find wonder in the ordinary and the normal that drives people to seek it in the extraordinary and the paranormal, and to experiment with such things as hallucinogenic drugs, pseudo-science and new-age cults. My hope is that if we could see knowledge as 'an unending adventure at the edge of uncertainty' (Jacob Bronowski, 1908–74) rather than a dull catalogue of facts to be swotted up for exams, we could reignite our sense of wonder in the everyday world.

Perhaps you will agree with me that in the end we should try to make sense of the world we live in not so much to reach a destination – for we will never have all the answers – as to travel with a different and altogether richer point of view. I hope you have a good journey!

Figure 20.10

Key points

- There are three main theories of truth: the correspondence theory, the coherence theory and the pragmatic theory.
- The correspondence theory says that a statement is true if it corresponds to a fact; but it is not clear in what sense facts exist, and the language in which we describe things will always fall short of reality.
- The coherence theory of truth says that a proposition is true if it fits in with our overall set of beliefs; but a set of beliefs can be coherent and yet untrue.
- The pragmatic theory of truth says that a proposition is true if it is useful or works in practice; but a proposition can be true but not useful, and useful but not true.
- We could try to combine the above theories and make a three-part test of truth, but there is still a gap between our picture of reality and reality itself.
- We cannot, however, dispense with the idea of truth, and it could be argued that the more perspectives we have on something the closer we get to the truth about it.
- Although it is generally considered good to seek the truth, it does not always make us happy, and the growth of modern technology, in particular, may make us wonder whether the costs sometimes outweigh the benefits.
- Beyond knowledge lies wisdom, which might be said to consist of: good judgement, breadth of vision, self-knowledge, responsibility and intellectual humility.
- Perhaps the ultimate point of trying to make sense of the world is not so much to reach a destination as to travel with a different point of view.

Key terms

circular reasoning
coherence theory of truth
communal reinforcement
correspondence theory of truth
cubist theory of truth
dogmatism
intellectual virtues
pragmatic theory of truth
problem of induction
rationalisation
relativism
selective attention

IB prescribed essay titles

1. To what extent is truth different in mathematics, the arts and ethics? (November 2009 / May 2010)
2. 'Context is all' (Margaret Atwood). Does this mean that there is no such thing as truth? (November 2007 / May 2008)

Further reading

Books

André Comte-Sponville, *The Little Book of Philosophy* (Heinemann, 2004), Chapter 12: 'Wisdom'. This short chapter contains many thoughtful insights on the nature of wisdom which, says the author, is best understood as 'the knowledge of how to live'.

Roger Shattuck, *Forbidden Knowledge* (St Martin's Press, 1996). Written by a literary critic, this book explores the question of whether we should pursue the truth at any price by considering various myths and literary texts, such as *Faust* and *Frankenstein*. You might enjoy dipping into some of the chapters.

Online articles

Robert Pirsig, 'Ghosts', in *Zen and the Art of Motorcycle Maintenance* (William Morrow, 1974).

Michael P. Lynch, 'Integrity', in *True to Life: Why Truth Matters* (MIT Press, 2005).

Part 5

ASSESSMENT

Introduction: The IB requirement

The TOK assessment consists of two elements:

- an essay
- and a presentation.

You must complete both of these elements to be eligible for the IB diploma. The essay and presentation are both marked out of 10, but the score for the essay is then doubled and added to that of the presentation. So the essay accounts for two-thirds of your overall TOK grade and the presentation for one-third. Your final grade for TOK ranges from A (excellent) to E (elementary). This is combined with the grade you get on your Extended Essay to determine the number of *bonus points* you receive as part of your total IB score. The maximum number you can get is 3, the minimum number is 0. This may sound complicated but it effectively means that you can get an extra 1½ points if you do a good job on your TOK assessment!

As regards the essay, you have to choose a title from a list of six *prescribed titles* which are set by the IB and released six months before you need to submit the essay. Your essay, which can be up to 1,600 words long, must be submitted electronically by your school to the IB and it will be graded by an external examiner. When it comes to the presentation, you must choose a 'real-life situation' as your focus and then subject it to TOK analysis. You can either do the presentation by yourself or with up to two other people. The timings are as follows:

- if you are doing the presentation by yourself, it should last about *ten minutes*
- if there are two of you, about *twenty minutes*
- with three people, it should last about *thirty minutes*.

Your presentation will initially be graded by your teacher, and if you do a group presentation you will each be given the same grade. You will also need to complete and submit various documents about your presentation, and the IB may use these to adjust your grade in a process known as *moderation*. Your school will explain to you the relevant deadlines and administrative details for TOK assessment.

Although there are some obvious differences between writing and speaking, there is considerable overlap in the skills you need to write the essay and those you need to give the presentation. In both cases the focus should be on TOK *analysis* rather than general description. The main difference between the two assessment tasks is that they move in opposite directions. The essay moves from the abstract – a prescribed title – to the concrete. The presentation, by contrast, moves from the concrete – a real-life situation – to the abstract.

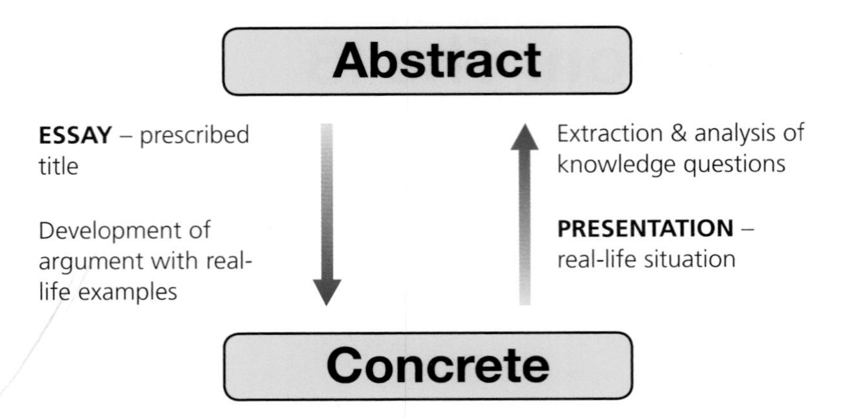

The aim of this final part of the book is to give you some practical tips so that you can do as good a job on the assessment tasks as possible. While advice and guidance are useful, you should keep in mind that there is no infallible formula for writing a good essay or giving a good presentation. So the points made in these two chapters should be seen not as a checklist that will guarantee success, but as a collection of tools that will help you to develop and refine your communication skills.

As a rational student who wishes to maximise their points, you might feel that with only 1½ points at stake you are wasting your time putting too much effort into your TOK assessment and that your energies are better focused elsewhere. This would be a great mistake. This is not only because *any* points are worth having, but also – and more importantly – because both the essay and presentation give you an opportunity to develop and demonstrate key skills that will serve you well in later life. Traditional education tended to put too much emphasis on the mere memorisation of material; but in the internet age, when everyone, it seems, is permanently connected, memorisation and repetition are no longer enough for success. Computers can do these things better than human beings. In the modern world the skills that are increasingly at a premium are **critical thinking**, **creativity**, **communication**, **cooperation** and **commitment**. These are precisely the skills that lie at the heart of TOK assessment. They will be crucial to your success should you move forward into higher education, and in the world of work. Developing these skills will not only make you more employable but also make you a more interesting person!

TOK tools

During the TOK course you will have acquired various thinking tools and the skills to apply them appropriately. In preparing for the essay and the presentation, you may find it helpful to review the following seven key 'TOK tools' which have been discussed at various points in this book. Keep in mind that you should only select a few of these tools that are relevant to your purpose. You might also find it useful to review the key point summaries at the end of any relevant chapters in this book.

1. *Knowledge questions.* You can begin to explore your topic by thinking about the seven 'high altitude' knowledge questions we mentioned in the Introduction to this book (see page ix).

Seven 'high altitude' knowledge questions

1. **What does it mean?**
   Definitions, metaphors, ambiguities, interpretations
2. **What counts as evidence?**
   WOKs, models, methodologies, explanations, underlying principles, paradigms
3. **How certain is it?**
   Quality and quantity of evidence: possible–probable, reasonable–unreasonable, generality, exceptions
4. **How else can we look at it?**
   Arguments and counter-arguments, cultural and historical perspectives
5. **What are the limitations?**
   Useful fictions, typical errors, associated prejudices, live controversies, hidden assumptions, ethical constraints, problems and mysteries
6. **Why does it matter?**
   Implications, consequences, practical value, social status, personal significance
7. **How similar/different is it to/from...?**
   Comparisons and connections with other WOKs and AOKs

Meaning
Evidence
Certainty
Perspective
Limitations
Value
Connections
How do you/ we know?

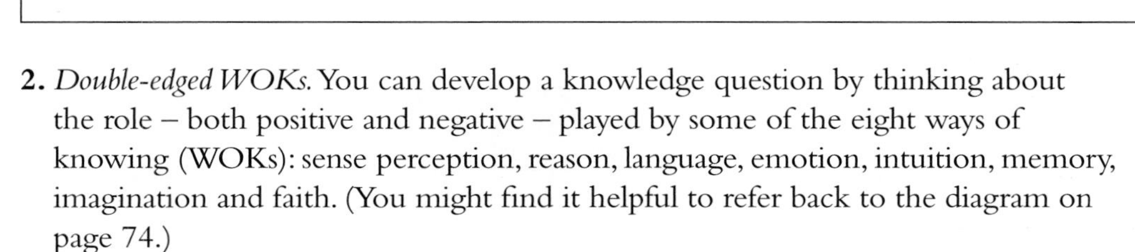

2. *Double-edged WOKs.* You can develop a knowledge question by thinking about the role – both positive and negative – played by some of the eight ways of knowing (WOKs): sense perception, reason, language, emotion, intuition, memory, imagination and faith. (You might find it helpful to refer back to the diagram on page 74.)

3. *Fallacy files.* Some of the fallacies discussed in Chapter 6 may be relevant to your analysis. (See, in particular, 'The ten deadly fallacies' on page 159.)

4. *Source evaluation.* You will probably need to evaluate the credibility of various secondary sources that you refer to in your presentation. (You may find it useful to look again at the 'Evaluating sources' diagram on page 69.)

5. *TOK concepts.* Where appropriate, use relevant TOK vocabulary. Listed below are some of the key TOK concepts you will probably have encountered during the course. (While your essay and presentation will doubtless make reference to some of these concepts, you should avoid using philosophical jargon in order to sound impressive or 'deep'.)

abstraction, ambiguity, analogy, anecdote, anomaly, argument, assumption, authority, axiom, belief, bias, causation, certainty, classification, coherence, common sense, concepts, confirmation, conjecture, consilience, context, controversy, convention, correlation, creativity, credulity, cultural imperialism, deduction, definition, dialogue, dogmatism, doubt, egocentricity, emotion, empathy, empiricism, evidence, experience, experiment, expertise, explanation, eye-witness testimony, fact, faith, fallacy, falsification, fantasy, generalisation, groupthink, heuristic, holism, hypothesis, illusion, imagination, indoctrination, induction, information, innate, intellectual virtues, interpretation, intuition, judgement, justification, know-how, knowledge, law, logic, memory, metacognition, metaphor, metaphysics, methodology, model, narrative, objective, opinion, paradigm, paradox, perspective, possibility, power, pragmatism, prejudice, principles, probability, proof, rationalism, realism, reason, reductionism, reflection, relativism, scepticism, sense perception, similarities and differences, stereotype, subjective, technology, theory, trend, trust, truth, understanding, universal, urban legend, value-judgment, wisdom, wish fulfilment.

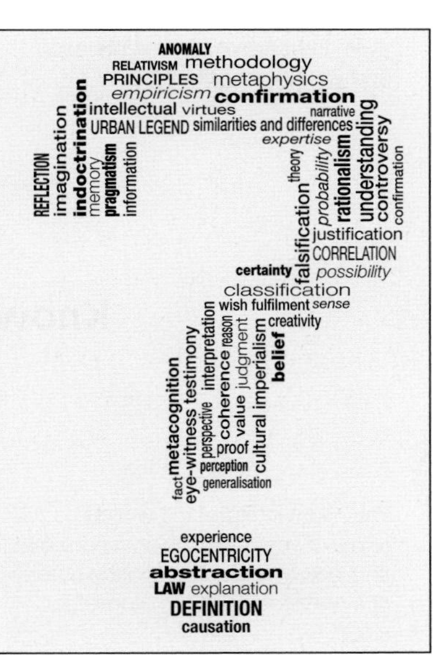

6. *Angles and perspectives.* Ask yourself: What's their angle? Where are they coming from? How might an X look at this? – where an X might be an old/young person, male/female, optimist/pessimist, scientist/artist, rich person / poor person, believer/atheist, someone from another culture, someone from the past/future, a Martian or God. (Note: take great care to avoid *stereotyping* when you consider different perspectives.)

Different perspectives

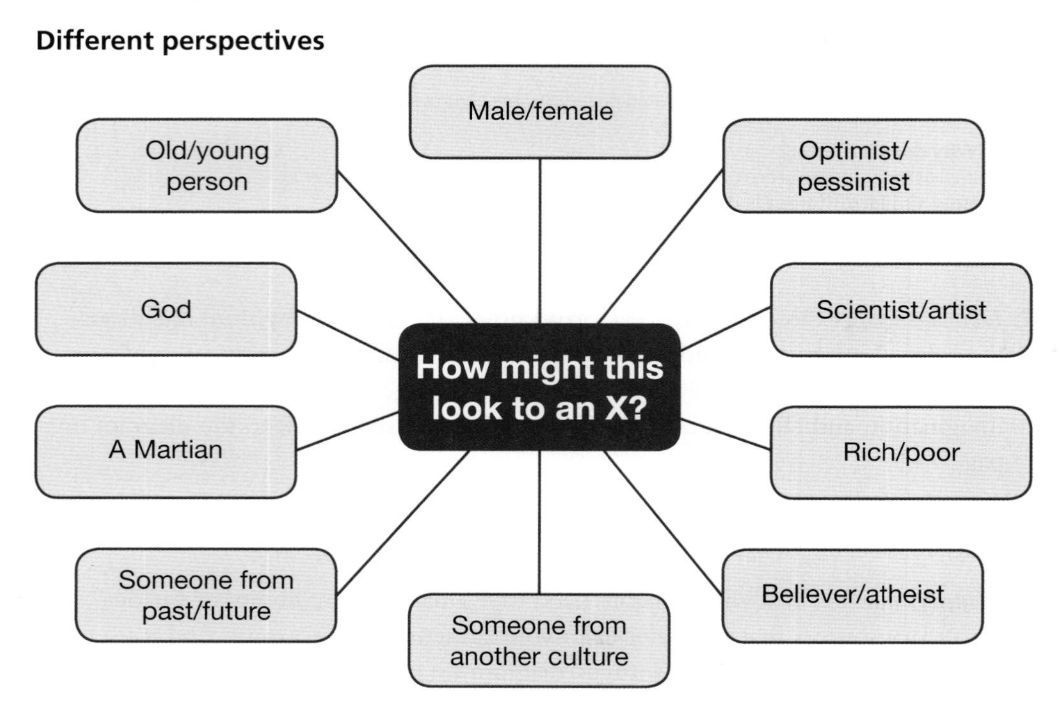

7. *Knowledge filters.* Consider how personal, subject-specific, cultural and psychological filters might influence your interpretation.

Knowledge filters

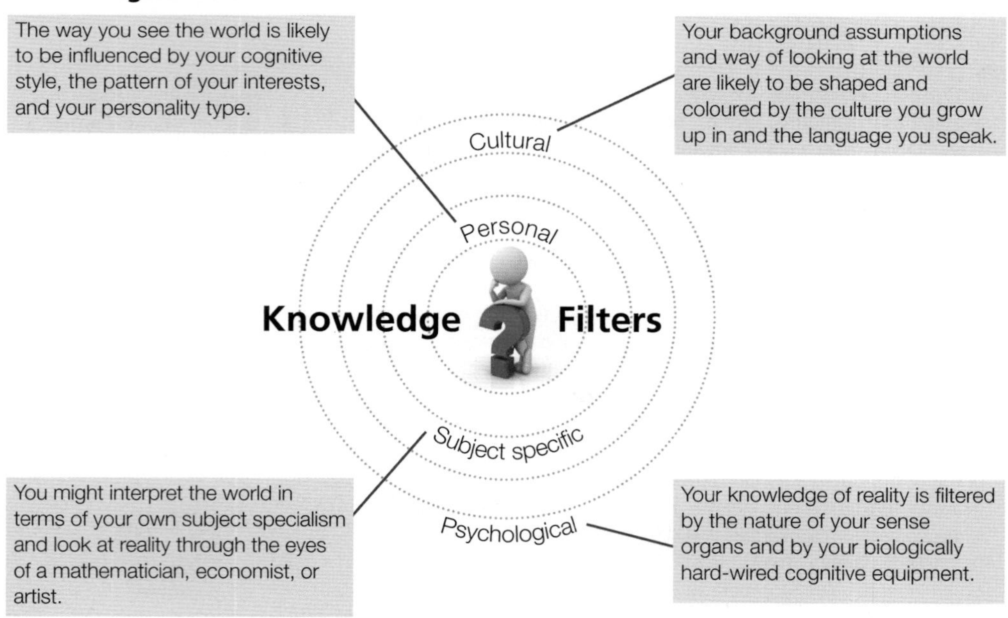

The TOK essay

21

Most people would rather die than think; in fact they do so.

Bertrand Russell, 1872–1970

You aren't going to have good ideas, unless you have lots of ideas and some principle of selection.

Linus Pauling, 1901–94

It is dangerous to read about a subject before we have thought about it ourselves... When we read another person thinks for us; we merely repeat his mental process.

Arthur Schopenhauer, 1788–1860

I write because I don't know what I think until I read what I say.

William Faulkner, 1897–1962

What is written without pain is read without pleasure.

Samuel Johnson, 1709–84

Have something to say, and say it as clearly as you can. That is the only secret of style.

Matthew Arnold, 1822–88

Deep people strive for clarity; those who wish to appear deep strive for obscurity.

Friedrich Nietzsche, 1844–1900

Thoughts obey the law of gravity to this extent, that they travel much more easily from head down to paper than they do from paper up to head, so that for the latter journey they require all the assistance we can give them.

Arthur Schopenhauer, 1788–1860

Everything should be made as simple as possible, but not simpler.

Albert Einstein, 1879–1955

Let no one say that I have said nothing new; the arrangement of the subject is new.

Blaise Pascal, 1623–62

Introduction

The word 'essay' comes from the French verb *essayer* meaning 'to try' or 'to attempt'. A French philosopher called Michel de Montaigne (1533–92) was the first person to use the word in its modern sense. The origin of the word is of interest here, because theory of knowledge (TOK) is concerned with questions that do not have definite answers, but this does not make such questions redundant. On the contrary, many of the most important questions in life do not have definite answers. When writing a TOK essay, it is helpful to think not so much in terms of answering a question as of *illuminating a problem*. That is what you are *trying* to do. A certain amount of humility is in order here. You are unlikely to come up with the definitive solution to the problem!

To illuminate a problem is to:

- explain what the problem is and why it matters
- clarify the meaning of key words
- consider different ways of thinking about the problem
- construct arguments and counter-arguments
- give examples
- assess supporting evidence
- explore implications
- make relevant connections
- uncover hidden assumptions.

Since it deals with open-ended questions, an essay has an important personal element to it. Other people may have come this way before, and you can doubtless learn a great deal from their explorations. However, your essay should be more than a summary of other people's opinions or simply a paraphrase of textbooks. You need to have the courage to strike out in your own direction; this is *your* attempt to illuminate the problem!

The IB requirement

Prescribed titles

You have to choose one from a list of six 'prescribed titles' which are set by the International Baccalaureate Organization (IB) and write an essay of up to 1,600 words on that title. These essays are cross-disciplinary. This means that you are expected to compare and contrast knowledge claims in different areas of knowledge (mathematics, natural sciences, human sciences, history, ethics, the arts, religious and indigenous knowledge systems), and, where appropriate, knowledge claims based on different ways of knowing (sense perception, language, reason, emotion, intuition, imagination, memory, faith). Here are two examples of recent prescribed titles:

1. Compare the roles played by reason and imagination in at least two areas of knowledge. (2007)

2. In what ways may disagreement aid the pursuit of knowledge in the natural and human sciences? (2013)

Assessment criteria

According to the IB, TOK essays 'should express the conclusions reached by students through a sustained consideration of knowledge questions'. Essays are graded in accordance with the IB assessment instrument, which is based on what is known as **global impression marking**. As the name suggests, this basically means that your essay is marked holistically (as a whole) rather than according to separate criteria which are then added together. Nevertheless, two key elements of assessment are distinguished:

1. understanding knowledge questions

2. quality of analysis of knowledge questions.

You will need to look carefully at what the IB itself says about the assessment of TOK essays, but you might find the following summary table useful.

UNDERSTANDING KNOWLEDGE QUESTIONS	ANALYSIS OF KNOWLEDGE QUESTIONS
Focus on knowledge questions	Justify main points
Show depth of understanding	Outline arguments and counter-arguments
Link to WOKs and AOKs	Explore assumptions and implications
Be aware of different perspectives	Use real-life examples

In addition to the above, the IB lists seven possible characteristics of an excellent essay:

cogent
accomplished
discerning
individual
lucid
insightful
compelling.

Keep these characteristics clearly in mind as you plan your essay.

Getting started

TOK notes

Throughout your TOK course, try to keep a good set of class notes. These will prove an invaluable resource when it comes to writing your essay. You should be clear about what it means to take notes. Simply going through handouts with a highlighter pen or cutting and pasting things from the internet is not enough. *You need to express things in your own words.* This will help you to digest the ideas you come across and is a good test of whether you really understand them. Here are two other pieces of advice:

1. As well as contributing to class discussions, try to keep track of them in your notes. The range of ideas and points of view that naturally come up in such discussions will help you to see how many different positions and perspectives can be taken on a topic.
2. Try to supplement your class notes with examples taken from your own experience, the subjects that you study and the media. You will be able to use some of these examples when it comes to writing your essay.

Choice of prescribed title

You will need to think carefully about which title to choose from the IB prescribed list. To avoid falling at the first hurdle, make sure that:

a. *You understand it.* You should be clear about what the question means, what knowledge questions it raises and what is and is not relevant to it.

b. *You are interested in it.* If *you* are not interested in the question, then you will find it difficult to get the reader excited about it. (However, if you feel too passionately about a topic, you may find it difficult to be objective.)

c. *You have something to say about it.* You should be confident that you can relate the question to the ideas you have covered in TOK, the subjects that you study, and your own experience.

Brainstorming

You might want to use standard brainstorming techniques to come up with ideas on your chosen question. Begin by scribbling down everything that comes to mind when you think about the question *without passing judgement on the quality of the ideas.* Then evaluate the ideas and discard those which are weak or irrelevant. Finally, think about how your ideas are related to one another and organise them into about six main points with related sub-points clustered around them. (You might find it useful to visualise the relationships between your ideas by making a 'mind map' or 'spider diagram'.)

Since a TOK essay is primarily a *reflective* essay, do not start by consulting a textbook, as you may be over-influenced by what you read and be inhibited from coming up with your own ideas. As the philosopher Arthur Schopenhauer (1788–1860) observed: 'It is dangerous to read about a subject before we have thought about it ourselves . . . When we read another person thinks for us; we merely repeat his mental process.' So have the confidence to think for yourself and try to map out your own response to the question before looking at what other people have said about it.

Practice

Since you can develop and improve your essay-writing skills only through practice, you will need to write at least one *practice essay* and look carefully at the feedback you get from your teacher. You should also read an *exemplar student essay* and make sure you understand why it received the grade it did.

Quick tip

Whenever you are working on your essay, have in front of you a brief summary of the key elements of the assessment criteria. This will help to keep you focused on what needs to be done.

How to write an essay

A necessary – but not sufficient – condition for a good TOK essay is that it is a good *essay*. An essay is more than a series of statements loosely connected to the question. A good essay in any subject should minimally be:

1. well structured
2. clearly written.

Structure

An essay's structure is what holds it together and gives it a sense of direction. You will need to think carefully about how to order your key points so that they flow naturally and help the reader to follow your argument. Here are some points you should keep in mind:

1. *Introduction*. An introduction can be thought of as a contract between writer and reader. You tell the reader what you are going to do and then in the body of your essay you go on and write what you have outlined. There are three things you should try to do in your introduction:

   - Get the reader's attention
   - Explain what you understand by the question
   - Briefly outline how you plan to tackle it.

   One way of arousing the reader's interest is to begin with something surprising or puzzling. Take, for example, the prescribed title, 'Compare the roles played by reason and imagination in at least two areas of knowledge'. You might begin with the following anecdote. When the German mathematician David Hilbert (1862–1943) was told that one of his students had given up mathematics to become a novelist, he said 'It is just as well – he did not have any imagination!' This is surprising because we usually identify mathematics with reason and literature with imagination. So we begin to wonder what Hilbert meant by this comment and how, if at all, it could be justified.

When it comes to explaining what you understand by the question, you might want to:

- reformulate it in your own words (but be careful not to change its meaning)
- indicate key terms that are unclear or ambiguous (for example, what is meant by 'reason' in question 1 on page 599?)
- say why the question is interesting or important (perhaps it challenges an entrenched stereotype).

You might also need to impose your own limits on the question. For example, if you tackle the question on reason and imagination, you might limit yourself to comparing the roles they play in mathematics and literature.

An introduction usually includes a *thesis statement*. This is the fundamental claim you are making in your essay and is the thread that runs through it and holds everything together. With reference to the first of the example essay titles on page 599, your thesis might be that reason and imagination play an important role in both mathematics and literature, but while the imaginative insights of mathematicians must ultimately be *provable*, those of novelists need only be *reasonable*. In planning your essay, the thesis will probably be the last thing you write and you may find that you modify it after writing your first draft. (Note that there is more than one way of writing a good essay: instead of putting your thesis in the introduction, you may decide to build to it and put it in your conclusion.)

2. *Paragraphs.* The point of breaking an essay into paragraphs is not to make the pages look neat, but to signal the introduction of major new points in your argument. A well-constructed paragraph typically consists of a cluster of arguments and evidence that bear directly on a specific sub-theme. You might think of it as a mini-essay with a beginning, middle and end and its own clear line of development. Ideally, you should begin with a *topic sentence* which, as the name implies, sets up a new topic for analysis, and end with a sentence which makes clear how it contributes to the development of the thesis.

   When it comes to the length and order of your paragraphs, there are three points to remember:

   a. Devote more space to important points and less to minor ones, and avoid getting sidetracked by minor or irrelevant details.
   b. Pay particular attention to the *transitions* between your paragraphs and organise them in such a way that one flows smoothly into the next.
   c. Think of your readers and help them by occasionally *signposting* where you are in the overall development of your argument.

3. *Conclusion.* To prevent your essay ending abruptly, you should write a conclusion which draws the various threads of the argument together and gives your reader a sense of closure. Rather than repeating what you have already said, try to find a new way of formulating your key insights. You might also mention unresolved issues and the broader implications of your argument. Think in particular about your final sentence: a striking and well-crafted last sentence acts as an effective full stop and helps to give your reader a positive overall impression of your essay.

Quick tip

Get someone to read the first and last sentence of each paragraph of your essay. If it is well structured, this should be enough to give them an idea of its main points.

Style

Different styles are appropriate to different tasks. In relation to a TOK essay, a good style can be summarised in three words:

- clarity
- economy
- precision

1. *Clarity.* Since your goal as a writer is to communicate, it is up to you to ensure that the reader can follow what you are saying. Some people confuse clarity with superficiality and obscurity with depth. Nothing could be further from the truth. In fact, it requires real depth to write with clarity and a great deal of hard work to make writing look easy. (As Samuel Johnson, 1709–84, once observed: 'What is written without pain is read without pleasure.') A pompous, convoluted, jargon-ridden style will not only lose your readers, it will also lose you marks; for you will get no credit for writing something that no one can understand!

2. *Economy.* Since you are writing to a 1,600-word limit, it is important that you make every word count. Although your essay should flow, you should try to express yourself succinctly and eliminate the extravagant use of adjectives and other unnecessary words. Guard in particular against the following:

   a. wordiness – writing a lot but saying little – especially in the introduction

   b. irrelevant padding

   c. pointless repetition.

   When you have written a first draft, go through each sentence and ask yourself: (i) Does it say anything? (ii) Is it relevant to my argument? If you cannot answer 'yes' to both questions you should delete the sentence from your essay.

3. *Precision.* Since there is a danger of a TOK essay floating off into empty abstractions, you should, where possible, try to be precise rather than vague. Three points to remember here:

   a. Avoid '*death by a thousand qualifications*'. While you may need to qualify some of your assertions, if you are too vague and hedge them around with too many qualifications, you will end up not saying anything!

   b. Choose your language with care and be aware of subtle differences in the meanings of words. For example, there is a difference between *belief* and *faith*; and a *generalisation* is not the same thing as a *stereotype*.

   c. Be particularly cautious with words like 'clearly', 'proves' and 'all' which are often misused or inadequately justified.

Quick tip

When you have finished your essay, read it out loud to yourself. This is a good way of seeing how well it flows and whether there is a natural rhythm to what you have written.

Figure 21.1

Factual accuracy and references

Since TOK can undermine accepted truths, it is important to keep in mind that there *is* a difference between a fact and an opinion: as the US senator Daniel Patrick Moynihan once observed, 'Everyone is entitled to his own opinion, but not his own facts.' In your essay you cannot simply help yourself to 'facts' that are patently false. At the same time, you should keep in mind that some alleged facts may turn out not to be facts at all. For example, despite being widely believed, it is not the case that we use only 10 per cent of our brains or that the Great Wall of China is the only man-made object visible from space.

You may need to include some references in your essay to show the source of your information. While there is no hard and fast rule about when this should be done, here are some guidelines:

a. You should reference surprising, counter-intuitive or little-known claims, but not things which are 'common knowledge', such as well-known facts or commonly held opinions. (What constitutes 'common knowledge' is itself an interesting TOK question!)

b. If you are closely following another person's line of argument – albeit it in your own words – it is intellectual good manners to acknowledge them.

c. If you are quoting someone's exact words, you should put the quotation in inverted commas and reference it.

d. Keep in mind that cultural references which are obvious to you may not be obvious to someone – such as an examiner – from another culture and they may need to be sourced.

You can use any accepted referencing system. All that matters is that the reader should be able to trace the source of your information and check its accuracy. Try to be consistent in the way you reference; and if you are citing a website, remember to include the date you accessed it.

Although the TOK essay is not primarily a research essay, you are expected to use sources such as books, articles, websites, etc. These should be listed in a bibliography. Only list sources that you actually refer to in your essay, or that have directly influenced it.

"I haven't read it yet, but I've downloaded it from the Internet."

Figure 21.2

Key features of a TOK essay

The points discussed so far in this chapter are relevant to writing a good essay in any subject. We will now consider more specifically what makes a good TOK essay.

TOK content

Despite being an unusual subject, TOK does have a specific content – not in the sense of a syllabus to be memorised and reproduced, but in the sense of a range of questions to be explored and reflected on.

From the start, you need to be clear about what distinguishes a TOK essay from a *subject-specific essay* on the one hand and a *general essay* on the other. Here are four key points about the nature of the questions that we consider in TOK:

1. *Knowledge questions.* The central question in TOK is *'How do you know?'* and the course asks you to assess the strengths and weaknesses of knowledge claims in various areas of knowledge.
2. *Second-order questions.* TOK is not primarily concerned with first-order questions *within* a subject – for example, 'What were the causes of the First World War?' – but with second-order questions *about* a subject – for example, 'How, if at all, can the past be known?'
3. *Open-ended questions.* Rather than having answers that can be memorised and reproduced without much thought, TOK questions are controversial and require personal thought and judgement.
4. *Comparative questions.* TOK typically asks you to compare and contrast various ways of knowing and areas of knowledge.

TOK toolbox

You will find it helpful to use some of the TOK tools mentioned in the introduction to Part 5 (see page 594). You should keep in mind that you will need to exercise judgement in selecting the appropriate tools for the essay you have chosen. Whatever essay title you select, you will only use a small number of the tools listed. The key thing that you should avoid is turning your essay into a shopping list which simply ticks off each of the ways of knowing, elements in the knowledge framework, and different perspectives.

Detailed understanding

To write an essay that is sufficiently rich in TOK content, you will be expected to demonstrate a *detailed understanding* of the ways of knowing and areas of knowledge you choose to discuss. In particular, ensure that you have a good grasp of the *methodologies* of any areas of knowledge you discuss and avoid vague, superficial, cliché-ridden characterisations of, say, the natural sciences or the arts. Remember – it is impossible to give a worthwhile analysis of a subject you do not understand properly.

Since a key element of TOK is *critical thinking*, you should also ensure that *description is always a prelude to analysis*. You might, for example, briefly describe the theory of evolution in order to analyse the extent to which it is a genuine scientific theory. But if you find yourself writing at length about Darwin's adventures on HMS *Beagle*, you will have drifted into descriptive irrelevance.

Personal thought

Quick tip

Ask yourself if your essay could have been written by someone who has not followed the TOK course. If the answer is 'yes', then it does not contain enough TOK content.

In writing a TOK essay a mixture of insecurity and inertia might tempt you to follow in another person's footsteps and do little more than recycle their thoughts and opinions. If you are aiming for a higher grade, this is something you should avoid. According to the IB, one of the characteristics of a weak essay is that it is 'derivative': a strong essay, by contrast, is 'individual'. This suggests that essays that merely rehash other people's arguments will do poorly, while those that demonstrate independent thinking and personal reflection will do better. Such reflection should, of course, be informed by a sound understanding of the relevant background ideas and theories. Indeed, one might say that a good TOK essay is the marriage of personal reflection and background understanding.

For an essay to be individual, it is not necessary that you come up with a Big Idea that no one has thought of before (unlikely) or summarise your personal philosophy of life, the universe and everything (undesirable). What is required is that you show personal thought in a variety of more modest ways – such as:

- the position you take
- the points you raise
- the way you organise them
- the comparisons you make
- your choice of examples
- your use of language
- your awareness of bias.

Keep in mind that an accumulation of small examples of personal thought such as those listed above will, when taken together, give your essay a distinctive voice. Once you start to focus on a specific question, you will find that new ideas occur to you in the process of planning and writing a draft, and you may be surprised by the freshness and originality of your final essay.

Definitions

There is a convention, with which you may already be familiar, that you should begin an essay by defining your terms. There are several dangers with this convention. The first is that rather than making a judgement about what needs definition, you simply define everything. The second is that you give simple dictionary definitions of key terms and then forget them. Part of the problem here is that many dictionary definitions are worthless. For example, defining knowledge as 'the state or fact of knowing' gets you nowhere because it is an empty truism. The main point to grasp is that TOK is full of what might be called *contested concepts*. The hallmark of such concepts is that they are both important and open to interpretation, in the sense that there are substantial disagreements about what they mean – disagreements that cannot be resolved simply by consulting a dictionary. There are numerous examples of such concepts: 'knowledge', 'science', 'art', 'democracy', 'justice', 'love', 'terrorism', etc. These concepts are worth arguing about because a lot depends on how we define them. If, for example, 'science' is defined in such a way that astrology can be described as a science, then why not teach astrology as an IB subject? If a liberation army consists of freedom fighters rather than terrorists, then why should we fight them?

What emerges from this discussion is that if you define a word you need to show why the definition matters and what depends on it. (If nothing depends on it, then it is probably not worth defining.) Furthermore, rather than trying to pin down the meaning of a word and drawing a circle round it, you should think of *analysing a concept*. While you might *begin* with a preliminary definition, you will probably need to refine it during the course of your essay. You might, for example, begin by saying that knowledge is commonly defined as justified true belief, and then find that you need to say more about what counts as an adequate justification. The point, in short, is that a definition should be the beginning rather than the end of reflection.

Instead of relying on a dictionary for the meaning of a concept, you might adopt the following three-part strategy:

1. Gather typical examples

2. Find common characteristics

3. Test your concept.

If, for example, you are trying to analyse the word 'art', think of some iconic works of art, such as Japanese writer Murasaki Shikibu's (c.978–1014) *Tale of Genji* (widely considered to be the world's first novel), or German composer Ludwig van Beethoven's (1770–1827) Symphony Number 5 (the opening of which is said to be one of the most recognisable melodies in the world), or Chinese painter Zhang Zeduan's (1085–1145) *Riverside Scene at Qingming Festival* (which has been described as China's *Mona Lisa*). Then ask yourself what such famous works of art have in common that justifies our calling them all 'art'. You might say that they all exemplify beauty, or show skill, or appeal to our emotions. So far, so good; but don't stop there. You now need to test your idea by trying to think of counter-examples. Can you think of examples of things that are not beautiful or skilful or emotionally engaging that you would still want to call art?. . . From this brief example, you will see that you are now on the way to a much richer discussion of the nature of art than anything that can be found in a dictionary.

Arguments

Some students do poorly in their TOK essay because they do not understand what an argument is. An argument is not a series of statements loosely related to a theme, but – to quote a well-known sketch from Monty Python (a 1970s British comedy group) – 'a connected series of statements intended to establish a definite

Figure 21.3

proposition'. While loosely related statements merely state things, an argument gives reasons (premises) to support a claim (conclusion). To see the difference, compare the following two sets of statements:

Quick tip

When you have finished your essay, go through it and make explicit all of the implicit 'therefores'. This will enable you to see how many arguments your essay contains.

1. Astrology is the belief that the position of the stars at the time of your birth affects your destiny. There are ten times more astrologers than astronomers in the United States. Despite its popularity, astrology cannot be classified as a science.
2. One of the hallmarks of a genuine science is that it makes testable predictions. Admittedly, astrologers do make predictions, but they are so vague that they cannot be verified or falsified. So, unlike astronomy, astrology cannot be classified as a science.

The difference between (1) and (2) is that while (1) makes three unrelated assertions about astrology, (2) makes a claim – 'Astrology cannot be classified as a science' – that is supported by reasons.

There is a simple test – called the *therefore test* – for determining whether or not a series of statements constitutes an argument. If you can put a *therefore* in front of one of the statements and the series makes sense, then it is an argument. (You may need to reorder the statements if the claim is in the beginning or the middle of the series.) You can see that while (2) passes the 'therefore' test, there is no way of ordering the statements in (1) so that it would make sense to put a 'therefore' in front of one of them. If you make such a series of unsubstantiated assertions in your essay, then – even if they are vaguely relevant to the title – you will get no credit for them.

Evidence

Even if the arguments in your essay are logically valid, they will only be as good as the reasons on which they are based. To return to argument (2) in the previous section – which is a valid argument – your readers will only find the conclusion convincing if they are willing to accept that science makes testable predictions and astrology does not. To give weight to your argument, you might want to flesh it out by comparing the kinds of predictions made in astronomy – for example, 'The next total solar eclipse will be on 20 March 2015' – with those made in astrology – for example, 'An ambition that you thought was just a dream comes into much sharper focus in the week ahead.'

Since you cannot justify every assertion you make without getting caught in an infinite regress, you will need to make a judgement about which assertions need to be supported with further evidence and which can be accepted as 'common knowledge'. As a rough guide, you should give supporting evidence if what you are saying is: (i) central to your argument, (ii) disputable or surprising. The more that hangs on an assertion and the more disputable it is, the more evidence you should give in support of it. (As the astronomer Carl Sagan once observed: 'Extraordinary claims require extraordinary evidence.')

You will also need to think about the *strength* of the evidence you appeal to. Some of it should be drawn directly from your own experience; but a lot will be derived from second-hand sources such as class notes, books, TV, newspapers, discussions with friends and acquaintances – and, of course, the internet. You should be careful here! Rather than accept the sources you use at face value, you should, where appropriate, be willing to question their reliability and trustworthiness. This is particularly necessary in the case of the internet, which is now where most people will look first when seeking information. Keep in mind that, despite the existence of many good websites, the internet is not an electronic oracle that can be relied upon to always give you the truth!

What is required when using any of these sources is that you approach them *critically*. Ask questions such as: Who says this? Do they have the relevant expertise? Are they trustworthy? Do they have a vested interest? What's the evidence? How plausible is it? Do they show both sides? Do they use emotive language? Do other experts agree?

Since evidence, whatever its source, is ultimately based on perception, reason or intuition, you may at some point want to discuss these ways of knowing in more detail. You might, for example, draw attention to the fallibility of perception, the limitations of reason, or the unreliability of intuition. However, it is important that you do not confuse critical thinking with destructive thinking; and you should, where appropriate, comment on the strengths as well as the weaknesses of any such sources of knowledge. In particular, you should avoid a kind of *idiot scepticism* which mindlessly questions everything. Your goal is not to reduce the edifice of knowledge to rubble, but to engage in the difficult task of distinguishing between more and less reasonable claims to knowledge.

Counter-arguments

Your TOK essay should not just consist of arguments backed up by evidence: you must also consider counter-arguments. In questioning the strength of your supporting evidence (as in the previous section), there is likely to be a natural movement from argument to counter-argument. To help this movement, try to think of your essay not so much as a monologue, but as a *dialogue*. Ideally, it should contain two (or more) voices: one proposing various arguments and the other opposing and suggesting alternatives. Since controversial issues are a key element of TOK, you should be able to find at least two sides to every question. If you have kept good notes from TOK class discussions, then you will have a preliminary bank of arguments and counter-arguments on which to draw. You should be able to supplement this through background reading, trying out arguments on friends, and – above all – personal thought. If you cannot think of any counter-arguments to what you are saying, then it is probably so obvious that it is not worth arguing for at all. You should, however, avoid the *straw man fallacy* of constructing and then demolishing weak or spurious counter-arguments. If you plan to take a position on an issue, the best way of carrying conviction with your reader is to show that it can withstand even the strongest criticism that can be levelled against it!

Once you have given a counter-argument, you will need to decide how it affects your original argument. There are two main types of response you can make:

a. *Refutation*. You reject the counter-argument by showing that it is mistaken, unlikely or unimportant.

b. *Concession*. You allow that there is some truth in the counter-argument and qualify your original argument to take account of it.

Here are two abbreviated examples to illustrate each of the above patterns of response:

a. We usually assume that human beings are capable of genuine altruism (*claim*); but it could be argued that even so-called altruists are simply doing what they most want to do – and so, in a sense, are being selfish (*counter-claim*). However, if everything anyone ever does is described as selfish, this effectively robs the word 'selfish' of its meaning (*refutation*).

b. The language of universal human rights reflects a widespread belief that values are objective (*claim*); but some people argue that the sheer diversity of moral practices means that there are in fact no objective values (*counter-claim*). Admittedly, different cultures have very different views about, for example, sexual morality (*concession*); but I would still argue that there are some core values common to all societies (*qualification of claim*).

These examples are just rough sketches and they would need to be fleshed out to carry any conviction in an essay; but they should at least give you an idea of how you might respond to counter-arguments.

Sound reasoning

The arguments you use in your essay will not get you much credit unless they are *good* arguments. To avoid sloppy reasoning, check that your claims are supported by the reasons you give for them. Guard, in particular, against the following common errors:

a. *Hasty generalisation.* This is the fallacy of generalising from insufficient evidence. Above all, avoid superficial caricatures of subject areas and cultures.

b. *Black and white thinking.* This is the fallacy of going from one extreme to the other. For example, just because we cannot achieve certainty, it does not follow that any opinion is as good as any other.

c. *Inconsistencies.* Check the overall consistency of your essay and ensure that your various points do not contradict one another.

Depth

Your TOK essay may be focused on knowledge questions and contain sound arguments supported by evidence; but if it comes across as *thin* it will still not achieve a high grade. You will need to give it *weight*. In general, the more good points you make, the better you are likely to do. (However, keep in mind that such points will only have value if they are crafted into a meaningful whole.)

Quick tip

Go through your essay and highlight every generalisation (for example, 'All scientists . . .', 'All Buddhists . . .'). Check that they have been properly justified.

In writing your essay, you might think of yourself as operating with two different lenses: a zoom for depth and a wide-angle for breadth.

Depth is about *taking your analysis to the next level.* Among the points you might think about here are:

1. *Depth of dialogue.* Try to extend your dialogues beyond the cursory ping-pong of argument and counter-argument and think of a response to the counter-argument and a counter-response to that. You will, of course, need to think about: (i) the quality as well as the quantity of such exchanges, and (ii) at what point to bring them to a close. (This is likely to depend on how important the particular argument is to your overall thesis.)

2. *Weight of evidence.* The more supporting evidence you can give for your arguments the more conviction they will carry. For example, if you are trying to argue that literature contributes to our knowledge of the world, then saying that it not only illuminates the human condition, but also teaches us sensitivity to language, is probably better than making only one of these points.

3. *Relevant distinctions.* Introducing relevant distinctions will add subtlety and finesse to your argument. You might, for example, distinguish between *knowing how* and *knowing that*, or between *inductive reasoning* and *deductive reasoning*, or between an *empirical proposition* and a *metaphysical proposition*. You should also be aware that when you talk about an area of knowledge, such as the arts, there are many different art forms and that what holds true of one will not necessarily hold true of another.

4. *Key implications.* By exploring the implications of your argument, you show that you are thinking around the issue. Ask yourself *what follows* from the point you are considering. For example, you might argue that:

- If knowledge is equated with certainty, then *it follows that* we know almost nothing.

- If all values are relative, then *it follows that* we can no longer speak of universal human rights.
- If human free-will is an illusion, then *it follows that* we can no longer hold people responsible for their actions.

5. *Background assumptions.* Ask yourself 'What assumptions am I making here?' and, where appropriate, be willing to question them. Since we often confuse what is cultural with what is natural, and unthinkingly assume that the practices we have grown up with are 'normal', you should pay particular attention to any cultural biases that may be influencing your analysis.

Quick tip

Although the IB does not stipulate a minimum number of words for the essay, the less you write the less depth you are likely to achieve. You should aim to write between 1,500 and 1,600 words.

Breadth

When it comes to breadth, you should think in terms of *making connections*. As was mentioned earlier, TOK essays are usually comparative in nature and you will be expected to consider the *similarities and differences* between different ways of knowing and different areas of knowledge. As a brainstorming exercise, you should be able to think of interesting links between all of the ways of knowing and areas of knowledge. (To get some ideas, look at the linking questions in the margins of this book.) This will help to get you thinking in a sufficiently broad way. You must then decide which of these connections are relevant to your chosen question. You will also need to ensure that you do not achieve breadth at the expense of depth. If, for example, you tackle the prescribed title mentioned earlier, 'Compare the roles played by reason and imagination in at least two areas of knowledge', you should consider two or three areas of knowledge, but do not try to cover all eight. To attempt to cover all eight in 1,600 words would produce an essay that is nothing more than a superficial survey of the territory.

Figure 21.4

As well as making connections within the TOK framework, you should also try to come up with some *different perspectives* on your chosen topic. To do this, you might ask yourself *How would an X look at this?*, where an X is someone of a different age, gender, profession, culture, or historical era. This will help you to think beyond the limits of your own viewpoint and may make you aware of hidden assumptions in your own thinking.

Examples

In your essay, you are expected to give 'varied and effective' examples. The IB places particular emphasis on the use of *real-life examples*, which may be drawn from your own academic or personal experience, or from the news and current affairs. Such examples will add interest and conviction to your writing and help the reader to grasp some of your more abstract points and see how they are related to the real world. There are a number of points you should keep in mind here:

1. *Hypothetical examples.* While occasional thought experiments have a place, real examples generally carry more conviction.
2. *Clichéd examples.* 'A bachelor is an unmarried man' is not the only example of a statement that is true by definition; and Copernicus' *revolutionary* claim that the earth goes round the sun rather than vice versa is not the only example of a paradigm shift.
3. *Representative examples.* Try not to distort your examples by focusing only on extreme cases.
4. *Varied examples.* Use examples drawn from different sources (for example, personal experience, the news media), different subject areas and different cultures.
5. *Brevity of examples.* Keep your examples relatively brief and make sure that they illustrate what they are supposed to illustrate.
6. *Examples vs statistics.* An attention-grabbing anecdote may be rhetorically convincing, but in some cases dry statistics are a more reliable guide to the truth.

Quotations

You may wish to include a few well-chosen quotations in your essay, but you should be aware of three common pitfalls:

1. *Cut-and-paste essays.* Make sure your essay does not become simply a cut-and-paste montage. While two or three short quotations are good, an essay that is stitched together using other people's words will get you no credit.
2. *Undigested quotations.* Rather than simply *parachuting* quotations into your essay, try to integrate them into the flow of your argument. In particular, keep in mind that *a quotation is a provocation not a proof* and that a telling quotation is not in itself enough to make an argument convincing. You should be willing to subject quotations to critical scrutiny. For example, if you quote John Keats' '"Beauty is truth, truth beauty," – that is all / Ye know on earth, and all ye need to know' you cannot simply let the quotation speak for itself and then start a new paragraph.

For, as it stands, it is clearly false. After all, there are many beautiful things – such as the famous Venus of Milo statue – that are not true, and many truths – such as the Holocaust – that are not beautiful. Perhaps there is a more interesting interpretation of what Keats said, but, if that is the case, you will need to convince the reader of it.

3. *Plagiarism*. According to the IB definition, *plagiarism* is 'the representation of the ideas or work of another person as the candidate's own'. If you are found to have plagiarised in the TOK essay you submit for assessment, you will not be awarded your diploma. To avoid plagiarism, the IB says that: 'Candidates must always ensure that they acknowledge fully and in detail the words and/or ideas of another person.' Be punctilious here and when you quote another person or source, be sure that you put their words in inverted commas and give appropriate references.

Just do it!

You may have planned your essay and have a good outline, yet still find it difficult to settle down to writing it. The best way to overcome the unsettling feeling of vertigo many of us experience when staring at a blank sheet of paper is to start filling it with words. Not only will this give you confidence – you will also find that new ideas occur to you in the very process of writing. Indeed, there is a sense in which *writing is a way of thinking*. (William Faulkner, 1897–1962, once said: 'I write because I don't know what I think until I read what I say.') So start getting words on paper as soon as you can; you can always go back later and revise them.

Throughout the writing process, try to keep in mind the key features of a successful TOK essay. As a quick summary and *aide-mémoire* you might find it useful to think in terms of the following four words:

CONTENT: *Think: addressing knowledge questions.*

CRITICAL THINKING: *Think: arguments and counter-arguments.*

CREATIVITY: *Think: personal reflection.*

CLARITY: *Think: well-structured essay.*

"It sort of makes you stop and think, doesn't it."

Figure 21.5

As we have seen, there is more to it than this; but if your essay focuses on knowledge questions, develops arguments and counter-arguments, shows personal reflection, and is clearly written and well structured, then you will definitely be on the right tracks.

Your essay will probably have to go through several *drafts* before you are happy with it, so make sure you start your writing well before the deadline. Try to become your own best critic. When you have a good draft, put it away for a few days; then return to it and read it with fresh eyes. This should help you to spot any outstanding weaknesses and errors in your work.

Keep in mind that you should write a maximum of 1,600 words and that you will automatically be penalised by one mark if you exceed the word limit. While you should focus on quality rather than quantity, the more top-quality work you produce, the more impressed the examiner is likely to be.

FREQUENTLY ASKED QUESTIONS	
1. How does a TOK essay differ from a general essay?	A TOK essay differs from a general essay in that it is focused on the question 'How do you know?' and deals with second-order knowledge questions using appropriate TOK tools and TOK language.
2. How does a TOK essay differ from a philosophy essay?	While there is some overlap between the questions asked in TOK and those asked in philosophy, your essay should not consist of lengthy explanation of 'what the philosophers said'. (In fact, it is not necessary to mention any philosophers at all.) The point is rather to apply TOK tools to your academic experience and the real world.
3. How much research should I do for my essay?	A TOK essay is not primarily a research essay which requires extensive background reading, but a reflective essay which requires personal thought. While some reference to authorities and key ideas in the field may be appropriate, they should not distract from your own voice.
4. How much can I rely on textbooks?	Textbooks should be a stimulus to, rather than a substitute for, personal thought. An occasional reference to a textbook is acceptable; simply paraphrasing chunks of it is not.
5. Must an essay include references?	There is a presumption, but no formal requirement, that your essay includes a few references – typically between three and five. (Remember that these are not included in the word count.)
6. What should I reference?	You should properly reference all quotations and paragraphs in which you paraphrase or closely follow someone else's ideas. You should also reference controversial or culturally specific claims, but need not reference claims which are considered 'common knowledge'.
7. What is included in the word count?	The word count includes everything in the main body of the essay, but it does not include footnotes or the bibliography. (Note that extensive footnotes are not considered appropriate and may not be read.)
8. What is the minimum I can write?	There is no minimum word count. Nevertheless, you are strongly advised to write between 1,500 and 1,600 words.
9. What happens if I exceed the word count?	An essay that is too long will lose one mark out of the possible ten available. (Remember that you have to state the number of words you have written in your essay.)
10. Is allowance made for non-native speakers?	Although you are not assessed on your language as such, if an examiner cannot understand what you are saying you will get no credit for what you have written.

The TOK presentation

22

The brain starts working the moment you are born and never stops until you stand up and speak in public.

Anonymous

The biggest problem with communication is the illusion that it has occurred . . .

George Bernard Shaw, 1856–1950

I believe that I shall never be old enough to speak without embarrassment when I have nothing to say.

Abraham Lincoln, 1809–65

As the stamp of great minds is to suggest much in few words, so, contrariwise, little minds have the gift of talking a great deal and saying nothing.

François de La Rochefoucauld, 1613–80

He is one of those orators, of whom it is well said, 'Before they get up, they do not know what they are going to say; when they are speaking, they do not know what they are saying; and when they have sat down, they do not know what they have said.'

Winston Churchill, 1874–1965

It usually takes more than three weeks to prepare a good impromptu speech.

Mark Twain, 1835–1910

All the great speakers were bad speakers at first.

Ralph Waldo Emerson, 1803–82

What matters is not saying as much as you can. It is thinking before you speak.

Tor Norretranders, 1955–

It is a sad thing when men have neither the wit to speak well, nor judgement to hold their tongues.

Jean de la Bruyère, 1645–96

The task

According to the IB, the TOK presentation requires you 'to identify and explore a knowledge question raised by a substantive real-life situation' (RLS) that interests you. The core idea is that you should apply some of the abstract TOK concepts you have acquired during the course to a concrete situation in the real world. The RLS will form the basis of your presentation. In a little more detail, the IB requires that you:

- describe your chosen RLS
- extract a central knowledge question (KQ)
- unpack subsidiary knowledge questions
- develop arguments and counter-arguments
- illustrate with examples
- explore different perspectives
- relate your analysis back to your original RLS
- show the broader relevance of your findings.

The IB has a useful diagram to illustrate how your presentation should move from the concrete to the abstract, and then relate your developed analysis back to the concrete. Below is a variation on that diagram. You might consider using this as a model to construct your own diagram, filling in specific details relevant to your own presentation.

When you give your presentation, you will also need to hand in a *presentation planning document* to your teacher. This is a summary of up to 500 words in bullet point or note form of your presentation. You can also include diagrams on this form, but you cannot exceed the space available. Your summary should cover the bullet points mentioned above.

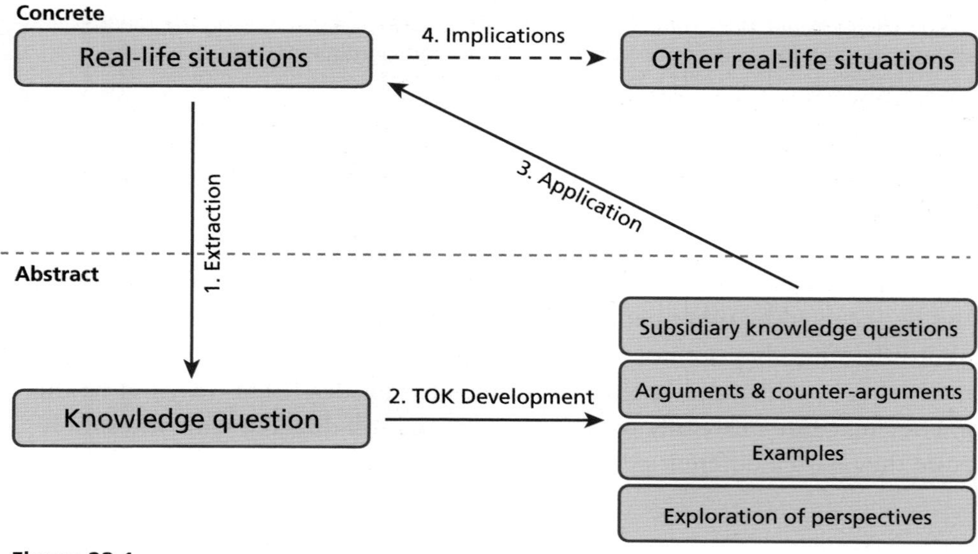

Figure 22.1

Here are a few other preliminary points about the presentation:

1. Each real-life situation and knowledge question can only be treated once by your year group. So you cannot pick the same RLS or KQ as any other students. Since there are literally hundreds of possible presentation topics, this should not be a problem.
2. Your teacher will determine the date for your presentation well in advance so that you have time to prepare.
3. Depending on your school, you may be able to do more than one presentation and have the marks for the best one submitted to the IB. However, you can treat neither the same RLS nor the same KQ more than once.
4. You will be able to have up to three meetings with your teacher to discuss your presentation and get advice.

Individual or group presentation?

You can either do your presentation alone or you can work in a group of up to three people. The required length of the presentation varies with the size of the group and should be roughly ten minutes per person. Some people prefer to do the presentation alone; others prefer to work in a group. There is no right or wrong choice, but there are pros and cons with either option. Among the points you might keep in mind are the following:

Pros and cons of working in a group

PROS	CONS
You can share ideas and perspectives on the topic.	You may find it difficult to meet together to plan.
You have more time, which enables you to go into more depth.	You may run out of ideas and struggle to fill the time.
You can use dramatic presentation methods, such as role-play, etc.	Your presentation may be fragmented and poorly coordinated.
You have more incentive to do a good job as a result of peer pressure.	You may end up working with students who are less engaged than you are.
You may find it a more sociable and enjoyable experience.	You may get distracted and find it difficult to stay on task.

One possible frustration of working in a group is that your suggestions may not always be accepted by other people. When people disagree with you it is easy to think it is because they are not really listening to what you say. (If only they listened properly they would appreciate the brilliance of your ideas!) This may not be the case. They may listen carefully to what you say and still disagree with you simply because they have a different perspective on the subject.

TOK talking point: *egocentric bias.*

According to research, when married couples estimate the percentage of household chores each of them does, the estimates usually sum to more than 120 per cent. In other words, each individual thinks that they do the lion's share of the work. Similar results have been found when students are asked to estimate their contribution to group work. This suggests that we all suffer from a degree of egocentric bias – something that is worth keeping in mind when you suspect that your friends are not pulling their weight in preparing for the presentation. This could just be your own (somewhat distorted) perspective. On the other hand, it could of course be true!

Despite the above point, there may be a marginal benefit in working in a group, and you may find it a more stimulating experience than working alone. If you do decide to work in a group, the next question to consider is who you should work with. Obviously, you will want to be in a group where you all get on with each other and feel that you can work well together. A group might also benefit from having members with complementary skills and/or backgrounds. For example, one of you may be good with multimedia and another may have dramatic flair; or you may have different subject specialisms or cultural backgrounds. This may make it easier for you to come up with different perspectives on your chosen topic.

You should also keep in mind the following three points if you decide to do a group presentation:

1. *Topic choice.* Since you have more time to fill, you will probably want to choose a topic that is somewhat broader or richer in TOK potential than if you are working alone.
2. *Individual contributions.* If you do a group presentation, you do not all need to speak for the same amount of time, but you should demonstrate that you have all been equally involved in the planning and delivery of the presentation.
3. *Presentation grade.* Since each group member will be given the same grade, it is particularly important that you feel in agreement when it comes to expectations about how much effort to put in to your presentation.

TOK talking point: *personal and shared knowledge.*

Evidence suggests that there is an element of truth in the Google slogan 'The many are smarter than the few'. According to a study of scientific papers in academic journals, those that were written by multiple authors were far more likely to be cited by other scientists than those written by single authors. This implies that the former papers were deemed to be of higher quality than the latter.

Choosing a topic

You have considerable freedom in your choice of presentation topic. You can choose something based on your personal experience, or something you came across via second-hand sources such as the internet, television, newspapers, magazines, books, novels, films, etc. Your RLS might be directly related to you or your local community, or it may have broader national or global significance. The only proviso is that your topic should be based on a specific situation which is suitable for a TOK presentation. The figure below gives you some ideas on how you might begin to focus in on a suitable RLS.

What is 'a substantive real-life situation'?

Since your presentation must be based on a 'real-life situation', it is important to be clear exactly what is meant by this phrase. Here are a few points to help you:

1. Although you may begin by thinking about a broad theme, such as world peace, or global warming, or scientific progress, these do not in themselves constitute real-life situations. If you are interested in such a theme, then choose a specific situation that is related to it. For example, you might look at the 2009 controversy known as 'Climategate' which centred round allegations that some scientists had manipulated climate data.
2. Your RLS cannot be a made-up example. It must be a real situation as opposed to an imaginary or hypothetical one. So you should not, for example, invent a personal dilemma that never actually happened to you as it is likely to lack conviction.

Personal experience
You might get ideas from an argument with friends, a CAS experience, an incident on vacation, or a personal dilemma. Or you might look for something related to your interests, e.g. music, photography or soccer.

Area of knowledge
You might consider something related to the subjects you study at school, for example, the uses and abuses of language; the difference between science and pseudo-sciences; or different interpretations of the same historical event.

News story
As the various headline prompts in this book suggest, news stories can be a rich source of ideas. The different slants rival media outlets put on the same story might naturally suggest taking different perspectives on it.

Broad theme
You might begin with a broad theme (e.g. knowledge and power, cultural differences, human rights, media bias, technology and society, health issues) and then look for a specific situation which exemplifies it.

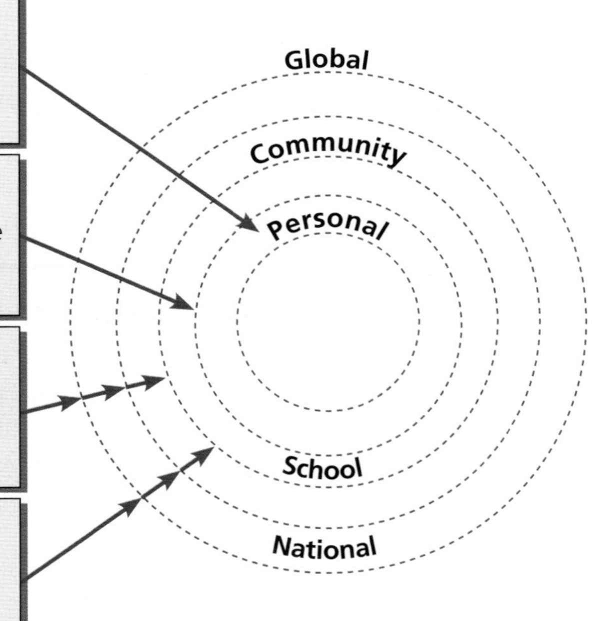

Figure 22.2 Choosing a presentation topic

3. You can, however, use incidents in books and films as your real-life situation. For example, you might use the famous scene in the 1999 movie *The Matrix* in which the hero, Neo, is given the choice between taking a red pill or a blue pill, to initiate a discussion about whether it is always good to seek the truth.
4. The RLS you choose does not have to be a contemporary one; it could be taken from the past. For example, you might look at the trial of Galileo in the seventeenth century and extract a knowledge question about the relation between science and religion.
5. Your RLS should be reasonably specific. For example, the Second World War is far too general, but a particular incident, such as the Allied bombing of Dresden, might be appropriate.
6. Avoid clichéd topics such as abortion or capital punishment. Instead, try to come up with something original which is more likely to stimulate creative thinking on your part.
7. While you should pick a topic that interests you, if you choose something you feel too passionately about there is a danger that the strength of your feelings will distort your analysis and make it difficult for you to be objective.
8. Avoid choosing an RLS that takes a lot of time to describe as this will not leave enough time for the TOK analysis, which should be the main focus of the presentation.

Quick tip

During the course, try to relate class discussion to the real world and integrate real-life examples into your notes. This will give you a bank of topics to choose from when it comes to doing your presentation.

Extracting a knowledge question

Your presentation should be built round a central knowledge question which you extract from the real-life situation and which will then generate further subsidiary knowledge questions. Knowledge questions can be elicited from almost any topic, and to a great extent the success of a presentation will depend not so much on *what* topic you choose as *how* you treat it.

Below are three points to help you to formulate knowledge questions. We will then look at some specific examples.

1. *Second order.* A knowledge question is one about the nature of a subject which cannot be answered within that subject (for more detail about this see pages vi and vii).
2. *General.* A knowledge question is directly related to the general question 'How do you know?' and requires analysis in TOK language rather than a descriptive response.
3. *Open-ended.* A knowledge question is open-ended and requires a judgement about a matter of degree ('To what extent . . .?') as opposed to a simple yes-or-no answer.

To summarise, we can say that a knowledge question is a second-order, how-do-you-know question which invites a sophisticated response expressed in TOK language.

The TOK presentation

One important point to keep in mind is that your presentation should be more than simply a discussion about a controversial topic. While it is true that all knowledge questions are controversial, it does not follow that all controversial questions are knowledge questions. If, for example, you simply debate the pros and cons of capital punishment, then you are operating at the wrong (first-order) level. Your analysis should, instead, be firmly focused on the underlying (second-order) knowledge questions – such as the nature and degree of certainty of the relevant evidence, different perspectives on the question, etc.

The following four examples illustrate how to extract knowledge questions from a real-life situation (RLS). You can find more examples in the appendix to this chapter. Each example begins with an RLS and is followed by descriptive, implicit, specific and generic questions. In each case, the descriptive question is *not* a knowledge question; and the implicit question is at best a *weak* knowledge question because it is not sufficiently explicit or clearly formulated. Both the specific and generic questions *are* knowledge questions, but at different levels of generality. The former is more closely tied to the RLS; the latter is broader in scope. It is a matter of judgement how specific or general to make your knowledge question: if it is too general, it will end up being 'How do we know anything?'; and if it is too specific it is in danger of lapsing into a question *within* rather than *about* a subject. In general, you should pitch your knowledge question at the level of the relevant area of knowledge, and your analysis should sit between the specific and the generic.

1. RLS: New Japanese history textbooks anger China

Descriptive Why has Japan published new textbooks?

Implicit Should the teaching of history in Japanese schools be more balanced and objective?

Specific What criteria might one use to determine whether or not history textbooks are biased?

Generic How is it possible to establish the truth about the past?

2. RLS: Mother of Boston bombers says she knows her sons are not terrorists

Descriptive Why do some parents always believe their children?

Implicit Does love sometimes cloud our judgement?

Specific To what extent can emotion both contribute to and detract from our knowledge of others?

Generic Can we ever really know another person?

3. RLS: You have dozens of digital photos of yourself at a party. You post the four best ones on social media and delete the rest.

Descriptive Why are people so obsessed with taking photos of themselves?

Implicit How do you decide which photos of yourself to keep and which to delete?

Specific Do the photos you post on social media create a misleading impression of 'the real you'?

Generic To what extent is it true that 'the camera never lies'?

4. RLS: Ecuador mixes folk and modern medicine

Descriptive	What is folk medicine?
Implicit	How effective is folk medicine?
Specific	How can we tell whether the benefits of medicine are genuine or the result of the placebo effect?
Generic	Should medical decisions be based on scientific evidence rather than anecdotal evidence?

Generating and developing ideas

Coming up with a good real-life situation and extracting an appropriate knowledge question is a crucial first step in planning a presentation, as it ensures that you set off in the right direction. However, it is only a starting point. You now need to generate and develop ideas. Although your presentation will begin with the description of your chosen RLS, you should move quickly to TOK analysis. This should occupy the majority of your presentation time.

To remind yourself what TOK analysis involves, look back at the seven key 'TOK tools' we discussed at the beginning of Part 5 on assessment (page 594).

Whether you are doing your presentation alone or in a group, it is important to discuss your ideas with other people, as this is likely to spark new thoughts and get your mind moving in new directions. If you are working in a group and you disagree about how to analyse the knowledge question, that need not be a problem. You can simply build your disagreements into your presentation in the form of arguments and counter-arguments.

Although the presentation is not primarily a research exercise, you may want to do some background reading to stimulate your thinking and flesh out your ideas. However, your presentation should not simply be a report of different people's opinions about your knowledge question. Try to keep the focus firmly on analysis and evaluation rather than mere description: How good is their argument? What more can be said in favour of it? What can be said against it? What are they assuming? And so on.

Quick tip

Do not turn your presentation into a 'shopping list' which simply ticks off TOK buzz words. Make a careful selection of TOK tools that are specifically relevant and will help to cast light on the knowledge question at the centre of your presentation.

Your presentation should not be a monologue which gives only one point of view. Try to ensure that it contains multiple voices with different perspectives on your knowledge question.

As with any form of assessment, you must acknowledge quoted material or segments of your presentation in which you are closely following someone else's ideas.

Structuring your presentation

Think carefully about both the form and organisation of your presentation.

Form

A presentation can take many different forms. A 'traditional' approach in which you engage with your audience and simply talk directly about your topic can work perfectly well, but you might also consider incorporating one or more of the following elements:

- *Role-play.* You might dramatise your RLS, or adopt different roles – such as scientist, artist, economist – and debate the issues, or have an interview scenario with a TV reporter talking to relevant individuals. (If you do this, ensure that you have a good understanding of the role you are playing to avoid superficial stereotypes.)
- *Multimedia.* You might incorporate multimedia, such as text, music, images, animations and video clips. If you include a video clip, this could be something from YouTube, or a short video you have made yourself.
- *Audience participation.* You might directly engage your audience by, for example, soliciting brief responses to questions. (But don't get the audience to do the work for you: it is your job to shed light on your knowledge question, not theirs!)

If you do choose one or more of the above options, be careful not to confuse means with ends. For example, if you do a role-play or make a short video, these should not be seen as ends in themselves, but as vehicles for the analysis of your knowledge question. If you get too carried away finding costumes and props, or shooting a video, you may get distracted from the main task of using TOK tools to cast light on a real-life situation.

Despite the variety of forms your presentation can take, the IB puts two limitations on these.

- The first is that the presentation cannot 'be simply an essay read aloud to the class'. (This applies not only to reading your text from paper, but also to reading it from a series of slides.) You can, of course, use prompts in the form of flash cards and bullet points on slides; but the key thing is that you should *present* rather than simply *read*.
- The second limitation is that the presentation 'must be a live experience and not a recording of the presentation'.

Quick tip

If you do a role-play, you will probably need to come 'out of character' at some point so that you can critique the various characters and evaluate the relative strengths of their arguments.

Indeed, as the name suggests, the presentation should consist primarily of you presenting. So if you do add colour and variety by including video clips and audience participation, they should not take up too much time. In the end you will be assessed on what *you* say. So if you rely too much on other people's voices and don't say much yourself you won't be credited for that.

Organisation

Much of the advice on how to structure an essay applies equally to giving a presentation. The key thing is that your presentation should have a beginning, a middle and an end, and a clear sense of direction and development. Consider the following points as you plan your presentation:

- Hit the ground running by starting with something which grabs your audience's attention, such as: 'In the time it takes to give this presentation, more than 50 million requests will be made to *Wikipedia* for information.'
- Steer a middle course and avoid the extremes of overloading your presentation or being too superficial. Devote more time to major points and less time to minor ones.

"I know so much that I don't know where to begin."

Figure 22.3

- Include occasional 'signposts' so that your audience has a sense of where you have come from and where you plan to go next. (This could be as simple as 'Having looked at *X*, we now turn to *Y*.')
- Leave your audience with a strong and memorable conclusion which shows the broader relevance of your topic and goes beyond a vague statement such as 'Therefore, we see there are many different points of view on this difficult question.'

As well as being easy to follow, your presentation should also be interesting and engaging. Try to include an element of variety and/or surprise – perhaps by incorporating some of the elements mentioned above (short role-plays, video clips, etc.). This is particularly important if your presentation lasts 30 minutes – which can seem like eternity if it is dull and uninteresting!

Quick tip

You might consider giving your audience a brief bullet-point summary of your RLS. This will enable you to explain it more quickly, and it will enable them to refer back to it during your presentation.

Delivering your presentation

Speaking in public comes high on many people's lists of biggest fears – perhaps because they are frightened of making a fool of themselves in front of other people. (This fear is known as *glossophobia*.) Since presenting is an extremely useful social skill, any fear you have is worth trying to overcome. Some people may appear to be 'naturals' at speaking and presenting in public; but, as with any ability, it actually requires a great deal of effort to make it appear relaxed, natural and spontaneous. As this suggests, public speaking is not so much a gift that you are born with as a skill that you can learn and develop.

Quick tip

Make sure that you have seen at least one good presentation so that you have a clear idea of what constitutes a good presentation.

Although your presentation skills are not formally assessed, they are likely to influence the overall impression that you make. If you mumble and your audience cannot follow what you are saying, then it will not be possible for you to get a good grade. Among the things to consider when delivering your presentation are:

- rhetoric
- body language
- presentation tools
- practice
- overcoming nerves.

Rhetoric

Rhetoric is concerned with the art of speaking persuasively. You will not persuade anyone of anything if your message is unclear and confused. Given this, you should use straightforward, accessible language and avoid pretentious jargon which may sound impressive but actually says nothing.

Among the rhetorical devices you should be aware of and might consider using are the following:

- *Tricolon.* A tricolon is a series of three parallel words or phrases. This can have a powerful effect. A famous example can be found in the US Declaration of Independence, which speaks of 'life, liberty, and the pursuit of happiness'.
- *Antithesis.* Antithesis is the balanced juxtaposition of two contrasting ideas. For example: 'Some people claim that faith complements and completes reason; other people insist that it contradicts and corrupts it.'
- *Analogy.* A good analogy can sometimes help to elucidate a difficult idea. However, be careful that you don't commit the fallacy of false analogy.
- *Rhetorical question.* A rhetorical question is one that does not expect an answer. Such questions are a good way of provoking your audience to think about the issue for themselves.
- *Humour.* Humour is a good way of getting the audience on your side and creating a relaxed atmosphere; but you should not turn your presentation into a comedy show!

Body language

'Body language' refers to such things as tone of voice, facial expression, eye contact, gesture and body posture, and it is the natural accompaniment of all face-to-face communication. To ensure that your presentation has maximum impact, you need to think not only about *what* you say, but also about *how* you say it. Keep in mind that a presentation is, at least in part, a *performance*, and that you therefore need to *act* and *project*.

Most advice in this area is common sense, but it is easy to forget it with the pressure of a presentation. With regard to your voice, speak slowly and clearly, emphasise key points and, where appropriate, pause for dramatic effect. Try to avoid using 'fillers' such as 'um', 'like', 'you know' and 'I mean'. Such habits can distract your audience and detract from the impact of your presentation. When it comes to other aspects of body language, face your audience at all times, make eye contact, and think carefully about your use of gestures.

TOK talking point: *body language*.

There is a great deal of mythology surrounding body language. According to one frequently quoted statistic, 93 per cent of face-to-face communication comes from non-verbal cues and only 7 per cent comes from what we actually say. Despite its popularity, this knowledge claim is almost certainly false. After all, if it were true, we should be able to communicate pretty well with foreigners whose language we do not speak – and this is clearly not the case! This misleading statistic derives from a misinterpretation of a 1960s study conducted by an American psychologist called Albert Mehrabian (1939–). Whatever validity it has is limited to situations in which people are expressing their feelings and there is a conflict between what they say and how they say it. For example, if someone says, 'You *are* awful', with a smile and a positive tone, your interpretation is much more likely to be influenced by their body language than their words. This is, however, irrelevant to the context of a TOK presentation. In that context, the thing to keep in mind is that while your style can help to convey the substance you wish to communicate, it is certainly not a substitute for it.

Figure 22.4

TOK talking point: *self-knowledge*.

The fact that we are often unaware of the way we come across to other people raises interesting questions about the extent of our self-knowledge. You might want to refer back to our comments on this issue in Chapter 9, page 237 and in Chapter 20 on page 587.

Presentation tools

Most people use a software program such as PowerPoint®, Keynote®, or Prezi® when giving a presentation. Sadly, such tools are often badly used. There can be few experiences more depressing than listening to a speaker who is simply reading text from a seemingly endless series of slides. Your audience can read – they don't need you to do it for them! So if you use one of these programs rule number one is: Don't subject your audience to 'death by PowerPoint'! Keep in mind that you are not, in any case, allowed to simply read out your presentation. Also, if you have too much text on your slides, you are likely not only to give a stilted performance, but also to make it harder for your audience to follow. This is because they can read four times faster than you can speak. So if you are speaking while they are reading this will interfere with their understanding. Here are a couple of key points to remember:

1. *Don't overload your slides with text.* A useful principle is the 1-7-7 rule: one main idea per slide, and a maximum of seven lines of text, and seven words per line.
2. *Use animations sparingly, if at all.* Having text fly in from all over the place may look good, but usually serves no purpose and can be very distracting.

Quick tip

Consider making an image-only slide presentation which contains no text at all. If you choose your images well, such a presentation can be very effective. Not only can it stimulate your audience, but it can also remind you of your next key point!

While PowerPoint might, understandably, give you some reassurance when you are standing in front of an audience, if you are only using it because you are worried that your mind will go blank and you will forget what to say, then it might be better for you to use flash cards. A PowerPoint presentation should, in fact, be more for the benefit of the audience than the speaker. In particular, it should help them to follow your line of argument and follow the overall structure of your presentation. Given what has been said, you should probably limit what you include on slides to **key words**, **bullet points**, **diagrams**, **pictures** – and perhaps a few short telling **quotes** that you want your audience to reflect on.

"I need someone well versed in the art of torture – do you know PowerPoint?"

Figure 22.5

"Great PowerPoint, Kevin, but the answer is no."

Figure 22.6

TOK talking point: *the medium and the message.*

According to the media guru Marshall McLuhin (1911–80), 'The medium is the message.' What he meant by this was that the form in which you communicate information subtly affects its content. With this in mind, it might be interesting to reflect on how, if at all, your use of PowerPoint shapes and influences what you say.

Practice

As with developing any skill, there is no doubt that practice makes perfect. Since the best way to feel comfortable speaking in front of your peers is to actually do it, you should take every opportunity available to you to give a presentation, or a mini-presentation. These are likely to arise in both TOK and in the other subjects you study.

When it comes to your assessed TOK presentation, you should rehearse it from start to finish at least once. This will allow you to check that you 'know your lines', that there are smooth transitions between the different parts, and that you have got the timing right and it is neither too long nor too short.

To ensure that there is a good flow to your presentation, you might find it helpful to write out what you plan to say in long-hand. Then reduce this to a list of key points, and focus on trying to memorise not the exact wording, but the flow of ideas. This will help to ensure that you do not overload your memory and that what you say sounds fresh and spontaneous.

Quick tip

Video yourself when you practise your presentation. This is a great way of getting feedback on how you are coming across to other people, and it may help you to spot and eliminate any undesirable linguistic or gestural habits.

Overcoming nerves

Most people experience a certain amount of stage-fright before giving any kind of public performance. This is normal and to some extent beneficial. There is probably an optimal degree of performance anxiety: too little and you may be insufficiently focused or energised; too much and you may choke and be unable to perform effectively. The key thing is to try to *manage* any nervousness you feel. The best way to combat nerves is to be well prepared and to practise your presentation – and then to think positively. However, positive thinking will not be much help if you are poorly prepared.

You will probably feel most nervous at the beginning of your presentation. Once you get into the flow of what you are saying, your anxiety is likely to disappear. With this in mind, you should make sure that you are particularly familiar with the opening part of your presentation.

Try to ensure that your audience do not pick up on your anxiety, as this will divert their attention away from your message. Breathe deeply, make eye contact, and smile. Remember that it is not a good idea to *tell* your audience that you are nervous, as this will create a tense atmosphere. You may, in fact, be able to overcome your nerves simply by acting as if you are not nervous! That, at least, was the view of American president Theodore Roosevelt (1858–1919): 'By acting as if I was not afraid I gradually ceased to be afraid.'

TOK talking point: *influencing emotions*.

You might relate Roosevelt's claim back to our discussion of the James–Lange theory in Chapter 7. According to this theory, bodily changes precede and elicit emotional changes. So if you smile, you may feel happier; and if you act confidently, you may actually feel more confident.

Summary: key tips on your presentation

1. Since you are supposed to show 'clear personal involvement' in your TOK presentation, try to pick a topic that interests and engages you.
2. Your presentation should focus on a specific real-life situation from which you can extract a clear knowledge question.
3. Keep in mind that the central question in TOK is 'How do you know?' This question should be at the centre of your presentation.
4. Do not spend too much time explaining your real-life situation and ensure that description is always a prelude to analysis of the relevant knowledge questions.
5. Demonstrate an awareness of different perspectives by asking yourself 'How would an X look at this?'
6. Where appropriate, show an awareness of your background assumptions and cultural biases.
7. Make sure that what you say is well structured and easy to follow by using effective signposting.
8. Do not simply read your notes, but face the audience and present to them. In particular, avoid death by PowerPoint!
9. If you include a skit or role-play, don't get so carried away with the costumes and characters that you forget about the knowledge questions you are analysing.
10. In your conclusion, show that you are aware of the broader implications of the topic and make clear why we should care about it.

Appendix: Extracting knowledge questions

1. RLS: *Teacher lied to protect children.*

Descriptive	Why do we lie?
Implicit	Is it wrong to lie?
Specific	How should we decide whether or not it is wrong to lie?
Generic	What role should reason and experience play in deciding what's right and wrong?

2. RLS: *The United Nations debate the meaning of the word 'terrorism'.*

Descriptive	Why are we worried about terrorism?
Implicit	What is the best definition of 'terrorism'?
Specific	Is the definition of 'terrorism' more a matter of objective fact or subjective opinion?
Generic	Why are some words so difficult to define and why does it matter?

3. RLS: *Stacy Synder denied teaching degree because of drunken pirate photo on internet.*

Descriptive	Why do people post embarrassing photos on the internet?
Implicit	Do institutions have the right to search for negative information about us online?
Specific	What reasons, if any, are there for thinking that some things are best forgotten?
Generic	To what extent is knowledge always a good thing?

4. RLS: *New national soccer training ground opens which monitors all aspects of performance.*

Descriptive	Why has the new soccer training ground been opened?
Implicit	Will the collection and analysis of data improve the performance of soccer players?
Specific	To what extent should soccer managers rely on data rather than intuition?
Generic	What is the role of intuition in a world of big data?

5. RLS: *Dutch psychology professor convicted of academic fraud.*

Descriptive	Why do some scientists cheat?
Implicit	Should we trust psychologists?
Specific	How should we decide whether to trust research in psychology?
Generic	To what extent is the scientific method self-regulating?

6. RLS: *Panel of astrologers predict president will win re-election.*

Descriptive Why do so many people believe in astrology?

Implicit How accurate have astrologers' predictions been in the past?

Specific Why does astrology fail to qualify as a genuine science?

Generic What distinguishes science from pseudo-science?

7. RLS: *Study shows that eating lots of candy can lead to violence.*

Descriptive How can we stop children eating so much candy?

Implicit How could a sugar rush cause violent behaviour?

Specific How can we distinguish a causal connection from a correlation?

Generic To what extent does the complexity of the subject-matter limit the acquisition of knowledge in the human sciences?

8. RLS: *Supermarket refuses to decorate a birthday cake with the name of a child called Adolf Hitler Campbell.*

Descriptive Why would anyone name their child after a mass murderer?

Implicit Should parents have the right to name their children as they wish?

Specific How might we determine whether 'a rose by any other name would smell as sweet' (William Shakespeare)?

Generic How, if at all, does language influence our perception of reality?

9. RLS: *'Mother Teresa's "40-year faith crisis".'*

Descriptive Why did Mother Teresa question her faith?

Implicit Did Mother Teresa really believe in God?

Specific Does the concept of faith imply being certain or is it consistent with doubt?

Generic How reliable are knowledge claims based on faith?

10. RLS: *Mother of toddler Freddie Linksky fools art world into buying his paintings.*

Descriptive Why did Freddie Linksky's mother try to fool the art world?

Implicit Are Freddie Linksky's paintings any good?

Specific To what extent should we trust the judgements of art experts?

Generic Are there any objective criteria for judging the value of a work of art?

11. RLS: *Oscar Pistorius is charged with the premeditated murder of his girlfriend, Reeva Steenkamp (February 2013).*

Descriptive What happened the night Reeva Steenkamp died?

Implicit Did Oscar Pistorius intend to kill his girlfriend?

Specific How can we know whether or not Oscar Pistorius is telling the truth?

Generic To what extent is it possible to establish the truth 'beyond reasonable doubt'?

12. RLS: *Politician Chris Grayling accused of using crime statistics to mislead public.*

Descriptive Why are people so willing to believe politicians?

Implicit Did Chris Grayling use misleading statistics?

Specific What are the main challenges involved in compiling accurate crime statistics?

Generic When should we trust statistics and when should we mistrust them?

13. RLS: *According to new research, the more money people think a bottle of wine costs, the better they think it tastes.*

Descriptive What determines the price of a bottle of wine?

Implicit Why do people think that the price of wine is a good indication of its quality?

Specific How do expectations influence our tastes?

Generic Given the influence of expectations on them, to what extent should we trust our senses?

Index

Index

Acknowledgments

The author and publishers are grateful for the permissions granted to reproduce materials in either the original or adapted form. While every effort has been made, it has not always been possible to identify the sources of all the materials used, or to trace all copyright holders. If any omissions are brought to our notice, we will be happy to include the appropriate acknowledgements on reprinting.

p. 20 from *White Noise* by Don DeLillo, copyright © 1984, 1985 by Don DeLillo. Used by permission of Viking Penguin, a division of Penguin Group (USA) LLC; p. 100 *Nineteen Eighty Four* by George Orwell (Copyright © George Orwell, 1949) by permission of Bill Hamilton as the Literary Executor of the Estate of the Late Sonia Brownell Orwell, and copyright © 1949 by Harcourt Brace Jovanovich, Inc and renewed 1977 by Sonia Brownell Orwell. Used by permission of Houghton Mifflin Harcourt Publishing Company. All rights reserved; p. 100 from *Word Play: What Happens When People Talk* by Peter Farb. Copyright © 1973 by Peter Farb. Used by permission of Brandt & Hochman Literary Agents, Inc. All rights reserved; p. 314 excerpt from *My Life As A Man* by Philip Roth. Copyright © 1970, 1971, 1973, 1974 by Philip Roth, used by permission of The Wylie Agency LLC; p. 378 script excerpt from Yes, Minister by Jonathan Lynn and Anthony Jay, series 1, episode 2, first aired on BBC2, January 1986, with permission from Alan Brodie Representation; p. 427 excerpt from *As I Please* by George Orwell (copyright © George Orwell, 1944) by permission of Bill Hamilton as the Literary Executor of the Estate of the Late Sonia Brownell Orwell, and from *The Collected Essays, Journals And Letters Of George Orwell, Volume III: As I Please*, 1943-1945. Copyright © 1968 by Sonia Brownell Orwell and renewed 1996 by Mark Hamilton. Used by permission of Houghton Mifflin Publishing Company. All rights reserved; The IB prescribed essay titles at the end of chapters throughout this book are reproduced by permission of the International Baccalaureate Organization.

The publishers would like to thank the following for permission to reproduce illustrations:

Cover: imageBROKER/Alamy; p. 6 *The Betrayal of Images: 'Ceci n'est pas une pipe'*, 1929 (oil on canvas), Magritte, Rene (1898-1967) / Los Angeles County Museum of Art, CA, USA / © DACS / Giraudon / The Bridgeman Art Library, © ADAGP, Paris and DACS, London 2014; pp. 7, 193, 198*r*, 209*t*, 358, 390, 427, 429, 483, 549 Getty Images; pp. 143*l*, 263*b* Photos 12/Alamy; p. 10 First_emotion/Shutterstock; p. 10 StockPhotosArt/Shutterstock; pp. 13, 105, 293*b*, 354, 516 Nick Kim from www.CartoonStock.com; p. 16*t*, 25 APTV/AP/Press Association Images; pp. 16*b*, 45, 56, 59*b*, 60, 85, 90, 120*t*, 137*t*, 166, 190, 201, 209*b*, 256, 257*t*, 267, 269, 276, 283, 294, 313, 356, 361, 378, 386*t*, 406, 414, 415, 438, 447*t*, 450*t*, *b*, 474, 486, 488, 489, 491, 497, 498*b*, 512*t*, 515, 520, 523*b*, 531*t*, *b*, 556, 579*b*, 582, 584, 585, 604, 608, 614, 625, 628, 629 The New Yorker Collection/The Cartoon Bank; pp. 27, 28, 47*b*, 338, 473, 589, 603, 612 Calvin and Hobbes © 1986, 1987, 1991, 1993, 1993, 1988, 1993 Watterson, dist. by Universal Uclick, reprinted with permission, all rights reserved; p. 30*tl* gnomeandi/ Shutterstock; p. 30*tc* toonman/Shutterstock; p. 30*tr*, *bl* Jorg Hackemann/Shutterstock; p. 30*bc* Viet Images/Shutterstock; p. 30*br* evantravels/Shutterstock; pp. 32, 245 © Punch Limited; p. 33 Dan Reynolds from www.CartoonStock.com; p. 35 AF archive/Alamy; p. 41 *The Thinker*, 1881, Auguste Rodin, (1840–1917)/Musee Rodin, Paris, France/Bridgeman Images; pp. 46, 596 amasterphotographer/Shutterstock; p. 47*t* Pukhov Konstantin/Shutterstock; p. 49*l*

Martin Thomas Photography/Alamy; p. 49*r* think4photop/Shutterstock; p. 52*t*, 200, 243 S. Harris from www.CartoonStock.com; p. 52*b* Hollywood Headshots/Alamy; p. 53 hamidisc/Shutterstock; p. 59*t* Pal Teravagimov/Shutterstock; p. 64 Ulrich Doering/Alamy; p. 66 Bejamin D. Hennig www.viewsoftheworld.net – Licensed under Creative Commons Attribution-Share Alike 3.0 via Wikimedia Commons CC BY-NC-ND 3.0; p. 68 AFP/Getty Images; p. 78 Evgeny Atamanenko/Shutterstock; p. 79 Huntstock, Inc/Alamy; p. 80*l* Getty Images/RunPhoto; p. 80*r* Getty Images/Jose Luis Pelaez; pp. 81, 179*t*, 317*b*, 319, 322*b*, 327, 345*t*, 586 Sidney Harris, ScienceCartoonPlus.com; p. 99 Horizons WWP/Alamy; p. 102 Getty Images/Frank Herholdt; p. 103 Antiques & Collectables/Alamy; p. 118 Getty Images/Jupiterimages; p. 119 Ivan Kuzmin/Shutterstock; p. 120*b* ZUMA Press, Inc./Alamy; p. 121 Darren Baker/Shutterstock; p. 124 Getty Images/AJA Productions; p. 130 www.eyewitnessid.com; pp. 141, 262*br* Pictorial Press Ltd/Alamy; p. 143*r* Getty Images/FOX Image Collection; p. 148 Randy Glasbergen www.glasbergen.com; p. 151 Paul Wishart/Shutterstock; pp. 154*l*, *r* CoraMax/Shutterstock; p. 154*c* Orla/Shutterstock; p. 157 Bizarro © 1993 Dan Piraro, Distributed by King Features Syndicate, Inc.; p. 158 ITAR-TASS Photo Agency/Alamy; p. 172 John McPherson from www.CartoonStock.com; p. 174*bl* Tyler Olson/Shutterstock; p. 174*tc* CREATISTA/Shutterstock; p. 174*bl* Gorich/Shutterstock; p. 174*tr* VikaValter/iStock; p. 174*bc* Jason Stitt/Shutterstock; p. 174*tr* Nicolas Hansen/iStock; p. 175*tl*, *bl* Eric Isselee/Shutterstock; p. 175*tr*, *br* Andy Bullock/Getty Images; p. 176*t*, 359 Peanuts Comic Strip © 1960, 1975 United Features Syndicate Inc.; p. 176*b* Klaus Vedfelt/Getty Images; p. 177*l* *The Scream*, 1893 (oil, tempera & pastel on cardboard), Munch, Edvard (1863-1944) / Nasjonalgalleriet, Oslo, Norway / © DACS / The Bridgeman Art Library and © Munch Museum/Munch - Ellingsen Group, BONO, Oslo/DACS, London 2014; p. 179*b* John McGrail/Getty Images; pp. 181, 278, 295, 297*tr*, 432, 472 AFP/Getty Images; p. 198*tl* Eddie Gerald/Alamy; p. 198*tc* kurhan/Shutterstock; p. 198*tr* Andrey_Popov/Shutterstock; p. 198 De Agostini/Getty Images; p. 198*b* *2nd from l* Kristoffer Tripplaar/Alamy; p. 198*b* *2nd from r* ClassicStock/Alamy; p. 205*l*, *r* vgstudio/Shutterstock; p. 206 NBCU Photo Bank via Getty Images; p. 207 Moviestore collection Ltd/Alamy; p. 210 *The Lac d'Annecy*, 1896 (oil on canvas), Paul Cezanne (1839–1906) / © Samuel Courtauld Trust, The Courtauld Gallery, London, UK / Bridgeman Images; p. 216 Gallo Images/Alamy; p. 224*t* niederhaus.galina/Shutterstock; pp. 224*b*, 238, 246 Chris Wildt from www.CartoonStock.com; p. 226*tl* Jeff Morgan 09/Alamy; p. 226*tr* WENN UK/Alamy; p. 234 Juriah Mosin/Shutterstock; p. 235*l* Andrew Holt/Alamy; p. 235*r* Cultura Creative (RF)/Alamy; p. 242 Tim Cordel from www.CartoonStock.com; p. 253 M. Moeller from www.CartoonStock.com; p. 254 don jon red/Alamy; p. 257*b* Mark Ishikawa from www.CartoonStock.com; p. 258 akg-images/picture-alliance; p. 259 Harris, T. Russell from www.CartoonStock.com; p. 262*t* Salvatore Cullari www.nvo.com/scullari; p. 262*bl* Greg Balfour Evans/Alamy; p. 263*tr* and *l* Burlington Police Department, NC, USA; p. 265 with permission of Asunta Rufino; p. 266, 380 Naf from www.CartoonStock.com; p. 268 Theresa McCracken from www.CartoonStock.com; p. 277 Gamma-Rapho via Getty Images; p. 279 Wiley Miller from www.CartoonStock.com; p. 292 epa european pressphoto agency b.v./Alamy; p. 293*t* ChameleonsEye/Shutterstock; pp. 296, 579*t* Non Sequitur ©2002 Wiley Ink, Inc. dist. by Universal Uclick, reprinted with permission, all rights reserved; p. 297*tl* muzsy/Shutterstock; p. 297*b* Mike Flanagan from www.CartoonStock.com; p. 298 Andrew Toos from www.CartoonStock.com; p. 299 Adrian Teal from www.CartoonStock.com; p. 314 with permission of Dan Everett; p. 315 James Peragine/Shutterstock; p. 323*c* Petr Malyshev/Shutterstock; p. 323*r* RAStudio/Shutterstock; p. 332 IxMaster/Shutterstock; p. 335 The LIFE Picture Collection/Getty Images; p. 336*t* Hellen Sergeyeva/Shutterstock; p. 336*b* anuphadit/Shutterstock; p. 342 RGB Ventures/SuperStock/Alamy; p. 344*l* Nomad_Soul/Shutterstock; p. 344*c* tankist276/Shutterstock; p. 344*r* cozyta/Shutterstock; p. 345*b* Skeptical Inquirer Magazine www.csicop.org; p. 348 Stuart Jenner/Shutterstock; p. 349 A. Barrington Brown/Science Photo Library; p. 363 The LIFE Images Collection/Getty Images; p. 366 © Union of Concerned Scientists/Steve Pauls,

2011 / www.ucsusa.org; p. 371 Betto Rodrigues/Shutterstock; p. 376*l* Serg Dibrova/ Shutterstock; p. 376*c* peters99/iStock; p. 376*r* FLPA/Alamy; p. 379 Clay Bennett © 2000 The Christian Science Monitor, reproduced with permission; p. 385 Commercial Eye/Getty Images; p. 386*b* Bruce Gilbert/Landov/Press Association Images; p. 389 Duke Downey/San Francisco Chronicle/Corbis; p. 396 National Geographic/Getty Images; p. 400 Aaron Bacall from www.CartoonStock.com; p. 401 Olivier Asselin/Alamy; p. 419*l*, *r* drawings from *Motel of the Mysteries* by David Macaulay © 1979 David Macaulay, reprinted by permission of Houghton Mifflin Company, all rights reserved; p. 420 Print Collector/Getty Images; p. 423*l*, 423*r* Ria Novosti; p. 425 Martha Campbell from www.CartoonStock.com; p. 436 Roger Viollet/Getty Images; p. 437, 561*l* Peter Horree/Alamy; p. 442, 445 Hemis/Alamy; p. 446 Ken Welsh/Alamy; p. 447*b* javarman/Shutterstock; p. 449*t* ROBIN UTRECHT/epa/ Corbis/; p. 449*b* Gjon Mili/Contributor/Getty Images / 'Bull's Head' by Pablo Picasso © Succession Picasso/DACS London 2014; p. 451 *Fountain, 1917/64 (ceramic), Duchamp, Marcel (1887-1968)/The Israel Museum, Jerusalem, Israel/Vera & Arturo Schwarz Collection of Dada and Surrealist Art* / Bridgeman Images / © DACS London 2014; p. 454*t The Lake, Petworth: Sunset, a Stag Drinking*, c.1829, Turner, Joseph Mallord William (1775-1851)/ Petworth House, Sussex, UK/The Bridgeman Art Library; p. 454*b The Mud Bath* 1914, David Bomberg © Tate, London 2011; p. 456 *America's Most Wanted* by Vitaly Komar and Alexander Melamid, 1994, oil and acrylic on canvas 24 x 32 inches, courtesy Ronald Feldman Fine Arts, New York www.feldmangallery.com; p. 457*t* Derwent Lakes, lithograph by I.C and S.A, from Charles Hullmadel's Ten Lithographic drawings of Scenery, 1826. ©V&A Images/Victoria and Albert Museum, London; p. 457*b View of Derwentwater* from 'The Silent Traveller in Lakeland' by Chiang Yee, Country Life, London 1938, used by permission of Mimi Chiang; p. 459 *Portrait of Gertrude Stein*, 1906 (oil on canvas), Picasso, Pablo (1881-1973)/Metropolitan Museum of Art, New York, USA/The Bridgeman Art Library © Succession Picasso/DACS, London 2014; p. 465*l*, 465*c*, 465*r* Bearded Slave and Young Slave, c.1520–23, The Awakening Slave, 1519-20 (marble), Buonarroti, Michelangelo (1475–1564) / Galleria dell'Accademia, Florence, Italy / Alinari / The Bridgeman Art Library; p. 480 Lisa F. Young/Shutterstock; p. 482 i4lcocl2/Shutterstock; p. 498*t* Bloomberg/Getty Images; p. 500 Harley Schwadron www.CartonStock.com; p. 511 LatinContent/Getty Images; pp. 512*b*, 542 Bule Sky Studio/Shutterstock; p. 513 Sistine Chapel Ceiling (1508–12): The Creation of Adam, 1511–12 (fresco) (post restoration), Buonarroti, Michelangelo (1475–1564)/Vatican Museums and Galleries, Vatican City, Italy/The Bridgeman Art Library; p. 523*t* Photo smile/Shutterstock; p. 534 David Jennings/Alamy; p. 547*l* Dr. Takahiko Masuda, University of Alberta; p. 547*r* Professor Richard E. Nisbett, University of Michigan; p. 555 UIG via Getty Images; p. 557*t* Robert Harding World Imagery/Alamy; p. 557*b* Universal Images Group/DeAgostini/Alamy; p. 558 YI-AN/Shutterstock; p. 559 Images of Africa Photobank/Alamy; p. 560 Coat of Arms of Niels Bohr by GJo. Licensed under Creative Commons Attribution-Share Alike 3.0 via Wikimedia Commons CC BY-SA 3.0; p. 561*r* Gamma-Rapho via Getty Images / 'Mother and Child' by Pablo Picasso © Succession Picasso/DACS London 2014; p. 563 Angelo Giampiccolo/Shutterstock; p. 581 *Portrait of Pablo Picasso*, 1912 (oil on canvas), Gris, Juan (1887–1927) / The Art Institute of Chicago, IL, USA/Bridgeman Images; p. 588 ChameleonsEye/Shutterstock.

Artwork on pp. 88, 114 and 203 by Mike Lacey (Beehive Illustration).

All other artwork by Jan and Peter Simmonett.

Design: Guido Caroti.